Lecture Notes in Computer Science   9916

Commenced Publication in 1973
Founding and Former Series Editors:
Gerhard Goos, Juris Hartmanis, and Jan van Leeuwen

Enqing Chen · Yihong Gong
Yun Tie (Eds.)

Advances in Multimedia Information Processing – PCM 2016

17th Pacific-Rim Conference on Multimedia
Xi'an, China, September 15–16, 2016
Proceedings, Part I

Springer

Editors
Enqing Chen
Zhengzhou University
Zhengzhou
China

Yun Tie
Zhengzhou University
Zhengzhou
China

Yihong Gong
Jiaotong University
Xi'an
China

ISSN 0302-9743   ISSN 1611-3349 (electronic)
Lecture Notes in Computer Science
ISBN 978-3-319-48889-9   ISBN 978-3-319-48890-5 (eBook)
DOI 10.1007/978-3-319-48890-5

Library of Congress Control Number: 2016956479

LNCS Sublibrary: SL3 – Information Systems and Applications, incl. Internet/Web, and HCI

This Springer imprint is published by Springer Nature
The registered company is Springer International Publishing AG
The registered company address is: Gewerbestrasse 11, 6330 Cham, Switzerland

Preface

The 17th Pacific-Rim Conference on Multimedia (PCM 2016) was held in Xi'an, China, during September 15–16, 2016, and hosted by the Xi'an Jiaotong University (XJTU). PCM is a leading international conference for researchers and industry practitioners to share their new ideas, original research results, and practical development experiences from all multimedia-related areas.

It was a great honor for XJTU to host PCM 2016, one of the most longstanding multimedia conferences, in Xi'an, China. Xi'an Jiaotong University, located in the capital of Shaanxi province, is one of the key universities run by the Ministry of Education, China. Recently its multimedia-related research has been attracting increasing attention from the local and international multimedia community. For over 2000 years, Xi'an has been the center for political and economic developments and the capital city of many Chinese dynasties, with the richest cultural and historical heritage, including the world-famous Terracotta Warriors, Big Wild Goose Pagoda, etc. We hope that our venue made PCM 2016 a memorable experience for all participants.

PCM 2016 featured a comprehensive program. The 202 submissions from authors of more than ten countries included a large number of high-quality papers in multimedia content analysis, multimedia signal processing and communications, and multimedia applications and services. We thank our 28 Technical Program Committee members who spent many hours reviewing papers and providing valuable feedback to the authors. From the total of 202 submissions to the main conference and based on at least three reviews per submission, the program chairs decided to accept 111 regular papers (54 %) among which 67 were posters (33 %). This volume of the conference proceedings contains the abstracts of two invited talks and all the regular, poster, and special session papers.

The technical program is an important aspect but only achieves its full impact if complemented by challenging keynotes. We are extremely pleased and grateful to have had two exceptional keynote speakers, Wen Gao and Alex Hauptmann, accept our invitation and present interesting ideas and insights at PCM 2016.

We are also heavily indebted to many individuals for their significant contributions. We thank the PCM Steering Committee for their invaluable input and guidance on crucial decisions. We wish to acknowledge and express our deepest appreciation to the honorary chairs, Nanning Zheng, Shin'chi Satoh, general chairs, Yihong Gong, Thomas Plagemann, Ke Lu, Jianping Fan, program chairs, Meng Wang, Qi Tian, Abdulmotaleb EI Saddik, Yun Tie, organizing chairs, Jinye Peng, Xinbo Gao, Ziyu Guan, Yizhou Wang, publicity chairs, Xueming Qian, Xiaojiang Chen, Cheng Jin, Xiangyang Xue, publication chairs, Jun Wu, Enqing Chen, local Arrangements Chairs, Kuizi Mei, Xuguang Lan, special session chairs, Jianbing Shen, Jialie Shen, Jianru Xue, demo chairs, Yugang Jiang, Jitao Sang, finance and registration chair, Shuchan Gao. Without their efforts and enthusiasm, PCM 2016 would not have become a reality. Moreover, we want to thank our sponsors: Springer, Peking University, Zhengzhou University,

Ryerson University. Finally, we wish to thank all committee members, reviewers, session chairs, student volunteers, and supporters. Their contributions are much appreciated.

September 2016

Meng Wang
Yun Tie
Qi Tian
Abdulmotaleb El Saddik
Yihong Gong
Thomas Plagemann
Ke Lu
Jianping Fan

Organization

Honorary Chairs

Nanning Zheng   Xi'an Jiaotong University, China
Shin'chi Satoh   National Institute of Informatics, Japan

General Chairs

Yihong Gong   Xi'an Jiaotong University, China
Thomas Plagemann   University of Oslo, Norway
Ke Lu   University of Chinese Academy of Sciences, China
Jianping Fan   University of North Carolina at Charlotte, USA

Program Chairs

Meng Wang   Hefei University of Technology, China
Qi Tian   University of Texas at San Antonio, USA
Abdulmotaleb EI Saddik   University of Ottawa, Canada
Yun Tie   Zhengzhou University, China

Organizing Chairs

Jinye Peng   Northwest University, China
Xinbo Gao   Xidian University, China
Ziyu Guan   Northwest University, China
Yizhou Wang   Peking University, China

Publicity Chairs

Xueming Qian   Xi'an Jiaotong University, China
Xiaojiang Chen   Northwest University, China
Cheng Jin   Fudan University, China
Xiangyang Xue   Fudan University, China

Publication Chairs

Jun Wu   Northwestern Polytechnical University, China
Enqing Chen   Zhengzhou University, China

Local Arrangements Chairs

Kuizi Mei   Xi'an Jiaotong University, China
Xuguang Lan   Xi'an Jiaotong University, China

Special Session Chairs

Jianbing Shen   Beijing Institute of Technology, China
Jialie Shen   Singapore Management University, Singapore
Jianru Xue   Xi'an Jiaotong University, China

Demo Chairs

Yugang Jiang   Fudan University, China
Jitao Sang   Institute of Automation, Chinese Academy of Sciences,
                     China

Finance and Registration Chair

Shuchan Gao   Xi'an Jiaotong University, China

Contents – Part I

Contents – Part II

Visual Tracking by Local Superpixel Matching with Markov Random Field

Heng Fan[1], Jinhai Xiang[2(✉)], and Zhongmin Chen[2]

[1] College of Engineering, Huazhong Agricultural University, Wuhan, China
[2] College of Informatics, Huazhong Agricultural University, Wuhan, China
jimmy_xiang@mail.hzau.edu.cn

Abstract. In this paper, we propose a novel method to track non-rigid and/or articulated objects using superpixel matching and markov random field (MRF). Our algorithm consists of three stages. First, a superpixel dataset is constructed by segmenting training frames into superpixels, and each superpixel is represented by multiple features. The appearance information of target is encoded in the superpixel database. Second, each new frame is segmented into superpixels and then its object-background confidence map is derived by comparing its superpixels with k-nearest neighbors in superpixel dataset. Taking context information into account, we utilize MRF to further improve the accuracy of confidence map. In addition, the local context information is incorporated through a feedback to refine superpixel matching. In the last stage, visual tracking is achieved via finding the best candidate by maximum a posterior estimate based on the confidence map. Experiments show that our method outperforms several state-of-the-art trackers.

Keywords: Visual tracking · Superpixel matching · Markov Random Field (MRF) · Local context information

1 Introduction

In computer vision field, object tracking plays a crucial role for its various applications, such as surveillance and robotics [14]. To develop a robust tracker, numerous algorithms have been proposed. Despite reasonable good results of these methods, visual tracking remains a challenge due to appearance variations caused by occlusion and deformation. To address these problems, a wide range of appearance models have been presented. In general, these appearance models can be categorized into two types: discriminative models [2,3,6,9,10,13,18,20] and generative models [1,5,7,8,15,16].

Discriminative algorithms focus on building online classifiers to distinguish the target from the background. These methods employ both the foreground and background information. In [2], an adaptive ensemble of classifier is trained to separate target pixels from background pixels. Kalal *et al.* [13] introduce a P-N learning algorithm for object tracking. However, this tracking method easily

E. Chen et al. (Eds.): PCM 2016, Part I, LNCS 9916, pp. 1–10, 2016.
DOI: 10.1007/978-3-319-48890-5_1

causes drift when object appearance varies. Babenko *et al.* [3] utilize the multiple instance learning (MIL) method for visual tracking, which can alleviate drift to some extent. Yang *et al.* [18] suggest a discriminative appearance model based on superpixels, which facilitates the tracking algorithm to distinguish the target from the background.

On the other hand, the generative models formulate tracking problem as searching for regions most similar to object. These methods are based on either subspace models or templates and update appearance model dynamically. In [16], the incremental visual tracking method suggests an online approach for efficiently learning and updating a low dimensional principal components analysis (PCA) subspace representation for the object. However, this representation scheme is sensitive to occlusion. Adam *et al.* [1] present a fragment-based template model for visual tracking. Mei and Ling [15] model the object appearance with sparse representation for visual tracking and achieve a good performance.

Though having achieved promising performance for object tracking, the aforementioned algorithms often suffer from drifting problems when substantial non-rigid and articulated motions are involved in the object.

To solve the problem of tracking non-rigid and/or articulated objects, we propose a novel tracking algorithm with local superpixel matching and markov random field (MRF). Our method mainly contains three stages. In the first stage, we construct a superpixel dataset by segmenting training frames into superpixels, and each superpixel in the dataset is represented with multiple features. Through this way, the appearance information of the object is encoded in the superpixel dataset. In the second stage, for each new frame, we represent it with its superpixels. We can compute its object-background confidence map by comparing its superpixels with their k-nearest neighbors in the superpixel dataset. In this process, the tracking task is treated as separating object pixels from background pixels. Taking the context information into consideration, we utilize MRF to further improve the accuracy of the confidence map. In addition, the local context information of each superpixel is incorporated through a feedback to refine superpixel matching. In the final stage, object tracking is achieved via searching the best candidate by maximum a posterior estimate based on the confidence map. When tracking is completed in each frame, we collect good tracking results to update the superpixel dataset. With the help of this update scheme, our tracker is able to adapt to the appearance changes of the target. Figure 1 illustrates the framework of the proposed method.

2   The Proposed Tracking Algorithm

2.1   Superpixel Dataset Construction

To build the superpixel dataset, we oversegment Q training frames to generate N superpixels by algorithm in [11]. For each superpixel s_i $(1 \leq i \leq N)$, we extract four kinds of features including SIFT histogram, RGB histogram, location histogram and PHOG histogram. These histograms are concatenated to represent a superpixel similar as in [19].

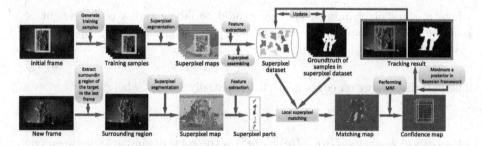

Fig. 1. Framework of the proposed method.

Let x_i denote the feature of s_i. We use y_i to represent its label, where $y_i \in \{0,1\}$ (0 and 1 represent the background and object labels respectively) and is determined by

$$y_i = \begin{cases} 1, & a_i \geqslant 95\,\% \\ 0, & otherwise \end{cases} \quad (1)$$

where a_i represents target area ratio of s_i. We then collect all the training superpixels into a database and obtain the superpixel database $D = \{s_i, x_i, y_i\}_{i=1}^N$.

2.2 Object-Background Confidence Map

For each new frame, we firstly extract the surrounding region[1] of the target in the last and then segment this region into superpixels with the same method in [11]. Let M be the number of its superpixels. For the ith superpixel s_j ($1 \leq j \leq M$), we are able to calculate its label cost by comparing its k-nearest neighbor $\mathcal{N}_k(j)$ in superpixel dataset D as follows

$$U(y_j = c | s_j) = 1 - \frac{\sum_{i \in \mathcal{N}_k(j), y_i = c} \mathcal{K}(x_j, x_i)}{\sum_{i \in \mathcal{N}_k(j)} \mathcal{K}(x_j, x_i)} \quad (2)$$

where x_j denotes the feature of s_j, $c \in \{0,1\}$ represents the label and $\mathcal{K}(x_j, x_i)$ is the intersection kernel between features x_j and x_i.

In this work, tracking is treated as separating object pixels from background pixels. In order to exploit the context relationship of object pixels and background pixels, we utilize MRF inference for contextual constraints. The energy function is given by

$$E(Y) = \sum_p U(y_p = c) + \lambda \sum_{pq} V(y_p = c, y_q = c') \quad (3)$$

---

[1] The surrounding region is a square area centered at the location of target X_t^c, and its side length is equal to $\lambda_s [X_s^t]^{\frac{1}{2}}$, where X_t^c represents the center location of target region X_t and X_t^s denotes its size. The parameter λ_s is a constant variable, which determines the size of this surrounding region.

where p, q are pixel indices, c, c' are candidate labels and λ is the weight of pairwise energy. The unary energy of one pixel is given by the superpixel it belongs to

$$U(y_p = c) = U(y_j = c|s_j), \ p \in s_j \tag{4}$$

The pairwise energy on edges is given by spatially variant label cost

$$V(y_p = c, y_q = c') = d(p, q) \cdot \mu(c, c') \tag{5}$$

where $d(p, q) = exp(-\|I(p) - I(q)\|^2/2\sigma^2)$ is the color dissimilarity between two adjacent pixels, and $\mu(c, c')$ is the penalty of assigning label c and c' to two adjacent pixels and defined by log-likelihood of label co-occurrence statistics

$$\mu(c, c') = -log[(P(c|c') + P(c'|c))/2] \times \sigma \tag{6}$$

Through this way, we can derive the labels of all pixels by performing MAP interference on $E(Y)$ with graph cut optimization in [4].

Taking into local context information of each superpixel into account, we adopt a simple yet effective feedback mechanism as in [19]. In the feedback process, we can obtain the pixel-wise classification likelihood of each pixel by

$$\ell(p, c) = \frac{1}{1 + exp(U(y_p = c))} \tag{7}$$

where $U(y_p = c)$ is the cost of assigning label c to pixel p in Eq. (4).

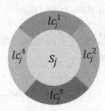

Fig. 2. Local context descriptor of superpixel.

For robust superpixel matching, we exploit the local context of each superpixel. For superpixel s_j, we divide its neighborhood into left, right, top, bottom four cells $\{lc_j^1, lc_j^2, lc_j^3, lc_j^4\}$ (see Fig. 2). For each cell lc_j^k ($1 \leq k \leq 4$), we compute its sparse context $h_j^k = [h_{j1}^k, h_{j2}^k]$ by

$$h_{ic}^k = \max_{p \in lc_i^k} \ell(p, c) \tag{8}$$

where $\ell(p, c)$ represents the pixel-wise classification likelihood obtained by Eq. (7). For superpixel s_i, we can obtain spatial context descriptor $h_j = [h_j^1; h_j^2; h_j^3; h_j^4]$. Thus we can classify the superpixels of the new frame by Eq. (2) with new feature $[x_j; h_j]$.

Through the above process, we are able to obtain the matching score $Score(j)$ for superpixel s_j by

$$Score(j) = \frac{U(y_j = 1|s_j) - U(y_j = 0|s_j)}{U(y_j = 1|s_j) + U(y_j = 0|s_j)} \tag{9}$$

and the confidence map C for each pixel on the entire current frame as follows. We assign every pixel whose label is object with 1, and every pixel whose label is background or outside the surrounding region with -1. Figure 3 shows the matching maps, confidence maps and tracking results of the target in video Iceskater by our method.

Iceskater ♯39   Iceskater ♯86   Iceskater ♯167   Iceskater ♯233

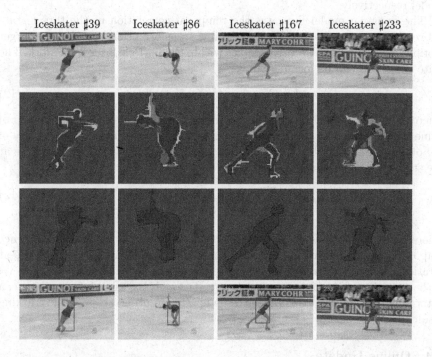

Fig. 3. Matching maps, confidence maps and tracking results on video Iceskater. First row: original images. Second row: matching maps of corresponding regions obtained by our local superpixel matching. Third row: confidence maps of corresponding regions derived by performing MRF on matching maps. Fourth row: the final tracking results of each frame (see details in Sect. 2.3).

2.3   Tracking Formulation

Our tracker is implemented within Bayesian framework. Given the observation set of targets $Z^t = \{z_1, z_2, \cdots, z_t\}$ up to the frame t, where z_τ ($\tau = 1, 2, \cdots, t$)

represents the observation of target in frame τ, we can obtain estimation $\widehat{X}_t$ by computing the maximum a posterior via

$$\widehat{X}_t = \underset{X_t^i}{\operatorname{argmax}} \ p(X_t^i|Y^t) \tag{10}$$

where $\widehat{X}_t$ denotes the ith sample at the state of X_t. The posterior probability $p(X_t^i|Z^t)$ can be obtained by the Bayesian theorem recursively via

$$p(X_t|Y^t) \propto p(z_t|X_t) \int p(X_t|X_{t-1})p(X_{t-1}|Z^{t-1})dX_{t-1} \tag{11}$$

where $p(X_t|X_{t-1})$ and $p(z_t|X_t)$ represent the dynamic model and observation model respectively.

The dynamic model indicates the temporal correlation of the target state between consecutive frames. We apply affine transformation to model the target motion between two consecutive frames within the particle filter framework. The state transition can be formulated as

$$p(X_t|X_{t-1}) = \mathcal{N}(X_t; X_{t-1}, \Psi) \tag{12}$$

where Ψ is a diagonal covariance matrix whose elements are the variance of affine parameters. The observation model $p(z_t|X_t)$ represents the probability of the observation z_t at state X_t. In this paper, the observation for i^{th} sample at the state of X_t is designed as in [18] by

$$p(z_t|X_t^i) \propto \sum_{(w,v)\in C_t^i} v_t^i(w,v) \times [S(X_t^i)/S(X_{t-1})] \tag{13}$$

where C_t^i is the confidence map of the ith candidate warped from confidence map of corresponding region, $v_t^i(w,v)$ denotes the confidence value of pixels at location (w,v), $S(X_t^i)$ represents the area size of the ith candidate and $S(X_{t-1})$ is the area size of the object in last frame. Through Bayesian inference, we can determine the candidate sample with the maximum observation as the tracking result.

2.4   Online Update

Before tracking, the target in the initial frame is manually labeled. The Q training samples utilized for constructing database are the same with the first frame and stored in a set T with fixed length L. Our strategy is to choose the latest good tracking result, add it into set T and remove the oldest element in T if T is full. In this way, when superpixel matching starts, the superpixel dataset can be effectively updated to adapt to the object appearance changes by the new set T.

Every H frames, we compute the occlusion coefficient O_t of the latest tracking result X_t by

$$O_t = 1 - \frac{\sum_{(w,v)\in C_t} v_t(w,v)/S(X_t)}{\sum_{(w,v)\in C_{t-1}} v_{t-1}(w,v)S(X_{t-1})} \tag{14}$$

When heavy occlusion happens, the occlusion coefficient O_t will be large, and thus it is unnecessary to add the tracking result into T. We set a threshold θ to determine whether the tracking result is added into T. If $O_t > \theta$, we skip this frame to avoid introducing noise into T. Otherwise, we add the tracking result into T and remove the oldest element from T if the number of elements in T is larger than L.

3 Experiments

We evaluate our tracker on eight challenging image sequences and compare it with seven state-of-the-art tracking methods. These algorithms are SPT tracking [18], CT tracking [20], SCM tracking [23], STC tracking [21], ASLA tracking [12], PCOM tracking [17], MTT tracking [22]. The proposed algorithm is implemented

Table 1. Average center location error (CLE) in pixel. The best and the second best results are shown in red and **blue** fonts.

Sequence	ASLA	CT	MTT	PCOM	SCM	STC	SPT	Ours
Bikeshow	182.7	82.2	190.0	135.1	193.2	148.4	**22.3**	6.8
David3	104.5	89.8	307.0	100.0	67.6	6.3	8.3	**8.1**
Gymnastics	**15.9**	24.7	100.0	102.1	16.5	17.7	25.3	11.9
Iceskater	21.6	45.3	86.9	125.6	144.7	130.1	**17.6**	12.7
Mottocross2	4.5	18.8	32.5	86.8	10.9	**4.6**	19.2	10.0
Skater	9.3	14.3	**7.6**	88.5	12.6	15.5	14.3	7.3
Skater2	28.4	41.0	76.3	107.6	88.5	28.4	**24.2**	9.1
Transformer	43.1	52.8	42.9	104.6	37.5	44.2	**15.6**	10.1
Average	51.3	46.1	105.4	106.3	71.4	49.4	**18.4**	9.5

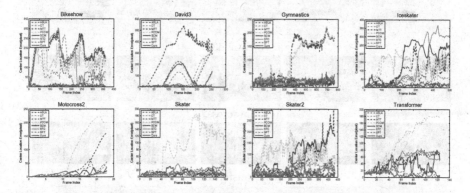

Fig. 4. Quantitative evaluation in terms of center location error in pixel. The proposed method is compared with seven state-of-the-art algorithms on eight challenging test sequences.

in MATLAB and runs at 1.5 frames per second on a 3.2 GHz Intel E3-1225 v3 Core PC with 8 GB memory. The parameters of the proposed tracker are fixed in all experiments. The number of neighbors k in Eq. (2) is set to 7. The number of particles in Bayesian framework is 300 to 600. The λ_s is set to 1.5. The number of initial training samples is 5. The length L of set T is fixed to 10, and H is set to 5. The threshold θ is 0.8.

3.1   Quantitative Comparison

We evaluate the above mentioned trackers by center location error (CLE) in pixels, and the comparing results are shown in Table 1. Figure 4 shows the center location error of utilized trackers on eight test sequences. Overall, the proposed tracker outperforms other state-of-the-art algorithms.

3.2   Qualitative Comparison

Deformation: Deformation is a disaster for a tracker because it is able to cause heavy appearance variations. Figure 5(a) and (d) demonstrate the tracking results in the presence of deformation. The proposed tracker is able to robustly locate the non-rigid object in these sequences we represent the object appearance with a robust superpixel database. With the help of update scheme, the

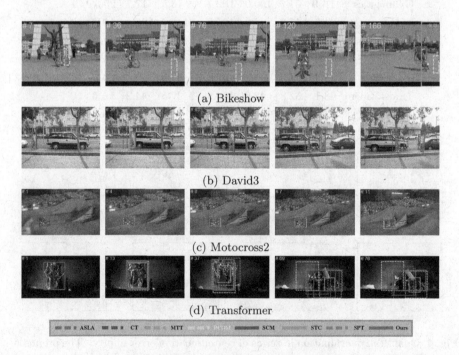

(a) Bikeshow

(b) David3

(c) Motocross2

(d) Transformer

Fig. 5. Screenshots of some sample tracking results.

superpixel database can be updated to adapt to object appearance changes, and thus our tracker is robust to deformation.

Occlusion: Occlusion is a common problem in visual tracking. Figure 5(b) shows the performance of our tracker in the presence of occlusion. When occlusion happens, object appearance will change because part of target is occluded. However, our tracker is still able to locate the object because our tracker can utilize the unoccluded part of the target for tracking with local superpixel matching.

Rotation: Figure 5(c) shows sampled experimental results of target with drastic rotation. In these sequence, the object suffers from not only rotation but also scale variation. Our methods demonstrates good performance to track the target owing to our appearance model. When rotation happens, the structure of object appearance will change. Nevertheless, our superpixel database can ignore this structure changes and distinguish the object superpixels from background superpixels via our matching method.

4 Conclusion

In this paper, we propose a novel method for object tracking, especially for the targets involved with non-rigid and articulated motions. This approach mainly consists of three stages. In the first stage, a superpixel database is constructed to represent the appearance of object. In the second stage, when a new frame arrives, it is firstly segmented into superpixels. Then we compute its confidence via superpixel matching and MRF. Taking context information into account, we utilize MRF to further improve the accuracy of confidence map. In addition, the local context information is incorporated through a feedback to refine superpixel matching. In the last stage, visual tracking is achieved through finding the best candidate by maximum a posterior estimate based on the confidence map. Experiments evidence the effectiveness of our method.

Acknowledgement. This work was primarily supported by Foundation Research Funds for the Central Universities (Program No. 2662016PY008 and Program No. 2662014PY052).

References

1. Adam, A., Rivlin, E., Shimshoni, I.: Robust fragments based tracking using the integral histogram. In: IEEE Conference on Computer Vision and Pattern Recognition (CVPR), pp. 798–805 (2006)
2. Avidan, S.: Ensemble tracking. IEEE Trans. Pattern Anal. Mach. Intell. (TPAMI) **29**(2), 261–271 (2007)
3. Babenko, B., Yang, M.-H., Belongie, S.: Robust object tracking with online multiple instance learning. IEEE Trans. Pattern Anal. Mach. Intell. (TPAMI) **33**(8), 1619–1632 (2011)
4. Boykov, Y., Veksler, O., Zabih, R.: Fast approximate energy minimization via graph cuts. IEEE Trans. Pattern Anal. Mach. Intell. (TPAMI) **23**(11), 1222–1239 (2001)

5. Fan, H., Xiang, J.: Robust visual tracking with multitask joint dictionary learning. IEEE Trans. Circ. Syst. Video Technol. **PP**, 1 (2016)
6. Fan, H., Xiang, J., Zhao, L.: Robust visual tracking via bag of superpixels. Multimedia Tools Appl. **75**, 8781 (2015)
7. Fan, H., Xiang, J., Liao, H., Du, X.: Robust tracking based on local structural cell graph. J. Vis. Commun. Image Represent. **31**, 54–63 (2015)
8. Fan, H., Xiang, J., Ni, F.: Multilayer feature combination for visual tracking. In: Asian Conference on Pattern Recognition (ACPR), pp. 589–593 (2015)
9. Fan, H., Xiang, J.: Patch-based visual tracking with two-stage multiple Kernel learning. In: Zhang, Y.-J. (ed.) ICIG 2015. LNCS, vol. 9219, pp. 20–33. Springer, Heidelberg (2015). doi:10.1007/978-3-319-21969-1_3
10. Fan, H., Xiang, J., Xu, J., Liao, H.: Part-based visual tracking via online weighted P-N learning. Sci. World J. (2014)
11. Felzenszwalb, P.F., Huttenlocher, D.P.: Efficient graph based image segmentation. Int. J. Comput. Vis. (IJCV) **59**(2), 167–181 (2004)
12. Jia, X., Lu, H., Yang, M.-H.: Visual tracking via adaptive structural local sparse appearance model. In: IEEE Conference on Computer Vision and Pattern Recognition (CVPR), pp. 1822–1829 (2012)
13. Kalal, Z., Mikolajczyk, K., Matas, J.: Tracking-learning-detection. IEEE Transactions on Pattern Analysis and Machine Intelligence (TPAMI) **34**(7), 1409–1422 (2012)
14. Liang, P., Blasch, E., Ling, H.: Encoding color information for visual tracking: algorithms and benchmark. IEEE Trans. Image Process. (TIP) **24**(12), 5630–5644 (2015)
15. Mei, X., Ling, H.: Robust visual tracking and vehicle classification via sparse representation. IEEE Trans. Pattern Anal. Mach. Intell. (TPAMI) **33**(11), 2259–2272 (2011)
16. Ross, D.A., Lim, J., Lin, R.S., Yang, M.-H.: Incremental learning for robust visual tracking. Int. J. Comput. Vis. (IJCV) **77**(1), 125–141 (2008)
17. Wang, D., Lu, H.: Visual tracking via probability continuous outlier model. In: IEEE Conference on Computer Vision and Pattern Recognition (CVPR), pp. 3478–3485 (2014)
18. Yang, F., Lu, H., Yang, M.-H.: Robust superpixel tracking. IEEE Trans. Image Process. (TIP) **23**(4), 1639–1651 (2014)
19. Yang, J., Price, B., Cohen, S., Yang, M.-H.: Context driven scene parsing with attention to rare classes. In: IEEE Conference on Computer Vision and Pattern Recognition (CVPR), pp. 3294–3301 (2014)
20. Zhang, K., Zhang, L., Yang, M.-H.: Fast compressive tracking. IEEE Trans. Pattern Anal. Mach. Intell. (TPAMI) **36**(10), 2002–2015 (2014)
21. Zhang, K., Zhang, L., Liu, Q., Zhang, D., Yang, M.-H.: Fast visual tracking via dense spatio-temporal context learning. In: Fleet, D., Pajdla, T., Schiele, B., Tuytelaars, T. (eds.) ECCV 2014. LNCS, vol. 8693, pp. 127–141. Springer, Heidelberg (2014). doi:10.1007/978-3-319-10602-1_9
22. Zhang, T., Ghanem, B., Liu, S., Ahuja, N.: Robust visual tracking via structured multi-task sparse learning. Int. J. Comput. Vis. (IJCV) **101**, 367–383 (2013)
23. Zhong, W., Lu, H., Yang, M.-H.: Robust object tracking via sparsity-based collaborative model. In: IEEE Conference on Computer Vision and Pattern Recognition (CVPR), pp. 1838–1845 (2012)

Saliency Detection Combining Multi-layer Integration Algorithm with Background Prior and Energy Function

Chenxing Xia and Hanling Zhang[⊠]

College of Information Science and Engineering,
Hunan University, Changsha 410000, China
{starry, jt_hlzhang}@hnu.edu.cn

Abstract. In this paper, we propose an improved mechanism for saliency detection. Firstly, based on a neoteric background prior selecting four corners of an image as background, color and spatial contrast with each super-pixel are being used to obtain a coarse map. Then, we put the Objectness labels as foreground prior based on part of information of the former map to construct another map. Further, an original energy function is applied to optimize both of them respectively and single-layer saliency map is formed by merging the above two maps. Finally, to settle the scale problem, we obtain our multi-layer saliency map by presenting an integration algorithm to take advantage of multiple saliency maps. Quantitative and qualitative experiments on three datasets demonstrate that our method performs favorably against the state-of-the-art algorithm.

Keywords: Corner · Objectness labels · Energy function · Multi-layer

1 Introduction

Saliency detection aimed at identifying the most important and conspicuous object regions in an image has attracted much attention in recent years. There are various applications for salient object detection, including image segmentation [1], object recognition [2], image compression [3], image retrieval [4], dominant color detection [5] and so on.

Recently, numerous bottom-up saliency detection methods have been proposed, which prefer to generate the saliency map by utilizing the boundary information. [8] uses the four boundaries of an image as background cues to get foreground queries via manifold ranking (MR). Generic object detection methods aim at generating the locations of all category independent objects in an image. We observe that generic object detection are closely related to saliency object segmentation. In [11], saliency is utilized as objectness measurement to generate object candidates. Apart From detecting salient objects in a single layer, salient object detection also has been extended to identifying common salient objects shared in multiple layers. [9] concludes six principles for effective saliency computation and fuse them into a single framework via combining with Bayesian framework. [10] proposes multi-layer Cellular Automata to

© Springer International Publishing AG 2016
E. Chen et al. (Eds.): PCM 2016, Part I, LNCS 9916, pp. 11–21, 2016.
DOI: 10.1007/978-3-319-48890-5_2

integrate multiple saliency maps into a better result under the Bayes framework. All of them achieve very good results demonstrating the effectivity of multi-layer in the accuracy of saliency detection.

2   Proposed Algorithm

In this section, we give the details about our model. To better capture intrinsic structure information and improve computational efficiency, an input image is over-segmented at M scales. At any scale m, an image is segmented into N small superpixels by the simple linear iterative clustering (SLIC) algorithm [7].

2.1   Contrast Background Saliency Map(CBSP)

The method of using four edges as background cannot deal well with the scene where some foreground noises may be in the border regions. It indicates that excessive using the edge information as background prior may result in the introduction of noise. Based on the observation that the probability of the case that the object appears at the corners is less than borders, we extract the superpixels along the four corners of an image as prior background regions. Figure 1 illustrates that this effects using corner prior are also pretty good as the same with boundary prior.

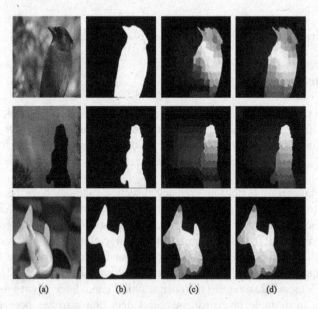

(a)   (b)   (c)   (d)

Fig. 1. Salient objects at different background prior. (a) Input image; (b) Ground truth; (c) Use boundary prior; (d) Use corner prior.

Our affinity between node i and node j is considered from the color and spatial characteristics. From the perspective of the color features, we define the affinity entry c_{ij} of node i to a certain node j as:

$$c_{ij} = \begin{cases} exp\left(-\frac{||c_i-c_j||}{2\sigma_1^2}\right) & j \in N(i) \, or \, i,j \in B \\ 0 & i = j \, or \, otherwise \end{cases} \tag{1}$$

where $||c_i - c_j||$ is the Euclidean Distance between the node i and j in CIELAB color space. σ_1 (here is 0.1) is a parameter controlling strength of the similarity. B denotes the set of background, $N(i)$ indicates the set of the direct neighboring nodes of superpixel i, as well as the direct neighbors of those neighboring nodes.

Similarly, from the perspective of the spacial features, we define the affinity entry s_{ij} of node i to a certain node j as:

$$s_{ij} = \begin{cases} exp\left(-\frac{||\gamma_i-\gamma_j||}{2\sigma_2^2}\right) & j \in N(i) \, or \, i,j \in B \\ 0 & i = j \, or \, withwise \end{cases} \tag{2}$$

where γ_i, γ_j are the coordinates of the superpixel i and j. σ_2 (here is 1.3) is a constant to control the strength of weight. Other abbreviations are same with Eq. 1.

Therefore, we define the affinity entry w_{ij} of node i to a certain node j as:

$$w_{ij} = \begin{cases} c_{ij} \times s_{ij} & j \in N(i) \, or \, i,j \in B \\ 0 & i = j \, or \, withwise \end{cases} \tag{3}$$

In order to normalize affinity matrix, a degree matrix $D = diag\{d_1,...,d_N\}$ is generated, where $d_i = \sum_j w_{ij}$. Finally, a row-normalized affinity matrix can be clearly calculated as follows: $G = D^{-1} \cdot W$.

It is too idealized that assuming the superpixels at the corners are possible background, because the salient object may connect with the image corner. To rectify this problem, we can define the saliency of a superpixel as its color and spacial contrasts to superpixels that on the four corners respectively. Let's take the left-up corner of the image as an example, we define its saliency value v_{lu} as:

$$v_{lu}(i) = \left(1-\frac{1}{n}\sum_j^n g_{ij}\right) \times \frac{1}{K_i}\sum_{p\in i} f(p) \tag{4}$$

Where g_{ij} is the affinity entry defined in G; n is the number of super-pixels on the left-up corner. Where K_i indicates the number of p pixels within region i. $f(p)$ is the value of p pixel. Hence, we can obtain four maps: v_{lu}, v_{ru}, v_{ld} and v_{rd} respectively with Eq. 4. Finally, we get CBSP by integrating the four maps according to the following equation:

$$v = v_{lu} \times v_{ru} \times v_{ld} \times v_{rd} \tag{5}$$

2.2 Objectness Foreground Saliency Map(OFSP)

As shown the middle row in Fig. 2(b), however, depending on the corner prior alone might lead to high saliency assignment to the background regions. This promotes me to use some foreground prior to improve the result. [12] proposes a Gaussian smoothing kernel of all sampling windowing to obtain the pixel-level objectness map $\widetilde{W}_p$ via combining over-lapping scores:

$$\widetilde{W}_p = \sum_{h=1}^{H} P_h \cdot \exp\left[-\left(\frac{(x_p - \rho_x)^2}{2\sigma_x^2} + \frac{(y_p - \rho_y)^2}{2\sigma_y^2}\right)\right] \tag{6}$$

The setting of the parameters can refer to [12]. Since saliency objects do not always appear at the image center as Fig. 3, the center-biased Gaussian model is not effectively and may include background pixels or miss the foreground regions. We use a new model W_p:

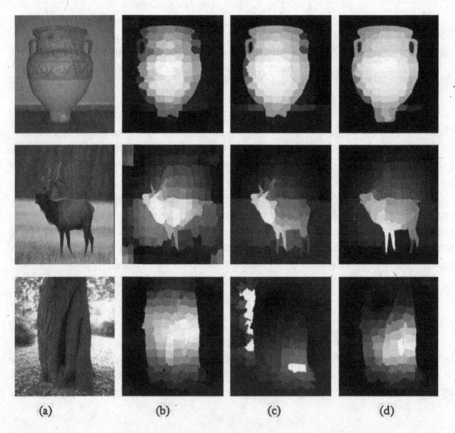

(a)   (b)   (c)   (d)

Fig. 2. Objectness integration. (a) Input image; (b) Corner prior map; (c) Objectness prior map; (d) Combine corner with objectness prior without using energy function.

$$W_p = \widetilde{W}_p * \frac{\sum_{x_p,y_p} lab_h(x_p,y_p) \times \upsilon(x_p,y_p)}{\sum_{x_p,y_p} lab_h(x_p,y_p) + \theta} \tag{7}$$

where $lab_h(x_p,y_p) = 1$ indicates that the pixel located at (x_p,y_p) of the input image belongs to the h-th object candidate, and $lab_h(x_p,y_p) = 0$ otherwise; $(x_p,y_p) \in [0,1]$ represents the CBSP value of pixel. In order to prevent the denominator is zero, we add a constant θ (here is 1) in the denominator. Based on the pixel-level objectness map $W(p)$, we generate the region-level objectness map $W(i)$ which is the average of pixels' objectness values within a region: $W(i) = \frac{1}{n_i}\sum_{p \in i} f(p)$.

Based on the fact that high values of region-level objectness score calculated by $W(i)$ can better indicate foreground areas. Figure 2(c) shows the saliency maps based on Objectness prior alone. The top and middle images effectively inhibit high values of the background saliency while the result of the bottom image is bad in some scenarios. It indicates that it is a good choice to combine corner prior map with objectness prior map.

2.3 Single-Layer Saliency Map(SLSP)

Since CBSP and OFSP are mingled with some noise, we optimize them with energy function respectively before incorporation. We binary the two maps with an adaptive threshold $th = mean(sal)$ [8], T_i denotes a certain node i, $T_i = 1$ when $sal_i >= th$, otherwise $T_i = 0$. Let S_i be the saliency value of the superpixel i, the normalized ζ_i denotes the saliency value of each super-pixel in the above maps. Our energy function is thus defined as:

$$\operatorname{argmin}_s \frac{1}{2}\left\{\sum_{i=1}^{N}[-\log(1-\zeta_i)]\cdot(s_i-1)^2 + \sum_{i=1}^{N}(1-T_i)\cdot s_i^2 + \sum_{i,j} w_{ij}\cdot(s_i-s_j)^2\right\} \tag{8}$$

The three terms define costs from different constraints. The first term encourages a superpixel i with large value ζ_i which is more likely to be foreground to take a large value s_i (close to 1). Similarly, the second term encourages a node i with small value T_i which is more likely to be background to take a small value s_i (close to 0). The last smoothness term encourages continuous saliency values. It indicates that a good saliency map should have similar saliency value between nearby super-pixels.

Fig. 3. Effect of different Gaussian smoothing kernel. (a) Input; (b) With $\widetilde{W}_p$; (c) With W_p.

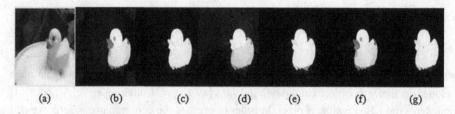

(a)   (b)   (c)   (d)   (e)   (f)   (g)

Fig. 4. Optimization and Integration. (a) Input image; (b) Corner prior map without optimization; (c) Corner prior map after optimization; (d) Objectness prior map without optimization; (e) Objectness prior map after optimization; (f) Integrate map(b) and map(d); (g) Integrate map(c) and map(e).

Hence, we obtain two optimized saliency maps. Both of the maps are complementary to each other. The CBSP can highlight the object more uniformly while the OFSP can better suppress the background noise. Therefore, we propose an integration mechanism to incorporate them into a unified formula:

$$\mathrm{SLSP} = \mathrm{CBSP} \cdot (1 - exp^{\eta \cdot OFSP}) \tag{9}$$

where η is a balancing factor between them which is empirically set to 6 in our experiments. Figure 4(g) shows the effect of integration of two maps which are optimized by energy function. We observe that our optimization scheme is better than without optimization operation in eliminating noise and suppressing background.

2.4   Multi-Layer Saliency Map (MLSP)

Most existing methods using single scale is not always the most optimal for different images which may result in the loss of many of the structural information. To deal with the scale problem, we generate multi-layer of superpixels with different granularities, where N = 100, 150, 200, 250, 300 respectively. We represent the saliency map at each scale as $\{SLSP^m\}$.

At first, we calculate the similarity SM_{ij} between two maps. The calculation of similarity is at the pixel-level, that is, the similarity plus 1 when the corresponding coordinates have the same value of pixel, and then the cumulative result is normalized to [0,1], namely: $SM_{ij} = \frac{\sum_{x,y} SM_{ij}^{xy}}{m \times n}$. Where x, y denote the coordinates of pixel p, x, y indicate two saliency maps. m, n are two parameters of the image size.

Because we choose five different scales, so we can get a similar matrix of 5x5 $[SM_{ij}]_{5 \times 5}$. Then what we will do is to find out the map m which is the biggest difference with others. So, an judgment vector $y = [y_1, \ldots, y_M]^T$ comes into being, where $y_m = \frac{1}{M} \sum_n SM_{mn}$. We find out the subscript m = index[min(y)]. Hence, we define our finally saliency map as:

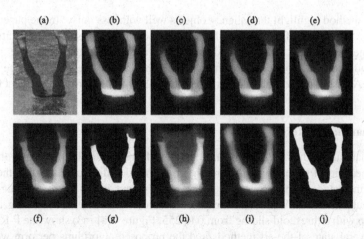

Fig. 5. Effect of our algorithm via multi-layer integration. (a) Input image; (b–f) Saliency maps with different superpixel N = 100, 150, 200, 250, 300; (g) SCA algorithm [10]; (h) MS algorithm [9]; (i) Ours; (j) Ground truth.

$$\text{MLSP} = \sum_{m=1}^{M} \widetilde{y}_m \cdot \text{SLSP}^m \qquad (10)$$

where vector $\widetilde{y}_m$ is same with vector except from the place $\widetilde{y}_m = 1$. We take full advantage of the characteristics of the five maps by increasing the weight of the least similar map. Finally, we further refine the saliency map with the guided filter [13]. Figure 5(g–i) show the saliency map with different algorithm via the way of integration. Figure 5(g–h) show that these algorithms lose a lot of information in fusion while Fig. 5(i) illustrates that our algorithm is of better robustness than other methods.

3 Experimental Results

We evaluate the proposed method on three datasets: MSRA10 K [21], SED1 [20], and ASD [1]. MSRA10 K contains 10,000 randomly-chosen images from the MSRA dataset. SED1 contains 100 images of a single salient object annotated manually by three users. ASD consists of 1000 images labeled with pixel-wise ground truth.

We compare our method with 8 state-of-the-art methods including the GS [15], SF [16], CP [17], PCA [18], CA [1], MB [19], MC [6], LPS [12] on the MSRA10 K, ASD and SED1 datasets.

3.1 Qualitative Results

We present some results of saliency maps generated by eight methods for qualitative comparison in Fig. 6. The result shows that the saliency maps generated by the proposed method highlight the saliency objects well with less noisy. In the paper, while we choose the corner information as the background, the result is good. In addition, we utilize objectness labels as foreground prior to generate foreground map. The detected foreground and background in our maps are smooth due to the import of the energy function. At last, the novel multi-layer integration algorithm improves the effect further.

3.2   Quantitative Results

We evaluate all methods by precision, recall and F-measure. The precious value represents the ratio of salient pixels correctly in all the identified pixels, while the recall value is indicated as the proportion of detected salient pixels corresponding to the ground-truth numbers. We obtain the precision-recall curves with binarizing the saliency map with a threshold sliding from 0 to 255. Figure 7(a1–a3) show the P-R curves where several state-of-the-art methods and the proposed algorithms perform well.

In addition, we measure the quality of the saliency maps using the F-Measure. The average precision and recall values are computed based on the generated binary masks and the ground truth while the F-Measure is computed by:

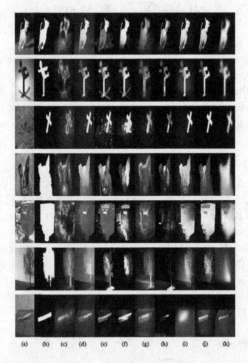

(a)   (b)   (c)   (d)   (e)   (f)   (g)   (h)   (i)   (j)   (k)

Fig. 6. Comparisons of saliency maps. (a) Input image; (b) Ground truth; (c) CA; (d) CP; (e) GS; (f) MB; (g) PCA; (h) SF; (i) MC; (j) LPS; (k) Ours.

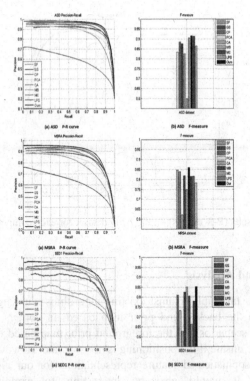

Fig. 7. Evaluation results on different datasets. From top to down: ASD, MSRA, SED1. From left to right: the P-R curves and F-measure.

$$F_\beta = \frac{(1+\beta^2) \cdot precision \cdot recall}{\beta^2 \cdot precision + recall} \qquad (11)$$

where we see $\beta^2 = 0.3$ to emphasize the precision [14]. Figure 7(b1–b3) show the F-Measure values of the evaluated methods on the three datasets. Overall, the proposed algorithms perform well.

3.3   Analysis of Designs Options

To demonstrate the effectiveness of our proposed algorithm, we test results on the standards dataset ASD. P-R curves in Fig. 8 show that: (1) the background-based maps and foreground-based maps are already satisfying; (2) Single-layer saliency map can greatly improve the precision of both of them; (3) Results integrated by Multi-layer algorithm are better. We note that each component more or less makes contributions to the final performance of the proposed method. These results also prove that it is all the components working together that lead to the best performance.

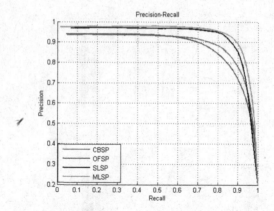

Fig. 8. Evaluation results (P-R curves) on the ASD dataset for each component of the proposed method.

3.4   Limitation and Analysis

Our model performs favorably against existing algorithms with higher precision and recall. However, as the background prior map based on corners feathers which is insufficient in some scenarios and the foreground prior map based on the locations of object which may be unsafe if the positioning is not accurate. However, we believe that investigating more sophisticated feature representations for our algorithm would be greatly beneficial. It would also be interesting to exploit top-down and category-independent semantic information to enhance the current results. We will leave these two directions as the starting point of our future research.

4   Conclusion

In this proposed a multi-layer integration for saliency detection based on selective background and objectness label. Firstly, based on a neoteric selective corner as background prior, we use color and spatial contrast with each superpixel to obtain CBSP. Then, we put the investigative object to prospect which employs the Objectness labels as foreground prior to construct OFSP. Taking into account the respective insufficient, an original energy function is applied to optimize both of them respectively, and SLSP is formed by merging the above twos. Finally, to deal with the scale problem, we generate multi-layer of superpixels with different granularities and present an integration algorithm to take advantage of MLSP. Experimental results demonstrate the effectiveness of our model. Our method achieves better performance in terms of different evaluation metrics, compared with the state-of-arts on three benchmark image datasets.

Acknowledgement. This work was supported by the Key Science and Technology Planning Project of Hunan Province, China (2014GK2007).

References

1. Goferman, S., Zelnik-Manor, L., Tal, A.: Context-aware saliency detection. In: CVPR, pp. 2376–2383 (2010)
2. Rutishauser, U., Walther, D., Koch, C., Perona, P.: Is bottom-up attention useful for object recognition? In: CVPR, pp. 37–44 (2004)
3. Itti, L.: Automatic foveation for video compression using a neurobiological model of visual attention. IEEE Trans. Image Process. 13, 1304–1318 (2004)
4. Chen, T., Cheng, M., Tan, P., Shamir, A., Hu, S.: Sketch2photo: internet image montage. ACM Trans. Graph. 28, 1–10 (2009). 124
5. Wang, P., Zhang, D., Wang, J., Wu, Z., Hua, X.-S., Li, S.: Color filter for image search. In: Proceedings of ACM Multimedia, pp. 1327–1328 (2012)
6. Jiang, B., Zhang, L., Lu, H., Yang, M., Yang, C.: Saliency detection via absorbing Markov chain. In: ICCV, pp. 1665–1672 (2013)
7. Achanta, R., Shaji, A., Smith, K., Lucchi, A., Fua, P., Süsstrunk, S.: SLIC Superpixels, Technical report (2010)
8. Yang, C., Zhang, L., Lu, H., Ruan, X., Yang, M.-H.: Saliency detection via graph-based manifold ranking. In: CVPR, pp. 3166–3173 (2013)
9. Tong, N., Lu, H., Zhang, L., Ruan, X.: Saliency detection with multi-scale superpixels. IEEE Sig. Process. Lett. 21, 1035–1039 (2014)
10. Yao, Q., Lu, H., Xu, Y., He, W.: Saliency detection via cellular automata. In: CVPR, pp. 110–119 (2015)
11. Alexe, B., Deselaers, T., Ferrari, V.: Measuring the objectness of image windows. In: PAMI, pp. 2189–2202 (2012)
12. Li, H., Lu, H., Lin, Z., Shen, X., Price, B.: Inner and inter label propagation: salient object detection in the wild. IEEE Trans. Image Process. 24, 3176–3186 (2015)
13. He, K., Sun, J., Tang, X.: Guided image filtering. In: Daniilidis, K., Maragos, P., Paragios, N. (eds.) ECCV 2010. LNCS, vol. 6311, pp. 1–14. Springer, Heidelberg (2010). doi:10.1007/978-3-642-15549-9_1
14. Achanta, R., Hemami, S., Estrada, F., Susstrunk, S.: Frequency tuned salient region detection. In: CVPR, pp. 1597–1604 (2009)
15. Wei, Y., Wen, F., Zhu, W., Sun, J.: Geodesic saliency using background priors. In: Fitzgibbon, A., Lazebnik, S., Perona, P., Sato, Y., Schmid, C. (eds.) ECCV 2012. LNCS, vol. 7574, pp. 29–42. Springer, Heidelberg (2012). doi:10.1007/978-3-642-33712-3_3
16. Perazzi, F., Krahenbuhl, P., Pritch, Y., Hornung, A.: Saliency filters: contrast based filtering for salient region detection. In: CVPR, pp. 733–740 (2012)
17. Yang, C., Zhang, L.H., Lu, H.C.: Graph-regularized saliency detection with convex-hull-based center prior. IEEE Sig. Process. Lett. 20, 1608–1623 (2013)
18. Margolin, R., Tal, A., Zelnik-Manor, L.: What makes a patch distinct? In: CVPR, pp. 1139–1146 (2013)
19. Zhang, J., Sclaro, S., Lin, Z., Shen, X., Price, B., Mch, R.: Minimum barrier salient object detection at 80 FPS. In: ICCV (2015)
20. Alpert, S., Galun, M., Basri, R., Brandt, A.: Image segmentation by probabilistic bottom-up aggregation and cue integration. In: CVPR, pp. 315–327 (2012)
21. Cheng, M., Zhang, G., Mitra, N.J., Huang, X., Hu, S.-M.: Global contrast based salient region detection. In: CVPR, pp. 409–416 (2011)

Facial Landmark Localization by Part-Aware Deep Convolutional Network

Keke He and Xiangyang Xue[✉]

Shanghai Key Lab of Intelligent Information Processing, School of Computer Science,
Fudan University, Shanghai, China
{kkhe15,xyxue}@fudan.edu.cn

Abstract. Facial landmark localization is a very challenging research task. The localization accuracy of landmarks on separate facial parts differ greatly due to texture and shape, however most existing methods fail to consider the part location of landmarks. To solve this problem, we propose a novel end-to-end regression framework using deep convolutional neural network (CNN). Our deep architecture first encodes the image into feature maps shared by all the landmarks. Then, these features are sent into two independent sub-network modules to regress contour landmarks and inner landmarks, respectively. Extensive evaluations conducted on 300-W benchmark dataset demonstrate the proposed deep framework achieves state-of-the-art results.

Keywords: Facial landmark localization · Deep learning

1 Introduction

Facial landmark localization is to automatically localize the facial key points including eyes, mouth, nose and other points on the face cheek. Due to its relevance to many facial analysis tasks like face recognition, face attribute analysis [10], 3D face modeling and etc., facial landmark localization has attracted increasing interests in the past years.

However, in an uncontrolled setting, face is likely to have large out-of-plane tilting, occlusion, illumination and expression variations. Facial landmark localization remains a challenging problem.

In general, existing methods to locate the facial landmarks can be divided into three categories: the first category is the ASM [6] and AAM [5] based methods, which fit a generative model by global facial appearance. However, these methods require expensive iterative steps and rely on good initializations. The mean shape is often used as the initialization, which may be far from the target position and hence inaccurate.

The second category is cascade regression based methods. The cascade regression framework has been proposed in recent works [17], which tries to estimate the facial landmark positions by a sequence of regression models. These methods obtain the coarse location first, and the following steps are to refine the initial

© Springer International Publishing AG 2016
E. Chen et al. (Eds.): PCM 2016, Part I, LNCS 9916, pp. 22–31, 2016.
DOI: 10.1007/978-3-319-48890-5_3

estimate, yielding more accurate results. Sun [13] proposed three-level cascaded deep convolutional networks. Zhou [19] designed a four-level coarse-to-fine network cascade to spread the network complexity and training burden of traditional convolutional networks. However these methods need to train individual systems for each group of the landmarks, the computational burden grows proportional to the group numbers and cascade levels. For example, this cascaded CNN method [13] needs to train 23 individual CNN networks.

Recently, a new framework based on multi-tasking has been proposed. The multi-task framework leverages other prior facial information like pose to assist landmark localization. Zhang [18] showed that learning the facial landmark localization task together with some correlated tasks, e.g., smile estimation would be beneficial. Yang [16] showed prior 3D head pose information will improve facial landmark localization accuracy. However these methods require auxiliary labels beyond landmarks and ignore the fact that landmarks on different facial parts have unbalanced localization difficulties. For instance, the detection of a mouth corner would be easy because there is abundant local information to capture. In contrast, the exact position of a landmark on the cheek is difficult to decide. As a consequence, it would be hard to optimize all the landmarks just in a single stage.

In this paper, we propose a novel end-to-end regression structure using deep convolutional neural network (CNN). Contrary to others, our method does not involve multiple individual models or require auxiliary labels. More importantly, the framework treats landmarks on different facial part differently which helps to learn discriminative features.

Our deep architecture first encodes the image into the feature maps shared by all the landmarks. Then, these shared features are sent into two individual sub-network modules to regress contour part landmarks and inner part landmarks respectively. The proposed method is called Part-Aware Convolutional Neural Network (PA-CNN).

To sum up, our main contributions are four-fold:

(1) We propose a novel end-to-end regression CNN model for facial landmark localization by incorporating a contour landmark sub-network and an inner landmark sub-network into a unified architecture.

(2) We clarify that all the landmarks sharing low level convolutional features and being independent in the latter layers can improve the accuracy and robustness.

(3) We demonstrate what the sub-network learns by visualizing intermediate layer activations.

(4) Finally, we show that the proposed network achieves state-of-the-art result on the 300-W [12] benchmark.

2   The Proposed Method

We will demonstrate our method in this section, describe the method in detail in Sect. 2.1 and analyze how to optimize our method in Sect. 2.2.

2.1   Architecture of PA-CNN

The proposed Part-Aware CNN (PA-CNN) framework integrates a contour landmark sub-network and an inner landmark sub-network, which handles the landmarks on different facial parts. Figure 1 illustrates the architecture of PA-CNN
in detail. We divide the total 68 landmarks into 2 categories because of the difference in texture and shape. The inner landmark denotes the 51 landmarks for
eyebrows, eyes, nose and mouth. The contour landmark is other 17 landmarks
on the face contour.

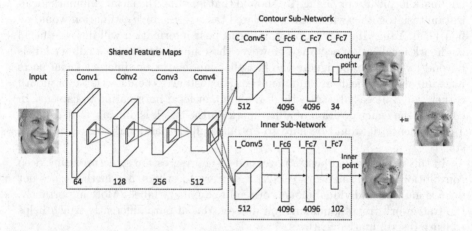

Fig. 1. PA-CNN network structure. This network structure uses cropped face detection
color image as input. After four shared convolutional layers, the network branches
into two sub-networks to localize contour landmarks and inner landmarks respectively.
Those sub-networks contain one convolutional layer and three fully connected layers.

The PA-CNN uses cropped face color image as input, then following 4 convolutional layers and 2 pooling layers extract feature maps. In these stages, all the
landmarks share the same weights. We have two concerns in designing bottom
sharing convolutional layers. First, all the landmarks can incorporate general
characteristics. By sharing input image and several convolutional layers, the
context over the face can be utilized to locate each landmark. At the same time,
all landmarks are implicitly encoded the geometric constraints. Second, sharing
bottom layers makes our model time efficiency. In the early stage of the network,
each layer extracts low level features. These features can be shared all across the
face. If we use individual models, one for predicting 17 contour landmarks and
another for predicting 51 inner landmarks, similar convolution modules need to
densely convolve the entire image twice, it would be very time consuming.

After shared layers, the proposed network branches into two sub-networks.
Each of the sub-networks takes the feature maps of the last shared convolutional
layer as input, then through one convolutional layer and two 4096 dimension
fully connected layers. For the contour landmark sub-network, the dimension of

the last fully connected layer is 34 because contour sub-network produces 17 landmarks and each landmark has x, y coordinates. The dimension of inner sub-network's last layer is calculated in the same way. The main concern of designing sub-networks is to impose our model to be specialized for specific landmarks. As inner landmarks and contour landmarks have unbalanced localization difficulties, learning to detect contour landmarks and inner landmarks respectively makes our model concentrate on the corresponding parts on the face. The integration of two sub-networks enables our PA-CNN to capture unique characteristics of landmarks. Later experiments in Sect. 3.3 will show this independence and share strategy is superior to optimal all landmarks in a single network stage. Finally, the outputs from the two sub-networks are combined to obtain the final result for each face.

2.2 Optimization

Let $x_i, y_i \in R$ be the x, y-coordinates of the i th facial landmark in an image I. Then the vector $[x_1, y_1, ..., x_N, y_N]^T$ denotes the coordinates of all the N facial landmarks in I, we take the vector P as the estimated landmarks and G as the ground truth landmarks. We define the landmark localization error as: $E = ||P - G||^2$. The predicted landmarks can be defined as

$$P = f(I; w) \tag{1}$$

f represents no-linear function, I donates the input image and w is the network weights. P can be calculated by network forward propagation. Finally, in a training batch, the network error can be represented as

$$E = \underset{w}{\mathrm{argmin}} \frac{1}{2} \sum_{i=1}^{N} ||f(I_i; w) - G_i||^2 \tag{2}$$

N donates the batch size, we set 70 in the training stage. The goal is to learn the optimal parameter w to minimize the loss function E by the training samples. According to the classical back propagate algorithm. For the exclusive layers like $conv5, fc1, fc2$, the weights are updated by the partial derivatives of loss with respect to weights $\Delta w = -r\frac{\partial E}{\partial w}$, r is the learning rate which controls the weight updating scale. For instance, the contour sub-network's $conv5$ layer can be updated by $\Delta w_{conv5} = -r\frac{\partial E_{con}}{\partial w_{conv5}}$, E_{con} is the loss of contour sub-network. The parameters in sub-network layers are only related to the sub-network loss. For the sharing layers like $conv1, ..., conv4$, the contour sub-network loss and the inner sub-network loss are back propagate together, can be represented as

$$\Delta w = -r\frac{\partial E_{con}}{\partial w} - \lambda * r\frac{\partial E_{inn}}{\partial w} \tag{3}$$

where E_{con} is the loss of contour sub-network, E_{inn} is the loss of inner sub-network, λ is the weight parameter to balance contour sub-network loss and inner sub-network loss, we choose 2 for our experiments.

3 Experiments

We conduct experiments on the 300-W dataset [12]. We will introduce this dataset in Sect. 3.1, describe the training detail in Sect. 3.2, and analyze the experiment results in Sects. 3.3, 3.4, 3.5 and 3.6.

3.1 Datasets

300-W is short for 300 Faces in-the-Wild [12]. It's a commonly used benchmark for facial landmark localization problem. It is created from existing datasets, including LFPW [1], AFW [20], Helen [9] and a new dataset called IBUG. Each image has been densely annotated with 68 landmarks. Our training set consists of AFW, the training sets of LFPW and the training sets of Helen, with 3148 images in total. Our testing set consists of IBUG, the testing sets of LFPW and the testing set of Helen, with 689 images in total. IBUG subset is extremely challenging because its images have large variations in face pose, expression and illumination. The IBUG is called Challenging, testing sets of LFPW and the testing set of Helen are called Common, and all the 689 images are called Fullset.

Data augmentation. We train our models only using the data from the training data without external sources. We employ two distinct forms of data augmentation to enlarge the dataset. The first form of data augmentation is image rotations. We do random rotation on images with angles range in $(-5°, 5°)$, $(-10°, 10°)$, $(-15°, 15°)$. The second form of data augmentation is random translation to right, left, up, down ranging in (-0.05, 0.05), which is a proportion of bounding box height or width. Finally, we enlarge the training data to 39561 images.

Evaluation. We evaluate the alignment accuracy by the popular mean error. The mean error is measured by the distances between the predicted landmarks and the ground truths, normalized by the inter-pupil distance, which can be represented as

$$err = \frac{1}{N} \sum_{i=1}^{N} \frac{\frac{1}{M} \sum_{j=1}^{M} |p_{i,j} - g_{i,j}|_2}{|l_i - r_i|_2} \tag{4}$$

where N is the total test image number, M is the landmark number, p is the predicted landmark position, g is the ground truth landmark position. l_i, r_i are the left eye position and right eye position of i th image.

3.2 Implementation Detail

We implement the proposed method based on the open source Caffe [7] framework. We first crop the image using the bounding box with 0.05 W padding on all sides (top, bottom, left, right), where W is the width of the bounding box. Then we resize the cropped image to 224 × 224.

We use the pre-trained VGG-S [4] model to initialize our network. The first four convolutional layers of the VGG-S network are used to initialize four shared convolutional layers. These shared layers are designed to produce feature maps from the entire input image. The rest layers of the VGG-S network are used to initialize both the contour sub-network and the inner sub-network. Our framework is learnt in an end-to-end way. We set min-batch size 70, the weight decay parameter 0.0001 and training learning rate 0.0001. We train our models by stochastic gradient descent with 0.9 momentum. Training continues until converge.

3.3 Performance Analysis

We compare our PA-CNN with two distinct network structures. One outputs all the landmarks in the last layer, named as One-CNN. Another uses individual network for contour and inner landmarks, named as Two-CNN. Figure 2 shows the network detailed structures.

Accuracy. Table 1 shows the localization error of contour landmarks and inner landmarks. PA-CNN has performance improvements on both two kinds of landmarks comparing to One-CNN, which shows sub-network helps to learn discriminative features. PA-CNN is also comparable to Two-CNN, which demonstrates sharing several convolutional layers will not hurt accuracy but help to capture general features.

Efficiency. Table 2 lists the testing time of each method. By sharing several convolution layers, PA-CNN is faster than Two-CNN.

Figure 3 shows the error curve of PA-CNN. Our PA-CNN which concentrates on different parts of the facial landmarks and does not involve multiple individual networks is both accurate and efficient.

(a)   (b)

Fig. 2. Other two network structures. (a). Left is One-CNN structure. (b). Right is Two-CNN structure.

Table 1. Error of Landmarks on Fullset.

Methods	Contour Error($\times 10^{-2}$)	Inner Error($\times 10^{-2}$)
One-CNN	9.02	5.04
Two-CNN	8.95	4.81
PA-CNN	**8.85**	**4.79**

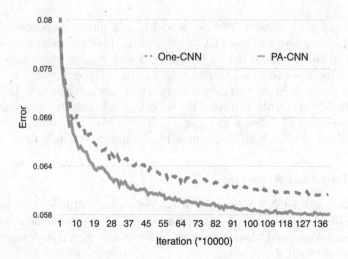

Fig. 3. Error Curve. Comparison of PA-CNN and One-CNN on FullSet test images. We can draw the conclusion that PA-CNN is superior to One-CNN on FullSet due to two sub-networks offering different concentrates on two kinds of facial landmarks.

Table 2. Comparison of testing time on Tesla K20 gpu.

Methods	One-CNN	Two-CNN	PA-CNN
Time(s/image)	0.0180	0.0359	0.0300

3.4 Intermediate Feature Visualization

We gain intuition about what our network learns by visualization intermediate features. We plot the feature map of $conv5$ layer at Fig. 4. Contour sub-network and inner sub-network have own $conv5$ layer. The first column is the input image. The second column is the activation of contour sub-network. The third column is the activation of inner sub-network. We can see that in contour sub-network's feature map, the high activations are always near the image contour, which indicates that contour sub-network concentrates on contour parts. In the inner sub-network, the high activation parts are corresponding to the eyes and nose parts, which reveal inner sub-network pays more attention on the inner facial parts. This result demonstrates that two sub-networks explore the different characteristics of landmarks on various parts dramatically and help to learn the discriminative features.

3.5 Comparison with State-of-the-Arts

In all previous analysis, we use VGG-S to pre-train our framework, and draw a conclusion that PA-CNN which shares the low-level convolutional features and uses two sub-network to localize different type of landmarks is superior to network in Fig. 2. We also compare the result of PA-CNN with the existing public

Fig. 4. The activation of sub-network. The first column is the input image. The second column is the activation of contour sub-network *conv*5 layer, high activation parts are around corner. The third column is the activation of inner sub-network *conv*5 layer, high activations are corresponding to the eyes and nose parts. (Best view in electronic form.)

methods, including PCRR [2], GN-DPM [14], CFAN [17], ESR [3], SDM [15], ERT [8], LBF [11]. The overall experimental results are reported in Table 3. We improve the performance on the 300-W dataset, especially on Challenging test set.

Table 3. The evaluation on 300-W dataset

Methods	Common($\times 10^{-2}$)	Challenging($\times 10^{-2}$)	Fullset($\times 10^{-2}$)
PCRR [2]	6.18	17.26	8.35
GN-DPM [14]	5.78	-	-
CFAN [17]	5.50	16.78	7.69
ESR [3]	5.28	17.00	7.58
SDM [15]	5.57	15.4	7.5
ERT [8]	-	-	6.4
LBF [11]	4.95	11.98	6.32
PA-CNN	**4.82**	**9.80**	**5.79**

3.6 Localization Results

Figure 5 shows the result of our localization method on the 300-W test images. Even the testing images have large head poses or occlusions, our method is accurate and robust.

Fig. 5. Facial landmark localization result on test images.

4   Conclusions

In this paper, we propose a novel end-to-end regression structure using convolutional neural network to deal with different facial landmarks. Our deep architecture first encodes the image into feature maps shared by all the landmarks. Then, these features are sent into two individual sub-network modules to regress contour landmarks and inner landmarks respectively. Experimental results on challenging 300-W dataset demonstrate our approach achieves state-of-the-art result. In future, we will extend the proposed PA-CNN to more facial parts.

Acknowledgments. This work was supported in part by two STCSM's Programs. (No. 15511104402 & 15JC1400103)

References

1. Belhumeur, P.N., Jacobs, D.W., Kriegman, D.J., Kumar, N.: Localizing parts of faces using a consensus of exemplars. IEEE Trans. Pattern Anal. Mach. Intell. **35**(12), 2930–2940 (2013)
2. Burgos-Artizzu, X.P., Perona, P., Dollár, P.: Robust face landmark estimation under occlusion. In: 2013 IEEE International Conference on Computer Vision (ICCV), pp. 1513–1520. IEEE (2013)
3. Cao, X., Wei, Y., Wen, F., Sun, J.: Face alignment by explicit shape regression. Int. J. Comput. Vis. **107**(2), 177–190 (2014)
4. Chatfield, K., Simonyan, K., Vedaldi, A., Zisserman, A.: Return of the devil in the details: delving deep into convolutional nets. arXiv preprint arXiv:1405.3531 (2014)
5. Cootes, T.F., Edwards, G.J., Taylor, C.J.: Active appearance models. In: Burkhardt, H., Neumann, B. (eds.) ECCV 1998. LNCS, vol. 1407, pp. 484–498. Springer, Heidelberg (1998). doi:10.1007/BFb0054760

6. Cootes, T.F., Taylor, C.J., Cooper, D.H., Graham, J.: Active shape models-their training and application. Comput. Vis. Image Underst. **61**(1), 38–59 (1995)
7. Jia, Y., Shelhamer, E., Donahue, J., Karayev, S., Long, J., Girshick, R., Guadarrama, S., Darrell, T.: Caffe: Convolutional architecture for fast feature embedding. arXiv preprint arXiv:1408.5093 (2014)
8. Kazemi, V., Sullivan, J.: One millisecond face alignment with an ensemble of regression trees. In: 2014 IEEE Conference on Computer Vision and Pattern Recognition (CVPR), pp. 1867–1874. IEEE (2014)
9. Le, V., Brandt, J., Lin, Z., Bourdev, L., Huang, T.S.: Interactive facial feature localization. In: Fitzgibbon, A., Lazebnik, S., Perona, P., Sato, Y., Schmid, C. (eds.) ECCV 2012. LNCS, vol. 7578, pp. 679–692. Springer, Heidelberg (2012). doi:10.1007/978-3-642-33712-3_49
10. Liu, Z., Luo, P., Wang, X., Tang, X.: Deep learning face attributes in the wild. In: Proceedings of the IEEE International Conference on Computer Vision, pp. 3730–3738 (2015)
11. Ren, S., Cao, X., Wei, Y., Sun, J.: Face alignment at 3000 fps via regressing local binary features. In: 2014 IEEE Conference on Computer Vision and Pattern Recognition (CVPR), pp. 1685–1692. IEEE (2014)
12. Sagonas, C., Tzimiropoulos, G., Zafeiriou, S., Pantic, M.: 300 faces in-the-wild challenge: the first facial landmark localization challenge. In: 2013 IEEE International Conference on Computer Vision Workshops (ICCVW), pp. 397–403. IEEE (2013)
13. Sun, Y., Wang, X., Tang, X.: Deep convolutional network cascade for facial point detection. In: 2013 IEEE Conference on Computer Vision and Pattern Recognition (CVPR), pp. 3476–3483. IEEE (2013)
14. Tzimiropoulos, G., Pantic, M.: Gauss-newton deformable part models for face alignment in-the-wild. In: 2014 IEEE Conference on Computer Vision and Pattern Recognition (CVPR), pp. 1851–1858. IEEE (2014)
15. Xiong, X., De la Torre, F.: Supervised descent method and its applications to face alignment. In: 2013 IEEE Conference on Computer Vision and Pattern Recognition (CVPR), pp. 532–539. IEEE (2013)
16. Yang, H., Mou, W., Zhang, Y., Patras, I., Gunes, H., Robinson, P.: Face alignment assisted by head pose estimation. arXiv preprint arXiv:1507.03148 (2015)
17. Zhang, J., Shan, S., Kan, M., Chen, X.: Coarse-to-fine auto-encoder networks (CFAN) for real-time face alignment. In: Fleet, D., Pajdla, T., Schiele, B., Tuytelaars, T. (eds.) ECCV 2014. LNCS, vol. 8693, pp. 1–16. Springer, Heidelberg (2014). doi:10.1007/978-3-319-10605-2_1
18. Zhang, Z., Luo, P., Loy, C.C., Tang, X.: Facial landmark detection by deep multi-task learning. In: Fleet, D., Pajdla, T., Schiele, B., Tuytelaars, T. (eds.) ECCV 2014. LNCS, vol. 8693, pp. 94–108. Springer, Heidelberg (2014). doi:10.1007/978-3-319-10599-4_7
19. Zhou, E., Fan, H., Cao, Z., Jiang, Y., Yin, Q.: Extensive facial landmark localization with coarse-to-fine convolutional network cascade. In: 2013 IEEE International Conference on Computer Vision Workshops (ICCVW), pp. 386–391. IEEE (2013)
20. Zhu, X., Ramanan, D.: Face detection, pose estimation, and landmark localization in the wild. In: 2012 IEEE Conference on Computer Vision and Pattern Recognition (CVPR), pp. 2879–2886. IEEE (2012)

On Combining Compressed Sensing and Sparse Representations for Object Tracking

Hang Sun[1], Jing Li[1(✉)], Bo Du[1], and Dacheng Tao[2]

[1] Computer School, Wuhan University, Wuhan 430072, China
sunhang0418@whu.edu.cn, {leejingcn,gunspace}@163.com
[2] Faculty of Engineering and Information Technology, University of Technology
Sydney, Sydney, NSW 2006, Australia
dacheng.tao@uts.edu.au

Abstract. The tracking algorithm of compressed sensing takes advantage of the objective's background information, but lacks the feedback mechanism towards the results. The 11 sparse tracking algorithm adapts to the changes in the objectives' appearances but at the cost of losing their background information. To enhance the effectiveness and robustness of the algorithm in coping with such distractions as occlusion and illumination variation, this paper proposes a tracking framework with the 11 sparse representation being the detector and compressed sensing algorithm the tracker, and establishes a complementary classifier model. A second-order model updating strategy has therefore been proposed to preserve the most representative templates in the 11 sparse representations. It is concluded that this tracking algorithm is better than the prevalent 8 ones with a respective precision plot of 77.15 %, 72.33 % and 81.13 % and a respective success plot of 77.67 %, 74.01 %, 81.51 % in terms of the overall, occlusion and illumination variation.

Keywords: Target tracking · Sparse representations · Compressed sensing · Classifier · Updating strategy

1 Introduction

As a classical research issue in the recent computer vision field [1,2], visual tracking has many practical applications such as automatic monitoring, human-computer interaction and identification. In the past decades, researchers have put forward many algorithms to cope with the problems occurring in the process of target tracking [3–13,15–23]. Nevertheless, restrained by some factors in specific video scenes such as pose transformation, illumination variation and occlusion to name just a few, target tracking still remains a challenging task. So far, there has been no single tracking algorithm which can successfully tackle all problems in different scenes. Hence, it is still challenging to come up with an effective target tracking system with robustness. The current tracking algorithms are mainly classified into two categories: discriminant model and generative model. The discriminant model regards target tracking as an online learning of binary classification whose main purpose is to distinguish the target from its background.

© Springer International Publishing AG 2016
E. Chen et al. (Eds.): PCM 2016, Part I, LNCS 9916, pp. 32–43, 2016.
DOI: 10.1007/978-3-319-48890-5_4

To deal with with the appearance transformations, Comanicu [3] integrated the trained SVM classifier into optical flow framework for tracking. In reference [4], a collection of online-learning weak classifier was used to distinguish whether the pixel belongs to the target or the background. Another method adopted is multiple-instance learning whose main idea is to package all ambiguous positive and negative samples and then learn the distinguishing model on-line [5]. In order to correct the mistakes found in the process of tracking, Kalal [6] presented a method guided by positive and negative constraints to distinguish the target from its background. Based on compressed sensing, Zhang et al. [7] put forward an effective tracking algorithm which is a real-time tracking and has made remarkable achievements in many videos.

The generative model sets an appearance model as its target by learning online. Then, it will locate the target within the searching area with a minimum error in the sequence of following videos. Recently, there have been many tracking algorithms based on sparse representations [8–13]. It is Mei and Lin [8] who firstly applied the sparse representations to the area of target tracking. Due to the computational complexity of solving multiple L1 problem, this algorithm fails to reach the real-time requirement. To enhance the runtime, reference [9] introduced the Minimum Error Boundary Cut which effectively reduced the amount of L1 minimization problems. Xu, in sequence, has adopted a structural model of partial sparse coding in reference [12]. This method subdivides all the target models into smaller image blocks which takes advantage of the local and space information. Afterwards, To further enhance the distinction of appearance models, Liu [13], on the basis of sparse coding, came up with an appearance model which is more distinguishable.

Although great achievements have been made in tracking algorithms based on discriminant and generative model in recent years, these two algorithms do have its own weakness. When tracking the target, the tracking results based on the discriminant model won't be evaluated by any detecting units. As a result, there will be disastrous tracking results in the following video sequence if the classifier fails to provide an accurate location. As for the tracking algorithm based on the generative model, it overlooks the background information significant in the discriminant model and adopts a single model for updating, which has a certain limitation. This paper, therefore, comes up with a pattern of compressed sensing tracking combined with the active detect feedback of L1 sparse representations. This algorithm uses the classifier in the discriminant model as its tracker and deploys the sparse representation in the generative model as its detector. During target tracking, the detector will evaluate the results collected by the tracker and then, according to the evaluation, selectively choose two classifiers to track the targets and update the classifiers with different strategies. At the same time, the results provided by the tracker can be the candidate updating templates for the dictionaries in the detector. And this paper decides to employ a two-stage updating temples to adapt to update the templates in dictionary when tracking with different classifiers.

2   Discriminant and Generative Tracking

2.1   Compressed Sensing Tracking Algorithm

In the process of target tracking under compressed sensing theory, the image $u \in R^n$ collected by the rectangular filter in high-dimensional space is projected to the low-dimensional space by random measurement matrix R under RIP circumstances. It can be described as $v = Ru$ with $m << n$. The main process is shown in Fig. 1.

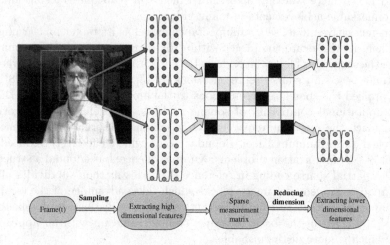

Fig. 1. Samples of compressed sensing

According to the compressed sensing tracking algorithm, multi-scale high-dimensional image features should first be acquired from positive and negative samples collected in current frame by rectangular filer. Then, these features will be projected to the low-dimensional compressed space from the high-dimensional space. After trained in the low-dimensional compressed space, the Bayes classifier will be finally used to identify the location of the targets in next frame. The appearance modeling through the Bayes filter is manifested below:

$$H(v) = log\left(\frac{\prod_{i=1}^{n} p(v_i|y=1)p(y=1)}{\prod_{i=1}^{n} p(v_i|y=0)p(y=0)}\right) = \sum_{i=1}^{n} log\left(\frac{p(v_i|y=1)}{p(v_i|y=0)}\right), \quad (1)$$

$$p(v_i|y=1) \sim N(\mu_i^1, \sigma_i^1), \; p(v_i|y=0) \sim N(\mu_i^0, \sigma_i^0) \quad (2)$$

In (1), v_i stands for the low-dimensional feature while y is the symbol of sample. In (2), (μ_i^1, σ_i^1) and (μ_i^0, σ_i^0) respectively represents the mean and variance of positive and negative samples.

The update of parameter for appearance model is shown as follow,

$$\mu_i^1 \leftarrow \lambda\mu_i^1 + (1-\lambda)\mu^1$$
$$\sigma_i^1 \leftarrow \sqrt{\lambda(\sigma_i^1)^2 + (1-\lambda)(\sigma^1)^2 + \lambda(1-\lambda)(\mu_i^1 - \mu^1)^2} \tag{3}$$

In (3), λ is the learning parameter which reflects the speed of model updating.

2.2 L1 Tracking Algorithm

Sparse representations tracking algorithm regards tracking as finding a sparse approximate in the subordinate space of templates. It first establishes a dictionary which is made up of m sets of target templates $T = \{t_1, \cdots, t_m\}$, n sets of positive trivial templates $I = \{i_1, \cdots, i_n\}$ as well as n sets of negative trivial templates $-I = \{-i_1, \cdots, -i_n\}$ ($m << n$). In the process of tracking, each potential target y is represented by a linear combination of the sample templates in the dictionary.

$$y = [T, I, -I] \begin{bmatrix} a \\ e^+ \\ e^- \end{bmatrix} = DC, \ s.t. \ C \geq 0 \tag{4}$$

The (4) is an undetermined system of equations. For a promising candidate target, there are only a few nonzero elements among the coefficient e^+ and e^-. Accordingly, this issue is transformed into a least square problem of L1 regularization which, as it's commonly accepted, conforms to sparse solution [15].

$$\min \|DC - y\|_2^2 + \lambda\|C\|_1 \tag{5}$$

The $\|\cdot\|_1$ and $\|\cdot\|_2$ in (5) stands for norm L1 and norm L2 respectively.

3   Proposed Framework

3.1   Decision-Making Model

The framework diagram of the tracking algorithm mentioned in this paper is shown in Fig. 2. In the framework of Fig. 2, after its initialization by the tracker and detector in the first frame, the detectors in each frame will evaluate the results of tracker. The decision-making model will activate two classifiers to identify targets, org_clf being the classifier for the initialization of the first frame and new_clf as the classifier of the new initialization of the decision-making model.

The output image of org_clf is defined as $y_o \in R^{d \times 1}$ and that of classifier new_clf $y_n \in R^{d \times 1}$ which is $y \in \{y_o, y_n\}$ in usual cases. For the frames in the beginning phase, the detector introduce the result of the tracker y_o into (5) and get the sparse solution $C = [c_1, ..., c_m, ..., c_{m+2n}]$. Among them, $C_{\text{primal}} = [c_1, ..., c_m]$ corresponds to the coefficient of template set in the dictionary

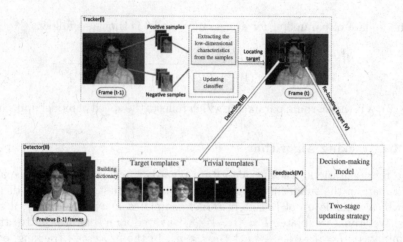

Fig. 2. Framework of the tracking by sparse representations detection

and $C_{\text{trivial}}=[c_{m+1}, ..., c_{m+2n}]$ corresponding to the coefficient of trivial template. The max value of the coefficient corresponds to m template sets is identified as,

$$C_m = \max\{[\min\|DC - y\|_2^2 + \lambda\|C\|_1] \cdot \alpha\} \qquad (6)$$

In (6), α is a column vector with a length of m+2n of which the first m values equal to 1 and the other 2n values equal to 0. After determining C_m, its corresponding template image is defined as $y_D \in R^{d\times 1}$. We set the condition parameter of the decision-making model as S which stands for the similarity between the output image y_O by classifier org_clf and its most relevant template y_D.

$$S = ar\cos\left\{\left[\frac{y_O}{\sqrt{Y_O}}\right]^T \cdot \left[\frac{y_D}{\sqrt{Y_D}}\right]\right\} \qquad (7)$$

In (7), $Y_O = \sum_{i=1}^{d} y_O$, $Y_D = \sum_{i=1}^{d} y_D$ and the image size of y_O and y_D is 12×15 and after transforming the image matrix into a column, it reaches the conclusion of $d = 180$. Among the two classifiers in the decision-making model–org_clf and new_clf, the similarity S is only able to measure the accuracy of the tracking results by classifier org_clf. To choose between these two classifiers and set its relative states, the corresponding reconstruction credibility to the result is,

$$\text{conf} = \exp(-\beta \cdot \|y - D_{1:m} \cdot C_{\text{prime}}\|_2) \qquad (8)$$

In (8), β is the constant and $D_{1:m}$ equals to the matrix formed by the first m templates. The respective tracking results of classifier org_clf and new_clf are y_o and y_n whose corresponding reconstruction credibility are conf_{org} and conf_{new} whose differential τ is the basis of classifier selection and relative states setting.

$$\tau = \text{sign}\,(\text{conf}_{\text{org}} - \text{conf}_{\text{new}}) \qquad (9)$$

In (9), $\tau \in \{-1, 0, 1\}$ and similarity S form the decision conditions. The process will be described in details in algorithm 1.

Algorithm 1. Decision-making model tracking

1: Input: the t frame in the videos
2: **if** $S > \theta$ *and* $\tau = 0$ **then**
3:     To preserve the relative state of classifier org_clf and then collect the positive and negative samples of the initialization classifier new_clf around the targets in t-1 frame.
4:     To update dictionary D by step 2 and the work out τ
5:     To update classifier new_clf according to (3) and the deal with the next frame.
6: **else if** $S > \theta$ *and* $\tau = -1$ **then**
7:     To identify targets using classifier new_clf according to (1) in t frame t
8:     To update dictionary D by step 2 and the work out τ
9:     To update classifier new_clf according to (3) and the deal with the next frame.
10: **else**
11:     To identify targets using classifier new_clf according to (1) in t frame t
12:     To update dictionary D and then set τ as 0
13:     To update classifier new_clf according to (3) and the deal with the next frame.
14: **end if**
15: Output: Tracking location l_t and the relative state of the classifiers

---

3.2   Strategies of Template Updating

Considering the characteristics of decision-making model in this paper, the template updating strategies would be divided into two stages-step 1 and step 2 for the sake of adaptive to our tracking algorithm. In the decision-making model of the algorithm in this paper, the tracker is responsible for locating targets while the main task of the detector is to dynamically reflect the changes in the target's appearances. Consequently, the template updating in this paper will be classified into two groups: one-class classifier(corresponding to step 1) and double classifiers (corresponding to step 2). Enlightened by the page replacement algorithm of the LRU in the operating system and combining the features of one-class classifier, then we would install a time-stamp $W = [w_1, \cdots, w_m]$ for each target template in dictionary D whose process is illustrated in Fig. 3.

In each frame, the detector would solve a coefficient $C_{\text{primal}} = [c_1, ..., c_m]$ according to the results given by the classifier org_clf. The nonzero coefficient c_i corresponds to template t_i whose times-tamp w_i will be set as 0, while for the coefficient $c_j = 0$, it corresponds to template t_j whose timestamp w_j is 1. The longer the template stays unused, the bigger its times-tamp will be. In order to avoid the redundant templates and unnecessary cost in time and storage space due to the excessive frequency in template updating, the we decides to update

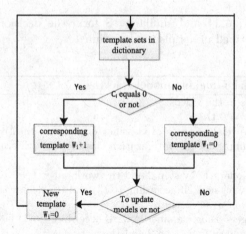

Fig. 3. Template updating process for step 1

the template with the biggest times-tamp in every k_1 frames. In each k_1 frames, there will be k_1 tracking results whose maximum coefficient is expressed in (10).

$$p = \max C_m^i, \quad i \in [1, k_1] \tag{10}$$

There will be k_1 coefficients $C_{\text{primal}} = [c_1, ..., c_m]$ in k_1 frames, and the biggest coefficient $C_m^i (i \in [1, k_1])$ in each frame can be concluded via (6). In this case, p is the biggest coefficient among C_m^i. Since the template won't be updated within k_1 frames, the biggest one among k_1 coefficients C_m^i of k_1 is concluded in the same dictionary. Among the tracking results in k_1 frames, the corresponding result of p is most representative, therefore it is used to replace the template with the biggest times-tamp. When tracking with the double classifiers, new_clf tracks the phony targets affected by the disturbing factors. The template sets will be updated by keeping its original version in case that a large amount of real target templates will be replaced by phony ones. Accordingly, m-1 increasing point sets $\hat{q}$ will be generated in the interval of [0,1].

$$\hat{q} = \frac{2n-1}{2^m+1}, \quad n \in [1, m-1] \tag{11}$$

By m-1 points, the interval [0,1] is divided into m subintervals increasing in length. In dictionary D, there are m target templates that corresponds to the m subintervals. Every time in updating, there will be a random number r in interval [0,1]. The template corresponding to the interval which r falls into will be eliminated and then a new template will be added to the end of the template set. In this way, it can be guaranteed that the old templates will be updated slowly while the new ones update at a faster speed. It is notable that the template sets will only be updated every $k_2 (k_2 < k_1)$ frames and the substitute templates are the same as those in step1 which is the corresponding tracking results of p.

4   Experimental Results and Analyses

In this section, the tracking framework mentioned in this paper will be compared with the 8 prevalent tracking algorithms in 10 standardized video sequences. These videos are mainly about some challenging problems including occlusion and illumination variation. And the 8 tracking algorithms are CT, MIL, LSK, CSK [16], Struck [17], CXT [18], L1APG [19], VTS [21]. Our experiments are carried out in the environment of Windows 7, matlab R2013a, and the computer configuration is Intel i5 2.8GHz CPU, 8G RAM.

4.1   Experiments Setups

In the experiment of our algorithms, the radius of target identifying areas is set as $\gamma = 20$ within which we collect samples. Specifically, for positive samples, radius is $\partial = 4$. For negative samples, inside radius is $\xi = 8$, external radius $\beta = 30$ and threshold $\theta = 60$. In every video sequence, the target location of the first frame is given manually. As for the template updating, the size of the target template is 12×15 in all experiments, of which, $k_1 = 9$ in step 1 and $k_2 = 6$ in step 2.

4.2   Quantitative Evaluation

In our experiment, Fig. 4 is about the precision plots and success rate plots for overall, occlusion and illumination variation. And Fig. 5 shows screenshots of some tracking results. At the same time, the overall average central location errors(ACLE), average bounding box overlap score(AOS) and average frames per second(FPS) shown by these algorithms in these ten video sequences are also included in this paper. As is depicted in Table 1 below, the boldface represents the first, the italic the second and the bold italic the third.

In Fig. 4, the precision plots of overall, occlusion and illumination variation in this paper takes up a respective percentage of 77.15, 72.33 and 81.13. Compared with other algorithms like CSK (71.68 %, 72 %, 70.3 %)and VTS(72.84 %, 67.96 %, 78.92 %), the precision in three metric of this paper is the highest within the 20-pixel threshold. Likewise, MIL and CT also adopt the Bayes classification, and they reach a precision of 63.29 %, 50.96 % in occlusion and 56.11 %, 46.38 % in illumination variation. It can be observed that they are better at coping with occlusion than illumination variation. By contrast, for the algorithm proposed in this paper, the precisions in these two metrics are 72.33 % and 81.13 %. Moreover, under the overlapping threshold S=0.5, the success rates of overall, occlusion and illumination variation by the proposed algorithm are 77.67 %, 74.01 % and 81.51 % respectively, ranking top among all algorithms. It is can be concluded from Table 1 that although this algorithm has advantages over others in terms of overall average central location errors and average bounding box overlap score in the ten video sequences, it takes only the fourth place in the list of average speed. It is because the results by the trackers in each frame would be used to work out the 11 least squares by detectors. Yet, the requirement for real-time can still be satisfied with the algorithm in this paper.

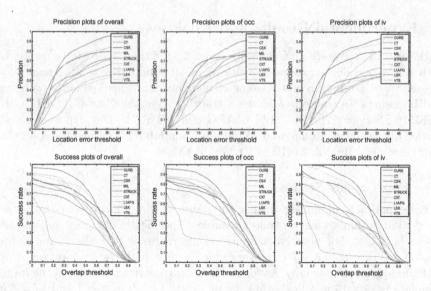

Fig. 4. Precision plots and success rate plots under the situation of overall, occlusion and illuminated

Table 1. Overall average center location errors (in pixel, Overall average bounding box overlap score(%) and FPS

Algorithm	Overall ACLE	Overall AOS	FPS
Ours	**12**	**64.58**	21.089
CT	38	45.75	*33.388*
CSK	36	*55.23*	**185.913**
MIL	*26*	52.16	*28.903*
Struck	41	48.52	7.948
CXT	105	34.47	12.418
L1apg	63	19.25	2.606
LSK	50	44.29	7.681
VTS	*31*	*57.43*	5.616

4.3 Qualitative Evaluation

Clustering of occlusion and background: as is illustrated in faceocc1 (Fig. 5(a)) and faceocc2 (Fig. 5(b)), the target subject in these two video sequences suffered from serious occlusion. Algorithm in this paper as well as other 8 algorithms has made favorable achievements, but as is shown in #293 in faceocc1, #730 in faceocc2 and #486 in #702, when under serious occlusion for a long time, the tracking results in algorithms MIL and CT would drift when the occlusion deviates from target subjects in that the classifiers are under continuous updating. When detecting serious occlusion, the algorithm in this paper would activate the new_clf to track targets and only update the new_clf. By observing #55 in subway (Fig. 5(c)), #99 in walking (Fig. 5(d)) and #28 in david3 (Fig. 5(e)), we can reach a conclusion that the algorithm CXT would lose its targets when coming across its first occlusion. In addition, for the targets in some frames in video david3, they are disturbed by the clusters of background. Many algorithms would lose their targets. It is the CSK algorithm and the VTS algorithm as well as the algorithm in this paper would correctly track its targets under the circumstances of occlusion and background clustering.

Fig. 5. Screenshots of some sampled tracking results

Illumination, Motion Blur and others: videos like basketball (Fig. 5(f)), shaking (Fig. 5(g)), tiger2 (Fig. 5(h)), boy (Fig. 5(i)), dudek (Fig. 5(j)) and faceocc2 (Fig. 5(b)) will be affected by many factors including illumination variation, occlusion, pose variation and motion blur. In video Basketball, targets were under the disturbance of illumination and occlusion and only algorithms like CT, CSK, VTS and algorithm in this paper were still able to lock the target. Although algorithm MIL is able to track targets in #700, it lost them in #625. It was not until the target moved into the sampling scope of MIL that it can track targets through learning. As is shown by shaking in Fig. 5(g) and tiger2 in Fig. 5(h), when it comes to acute changes in illumination and target's pose, many algorithms either lose their targets or make relatively big location errors.

The algorithm in this paper, by contrast, is capable of identifying targets correctly which can be verified by #66, #111 and #353 in shaking and #214, #296 and #396 in tiger2. It is because the detector–L1 sparse representations that updates the dictionary according to step 1, is able to precisely detect the acute changes in illumination and pose and then locate the target correctly based on the decision-making model.

5 Conclusion

On Combining Compressed Sensing and Sparse Representations proposed in this paper is simple in operation with great robustness. According to the experiments conducted on 10 challenging video sequences and 8 prevalent algorithms, the algorithm has made remarkable achievements in such aspects as serious occlusion, illumination variation and background similarity. To make it more reliable and to gain wider applications, the we would set sights on researching such challenging issues as scale variation and targets relocating under the generative and discriminant tracking model.

References

1. Cannons, K.: A review of visual tracking. Technical report CSE 2008–07, York University, Canada (2008)
2. Yilmaz, A., Javed, O., Shah, M.: Object tracking: a survey. ACM Comput. Surv. **38**(4), 1–45 (2006)
3. Comaniciu, D., Ramesh, V., Meer, P.: Kernel-based object tracking. IEEE Trans. Pattern Anal. Mach. Intell. **25**(5), 564–577 (2003)
4. Avidan, S.: Ensemble tracking. IEEE Trans. Pattern Anal. Mach. Intell. **29**(2), 261–271 (2008)
5. Babenko, B., Yang, M.-H., Belongie, S.: Visual tracking with online multiple instance learning. In: IEEE Conference on Computer Vision and Pattern Recognition, pp. 983–990 (2009)
6. Kalal, Z., Matas, J., Mikolajczyk, K.: P-N learning: bootstrapping binary classifiers by structural constraints. In: IEEE Conference on Computer Vision and Pattern Recognition, pp. 49–56 (2010)
7. Zhang, K., Zhang, L., Yang, M.-H.: Fast compressive tracking. IEEE Trans. Pattern Anal. Mach. Intell. **36**(10), 2002–2015 (2014)
8. Mei, X., Ling, H.: Robust visual tracking using L1 minimization. In: IEEE International Conference on Computer Vision, pp. 1436–1443 (2009)
9. Mei, X., Ling, H., Wu, Y., et al.: Minimum error bounded efficient L1 tracker with occlusion detection. IEEE Trans. Image Process. **22**(7), 2661–2675 (2013)
10. Zhang, T., Ghanem, B., Liu, S., Ahuja, N.: Robust visual tracking via Structured multitask sparse learning. Int. J. Comput. Vis. **101**, 367–383 (2013)
11. Zhong, W., Lu, H., Yang, M.-H.: Robust object tracking via sparsity-based Collaborative model. In: IEEE Conference on Computer Vision and Pattern Recognition, pp. 1838–1845 (2012)
12. Jia, X., Lu, H., Yang, M.-H.: Visual tracking via adaptive structural local sparse appearance model. In: IEEE Conference on Computer Vision and Pattern Recognition, pp. 1822–1829 (2012)

13. Liu, B., Huang, J., Yang, L., Kulikowsk, C.: Robust tracking using local sparse appearance model and K-selection. IEEE Trans. Pattern Anal. Mach. Intell. **35**(12), 2968–2981 (2013)
14. Wu, Y., Lim, J., Yang, M.-H.: Online object tracking: a benchmark. In: IEEE Conference on Computer Vision and Pattern Recognition, pp. 2411–2418 (2013)
15. Wright, J., Yang, A.Y., Ganesh, A., Sastry, S.S., Ma, Y.: Robust face recognition via sparse representation. IEEE Trans. Pattern Anal. Mach. Intell. **31**(1), 210–227 (2009)
16. Henriques, J.F., Caseiro, R., Martins, P., Batista, J.: Exploiting the circulant structure of tracking-by-detection with kernels. In: Fitzgibbon, A., Lazebnik, S., Perona, P., Sato, Y., Schmid, C. (eds.) ECCV 2012. LNCS, vol. 7575, pp. 702–715. Springer, Heidelberg (2012). doi:10.1007/978-3-642-33765-9_50
17. Hare, S., Saffari, A., Torr, P.H.S.: Struck: structured output tracking with kernels. In: IEEE International Conference on Computer Vision, pp. 263–270 (2011)
18. Dinh, T.B., Vo, N., Medioni, G.: Context tracker: exploring supporters and distracters in unconstrained environments. In: IEEE Conference on Computer Vision and Pattern Recognition, pp. 1177–1184 (2011)
19. Li, H., Shen, C., Shi, Q.: Real-time visual tracking using compressive sensing. In: IEEE Conference on Computer Vision and Pattern Recognition, pp. 1305–1312 (2011)
20. Sun, H., Li, J., Chang, J., et al.: Efficient compressive sensing tracking via mixed classifier decision. Sci. China Inf. Sci. **59**(7), 1–15 (2016)
21. Kwon, J., Lee, K.M.: Tracking by sampling trackers. In: IEEE International Conference on Computer Vision, pp. 1195–1202 (2011)
22. Henriques, J.F., Caseiro, R., Martins, P., Batista, J.: High-speed tracking with kernelized correlation filters. IEEE Trans. Pattern Anal. Mach. Intell. **37**(3), 583–596 (2015)
23. Zhang, K., Liu, Q., Wu, Y., Yan, M.-H.: Robust visual tracking via convolutional networks without training. IEEE Trans. Image Process. **25**(4), 1779–1792 (2016)

Leaf Recognition Based on Binary Gabor Pattern and Extreme Learning Machine

Huisi Wu[1], Jingjing Liu[1], Ping Li[2], and Zhenkun Wen[1(✉)]

[1] College of Computer Science and Software Engineering,
Shenzhen University, Shenzhen, China
wenzk@szu.edu.cn
[2] Department of Mathematics and Information Technology,
The Hong Kong Institute of Education, Hong Kong, China

Abstract. Automatic plant leaf recognition has been a hot research spot in the recent years, where encouraging improvements have been achieved in both recognition accuracy and speed. However, existing algorithms usually only extracted leaf features (such as shape or texture) or merely adopt traditional neural network algorithm to recognize leaf, which still showed limitation in recognition accuracy and speed especially when facing a large leaf database. In this paper, we present a novel method for leaf recognition by combining feature extraction and machine learning. To break the weakness exposed in the traditional algorithms, we applied binary Gabor pattern (BGP) and extreme learning machine (ELM) to recognize leaves. To accelerate the leaf recognition, we also extract BGP features from leaf images with an offline manner. Different from the traditional neural network like BP and SVM, our method based on the ELM only requires setting one parameter, and without additional fine-tuning during the leaf recognition. Our method is evaluated on several different databases with different scales. Comparisons with state-of-the-art methods were also conducted to evaluate the combination of BGP and ELM. Visual and statistical results have demonstrated its effectiveness.

Keywords: Leaf recognition · Binary Gabor Pattern · Extreme Learning Machine · Leaf recognition processing batch

1 Introduction

As the most widely distributed large species on the earth, plants are playing important role in human survival and development process. Botanists usually recognize different kinds of plants according to their leaves, flowers, or vein structures. As flowers cannot be easily captured for most of time in a year, more plant researchers are using leaf features to identify species. However, when facing with a huge amount of species, it is impossible for human to remember all the names of the leaves and their details of leaf features. Furthermore, a manually leaf recognition also turns out time-consuming and error-prone. Thus it is a very emergent and important task in the area of computer vision and machine learning to develop an automatic leaf recognition system for the botanists.

© Springer International Publishing AG 2016
E. Chen et al. (Eds.): PCM 2016, Part I, LNCS 9916, pp. 44–54, 2016.
DOI: 10.1007/978-3-319-48890-5_5

With the rapid development of information technology, we can easily capture leaf images. However, leaf properties can be affected by color, shape, texture which is not same in different growth stages. For different image databases, it is a difficult issue to evaluate which is the main factor to solve the problem of leaf recognition. Actually for this series of problems, researchers have proposed several representative methods for solving plant classification problem. Researchers usually are tending to recognize plants by extracting leaf features for automatic leaf recognition including external shape or internal texture features. Relying on shape features, Wang *et al.* [1] presented an efficient approach for leaf recognition by using two shape features including centroid-contour distance (CCD) curve, eccentricity and angle code histogram (ACH). Wang *et al.* [2] also proposed a method for recognizing leaf images based on shapes features and hyper-sphere classifier. Zhang *et al.* [3] presented a special shape descriptor in detail for leaf identification. McNeill *et al.* [4] also developed an improved method by hierarchical analyze matching for shape retrieval. Ling *et al.* [5] adopt shape classification by using inner distance. On the other hand, several researchers have focused on extracting texture feature not just single shape feature. Wu *et al.* [6] proposed a rotation invariant shape context (RISC) for automatic leaf recognition. Ojala *et al.* [7] proposed the Local Binary Pattern (LBP) method, which utilized a set of binary patterns to represent the image. Li *et al.* [8] has proposed robust feature extraction by maximum margin criterion. In addition, neural network methods and machine learning methods are also applied to leaf recognition, such as BP network, radial basis function network (RBF) and SVM. The improved version for the SVM is developed in LIBSVM [19]. Wu *et al.* [9] further employed Probabilistic Neural Network (PNN) with image processing techniques for automatic recognition. However, most of existing automatic leaf recognition methods still cannot be used in the real applications due to their limitation in the accuracy or speed performances. For existing feature-based methods, they usually only consider feature matching as the key step for leaf recognition, which cost too much time in matching feature vectors one by one. For most learning based methods, they also easily incur low accuracy or time consuming according the number of iterations during optimizations.

In this paper, we proposed a novel method for automatic leaf recognition based on binary Gabor pattern (BGP) and extreme learning machine (ELM). Compared to the traditional feature-based methods or learning-based methods, our method emphasizes both BGP feature and extreme learning machine in the leaf recognition. Due to our BGP feature can be extracted offline, our method can achieve almost real-time performance based on the rapid ELM. In addition, our method also do not require training network iteratively to obtain local minimum convergence. The proposed method was evaluated with extensive experiments on leaf databases with different size. Experimental results demonstrated that our method generally outperformed state-of-the-art methods in both accuracy and running-time.

The rest of this paper is organized as follows. In Sect. 2, the recognition algorithms are described in detail. The experimental results are provided in Sect. 3 with conclusions in Sect. 4.

2 Methodology

To achieve a more efficient and robust system for leaf recognition, we combine BGP feature extraction with ELM classifier in our novel framework. The overview of our system is as shown in Fig. 1. A cropping preprocess is conducted before extracting BGP feature. According to the whole cropped texture, we use a Gabor Filter algorithm with 8 direction to acquire a feature vector (1×216), which is represented with a BGP histogram. We also build a feature database to form a $N \times 216$ (N is the number of training leaf image) dimensional vector. Finally, ELM is applied to recognize the input image according to its BGP vector.

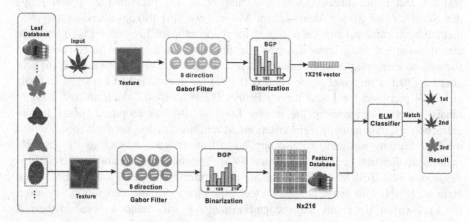

Fig. 1. Overview of our leaf recognition system

2.1 Preprocessing

Given an input leaf image, we have to convert it to gray before extracting BGP feature. We also need to crop the leaf with a rectangle to remove the unrelated regions. In our implementation, a morphology method and Otsu's method were applied to accurately crop the leaf exactly from the input image, as shown in Fig. 2.

2.2 BGP Feature Extraction

Based on the cropped leaf rectangle, we apply Binary Gabor Pattern (BGP) algorithm [10] to extract texture feature. Different from traditional method local binary pattern (LBP), BGP feature is a global texture feature with more distinguish description ability. In addition, BGP is a training-free rotation invariant texture feature based on difference between two regions. Obviously, such an implementation is much more robust than the method based on difference between two pixels.

The first step of BGP is applying a Gabor filter to every pixel in the image. In spatial domain, a 2D Gabor filter is a Gaussian kernel function modulated by a

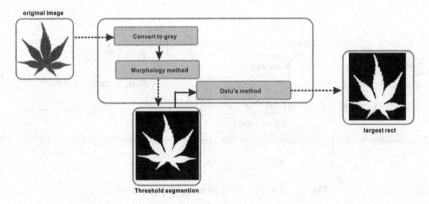

Fig. 2. Leaf cropping based on morphology and Otsu's method

sinusoidal plane wave, which can be written with even-symmetric and odd-symmetric forms as follows:

$$g_g(x,y) = \exp\left(-\frac{1}{2}\left(\frac{x'^2}{\sigma^2} + \frac{y'^2}{(\gamma\sigma)^2} \right) \right) \cos\left(\frac{2\pi}{\lambda}x' \right) \tag{1}$$

$$g_g(x,y) = \exp\left(-\frac{1}{2}\left(\frac{x'^2}{\sigma^2} + \frac{y'^2}{(\gamma\sigma)^2} \right) \right) \sin\left(\frac{2\pi}{\lambda}x' \right) \tag{2}$$

Where $x' = x\cos\theta + y\sin\theta$ and $y' = -x\sin\theta + y\cos\theta$. λ is the wavelength of the sinusoid factor. θ is the orientation of the normal to the parallel stripes of the Gabor function. σ is the sigma of the Gaussian envelope and γ is the spatial aspect ratio. We extract feature from the image under three different resolutions with eight different directions. For each resolution, we set the same parameters for the Gabor filter but with a different orientation. Let R denote the filter radius for the given leaf image. We give J different orientations correspond to $g_0 \sim g_{J-1}$, which represent a special J Gabor filter. Then the BGP algorithm utilizes formula (1) and (2) on a circular region of leaf image. The approach we adopt is applying $g_0 \sim g_{J-1}$ to the leaf image with a point-wise manner. We sum up all the responses in the circular region.

After applying $g_0 \sim g_{J-1}$ to the leaf image, we can get a response vector $r = \{r_j : |j = 0 \sim J - 1\}$. So the second step is to binarization. After changing the parameter θ in formula (1) and (2) J times, we can get a binary vector $b = \{b_j : |j = 0 \sim J - 1\}$ (the b_j is 1 if the sum is above zero) by comparing the sum with zero. We can finally get the Binary Gabor Pattern that characterizes the texture feature of local leaf image by assigning each b_j a binomial factor 2^j.

$$BGP = \sum_{j=0}^{J} b_j 2^j \tag{3}$$

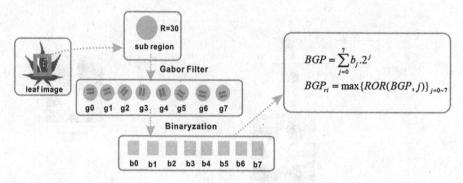

Fig. 3. The steps of generating feature vector

According to formula (3), there will produce 2^J different patterns. In order to achieve rotation invariance, the third step is adopting an analogous strategy as used in LBP. So the BGP algorithm define the rotation invariant BGP (BGP_{ri}) as

$$BGP_{ri} = \max\{ROR(BGP, j)| j = 0 \sim J - 1\} \tag{4}$$

Where $ROR(x, j)$ executes a circular bitwise right shift on x j times, the suffix ri indicates "rotation invariant" and BGP_{ri} is the maximum of shifting results. If $J = 8$, BGP_{ri} will generate 36 different values. The integral calculation process of BGP and BGP_{ri} through an example is shown in Fig. 3.

2.3 Classification Based on Extreme Learning Machine

For eigen vector obtained by BGP, we put them into classifier for training. So we can predict the unknown leaf species. Before this, we also extract BGP features in advance and save in the database off-line to accelerate training and recognition. We applied a simple learning algorithm for single-hidden-layer feedforward neural networks (SLFNs), which is also named extreme learning machine (ELM) [11]. Its learning speed can be thousands of times faster than traditional feedforward network learning algorithm and also obtain a better generalization performance. In addition, ELM can be easily implemented.

For N arbitrary training samples (x_i, t_i), where $x_i = [x_{i1}, x_{i2}, \ldots, x_{in}]^T$ is the feature vector and $t_i = [t_{i1}, t_{i2}, \ldots, t_{im}]^T$ is the label of training species. The mathematical model of ELM is:

$$\sum_{i=1}^{\tilde{N}} \beta_i g_i(x_j) = \sum_{i=1}^{\tilde{N}} \beta_i g(a_i x_j + b_i) = o_j, j = 1, \ldots, N \tag{5}$$

$$X_i \in R^m, \tilde{N} : \text{hidden nodes}$$

Where $g(x)$ is activation function, $w_i = [w_{i1}, w_{i2}, \ldots, w_{im}]^T$ is the weight vector connecting the i th hidden node and the input nodes $\beta_i = [\beta_{i1}, \beta_{i2}, \ldots, \beta_{im}]^T$ is the weight vector connecting the i th hidden nodes and the output nodes. b_i is hidden layer biases. $a_i * x_j$ denotes the inner product. o_j is the actual output. Our goal is to make the minimum error between actual output and desired output, so the objective function is

$$\sum_{j=1}^{\tilde{N}} \| O_j - t_j \| = 0 \qquad (6)$$

The above (5) equations can be written compactly as $H\beta = T$ where H denote the hidden layer output matrix of the neural network. The method presented here is fixed randomly selected input weights a_i and hidden layer threshold b_i training this network. It is equivalent to solving linear systems of $H\beta = Y$ least squares solution $\hat{\beta}$ which is the output weights. In the training phase, we get the weights of output for applying in $H\beta = Y$ to obtain actual output Y in the predict phase. The principle of obtaining output weights is:

$$\| H(a_1, \ldots, a_{\tilde{N}}, b_1, \ldots, b_{\tilde{N}})\hat{\beta} - Y \| = \min \| H(a_1, \ldots, a_{\tilde{N}}, b_1, \ldots, b_{\tilde{N}})\beta - Y \| \qquad (7)$$

According to Huang et al. [12], the minimum least squares solution of these linear systems should satisfy three conditions: (1) $\hat{\beta} = H^{-1}Y$, here H^{-1} is the Moore-Penrose generalized inverse of matrix H, (2) the minimum least squares solution $\hat{\beta} = H^{-1}Y$ is unique, (3) the minimum weight and the best generalization performance can be written as:

$$\| \hat{\beta} \| = \| H^{-1}Y \| \leq \| \beta \|, \forall \beta \in \{\beta : \| H\beta - Y \| \leq \| Hz - Y \|, \forall z \in R^{n*m}\} \qquad (8)$$

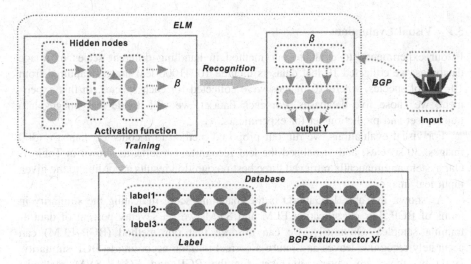

Fig. 4. The work flow of ELM

It is worth to mention that the relationship between hidden nodes and the number of samples satisfies $\tilde{N} \leq N$. Specifically, activation function can be a sine function, a cosine function, a sigmoid function, a threshold function or a RBF function in the mathematical model of the ELM. In our system, we selected sigmoid function as activation function and adopt basic ELM to randomly generate both input weights and bias. Our classification procedure of ELM is shown in Fig. 4.

3 Results

We have implemented our novel method using MATLAB R2012a on a Windows 7 operating system. To test the both accuracy and speed of our proposed method, we also applied our system to leaf database with hundreds of images (Fig. 5).

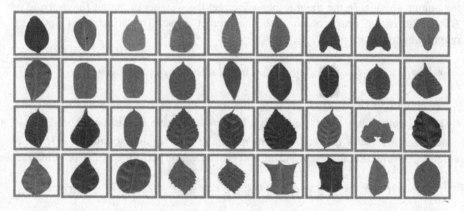

Fig. 5. Typical leaf image examples in our database

3.1 Visual Evaluations

In our experiments, to evaluate our method in handling different scales of image databases, we collected 10 leaf datasets include 100–1000 leaf images captured from 10–100 of species, where 10 images were collected for each species. In this experiment, we chose five databases. For each dataset, we will divide leaf images into training set and prediction set for experiments.

For visual evaluations, we run our proposed method to a collected database (300 images, 30 species) and visualized the leaf recognition results, as shown in Table 1. Our system automatically retrieved three best recognition results according to the given input leaf image.

As shown in Table 1, GaborD is the matching score indicating the similarity in terms of BGP. For classification ELM and SVM, we set seventy percent of data as training samples. Obviously, we can observe that our method (BGP+ELM) can accurately recognize leaves and return a correct ranking according to BGP similarity. However, there are several mistakes for the BGP and BGP + SVM methods.

Table 1. Comparison with different methods on a collected database (300 images, 30 species)

Input image	Method	Results		
		1	2	3
	BGP			
		GaborD=0.0061	GaborD=0.0069	GaborD=0.0073
	BGP+SVM			
	BGP+ELM			
	BGP			
		GaborD=0.0064	GaborD=0.0076	GaborD=0.0081
	BGP+SVM			
	BGP+ELM			

Our method can still recognize correct results even when the leaf image has occlusion or noise regions (the yellow regions in the Table 1).

3.2 Statistical Evaluation

Besides the visual evaluations, we also performed a statistical evaluation for our method to test the effectiveness of the ELM. By considering both BGP and ELM during the leaf recognition, our method should outperform the traditional leaf recognition methods that usually only extracted features to identify the leaf. To verify the running-time and accuracy of different methods on different scales of databases, we also designed different leaf databases with different numbers of leaves. Specifically, we used five databases (A, B, C, D, E) which including 100, 200, 300, 400 and 500 leaf images to evaluate the performance of our method on different scales of databases. In addition, three state-of-the-art methods were also implemented to compare with our method in leaf recognition, including RISC, BGP, BGP+SVM. Average accuracy and running time statistics for different methods over the five datasets are as shown in Tables 2 and 3.

From the statistical results in Table 2, we can see that our method generally outperformed the other competitors with a higher average accuracy rate for all five

Table 2. Average accuracy statistics for different methods over five datasets

Dataset	Leaf Recognition Accuracy(%)			
	RISC	BGP	BGP+SVM	BGP+ELM
DatabaseA	80.3	90.5	87.1	94.2
DatabaseB	81.8	82.4	86.5	90.5
DatabaseC	80.7	83.6	85.0	84.4
DatabaseD	83.1	82.1	84.2	90.1
DatabaseE	82.5	81.2	83.4	90.8

Table 3. Average running time statistics for different methods over five datasets

Dataset	Average Running Time(s)			
	RISC	BGP	BGP+SVM	BGP+ELM
DatabaseA	180.605	186.693	0.321	0.295
DatabaseB	280.281	286.724	0.599	0.566
DatabaseC	340.424	341.258	0.875	0.885
DatabaseD	600.200	615.372	1.018	1.026
DatabaseE	1000.561	1005.861	1.173	1.244

databases, which points out that the combination of BGP and ELM is effective in improving the robustness of automatic leaf recognition. Also, if only comparing our method with the methods RISC and BGP which only considering feature matching for leaf recognition, the advantage of our method is especially outstanding.

From the statistical results in Table 3, we can clearly see that running time grows with the scale increasing for all competitors. However, our method is still faster than all other three competitors. As the BGP features can be extracted off-line for our method, the recognition running time for ELM turns out to be almost real-time performance, indicating that our method has potential to be used in the real applications. Furthermore, we also plotted the average accuracy statistics for different methods over the five datasets to visualize the effectiveness and efficiency of our method when comparing with the other competitors, as shown in Fig. 6.

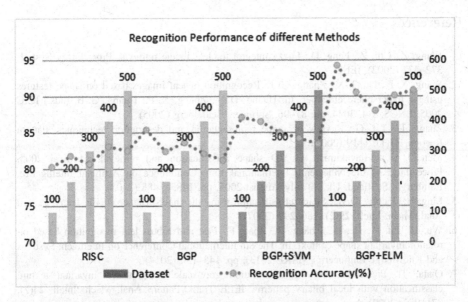

Fig. 6. Average accuracy comparisons for different methods over the five datasets

4 Conclusion

In this paper, we presented a novel method for leaf recognition based on BGP and ELM. To the best of our knowledge, our system is the first to combine BGP and ELM in automatic leaf recognition. By extracting the BGP to form distinguish feature vector sets in an offline manner, our method greatly saves the matching and training time. In virtue of batching images, we can deal with large database. By learning and recognizing the leaf specie using an ELM, our method can accurately identify the final results almost in real-time. Without the limitations of local minima and over-fitting, ELM has better generalization performance than gradient-based learning and SVM. ELM requires less parameters contrast than SVM in fine-turning of the optimization that also make our method to be much more user-friendly. Our method is evaluated in different datasets with different scales, and under different occlusion or noise conditions. Experimental results demonstrated the effectiveness and efficiency of the combination of BGP and ELM. Comparison with state-of-the-art methods were also conducted to show the advantages and improvements of our method in terms of accuracy and running time.

Acknowledgments. This work was supported in part by grants from the National Natural Science Foundation of China (No. 61303101), the Shenzhen Research Foundation for Basic Research, China (Nos. JCYJ20150324140036846), the ShenzhenPeacock Plan (No. KQCX20130621101205783) and the Start-up Research Fund of Shenzhen University (Nos. 2013-827-000009).

References

1. Wang, Z., Chi, Z., Feng, D.: Fuzzy integral for leaf image retrieval. Proc. Fuzzy Syst. **1**, 372–377 (2002). IEEE
2. Wang, X.-F., Du, J.-X., Zhang, G.-J.: Recognition of leaf images based on shape features using a hypersphere classifier. In: Huang, D.-S., Zhang, X.-P., Huang, G.-B. (eds.) ICIC 2005. LNCS, vol. 3644, pp. 87–96. Springer, Heidelberg (2005)
3. Zhang, D., Lu, G.: Review of shape representation and description techniques. Pattern Recogn. **37**(1), 1–19 (2004)
4. Mcneill, G., Vijayakumar, S.: 2D shape classification and retrieval. In: Ijcai 2005, Proceedings of the Nineteenth International Joint Conference on Artificial Intelligence, Edinburgh, Scotland, Uk, 30 July–August 2005, pp. 1483–1488 (2005)
5. Ling, H., Jacobs, D.W.: Shape classification using the inner-distance. IEEE Trans. Pattern Anal. Mach. Intell. **29**(2), 286–299 (2007)
6. Wu, H., Pu, P., He, G., Zhang, B., Zhao, F.: Fast and robust leaf recognition based on rotation invariant shape context. In: The 8th International Conference on Intelligent Systems and Knowledge Engineering (ISKE 2013), pp. 145–154 (2014)
7. Ojala, T., Pietikinen, M.: Multi-resolution gray-scale and rotation invariant texture classification with local binary patterns. IEEE Trans. Pattern Anal. Mach. Intell. **24**(7), 971–987 (2002)
8. Li, X.R., Jiang, T., Zhang, K.: Efficient and robust feature extraction by maximum margin criterion. IEEE Trans. Neural Netw. **17**(1), 157–165 (2006)
9. Wu, S.G., Bao, F.S., Xu, E.Y.: A leaf recognition algorithm for plant classification using probabilistic neural network. Comput. Sci. **2007**, 11–16 (2007)
10. Zhang, L., Zhou, Z., Li, H.: Binary gabor pattern: an efficient and robust descriptor for texture classification. In: 2012 19th IEEE International Conference on Image Processing (ICIP). IEEE (2012)
11. Huang, G.B., Zhu, Q.Y., Siew, C.K.: Extreme learning machine: theory and applications. Neurocomputing **70**(1–3), 489–501 (2006)
12. Huang, G.B.: Learning capability and storage capacity of two hidden-layer feed forward networks. IEEE Trans. Neural Netw. **14**(2), 274–281 (2003)
13. Wu, Q., Zhou, C., Wang, C.: Feature extraction and automatic recognition of plant leaf using artificial neural network. In: Proceedings of Advances in Artificial Intelligence (2003)
14. ArunPriya, C., Balasaravanan, T., Thanamani, A.: An efficient leaf recognition algorithm for plant classification using support vector machine. In: Proceedings of the International Conference on Pattern Recognition. Informatics and Medical Engineering, pp. 428–432 (2012)
15. Song, M.: Combination of local descriptors and global features for leaf recognition. Sig. Image Process. **2**(3), 23 (2011)
16. Zulkifli, Z., Saad., P., Mohtar, I.A.: Plant leaf identification using moment invariants & general regression neural network. In: 2011 11th International Conference on Hybrid Intelligent Systems (HIS), pp. 430–435. IEEE (2011)
17. Zhang, L., Zhang, D., Guo, Z.: MONOGENIC-LBP: a new approach for rotation invariant texture classification 2010, pp. 2677–2680 (2010)
18. Ohtsu, N.: A threshold selection method from gray-level histograms. IEEE Trans. Syst. Man Cybern. **9**(1), 62–66 (1979)
19. Chang, C.-C., Lin, C.-J., et.al.: LIBSVM: a library for support vector machines. Department of Computer Science. National Taiwan University, Taipei, Taiwan (2001)

Sparse Representation Based Histogram in Color Texture Retrieval

Cong Bai[1], Jia-nan Chen[1], Jinglin Zhang[2(✉)], Kidiyo Kpalma[3],
and Joseph Ronsin[3]

[1] College of Computer Science, Zhejiang University of Technology, Hangzhou, China
[2] School of Atmospheric Science,
Nanjing University of Information Science and Technology, Nanjing, China
`jinglin.zhang@nuist.edu.cn`
[3] IETR UMR CNRS 6164, INSA de Rennes, Université Européenne de Bretagne,
Rennes, France

Abstract. Sparse representation is proposed to generate the histogram of feature vectors, namely sparse representation based histogram (SRBH), in which a feature vector is represented by a number of basis vectors instead of by one basis vector in classical histogram. This amelioration makes the SRBH to be a more accurate representation of feature vectors, which is confirmed by the analysis in the aspect of reconstruction errors and the application in color texture retrieval. In color texture retrieval, feature vectors are constructed directly from coefficients of Discrete Wavelet Transform (DWT). Dictionaries for sparse representation are generated by K-means. A set of sparse representation based histograms from different feature vectors is used for image retrieval and chi-squared distance is adopted for similarity measure. Experimental results assessed by Precision-Recall and Average Retrieval Rate (ARR) on four widely used natural color texture databases show that this approach is robust to the number of wavelet decomposition levels and outperforms classical histogram and state-of-the-art approaches.

Keywords: Sparse representation · Feature representation · Color texture retrieval

1 Introduction

Digital image collections bring more and more information. In the meantime, the difficulty for an efficient use of images is also growing, unless we can browse, search and retrieve the desired images easily [20]. Therefore, it brings the need of content-based image retrieval (CBIR). The term CBIR [11] refers to indexing images with their own visual contents. The fields of application are very diverse, for example, web search, arts and museums, medical imaging and criminal prevention. The core or the key problem of CBIR is that both a proper representation of the images by gathering their visual features and a measure

© Springer International Publishing AG 2016
E. Chen et al. (Eds.): PCM 2016, Part I, LNCS 9916, pp. 55–64, 2016.
DOI: 10.1007/978-3-319-48890-5_6

that can determine how similar or dissimilar the images are from the query are needed in order to find images that are visually similar to a given query [19].

Feature extraction, which is a process of transferring the input image into a set of features, namely feature descriptors, is the basis of CBIR [21]. Two main categories of feature descriptors can be used for image retrieval: intensity-based, in which color or/and texture information is used, and geometry-based, in which shape information is used. However, it is reasonable to describe an image by a distribution of vectors instead of individual vectors. Among them, histogram is an efficient manner for representing the distribution of data. In the perspective of feature representation, one vector is represented by one element vector in traditional histogram. As an intuitive idea, histogram could be modified by improving the mode of feature representation. This work is motivated by the fact that sparse representation is proven to be an efficient representation manner in computer vision and pattern recognition [22].

In this paper, a sparse representation based histogram (SRBH) is proposed. In SRBH, one feature vector is represented by a number of basis vectors with different weights, which provides more information on the relations between a vector and its related basis vectors than classical histogram based approach in which one feature vector is represented by only one basis vector. The proposed histogram is generic since it allows the use of any kind of feature vectors for image retrieval. Such feature vectors can be selected with the knowledge from different studies to meet the requirement of retrieval task at hand. In our research, feature vectors constructed directly from DWT domain is picked up for color texture retrieval.

Experimental results obtained from four natural color texture image databases indicate that the histogram generated from sparse representation gives a more accurate feature descriptor, which leads to higher retrieval accuracy in color texture retrieval. The advantage of this modification is confirmed by the reconstruction errors measured by Mean Square Error (MSE). Furthermore, the proposed approach is robust to the decomposition levels of wavelet transform.

The rest of the paper is organized as follows. The proposed sparse representation based histogram is detailed in Sect. 2, and the description of application in color texture retrieval is shown in Sect. 3. Experimental results are shown in Sect. 4 and a conclusion with discussions are given in the last section.

2   Sparse Representation Based Histogram

Histogram generated from sparse representation is described in this section. Two key aspects should be considered for applying SRBH: histogram construction and dictionary learning.

2.1   Histogram Construction

Let $\mathbf{X}_I$ be the matrices of feature vectors extracted from images. Then matrix $\mathbf{X}_I$ can be represented by a linear combination of a few basis vectors from dictionary $\mathbf{D}_I$, and the coefficients in each row of $\mathbf{C}_I$ can be seen as the weighting parameters of corresponding basis vectors:

$$\arg \min_{\mathbf{D}_I, \mathbf{C}_I} \|\mathbf{X}_I - \mathbf{D}_I \mathbf{C}_I\|_{\ell_2} + \lambda \|\mathbf{C}_I\|_{\ell_1} \tag{1}$$

$$s.t. \ \mathbf{C}_I \succeq 0.$$

Many kinds of mathematic methods have been proposed to solve $\mathbf{C}_I$. In our proposal, LARS algorithm [5] provided by the toolbox SPAMS [6] is choosen.

Inspired from our previous work [23], the sparse representation based histogram $H_I = \{h_I(j)\}$ for the set of feature vectors A is proposed as:

$$h_I(j) = \sum_{i=1}^{M} \mathbf{C}_I(i, j) \tag{2}$$

where $\mathbf{C}_I(i, j)$ is the coefficient of $\mathbf{C}_I$ and $h_I(j)$ indicates the value of the jth bin in the histogram, $j = \{1, 2, \ldots, K_A\}$, and M is the total number of feature vectors in matrix $\mathbf{X}_I$. In this way, the bin value represents the total weight of corresponding basis vectors in the sparse representation of feature vector matrix. Therefore, one feature vector is represented not by only one basis vector but by a few basis vectors with different weights in SRBH.

2.2 Dictionary Learning

Dictionary learning has proven to be critical to achieve good results in signal and image processing [9]. Different dictionaries may lead to different performances. In our work, we choose the widely used unsurprised learning method, K-means for its simplicity, efficiency and ease of implementation [18]. The cluster centers resulting from K-means are used as the dictionary.

3 Color Texture Retrieval Using SRBH

The procedure of SRBH in color texture retrieval is detailed in this section, including vector construction and similarity measurement.

3.1 Multiresolution Feature Vectors

Color images are converted to YCbCr color space firstly, whose components are denoted by I_Y, I_{Cb} and I_{Cr}. Then each component is decomposed with N-level Discrete Wavelet Transform (DWT). Wavelet subbands are represented by W_S^{mn}, where $S \in \{Y, Cb, Cr\}$ denotes the component, $m \in \{LL, HL, LH, HH\}$ the subband orientation and $n \in \{1, 2, \ldots, N\}$ the wavelet decomposition level. In the proposed approach, we choose CDF 9/7 wavelet used in JPEG2000. Subbands can be classified into two categories: approximation subband W_S^{LLN} and detail subbands W_S^{HLn}, W_S^{LHn} and W_S^{HHn}. The approximation subband W_S^{LLN} is the lowest resolution version of the original image.

The detail subbands W_S^{HLn}, W_S^{HLn} and W_S^{HHn} reflect local variations of horizontal, vertical and diagonal directions in the image respectively. The feature vectors constructed with the coefficients from subbands can also be categorized into two kinds: approximation vector A and detail vector T_n. A is constructed from W_S^{LLN} whose elements are the coefficients at the same location in each component. At decomposition level n, T_n is constructed from three detail subbands in each component and its elements are the coefficients at the same location in each of the horizontal, vertical and diagonal subbands.

$$
\begin{aligned}
A =\ & [W_Y^{LLN}(x_a, y_a),\ W_{Cb}^{LLN}(x_a, y_a),\ W_{Cr}^{LLN}(x_a, y_a)] \\
T_n =\ & [W_Y^{HLn}(x_n, y_n),\ W_Y^{LHn}(x_n, y_n),\ W_Y^{HHn}(x_n, y_n), \\
& W_{Cb}^{HLn}(x_n, y_n),\ W_{Cb}^{LHn}(x_n, y_n),\ W_{Cb}^{HHn}(x_n, y_n), \\
& W_{Cr}^{HLn}(x_n, y_n),\ W_{Cr}^{LHn}(x_n, y_n),\ W_{Cr}^{HHn}(x_n, y_n)]
\end{aligned}
\tag{3}
$$

where $n = \{1, 2, \ldots, N\}$ and (x_a, y_a) and (x_n, y_n) indicate the coordinates of the coefficients in the corresponding subbands. For N decomposition levels, we have one set of A and N sets of T_n for one image.

For approximation vector A and detail vector T_n, the histogram H_A and H_{T_n} are constructed as mentioned in the previous section, where $n = \{1, 2, \ldots, N\}$, and thus $N + 1$ sparse representation based histograms $H_A, H_{T_1}, \ldots, H_{T_N}$ can be obtained for one image.

3.2   Similarity Measure

To measure the similarity between the histogram H_Q of query image and the histogram H_I of image from the database, χ^2 distance is chosen, which is defined as:

$$
DS(Q, I) = \sum_{j=1}^{K} \frac{(H_Q(j) - H_I(j))^2}{H_Q(j) + H_I(j)}
\tag{4}
$$

where K indicates the number of bins in the histogram.

For each image, $N + 1$ sparse representation based histograms $H_A, H_{T1}, \ldots, H_{TN}$ have been constructed, so the fusion of respective distances DS_A, $DS_{T1}, \ldots, DS_{TN}$ is used to measure the similarity between images. The global distance used to evaluate the similarity between the query image Q and an image I_i in the database is then given by:

$$
DS_G(Q, I_i) = \alpha \cdot DS_A(Q, I_i) + (1 - \alpha) \cdot DS_T(Q, I_i)
\tag{5}
$$

where $(0 \leq \alpha \leq 1)$ is a weighting parameter that balance the impacts between the histogram of approximation vectors and that of the detail vectors in the process of retrieval and $DS_T = \sum_{n=1}^{N} DS_{Tn}$.

4   Experimental Results

The experiments are performed on the following two purposes: (1) Comparing SRBH with classical histogram. (2) Comparing the proposed method with state-of-the-art methods.

4.1   Image Databases

Our method is evaluated on MIT Vision Texture Database (VisTex) [10], Amsterdam Library of Textures (ALOT) [3] and Salzburg Textures (STex) [16]. The protocol of using such databases is the same with [4,7,17].

4.2   Evaluation Measures

In image retrieval experiments, for all data sets, each subimage in the database is used once as a query. The Precision-Recall and Average Retrieval Rate (ARR) [15] are then used to evaluate the performance. Relevant images for each query consists of all the subimages from the same original texture.

4.3   Parameters Setting

A random selection of a quarter of images from each image database is chosen as the training set for generating the corresponding dictionaries $\mathbf{D}_A$ and $\mathbf{D}_{T1}, \ldots, \mathbf{D}_{TN}$. The number of basis vectors in the dictionaries, K_A and $K_{T_1} \ldots, K_{T_N}$,, are fixed to 400 and 1000 respectively (otherwise specified particularly), which were found experimentally.

We should also emphasize that for different value of α in Eq. (5), different retrieval performance can be obtained because α controls the contributions of the histogram of approximation feature vector and that of detail feature vector in the process of retrieval. To avoid over-optimization of this parameter for different data sets, all the results presented below are the result for $\alpha = 0.3$, assuring a good performance that we can experimentally get in all database.

4.4   Comparison with Classical Histogram

To evaluate the effectiveness of SRBH, comparison is performed with classical histogram firstly. In classical histogram method [1,2], vectors in the dictionary are treated as the centers of partitions of feature vectors, and the values of bins are defined as the number of feature vectors that fall into the corresponding partitions.

Furthermore, for a complete comparison, retrieval is performed on different decomposition levels $N = \{1, 2, 3, 4, 5\}$ and the fusion of the distances of H_A, $H_{T_1} \cdots H_{T_N}$ using Eq. (5) is exploited to measure the similarity of images. Precision-Recall and ARR are computed. The Precision-Recall on Small VisTex, Whole VisTex, ALOT and STex databases are shown in Figs. 1, 2, respectively.

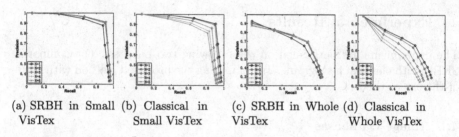

(a) SRBH in Small VisTex (b) Classical in Small VisTex (c) SRBH in Whole VisTex (d) Classical in Whole VisTex

Fig. 1. The Precision-Recall pair of two kinds of histograms on different decomposition levels on VisTex

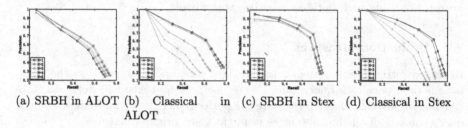

(a) SRBH in ALOT (b) Classical in ALOT (c) SRBH in Stex (d) Classical in Stex

Fig. 2. The Precision-Recall pair of two kinds of histograms on different decomposition levels on ALOT and STex

Table 1 shows the numerical comparison of ARR between the SRBH and classical histogram on these four databases.

From Table 1 and Figs. 1 to 2, we can notice that the performance of classical histogram decreases significantly when the decomposition level N increases, while SRBH keeps a smaller standard deviation (δ) of ARR when N changes. It means that the proposed method is robust to the number of decomposition levels. We can also conclude that the overall performance of the proposed approach is better than that of classical histogram method. This conclusion comes from two-fold facts. On one hand, our method outperforms classical histogram method when the retrieval is performed with the same decomposition level. On the other hand, the mean value of ARR on different decomposition level of SRBH, as marked bold in Table 1, is higher than that of classical histogram method.

Until now, we could get the conclusion that SRBH method is better than classical histogram method in the context of color texture retrieval. However, as the retrieval is performed by the fusion of the distances of $H_A, H_{T_1} \cdots H_{T_N}$, to make the advantage of SRBH to be more solid, only the histograms constructed from one kind of feature vectors is used to perform the retrieval. Since the set of detail vectors T_1 is the same for different decomposition level N, the histograms constructed by SRBH and classical histogram method are chosen, namely H_{ST_1} and H_{CT_1} respectively. In the experiments, the multiresolution feature vectors extracted from images and basis vectors in the dictionary used for constructing these two types of histograms are the same and we change the number of basis vectors K_{T_1} from 10 to 100 (using 10 as interval) and from 100 to 1500 (using 100 as interval). The results are shown in Fig. 3.

Table 1. Comparison of ARR [%] on five decomposition levels of different histograms with different number of top matches considered

Z	N	Small VisTex		Whole VisTex		Alot		STex	
		Classical	Sparse	Classical	Sparse	Classical	Sparse	Classical	Sparse
Z=16	N=1	90.75	87.88	65.82	65.09	61.59	54.22	67.39	68.94
	N=2	89.80	90.21	63.57	68.69	60.73	58.26	65.87	72.12
	N=3	86.43	91.03	58.79	69.60	51.56	59.12	59.42	72.94
	N=4	83.49	91.48	54.64	69.16	42.78	56.22	43.14	69.09
	N=5	81.62	91.45	52.17	68.80	37.48	54.19	48.85	68.11
	Average ARR	86.42	**90.41**	59.00	**68.27**	50.83	**56.40**	56.93	**70.24**
	δ of ARR	3.93	**1.50**	5.77	**1.81**	10.69	**2.27**	10.62	**2.14**
Z=60	N=1	97.93	96.01	86.63	85.89	80.37	72.96	80.23	83.18
	N=2	95.65	96.87	82.43	87.42	80.37	76.84	80.23	83.18
	N=3	94.00	97.3	86.63	87.62	68.22	77.63	76.89	84.91
	N=4	93.18	97.3	75.25	87.08	59.98	74.94	65.81	83.18
	N=5	92.78	97.29	73.89	86.91	55.07	74.29	62.95	81.65
	Average ARR	94.71	**96.95**	80.97	**86.98**	68.80	**75.33**	73.22	**83.22**
	δ of ARR	2.11	**0.56**	6.10	**0.67**	11.56	**1.90**	8.25	**1.15**

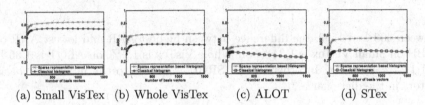

(a) Small VisTex   (b) Whole VisTex   (c) ALOT   (d) STex

Fig. 3. ARR (Z=16) of classical histogram and SRBH on four data sets

From these four figures, we can get two observations. The first one is that SRBH still outperforms classical histogram. This advantage mainly comes from the modification of feature representation in SRBH. This conclusion is supported by the reconstruction errors of these two types of histograms as shown in Table 2. The reconstruction errors are evaluated by the Mean Square Error (MSE) between the feature vectors extracted from the images and the basis vectors used in the histogram to represent these feature vectors. We can observe that the MSE of SRBH is significantly lower than that of classical histogram, which means that SRBH is a more accurate representation of feature vectors than the classical histogram. From the point of view of feature representation, one feature vector is represented by one basic vector in classical histogram but it is represented by several basic vectors in SRBH. Based on the MSEs in Table 2, we can conclude that this modification makes the SRBH to be a more accurate representation of feature vectors than the classical histogram, which leads to a better retrieval performance.

The second conclusion is that if the number of basis vectors is in a reasonable range, it will not have much effect on the performance. When K_{T_1} is in the range

Table 2. Comparison of reconstruction errors (MSE) of classical histogram and SRBH on four databases

Histogram	Small Vistex	Whole VisTex	Alot	Stex
Classical	0.232	0.1771	0.1816	0.2394
SRBH	**0.042**	**0.0407**	**0.035**	**0.0515**

Table 3. ARR on VisTex, ALOT and STex (N=3, Z=16) [%]

	Small VisTex	Whole VisTex	ALOT	STex
DWT [4]	82.0	53.2	42.3	49.3
MGG [17]	**91.2**	69.3	49.3	71.3
GCWD [7]	89.5	63.0	54.1	70.6
LBP [12]	90.54	66.32	46.05	68.36
MTH [8]	76.2	50.0	43.6	52.6
SRBH	91.03	**69.6**	**59.12**	**72.94**

between 400 and 1500, the difference between highest ARR and lowest ARR of SRBH on Small VisTex is 1.34 %, on Whole VisTex is 1.2 %, on ALOT is 1.35 % and 1.34 % on STex. In other words, SRBH is robust to the number of basis vectors in the dictionaries.

4.5 Comparison with State-of-the-art Methods

Finally the comparison is conducted between the proposed approach and referred methods including state-of-the-art methods [4,7,8,12,17] on four data sets for a complete evaluation: Small VisTex, Whole VisTex, ALOT and STex. Retrievals are performed by using the fusion of distances of H_A, $H_{T_1} \cdots H_{T_N}$ as defined in Eq. (5).

Since the decomposition level N has the effect on the retrieval performance, for objective comparison, N is set to 3, which is the same as that used in [4,7,17]. Table 3 presents the retrieval performance on four databases. From Table 3, we can notice that the proposed approach consistently outperforms DWT [4], GCWD [7], LBP [12] and MTH [8]. Considering approach MGG [17], the proposed approach could obtain similar performance in two relatively small data sets, Small VisTex and Whole VisTex, but it outperforms on ALOT and STex, two relatively big data sets.

5   Conclusion and Discussion

We have proposed a novel sparse representation based histogram (SRBH) and verified it in the field of color texture retrieval. In SRBH, one feature vector is represented by a number of basis vectors instead of by only one basis vector in classical histogram. The values of bins in sparse representation based histogram indicate the total weight of corresponding basis vectors in the sparse representation of feature vectors. According to the MSEs of reconstruction errors, we can confirm that this modification allows SRBH to be more accurate than the classical histogram and thus leads to a higher accuracy in color texture retrieval. Results show that the proposed approach is robust to the number of wavelet decomposition levels and improves retrieval rate compared to classical histogram methods and state-of-the-art methods in color texture retrieval.

Although our approach is only verified for color texture retrieval in which color and texture feature are used to generate SRBH, it should be noted that the proposed histogram could be applied to other retrieval task by integrating other features if they could be represented by a set of J-dimensional feature vectors. Furthermore, as a start-up work of using sparse representation to generate histograms, the widely used unsupervised learning method, K-means is adopted for dictionary learning in this work. However, more compact and more accurate dictionaries will be expected with different dictionary learning methods [13,14].

Acknowledgement. Part of this work was done while Cong Bai worked as a Ph.D student in IETR UMR CNRS 6164, INSA de Rennes, Université Européenne de Bretagne, France. This work is now supported by Natural Science Foundation of China under Grant No. 61502424, 61402415, U1509207 and 61325019, Zhejiang Provincial Natural Science Foundation of China under Grant No. LY15F020028, LY15F030014, LY16F020033 and Zhejiang University of Technology under Grant No.2014XZ006. The work of Jinglin Zhang is supported by the Scientific Research Foundation of Nanjing University of Information Science and Technology(Grant No.S8113055001),Natural Science Foundation of JiangSu province (Grant No.SBK2015040336) and Special Program for Applied Research on Super Computation of the NSFC-Guangdong Joint Fund (the second phase).

References

1. Bai, C., Zhang, J., Liu, Z., Zhao, W.L.: K-means based histogram using multiresolution feature vectors for color texture database retrieval. Multimedia Tools. Appl. **74**(4), 1469–1488 (2014)
2. Bai, C., Zou, W., Kpalma, K., Ronsin, J.: Efficient colour texture image retrieval by combination of colour and texture features in wavelet domain. Electron. Lett. **48**(23), 1463–1465 (2012)
3. Burghouts, G.J., Geusebroek, J.M.: Material-specific adaptation of color invariant features. Pattern Recogn. Lett. **30**(3), 306–313 (2009)
4. Do, M., Vetterli, M.: Wavelet-based texture retrieval using generalized gaussian density and kullback-leibler distance. IEEE Trans. Image Process **11**(2), 146–158 (2002)
5. Efron, B., Hastie, T., Johnstone, I., Tibshirani, R.: Least angle regression. Ann. Stat. **32**, 407–499 (2004)
6. Mairal, J., Bach, F., Ponce, J.: SPArse Modeling Software. http://spams-devel. gforge.inria.fr/index.html. Accessed June 2011

7. Kwitt, R., Meerwald, P., Uhl, A.: Efficient texture image retrieval using copulas in a bayesian framework. IEEE Trans. Image Process **20**(7), 2063–2077 (2011)
8. Liu, G.H., Zhang, L., Hou, Y.K., Li, Z.Y., Yang, J.Y.: Image retrieval based on multi-texton histogram. Pattern Recogn. **43**(7), 2380–2389 (2010)
9. Mairal, J., Bach, F., Ponce, J., Sapiro, G.: Online learning for matrix factorization and sparse coding. J. Mach. Learn. Res. **11**, 19–60 (2010)
10. Media Laboratory, M.: Vistex database of textures. http://vismod.media.mit.edu/vismod/imagery/VisionTexture/. Accessed Dec 2010
11. Mei, T., Rui, Y., Li, S., Tian, Q.: Multimedia search reranking. ACM Comput. Surv. **46**(3), 1–38 (2014)
12. Ojala, T., Pietikäinen, M., Harwood, D.: A comparative study of texture measures with classification based on featured distributions. Pattern Recogn. **29**(1), 51–59 (1996)
13. Ophir, B., Lustig, M., Elad, M.: Multi-scale dictionary learning using wavelets. IEEE J. Sel. Top. Sig. Process. **5**(5), 1014–1024 (2011)
14. Patel, V., Chellappa, R.: Dictionary learning. In: Patel, V.M., Chellappa, R. (eds.) Sparse Representations and Compressive Sensing for Imaging and Vision, pp. 85–92. Springer, New York (2013)
15. Picard, R., Kabir, T., Liu, F.: Real-time recognition with the entire brodatz texture database. In: IEEE International Conference on Computer Vision Pattern Recognition (CVPR), pp. 638–639, June 1993
16. University of Salzburg: Salzburg texture image database. http://www.wavelab.at/sources/STex/. Accessed Sep 2012
17. Verdoolaege, G., De Backer, S., Scheunders, P.: Multiscale colour texture retrieval using the geodesic distance between multivariate generalized gaussian models. In: Proceedings of the IEEE International Conference on Image Processing (ICIP), pp. 169–172, October 2008
18. Wang, M., Fu, W., Hao, S., Tao, D., Wu, X.: Scalable semi-supervised learning by efficient anchor graph regularization. IEEE Trans. Knowl. Data Eng. **28**(7), 1864–1877 (2016)
19. Wang, M., Gao, Y., Lu, K., Rui, Y.: View-based discriminative probabilistic modeling for 3d object retrieval and recognition. IEEE Trans. Image Process. **22**(4), 1395–1407 (2013)
20. Wang, M., Li, H., Tao, D., Lu, K., Wu, X.: Multimodal graph-based reranking for web image search. IEEE Trans. Image Process. **21**(11), 4649–4661 (2012)
21. Wang, M., Li, W., Liu, D., Ni, B., Shen, J., Yan, S.: Facilitating image search with a scalable and compact semantic mapping. IEEE Trans. Cybern. **45**(8), 1561–1574 (2015)
22. Wright, J., Ma, Y., Mairal, J., Sapiro, G., Huang, T., Yan, S.: Sparse representation for computer vision and pattern recognition. Proc. IEEE **98**(6), 1031–1044 (2010)
23. Zou, W., Kpalma, K., Ronsin, J.: Semantic segementation via sparse coding over hierarchical regions. In: Proceedings of the IEEE International Conference on Image Processing (ICIP), pp. 2577–2580, October 2012

Improving Image Retrieval by Local Feature Reselection with Query Expansion

Hanli Wang[1,2(✉)] and Tianyao Sun[1,2]

[1] Department of Computer Science and Technology,
Tongji University, Shanghai, China
{hanliwang,1333783_sty}@tongji.edu.cn
[2] Key Laboratory of Embedded System and Service Computing,
Ministry of Education, Tongji University, Shanghai, China

Abstract. A novel approach related to query expansion is proposed to improve image retrieval performance. The proposed approach investigates the problem that not all of the visual features extracted from images are appropriate to be employed for similarity matching. To address this issue, we distinguish image features as effective features from noisy features. The former is benefit for image retrieval while the latter causes deterioration, since the matching of noisy features may rise the similarity score of irrelevant images. In this work, a detailed illustration of effective and noisy features is given and the aforementioned problem is solved by selecting effective features to enhance query feature set while removing noisy features via spatial verification. Experimental results demonstrate that the proposed approach outperforms a number of state-of-the-art query expansion approaches.

Keywords: Image retrieval · Query expansion · Feature reselection

1 Introduction

The last decade has witnessed an astonishing development in image retrieval, which is a fundamental but challenging task in computer vision. Among the image retrieval techniques, the Bag-of-Words (BoW) [1] representation is one of the most effective models, which detects local key points from images with feature detectors such as the Hessian-Affine [2] detector and described using feature descriptors, *e.g.*, the Scale Invariant Feature Transform (SIFT) [3] descriptor. Based on the BoW model, an index consisting of K_c-size visual vocabulary is generated by splitting all features into K_c visual clusters. Then, the inverted file index technique can be further employed to accelerate similarity matching by

This work was supported in part by the National Natural Science Foundation of China under Grant 61472281, the "Shu Guang" project of Shanghai Municipal Education Commission and Shanghai Education Development Foundation under Grant 12SG23, and the Program for Professor of Special Appointment (Eastern Scholar) at the Shanghai Institutions of Higher Learning under Grant GZ2015005.

E. Chen et al. (Eds.): PCM 2016, Part I, LNCS 9916, pp. 65–74, 2016.
DOI: 10.1007/978-3-319-48890-5_7

means of the sparsity of BoW representation. For a query image, its features are extracted and the similarity scores between the query image and reference images are calculated given a specific similarity matching metric.

To improve image retrieval performance, query expansion is introduced to partly address the problem of low recall such as [4]. In general, most of the successful image retrieval systems employ query expansion to achieve state-of-the-art performances. Query expansion is aimed to select out good matching features from top relevant images and re-issue them to the initial query set. The initial query feature set is enriched by adding additional information from relevant images to boost recall. The enriched features can not only compensate the initial detection failure but also expand relevant information which do not appear in the query image. As a consequence, more effective features are searched and a higher recall will be achieved. Moreover, to verify true matches, spatial verification methods have been introduced to image retrieval such as [5–7], most of which combine query expansion with spatial verification by re-ranking the retrieval results to pick out more reliable images. In general, the top ranked candidate image features are spatially verified and the images with the number of inliers above a predefined threshold are chosen as reliable images.

In fact, a large amount of aforementioned query expansion strategies pay attention to the method of feature reselection from top relevant images. As the development of research on query expansion, spatial verification has also been involved to remove spatially inconsistent matches in some state-of-the-art query expansion strategies such as [8]. Unlike these query expansion methods, in this work, we propose to not only select effective features from reliable images but also abandon noisy features extracted from initial images and judge the effectiveness of each feature without re-ranking. To this aim, the RANSAC algorithm [9] is utilized to select out verified features. Base on these verified features, noisy features are removed while reliable features are added to the query representation and a weight attribute is introduced to judge the effectiveness of each feature. As a consequence, a novel feature reselection approach is proposed to enhance the quantity and quality of the initial query feature representation.

The rest of the paper is structured as follows. The proposed feature reselection approach is detailed in Sect. 2. Comparative experimental results are presented in Sect. 3 to demonstrate the effectiveness of the proposed approach. Finally, Sect. 4 concludes this work.

2   Proposed Feature Reselection Based Query Expansion

In this section, the main idea of the proposed feature reselection based query expansion approach is introduced in Sect. 2.1. Then, Sect. 2.2 discusses how to incorporate the proposed feature reselection based query expansion approach into the powerful Aggregated Selective Match Kernel (ASMK) [10] method. Considering spatial verification is a little bit time consuming, we also design a simplified version of the proposed approach as presented in Sect. 2.3.

Query image

Reference images

Fig. 1. Illustration of effective (red oval) and noisy (yellow oval) features. All the images are from the Oxford5k image database with the leftmost image being the query image, the right images with the red frame are good matched images while the others with the yellow frame are mismatched ones. It can be seen that the features marked by the red oval are effective, which can depict the characteristics of the query image. On the other hand, the features marked by the yellow oval tend to be noisy which may probably lead to mismatching. (Color figure online)

2.1 K-nearest Neighbors Query Expansion (KQE)

In general, not all of the features extracted from the initial query image are effective to be used. In most cases, the initial query image is only partially similar to its revelent images. Figure 1 is shown to illustrate this phenomenon, where a representative query image and a number of its related images from the benchmark Oxford5k image database are employed for demonstration. As shown in Fig. 1, the features extracted from the characteristic structure of the leftmost query image are effective (which are marked by red oval) while the other features (yellow oval) are less important or even noisy. In order to filter out noisy features, the technique of spatial verification is used via the RANSAC algorithm [9], which can detect the main characteristic structure of similar images. The details of the proposed approach for effective feature reselection are given below.

Assume an image retrieval approach has already been carried out given a query image denoted as I_q and there is a list of retrieved images from which the top ranked N_L images are used to construct a candidate image set S_L^I. Then for each of the images belonging to S_L^I: $I_r^i \in S_L^I$, $N_L \geq i \geq 1$, the RANSAC algorithm is used to perform spatial verification between the features of I_r^i and I_q. According to the spatial verification results, a relevant image set S_R^I is constructed consisting of all the images that have their own number of spatially verified features larger than a predefined threshold (which is set to 4 empirically). Moreover, all the spatially verified features extracted from S_R^I are considered as effective and forms a feature set S_R^F. Therefore, we obtain S_R^F as a benchmark feature set to enrich query expansion in the following processes.

On the other hand, the traditional query expansion technique is also considered, so that the top ranked N_H images from the initial image retrieval list are employed to form the image set S_H^I and all the features extracted from S_H^I are utilized to generate the feature set S_H^F. Based on the feature set S_H^F, we consider to enlarge the effective feature set S_R^F by exploring the relation of features between S_R^F and S_H^F. Specifically, for each feature $f_R^i \in S_R^F$, $\#S_R^F \geq i \geq 1$ (where $\#$ stands for the cardinality of a set), its K_n-nearest neighbor features from S_H^F in terms of the ℓ_2 Euclidean distance in the feature space are kept to form an improved feature set S_E^F. Intuitively, the features in S_E^F will be more similar than that of S_H^F to I_q's features. Moreover, a weight attribute is introduced to represent the effectiveness of the features in S_E^F with the following formula as

$$w_E^{i,j} = e^{[d(f_R^i, f_H^{i,j}) - d(f_R^i, f_H^{i,1})]^{-0.5}}, \tag{1}$$

where f_R^i is the ith feature of S_R^F, $f_H^{i,j}$ is the jth neighbor feature of f_R^i selected from the feature set S_H^F, $\#S_R^F \geq i \geq 1$ and $K_n \geq j \geq 1$. The function of $d(x,y)$ calculates the ℓ_2 Euclidean distance between feature x and y in the feature space. Moreover, we consider all the features in S_R^F are effective such that $w_R^i = 1$, $\#S_R^F \geq i \geq 1$.

Since the features in S_R^F and S_E^F are closely related to the features extracted from the query image I_q, we further propose to generate the final effective feature set S_*^F as

$$S_*^F = S_R^F \cup S_E^F. \tag{2}$$

As a result, four candidate feature sets are available for query expansion, including S_R^F, S_H^F, S_E^F and S_*^F. Theoretically speaking, the performance based on S_*^F should be better than that of S_R^F and S_E^F based on Eq. (2), which will also be verified by the comparative experiments presented in Sect. 3.

2.2   KQE with Aggregated Selective Match Kernel (ASMK)

The proposed feature reselection method as discussed in Sect. 2.1 can be applied to query expansion regardless of the underlying image retrieval approach. In this work, the state-of-the-art Aggregated Selective Match Kernel (ASMK) [10] is employed as the testbed to evaluate the proposed query expansion approach. ASMK [10] is an efficient strategy for image retrieval to solve the burstiness phenomenon [11] by keeping only one representative instance of all similar descriptors. The details of the incorporation of the proposed feature reselection approach via the feature set S_*^F into ASMK are presented below.

As aforementioned, the enriched query image representation can be described by the feature set $S_*^F = \left\{ f_*^1, f_*^2, \cdots, f_*^{\#S_*^F} \right\}$, and all these features are quantized by a K-Means quantiser as

$$q : \mathbb{R}^d \to \mathcal{C} \subset \mathbb{R}^d,$$
$$f_*^i \mapsto q(f_*^i), \tag{3}$$

where d is the feature dimension of f_*^i, $\mathcal{C} = \{c_1, c_2, \cdots, c_{K_c}\}$ denotes the visual vocabulary of K_c words. Then, the feature subset of S_*^F which are assigned to the jth visual word c_j is defined as

$$S_*^{F,j} = \{f_* \in S_*^F : q(f_*) = c_j, c_j \in \mathcal{C}\}. \tag{4}$$

Then, for each image $I_R^u \in S_R^I$, $\#S_R^I \geq u \geq 1$, its aggregation of feature subset $S_*^{F,j}$ in terms of quantization residual is calculated as

$$A_u^j\left(S_*^{F,j}\right) = \sum_{f_*^{u,v} \in S_*^{F,j}} (w_*^{u,v})^\alpha (f_*^{u,v} - c_j), \tag{5}$$

where the index of u stands for the image I_R^u and v represents the index of feature belonging to $S_*^{F,j}$, $w_*^{u,v}$ is the weight attribute of the feature $f_*^{u,v}$ which is obtained via Eq. (1). α is a control parameter with its typical value equal to 3, which will be demonstrated in Sect. 3. The aggregated residual $A_u^j\left(S_*^{F,j}\right)$ is subsequently ℓ_2-normalized to ensure that it lies in the range $[-1, +1]$ as

$$\widehat{A_u^j\left(S_*^{F,j}\right)} = \frac{A_u^j\left(S_*^{F,j}\right)}{\left\|A_u^j\left(S_*^{F,j}\right)\right\|_2}. \tag{6}$$

For a reference image I_y, we can extract its feature set denoted as S_y^F. Similar to Eqs. (5) and (6), the normalized aggregated residual of I_y related to the visual word c_j is calculated as $\widehat{A_y^j\left(S_y^{F,j}\right)}$ by setting all the weights to 1. Therefore, the match kernel $\mathcal{K}$ can be written as

$$\mathcal{K}(S_*^{F,j}, S_y^{F,j}) = \sum_u \sigma\left(\left[\widehat{A_u^j\left(S_*^{F,j}\right)}\right]^\mathsf{T} \widehat{A_y^j\left(S_y^{F,j}\right)}\right), \tag{7}$$

where $\sigma(\cdot)$ is a polynomial selectivity function defined as

$$\sigma(x) = \begin{cases} \operatorname{sign}(x)|x|^\beta, & if \ x > \tau \\ 0, & otherwise \end{cases}, \tag{8}$$

where β balances strong and weak matches and τ is a threshold to filter out weak matches. In this work, we set $\beta = 3$ and $\tau = 0$. As compared with the original ASMK approach, the proposed KQE+ASMK method introduces the weight attribute for matching kernel computation, which embodies the effectiveness of each query feature. Moreover, the enriched query feature set S_*^F is used instead of the feature set which is only extracted from the initial query image I_q.

2.3   Simplified KQE

As discussed in Sect. 2.1, the RANSAC algorithm is employed to perform spatial verification to generate the feature set S_R^F, which will introduce several geometry computations. Alternatively, we design a simplified version of the proposed S_R^F generation method, that is, the feature set S_q^F which is extracted from the initial query image I_q is used to substitute S_R^F. As a consequence, the process of spatial verification is removed from the proposed KQE approach. A comparison of the proposed KQE approach with and without spatial verification will be made in the following Sect. 3.

3 Experimental Results

In order to evaluate the proposed KQE approach, three benchmark datasets including Oxford5k, Paris6k and Oxford105k are employed for experiments. The mean Average Precision (mAP) is used as the evaluation criterion of image retrieval accuracy. Moreover, in order to make a fair comparison with up-to-date techniques, we follow the experimental implementations of [10]. In particular, the implementation details are listed as follows.

- The modified Hessian-Affine detector [12] and the SIFT descriptor are used for feature detection and description. As the same as in [10], both the settings of small set and large set of features are employed to evaluate the performance on Oxford5k.
- The K-Means clustering algorithm is applied to generate visual vocabularies, and the vocabularies used for Oxford5k are trained on Paris6k, and vice versa, which follows [10].
- The query-side Multiple Assignment (MA) [13] is applied to further reduce the impact of quantization error. In order to perform MA, each descriptor is assigned to N_{ma} nearest visual words.
- When generating the query feature sets S_R^F and S_H^F, we set $N_L = 100$ and $N_H = 10$ empirically.

Firstly, we valuate the impact of vocabulary size of K_c used by K-Means clustering on our proposed approach as shown in Fig. 2, where the term of 'SV' stands for spatial verification and ASMK+KQE+SV indicates the proposed KQE approach with SV enabled while ASMK+KQE represents the simplified KQE approach without SV. From the results in Fig. 2, it can be observed that along with the increment of vocabulary size K_c, the mAP performances have

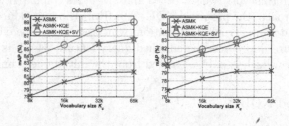

Fig. 2. Impact of vocabulary size K_c with different kernels on Oxford5k and Pairs6k.

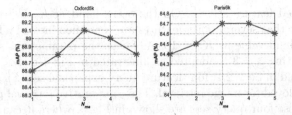

Fig. 3. Impact of the parameter N_{ma} on the performance of multiple assignment.

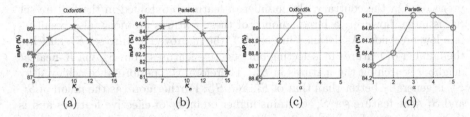

(a)   (b)   (c)   (d)

Fig. 4. Impacts of the number of nearest neighbors K_n and the parameter α in Eq. (5). (a) Impact of K_n on Oxford5k. (b) Impact of K_n on Paris6k. (c) Impact of α on Oxford5k. (d) Impact of α on Paris6k.

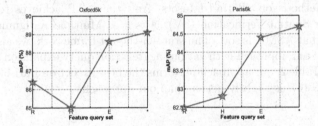

Fig. 5. Performance comparison of the four feature query expansion sets, including S_R^F (denoted as 'R'), S_H^F (denoted as 'H'), S_E^F (denoted as 'E') and S_*^F (denoted as '*').

been improved by all the three competing approaches. In the following experiments, we keep $K_c = 65k$. Regarding the MA technique, Fig. 3 shows the effect of N_{ma} on the mAP performances, where the best performances can be achieved when $N_{ma} = 3$. Therefore, we set $N_{ma} = 3$ in the following experiments.

Moreover, we evaluate the two parameters related to the proposed KQE approach. One is the parameter K_n which is the number of nearest neighbors to generate the feature set S_E^F, and the other is the parameter α which is used to regulate the weight contribution for feature aggregation as employed in Eq. (5). Their effects are demonstrated in Fig. 4, respectively. As observed from the comparison shown in Fig. 4(a–b), the mAP performance is sensitive when K_n changes. If K_n is too small, a number of effective features will be missed to be included into the enriched feature set S_E^F. On the other hand, if K_n is too large, it is highly probable that several noisy features are contained into S_E^F. Therefore, we choose the optimal value as $K_n = 10$. As far as the parameter α is concerned, the optimal setting $\alpha = 3$ is adopted as illustrated in Fig. 4(c–d).

As mentioned in Sect. 2.1, four feature query expansion sets S_R^F, S_H^F, S_E^F and S_*^F can be employed for image retrieval. The comparative retrieval performances achieved by these four query sets are shown in Fig. 5, where it can be seen that the feature sets S_E^F and S_*^F performs much better than S_R^F and S_H^F. Even though all features included in the feature set S_R^F are considered to be effective, the number of the query features in S_R^F is relatively small which leads to a low precision. On the contrary, the number of features contained in the feature set S_H^F is large, however, a large amount of these features are noisy also resulting in a low precision. As detailed in Sect. 2.1, the improved feature set S_E^F enriches the number of features by selecting out effective features from S_H^F via K-nearest neighbor searching the features in S_R^F. Therefore, the performance achieved by S_E^F is generally better than that of S_R^F and S_H^F. Furthermore, as the union of S_R^F and S_E^F, the feature set S_*^F contains higher quantity of effective features and is thus surely to perform the best.

Next, we compare the proposed KQE approach with a number of state-of-the-art methods in Table 1, where the small set of feature configuration is used which follows the benchmark comparison in [10]. From the results in Table 1, it can be observed that the proposed KQE approach outperforms all the other competing methods on all the datasets. And the mAP achieves to the best by employing Spatial Verification (SV) as well as Multiple Assignment (MA). Considering that ASMK is sort of an state-of-the-art framework, we also give the comparison of our approach with various aggregation query expansion strategies. As shown in Table 2, our approach performs the best except on Paris6k on which Q.adap+RNN [17] is slightly better than our approach.

Table 1. Performance comparison with state-of-the-art methods when the small set of feature configuration is applied.

Methods	SV	MA	Oxford5k	Paris6k	Oxford105k
Perdoch [12]	×	×	0.822	-	0.772
Mikulík [14]	×	×	0.849	0.824	0.795
Chum [4]	×		0.827	0.805	0.767
Arandjelovic [15]	×		0.809	0.765	0.722
Tolias [16]		×	0.838	0.828	-
Tolias [16]	×	×	0.880	0.828	0.840
ASMK [10]		×	0.817	0.782	-
ASMK+KQE		×	0.866	0.840	-
ASMK+KQE	×		0.884	0.844	-
ASMK+KQE	×	×	**0.891**	**0.847**	**0.855**

Table 2. Comparison of various aggregation query expansion methods.

Method	MA	Oxford5k	Paris6k	Oxford105k
Total recall II [8]		0.827	0.805	0.767
Fine voc+QE [18]	×	0.849	0.824	0.795
Q.adap+RNN [17]	×	0.850	**0.855**	0.816
i-ASMK*+HQE [19]	×	0.869	0.851	0.853
ASMK+KQE	×	**0.891**	0.847	**0.855**

Table 3. Performance comparison of the proposed KQE approach when spatial verification is enabled or disabled with both the small and large set of feature configurations on Oxford5k.

Methods	Small	Large
ASMK	0.817	0.838
ASMK+KQE	0.866	0.873
ASMK+KQE+SV	0.891	**0.897**

Moreover, we adjust the feature detector threshold lower to extract more features to perform the large set of feature configuration as suggested in [10] with the comparative results shown in Table 3, where it can be observed that the best mAP performance (*i.e.*, 0.897) is achieved when the large set of feature configuration is used. In addition, it can also be seen from Table 3 that the simplified KQE approach without spatial verification (*i.e.*, ASMK+KQE in Table 3) will degrade the retrieval performance as compared with the ASMK+KQE+SV approach with spatial verification implemented.

4   Conclusion

In this work, a novel feature reselection technique is proposed to improve the query expansion performance for image retrieval. To this aim, effective features are selected out to form an enriched feature query set which is able to depict the main characteristics of a query image. Moreover, the effectiveness of these selected features is quantitatively expressed as a weight attribute. The proposed feature reselection approach is combined with the state-of-the-art ASMK method, and the comparative experimental results have demonstrated the advantage of the proposed approach. In the future, we will further investigate the applicability of the proposed approach with other up-to-date image retrieval techniques.

References

1. Sivic, J., Zisserman, A.: Video google: a text retrieval approach to object matching in videos. In: Proceedings of the ICCV 2003, pp. 1470–1477, October 2003
2. Mikolajczyk, K., Schmid, C.: Scale and affine invariant interest point detectors. Int. J. Comput. Vis. **60**(1), 63–86 (2004)
3. Lowe, D.: Distinctive image features from scale-invariant keypoints. Int. J. Comput. Vis. **60**(2), 91–110 (2004)
4. Chum, O., Philbin, J., Sivic, J., Isard, M., Zisserman, A.: Total recall: automatic query expansion with a generative feature model for object retrieval. In: Proceedings of the ICCV 2007, pp. 1–8, October 2007
5. Jegou, H., Douze, M., Schmid, C.: Hamming embedding and weak geometric consistency for large scale image search. In: Forsyth, D., Torr, P., Zisserman, A. (eds.) ECCV 2008. LNCS, vol. 5302, pp. 304–317. Springer, Heidelberg (2008). doi:10.1007/978-3-540-88682-2_24
6. Philbin, J., Chum, O., Isard, M., Sivic, J., Zisserman, A.: Object retrieval with large vocabularies and fast spatial matching. In: Proceedings of the CVPR 2007, pp. 1–8, June 2007
7. Wang, W., Zhang, D., Zhang, Y., Li, J.: Fast and robust spatial matching for object retrieval. In: Proceedings of the ICASSP 2010, pp. 1238–1241, March 2010
8. Chum, O., Mikulik, A., Perdoch, M., Matas, J.: Total recall II: query expansion revisited. In: Proceedings of the CVPR 2011, pp. 889–896, June 2011
9. Fischler, M.A., Bolles, R.C.: Random sample consensus: a paradigm for model fitting with applications to image analysis and automated cartography. Commun. ACM **24**(6), 381–395 (1981)
10. Tolias, G., Avrithis, Y., Jégou, H.: To aggregate or not to aggregate: Selective match kernels for image search. In: Proceedings of the ICCV 2013, pp. 1401–1408, December 2013
11. Jégou, H., Douze, M., Schmid, C.: On the burstiness of visual elements. In: Proceedings of the CVPR 2009, pp. 1169–1176, June 2009
12. Perdoch, M., Chum, O., Matas, J.: Efficient representation of local geometry for large scale object retrieval. In: Proceedings of the CVPR 2009, pp. 9–16, June 2009
13. Verbeek, J., Harzallah, H., Schmid, C., Jégou, H.: Accurate image search using the contextual dissimilarity measure. IEEE Trans. Pattern Anal. Mach. Intell. **32**(1), 2–11 (2010)
14. Mikulík, A., Perdoch, M., Chum, O., Matas, J.: Learning a fine vocabulary. In: Daniilidis, K., Maragos, P., Paragios, N. (eds.) ECCV 2010. LNCS, vol. 6313, pp. 1–14. Springer, Heidelberg (2010). doi:10.1007/978-3-642-15558-1_1
15. Arandjelovic, R., Zisserman, A.: Three things everyone should know to improve object retrieval. In: Proceedings of the CVPR 2012, pp. 2911–2918, June 2012
16. Tolias, G., Jégou, H.: Visual query expansion with or without geometry: refining local descriptors by feature aggregation. Pattern Recog. **47**(10), 3466–3476 (2014)
17. Qin, D., Wengert, C., Gool, L.V.: Query adaptive similarity for large scale object retrieval. In: Proceedings of the CVPR 2013, pp. 1610–1617, June 2013
18. Mikulík, A., Perdoch, M., Chum, O., Matas, J.: Learning vocabularies over a fine quantization. Int. J. Comput. Vis. **103**(1), 163–175 (2013)
19. Tolias, G., Avrithis, Y., Jégou, H.: Image search with selective match kernels: aggregation across single and multiple images. Int. J. Comput. Vis. **116**(3), 247–261 (2016)

Sparse Subspace Clustering via Closure Subgraph Based on Directed Graph

Yuefeng Ma and Xun Liang[(✉)]

Department of Computer Science, Renmin University, Beijing, China
{rzmyf1976,xliang}@ruc.edu.cn

Abstract. Sparse subspace clustering has attracted much attention in the fields of signal processing, image processing, computer vision, and pattern recognition. We propose an algorithm, sparse subspace clustering via closure subgraph (SSC-CG) based on directed graph, to accomplish subspace clustering without the number of subspaces as prior information. In SSC-CG, we use a directed graph to express the relations in data instead of an undirected graph like most previous methods. Through finding all strongly connected components with closure property, we discovery all subspaces in the given dataset. Based on expressive relations, we assign data to subspaces or treat them as noise data. Experiments demonstrate that SSC-CG has an exciting performance in most conditions.

Keywords: Sparse subspace clustering · Directed graph · Closure subgraph · Strongly connected component

1 Introduction

Subspace clustering has received a widespread attention in many areas such as machine learning, signal and image processing, computer vision, pattern recognition, bioinformatics, etc. [1]. In general, the main target of subspace clustering is to separate high-dimensional data into different subspaces according to their natural space. Based on their methods, there are four main categories in subspace clustering research. They are iterative subspace clustering [2], statistical methods [3], algebraic algorithms [4], and the spectral methods [5, 6].

In spectral methods, with a novel data representation method developed, compressed sensing [7, 8], a competitive method named sparse subspace clustering (SSC) was proposed in recent years [9, 10]. Similar to other spectral methods, SSC also includes two steps to accomplish clustering. In its first step, SSC builds a symmetric similarity matrix through solving convex optimization problems based on self-expressiveness property. In the second step, a general spectral clustering method is applied on a symmetric similarity matrix with the given number of subspaces [11]. The main development of SSC focused on its first step in most researches. To reduce the computational complexity of obtaining the sparse representation, latent space sparse subspace clustering was presented based on kernel method in the first step [12, 13]. In order to improve the performances of SSC on computational time and memory requirement in a large scale dataset, a scalable SSC method was proposed by using

E. Chen et al. (Eds.): PCM 2016, Part I, LNCS 9916, pp. 75–84, 2016.
DOI: 10.1007/978-3-319-48890-5_8

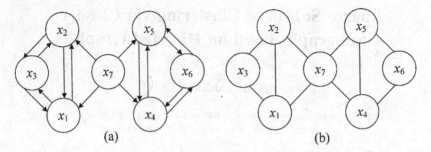

(a)   (b)

Fig. 1. An example of subspace clustering using directed and undirected graph.

sampling technology [14]. Using a kernel trick, SSC is extended to non-linear manifolds, and the alternating direction method of multipliers is used to efficiently obtain kernel sparse representations [15]. A linear-time subspace clustering was introduced to develop SSC through combining sparse representation and bipartite graph model [16].

Although SSC and its other variants achieved impressive progress, there are some limitations in the SSCs. The first limitation is that they cannot deal with the situation that there is only one subspace in the given dataset. The second limitation is that an exact number of subspaces must be given as prior information to use spectral clustering method. The third limitation is that the complexity of spectral clustering is very high in both computational complexity and memory cost. These limitations are caused mainly by using spectral clustering method which is based on a symmetric relation in data. Figure 1 displays a schematic diagram for these problems. Figure 1(a) describes the expressive relations in data. For example, point x_1 is expressed by a linear combination with points x_2 and x_3. Clearly, point x_7 is an outlier which is expressed by points from two subspaces. If regarding the relations as symmetric relations, we can obtain Fig. 1(b). In Fig. 1(b), point x_7 becomes the center point in the graph. It will lead to a wrong separation using graph like Fig. 1(b) in most conditions. So it may not be a perfect way to use an undirected graph in sparse subspace clustering. In this paper we propose a method called Sparse Subspace Clustering via Closure subGraph (SSC-CG) based on a directed graph.

Our contributions are listed as follows. Firstly, we demonstrate the closure property of sparse subspace. Secondly, SSC-CG adopts a directed graph to represent the expressive relationship in data. That is different with other sparse subgraph clustering algorithms. Using the directed graph we effectively reduces both the computation complexity and memory cost. The reason is that SSC-CG avoids using singular value decomposition (SVD). Thirdly, SSC-CG does not need the number of subspaces as prior information and the number can be obtained by itself. This advantage gives SSC-CG capacity to discover a subspace from a dataset which includes only one subspace especially when the number of data in the subspace is small.

2   Sparse Subspace Clustering

Let $X = \{x_i \in R^M, i = 1, ..., N\}$ be a dataset in which each column is a datum drawn from a union of L independent linear subspaces, $S = \{S_l, l = 1, ..., L\}$. S_l is a set including all data which belong to the lth subspace with the unknown dimensions d_l.

The problem of subspace clustering is to find L, their dimensions d_l, and assign each datum in X to a subspace or treat it as an outlier.

In SSCs, a special property, named self-expressiveness property, is used to determine whether a datum is in a subspace or not [10]. This property means that if a datum lies in one subspace, then it can be represented as a linear combination of other data in the same subspace. In general, we can obtain a sparse expression of x_i through solving an optimization problem as follows,

$$\min_{c_i} \|c_i\|_0 \, s.t. \, x_i = Xc_i, \, c_{ii} = 0, \tag{1}$$

where $\|\bullet\|_0$ is the l_0-norm, and c_i is the sparse expressive coefficient of x_i in X. Problem (1) is an NP-hard problem to find the sparsest representation of x_i using l_0-norm [17]. In order to efficiently get the sparse expression of data, it is a general way by replacing the objective function of (1) with a relaxation variant. To achieve more information about variants of (1), one can read relative references [1, 13, 18, 19].

After all sparse expressive coefficients of data are achieved, a weighted undirected graph is constructed in different ways. Generally, the graph includes all data in X as its vertexes and uses a symmetric nonnegative matrix W as its adjacent matrix. The value of w_{ij} is the weight of the edge between x_i and x_j. In different methods, the way to construct W is different. Based on the adjacent matrix and the given number of subspaces, a general spectral method is used to complete clustering.

3   SSC-CG

The basic idea of SSC-CG can be simple presented as follows. We treat x_i as a point in a directed graph which includes all data in X. If the number of data from one subspace is enough to satisfy self-expressiveness property, these points in the directed graph should include at least one strongly connected component which is a closure subgraph. In turn, if a strongly connected component is a closure subgraph, the points in it should lie in a subspace. Based on this feature, we can discover all existing subspaces in three steps. The first step is to find all strongly connected components in the directed graph. In the next step, these data in same subspaces will be selected by the property of closure. Regarding these data as subspaces' bases, we separate the data into different clusters in the last step. In SSC-CG, the property of closure subgraph is important. In order to describe the property clearly, we give some definitions in the following,

Definition 1 (Arc Rear Set). Let $G = <V, E>$ be a directed graph, V' be a subset of V, and (v_i, v_j) be an arc in E. An arc rear set of V' is defined as follows,

$$R_{V'} = \{v_j| \, (v_i, v_j) \in E, v_i \in V', v_j \in V\}. \tag{2}$$

Obviously, $R_{V'}$ is the set of points which have directed connection with V'.

Definition 2 (Closure Subgraph). Let G be a directed graph and $G' = <V', E'>$ be a subgraph of G. G' is a closure subgraph if and only if G' satisfies that $V' = R_{V'}$.

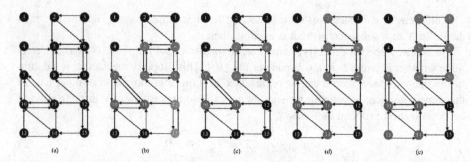

Fig. 2. An exhibition of the process of SSC-CG. (a) Constructing G using relations as arcs. (b) Finding all strongly connected components to construct S. (c) Removing subgraphs without closure property from S. (d) and (e) Adding points into S. (Color figure online)

Clearly, a closure subgraph has no relation with the outward. Any arc starting from point in a closure subgraph always ends in the same closure subgraph. Obviously, G and empty set are closure subgraphs which we call trivial closure subgraphs. In the following discussion we do not consider trivial closure subgraphs.

After obtaining the optimal solution of sparse expression optimization model, we can construct a directed graph $G = <X, E>$. Considering the situations that some outlier cannot be represented as any data combination and the computational error, we set e_{ij} using the following formula,

$$e_{ij} = \begin{cases} 1, & |c_{ij}| \geq \varepsilon \\ 0, & otherwise, \end{cases} \tag{3}$$

where ε is a threshold to filter computational error. So G is a directed graph without weights. G presents the expressive relations in X. Figure 2(a) gives an example of G.

We divide its points into three classes after obtaining G. The first one is that a point have no any relations with other points, such as point 1 in Fig. 2(a). This situation indicates that the point cannot be represented by any combination of others. So we can regard points in this type as outliers. The second class is that a point can be represented by others but it cannot be used to express other points. We regard these points as border points. Their subspaces can be determined by other points. For example, points 3, 4, and 13 belong to this class in Fig. 2(a). The last situation is that a point not only can be expressed by other points but also can express other points. These points are important and they can determine segments of the others. We call these points as core points. Obviously, the points are core points in Fig. 2(a) except for points 1, 3, 4 and 13.

Then the key problem of SSC-CG is to identify these core points and assign them to the subspaces which they belong to. Obviously the core points belonging to one subspace have a special character that these points have no arc pointing out the set which only include themselves. In other words, their expressions do not depend on points in other subspace. So a subgraph which only includes core points in one subspace is a closure subgraph of G. In general, if a strongly connected component is a closure subgraph, it must be a minimal closure subgraph. A minimal closure subgraph is a strongly connected component meanwhile. These core points from a same subspace will form at least one closure subgraph. But it is difficult to find subspace using closure property straightforward. We observe that the core points in one subspace will construct strongly connected components. These components can be closure or not. In most conditions, if we choose a suitable optimal model for the dataset and the solutions of the optimal model are accurate enough, one linear subspace will only include one strongly connected component which is closure subgraph and one strongly connected component which is closure will belong to one subspace. Then, the number of subspaces is equal to the number of strongly connected components which are closures in G. Based on the feature, we can find all strongly connected component of G in the first step. Then these components which are not closures will be removed. Based on the reminding strongly connected components which are closures, we add points to them and keep their closure property step by step. When the process ends, the segment will be achieved. Figure 2 demonstrates the process.

Figure 2(a) displays a directed graph constructed by solving one of the optimization problems and using formulas (3). In Fig. 2(b), we identify points in different strongly connected components by different colors. The points in red, green, and blue construct three strongly connected components, respectively. Figure 2(c) shows that the strongly connected component {12, 15} is abandoned because it is not a closure. Figure 2(d) and (e) shows a process to add points on the reserved components to accomplish the clustering. SSC-CG is listed in Algorithm 1.

Algorithm 1. Sparse Subspace Clustering via Closure subGraph (SSC-CG)

Inputs: Dataset X and parameters.

Outputs: Subspace set S.

1. $S=\{\}$;
2. Obtain sparse coefficient matrix C^* by solving an optimization model of sparse representation;
3. Construct direct graph G from C^* using (3);
4. $S=\{S_i \mid S_i$ is a strongly connected component which is a closure subgraph$\}$;
5. **while** S is changed
6.   Select point $p_j \in X$ which could keep closure property for S_i;
7. $S_i=S_i \cup p_j$;
8. $X=X-p_j$;
9. **end while**

The main difference between SSC [10] and SSC-CG is how to accomplish the separation of data into subspaces based on graph. Then we analyze the complexity of computation and memory on this part. Obviously, SSC-CG includes two main steps to obtain the clusters. The first one is to find all strongly connected components of G. It costs about $O(n + e)$ where n and e are the numbers of the vertexes and arcs of G, respectively. In the worst condition, $e \approx nd_{max}$ where d_{max} is the maximum value of d_l. So the computational complexity is $O(n)$. The second one is to assign points to subspaces with $O(n)$ computational complexity. Totally, SSC-CG costs $O(n)$ to accomplish subspace discovery. On the memory requirement, the main cost is in the storage of G. Because G can be stored using sparse method, the memory cost of SSC-CG is $O(n)$ which is much lower than $O(n^3)$ of SSC.

4 Experimental Analysis

4.1 Experimental Design

In this section we evaluate our proposed method. We compared our method with SSC [10] and K-mean. All experiments were conducted on a window 7 system with 2.0 GHz Intel Core i5 processor. The soft platform was Matlab 2012a. We used CVX optimization package to solve optimization problems in our experiments. Experiments under same parameters were executed for twenty times.

We evaluate three aspect performances of algorithms. They are clustering accuracy (AC) and standard deviation of AC (Std. AC), computation time (CT) and standard deviation of CT (Std. CT), assignment time (AT) and standard deviation of AT (Std. AT). CT is the time from loading dataset into memory to accomplish subspace clustering, and AT is the time from obtaining coefficient matrix to give subspace segments.

To evaluate the performances of SSC-CG, we designed two experiments in different scenes. The first experiment was to discover a subspace from a dataset which includes only one subspace and noise data. The second one was to discover a subspace with small number of data from a dataset that includes another subspace with a large scale data and some noise data. In the two experiments, we set $M = 20$ and the dimension of each subspace to be 5. The noise data lay in the space by uniform distribution.

In the first experiment, we randomly generated N_s data in the single subspace with d-dimension firstly. Then we added noise data which was randomly generated in uniform distribution into the dataset. Figures 3 and 4 display the results of the first experiment on accuracy and computational time respectively.

In the second experiment, we evaluated the performance of obtaining a small subspace from a dataset which includes two subspaces and some noise points. One subspace is the main subspace with large quantity points and another subspace is minor subspace with small quantity data. We fix the size of the main subspace and the number

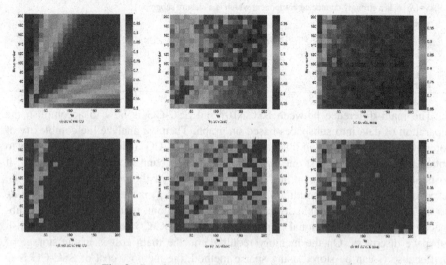

Fig. 3. Results on accuracy in the first experiment.

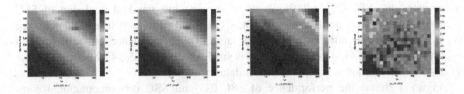

Fig. 4. Results on computational time in the first experiment.

of noise point. Let the size of the main subspace keep 100 and the size of noise be 10. The size of the minor subspace changed from 10 to 50. With changing the size of the minor subspace, we also change the angel between the two subspaces. The angel of the two subspace, θ, is defined as follows,

$$\cos(\theta) = \max_{x \in S_1, y \in S_2} \frac{x^T y}{\|x\|_2 \|y\|_2} \tag{4}$$

where $(\cdot)^T$ is transposition of $(\cdot)$.

4.2   Experimental Results

4.2.1   Results of the First Experiment

In Fig. 3(a), (b), and (c) give the mean values of AC for SSC-CG, SSC, and K-mean, respectively. In Fig. 3(d), (e), and (f) are the standard deviation values of AC for SSC-CG, SSC, and K-mean.

From (a), (b), and (c), we observe the following phenomenon. When the number of noise data is larger than the number of data in subspace, SSC-CG has a highest accuracy in the three algorithms. For example, when N_s is 10, 2 times of dimension of the subspace, and the number of noise reached 200, 10 times of N_s, the accuracy of SSC-CG achieves about 95 % while SSC reaches 80 % and K-mean only gets 65 %. It manifests that SSC-CG has an exciting performance on discovering subspace when a subspace with a small number of data hides in a large number chaotic data. In another words, SSC-CG is more suitable to discover a subspace than SSC. With N_s increase, the accuracy of SSC-CG drops gradually and the others increase stepwise. After N_s exceeds a certain value, SSC and K-mean will reach high accuracy. SSC-CG displays an exciting performance when the difference of number between subspace data and noise is large. When the difference is very little, SSC-CG cannot make a significant segment. The reason lies in that when the N_s and the number of noise are very large, some noise data can be represented by other noise data or some noise data can be represented by data in subspace. It will lead to an undesirable result that the closure character of subspace to be broken by noise. So the accuracy of SSC-CG decline.

The robustness of the three algorithms are also different in different conditions. In general, SSC-CG holds the lowest standard deviation of the three algorithms in each pair of N_s and number of noise in most conditions. When the number of noise is small, the three algorithms show a similar performance on robustness. While the number of noise increases, SSC-CG still shows its steady and the standard deviation of SSC increase. An important performance of SSC-CG lies in that it holds its robustness when N_s is small and the number of noise is large. The performance on accuracy and robustness of SSC-CG in condition of N_s is small shows that SSC-CG is very suitable to discover an unknown subspace from a dataset.

Figure 4 shows the performance of SSC-CG and SSC on computational complexity. From (a) and (b), results on CT of SSC-CG and SSC respectively, we can find two phenomena. Firstly, the results on CT are almost equal between SSC-CG and SSC, but they are much larger than K-mean. The results of K-mean on CT are about 10^{-2} s in almost conditions. The results of SSC-CG and SSC are about 1000 times of K-mean. The main reason lies in that the computation of the coefficient matrix has a very large ratio in CT with about 99 %. It is very time-consuming to solve an optimization problem. The expensive cost leads to a predicament that an algorithm cannot be suitable to a large scale dataset with solving optimization problem. Secondly, the results of CT increase with the growth of the number of data in general condition and do not care about data is subspace or noise. That means the computational complexities of the two algorithms, SSC-CG and SSC, are not sensitive to the character of the data.

The advantage of SSC-CG in AT is very clear in Fig. 4(c) and (d). In most situations, SSC-CG has a 1 % time cost of SSC in the assignment process. It is because that SSC needs to do a SVD operation on the coefficient matrix which is about $O(n^3)$. Otherwise, SSC-CG needs only to do two processes with computational time $O(n)$. One process is to find all strongly connected components and another one is assignment process. The two processes are all linear. So the difference between SSC-CG and SSC is very large on assignment time. At the same time, the assignment time of SSC-CG is only depended on the number of data. The ratio of numbers between subspace and noise does not influenced its assignment time.

4.2.2 Results of the Second Experiment

Figures 5 and 6 show the results in the second experiment. Figure 5 gives comparisons on mean values and standard deviations of accuracy for the three algorithms in different pair of N_s and θ. Figure 6 gives contrast on CT and AT for SSC-CG and SSC while the computation time of K-mean is very little in the experiment.

From (a), (b), and (c) in Fig. 5, we can obtain three conclusions. Firstly, in most conditions, SSC-CG has the best performance among the three algorithms. Secondly, the accuracy of SSC-CG does not vary with the angle variation while the other algorithms are greatly influenced by the alteration of angle. The accuracy of SSC-CG stably lies in a very small interval with the size about 0.02, and range of the other algorithms are about 0.2. Thirdly, when the angle is fixed, the growth of N_s does not influence the accuracy of the three algorithms. In other words, the accuracy has no distinct relation with accuracy when a subspace is fixed and the dataset includes noise. Finally, with the change of angle, different algorithms show different.

SSC-CG is not influenced by the angel when N_s is fixed on the mean and standard deviation matrices. SSC and K-mean are influenced greatly when the angle changes. So SSC-CG demonstrates a better performance than the other algorithms on accuracy. Figure 6 displays computational time and assignment time of SSC-CG and SSC. From (a) and (b), CT of SSC-CG and SSC, respectively, we can find that the integrated

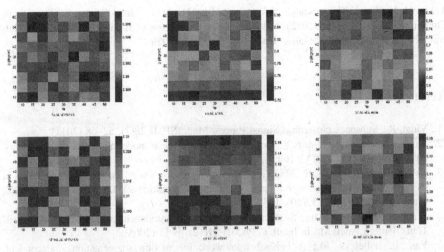

Fig. 5. Results on accuracy in the second experiment.

Fig. 6. Results on computational time in the second experiment.

computational time is very similar between the two algorithms. From (c) and (d), the assignment time of SSC-CG is about 1 % of SSC in the same condition. To complete assignment of 160 data, SSC-CG needs about 0.002 s while SSC needs about 0.3 s. The AT of SSC-CG and SSC are declined with the angle declining. For SSC-CG, the increase of N_s influences scarcely on the AT, and the increase of AT is very little.

5   Conclusion

In this paper, we proposed a novel sparse subspace clustering algorithm, SSC-CG. Using a directed graph instead of an undirected graph, we can accomplish subspace clustering without the number of subspaces given as prior information. After obtaining the coefficients of data, we transform the coefficients into a directed graph. Through finding closure strongly connected components, we can determine the number of subspaces, and the core points of each subspace. Based on these core points, the reminder data can be assigned to a subspace or regarded as outlier. Using directed graph, we success to decline the computation complexity from $O(n^3)$ down to $O(n)$ in assignment step with holding a high accuracy in most conditions. Based on the performances of SSC-CG, we can extend it into many domain such as stream, online subspace discovery, and large scale subspace clustering.

Acknowledgments. This research was supported by National Natural Science Foundation of China (nos. 71271211, 71531012), Natural Science Foundation of Beijing (no. 4132067), Natural Science Foundation of Renmin University (no. 10XN1029).

References

1. Vidal, R.: Subspace clustering. Signal Proces. Mag. (SPM) **28**(2), 52–68 (2011)
2. Zhang, T., Szlam, A., Wang, Y., Leaman, G.: Hybrid linear modeling via local best-fit flats. Int. J. Comput. Vis. (IJCV) **100**(3), 217–240 (2012)
3. Rao, S., Tron, R., Vidal, R., Ma, Y.: Motion segmentation via robust subspace separation in the presence of outlying, incomplete, or corrupted trajectories. IEEE Trans. Pattern Anal. Mach. Intell. (TPAMI) **32**(10), 1832–1845 (2010)
4. Vidal, R., Ma, Y., Sastry, S.: Generalized principal component analysis (GPCA). IEEE Trans. Pattern Anal. Mach. Intell. (TPAMI) **27**(12), 1–15 (2005)
5. Yan, J., Pollefeys, M.: A general framework for motion segmentation: independent, articulated, rigid, non-rigid, degenerate and non-degenerate. In: Leonardis, A., Bischof, H., Pinz, A. (eds.) ECCV 2006. LNCS, vol. 3954, pp. 94–106. Springer, Heidelberg (2006). doi:10.1007/11744085_8
6. Chen, G., Lerman, G.: Spectral curvature clustering. Int. J. Comput. Vis. (IJCV) **81**(3), 317–330 (2009)
7. Candès, E., Romberg, J., Tao, T.: Robust uncertainty principles: exact signal reconstruction from highly incomplete frequency information. IEEE Trans. Inf. Theory (TIT) **52**(2), 489–509 (2006)
8. Donoho, D.: Compressed sensing. IEEE Trans. Inf. Theory (TIT) **52**(4), 1289–1306 (2006)
9. Elhamifar, E.: Vidal, R.: Sparse subspace clustering. In: Computer Vision and Pattern Recognition (CVPR) (2009)
10. Elhamifar, E., Vidal, R.: Sparse subspace clustering: algorithm, theory, and applications. IEEE Trans. Pattern Anal. Mach. Intell. (TPAMI) **35**(11), 2765–2781 (2013)
11. Luxburg, U.V.: A tutorial on spectral clustering. Stat. Comput. **17**, 395–416 (2007)
12. Patel, V.M., Nguyen, H.V., Vidal, R.: Latent space sparse subspace clustering. In: International Conference on Computer Vision (ICCV) (2013)
13. Patel, V.M., Nguyen, H.V., Vidal, R.: Latent space sparse and low-rank subspace clustering. IEEE J. Sel. Top. Signal Proces. **9**(4), 691–701 (2015)
14. Peng, X., Zhang, L., Yi, Z.: Scalable sparse subspace clustering. In: Computer Vision and Pattern Recognition (CVPR) (2013)
15. Patel, V.M., Vidal, R.: Kernel sparse subspace clustering. In: International Conference on Image Processing (ICIP) (2014)
16. Adler, A., Elad, M., Hel-Or, Y.: Linear-time subspace clustering via bipartite graph modeling. IEEE Trans. Neural Netw. Learn. Syst. (TNNLS). **26**(10), 2234–2246 (2015)
17. Amaldi, E., Kann, V.: On the approximability of minimizing nonzero variables or unsatisfied relations in linear systems. Theor. Comput. Sci. **209**, 237–260 (1998)
18. Candès, E., Tao, T.: Decoding by linear programming. IEEE Trans. Inf. Theory (TIT) **51**(12), 4203–4215 (2005)
19. He, R., Zhang, Y., Sun, Z., Yin, Q.: Robust subspace clustering with complex noise. IEEE Trans. Image Process. (TIP) **24**(11), 4001–4013 (2015)

Robust Lip Segmentation Based on Complexion Mixture Model

Yangyang Hu[1], Hong Lu[1], Jinhua Cheng[2], Wenqiang Zhang[2(✉)], Fufeng Li[3],
and Weifei Zhang[3]

[1] Shanghai Key Lab of Intelligent Information Processing,
School of Computer Science, Fudan University, Shanghai, People's Republic of China
[2] School of Computer Science, Shanghai Engineering Research Center for Video
Technology and System, Fudan University, Shanghai, People's Republic of China
wqzhang@fudan.edu.cn
[3] Shanghai University of Traditional Chinese Medicine, Shanghai 201203, China

Abstract. Lip image analysis plays a vital role in Traditional Chinese Medicine (TCM) and other visual and speech recognition applications. However, if the lip images contain weak color difference with background parts or the background is complicated, most of the current methods are difficult to robustly and accurately segment the lip regions. In this paper, we propose a lip segmentation method based on complexion mixture model to resolve this problem. Specifically, we use the pixels' color of the upper (lip-free) part of the face as training data to build a corresponding complexion Gaussian Mixture Model (GMM) for each face image in *Lab* color space. Then by iteratively removing the complexion pixels not belonging to the lip region in the lower part of the face based on the GMM, an initial lip can be obtained. We further build GMMs on the initial lip and non-lip regions, respectively. The background probability map can be obtained based on the GMMs. Finally, we extract the optimal lip contour via a smooth operation. Experiments are performed on our dataset with 1000 face images. Experimental results demonstrate the efficacy of the proposed method compared with the state-of-art lip segmentation methods.

Keywords: Lip segmentation · Complexion mixture model

1 Introduction

In Traditional Chinese Medicine (TCM), lip diagnosis is one of the most important diagnostic methods of medical inspection, which can be used to reflect the human's healthy status. The lip is analyzed by an experienced doctor's naked eyes in traditional diagnostic method. This method is particularly inefficient when dealing with a large number of lip images. Therefore, it is necessary to robustly and accurately segment lip regions from face images for TCM. However, if the lip images contain weak color difference with background parts or the

© Springer International Publishing AG 2016
E. Chen et al. (Eds.): PCM 2016, Part I, LNCS 9916, pp. 85–94, 2016.
DOI: 10.1007/978-3-319-48890-5_9

background is complicated, lip segmentation is difficult. On the other hand, lip detection is widely used in many applications such as face detection, lip reading, and speech recognition [1–5].

In general, the color difference between the lip region and the facial skin background vary a lot for different people. Thus it is necessary to propose a lip segmentation method to adapt to various color differences. Many methods for lip image segmentation have been proposed. Specifically, [6] proposes a lip segmentation method based on facial complexion template. First, the largest bins in H and S components of upper-part of the detected face are used as the template of the pure-face region in HSV color space. Then it removes the non-lip pixels based on the constructed template in the lower-part of the face image. The lip segmentation result highly relies on the template. However, a single H and S value can not well represent the facial complexion.

[7,8] propose clustering methods to resolve the problem. In the methods, the number of clusters needs to be determined first. Thus the methods can not adapt to diverse lip images. Especially, when dealing with lip images with complex background such as mustaches or beards, it is difficult to accurately segment the lip regions. [9] proposes a multi-class, shape-guided Fuzzy C-Means (FCM) clustering algorithm for lip segmentation.

Another class of widely-used methods are based on a color transformation or color filter to enhance the contrast between lip region and non-lip region [10,11]. For images with weak color difference between lip and non-lip regions, or the image with complicated background, these methods can not obtain satisfactory results. On the other hand, a single-Gaussian model is used for the non-lip region in [11]. Since the background region is normally inhomogeneous, single-Gaussian can not well model the background.

In this paper, we address the challenge of accurate lip segmentation by constructing a complexion mixture model. In recent years, Gaussian Mixture Model (GMM) has been widely used in image segmentation due to its efficacy. It accurately segment the objects in a probabilistic manner. The applications include GrabCut [12], Video SnapCut [13], and Soft Scissors [14], etc. We adopt GMM in lip segmentation. The framework is shown in Fig. 1. Specifically, we first use the pixels' color of the upper (lip-free) part of the face as training data to build a corresponding complexion GMM for each face image in Lab color space. Then by iteratively removing the complexion pixels not belonging to the lip region in the lower part of the face based on the GMM, an initial lip can be obtained. We further build GMMs on the initial lip and non-lip regions, respectively. The background probability map can be obtained based on the GMMs. Finally, we extract the optimal lip contour via a smooth operation.

2   Building the Complexion GMM

First of all, we utilize Haar classifier [15] to detect human face from the input image. If the input image is large, we scale the image to accelerate face detection.

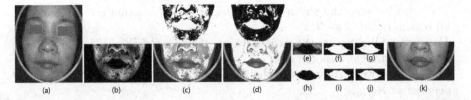

Fig. 1. Illustration of the proposed lip segmentation method. (a) The detected face image. (b) The complexion probability map of the lower part of the face. The results after the 2nd iteration (c), and 5th iteration (d) where the lip region is obtained. (e) The region-of-interest (ROI) of the lip obtained from (b). The results after 6th iteration (f), and 8th iteration (g) where the initial lip is obtained. (h) The background probability map. (i) The binary image obtained. (j) The optimal lip mask obtained by "k-points method". (k) The final lip contour.

Then we can obtain the face part and remove the non-face background. Actually, the accuracy of removing the non-face background has little effect on obtaining the final lip segmentation result. We use the pixels' color of the upper (lip-free) part of the face as the training data to build a GMM for facial skin in *Lab* color space. Here *Lab* color space is selected due to its persistency with human perception. The number of components in GMM is set to 3 based on our empirical study.

3 Lip Detection

The complexion mixture model has been constructed in the *Lab* color space. Then for each pixel j in the lower part of the face with its color value $x_j = (l_j, a_j, b_j)^T$, its complexion probability generated from the complexion mixture model is computed as

$$p(x_j) = \sum_{k=1}^{3} \pi_k \frac{1}{(2\pi)^{\frac{3}{2}} |\Sigma_k|^{\frac{1}{2}}} \times \exp\{-\frac{1}{2}(x_j - \mu_k)^T \Sigma_k^{-1}(x_j - \mu_k)\} \quad (1)$$

where π_k, μ_k, Σ_k are the weight, mean and the covariance of the k_{th} Gaussian component in the mixture model, respectively. A complexion probability map of the lower part of the face can be obtained.

3.1 Prior Knowledge of the Lips

Based on the large amounts of lip images in our dataset, we can obtain the statistical information on the size and position of lips in the lower part of the face images.

– The ratio between the width and the height of the external rectangle of the lip region, denoted as R_{wh}.
– The target fill rate, i.e. the ratio between the areas of the lip region and its external rectangle, denoted as R_{fill}.
– The ratio between the areas of the lip region and the lower part of the face, denoted as R_{area}.
– The center position of the lip region, denoted as $l_c = \{l_x, l_y\}$.

In the experiment, $R_{wh} \in [1, 6]$, $R_{fill} \in [0.3, 1)$, $R_{area} \in [0.03, 0.15]$. l_x ranges from one-third to two-thirds of the width of the lower part of the face. l_y is larger than one-third of the height of the lower part of the face.

3.2   Detecting Lip Region

In traditional lip detection methods, normally a fixed threshold is used to estimate the pixels belonging to lip region or not. However, the color difference between the lip and the facial skin background around the lip vary a lot for different people. Also, in some cases, the difference is weak. We address the problem by an iterative detection method. First, we set an iterative threshold array as $it\,[14] = \{0.6, 0.5, 0.4, 0.3, 0.2, 0.1, 0.05, 0.01, 0.005, 0.001, 0.0005, 0.0001, 0.00005, 0.00001\}$. The values in the array are set based on our empirical study. Figure 2 shows an example of iteratively detecting the lip region for Fig. 1.

Iteratively Detecting the Lip. We use the iterative method to detect the lip region in the complexion probability map of the lower part of the face as below.

1. Initialization: set $i = 0$, i.e., the iterative value takes $it[0]$.
2. Remove the complexion pixels: for each pixel j in the complexion probability map, if $p(x_j) \geq it[i]$, it means the pixel is similar to facial complexion, then remove the pixel, else reserve the pixel.
3. Find the number of the candidate lip regions in the lower part of the face by using the prior knowledge of the lips, denoted as lip_{cnt}.
4. If $lip_{cnt} \equiv 1$, it means the lip region is found, then set $i_t = i$, get the region-of-interest (ROI) of the lip, and go to iteratively optimizing the lip region. Else if $lip_{cnt} \neq 1$ and $i < 14$, then increase i and go to Step 2. Else no lip region is found, and exit.

Figure 1(c) shows the result of the 2nd iteration. Figure 1(d) shows the result of the 5th iteration where the lip region is found. Figure 1(e) shows the ROI of the lip region.

Iteratively Optimizing the Lip Region. Normally the brightness of complexion pixel is higher than non-complexion pixel in the complexion probability map. The self-adaptive threshold value computed by the iterative method should be able to distinguish between complexion pixels and non-complexion pixels. Intuitively, with the decrease of the threshold $it[i]$, i.e., the increase of i, the area of the detected complexion region is increased. However, the increment is not large in a certain scope. It is due to most of the complexion pixels have been detected at this stage, and most of the non-complexion pixels have not been mistakenly regarded as complexion pixels. But if we continue reducing the threshold $it[i]$, i.e., increasing i, the area of the detected complexion region will be increased dramatically since many non-complexion pixels will be regarded as complexion pixels. Then we need to set the optimal threshold where the growth rate of the detected complexion pixels relatively low.

Specifically, we start with $i = i_t$ to iteratively remove the complexion pixels in the complexion probability map of the lip's ROI. In the iteration, we obtain the first local minimum of the growth rate and set the optimal threshold as the corresponding $it[i]$, i.e. $T = it[i]$. If no local minimum of the growth rate is found, $T = it[i_t]$. Then in the complexion probability map of the lip's ROI, we use the determined threshold T to remove the complexion pixels and obtain a binary image of the initial lip region. Figure 1(f) shows the result of the 6th iteration. Figure 1(g) shows the obtained initial lip region.

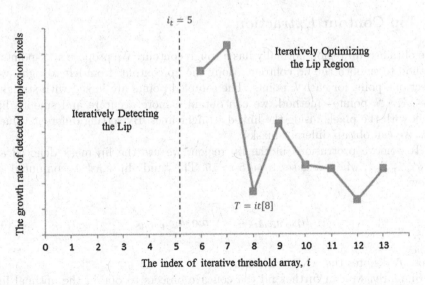

Fig. 2. Illustration of iteratively detecting the lip region for Fig. 1. For iteratively detecting the lip, the lip is found in the 5th iteration, $i_t = 5$. For iteratively optimizing the lip region, the first local minimum of growth rate is obtained in the 8th iteration, $T = it[8]$.

4   Optimization

Normally the initial lip region is not the optimal one. It contains some skin pixels. Some lip pixels are also wrongly eliminated in the initial lip. To further resolve the problem, we propose an optimization method. Specifically, in *Lab* color space, we use the color of the pixels in the initial lip and non-lip regions to build refined GMMs, respectively. The initial lip and non-lip regions are shown in the block of Fig. 1(g). The number of the component in each GMM is set to 3 based on our empirical study. We use the two GMMs to compute the background probability map. For each pixel j with its color value $x_j = (l_j, a_j, b_j)^T$ in the initial lip image, its background probability generated from the two GMMs is computed as below.

$$p_B(x_j) = \frac{p(x_j|non\_lip)}{p(x_j|non\_lip) + p(x_j|lip)} \tag{2}$$

where $p(x_j|lip)$ and $p(x_j|non\_lip)$ are the corresponding probabilities computed from the two GMMs. A background probability map obtained in this method is shown in Fig. 1(h). We further use the Otsu's method [16] to obtain an binary image. Then we find the largest connected region to obtain the lip region. The obtained lip region is shown in Fig. 1(i).

5   Lip Contour Extraction

The obtained lip region normally has a rough contour. We propose a "k-points" method to smooth the lip contour. Along the lip contour, from left to right, we select one point for each k points. The sampled points are linked with straight lines. By "k-points" method, we can obtain a more accurate and smooth lip mask with the pixels inside the linked straight lines. By setting different values of k, we can obtain different masks.

To remove protrusions in the lip region, we use the lip mask denoted as $mask_{k-points}$, where k is set from 5 to 15. The "and" lip mask is computed as below.

$$lip_{and\_mask} = \bigwedge_{k=5}^{15} mask_{k-points} \tag{3}$$

where $\bigwedge$ denotes the AND operation.

Similarly, we can further fill the concave objects to obtain the optimal lip mask denoted as $lip_{optimal\_mask}$ by using the OR operation. The optimal lip mask is computed as below.

$$lip_{optimal\_mask} = \bigvee_{k=5}^{10} (lip_{and\_mask})_{k-points} \tag{4}$$

where $\bigvee$ denotes the OR operation, and k is set from 5 to 10. Finally, based on the optimal lip mask, the optimal contour of the lip can be obtained. The optimal lip mask obtained by "k-points" method is shown in Fig. 1(j). Figure 1(k) shows the final lip contour.

6   Experiment

6.1   Experimental Data and Setting

We use the dataset which contains 1131 face images. The images are captured in the Shanghai Shuguang Hospital. The images are in size of 2816×2112. We randomly sample 1000 images from the dataset and manually annotate the images as ground truth. We compare the proposed lip detection method with Sun's [6] and Li's [11] methods. In the evaluation, two criteria of OL and SE are used in [6,11]. Specifically, OL measures the area overlap of the detection result with the ground truth. The larger the OL value, the better the performance. SE is defined to measure the segmentation error. The lower the value, the better the performance.

6.2   Experimental Results

Table 1 illustrates the comparison of our proposed method with the state-of-art methods [6,11]. It can be observed from Table 1 that our method can obtain better performance than the compared methods.

Figures 3 and 4 shows some lip contour extraction results for the images in the dataset. From Figs. 3 and 4, we can see that the lip segmentation results by using our method are more accurate than that obtained by the compared methods. Even for lip images with weak color difference, our method can also well segment the lip regions.

For lip images with mustaches or beards, the background region becomes complicated. Normally the current methods can not well detect the lip regions. On the other hand, our proposed method can well resolve the problem. When we build the complexion GMM based on the upper (lip-free) part of the face, the training data can reserve some pixels belonging to the eyebrows and the hair.

Table 1. Comparison of lip segmentation methods

Method	Li's [11]	Sun's [6]	Ours
Average OL (%)	85.87	87.05	96.76
Average SE (%)	16.46	11.25	3.29

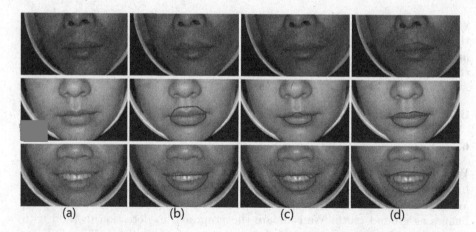

Fig. 3. Lip contour extraction results. (a) Original lip images. The results obtained by Li's method [11] (b), Sun's method [6] (c), and the proposed method (d). (Color figure online)

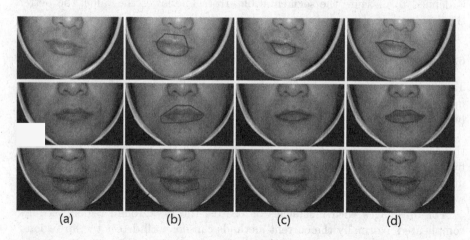

Fig. 4. Lip contour extraction results. (a) Original lip images. The results obtained by Li's method [11] (b), Sun's method [6] (c), and the proposed method (d). (Color figure online)

Since the color of the eyebrows and the hair is similar to the color of mustaches or beards in the lower part of the face, the mustaches or beards can be removed by the complexion mixture model. Figure 5 shows some segmentation results for lip images with mustaches or beards. Comparing the corresponding three output images, we can see that our method outperforms the other two methods for lip images with complex background.

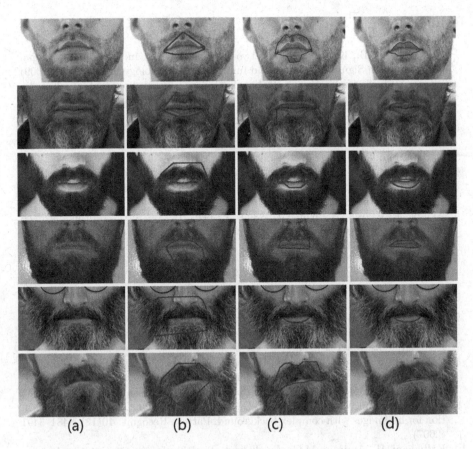

(a)   (b)   (c)   (d)

Fig. 5. Lip segmentation results for lip images with mustaches or beards. (a) Original lip images. (b) Li's method [11]. (c) Sun's method [6]. (d) the paper's method. (Color figure online)

7 Conclusions

In this paper, we propose a complexion mixture model for robust and accurate lip segmentation. It is in a probabilistic manner. We formulate a corresponding complexion GMM for each face image. For lip images with weak color difference or complicated background, the proposed method can well segment the lip regions. Experimental results demonstrate that the proposed method can obtain promising performance. The lip segmentation results can be served for TCM and other applications such as lip reading, speech recognition, etc.

Acknowledgements. This work was supported in part by the National Natural Science Foundation of China (No. 81373555), and Shanghai Committee of Science and Technology (14JC1402202 and 14441904403).

References

1. Shin, J., Jun, B., Kim, D.: Robust two-stage lip tracker. In: IEEE International Symposium on Signal Processing and Information Technology, pp. 265–270 (2009)
2. Zhang, Y., Levinson, S., Huang, T.: Speaker independent audio-visual speech recognition. In: IEEE International Conference on Multimedia and Expo, vol. 2, pp. 1073–1076 (2000)
3. Lucey, S., Sridharan, S., Chandran, V.: Initialised eigenlip estimator for fast lip tracking using linear regression. In: IEEE International Conference on Pattern Recognition, vol. 3, pp. 178–181 (2000)
4. Rabi, G., Lu, S.: Visual speech recognition by recurrent neural networks. In: Engineering Innovation: Voyage of Discovery Electrical and Computer Engineering, vol. 1, pp. 55–58. IEEE (1997)
5. Ngiam, J., Khosla, A., Kim, M., Nam, J., Lee, H., Ng, A.Y.: Multimodal deep learning. In: Proceedings of the 28th International Conference on Machine Learning, pp. 689–696 (2011)
6. Sun, C., Lu, H., Zhang, W., Qiu, X., Li, F., Zhang, H.: Lip segmentation based on facial complexion template. In: Ooi, W.T., Snoek, C.G.M., Tan, H.K., Ho, C.-K., Huet, B., Ngo, C.-W. (eds.) PCM 2014. LNCS, vol. 8879, pp. 193–202. Springer, Heidelberg (2014). doi:10.1007/978-3-319-13168-9_20
7. Ghaleh, V.E.C., Behrad, A.: Lip contour extraction using RGB color space and fuzzy c-means clustering. In: IEEE International Conference on Cybernetic Intelligent Systems, pp. 1–4 (2010)
8. Rahman, F.S., Nath, R., Nath, S., Basak, S., Audin, S.I., Fattah, S.A.: Lip contour extraction scheme based on k-means clustering in different color planes. In: IEEE International Conference on Informatics, Electronics & Vision, pp. 1–4 (2014)
9. Wang, S.-L., Lau, W.-H., Liew, A.W.-C., Leung, S.-H.: Robust lip region segmentation for lip images with complex background. Pattern Recognit. 40(12), 3481–3491 (2007)
10. Kalbkhani, H., Amirani, M.C.: An efficient algorithm for lip segmentation in color face images based on local information. J. World Elect. Eng. Technol. 1(1), 12–16 (2012)
11. Li, M., Cheung, Y.: Automatic segmentation of color lip images based on morphological filter. In: Diamantaras, K., Duch, W., Iliadis, L.S. (eds.) ICANN 2010. LNCS, vol. 6352, pp. 384–387. Springer, Heidelberg (2010). doi:10.1007/978-3-642-15819-3_51
12. Rother, C., Kolmogorov, V., Blake, A.: "Grabcut": interactive foreground extraction using iterated graph cuts. ACM Trans. Graph. 23(3), 309–314 (2004)
13. Bai, X., Wang, J., David, S., Sapiro, G.: Video snapcut: robust video object cutout using localized classifiers. ACM Trans. Graph. (TOG) 28(3) (2009)
14. Wang, J., Agrawala, M., Cohen, M.F.: Soft scissors: an interactive tool for realtime high quality matting. In: ACM Transactions on Graphics (TOG), vol. 26. ACM (2007)
15. Viola, P., Jones, M.: Rapid object detection using a boosted cascade of simple features. In: Proceedings of the IEEE Computer Society Conference on Computer Vision and Pattern Recognition, CVPR 2001, vol. 1, pp. I-511 (2001)
16. Otsu, N.: A threshold selection method from gray-level histograms. Automatica 11(285–296), 23–27 (1975)

Visual BFI: An Exploratory Study for Image-Based Personality Test

Jitao Sang[1(✉)], Huaiwen Zhang[1,2], and Changsheng Xu[1,2]

[1] Institute of Automation, Chinese Academy of Sciences, Beijing, China
{jtsang,zhanghuaiwen2016,csxu}@nlpr.ia.ac.cn
[2] University of Chinese Academy of Sciences, Beijing, China

Abstract. This paper positions and explores the topic of image-based personality test. Instead of responding to text-based questions, the subjects will be provided a set of "choose-your-favorite-image" visual questions. With the image options of each question belonging to the same concept, the subjects' personality traits are estimated by observing their preferences of images under several unique concepts. The solution to design such an image-based personality test consists of concept-question identification and image-option selection. We have presented a preliminary framework to regularize these two steps in this exploratory study. A demo version of the designed image-based personality test is available at http://www.visualbfi.org/. Subjective as well as objective evaluations have demonstrated the feasibility of accurately estimation the personality of subjects in limited round of visual questions.

1 Introduction

Personality refers to a type of psychological traits explaining human behaviors in terms of a few, stable and measurable individual characteristics [1]. Different from demographic attributes, personality traits explain and predict behavior differences from the internal psychological perspective. One of the most popular personality models is Big Five (BF) or Five-Factor Model (FFM) [2], which defines personality along five dimensions, i.e., *Openness, Conscientiousness, Extraversion, Agreeableness* and *Neuroticism*. Accurately estimating these personality traits has wide applications including occupational assistance, target advertisement, personalized recommender system, disease detection and prevention, and even human-robot interaction [3,4].

Traditionally, standard personality tests, e.g., Big-Five Inventory (BFI), are used to gauge one's personality score in each dimension. In these tests, psychological experts design text-based questionnaires to ask subjects make self-assessment by responding the level of agreement to each question. The left of Fig. 1 illustrates a shorter version of the BFI comprising of 10 questions (i.e., BFI-10). The suffix "O, C, E, A, N" is the abbreviation of five personality dimensions, indicating which dimension the question contributes to. Despite the wide utilization of BFI, the current text-based personality tests are subject to several limitations: (1) The subjects need to read and understand each question

E. Chen et al. (Eds.): PCM 2016, Part I, LNCS 9916, pp. 95–106, 2016.
DOI: 10.1007/978-3-319-48890-5_10

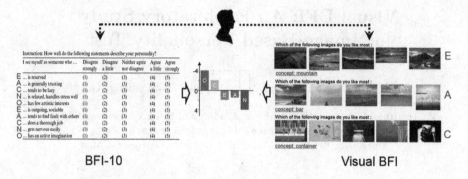

BFI-10 Visual BFI

Fig. 1. Personality test: text-based BFI-10 vs. visual BFI.

thoroughly before making responses. This is time consuming and can be a huge burden to the subjects especially in long personality tests [5] (e.g., BFI-44 with 44 questions, NEO-PI-R with 240 questions). Moreover, the text-based personality tests are built on the assumption that the subjects "have access to the psychological property to be measured" and know enough about themselves to make accurate response [6]. This is impractical in many cases and significantly limits the scope of applicability. (2) The text-based questions convey clear meanings to portray the subjects. With the predisposition toward self-enhancement, the subjects are likely to respond in a way presenting themselves more favorable [7]. For example, regarding the question "I see myself as someone who tends to be lazy" in BFI-10, most subjects will have "disagree" response to maintain positivity about themselves even at the expense of being unrealistic. This easily leads to response biases and inaccurate personality estimation. (3) Text-based questionnaires are language-sensitive. Language-specific models need to be carefully developed by experts and professionals, instead of just translating a reference model into a destination language [8]. For example, "calm" is used to measure *Neuroticism* in English-based BFI. The direct translation of "calm" in German is "ruhlg". However, "ruhlg" in German actually has both correlation with *Neuroticism* and *Extraversion*.

Recently has witnessed some studies attempting to automatically infer personality traits from users' social media interactions with images. Cristani et al. proposed to assess the personality of users by looking at their favorite images [9]. 300 Flickr users are examined with each consisting of 200 favorite images. Following this, in [10], more image features are extracted for personality prediction. Based on the derived personality traits, the application of image recommendation is investigated. These attempts suggest that people's image favorite behavior promisingly reflects their personality traits. Inspired by this, to address the above-mentioned problems in text-based personality tests, we propose to research on image-based personality test, by exploring the underlying correlation between subjects' visual preferences and personality traits to select and organize discriminative images for questionnaire design.

Language psychology shows that the choice of words is driven not only by meaning, but also by speakers'/writers' psychological characteristics such as emotions and personality traits [11]. In other words, when expressing the same meaning, it is highly possible the different psychological characteristics that leads to different word choices. We are motivated to make an analogy in the scenario of image choice, and predict the subjects' personality traits by investigating their preferences of images belonging to the same concept. In particular, *the goal is to design a set of "choose-your-favorite-image" questions, with each question corresponding to one concept and options for each question corresponding to different patterns of images under this concept.* On the right of Fig. 1 we show three example questions in our designed visual BFI. This visual BFI preferably solves the three problems in text-based personality tests: (1) Image is recognized as more natural interaction means than text. With less sense of task-performing, subjects are expected to answer the questionnaire in a more relaxed way. (2) The intent behind choosing images is not clear, which is less offensive to the subjects. Subjects therefore make objective responses based on their realistic perceptions. (3) People's perception to visual information is universal regardless of their mother tongue. Aside from cultural differences, we hope the image-based personality test is applicable to subjects in different languages.

Designing the image-based personality test consists of concept-question identification for each personality dimension, and image-option selection for each question. In the remainder of this paper, Sect. 2 explores the potential of individual concept in personality prediction. In Sect. 3, we introduce how to combine several concepts and develop boosted regressor in predicting each dimension of personality, and how to select images from these concepts to construct questions and options for questionnaire design. Section 4 presents experimental results of both the proposed boosted regressor in automatical personality prediction, and the designed image-based questionnaire on real-world personality test via Amazon Mechanical Turk.

2 Exploring Single Concept for Personality Prediction

Our study is based on the PsychoFlickr dataset provided in [9]. This dataset consists of 300 Flickr users, with each user associating with his/her 200 favorite images and the self-assessed personality traits in five dimensions. 82-dimension aesthetics and content feature has been extracted for each image. The first step of the study is to generate a candidate concept list. As illustrated in Fig. 2(a), for each of the 60,000 images, GoogleNet [12] was used to obtain the confidence score over 1,000 ImageNet categories and the top-5 categories with confidence score larger than 0.1 are remained. The 1,000 ImageNet categories construct our original concept set at level 1. To expand the candidate concepts, for each of 1,000 concepts at level 1, its hypernym in WordNet is traced and added into the included concepts for corresponding images. We repeat this process three times to obtain totally 1,789 concepts at four levels. Figure 2(b) shows an example concept hierarchy and the number of traced unique concepts at each level.

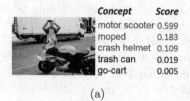

Concept	Score
motor scooter	0.599
moped	0.183
crash helmet	0.109
trash can	0.019
go-cart	0.005

	level1	level2	level3	level4
Example	motor scooter	wheeled vehicle	vehicle	conveyance, transport
#Concept	1,000	558	123	108

(a)   (b)

Fig. 2. Candidate concept generation: (a) GoogleNet-based concept detection (the remained concepts are highlighted with blue); (b) the example and statistic for hypernym-based concept expansion (Color figure online)

Table 1. Personality prediction accuracy in terms of RMSE.

Trait	SVR			LASSO			CART			CG+LASSO [9]
O	1.624	1.639	1.656	**1.612**	1.622	1.638	1.621	1.625	1.630	1.698
C	**1.729**	1.745	1.768	1.730	1.742	1.749	1.808	1.813	1.817	1.789
E	2.124	2.154	2.166	2.111	2.121	2.133	2.106	2.182	2.228	**2.077**
A	1.612	1.639	1.653	1.610	1.617	1.632	**1.606**	1.614	1.631	1.669
N	**2.148**	2.160	2.172	2.181	2.207	2.225	2.183	2.239	2.314	2.208

The images including concept c construct a image set $\mathcal{I}_c$, and the users who has favored image $I_i \in \mathcal{I}_c$ constructs a user set $\mathcal{U}_c$. Our goal in this section is to examine the potential of personality prediction based on users' favorite images belonging to single concept. To this goal, among the 1,789 concepts, we first identified 235 concepts that are favored by at least 104 users[1], i.e., $\forall c \in \mathcal{C}_1, |\mathcal{U}_c| \geq 104$. For one concept $c \in \mathcal{C}_1$, we assume each user $u \in \mathcal{U}_c$ only have one favorite image and utilize the 82-dimension image feature as user representation $\mathbf{x}_u^{(c)}$. Different personality traits are treated separately, and for each personality trait $p \in \{O, C, E, A, N\}$, we need to build a set of concept-based regressors: 104 user samples for each concept, with each sample's input as the user's favorite image feature vector $\mathbf{x}_u^{(c)}$, and the output as the user's personality score p_u (integer value from -4 to 4).

Three standard regression methods are utilized: Support Vector Regression (SVR), LASSO regression, Classification And Regression Tree (CART). Considering the small scale of samples, 10 times of 10-fold cross validation is conducted and only statistically significant (p-value $< 5\%$) results are reported. Table 1 shows the prediction accuracy of top-3 single concepts for each method. For comparison, the performance based on the method proposed in [9] is also shown and denoted as CG+LASSO. Note that the study in [9] considered 200 favorite images for each user. While, the results reported under SVR, LASSO and CART only considered at most 5 favorite images for each user. It is demonstrated from

---

[1] For those concepts favored by more than 104 users, 104 random users are selected to construct the sample set for this concept. We fix the sample number as 104 to facilitate the performance comparison with solutions in the next section.

Algorithm 1. View-based Gradient Boosted Decision Tree (vGBDT)

Input: User's personality score at certain trait $p_i \in [-4, 4]$, and his/her K-view
representation $\mathbf{x}_i \in \mathbb{R}^{Kd}$, $i = 1, \cdots, N$ (N is the number of training
samples).

Output: The strong regressor $F : \mathbf{x} \to p$.

1   $F_0 = \frac{1}{N} \sum_{i=1}^{N} p_i$

2   **for** $m = 1$ *to* M **do**

3     $r_i = p_i - F_{m-1}(\mathbf{x}_i), i = 1, \cdots, N$

4     $(V_m, R_m, A_m) = \arg\min_{V,R,A} \sum_{i=1}^{N} ||r_i - T(\mathbf{x}_i; V, R, A)||_2^2$

5     $F_m(\mathbf{x}) = F_{m-1}(\mathbf{x}) + \upsilon T(\mathbf{x}; V_m, R_m, A_m)$

6 **Return**: $F = F_M$.

---

the results that, by examining users' favorite images belonging to few selective concepts, we can achieve comparable, if not better prediction accuracy than that based on much more unorganized favorite images.

3 Combining Multiple Concepts for Personality Test

The previous section has proved the feasibility of automatic personality prediction by only examining user's image favorite behavior under single concept. This section further this study by introducing: (1) how to combine users' image favorite behavior under multiple concepts to improve the prediction accuracy, and (2) how to exploit the developed prediction model for image-based personality test design.

3.1 vGBDT-Based Multiple Concept Combination

A natural way to combine different base models is ensemble learning. Considering totally K concepts, each user can be seen as a K-view sample represented as $\mathbf{x} = (\mathbf{x}^{(1)}, \cdots, \mathbf{x}^{(i)}, \cdots, \mathbf{x}^{(K)}]^{\mathrm{T}}$, where $\mathbf{x}^{(i)} = [x_{i(d-1)+1}, \cdots, x_{id}]$ indicates his/her favorite image features under the ith concept. To facilitate the questionnaire design, each base regressor is expected to correspond to one single concept, so as to collect user's image favorite response for one concept in each round of question. This means only one view in user's representation will be utilized in one base regressor and then contribute to the final personality trait estimation.

Standard ensemble learning methods cannot be directly applied in this scenario. For example, Gradient Boosted Decision Tree (GBDT) select the best base CART from a unique feature space to fit to the residual. In this study, we modify the standard GBDT and introduce a view-based GBDT (vGBDT) to address this problem. Specifically, in the training phase, for each round of base regressor, vGBDT not only tune the optimal partitions and the output leaf value, but identify which view of features will be utilized. The base regression tree is denoted

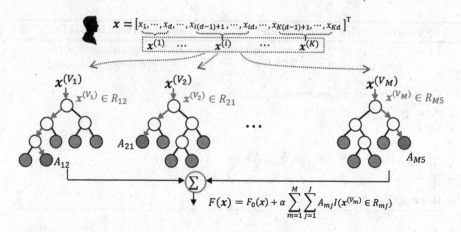

Fig. 3. vGBDT-based personality prediction by combining multiple concepts.

as $T(\mathbf{x}; V_m, R_m, A_m) = \sum_{j=1}^{J} A_{mj} \cdot \mathbb{I}(\mathbf{x}^{(V_m)} \in R_{mj})$, where $\mathbb{I}(\cdot)$ is the indicator function, J is the number of leaf nodes, V_m, R_m, A_m indicates the selected view of feature, learned disjoint partitions, and output leaf values respectively. The training phase of vGBDT is summarized in Algorithm 1. Assuming M base regressors (concepts) are considered, the final strong regressor can be expressed as an ensemble of regression trees T:

$$F(\mathbf{x}; \boldsymbol{\Theta}) = F_0 + v \sum_{m=1}^{M} T(\mathbf{x}; V_m, R_m, A_m) \tag{1}$$

where F_0 is the mean value of all training samples, v is the shrinkage parameter. In the testing phase, as illustrated in Fig. 3, user's V_m^{th} view feature is used as input to the mth regressor and the final personality score is calculated according to Eq. (1).

3.2 Image-Based Personality Test Design

After training vGBDT for each personality trait, M concepts are identified for the M corresponding questions in the personality questionnaire. For each concept-question, we need then to select J representative images as options for subjects to choose from.

Assuming the mth concept in predicting personality trait p is c_m^p, each image $I_i \in \mathcal{I}_{c_m^p}$ can be assigned to one of the J leaf nodes by running the base regressor $T(V_m^p, R_m^p, A_m^p)$. This is illustrated in the top of Fig. 4 ($J = 5$ in this case, where each image is assigned a label $l_i \in [1,5]$). To reduce the distractors that influence subjects' choice, it is critical to make the J image-options as similar as possible, e.g., at the similar aesthetic level, all w/ or w/o faces in the images, etc. Therefore, we conduct Affinity Propagation (AP) on the image set $I_i \in \mathcal{I}_{c_m^p}$

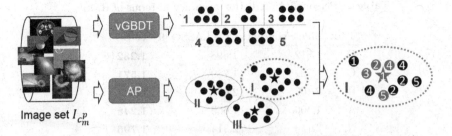

Fig. 4. Illustration for image-option selection (the red ones are selected). (Color figure online)

to obtain several image clusters. Within the largest image cluster (cluster I)[2], for each label from $\{1, 2, \cdots, J\}$, the image nearest to the cluster center is selected as the option image (see the bottom of Fig. 4).

During the personality test, for each personality trait p, the subjects will be asked to sequentially answer M questions, with each question consisting of J image-options to choose from. The subject's final personality score for p is calculated by collecting his/her choices:

$$F = F_0 + v \sum_{m=1}^{M} A_{m\pi_m} \tag{2}$$

where π_m records the option index of subject's choice for the mth question. An online version of the designed image-based personality test is available at http://www.visualbfi.org/. The personality test is expected to be finished within 5 min.

4 Experiments

4.1 Evaluation on Automatic Personality Prediction

To evaluate the performance of combining multiple concepts for personality prediction, among the 1,789 concepts, we identified 36 concepts that are co-favored by 104 users to construct he candidate concept set $\mathcal{C}_2$, i.e., $|\bigcap_{c \in \mathcal{C}_2} \mathcal{U}_c| = 104$. With the view number $K = 36$, the task of vGBDT is to select and construct M concept-based base regressors by examining the training users' favorite images over 36 concepts.

For parameter setting, considering the practical application in personality test, we choose a small number of base regressors (concept-questions) $M = 5$, i.e., the designed personality test will totally consist of $5 \times 5 = 25$ concept-questions. For each question, the number of image-options is chosen as $J = 5$. A large shrinkage weight is selected as $v = 0.5$ to value the contribution of each

---

[2] In practical implementation, we can select images from different clusters to design several versions of questionnaires.

Table 2. Personality prediction accuracy in terms of RMSE.

Trait	Single concept	CG+LASSO [9]	vGBDT
O	1.612	1.698	**1.232**
C	1.729	1.789	**1.571**
E	2.106	2.077	**1.601**
A	1.606	1.669	**1.248**
N	2.148	2.314	**1.796**

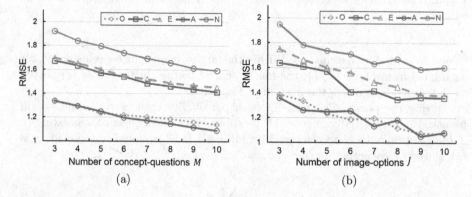

Fig. 5. Influence of vGBDT parameters: (a) the number of concept-questions M, (b) the number of image-options J.

question. 10 times of 10-fold cross validation are conducted, with the average personality prediction accuracy reported in Table 2. *Single Concept* indicates the best performance of single content for each personality trait in Table 1. It is shown that by combining users' image favorite responses over multiple concepts, vGBDT achieves significant performance gains.

We also examined the influence of concept-question and image-option numbers on prediction performance. Figure 5(a) shows the personality prediction RMSE with fixed image-option number $J = 5$ and different concept-question numbers M for each trait. The RMSE consistently decreases as the number of concept-questions increases, to achieve a low RMSE around 1.1 for the trait *Agreeableness* and *Openness* with $M = 10$ concept-questions. This basically indicates that in the personality test, the more users' favorite choices over concepts are observed, the more accurate personality estimation results can be obtained. Figure 5(b) shows the prediction RMSE with fixed concept-question number $M = 5$ and different image-option numbers J. Different from that of Fig. 5(a), there exists no monotonically decreasing tendency in Fig. 5(b). For an acceptable personality test, we fix the number of image-options $J = 5$ and the number of concept-questions $M = 5$ in the questionnaire design and the later real-world evaluation.

4.2 Evaluation on Real-World Personality Test

We conducted a real-world evaluation by recruiting 67 master workers from Amazon Mechanical Turk (MTurk). Each subject was asked to answer four questionnaires: two versions of the proposed visual BFI (vBFI), one BFI-10 and one BFI-44. To guarantee the credibility of the responses, we examined the stableness between subjects' derived traits from BFI-10 and BFI-44. 40 MTurk subjects were kept for evaluation who had RMSE in BFI-10 vs. BFI-44 lower than 1.2.

We first compared between the personality traits derived from the first version of visual BFI (vBFI_1) and BFI-10. The results are shown in the second column of Table 3. We see a higher RMSE between 1.5 to 2.0 than that in Table 2. We ascribe this decreased accuracy to two reasons: (1) different sample distribution between the training Flickr users and the testing MTurk workers (e.g., the different mean value); and (2) the coarser user division by locating subjects in fixed and limited image-options. It leaves us space for improvement by considering these two issues in the future work.

Although text-based personality test like BFI-10 has recognized accuracy and is utilized as the ground-truth in our previous studies, it should be noted that the goal of image-based personality test is not to fit to the text-based test results, but to match with the subjects' own perception. Therefore, in addition to comparing with BFI-10, we also solicited the subjects' perception of the derived traits. After finishing vBFI_1, we presented the estimated personality results from vBFI[3] to the subjects with the detailed explanation for each trait. Each subject rated how accurate they thought the derived traits were on a seven-likert scale (1 being worse and 7 being best). The mean of the resultant ratings is 5.150 ($std = 1.494$), suggesting that the derived traits from vBFI generally matched well with their own perceptions.

Finally the robustness of the designed visual BFI is examined. Following the comparison between vBFI and BFI-10, we compared between the derived traits from the two versions of visual BFI (vBFI_1 and vBFI_2). Note that vBFI_2 is designed by selecting image-options from the second-largest cluster as footnoted in Sect. 3.2. Results shown in the last column of Table 3 achieve a relative low

Table 3. Real-world evaluation results from MTurk.

Trait	vBFI_1 vs. BFI-10 (RMSE)	Rate (mean/std.)	vBFI_1 vs. vBFI_2 (RMSE)
O	1.647	5.150/1.494	0.872
C	1.859		1.004
E	2.059		1.101
A	1.506		0.866
N	2.075		1.300

---

[3] Note that the subjects were never given their personality test results from text-based BFI-10 or BFI-44 to avoid the interaction effect of different tests.

RMSE around 1. This robustness demonstrates the feasibility of visual BFI in accurately personality estimation from another perspective.

5 Conclusion, Discussion and Future Work

In this paper we position the topic of image-based personality test design and present our first exploratory study under this topic. Subjective as well as objective evaluations have demonstrated the feasibility of personality estimation by observing subjects' "choose-your-favorite-image" responses over few concept-questions.

Under the topic of image-based personality test design, this work can be extended along several directions in the future: (1) The relative small scale of subjects limits the number of explored concepts in current study. We are working towards collecting the personality traits as well as their favorite image behaviors from more subjects, so as to explore more concepts for personality test design. (2) Regarding the task of personality estimation, the image feature should reflect the style of users who favorite it, instead of indicating the image semantics. Since it is difficult to pre-define what features contribute to the discrimination of user personality, the second future direction is to combine deep learning to extract and discover the most contributive features. (3) The current personality test is based on a static questionnaire. An interesting extension is to formulate the personality test as a dynamic decision making process and develop solutions for more efficient dynamic questionnaires: given subject's previous responses, to dynamically select subsequent questions with goal of accurate personality estimation in as few steps as possible. (4) It is also significant to investigate into the mechanism behind the correlation between the visual preference behaviors and personality traits from a psychological perspective. Taking Fig. 6 as example: why different image favorites on the concept "mountain" discriminates the trait of *Extraversion*, and why favoring certain style of "mountain" images contribute most to the score calculation (with most positive output leaf value). (5) We realized that personality is only one of the factors leading to the visual preference difference. Therefore, a critical future direction is to exclude the other influencing factors like age, gender and cultural background, by restricting the subjects' to fall into certain group. The ideal solution is to develop a unified visual personality test model, and optimize model parameter settings for different groups of subjects.

Trait: Neuroticism   (*concept: mountain*)

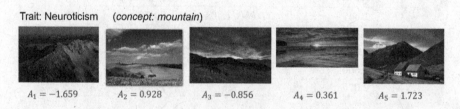

$A_1 = -1.659$ $A_2 = 0.928$ $A_3 = -0.856$ $A_4 = 0.361$ $A_5 = 1.723$

Fig. 6. Example of image-options with the corresponding output leaf value A.

In addition to image-based personality test design, this work is potentially interest-provoking to two closely-related problems: (1) Data-driven questionnaire design. Questionnaire design has long been viewed as more of an art than a science [13], where questions are initialized by professionals and then modified according to the collected responses from surveys. In the era of big data, as demonstrated in this study, it has great potential in exploring correlations from historic data to shed light on question development, or completely automating questionnaire design by formulating an optimization problem. (2) Active user modeling. Users are basically willing to answer few questions if more accurate user profiles and improved personalized services are promised [14]. Therefore, actively collecting users' responses to carefully-designed questions can serve as important supplements to traditional user modeling based on numbers of noisy and low-quality passive data. Similar to the personality test problem, the key in active user modeling is the trade-off between efficiency and effectiveness: to achieve an acceptable user modeling accuracy in minimum questions before annoying the user.

Acknowledgments. The authors thank Cristina Segalin for providing the PsychoFlickr dataset and the code of *CG+LASSO*. This work is supported by National Basic Research Program of China (No. 2012CB316304), National Natural Science Foundation of China (No. 61432019, 61225009, 61303176, 61272256, 61373122, 61332016).

References

1. Matthews, G., Deary, I.J., Whiteman, M.C.: Personality Traits. Cambridge University Press, Cambridge (2003)
2. McCrae, R.R., John, O.P.: An introduction to the five-factor model and its applications. J. Personal. **60**(2), 175–215 (1992)
3. Tkalcic, M., Tasic, J., Košir, A.: Emotive and personality parameters in multimedia recommender systems. In: Affective Computing and Intelligent Interaction. ACII 2009, p. 33 (2009)
4. Chittaranjan, G., Blom, J., Gatica-Perez, D.: Who's who with big-five, analyzing and classifying personality traits with smartphones. In: 2011 15th Annual International Symposium on Wearable Computers (ISWC), pp. 29–36. IEEE (2011)
5. Paulhus, D.L., Vazire, S.: The self-report method. In: Handbook of Research Methods in Personality Psychology, pp. 224–239 (2007)
6. McDonald, J.D.: Measuring personality constructs: the advantages and disadvantages of self-reports, informant reports and behavioural assessments. Enquire **1**(1), 1–19 (2008)
7. Fiske, S.T., Taylor, S.E.: Social Cognition. McGraw-Hill, New York (1991)
8. De Raad, B., Perugini, M., Hrebíčková, M., Szarota, P.: Lingua franca of personality taxonomies and structures based on the psycholexical approach. J. Cross Cult. Psychol. **29**(1), 212–232 (1998)
9. Cristani, M., Vinciarelli, A., Segalin, C., Perina, A.: Unveiling the multimedia unconscious: implicit cognitive processes and multimedia content analysis. In: Proceedings of the 21st ACM international conference on Multimedia, pp. 213–222. ACM (2013)

10. Guntuku, S.C., Roy, S., Weisi, L.: Personality modeling based image recommendation. In: He, X., Luo, S., Tao, D., Xu, C., Yang, J., Hasan, M.A. (eds.) MMM 2015. LNCS, vol. 8936, pp. 171–182. Springer, Heidelberg (2015). doi:10.1007/978-3-319-14442-9_15
11. Tausczik, R.Y., Pennebaker, J.W.: The psychological meaning of words: LIWC and computerized text analysis methods. J. Lang. Soc. Psychol. 29(1), 24–54 (2010)
12. Szegedy, C., Liu, W., Jia, Y., Sermanet, P., Reed, S., Anguelov, D., Erhan, D., Vanhoucke, V., Rabinovich, A.: Going deeper with convolutions. In: Proceedings of the IEEE Conference on Computer Vision and Pattern Recognition, pp. 1–9 (2015)
13. Rattray, J., Jones, M.C.: Essential elements of questionnaire design and development. J. Clin. Nurs. 16(2), 234–243 (2007)
14. Birlutiu, A., Groot, P., Heskes, T.: Efficiently learning the preferences of people. Mach. Learn. 90(1), 1–28 (2013)

Fast Cross-Scenario Clothing Retrieval Based on Indexing Deep Features

Zongmin Li[✉], Yante Li, Yongbiao Gao, and Yujie Liu

College of Computer and Communication Engineering,
China University of Petroleum (East China), Beijing, China
lizongmin@upc.edu.cn

Abstract. In this paper, we propose a new approach for large scale daily clothing retrieval. Fast clothing image search in cross scenarios is a challenging task due to the large amount of clothing images on the internet and visual differences between street photos (pictures of people wearing clothing taken in our daily life with complex background) and online shop photos (pictures of clothing items on people, captured by professionals in more controlled settings). We tackle the problem of cross-scenario clothing retrieval through clothing segmentation based on coarse-fine hierarchical superpixel segmentation and pose estimation to remove the background of clothing image and employ deep features representing the clothing item aimed at describing various clothing effectively. In addition, in order to speed up the retrieval process for large scale online clothing images, we adopt inverted indexing on deep feature by regarding deep features as Bag-of-Word model. In this way, we obtain similar clothing items far faster. Experiments demonstrate that our method significantly outperforms state-of-the-art approaches.

Keywords: Clothing retrieval · Over segmentation · Cross-scenario · Deep learning · Inverted index · Bag-of-Words

1 Introduction

Nowadays, online clothing shopping is becoming an increasingly popular shopping way. Billions of on-line clothing in various styles make it a challenging task to retrieve them accurately and efficiently. In most cases, due to the diversity of clothing, describing clothing by some keywords, such as white, sleeveless, leather, can't help customers exactly find their favorite clothing. So, the content based clothing retrieval is proposed. There are many researches focus on improving the clothing retrieval accuracy in the past decade [6, 8, 9, 11, 12, 19].

Cross-scenario clothing retrieval has been a hot spot in recent years, where the input query clothing image and the images in dataset belong to different scenes. The query images are always taken in our daily life with clutter scenes while the related products we search online tend to be taken in particular environments with clean background. Segmenting clothing from complex surroundings is a critical step for accurate clothing retrieval. Superpixel segmentation combined with pose estimation [7] is the common

© Springer International Publishing AG 2016
E. Chen et al. (Eds.): PCM 2016, Part I, LNCS 9916, pp. 107–118, 2016.
DOI: 10.1007/978-3-319-48890-5_11

method to segment clothing items to reduce the influence of background. However, simply segmenting the clothing once always fail to obtain accurate clothing segmentation, because of the diversity of the clothing and complex surroundings. Accordingly, we propose a coarse-fine superpixel segmentation in order to improve the segmentation accuracy. And due to the complex attributes of the clothing, we extract deep features containing rich high level context information, instead of the traditional features e.g. SIFT [2], on segmented clothing item which proved effective to describe the clothing.

Although deep features are more discriminative and compact than most of traditional features, it still cannot efficiently deal with large-scale image search issues as the high dimensions of deep feature. When the database is large-scale, both the computational and storage efficiency will deteriorate sharply. To speed up the searching process, various indexing schemes have been studied sufficiently. Among these methods, inverted indexing based on bag-of-words (BOW) model is the current state-of-the-art method. In this paper, we use the work of Ruoyu Liu [20] for reference, regarding deep feature as BOW model, adopting inverted table to deep feature indexing to improve the computational and storage efficiency. Moreover, since deep features are not sparse, using inverted index directly can't accelerate retrieval speed effectively, we preprocess deep features to sparse firstly.

Our contributions can be concluded as two main points: (1) a clothing segmentation based on coarse-fine super pixel. (2) improving clothing retrieval speed by converting the sparse deep feature in to inverted table. The rest of this paper is organized as follows. We introduce the related works in Sect. 2. In Sect. 3, we present our clothing segmentation and indexing feature method is proposed in Sect. 4. In Sect. 5, we evaluate the proposed method by experiment. Finally, we conclude our paper in Sect. 6.

2 Related Work

There is a large body of research literatures on the similar clothing retrieval. In the early times, most of the researches locate the clothing parts approximately through face recognition and skin detection. As the pose estimation [7] is proposed, Chen [11] adopted a pose adaptive feature extraction algorithm on the basis of Grabcut algorithm [5] and employed Conditional Random Field to calculate the semantic attributes of the clothing. Kalantidis firstly over-segmented clothing item through Graphcut [14] and merged the segmented parts by AGM [22] clustering method. Di [10] presented a fine-grained clothing style recognition and retrieval system. But these works are within-scenario clothing retrieval.

Cross-scenario clothing retrieval was proposed by Liu [6]. In cross-scenario clothing retrieval, the input query clothing image (street photos) and the images in database (online photos) belong to different scenes. Liu adopted pose estimation [7] to gain body patches and employed two step sparse coding approach to realize the cross scenario clothing retrieval. Fu [9] expanded the work of Liu and sparse coding was used to filter the background. When we pay attention to clothing, we will appreciate the whole appearance first and then the details. So it is essential to segment the clothing precisely. However, the popular superpixel based methods, such as Grabcut and Graphcut, fail to segment clothing items accurately from complex surroundings at times. Other than above methods, we occupied the intact segmented clothing for retrieval by using coarse-fine hierarchical superpixel segmentation we proposed in this paper in order to improving the segmentation accuracy.

In all of the above methods, clothing items are represented by the combination of traditional local and global features, such as LAB, SIFT. The mix of different features may have negative effect with each other. With the proposal of deep learning (DL) [15], Kiapour [17] adopted RCNN [18] to compute the deep feature to represent clothing items, encoding the high-level semantic meaning of image into a high dimensional vector. However, due to the diversity of the clothing, the selective search [21] method in RCNN can't segment the clothing item accurately and lead to a bad performance. Considering this problem, we preprocess a clothing segmentation algorithm first, followed by computing deep features on the segmented clothing. In our work, we extract the image features by using the deep convolutional neural networks toolkit, named Matcovnet. The network of Matcovnet takes segmented clothing images as the input and generates a feature vector of 4096 or 1000 dimensions as output.

Indexing is the common method to improve the computational and storage efficiency. Initially, the inverted table is used to index text documents in text retrieval. For facilitating the image matching on basis of local features, Sivic [3] extended this technique to image indexing via the BOW model [3]. Recently, Ruoyu Liu [20] presented BOW model [16] and inverted table [15] to deep feature indexing. Inspired by Ruoyu Liu's work, we convert CNN vector into discrete words and generate inverted table to index the feature which accelerate similar clothing retrieval sharply (Fig. 1).

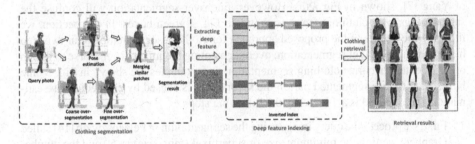

Fig. 1. The whole framework of the system

3   Clothing Segmentation

The query images are pictures of people wearing clothing in everyday uncontrolled settings while the related products we search online tend to be taken in particular environments with clean background and uniform illumination. So, there is a bridge between the street images and online images which lead to an inferior result. Eliminating the background can solve this problem to some degree. In this section, we introduce a novel approach for clothing detection and segmentation on the query image. For the input image, we first over-segment the image to visually coherent superpixels by two step coarse-fine image over-segmentation shown in Fig. 2 and then merge the similar superpixels on body patches. What is worth mentioning is that our approach guarantees the integrity of the clothing regions by merging spatially distant ones according to the similarity of their visual features.

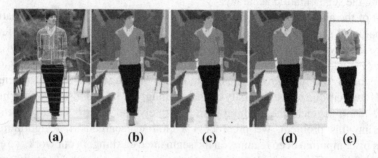

(a)   (b)   (c)   (d)   (e)

Fig. 2. The introduction of clothing segmentation. (a) Pose estimation. (b) Coarse superpixel segmentation. (c) Fine superpixel segmentation. (d) Merge the similar patches on body. (e) Segmented clothing.

3.1   Clothing Segmentation

Segmenting clothing from complex surroundings is a critical step for accurate clothing retrieval. Common segmentation methods based on superpixel always fail to segment clothing accurately when the background is relatively complex. Coarse over-segmentation makes it harder to identify intact clothing items through pose estimation algorithm of Yang [7], shown in Fig. 2(a). However, fine over-segmentation will confuse the surroundings with clothing items, as shown in Fig. 3 green boxes. In this section, we illustrate the details of the proposed approach for clothing segmentation. Our two step hierarchical superpixel segmentation, over-segmenting the image from coarse to fine in order to obtain accurate clothing segmentation and examples are shown in Fig. 3 blue boxes. The failure segmented part in the second row is caused by erroneous pose estimation. Our method is achieved by the following steps.

1. First, we process the query image using the segmentation of Felzenszwalb [14] called Graphcut, setting the minimum size of superpixel (min_size) as 50 and the number of superpixel (num_superpixel) as 400. After the first Graphcut segmentation, we obtain an initial superpixel image which is coarse, shown in Fig. 2(b).
2. As the initial superpixel image is coarse and scattered. Graphcut segmentation with fine parameters (min_size = 150; num_superpixel = 100) is applied again to acquire a relative neat and unbroken superpixel image segmentation. This is helpful to get accurate and complete clothing segmentation in following steps.
3. Merging the similar regions on the human body which can be estimated by pose estimation. We calculate the similarity matrix (Euclidean distance) of the superpixels in S in Color Naming feature space and set a fix value 0.12 to determine merging.

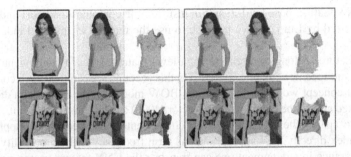

Fig. 3. The comparison between Graphcut segmentation and coarse-fine Graphcut segmentation. The leftmost image is the original image. The middle images in green boxes are segmentation results of Graphcut algorithm. While the rightmost images in blue boxes illustrate the procedure of coarse-fine Graphcut segmentation. (Color figure online)

Finally, we refined the segments through employing the exemplar-SVM (ESVM) templates proposed by Malisiewicz [13], then, we cut out the original clothing image according to the segmentation. As so far, we can obtain the intact clothing item.

4   The Index of Deep Feature on Clothing

In this paper, we propose to extract deep feature on the segmented clothing followed by indexing deep feature. Attention, all the segmented clothing images need to be resized to the fix size to compute deep features. Deep features obtained through training billions of images are more compact and discriminative than the combination of traditional features (e.g. SIFT, LAB). And different features combined together may have negative effect with each other. Hence, deep feature is suitable to represent clothing which possesses multiple characteristics and changes with variations in styles. The experiments in Sect. 5 confirm that deep features do have perfect performance on clothing representation. Moreover, indexing deep feature addresses the problem where the database is too large to be retrieved effectively by direct search.

In this paper, we employ the imagenet-vgg-f model, which is simple and memory-efficient, but has been proved to be effective for image representation. The imagenet-vgg-f model is learned through 5 convolutional layers and 3 fully-connected layers, pre-trained for image classification on ImageNet. The 20th layer which is fully trained is used as our feature representation for clothing representation. And the 20th layer does perform superior on clothing representation than other layers according to our experiments in Sect. 5. The CNN feature is just computed on the clothing region for query images (street photos) and images in database (shop photos). Therefore, we can assure the accuracy of the feature representation.

However, the shortcoming of employing CNN feature is that the high dimension of FC3 (4096 dimension) leading to low retrieval efficiency and large storage space even in a small image dataset. When the scale of the dataset is large, clothing search system CNN feature-based will result in insufferable computational cost and storage usage. Inspired by Liu [20], we propose to use the method of inverted index as our solution.

CNN features belong to a relative high-level feature, so each component of CNN contains some specific semantic content. On this account, we can treat each component as a virtual concept word. In this way, the BOW model can be used and a dictionary with the fixed size of the length of CNN vector (4096) can be constructed. But, the CNN feature is not sparse (the frequency of every component appearance is high), approaching inverted index directly isn't appropriate. As term frequency is the probability of each word appearance in a document, we can translate the CNN feature vector into a term frequency (probability) vector.

In our scheme, given a CNN feature vector $x = \{x_1, x_2, \ldots x_D\}$, we deal with each component by using the following softmax function:

$$\sigma(x_i)_i = \frac{e^{x_i}}{\sum_{j=1}^{D} e^{x_j}} \tag{1}$$

Through this approach, a CNN feature vector can be translated to a histogram $x = \{x_1, x_2, \ldots x_D\}$. Each bin in the histogram indicates the probability of corresponding word appearance in the image. Considering the top value bins describe the main content of the image, we maintain only the words corresponding to top S bin values taken into account. Although, it will lose some spatial information from initial segmentation, the local feature is much more important for clothing representation. The clothing retrieval precision decreases a little, which is absolutely in acceptable degree, while the speed of retrieval improves sharply and makes it suitable for large scale datasets. Our experiment shows that top 80 value bins is able to describe the clothing well in the following Sect. 5.4. Using the method mentioned above, only a small-scale dictionary with 4096 entries can be used to construct the inverted table. As for the construction of inverted table, for each visual word, we build a list in which the ID and Term frequency information of images that contains the visual word is inserted. In the search phase, a voting process is performed to measure the similarity between query and dataset images. The details of the inverted index are shown in Fig. 4.

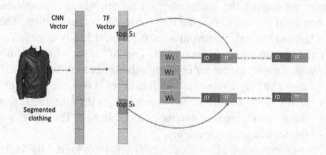

Fig. 4. The illustration of indexing structure. TF vector is the term frequency of CNN vector. Only the words corresponding to top S bin values in TF vector are converted into inverted table.

5   Experiments

5.1   Experimental Setting

In this section, we evaluate the performance of the proposed approaches on three data-sets: Product Clothing Dataset (PC), Daily Clothing Dataset (DC) and Fashionista Dataset [4]. PC Dataset and DC Dataset are built by us, where the images are selected from 1.5 billion product clothing images online and well labeled. The details of PC Dataset and DC Dataset are as follow:

Product Clothing Dataset (PC): includes 15,690 different clothing images in various colors and styles.

Daily Clothing Dataset (DC): includes 6500 people daily photos in various scenarios with arbitrary human gestures in complex backgrounds.

Fashionista Dataset [4]: consists of 158,235 photographs. 53 different clothing items are selected as ground truth data set, which are annotated by 56 labels.

Evaluation Criterion for clothing retrieval: In clothing retrieval, all features were computed on the segmented clothing items. We performed experiments on the CNN features. And we follow the evaluation criterion of [6]. Given a query image q, we evaluate a ranking of top k retrieved images with respect to a query q by a precision:

$$Precision_k = \frac{\sum_i^k Rel(i)}{N} \tag{9}$$

where N is a normalization constant and $Rel(i)$ presents the correct attributes between the ith image and q. Mean Average Precision (MAP) is used as the accuracy measure.

5.2   Clothing Segmentation

For experiments on clothing segmentation, we use the ground truth data set of Fashionista Dataset [4] to test the average score of recall, precision and F-measure. Performance of the proposed clothing segmentation approach in comparison with the methods using Graphcut and Grabcut [5] segmentation algorithms are shown in Fig. 5(a). The experimental results show that the approach proposed in this paper is more precise than other methods while the recall is a little lower than the Grabcut. Since the application we care about is clothing suggestion, we have far more interest in segmentation precision than recall. So, our method is suitable for clothing segmentation. More examples of clothing segmentation are shown in Fig. 5(b).

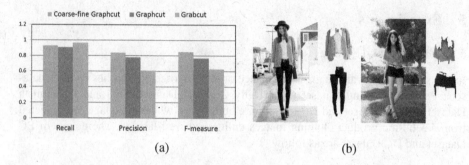

(a)   (b)

Fig. 5. (a) The performances of different clothing segmentation algorithms. The results are the average score of the upper body and the lower body. (b) Examples of clothing segmentation.

5.3   Different Layers in the imagenet-vgg-f Model

In our work, we employed the 20th layer of the imagenet-vgg-f model as the clothing feature. We test the performance from the 17th layer to the 20th layer on 300 images in DC follow the criterion (9) and the results are shown in Fig. 6. The results show that the 20th layer feature performs superior than other layers. Because the 20th layer is fully trained compared with other layer, it is reasonable to take the 20th layer as clothing representation.

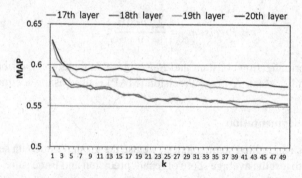

Fig. 6. The comparison of performances though employing different layers in imagenet-vgg-f model on top k item retrieval.

5.4   Inverted Index on CNN Feature

In this section, we test the effect of factor S (the number of top bin values in CNN taken into account) on 400 images in DC. The MAP score change curve with S is shown in Fig. 7(a), demonstrating that S going up to large value (e.g. 80), the performance tends to be stable. This means that the top 80 components of CNN feature mostly describe an image. So, 80 dimension inverted table is adopted in our paper.

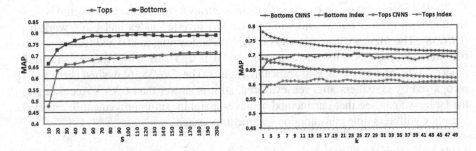

Fig. 7. (a) The accuracy sensitivity of factor S. S represents the number of top bin values in CNN taken into account. (b) The performances of top-k cross-scenario clothing item retrieval with and without indexing.

To validate the effectiveness of our proposed indexing method, we perform the experiment comparing the performance of retrieval directly and based on index. The evaluation of clothing retrieval accuracy on 800 images in DP dataset is shown in Fig. 7(b). Although the accuracy decrease a little, the time cost reduce sharply by around 7 times shown in Table 2.

5.5 Clothing Retrieval

In the experiment for Clothing retrieval, 500 Daily Clothing images were chosen to test the retrieval performance. The results are shown in Fig. 8 where *Tops index* and *Bottoms index* represent the upper-body and lower-body clothing retrieval results through our method, *Tops CROSS* and *Bottoms CROSS* are the results of [6]. The horizontal axis represents the number of returned similar images. Our method performs better and achieves 62% and 71% for upper-body and lower-body datasets.

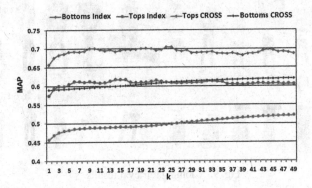

Fig. 8. The cross-scenario retrieval performance comparison. The "*Index*" represents our method and the "*CROSS*" represents the method proposed by Liu [6].

Table 1 shows the memory usage as well as retrieval time of the three methods: our method with (*CNNS Index)* and without (*CNNS*) inverted index and Liu's work [6] (*CROSS*). The Memory usage consists of two parts: learning model and feature set. In our methods, the CNN model (imagenet-vgg-f) is 233 MB while the classification models in [6] occupy 299 MB as shown in Table 2. The *CROSS* [6] method needs to be recognized by classifiers after retrieval step, so it is slower than *CNNS*. According to the table, we can see that our method achieves a significant improvement in retrieval accuracy with less time consumption and memory usage.

Table 1. Comparsion memory usage and average retrieval time. The memory usage consists of learning model and feature sets shown in brackets.

Approach	Storage	Memory usage	Retrieval timtime
CNNS Index	Inverted Index	255 MB (233 + 22)	0.009 s
CROSS [6]	Auxiliary Set	491 MB (299 + 192)	0.114 s
CNNS	Auxiliary Set	447 MB (233 + 214)	0.071 s

Table 2. Clothing retrieval results on 20 returned images.

Approach on tops	Precision (%)	Approach on bottoms	Precision (%)
CNNS	61.8	CNNS	71.9
CNNS Index	59.6	CNNS Index	68.1
RCNN [17]	39.1	RCNN [17]	45.9
CROSS [6]	49.3	CROSS [6]	61.1

In Table 2, we compare the evaluation results of our method on 20 returned images with two state-of-the-art methods. The evaluation results tell us that our methods outperforms Cross [6] and RCNN [17]. More retrieval results are shown in Fig. 9.

Fig. 9. Clothing retrieval results.

6 Conclusion

In this paper, we propose a new approach for fast cross-scenario clothing retrieval in large scale. We present a coarse-fine clothing segmentation approach to segment the clothing more precise and employ deep feature, which is compact and discriminative, as the representation of clothing. Furthermore, BOW model and inverted indexing is approached in order to improve the retrieval efficiency and it is significant for large scale clothing retrieval. The experiments show that our approach outperforms the state-of-the-art approach on the performance of retrieval accuracy, memory usage and retrieval time.

Acknowledgment. The authors would like to thank the support of National Natural Science Foundation of China, the Scientific Research Foundation for the Excellent Middle-Aged and Youth Scientists of Shandong Province of China.

References

1. Deng, J., Dong, W., Socher, R, Li, L.-J., Li, K., Fei-Fei, L.: ImageNet: a large-scale hierarchical image database. In: IEEE Conference on Computer Vision and Pattern Recognition, pp. 248–255 (2009)
2. Lowe, D.G.: Distinctive image features from scale-invariant keypoints. Int. J. Comput. Vis. **60**(2), 91–110 (2004)
3. Sivic, J., Zisserman, A.: Video Google: a text retrieval approach to object matching in videos. In: International Conference on Computer Vision, pp. 1470–1477 (2003)
4. Yamaguchi, K., Kiapour, M.H., Ortiz, L.E., Berg, T.L.: Parsing clothing in fashion photographs. In: IEEE Conference on Computer Vision and Pattern Recognition, pp. 3570–3577 (2012)
5. Rother, C., Kolmogorov, V., Blake, A.: Grabcut - interactive foreground extraction using iterated graph cuts. ACM Trans. Graph. (TOG) **23**, 309–314 (2004)
6. Liu, S., Song, Z., Liu, G.: Street-to-shop: cross-scenario clothing retrieval via parts alignment and auxiliary set. In: IEEE Conference on Computer Vision and Pattern Recognition, pp. 3330–3337 (2012)
7. Yang, Y., Ramanan, D.: Articulated pose estimation with flexible mixtures-of-parts. In: IEEE Conference Computer Vision and Pattern Recognition, pp. 1385–1392 (2011)
8. Liu, S., et al.: Hi, magic closet, tell me what to wear! In: Proceedings of the 20th ACM International Conference on Multimedia, pp. 619–628 (2012)
9. Fu, J., Wang, J., Li, Z., et al.: Efficient clothing retrieval with semantic preserving visual phrases. In: Proceedings of 11th Asian Conference on Computer Vision, pp. 420–431 (2013)
10. Di, W., Wah, C., Bhardwaj, A., Piramuthu, R., Sundaresan, N.: Style finder: fine-grained clothing style recognition and retrieval. In: Computer Vision and Pattern Recognition Workshops, pp. 8–13 (2013)
11. Chen, H. Gallagher, A. Girod, B.: Describing clothing by semantic attributes. In: Proceedings of the 12th European Conference on Computer Vision, pp. 609–623 (2012)
12. Kalantidis, Y., Kennedy, L., Li, L.J.: Getting the look: clothing recognition and segmentation for automatic product suggestions in everyday photos. In: The 3rd ACM Conference on International Conference on Multimedia Retrieval, pp. 105–112 (2013)

13. Malisiewicz, T., Gupta, A., Efros, A.A.: A. Ensemble of exemplar-SVMs for object detection. In: International Conference on Computer Vision, pp. 89–96 (2011)
14. Sutskever, I., Krizhevsky, A., Hinton, G.: Imagenet classification with deep convolutional neural networks. In: Neural Information Processing Systems, pp. 1097–1105 (2012)
15. Babenko, A., Lempitsky, V.: The inverted multi-index. In: IEEE Conference on Computer Vision and Pattern Recognition, pp. 3069–3076 (2012)
16. Jurie, F., Nowak, E., Triggs, B.: Sampling strategies for bag of features image classification. In: European Conference on Computer Vision, pp. 490–503 (2006)
17. Kiapour, M.H., Lazebnik, S., Han, X.: Where to buy it: matching street clothing photos in online shops. In: IEEE International Conference on Computer Vision, pp. 3343–3351 (2015)
18. Girshick, R., Donahue, J., Darrell, T.: Region based convolutional networks for accurate object detection and semantic segmentation. IEEE Trans. Pattern Anal. Mach. Intell. **38**, 142–158 (2015)
19. Kuang, Z., Li, Z., Lv, Q.: Modal function transformation for isometric 3D shape representation. Comput. Graph. **46**, 209–220 (2015)
20. Liu, R., Zhao, Y., Wei, S., Zhu, Z., Liao, L., Qiu, S.: Indexing of CNN features for large scale image search. CoRR, abs/1508.00217 (2015)
21. Uijlings, J., van Sande, K.E.A.: Selective search for object recognition. Int. J. Comput. Vis. **104**, 154–171 (2013)
22. Avrithis, Y., Kalantidis, Y.: Approximate Gaussian mixtures for large scale vocabularies. In: Fitzgibbon, A., Lazebnik, S., Perona, P., Sato, Y., Schmid, C. (eds.) ECCV 2012. LNCS, vol. 7574, pp. 15–28. Springer, Heidelberg (2012). doi:10.1007/978-3-642-33712-3_2

3D Point Cloud Encryption Through Chaotic Mapping

Xin Jin[1,2(✉)], Zhaoxing Wu[1,2], Chenggen Song[1,2],
Chunwei Zhang[1,2], and Xiaodong Li[1,2(✉)]

[1] Beijing Electronic Science and Technology Institute, Beijing 100070, China
{jinxin,lxd}@besti.edu.cn
[2] GOCPCCC Key Laboratory of Information Security, Beijing 100070, China

Abstract. Three dimensional (3D) contents such as 3D point clouds, 3D meshes and 3D surface models are increasingly growing and being widely spread into the industry and our daily life. However, less people consider the problem of the privacy preserving of 3D contents. As an attempt towards 3D security, in this papers, we propose methods of encrypting the 3D point clouds through chaotic mapping. 2 schemes of encryption using chaotic mapping have been proposed to encrypt 3D point clouds. (1) 3 random sequences are generated by the logistic chaotic mapping. Each random vector is sorted to randomly shuffler each coordinate of the 3D point clouds. (2) A random 3×3 invertible rotation matrix and a 3×1 translate vector are generated by the logistic mapping. Then each 3D point is projected to another random place using the above random rotation matrix and translate vector in the homogeneous coordinate. We test the above 2 encryption schemes of 3D point cloud encryption using various 3D point clouds. The 3D point clouds can be encrypted and decrypted correctly. In addition, we evaluated the encryption results by VFH (Viewpoint Feature Histogram). The experimental results show that our proposed methods can produce nearly un-recognized encrypted results of 3D point clouds.

Keywords: 3D point clouds · Encryption · Chaotic mapping · Point feature histogram · View feature histogram

1 Introduction

Nowadays, tremendous visual contents such as images, videos and 3D models are transmitted to thousands of people by social network software and cloud storages. Besides images and videos, the 3D models are increasingly growing with the image based 3D modeling and 3D print technologies. Some Apps on the smartphone such as Autodesk 123D Catch[1] allow users to shot photos of one subject from various views and upload all the photos to Autodesk cloud server. Then the 123D service on the cloud server will return a 3D model of subject to the users. Desktop software such as Google Sketchup[2] also makes one editing 3D models easily. The 3D models are going into our daily life

---

[1] http://www.123dapp.com/.
[2] http://www.sketchup.com/.

© Springer International Publishing AG 2016
E. Chen et al. (Eds.): PCM 2016, Part I, LNCS 9916, pp. 119–129, 2016.
DOI: 10.1007/978-3-319-48890-5_12

step by step. In the industry, the virtual reality technology is now a hot topic, which needs plenty of 3D models to build the virtual world. The governments are scanning the whole city into 3D virtual city models by laser scanners and multi-view cameras.

Previous Work. The image encryption and video encryption technologies have been studied for a long time. The particular properties of chaos [1, 2], such as sensitivity to initial conditions and system parameters, pseudo-randomness, ergodicity and so on, have granted chaotic dynamics as a promising alternative for the conventional cryptographic algorithms. The inherent properties connect it directly with cryptographic characteristics of confusion and diffusion, which is presented in Shannon`s works. Chaotic system is reliable to design secure image and video encryption scheme because of its high complexity [3–9].

However, less people consider the problem of the encryption of 3D contents. The 3D digitalized objects are defined by means of two types of 3D contents: 3D solid models and 3D shell (boundary) models. A solid model defines the volume of the physical object that represents, whereas a shell model represents the surface, not the volume. In [10], Rey has addressed the encryption of 3D solid models, however, the encryption of 3D shell model has not appeared in the literature.

Thus 3D shell model encryption technologies are required in order to accomplish a high level of security, integrity, confidentiality and to prevent unauthorized access of sensitive 3D models during the storage or transmission over an insecure channels. The 3D contents contains of various types such as 3D point clouds, 3D meshes and 3D models with textures. Different 3D types should correspond to different encryption methods. To the best of our knowledge, there is little work that considering encryption of 3D shell models [12].

Different from text encryption techniques, visual data has some special characteristics, such as bulk data capacity and high correlation among pixels or points. Traditional encryption algorithms, such as Data Encryption Standard (DES), International Data Encryption Algorithm (IDEA) and Advanced Encryption Standard (AES), etc., are not suitable for visual data encryption. Different from images or videos, the 3D contents contains points, meshes and textures in 3D space. The traditional image or video encryption method are not suitable for 3D contents. Thus, new method of 3D content encryption should be proposed.

Our Approach. As an attempt towards 3D security, in this papers, it is the first time for the 3D point clouds to be encrypted by chaotic mapping, as shown in Fig. 1. 2 schemes of encryption using chaotic mapping have been proposed to encrypt 3D point clouds. According to the first scheme, three random sequences are generated by the logistic chaotic mapping. Each random vector is sorted to randomly shuffler each coordinate of the 3D point clouds. According to the second scheme, a random 3×3 invertible rotation matrix and a 3×1 translate vector are generated by the logistic mapping. Then each 3D point is projected to another random place using the above random rotation matrix and translate vector in the homogeneous coordinate. We test the above 2 encryption schemes of 3D point cloud encryption using various 3D point clouds. The 3D point clouds can be encrypted and decrypted correctly. In addition, we evaluated the encryption results by VFH (Viewpoint Feature Histogram). The experimental results show that our proposed methods can produce nearly un-recognized encrypted results of 3D point clouds. The **contributions** of this work includes:

1. The first work that addresses the 3D point cloud encryption.
2. Two schemes of 3D point cloud encryption using the logistic chaotic mapping.
3. Using VFH to evaluate the encryption result of 3D point cloud.

Input 3D Point Cloud   The Encrypted 3D Point Cloud

Fig. 1. The encryption of 3D point cloud

2 Cryptography Primitive

In this section we briefly introduce the cryptography primitive we used in this paper. The simple but efficient chaotic mapping (logistic) is defined as follows:

$$
\begin{aligned}
&x_{n+1} = \mu x_n(1 - x_n) \\
&3.569945672\ldots < \mu \le 4 \\
&0 \le x_n \le 1 \\
&n = 0, 1, 2, \ldots
\end{aligned}
\tag{1}
$$

When the parameter μ and the initial value x_0 follow the Eq. 1, the outputs of this chaotic mapping x_n become chaotic state and have good potential to form a random sequence.

3 Point Cloud Encryption via the Logistic Mapping

We propose 2 schemes for point cloud encryption via the logistic mapping. In the first scheme, we use the logistic mapping to generate 3 random vectors to shuffle the 3 coordinates of the point clouds. In the second, we generate a random transformation matrix for each 3D point using the logistic mapping. We will describe the details of these to encryption scheme in this section and compare them in the next 2 sections.

3.1   Scheme 1: Random Vector (RV)

In the 3D Euclidean space, each point has 3 coordinates. Thus, we generate 3 random vectors using the logistic mapping for the 3 coordinates. As shown in Fig. 2, each coordinate of each point is corresponded to a random number in the random vector. Then, the random vectors are sorted to new orders. The corresponding coordinates are reordered by the new orders of the random vectors. Then the coordinates of each point are confused to form the final encrypted 3D points. The decryption is the inverse procedure of encryption. The encrypted coordinates are resorted to the original position according the logistics mapping with the same key used in the encryption.

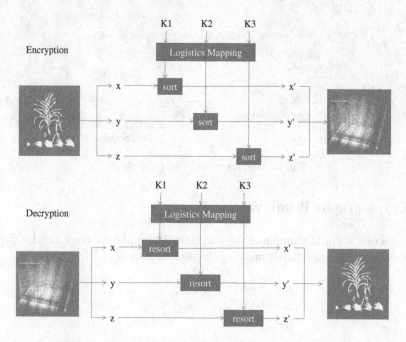

Fig. 2. Random vector based encryption and decryption

A 3D point can be represented as $p = (x, y, z)$. A point cloud consists of a set of 3D points: $P = \{p_1, p_2, \ldots, p_n\}$. The 3 coordinates of the 3D point cloud can be represented as $X = \{x_1, x_2, \ldots, x_n\}, Y = \{y_1, y_2, \ldots, y_n\}, Z = \{z_1, z_2, \ldots, z_n\}$. We use the logistic mapping to randomly shuffle the three vector X, Y, Z for encryption and obtain 3 new vectors: $X' = \{x'_1, x'_2, \ldots, x'_n\}, Y = \{y'_1, y'_2, \ldots, y'_n\}, Z = \{z'_1, z'_2, \ldots, z'_n\}$. The decryption procedure is to remap X', Y', Z' to X, Y, Z so as to obtain the original point cloud.

3.2   Scheme 2: Random Transformation Matrix (RTM)

A point in the 3D Euclidean space can be transformed to another location using the translate and rotation operations A 4×4 transformation matrix T consists of a 3×3 rotation matrix R and a 3×1 translate matrix $t = (t_x, t_y, t_z)$. A 3D point can be represented as a homogeneous coordinate: $p = (x, y, z, 1)$. Then the transformation of a 3D point is shown in Eq. (2).

$$\begin{pmatrix} x' \\ y' \\ z' \\ 1 \end{pmatrix} = \begin{bmatrix} R[0,0] & R[0,1] & R[0,2] & t_x \\ R[1,0] & R[1,1] & R[1,2] & t_y \\ R[2,0] & R[2,1] & R[2,2] & t_z \\ 0 & 0 & 0 & 1 \end{bmatrix} \begin{pmatrix} x \\ y \\ z \\ 1 \end{pmatrix} \tag{2}$$

where $p' = (x', y', z', 1)$ is the transformed point of the original 3D point. As shown in Fig. 3, we use the logistic mapping to generate random and invertible matrix T. All the 3D points are transformed to another position randomly. In the decryption phase, we use the invert matrix T^{-1} to re-transform each point to the original position to obtain the original 3D point cloud.

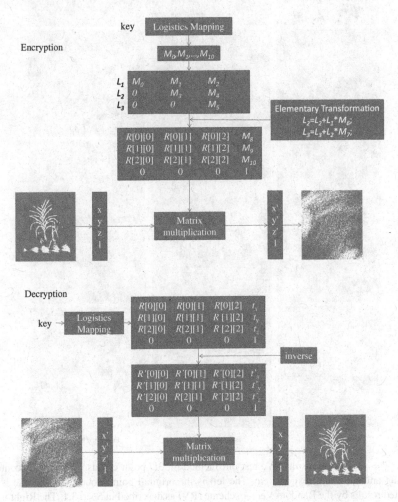

Fig. 3. Random transformation matrix based encryption and decryption

4 Simulation Results

We use plenty of plain 3D point clouds to test our method, as shown in Fig. 4, with secret keys. The 3D point clouds with various contents are tested. All the encryption results can be correctly decrypted to the original plain 3D point clouds with the correct keys. The simulation results are quite satisfactory.

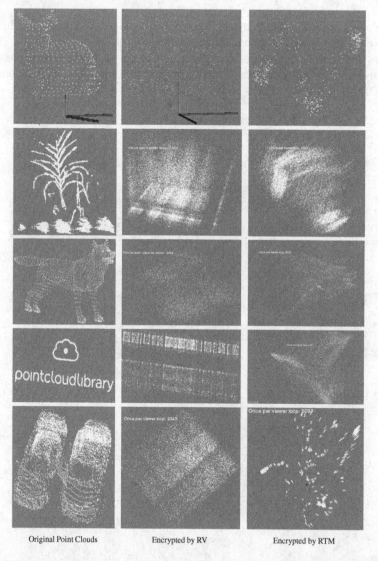

Original Point Clouds   Encrypted by RV   Encrypted by RTM

Fig. 4. The simulation results. We test our method on 3D point clouds with various contents including animal, plant, text, car etc. The left is the original point clouds. The middle is the encrypted results by the Random Vector scheme (RV) as described in Sect. 3.1. The Right is the encrypted results by the Random Transformation Matrix (RTM) as described in Sect. 3.2.

5   Security and Performance Analysis

A well designed image encryption scheme should be robust against different attacks, such as brute-force attack and statistical attack. In this section, we analyze the security of the proposed encryption methods using various 3D point clouds.

5.1   Resistance to the Brute-Force Attack

Key Space. The key space of the image encryption scheme should be large enough to resist the brute-force attack, otherwise it will be broken by exhaustive search to get the secret key in a limited amount of time. The key space of our method is described as follow:

The Random Vector (RV) scheme. We give each coordinate vector of point clouds a pair of key for the logistic mapping:

$$3.569945672\ldots < \mu_x, \mu_y, \mu_z \leq 4$$

$$0 \leq x_0^x, x_0^y, x_0^z \leq 1$$

The Random Transformation Matrix (RTM) scheme. We give each point a pair of key for the logistic mapping:

$$3.569945672\ldots < \mu_0, \mu_1, \ldots, \mu_N \leq 4$$

$$0 \leq x_0^0, x_0^1, \ldots, x_0^N \leq 1$$

where, N is the number of the point in a point cloud. The precision of 64-bit double data is 10^{-15}. Thus, the key space of the RV scheme is about $(10^{15})^6 = 10^{90} \approx 2^{224}$, which is nearly equal to the max key space (2^{256}) of practical symmetric encryption of the AES. The key space of the RTM scheme is about $(10^{15})^{2N} = 10^{30N} \approx 2^{75N}$. If $N > 3$, the key space will be much larger than the max key space of AES. Our key space is large enough to resist brute force attack.

Sensitivity of Secret Key. The chaotic system are extremely sensitive to the system parameter and initial value. A light difference can lead to the decryption failure. To test the secret key sensitivity of our 3D point cloud encryption scheme, we change the secret key as follow:

The RV scheme:

$$\mu_x \text{ from } 3.86 \text{ to } 3.8600001$$

$$\mu_y \text{ from } 3.77 \text{ to } 3.7700001$$

$$\mu_z \text{ from } 3.91 \text{ to } 3.9100001$$

The RTM scheme:

$$\mu_i = \mu_i + 0.0000001, i = 1, 2, \dots, N$$

We use the change key to decrypt the encrypted 3D point cloud in Fig. 5 by the RV and the RTM scheme, respectively, while the other secret keys remain the same. The decryption results are shown in Fig. 5. The decrypted 3D point clouds are completely different from the original 3D point cloud. The test results of the other secret key are similar. The experiments show that both the 2 schemes are quite sensitive to the secret key, which also indicates the strong ability to resist exhaustive attack.

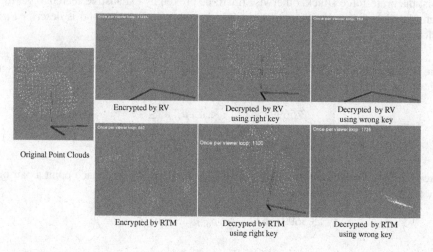

Fig. 5. We slightly change the key and get the completely wrong decrypted results.

5.2 Resistance to the Statistic Attack

The Point Feature Histograms (PFH) are informative pose-invariant local features which represent the underlying surface model properties at a point.

The Viewpoint Feature Histogram (VFH) descriptor is a novel representation for point clusters for the problem of Cluster (e.g., Object) Recognition and 6 DOF Pose Estimation. The major difference between the PFH descriptors and VFH, is that for a given point cloud dataset, only a single VFH descriptor will be estimated, while the resultant PFH data will have the same number of entries as the number of points in the cloud [11]. We use the VFH for the evaluation of our 3D point cloud encryption. As shown in Fig. 6, the VFHs of the encrypted results by both the RV scheme and the RTM scheme are completely different from the VFH of the original point cloud, which makes statistical attacks impossible.

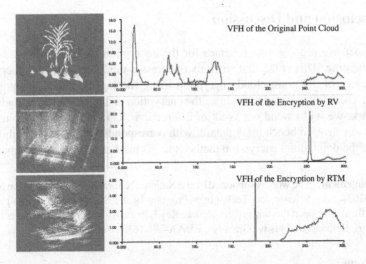

Fig. 6. The VFH of the original point cloud, the encrypted result by RV and RTM

5.3   The Speed of the Encryption and Decryption

The image encryption scheme is implemented by C++ and the PCL library[3] on personal computer with AMD A10 PRO-7800B R7, 12 c, 4 c + 8 G 3.5 GHz and 4.00 G RAM. The consumption time encryption and decryption is recorded for different number of points in the cloud. The larger the number is, the more time it needs for encryption and decryption.

As shown in Fig. 7, we test the speed of the encryption and decryption progress using the two proposed schemes for point cloud encryption. The RTM scheme is less time consuming than the RV scheme.

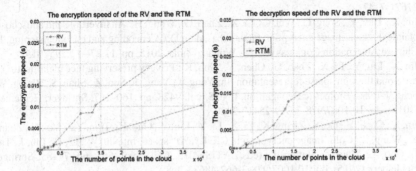

Fig. 7. The speed of the encryption and decryption of the RV and the RTM scheme.

---

[3] http://www.pointclouds.org/.

6   Conclusion and Discussion

In this paper, we propose two schemes for the encryption of 3D point clouds using chaotic mapping. This is the first work that addresses the 3D point cloud encryption. Two schemes of 3D point cloud encryption using the logistic chaotic mapping are proposed. The VFH are used to evaluate the encryption result of 3D point cloud. In the future work, we will extend our work in 2 directions: (1) building a 3D point cloud encryption evaluation bench mark dataset with corresponding evaluation methods, (2) extending the point cloud encryption methods to 3D meshes and 3D surface models.

Acknowledgement. The work is supported by the National Natural Science Foundation of China (No. 61402021), the Science and Technology Program of the State Archives Administration (2015-B-10), and the open funding project of State Key Laboratory of Virtual Reality Technology and Systems, Beihang University (Grant No. BUAA-VR-16KF-09).

References

1. Huang, C., Nien, H.: Multi chaotic systems based pixel shuffle for image encryption. Opt. Commun. **282**, 2123–2127 (2009)
2. Lian, S., Sun, J., Wang, Z.: A block cipher based on a suitable use of the chaotic standard map. Chaos Soliton. Fract. **26**(1), 117–129 (2005)
3. Zhen, P., Zhao, G., Min, L.Q., Jin, X.: Chaos-based image encryption scheme combining DNA coding and entropy. Multimedia Tools Appl. (MTA) **75**, 6303–6319 (2015)
4. Wang YZ., Ren GY., Jiang JL., Zhang J., Sun L.J.: Image encryption method based on chaotic map. In: 2nd IEEE Conference on Industrial Electronics and Applications (ICIEA), pp. 2558–2560 (2007)
5. Jin, X., et al.: Private video foreground extraction through chaotic mapping based encryption in the cloud. In: Tian, Q., Sebe, N., Qi, G.-J., Huet, B., Hong, R., Liu, X. (eds.) MMM 2016. LNCS, vol. 9516, pp. 562–573. Springer, Heidelberg (2016). doi:10.1007/978-3-319-27671-7_47
6. Jin, X., Tian, Y., Song, C., Wei, G., Li, X., Zhao, G., Wang, H.: An invertible and anti-chosen plaintext attack image encryption method based on DNA encoding and chaotic mapping. In: Chinese Automation Congress (CAC), Wuhan, China, 2015, pp. 11.27– 11.29 (2015)
7. Jin, X., Liu, Y., Li, X., Zhao, G., Chen, Y., Guo, K.: Privacy preserving face identification in the cloud through sparse representation. In: Yang, J., Yang, J., Sun, Z., Shan, S., Zheng, W., Feng, J. (eds.) Biometric Recognition. LNCS, vol. 9428, pp. 160–167. Springer, Heidelberg (2015). doi:10.1007/978-3-319-25417-3_20
8. Jin, X., Chen, Y., Ge, S., Zhang, K., Li, X., Li, Y., Liu, Y., Guo, K., Tian, Y., Zhao, G., Zhang, X., Wang, Z.: Color image encryption in CIE L*a*b* space. In: Niu, W., Li, G., Liu, J., Tan, J., Guo, L., Han, Z., Batten, L. (eds.) ATIS 2015. CCIS, vol. 557, pp. 74–85. Springer, Heidelberg (2015). doi:10.1007/978-3-662-48683-2_8
9. Li, Y., et al.: An image encryption algorithm based on Zigzag transformation and 3-Dimension chaotic Logistic map. In: Niu, W., Li, G., Liu, J., Tan, J., Guo, L., Han, Z., Batten, L. (eds.) ATIS 2015. CCIS, vol. 557, pp. 3–13. Springer, Heidelberg (2015). doi: 10.1007/978-3-662-48683-2_1

10. del Rey, A.M.: A method to encrypt 3D solid objects based on three-dimensional cellular automata. In: Onieva, E., Santos, I., Osaba, E., Quintián, H., Corchado, E. (eds.) HAIS 2015. LNCS (LNAI), vol. 9121, pp. 427–438. Springer, Heidelberg (2015). doi:10.1007/978-3-319-19644-2_36
11. Rusu, R.B., Blodow, N., Beetz, M.: Fast point feature histograms (FPFH) for 3D registration. In: IEEE International Conference on Robotics and Automation (2009)
12. Éluard M., Maetz Y., Doërr G.: Geometry-preserving encryption for 3D meshes. In: Compression Et Représentation Des Signaux Audiovisuels (2013)

Online Multi-Person Tracking Based on Metric Learning

Changyong Yu, Min Yang, Yanmei Dong, Mingtao Pei[✉], and Yunde Jia

Beijing Laboratory of Intelligent Information Technology,
School of Computer Science, Beijing Institute of Technology,
Beijing 100081, People's Republic of China
{yuchangyong,yangminbit,dongyanmei,peimt,jiayunde}@bit.edu.cn

Abstract. The correct associations of detections and tracklets are the key to online multi-person tracking. Good appearance models can guide data association and play an important role in the association. In this paper, we construct a discriminative appearance model by using metric learning which can obtain accurate appearance affinities with human appearance variations. The novel appearance model can significantly guide data association. Furthermore, the model is learned incrementally according to the association results and its parameters are automatically updated to be suitable for the next online tracking. Based on an online tracking-by-detection framework, our method achieves reliable tracking of multiple persons even in complex scenes. Our experimental evaluation on publicly available data sets shows that the proposed online multi-person tracking method works well.

Keywords: Online tracking · Metric learning · Multi-person tracking · Appearance model

1 Introduction

Multi-person tracking aims to estimate the states of multiple persons while conserving their identifications under appearance and motion variations over time. As the development of human detectors [2,19], *tracking-by-detection* technique [1,2,10,14,21] has got substantial improvement. However, in complex scenes, it is still a very challenging problem to track multiple persons due to frequent occlusion caused by clutter, other objects or other persons with similar appearances, etc.

Online tracking method is a crucial method in multi-person tracking and can be applied to real-time applications. These methods [3,12,15,17,18] sequentially build trajectories based on frame-by-frame association using online information up to the present frame. For online methods, trajectories and detections should be associated correctly to achieve good tracking results. Accordingly, online multi-person tracking is formulated as a data association problem. The affinity measurement between a trajectory and a detection is the core to finding correct association. Appearance model plays an important role in distinguishing different individuals, and thus is a critical cue for affinity measurement.

© Springer International Publishing AG 2016
E. Chen et al. (Eds.): PCM 2016, Part I, LNCS 9916, pp. 130–140, 2016.
DOI: 10.1007/978-3-319-48890-5_13

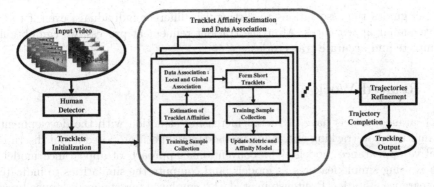

Fig. 1. Overview of our method. We collect positive and negative samples first. After obtaining tracklet affinities, the next step is data association, which includes local and global association. Then we update our metric and affinity model by training samples for next tracking.

Many multi-person tracking methods have designed good appearance models [1,9,11,12]. These methods tend to learn the discriminativeness among targets and show impressive tracking results. Inspired by these methods, we focus on learning an effective appearance model based on metric learning to obtain good tracking performance. Metric learning method has great advantage in terms of similarity measurement. It can exploit human appearance information to distinguish different individuals, even when they have similar appearances at some times. This makes it possible to accurately identify persons even under significant pose and appearance changes and long-term occlusion. Therefore, our method is especially applicable to multi-person tracking

In this paper, we propose an online updating discriminative appearance model based on metric learning. Our appearance model learns a Mahalanobis distance function over input data to guide the association. After associations, the model is automatically updated by positive and negative samples collected from the last association, so the discrimination of the model will be improved after every association. Experimental results show that our appearance model is much more effective than other models in terms of computation cost and identification accuracy. Some tracking methods [13,20,22] have utilized metric learning and achieved impressive performance. For example, Wang et al. [22] applies metric learning to tracklets association by network flow optimization for long-term multi-person tracking. Different from that, based on online metric learning, we focus on appearance modeling and make the discrimination of appearance model more effective.

The overview of our method is illustrated in Fig. 1. The estimation of tracklet affinities process incorporates multi-person tracking cues, such as appearance, shape and motion. In contrast to the traditional metric learning applications, the proposed method doesn't need off-line training. We utilize local and global association to solve the trajectory recovery problem. Furthermore, our appearance model guides the associations to distinguish different individuals, even if they have similar appearances. After the tracklet refinement process, we can obtain complete and accurate trajectories.

2 Related Work

Appearance models have attracted increasing attention with the development of multi-person tracking and many methods have been proposed about discriminative appearance models. The conventional approach of appearance modeling is using simple features as models, and compute the similarities to indicate appearance affinities. Breitenstein et al. [12] employed target specific appearance models with online learning. This appearance model is trained for distinguishing a person from the background. To learn appearance models for discriminating different persons, Kuo et al. [1] and Yang et al. [11] collected positive samples from the same tracklets and negative samples from other tracklets, and the models were simultaneously learned using standard AdaBoost [1] or MIL instance learning [11] methods. They also used online-trained classifiers to estimate the appearance affinity between two short trajectories and improved both target-specific and global appearance models for tracklets association. However, these learning methods are learned in a batch manner. Due to the significant temporal delay and time-consuming iterative process, it is difficult to apply these methods to time-critical applications. To learn appearance models online, Bae et al. [9] employed incremental linear discriminant analysis method to update appearance model. They aim to find a projection that can gather the appearances from the same target and at the same time separates the appearances from different targets at the same time. As a result, they can significantly reduce the computational complexity in appearance learning.

Our work focuses on building an effective appearance model for online multi-person tracking, which only considers observations up to the current frame and outputs trajectories without temporal delay. The effective approach of appearance modeling is using descriptors, such as color histograms [2,3,14], to represent the targets, and compute the similarities between descriptors to indicate appearance affinities. Our method also chooses color histograms as the descriptor to represent the targets because color histograms is a traditional and efficient descriptor. In addition, our appearance model computes Mahalanobis distance of targets to estimate their affinities, thus, it can restore the complete and accurate trajectories.

3 Discriminative Appearance Learning

In this section, we present our online metric learning method and build the online learning appearance model. In the discriminative appearance learning process, we take two important steps: (a) collect online training samples, (b) construct appearance model by applying metric learning.

3.1   Online Metric Learning

We restrict our method to learning a Mahalanobis distance function over input data, which is a distance function parameterized by a $d \times d$ positive definite matrix A. Given d-dimensional vectors u and v, the squared Mahalanobis distance between them is defined as

$$d_A(u,v) = (u,v)^T A(u,v). \tag{1}$$

Positive definiteness of A assures that the distance function will return positive distances.

   In general, learning a Mahalanobis distance is substantially learning the appropriate positive definite matrix A based on constraints over the distance function. In contrast to offline approaches assuming that all constraints are provided up front, online algorithms assume that constraints are received one at a time. We assume that at time step t, there exists a current distance function parameterized by A_t. We consider a variant of the model where the input is a quadruple (u_t, v_t, y_t, b_t), if $b_t = 1$ indicates that the distance between u_t and v_t be less than or equal to y_t, and $b_t = -1$ indicates that the distance between u_t and v_t be greater than or equal to y_t, and incur a loss $\ell(\hat{y}_t, y_t)$. To improve the discriminativeness of matrix A, we update A_t to A_{t+1}. The goal is to minimize the sum of the losses over all time steps. The corresponding loss function is $\ell(\hat{y}_t, y_t, b_t) = max(0, \frac{1}{2}b_t(\hat{y}_t - y_t))^2$. A typical approach [4] for the above given online learning problem is to solve for A_{t+1} by minimizing a regularized loss at each step:

$$A_{t+1} = \underset{A \succ 0}{argmin} D(A, A_t) + \eta\ell(d_A(u_t, v_t), y_t), \tag{2}$$

where $D(A, A_t)$ is a regularization function and η is the regularization parameter. The algorithm minimizes (2) to solve for the updated parameters A_{t+1}. As in [4], we use the LogDet divergence $D_{\ell d}(A, A_t)$ as the regularization function.

   Using straightforward algebra and the Sherman-Morrison inverse formula, the solution to the minimization of (2) is

$$A_{t+1} = A_t - \frac{\eta(\overline{y} - y_t)A_t z_t z_t^T A_t}{1 + \eta(\overline{y} - y_t)z_t^T A_t z_t}, \tag{3}$$

where $z_t = u_t - v_t$ and $\overline{y} = d_{A_{t+1}}(u_t, v_t) = z_t^T A_{t+1} z_t$. By multiplying the update in (3) on the left by z_t^T and on the right by z_t and noting that $\hat{y}_t = z_t^T A_t z_t$, we obtain

$$\overline{y} = \frac{\eta y_t \hat{y}_t - 1 + \sqrt{(\eta y_t \hat{y}_t - 1)^2 + 4\eta\hat{y}_t^2}}{2\eta\hat{y}_t}. \tag{4}$$

We solve for $\overline{y}$ using this formula, and then plug this into the Eq. (3) to update A_t to A_{t+1}.

3.2   Appearance Model Based on Metric Learning

An effective affinity measurement can make great contribution to the recognition of different persons. Compared to the shape and motion information of people, human appearance can provide richer information. According to this, appearance model is a critical cue for affinity measurement and is the core of our algorithm. The one we used can be expressed as

$$\Lambda^A(X, Y) = exp(-\lambda * \hat{d}), \tag{5}$$

where $\hat{d}$ is the Mahalanobis distance. We plug (1) into (5) and make $\hat{d} = (X_f - Y_f)' * A * (X_f - Y_f)$, where X_f and Y_f represents u and v. X_f and Y_f are the features of X and Y, where X and Y are tracklets or detections. We initialize matrix A as a unit matrix. With the association of tracklets and detections, our method automatically updates matrix A according to the results of association. Next, we will describe the update of matrix A.

By plugging Mahalanobis distance $\hat{d}$ and target distance d into (4), we obtain

$$\overline{d} = \frac{\eta d\hat{d} - 1 + \sqrt{\left(\eta d\hat{d} - 1\right)^2 + 4\eta\hat{d}^2}}{2\eta\hat{d}}. \tag{6}$$

Target distance d corresponds to y_t in the quadruple (u_t, v_t, y_t, b_t). To update matrix A_{t+1}, we plug $\overline{d}$, X_f and Y_f into (3), then the updated matrix A_{t+1} is as follows:

$$A_{t+1} = A_t - \frac{\eta(\overline{d} - d)(A_t(X_f - Y_f)'(X_f - Y_f)A_t)}{1 + \eta(\overline{d} - d)}. \tag{7}$$

With the update, matrix becomes more discriminative.

To update matrix A, we collect training samples from tracklets after every data association. Figure 2 shows training samples collected form tracklets with high confidence and low confidence. Image frames are on the left side of the

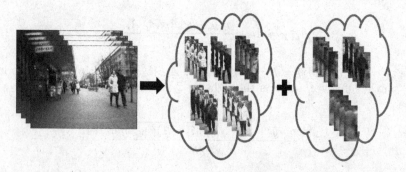

Fig. 2. Training samples with high confidence (red) and low confidence (blue). (Color figure online)

figure, and the right side is training samples extracted from tracklets with high confidence (red) and low confidence (blue).

For each image patch (i.e., sample), we create a low level color histogram feature f_l extracted from HSV color channel images. A set $B = \{(f_l, y_l)\}_{l=1}^{N}$ consisting of features f_l and the labels of tracklets (i.e. ID) y_l is constructed. We use the tracklets with the same label and different labels to update our appearance model separately. In our method, the patch is resized to 96×32. Since the feature dimension is very high, directly exploiting the high-dimensional feature to distinguish each object is not effective. Therefore, we reduce the dimension of feature to 192.

At each frame, after local and global associations, we obtain the distances between tracklets and detections. If the distance of these tracklets is close, they have the same label. Otherwise, they have different labels. Tracklets have the same label are one kind of trajectory while tracklets have different labels belong to different trajectories. We use these tracklets to update discriminative matrix A next. At next frame, the distance between similar tracklets and detections will be closer, and distance between different tracklets and detections will be farther. By updating matrix A, tracklets that have same label can be accumulated in the process of association. Short tracklets gradually form long tracklets and finally they form complete trajectories.

4 Online Tracking with Confidence

The confidence of tracklets is important to the tracking-by-detection framework [9]. According to the level of tracklet confidence, the framework will utilize different association methods. Tracklets with high confidence are locally associated with online-provided detections, while tracklets with low confidence are globally associated with the other tracklets and detections.

4.1 Tracklet Confidence

Tracklet confidence is how well the constructed tracklet matches the real trajectory of the person. When a detection of the object is not reliable, the confidence of a tracklet is decreased. Since the tracklet confidence lies in $[0, 1]$, we consider a tracklet as a reliable tracklet with high confidence when confidence >0.5, otherwise it is considered as the fragmented tracklet with low confidence.

4.2 Affinity Model

We describe a tracklet T_i with three elements $\{A^i, S^i, M^i\}$, where A^i, S^i and M^i represent appearance, shape, and motion models, respectively. An affinity measure to determine how well two tracklets (or a tracklet and a detection) are matched is then defined as

$$\Lambda(X, Y) = \Lambda^A(X, Y)\Lambda^S(X, Y)\Lambda^M(X, Y), \tag{8}$$

where X and Y are tracklets or detections. The affinity score is computed based on the affinities of appearance, shape, and motion models. The appearance model $\Lambda^A(X, Y)$ is given in Sect. 3.2. The shape affinity $\Lambda^S(X, Y)$ is calculated with the height h and width w of objects and $\Lambda^M(X, Y)$ is the motion affinity between X tail (i.e. the last refined position) and Y head (i.e. the first refined position) with the frame gap.

4.3   Data Association

Data association includes local association and global association. In local association, tracklets with high confidence $T^{i(hi)}$, are sequentially grown with a set of detections at frame t, Z_t. Pairwise association is performed to associate detection responses with tracklets. At frame t, we define a score matrix to compute the association of tracklets with high confidence and detections. Then, we determine tracklet-detection pairs using the Hungarian algorithm. This will ensure the total affinity in score matrix is maximized, thus make the association more reliable. If the association cost of a tracklet-detection pair is less than a pre-defined threshold, z_t^j is associated with $T^{i(hi)}$.

In global association, tracklets with low confidence $T^{i(lo)}$ are globally associated with other tracklets and detections. Suppose that there exist h and l tracklets with high and low confidence, respectively. Since association events are mutually exclusive, we only consider n detections and Y_t in associating $T^{i(lo)}$, where Y_t is a set of detections not associated with any $T^{i(hi)}$ in the local association. We consider one of the following three events: $T^{i(lo)}$ is associated with $T^{i(hi)}$, $T^{i(lo)}$ is terminated or $T^{i(lo)}$ is associated with y_t^j. Based on these three events, we define a cost matrix and also use the Hungarian algorithm to maximize the total affinity. The same threshold θ used in the local association is also employed to select a reliable association pair having a high affinity score.

5   Experiments

In this section, we perform an extensive experimental evaluation on various datasets to validate the effectiveness and the superiority of our method. We give the detailed description of datasets, evaluation metrics and parameter settings. Then we compare our method with a number of online multi-person tracking methods and analyze the experimental results.

5.1   Datasets and Evaluation Metrics

The publicly available video sequences we used are collected in unconstrained environments for experimental evaluation: ADL-Rundle-6 [5], PETS09-S2L1 [6], TUD-Stadtmitte [7], ETH-Bahnhof [8].

We use the widely accepted CLEAR performance metrics [4] for quantitative evaluation: the multiple object tracking precision (MOTP↑) that evaluates average overlap rate between true positive tracking results and the ground truth, and the multiple object tracking accuracy (MOTA↑) which indicating the accuracy composed of false positives (F.P↓), false negatives (F.N↓) and identity switches (IDS↓). Additionally, the measures also include the percentage of mostly tracked (MT↑) and mostly lost (ML↓) ground truth trajectories, the number of trajectories in the ground truth (GT), as well as the number of track fragments (FG↓). The false positive ratio is also measured by the number of false alarms per frame (FAF↓). Here,↑ means that higher scores indicate better results, and ↓ represents that lower is better.

5.2   Parameter Settings

All parameters of our method are found experimentally and remain unchanged for all datasets. In (6) and (7), $\eta = 1/8$. In updating process, we make the target distance $d = 2$ to update matrix A if the tracklets have the same label. The target distance should be no great than 2. We make the target distance $d = 8$ to update matrix A if the tracklets have different labels. In this case, the target distance should be no less than 8. The same threshold $\theta = 0.4$ is used for the local and global association.

5.3   Quantitative Comparison

As mentioned, appearance modeling draws increasing attention and methods TC_ODAL [9], TBD [10] and SMOT [16] make much progress in appearance modeling. Among these methods, TC_ODAL tracker is an online algorithm, while TBD and SMOT trackers are offline tracking methods. In order to ensure a effective comparison, we choose these methods which also build good appearance models to compare with our method.

In Table 1, a quantitative comparison between our method and other proposed approaches is given. Overall, our method outperforms other state-of-the-art methods. Our method achieves the lowest identity switch (IDS) while achieving the highest detection accuracy (lowest FP and FN) and tracking consistency (highest MT and lowest ML). In addition, it achieves better performance in terms of MOTP and MOTA. The quantitative evaluation results imply that our system can robustly construct trajectories under challenging conditions.

The experimental results show that our method outperforms the others compared with the existing multi-person tracking algorithms. Several qualitative examples of tracking results are shown in Fig. 3.

Table 1. Quantitative evaluation accuracy of our method and other proposed approaches

	MOTA[%]↑	MOTP[%]↑	F.P↓	F.N↓	IDS↓	MT[%]↑	ML[%]↓	FG↓	GT	FAF↓
Ours	16.3	76.6	10677	17191	487	7.1	46.3	20	500	1.9
TC_ODAL [9]	11.4	71.4	13961	19059	637	3.2	55.8	25	500	2.5
TBD [10]	13.2	72.1	11964	19288	1372	6.4	47.9	33	500	2.1
SMOT [16]	15.1	73.2	11542	18455	1043	4.2	53.7	28	500	2.0

Fig. 3. Sample tracking results of our method on four publicly available video sequences. At each frame, persons with different IDs are indicated by bounding boxes.

6   Conclusion

In this paper, we have proposed an online multi-person tracking method based on metric learning. We construct an novel online discriminative appearance model, which is the core part of affinity measurement. Owing to the accuracy of the affinity measurement, we gain optimal trajectories by sequentially linking tracklets and detections. The proposed online appearance learning allows us to discriminate multiple persons even in complex scene. Experimental results compared with other methods show the superiority and robustness of our method.

Acknowledgments. This work was supported in part by the Natural Science Foundation of China (NSFC) under Grant No. 61472038 and No. 61375044, and Beijing Key Laboratory of Advanced Information Science and Network Technology (No. XDXX1601).

References

1. Kuo, C.H., Nevatia, R.: How does person identity recognition help multi-person tracking? In: 2011 IEEE Conference on Computer Vision and Pattern Recognition (CVPR), pp. 1217–1224. IEEE (2011)

2. Wu, B., Nevatia, R.: Detection and tracking of multiple, partially occluded humans by Bayesian combination of edgelet based part detectors. Int. J. Comput. Vis. **75**(2), 247–266 (2007)

3. Poiesi, F., Mazzon, R., Cavallaro, A.: Multi-target tracking on confidence maps: an application to people tracking. Comput. Vis. Image Underst. **117**(10), 1257–1272 (2013)

4. Davis, J.V., Kulis, B., Jain, P., et al.: Information-theoretic metric learning. In: Proceedings of the 24th International Conference on Machine learning, pp. 209–216. ACM (2007)

5. Leal-Taix, L., Milan, A., Reid, I., et al.: Motchallenge 2015: towards a benchmark for multi-target tracking. arXiv preprint arXiv:1504.01942 (2015)

6. Ferryman, J., Shahrokni, A.: PETS2009: dataset and challenge. In: 2009 Twelfth IEEE International Workshop on Performance Evaluation of Tracking and Surveillance (PETS-Winter), pp. 1–6. IEEE (2009)

7. Andriluka, M., Roth, S., Schiele, B.: Monocular 3D pose estimation and tracking by detection. In: 2010 IEEE Conference on Computer Vision and Pattern Recognition (CVPR), pp. 623–630. IEEE (2010)

8. Ess, A., Leibe, B., Gool, L.V.: Depth and appearance for mobile scene analysis. In: IEEE 11th International Conference on Computer Vision, ICCV 2007, pp. 1–8. IEEE (2007)

9. Bae, S.H., Yoon, K.J.: Robust online multi-object tracking based on tracklet confidence and online discriminative appearance learning. In: 2014 IEEE Conference on Computer Vision and Pattern Recognition (CVPR), pp. 1218–1225. IEEE (2014)

10. Geiger, A., Lauer, M., Wojek, C., et al.: 3D traffic scene understanding from movable platforms. IEEE Trans. Pattern Anal. Mach. Intell. **36**(5), 1012–1025 (2014)

11. Yang, B., Nevatia, R.: Multi-target tracking by online learning of non-linear motion patterns, robust appearance models. In: 2012 IEEE Conference on Computer Vision and Pattern Recognition (CVPR), pp. 1918–1925. IEEE (2012)

12. Breitenstein, M.D., Reichlin, F., Leibe, B., et al.: Online multiperson tracking-by-detection from a single, uncalibrated camera. IEEE Trans. Pattern Anal. Mach. Intell. **33**(9), 1820–1833 (2011)

13. Wu, Y., Ma, B., Yang, M., et al.: Metric learning based structural appearance model for robust visual tracking. IEEE Trans. Circuits Syst. Video Technol. **24**(5), 865–877 (2014)

14. Yoon, J.H., Yang, M.H., Lim, J., et al.: Bayesian multi-object tracking using motion context from multiple objects. In: 2015 IEEE Winter Conference on Applications of Computer Vision (WACV), pp. 33–40. IEEE (2015)

15. Yang, M., Jia, Y.: Temporal dynamic appearance modeling for online multi-person tracking. In: Computer Vision and Image Understanding (2016)

16. Dicle, C., Camps, O., Sznaier, M.: The way they move: tracking multiple targets with similar appearance. In: Proceedings of the IEEE International Conference on Computer Vision, pp. 2304–2311 (2013)

17. Solera, F., Calderara, S., Cucchiara, R.: Learning to divide and conquer for online multi-target tracking. In: International Conference on Computer Vision (ICCV), pp. 4373–4381 (2015)

18. Possegger, H., Mauthner, T., Roth, P., et al.: Occlusion geodesics for online multi-object tracking. In: Proceedings of the IEEE Conference on Computer Vision and Pattern Recognition. 1306–1313 (2014)

19. Dollr, P., Appel, R., Belongie, S., et al.: Fast feature pyramids for object detection. IEEE Trans. Pattern Anal. Mach. Intell. **36**(8), 1532–1545 (2014)

20. Yang, M., Pei, M.T., Wu, Y.W., et al.: Learning online structural appearance model for robust object tracking. Sci. China Inf. Sci. **58**(3), 1–14 (2015)
21. Yang, M., Pei, M., Shen, J., Jia, Y.: Robust online multi-object tracking by maximum a posteriori estimation with sequential trajectory prior. In: Arik, S., Huang, T., Lai, W.K., Liu, Q. (eds.) ICONIP 2015. LNCS, vol. 9489, pp. 623–633. Springer, Heidelberg (2015). doi:10.1007/978-3-319-26532-2_69
22. Wang, B., Wang, G., Chan, K., et al.: Tracklet association with online target-specific metric learning. In: Proceedings of the IEEE Conference on Computer Vision and Pattern Recognition, pp. 1234–1241 (2014)

A Low-Rank Tensor Decomposition Based Hyperspectral Image Compression Algorithm

Mengfei Zhang[1], Bo Du[1], Lefei Zhang[1(✉)], and Xuelong Li[2]

[1] School of Computer, Wuhan University, Wuhan, China
{mzhang,remoteking,zhanglefei}@whu.edu.cn
[2] Center for OPTIMAL, State Key Laboratory of Transient Optics
and Photonics, Xi'an Institute of Optics and Precision Mechanics,
Chinese Academy of Sciences, Xi'an, China
xuelong_li@opt.ac.cn

Abstract. Hyperspectral image (HSI), which is widely known that contains much richer information in spectral domain, has attracted increasing attention in various fields. In practice, however, since a hyperspectral image itself contains large amount of redundant information in both spatial domain and spectral domain, the accuracy and efficiency of data analysis is often decreased. Various attempts have been made to solve this problem by image compression method. Many conventional compression methods can effectively remove the spatial redundancy but ignore the great amount of redundancy exist in spectral domain. In this paper, we propose a novel compression algorithm via patch-based low-rank tensor decomposition (PLTD). In this framework, the HSI is divided into local third-order tensor patches. Then, similar tensor patches are grouped together and to construct a fourth-order tensor. And each cluster can be decomposed into smaller coefficient tensor and dictionary matrices by low-rank decomposition. In this way, the redundancy in both the spatial and spectral domains can be effectively removed. Extensive experimental results on various public HSI datasets demonstrate that the proposed method outperforms the traditional image compression approaches.

Keywords: HSI · Compression · Reconstruction · Tensor representation · Low-rank decomposition

1 Introduction

Hyperspectral imaging systems record per-pixel reflectance spectroscopy in a number of narrow wavelength bands over a wide range of the electromagnetic spectrum, thereby providing a much higher spectral resolution than the typical gray-level and RGB images, and are thus able to better capture material-specific information. More recently, thanks to the development and decreasing cost of the latest hyperspectral cameras, they have become affordable and popular in many computer vision and multimedia applications [1] such as face recognition, iris recognition, and medical diagnosis [2–4], etc.

However, the provided numerous spectral bands have led to some problems [5]. Compared to the conventional gray-level and RGB images, despite possessing much

© Springer International Publishing AG 2016
E. Chen et al. (Eds.): PCM 2016, Part I, LNCS 9916, pp. 141–149, 2016.
DOI: 10.1007/978-3-319-48890-5_14

more information, HSIs are trapped in increased computational and time cost owning to the large number of spectral bands. Thus it's quite important to find a way to efficiently process and analyze these HSIs which have hundreds of thousands of contiguous spectral bands. As an ideal solution, image compression algorithms played a great role in solving this problem.

There are many conventional and classical image compression methods that can solve aforementioned problems. Pixel coding-based methods such as JPEG [6], SPIHT [7] and EZW [8] are most widely applied compression methods. Du [9] proposed to deploy PCA [10, 11] in JPEG 2000 for gray-level image processing. 3D coding based algorithms such as the 3D reversible integer lapped transform [12] and the DWT coupled with tucker decomposition [13] are proved to be effective for both spectral and spatial information. However, these methods do not consider the internal characteristics of the HSI, which might result in a loss of the important information in the subsequent image analysis (e.g., classification and recognition). To address this issue, tensor [14] was applied in image compression method to preserve both neighborhood relationship across the spatial dimension as well as global correlation among the spectral dimension. Typical examples are multilinear principal component analysis [15] (MPCA) generalized by PCA, concurrent subspace analysis [16], tensor canonical correlation analysis [17], and some other tensor based HSI compression methods [18, 19]. Although, at first glance, these methods may appear suitable for HSI compression, they were actually designed for a group of tensor objects, and they may not be effective for single tensor data based image compression.

Conventional compression methods usually process the HSI by spectral channel or by pixel, while it is quite different in our framework. To fully exploit the advantages of HSI, we propose a novel patch-based low-rank tensor decomposition (PLTD) method, combining patch-based tensor representation and the tensor extension of dictionary learning [20]. Firstly, HSI is blocked into local tensor patches. Then, by exploring the nonlocal similarity over the spatial domain [21, 22], similar tensor patches are grouped together by clustering method, and a fourth-order tensor are constituted for each cluster. Since the tensor data is assumed to be redundant, each big tensor can be finally low-rank decomposed into low-dimensional coefficient tensor and dictionary matrices. In this way, both spatial and spectral redundancy are optimally removed by our proposed framework.

The remainder of this paper is organized as follows. Section 2 presents the detailed PLTD algorithm for HSI compression and reconstruction. Experiments and analysis are provided in Sect. 4. The last section is a conclusion.

2 Patch-Based Low-Rank Tensor Decomposition (PLTD) for HSI Compression

The compression process of the PLTD framework can be summarized as blocking, clustering, tensor dictionary learning and low-rank decomposition. It can realize simultaneous compression of both the spatial and spectral modes. The reconstructed HSI can be simply obtained by combining the recovered patches which are the tensor product of coefficient tensor and dictionaries per cluster. The overall process is illustrated in the

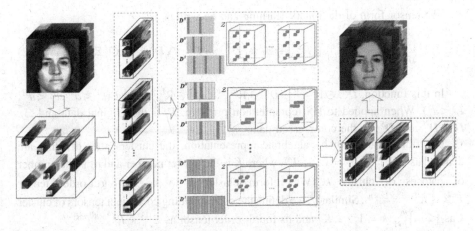

Fig. 1. Flow chart of the PLTD algorithm.

flow chart in Fig. 1. The detailed theory of the framework are given in the following sections, in which notations and multilinear algebras can refer to paper [23].

2.1   Patch-Based Tensor Representation

Given a third-order tensor HSI $\mathcal{I} \in \mathbb{R}^{L^W \times L^H \times L^S}$, we divide it by block size $l^W \times l^H$ ($l^W < L^W$, $l^H < L^H$) and consider there is no overlap between patches. We can then construct a group of 3D patches $\{\mathcal{P}_{ij}\}_{1 \leq i \leq n^W, 1 \leq j \leq n^H} \subset \mathbb{R}^{l^W \times l^H \times l^S}$, where $n^W = L^W / l^W$ and $n^H = L^H / l^H$, and the patch number n is equal to $n = n^W n^H$. Each patch is a cube preserving all the spectral information of the original HSI.

To make full use of the local information in the spatial and spectral domain and to simplify the deduction of the algorithm, we divide the patches into several clusters according to nonlocal similarity. After that, each cluster is reformed as a fourth-order tensor and can be resolved individually.

2.2   Tensor Dictionary Learning

Dictionary learning was originally used for image restoration. The objective function of the dictionary learning model can be given as:

$$\min_{D,Z} \| A - DZ \|, s.t. \mathcal{O}(z_i) \leq s \tag{1}$$

where $D = [d_1, \ldots, d_m] \in \mathbb{R}^{d \times m}, m > d$ is a redundant dictionary; and $A = [a_1, \ldots, a_n] \in \mathbb{R}^{d \times n}$ is a collection of n sample images, each image is originally 2D and is vectorized to a long vector a_i. $Z = [z_1, \ldots, z_n] \in \mathbb{R}^{m \times n}$ is the coefficient matrix. $\mathcal{O}(\cdot)$ denotes a sparsity controlling operator such as the l_0 or l_1 norm.

The tensor form of dictionary learning can be written as:

$$\min_{D^W,D^H,D^S,\mathcal{Z}_i} \sum_{k=1}^{K} \| \mathcal{P}^{(k)} - \mathcal{Z}_i \times_1 D^W \times_2 D^H \times_3 D^S \|, s.t. \mathcal{O}(\mathcal{Z}_i) \leq s \qquad (2)$$

In this function, $D^W \in R^{l^W \times d^W}$, $D^H \in R^{l^H \times d^H}$, $D^S \in R^{L^S \times d^S}$, and ($l^W < d^W$, $l^H < d^H$, $L^S < d^S$). When applied to HSI compression problem, $\mathcal{P}_i$ is the original data and $\mathcal{Z}_i$, D^W, D^H and D^S are the compressed data.

Describing clustering by algebraic representation, the clusters after dividing are denoted as $\{\mathcal{P}_{k,j}\}_{j=1}^{n_k} (k = 1, \ldots, K)$, where K is the cluster number and n_k is the number of patches of cluster k. We reform cluster k to be a fourth-order tensor $\mathcal{P}^{(k)} \in R^{l^W \times l^H \times L^S \times n_k}$. Similarly, we define the corresponding coefficient tensors of cluster k as $\{\mathcal{Z}_{k,j}\}_{j=1}^{n_k} (k = 1, \ldots, K)$ and its fourth-order tensor as $\mathcal{Z}^{(k)} \in R^{d^W \times d^H \times d^S \times n_k}$.

In addition, it is verified that for an nth-order tensor $\mathcal{T}$ there is a smallest subset $I^1, \ldots, I^n (I^i|_{i=1,\ldots,n} \in R^{m^i})$ satisfying that the tensor value $t(i_1, \ldots, i_n) = 0$ for all $(i_1, \ldots, i_3) \notin [I^1, I^2, \ldots, I^{n-1}]$. On this condition, the tensor $\mathcal{T}$ is sparse [24, 25]. We can denote $idt(\mathcal{T})$ as an intrinsic dense tensor of $\mathcal{T}$ composing of all the nonzero entries from $\mathcal{T}$. According to this analysis, the objective function can then be reformed as follows:

$$\min_{D^W,D^H,D^S,\mathcal{Z}^{(k)}} \sum_{k=1}^{K} \| \mathcal{P}^{(k)} - \mathcal{Z}^{(k)} \times_1 D^W \times_2 D^H \times_3 D^S \|$$
$$s.t. \mathcal{O}_t(\mathcal{Z}_{k,j}|_{j=1,\ldots,n_k, k=1,\ldots,K}) \prec (m_k^W, m_k^H, m_k^S) \qquad (3)$$

The constraint means that the number of nonzero elements of first three modes are less than m_k^W, m_k^H, and m_k^S, respectively, while the fourth-order is unchanged. Thus constraining the tensor $\mathcal{Z}^{(k)}$ to be sparse in the spatial and spectral domains.

2.3   Low-Rank Tensor Decomposition

Each patch is linearly combined by a rather small number of dictionary atoms, leading to high redundancy of the three dictionaries. Considering this fact, we split the dictionaries so that each sub-dictionary consists of only those atoms that are utilized by a single cluster. For example, the dictionaries of cluster k can be reformulated as: $D_k^W \in R^{l^W \times m_k^W}, D_k^H \in R^{l^H \times m_k^H}, D_k^S \in R^{L^S \times m_k^S}$, where m_k^w, m_k^H and m_k^S represent the number of atoms that are utilized in cluster k along the width, height, and spectral modes, respectively. In the same time, we can replace the coefficient tensor with its intrinsic dense tensor. As a result, the objective function can be reformulated like:

$$\min_{D_k^W,D_k^H,D_k^S,idt(\mathcal{Z}^{(k)})} \sum_{k=1}^{K} \| \mathcal{P}^{(k)} - idt(\mathcal{Z}^{(k)}) \times_1 D_k^W \times_2 D_k^H \times_3 D_k^S \| \qquad (4)$$

The size of coefficient tensor and dictionaries in each cluster are much smaller than the original ones, and the coefficient tensor is dense now so there is no longer any need to impose the sparsity constraint on the values. After replacing $idt(\mathcal{Z}^{(k)})$ with $\mathcal{S}^{(k)}$ for simplification, the objective function is equivalent to the following:

$$\min_{D_k^W, D_k^H, D_k^S, \mathcal{S}^{(k)}} \sum_{k=1}^{K} \| \mathcal{P}^{(k)} - \mathcal{S}^{(k)} \times_1 D_k^W \times_2 D_k^H \times_3 D_k^S \| \tag{5}$$

This problem is much easier since it has no constraints. Considering that there are only three dictionaries for the fourth-order core tensor, this function can be approximated as a low-rank tensor decomposition problem by adding a matrix:

$$\min_{U_k^{(1)}, U_k^{(2)}, U_k^{(3)}, U_k^{(4)}, \mathcal{G}^{(k)}} \sum_{k=1}^{K} \| \mathcal{X}^{(k)} - \mathcal{G}^{(k)} \times_1 U_k^{(1)} \times_2 U_k^{(2)} \times_3 U_k^{(3)} \times_4 U_k^{(4)} \| \tag{6}$$

Matrices $U_k^{(1)}, U_k^{(2)}$ and $U_k^{(3)}$ are three dictionaries, and the result of $\mathcal{G}^{(k)} \times_4 U_k^4$ is equal to coefficient tensor $\mathcal{S}^{(k)}$. Note that $U_k^3 \in R^{L^S \times m_k^S}$ and $L^S > m_k^S$, so the spectral bands are compressed. Therefore, the redundant spectral information is removed. The detailed steps are exhibited in the following Algorithm 1.

Algorithm 1: The PLTD algorithm for HSI reconstruction

Input: HSI $\mathcal{J} \in R^{L^W \times L^H \times L^S}$

Output: dictionaries $D^W = [D_1^W, \cdots, D_K^W]$, $D^H = [D_1^H, \cdots, D_K^H]$, $D^S = [D_1^S, \cdots, D_K^S]$, coefficient tensors $\mathcal{Z}^{(k)}$, and the reconstructed HSI $\mathcal{R} \in R^{L^W \times L^H \times L^S}$.

1   Split the HSI into patches $\{\mathcal{P}_{i,j}\}_{1 \leq i \leq L^W / l^W, 1 \leq j \leq L^H / l^H}$.

2   Group all the patches into K clusters $\{\mathcal{P}_{k,j}\}_{j=1}^{n_k} (k = 1, \cdots, K)$.

3   For $k=1:K$

4   Given m_k^W, m_k^H, m_k^S of cluster k.

5   According to the Tucker decomposition, compute (6) to tain $\mathcal{G}^{(k)}, U_k^{(1)}, U_k^{(2)}, U_k^{(3)}$, and $U_k^{(4)}$ of cluster k.

6   Calculate the three dictionaries and the coefficient tensor of cluster k by $D_k^W = U_k^{(1)}$, $D_k^H = U_k^{(2)}$, $D_k^S = U_k^{(3)}$, and $idt(\mathcal{Z}^{(k)}) = \mathcal{G}^{(k)} \times_4 U_k^{(4)}$.

7   End for

8   Compute the reconstructed fourth-order tensor patch group by $\mathcal{R}^{(k)} = \mathcal{G}^{(k)} \times_1 U_k^{(1)} \times_2 U_k^{(2)} \times_3 U_k^{(3)} \times_4 U_k^{(4)}$.

9   Combine the reconstructed patches $\{\mathcal{R}^{(k)}\}$.

10   Output $D^W, D^H, D^S, \mathcal{Z}^{(k)}$, and $\mathcal{R}$.

---

3   Experiments and Analysis

In this section, we present the experiments undertaken on a natural scene hyperspectral dataset and provide the experimental analysis.

3.1   Experimental Setup

We employed five image compression methods for comparison: MPCA [15], PCA [10], JPEG [6], PCA+JPEG, and KSVD [26]. Among which, JPEG and KSVD are originally proposed for gray-level image processing. When dealing with HSIs, JPEG treats them as a group of gray-level images and compresses one by one. PCA treats all the spectral values of one pixel as a sample, *i.e.*, PCA compresses the band information only. MPCA takes the gray-level image of each band as a sample and compress the spatial redundancy only. For the PCA+JPEG method, this method involves successively compressing an image by PCA and JPEG.

The HSI has to be clipped so that the spatial dimension is divisible by the patch size. For JPEG, the spatial dimension size has to be divisible by 8×8 since the DCT translation splits the original gray-level image into 8×8 data blocks. Considering these limitations, we adopt the clipping step in all the comparison methods. Furthermore, to alleviate the influence caused by data diversity, we normalized the hyperspectral data to keep all the values in the interval [0, 255].

We employed five indices for the image compression performance evaluation: the peak signal-to-noise ratio (PSNR), the structural similarity (SSIM) index, the feature similarity (FSIM) index, the erreur relative globale adimensionnelle de synthese (ERGAS) [27], and the spectral angle mapper (SAM) [28]. For PSNR, SSIM, and FSIM, the larger the values, the better the performance of the algorithm. The opposite goes for ERGAS and SAM.

3.2   Performance on Natural Scene HSI

To begin with, we choose an image from a natural scene HSI database for compression, the HSI is named scene 8 in this paper. The original dimension of scene 8 is $1018 \times 1340 \times 33$. We clip it into the size of $512 \times 512 \times 33$. Then, we normalize it to keep its value be within the scope 0–255. The results and comparison are listed in Table 1. The compression ratio is the ratio between the size of the original data and the sum of the compressed data size. It is reasonable that the compression ratio of the six methods could not be completely the same; however, we tried as far as possible to keep them approximately equal.

Note that the above comparisons were carried out at only one compression ratio. So what would the situation be with other compression ratios? Would the other methods outperform the PLTD algorithm? To answer these questions, we varied the compression ratio and tested the compression results. We changed the ratio from 0 to 0.25, which was adequate to test these methods. The comparisons are exhibited in Fig. 2.

Table 1. Comparision of compression and reconstruction results on hyperspectral scene 8.

	Proposed	MPCA	PCA	JPEG	PCA+JPEG
Rate	0.0441	0.0467	0.0445	0.0465	0.0467
PSNR	**43.1343**	39.1176	39.3904	37.5290	33.5215
SSIM	**0.9836**	0.9666	0.9637	0.9511	0.8984
FSIM	**0.9980**	0.9960	0.9909	0.9764	0.9526
ERGAS	**24.7816**	42.6079	37.5006	46.2918	81.4623
MSAM	**0.0351**	0.0498	0.0648	0.0465	0.1871
Time	10.56	14.58	128.72	1.06	235.90

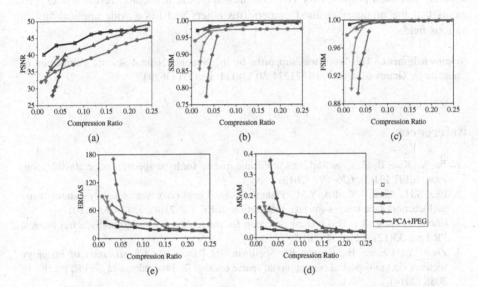

Fig. 2. Comparison of the compression and reconstruction results when the compression ratio varies from 0 to 0.25.

According to Fig. 2, despite the certain interval within which the MPCA algorithm or the PCA algorithm perform better than the PLTD algorithm, the PLTD algorithm obtains the best performance in most cases. Exceptions occur because the PCA algorithm only compresses the spectral information, and MPCA only compresses the spatial information, while PLTD compresses both the spatial and spectral information. Therefore, most of the time, the tensor-based PLTD algorithm performs better than the other methods.

To sum up the experiments, we implemented enough experiments on the hyperspectral scene 8 image to confirm that the proposed method outperforms all the other methods.

4 Conclusion

In this paper, a new compression method called patched-based low-rank tensor decomposition (PLTD) have been proposed. The new method employs tensor patch representation, nonlocal similarity, tensor dictionary learning together to solve the problem of effectively compressing HSIs. According to the paper, by clustering, a big data problem is decomposed into several small data problems which can be quickly solved by low-rank decomposition algorithm. Since the decomposed data discard both the spectral and spatial redundancy, and only retain the most discriminant information, the data after compression can better improve the efficiency and accuracy for the subsequent analysis. As far as we know, this is the first time that a patch-based tensor structure has been proposed for HSI compression. And it is confirmed in the experiments that the proposed method outperforms others and has a wide applicability in various fields.

Acknowledgment. This work was supported by the National Natural Science Foundation of China under Grants 61401317, 61471274, 91338111, and U1536204.

References

1. Jia, X., Kuo, B.-C., Crawford, M.M.: Feature mining for hyperspectral image classification. Proc. IEEE **101**(3), 676–697 (2013)
2. Lee, S.H., Choi, J.Y., Ro, Y.M., Plataniotis, K.: Local color vector binary patterns from multichannel face images for face recognition. IEEE TIP **21**(4), 2347–2353 (2012)
3. Chen, R., Ding, X.L.T.: Liveness detection for iris recognition using multispectral images. PR Lett. **33**(12), 123–134 (2012)
4. Zhou, Y., Chang, H., Barner, K., Spellman, P., Parvin, B.: Classification of histology sections via multispectral convolutional sparse coding. In: Proceedings of CVPR, pp. 3081–3088 (2014)
5. Holloway, J., Priya, T., Veeraraghavan, A., Prasad, S.: Image classification in natural scenes: are a few selective spectral channels sufficient? In: Proceedings of ICIP, pp. 655–659 (2014)
6. Wallace, G.: The jpeg still picture compression standard. IEEE TCE **38**(1), 18–34 (1992)
7. Said, A., Pearlman, W.A.: A new fast and efficient image codec based on set partitioning in hierarchical trees. IEEE TCSVT **6**(6), 243–250 (1996)
8. Shapiro, J.M.: Embedded image coding using zero-trees of wavelet coefficients. IEEE TSP **41**(12), 3445–3462 (1993)
9. Du, Q., Fowler, J.E.: Hyperspectral image compression using jpeg2000 and principal component analysis. Geosci. Remote Sens. Lett. **4**(2), 201–205 (2007)
10. Jolliffe, I.T.: Principal Component Analysis. Springer, Heidelberg (2002)
11. Guo, Y., Lin, X., Teng, Z., Xue, X., Fan, J.: A covariance-free iterative algorithm for distributed principal component analysis on vertically partitioned data. PR **45**(3), 1211–1219 (2011)
12. Wang, L., Jiao, L., Bai, J., Wu, J.: Hyperspectral image compression based on 3D reversible integer lapped transform, electron. Electron. Lett. **46**(24), 1601–1602 (2010)

13. Karami, A., Yazdi, M., Mercier, G.: Compression of hyperspectral images using discrete wavelet transform and tucker decomposition. IEEE JSTARS **5**(2), 444–450 (2012)

14. Lathauwer, L.D.: Signal Processing Based on Multilinear Algebra. Katholieke Universiteit Leuven (1997)

15. Lu, H., Plataniotis, K.N., Venetsanopoulos, A.N.: Mpca: multilinear principal component analysis of tensor objects. IEEE SPM **19**(1), 18–39 (2008)

16. Xu, D., Yan, S., Zhang, L., Lin, S.: Reconstruction and recognition of tensor-based objects with concurrent subspaces analysis. IEEE TCSVT **18**(1), 36–47 (2008)

17. Luo, Y., Tao, D., Wen, Y., Ramamohanarao, K., Xu, C., Wen, Y.: Tensor canonical correlation analysis for multi-view dimension reduction. IEEE TKDE **27**(11), 3111–3124 (2015)

18. Zhang, L., Zhang, L., Tao, D., Huang, X., Du, B.: Compression of hyperspectral remote sensing images by tensor approach. Neurocomputing **147**, 358–363 (2015)

19. Zhang, L., Zhang, L., Tao, D., Huang, X.: Tensor discriminative locality alignment for hyperspectral image spectral-spatial feature extraction. IEEE TGRS **51**(1), 242–256 (2013)

20. Yang, C., Shen, J., Peng, J., Fan, J.: Image collection summarization via dictionary learning for sparse representation. PR **46**, 948–961 (2013)

21. Buades, A., Coll, B., Morel, J.-M.: A non-local algorithm for image denoising. In: Proceedings of CVPR, pp. 60–65 (2005)

22. Zhou, C., Güney, F., Wang, Y., Geiger, A.: Exploiting object similarity in 3D reconstruction. In: Proceedings of ICCV (2015)

23. Lu, H., Plataniotis, K.N., Venetsanopoulos, A.N.: A survey of multilinear subspace learning for tensor data. PR **44**(7), 1540–1551 (2011)

24. Peng, Y., Meng, D., Xu, Z., Gao, C., Yang, Y., Zhang, B.: Decomposable nonlocal tensor dictionary learning for multispectral image denoising. In: Proceedings of CVPR, pp. 4321–4328 (2014)

25. Zhang, Z., Xu, Y., Yang, J., Li, X., Zhang, D.: A survey of sparse representation: algorithms and applications. CoRR abs, **3**, 490–530 (2015)

26. Aharon, M., Elad, M., Bruckstein, A., Katz, Y.: K-SVD: an algorithm for designing over complete dictionaries for sparse representation. IEEE TSP **54**(11), 4311–4322 (2006)

27. Wald, L.: Data Fusion: Definitions and Architectures: Fusion of Images of Different Spatial Resolutions. Les Presses Ecole des Mines, Paris (2002)

28. Yuhas, R.H., Boardman, J.W., Goetz, A.F.H.: Determination of semi-arid landscape endmembers and seasonal trends using convex geometry spectral unmixing techniques. Ratio **4**(22) (1990)

Moving Object Detection with ViBe and Texture Feature

Yumin Tian, Dan Wang, Peipei Jia[✉], and Jinhui Liu

School of Computer Science and Technology, Xidian University, Xi'an 710071, Shannxi, China
ymtian@mail.xidian.edu.cn, jiapei_608@163.com

Abstract. In the field of computer vision, moving object detection in complicated environments is challenging. This study proposes a moving target detecting
algorithm combining ViBe and spatial information to address the poor adaptability of ViBe in complex scenes. The CSLBP texture descriptor was improved
to more accurately describe background features. An adaptive threshold was
introduced, and thresholding on absolute difference was applied to obtain binary
string descriptors using comparisons of pixels from the same region or different
images. Afterwards, by adding spatial features to ViBe, a background model
based on color and texture feature was obtained. Experimental results show that
the proposed method addresses the deficiency of ViBe's feature representation
and improves its adaptability in complex video scenes with shadow, background
interference and slow-moving targets. This adaptability allows the precision of
detection to improve.

Keywords: Moving object detection · ViBe · CSLBP · Background modeling

1 Introduction

In recent years, moving object detection has been an important topic in the field of
computer vision. It is also a crucial part of intelligent monitoring systems and has broad
prospective applications in many other fields, including pattern recognition, medical
image processing and human-computer interaction. Object detection's rise in importance has directly influenced the kind of research pursued, such as target classification,
tracking identification and behavior analysis.

The methods of moving target detection can be divided into three categories: frame
difference algorithms [1], optical flow method [2] and background subtraction methods
[3, 4], which are widely used in motion detection. The method extracts moving regions
by calculating the differences between the current image and the background model.
The quality of the background model is directly related to the performance of target
detection, so this kind of method must set up and continuously update its background
models through machine learning. At present, most background modeling methods are
based on changes of pixels over time. Wren et al. [5] proposed the Single Gaussian
model for object detection, which can be used for single mode scenes. However, when
there are interference factors in the background, such as leave rustling or camera shaking,
false detections may occur. Stauffer et al. [6] used the Gaussian mixture model to
describe the state of pixels, which can be used for scenes with background disturbance,

© Springer International Publishing AG 2016
E. Chen et al. (Eds.): PCM 2016, Part I, LNCS 9916, pp. 150–159, 2016.
DOI: 10.1007/978-3-319-48890-5_15

but the detection results are not ideal when scenes change frequently. Elgammal et al. [7] presented the nonparametric kernel density estimation method (KDE) for background modeling, which does not need to assume the probability model of the background, although it requires a large number of calculations. PBAS (Pixel-Based Adaptive Segmenter) [8] is based on the ViBe method which will be explained in more detail later on. It realizes a nonparametric detection algorithm by making the foreground decision threshold and the update rate of background model adaptive. However, the process of background modeling is very complex, and the identified algorithms all ignore the characteristics of pixels in the spatial domain. As a result, the description of background features is not accurate in their motion detection outputs. To solve this problem, Heikkil et al. [9] have taken LBP (Local Binary Patterns) histograms as features to generate background models. This method is appropriate for illumination changes and shadow areas, but its high dimensional histograms lead to a large amount of computing, significantly slowing down the target detection speed.

To improve the robustness of motion detection algorithm, a new strategy based on the combination of ViBe and texture features is presented, which considers the information of both space and time for the pixels in the background models. To describe these features more accurately, the CSLBP (Center-Symmetric Local Binary Patterns) texture descriptor is improved by adding an absolute difference operation and using comparison strategies of pixels from both the same and different regions. Additionally, the adaptive similarity threshold is introduced to enhance the adaptive capacity of the object detection algorithm to cases of illumination variation. In the background modeling phase, the improved texture descriptor is added to the ViBe model, which describes the changes in background and color feature simultaneously and can produce background models based on both color and texture features.

2 ViBe Method and Texture Model

2.1 ViBe Method

The ViBe method [10, 11] is a universal foreground detection algorithm developed in recent years. It is suitable for a variety of video formats, scenes and colors spaces. In the ViBe approach, the first frame of a video is regarded as an approximation of the background image, so it is used to initialize the ViBe background model. For a pixel in the first frame, we randomly select the values of N neighboring pixels (using a predefined pattern) as sampling values, so that each pixel corresponds to a set of samples with N-pixel capacity.

After the establishment of the initial background model, moving targets can be detected starting from the second frame of a sequence. $v(\mathrm{x})$ is a pixel value at position x in a new frame, and $M(x) = (v_1, v_2, \ldots, v_N)$ is the pixel model, where $v_i, i = 1, 2, \cdots, N$ are the sampling values in the model. In order to classify pixels, we defines a sphere $S_R(v(x))$ of radius R centered on $v(x)$. # is defined as the number of elements in the intersection of the background model $M(x)$ and the sphere $S_R(v(x))$, and it can be represented as:

$$\#\{S_R(v(x)) \cap \{V_1, V_2, \ldots, V_N\}\} \tag{1}$$

The above formula reflects the similarity of the current pixel and background model. If it is greater than the given threshold $\#_{min}$, the pixel value $v(x)$ will be classified as belonging to the background, and if not, it is considered part of the foreground. Figure 1 shows the comparison process of the set of samples and the pixel value $v(x)$ in two-dimensional Europe-type color space.

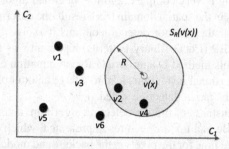

Fig. 1. The comparison of the set of samples and the sphere $S_R(v(x))$

The ViBe algorithm adopts a novel strategy to update its background model consisting of a random replacement policy, a spatial information propagation method and a random time subsampling. It defines a time subsampling factor Φ to enlarge the size of the time window covered by the background model. When a pixel value is considered to be part of the background, it has a one in Φ chance to update a sample in the corresponding pixel model. It also has the same probability to update a model from one of its neighboring pixels. The sample be updated is randomly selected, which allows background samples to be spread out and ghost areas to be quickly identified and restored.

2.2   Texture Model

A local binary pattern (LBP) is a type of effective texture feature representation. It calculates the texture eigenvalue of a pixel through the comparison of gray values between a center pixel and pixels in its neighborhood. The computation formula of the LBP texture descriptor is:

$$LBP_{P,R}(x_c, y_c) = \sum_{i=0}^{P-1} s(n_i - n_c)2^i, \quad s(x) = \begin{cases} 1 & x \geq 0 \\ 0 & x < 0 \end{cases} \tag{2}$$

where n_c represents the gray value of the center pixel located at the position of (x_c, y_c) in an image and n_i is the intensity of pixel i in the local area. $LBP_{P,R}(x_c, y_c)$ stands for the texture feature of the center pixel.

When an LBP is applied to background subtraction, it mainly use LBP histograms, which contain local neighborhood relationships that represent the background model.

A local area consisting of P pixels needs a 2^P dimensional histogram to describe it, so the dimension of the LBP histogram is usually too high, and the feature is also sensitive to noise. To solve this problem, Heikkila et al. [12] proposed the Center-Symmetric Local Binary Pattern (CSLBP), a more compact binary feature descriptor. It replaces the comparison between a center pixel and pixels in its neighborhood with the difference operation between the pixels that are symmetric about the center pixel. The CSLBP operator is defined as:

$$CS - LBP_{P,R,T}(x_c, y_c) = \sum_{i=0}^{P/2-1} s(n_i - n_{i+P/2})2^i, \quad s(x) = \begin{cases} 1 & x > T \\ 0 & x \leq T \end{cases} \tag{3}$$

where T is the similarity threshold. The comparison of the LBP and CSLBP is shown in Fig. 2.

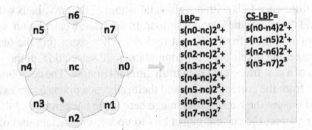

Fig. 2. The comparison of LBP and CSLBP

3　Moving Object Detection Based on ViBe and Texture

Although ViBe performs well in simple scenarios with little background interference, it does not work under the conditions of background disturbance or illumination changes. However, the CSLBP feature can effectively address these problems: it is effective in scenes with illumination changes or background interference, and can also compensate for a certain amount of noise. Therefore, the current study examines and improves the CSLBP texture, and puts forward a binary string descriptor suitable for background modeling. By putting the improved feature descriptor into ViBe, we can implement a new object detection method combining ViBe and spatial information.

3.1　The Improved Texture Descriptor

There are two main problems when CSLBP descriptors are used for background modeling. One is that adjacent pixels in an image tend to share a similar color and brightness distribution. However, the CSLBP descriptor is computed by comparing the grey values of pixels in the same area, which easily causes the background area and motion area to correspond to the same feature value and lead to a residual phenomenon. The other issue is that the CSLBP descriptor directly compares gray scale difference with the threshold T: if the difference value is greater than T, $s(x)$ will be set to 1, and otherwise it will be set to 0. This comparison method can show the relative size of pixels, but cannot effectively reflect their similarity, which affects the accuracy of detection results.

For these reasons, the CSLBP feature was improved in this study. We put forward a new texture feature named CSLBSP (Center-Symmetric Local Binary Similarity Pattern), which is applicable to background modeling. The improved feature descriptor is defined as:

$$CSLBSP_{P,R,T}(x_c, y_c) = \sum_{i=0}^{P-1} s(n_i - b_r)2^i, \quad s(x) = \begin{cases} 1 & |x| \leq T \\ 0 & |x| > T \end{cases} \tag{4}$$

where b_r is the pixel corresponding to n_i. In order to better reflect the similarity between pixels, we introduce the absolute difference operation in the process of feature extraction. If the absolute difference falls within a given threshold T, the two pixels will be considered similar, and otherwise they are not similar. In the feature calculation, we add a new strategy to compare pixels from different regions. When extracting the features of the background image, the pixels used for computation are selected from the same region, but the features of a new frame are taken from different images. The neighborhood pixels n_i are extracted from the current image, and their reference pixels b_r are extracted from the background image (the background image here is the background of the last frame, which is used to detect the current object and to update the background of the current frame).

The value of the similarity threshold T is generally associated with the intensity of pixels. For regions with large intensity, the range of its background pixel value is relatively large. In this study, with reference to the literature [13], the texture descriptor is revised on the basis of the Formula (4) by introducing the adaptive threshold:

$$CSLBSP_{P,R,T}(x_c, y_c) = \sum_{i=0}^{P-1} s(n_i - b_r)2^i, \quad s(n_i - b_r) = \begin{cases} 1 & |n_i - b_r| \leq T_r \cdot b_r \\ 0 & otherwise \end{cases} \tag{5}$$

where $T_r \cdot b_r$ is the similarity threshold. The improved descriptor can reasonably set the similarity threshold according to illumination variation cases, improving its adaptability to illumination changes.

3.2   Background Modeling Based on ViBe and Texture

The ViBe method builds the background model largely according to the changing color features of pixels in a sequence. To improve its accuracy under the conditions of shadow, light changes and background interference, this study puts the improved texture descriptors in the ViBe approach and describes the changes of the background and color feature.

We built background models and detected foreground objects based mainly on the ViBe algorithm. The random selection policy is adopted during the background model initialization. For a given pixel in the first frame of a video, N neighboring pixels are randomly selected, and their color and texture features are chosen as samples of the pixel model. Moving objects can be extracted from the second frame. The similarities of color and texture can be discovered by calculating the differences between the current image and the background model, according to Formulas (6) and (7):

$$ColorDist(v_{x,y}, MColor_{x,y}) = L1Dist(v_{x,y}, MColor_{x,y}) \tag{6}$$

$$DescDist(CSLBSP(x,y), MDesc_{x,y}) = CSLBSP(x,y) \oplus MDesc_{x,y} \tag{7}$$

where $v_{x,y}$ and $CSLBSP(x, y)$ respectively represent the color and texture information at position (x, y) in the current image, $MColor_{x,y}$ and $MDesc_{x,y}$ calculate the color and texture descriptor of the (x, y) pixel in the background image. L1 distance and Hamming distance are used for color and texture similarity measurement. Afterwards, we look for samples matching the current pixel according to the following formula, and calculate the number of them as $S(x)$:

$$ColorDist(v_{x,y}, MColor_{x,y}) \leq T_{color} \tag{8}$$

$$DescDist(CSLBSP(x,y), MDesc_{x,y}) \leq T_{desc} \tag{9}$$

where T_{color} and T_{desc} are the similarity thresholds of color and texture descriptor, respectively. To determine the category of the current pixel, the total number of samples meeting the above conditions $S(x)$ are compared to the given threshold $\#_{min}$. If it is greater than the threshold, the pixel will be classified as a background pixel, and otherwise it will belong to the foreground.

The updated strategy of the ViBe method applied in this study contains the memoryless update policy and the time subsampling and spatial propagation methods. When a pixel value is classified as background, it has a one in Φ chance to update not only its own pixel model but also one of its neighboring pixels' models.

4   Experimental Results

In order to evaluate the performance of the proposed method, we tested and compared it with the ViBe, LBP and PBAS algorithms. Of these, the PBAS method improves upon ViBe. To handle scene changes, it adds the adaptive foreground decision threshold and the adaptive background update rate on the basis of ViBe, which realizes a nonparametric moving object detection algorithm. We make evaluation on the CDNet dataset and select several representative detection results of the videos of a canoe, an office and a bus station to demonstrate, which are shown in Fig. 3.

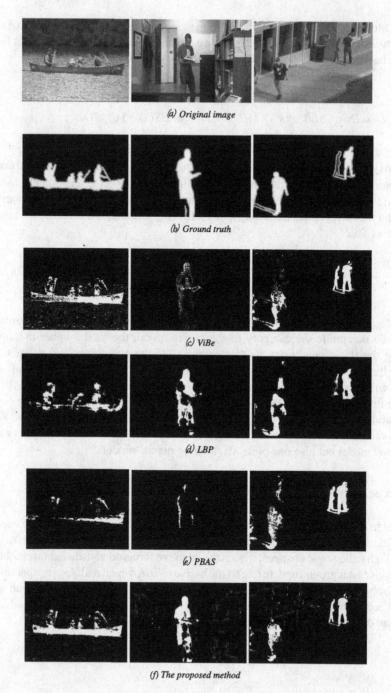

(a) Original image

(b) Ground truth

(c) ViBe

(d) LBP

(e) PBAS

(f) The proposed method

Fig. 3. Moving object detection results of 4 methods

Experimental Setup: the experimental conditions are a personal computer (2.93 GHZ Intel Xeon CPU, 2 cores, 12 GB) and Visual Studio 2010 platform with the OpenCV2.4 library. The parameters used in experiments are shown in Table 1.

Table 1. Parameters used in experiments

Parameter	T_r	T_{color}	T_{desc}	$\#_{min}$
Value	0.4	35	6	40

The canoe video is a lake scene video. It can be seen in Fig. 3 that there are different degrees of noise, caused by fluctuations of the water's surface that exist in the results of both ViBe and the proposed approach. Our method can better suppress background interference than ViBe can, and its foreground object is more complete. Although the foreground images of the LBP and PBAS methods are "clean", the omission phenomenon is very obvious, leading to unsatisfactory results.

The office video has an uneven distribution of light and slow-moving targets. Therefore, PBAS and ViBe fail to completely extract moving objects, and a large area of void space exists in their foreground regions. The contour of the target detected by LBP is also inaccurate. Although the proposed method produces some noise points, its foreground image is the closest to the ground truth image and ensures the integrity of targets.

The bus station video contains a largely outdoor scene. Targets constantly enter, stop and leave the video, and shadows also exist in the scene. In this case, the improved algorithm and the LBP method have advantages over the other two methods in the integrity of targets. However, the LBP algorithm calculates texture features in a large area, and it is easy to mistake the background pixels in the targets' neighborhood as foreground pixels, leading to the expansions of the target edges. By contrast, the improved algorithm in this study can handle this problem effectively, and the target contours are closer to the real targets.

Table 2 shows the average values in precision, recall and F-measure of the four background modeling algorithms for the CDNet dataset. Based on the evaluation indicators, it is clear that our method outperforms the others. Its precision is within the acceptable range, and it has significantly higher values in recall and F-measure than other methods. Meanwhile, our proposed method is especially adaptive to the background with large interference, and can better suppress background interference than other method can. Although the detection results of our method will have few noise in some scenes, but our method can detect more foreground pixels and is the closest to the ground truth image compared with the other three contrast method.

Table 2. The evaluation of four background modeling methods

Methods	Recall	Precision	F-measure
ViBe	0.45	0.76	0.52
LBP	0.50	0.89	0.62
PBAS	0.35	0.91	0.49
The proposed method	0.57	0.82	0.66

5   Conclusion

In this study, we present a background modeling algorithm combining ViBe and texture features. This method modifies the CSLBP descriptors by introducing the comparison between different regions and thresholding on absolute difference operations, making the representations of features more accurate. The adaptive similarity threshold is initially introduced to enhance the adaptability of the algorithm to illumination variations. In order to improve the adaptability of ViBe to complex scenes, this study combines the improved descriptors and the ViBe method, achieving a novel moving object detection approach based on color and texture. Experimental results demonstrate that the proposed method can clearly improve the quality of target detection, proving the effectiveness of this algorithm.

Acknowledgments.   This paper was supported by the NSFC under grant 61303034, the Aeronautical Science Foundation of China under grant 2013ZD31007, and Science and technology project of Shaanxi province (Grant No. 2016GY-033).

References

1. Chaohui, Z., Xiaohui, D., Shuoyu, X., et al.: An improved moving object detection algorithm based on frame difference and edge detection. In: Fourth International Conference on Image and Graphics, ICIG 2007, pp. 519–523. IEEE (2007)
2. Horn, B.K.P., Schunck, B.G.: determining optical flow. Artif. Intell. **17**(81), 185–203 (2004)
3. Lucia, M., Alfredo, P.: A self-organizing approach to background subtraction for visual surveillance applications. IEEE Trans. Image Process. **17**(7), 1168–1177 (2008)
4. Bilodeau, G.A., Jodoin, J.P., Saunier, N.: Change detection in feature space using local binary similarity patterns. In: International Conference on Computer & Robot Vision. IEEE Computer Society, pp. 106–112 (2013)
5. Wren, C.R., Azarbayejani, A., Darrell, T., et al.: Pfinder: real-time tracking of the human body. IEEE Trans. Pattern Anal. Mach. Intell. **19**(7), 780–785 (1997)
6. Stauffer, C., Grimson, W.E.L.: Adaptive background mixture models for real-time tracking. In: Proceedings of Cvpr, vol. 2, pp. 22–46 (1999)
7. Elgammal, A., Duraiswami, R., Harwood, D., et al.: Background and foreground modeling using non-parametric kernel density estimation for visual surveillance KDE. Proc. IEEE **90**(7), 1151–1163 (2002)
8. Hofmann, M., Tiefenbacher, P., Rigoll, G.: Background segmentation with feedback: the pixel-based adaptive segmenter. In: 2012 IEEE Computer Society Conference on Computer Vision and Pattern Recognition Workshops (CVPRW). IEEE, pp. 38–43 (2012)
9. Marko, H., Matti, P.: A texture-based method for modeling the background and detecting moving objects. IEEE Trans. Pattern Anal. Mach. Intell. **28**(4), 657–662 (2006)
10. Barnich, O., Vanogenbroeck, M.: ViBE: a powerful random technique to estimate the background in video sequences. In: IEEE International Conference on Acoustics, Speech & Signal Processing, pp. 945–948 (2009)
11. Olivier, B., Marc, V.: ViBe: a universal background subtraction algorithm for video sequences. IEEE Trans. Image Process. A Publ. IEEE Sig. Process. Soc. **20**(6), 1709–1724 (2011)

12. Heikkilä, M., Pietikäinen, M., Schmid, C.: Description of interest regions with center-symmetric local binary patterns. In: Kalra, Prem, K., Peleg, S. (eds.) ICVGIP 2006. LNCS, vol. 4338, pp. 58–69. Springer, Heidelberg (2006). doi:10.1007/11949619_6

13. Liao, S., Zhao, G., Kellokumpu, V., et al.: Modeling pixel process with scale invariant local patterns for background subtraction in complex scenes. In: 2010 IEEE Conference on Computer Vision and Pattern Recognition (CVPR), pp. 1301–1306. IEEE (2010)

Leveraging Composition of Object Regions for Aesthetic Assessment of Photographs

Hong Lu[1], Zeping Yao[1], Yunhan Bai[1], Zhibin Zhu[1], Bohong Yang[2], Lukun Chen[3], and Wenqiang Zhang[2]([✉])

[1] Shanghai Key Laboratory of Intelligent Information Processing, School of Computer Science, Fudan University, Shanghai, China
[2] Shanghai Engineering Research Center for Video Technology and System, School of Computer Science, Fudan University, Shanghai, China
wqzhang@fudan.edu.cn
[3] College of Information Science and Technology, Nanjing Agricultural University, Nanjing, China

Abstract. Evaluating the aesthetic quality of photos automatically can be considered as a highly challenging task. In this paper, we propose and investigate a novel method for the aesthetic assessment of photos. We integrate photo composition of salient object regions into the assessment. Specifically, we first evaluate the objectness of regions in photos by considering the spatial location and shape of the image salient object regions. Then, we extract features based on the spatial composition of objects. The proposed features fuse aesthetics rules with composition of semantic regions. The proposed method is evaluated on a large dataset. Experimental results demonstrate the efficacy of the proposed method.

Keywords: Computer aesthetic assessment · Photo composition · Salient object region feature · Objectness

1 Introduction

With the fast growing and wide spreading of computer and communication network, the digital media develop so dramatically that it changes the way people enjoy and feel beauty. The world is filled with beauty. There is no doubt that people pursue beauty, prefer things that are more fascinating than others.

As a consequence, assessing the aesthetic quality of diverse photos becomes an attractive topic. Recently, a good deal of work related to aesthetic assessment have drawn significant attention [9].

The key part of assessment is to evaluate the underlying aesthetic properties of photos by leveraging universal or traditional metric. In this work, we consider incorporating the photo composition and the objectness of salient object regions into the assessment. Naturally, it is necessary to evaluate different categories of photographs objectively. Hence, we develop a universal method to score various photos.

© Springer International Publishing AG 2016
E. Chen et al. (Eds.): PCM 2016, Part I, LNCS 9916, pp. 160–169, 2016.
DOI: 10.1007/978-3-319-48890-5_16

The contributions of the paper are as follows.

- We obtain salient object regions for aesthetic assessment of photographs by clustering and optimization algorithms
- We propose novel features extracted from the object regions and fuse for better performance
- We experimentally validate our method and demonstrate that it can rate different categories of photographs

2   Related Works

Automatic aesthetic assessment of photographs through computer is a kind of objective task. Its procedure is as follows.

1. Select relevant photo features to represent aesthetic value.
2. Quantify the aesthetic value of the photo by combining features with some certain rules.
3. The data is fed into a classifier, e.g. support vector machine (SVM), to improve the performance of the classifier.
4. Finally, the aesthetic value could be evaluated by the trained classifier.

Previous relevant work has focused on extracting features from regions. Specifically, [6] extracts features to represent both global characteristic and local characteristic. [9] proposes content-based photograph quality assessment using regional and global features. And [11] utilizes some combined local features for the task. [5] takes the local area features and the impact of visual saliency into consideration.

Aside from low level features, such as color, texture, shape, etc., [2] leverages the high level features. Composition is one of high level features. [9] makes use of the rule of thirds to improve the harmonious degree of the whole photo. In this paper, we take advantage of other high level features, such as diagonal rule, proportionality principle. More details are given in the following sections.

3   Method

In this section, we describe our proposed method on aesthetics assessment of photographs.

3.1   Objectness

The objectness measure, as an object detector, could quantify how likely it is for an image window to contain an object of any class opposed to backgrounds. The class includes fish, cat, etc. Therefore it can help us to locate the underlying object regions. In this section, we introduce our method that performs clustering and optimization over the object proposals by Binarized Normed Gradients method, i.e. BING [1]. The object regions are necessary for aesthetic assessment of photographs.

BING. Generally, the object is quite dissimilar from background within a fixed size of window in gradient mode. Specifically, the gradient distribution of objects appears uncertain and stochastic. On the contrary, the gradient distribution of the background is neat and simplex.

We leverage BING [1] to obtain candidate object windows. The windows can be resized into 8×8. Each candidate window is required to be flattened to a 64-dimension normed gradient feature vector. The features are fed into a linear classifier. The normed gradient's interval is [0, 255]. Then a feature vector could be stored within a byte. Obviously, bit operation can speed up the computation.

Clustering and Optimizing Object Regions. After performing the BING algorithm, there are plentiful proposal windows. The examples are shown in Fig. 1(a). These proposal windows corresponding to duplicates for image objects, such as red and green boxes as shown in Fig. 1(b), can be determined by clustering. We perform k-means clustering [4] on the proposal windows. For similarity measure, we use the area overlapping defined as below.

$$Sim(S_i, S_j) = \frac{S_i \cap S_j}{S_i \cup S_j} \tag{1}$$

where S_i and S_j denote areas of the i-th and j-th region. The distance is computed as $D(S_i, S_j) = 1 - Sim(S_i, S_j)$.

For initialization, we first compute the pairwise distance matrix for proposal regions. Then we define the weight of i-th region as $\sum_k Sim(S_i, S_k)$. And we select the top k regions ranked by weight as the initial centroids for clustering.

After initialization, we perform two steps. The first step is to assign each region to its nearest centroid. The second step is to refine the new cluster centroids according to the member belonging to that cluster. The number of clusters is set empirically.

After k-means clustering, we cluster the proposal windows into k clusters. We select $\alpha\%$ proposal windows from the same cluster, where α is a parameter to be determined in experiment. Then we find the bounding box of several selected proposal windows as the object regions. The results are shown as blue boxes in Fig. 1(c). Furthermore, we perform denoising step to eliminate the boxes with small areas which have overlapping with that of large areas. The final obtained regions are shown in Fig. 1(d).

3.2   Feature Extraction

In order to extract features from object regions, we need to employ some aesthetic principles. The rule of thirds, the diagonal rule and proportional balance principle are included in our evaluation. By using these principles, the result of assessment is more objective and accurate. In this section, we describe how to implement these principles.

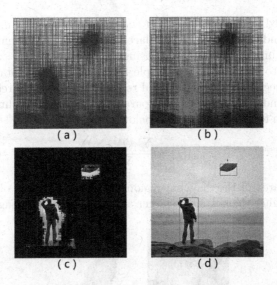

Fig. 1. Clustering and optimizing on the object regions. (Color figure online)

Position Feature. The rule of thirds, as one of most well known principles of photographic composition, can be applied to the process of composing digital images. It is about where to put the salient or main elements in a scene. The rule is based on the fact that human eyes are naturally drawn to a point about two-thirds up a page. What' more, the rule suggests that an image will look more aesthetically pleasing if you place the important parts in the target area.

The image is equally divided into nine square parts by two equally horizontal and two equally vertical straight lines. Then, the most important compositional elements are supposed to appear along these lines or their intersections. The four intersections of these lines which are called golden sections play a great significance in aesthetic assessment. Generally, the more number of object centers located in the golden section points, the more pleasure we will obtain. As in [3] considered, we also use the feature as follows:

$$E_{pos}(I) = \frac{1}{\sum_i S_i} \sum_i S_i \cdot \cos((\frac{\|p_{ix} - p_{ix}^s\|}{w/3} + \frac{\|p_{iy} - p_{iy}^s\|}{h/3}) \cdot \frac{\pi}{2}) \tag{2}$$

where S_i is the area of an object region $R_i.p_i$ and p_i^s are the center of mass of R_i and the closest golden section point to p_i, respectively. In the above formula, E_{pos} is the distance between the image object region and the closest golden section point. Accordingly, the distance is normalized into the interval $[-1, 1]$.

Angle Feature. The diagonal rule is another principle for image aesthetics assessment. It concentrates on extracting angle feature of the image. As indicated in [10], the image composition is more harmonious and the eyes are pleasant if most objects are parallel to the diagonal direction. Specifically, if the important objects are placed around the two diagonal lines, the image is more attractive. On the other hand, if the objects are placed on the top or bottom of the image, the image looks unbalanced and unpleasing.

We propose to quantify this principle by computing the total area covered by both object regions and the diagonal regions. The diagonal region is defined by the area bounded by the two lines parallel to the diagonal line as shown in Fig. 2. The angle feature is defined as below.

$$E_{ang}(I) = \frac{\sum_i (T \cap S_i))}{\sum_i S_i} \qquad (3)$$

where T is the area of the diagonal region, S_i the area of i-th object region of image I. The higher the score, the larger aesthetic score the image has.

Fig. 2. Diagonal region feature extraction.

Area Feature. To meet the proportionality principle, it is necessary to maintain the ratio between the object area and the whole image in a reasonable range. We propose to use the area of the proposal box covered by the corresponding object for evaluation. We define the area feature as below.

$$E_{area}(I) = \frac{\sum_i (w_i \cdot h_i)}{W \cdot H} \qquad (4)$$

where w_i and h_i are the width and the height of object window i, W and H are the width and the height of the whole image. Specifically, the formulation computes the ratio between areas of the object and the whole image.

Shape Feature. To meet the proportional balance principle, only considering the object's relative area is not enough. We also take the shape of the object into consideration. It is difficult to describe the shape of an irregular region. We adopt the average product of the width and height of the regions as the measure. The feature is defined as below.

$$E_{shape}(I) = \frac{\sum_i (w_i \cdot h_i)}{n \cdot W \cdot H} \qquad (5)$$

where n is the number of the object windows.

Depth of Field Feature. Depth of Field (DoF) is the zone of acceptable sharpness within a photo that will appear in focus. Namely, DoF indicates whether the salient object and background can be sharply focused simultaneously. In image composition, an object with high clarity tends to have high aesthetic value. We propose to employ a traditional method which uses the rate of gray level to quantify the clarity. Specifically, the rate of gray level is defined as below.

$$I_{i,j} = \sum_{l=-1}^{1} \sum_{m=-1}^{1} \frac{|p_{i,j} - p_{i+l,j+m}|}{\sqrt{||l|| + ||m||}} \tag{6}$$

And the DoF feature is defined as below.

$$E_{dof}(I) = \frac{\sum_{k=1}^{n} \sum_{(i,j) \in S_k} I_{i,j}/n}{\sum_{k=1}^{n} S_k} \tag{7}$$

where n is the number of the object windows.

3.3 Assessment Method

Our method on image aesthetics assessment is as below.

1. Use the BING [1] method as well as clustering and optimization to obtain the object regions.
2. Extract features as described above based on the detected object regions for aesthetics assessment. The features can be used separately and in a fusion manner.

4 Experiments

4.1 Experimental Dataset

To validate our method, we use the AVA dataset provided by [8]. The dataset is a large-scale dataset used for aesthetic assessment. It contains over 250,000 images. The images are from DPChallenge[1]. Each image in the dataset has a large number of aesthetic scores. The higher the score, the better aesthetics quality the image has.

In order to estimate the aesthetic score of each image has, we pick a random sample of 200 independent scores within the photo's score set and take the average of these scores as the ground truth score. Besides, the image data are split into two sets. The two sets contain the images with aesthetic scores above 5.5 and with scores equal to or below 5.5. These two image sets form the high quality and low quality image sets, respectively. Inspired by [7,8], we form three data groups from AVA dataset. The first group contains twenty thousand images from six categories, i.e. animal, architecture, floral, landscape, portrait, and still

---

[1] DPChallenge. http://www.dpchallenge.com/.

life. The second group is randomly sampled from the first group and contains 4000 images. And according to the aesthetics scores, the second group is divided into several sets respectively as the training set. Each set contain same number of images, i.e. 800 images in each set. 1000 images are sampled as testing set. Table 1 shows the set with the corresponding aesthetic score. The third group contains images with 15 % top and 15 % bottom scores in the whole dataset as training set, 6000 samples with aesthetic scores of gaussian distribution as testing set.

Table 1. The training set with the corresponding aesthetic score.

Training set ID	Score distribution
1	$[5.0, 6.0]$
2	$[4.5, 5.0) \cup (6.0, 6.5]$
3	$[4.0, 4.5) \cup (6.5, 7.0]$
4	$[3.5, 4.0) \cup (7.0, 7.5]$
5	$[1.0, 3.5) \cup (7.5, 10]$

4.2   Experiments

Effects of the Distribution of the Aesthetic Scores. In AVA dataset, human label the aesthetic score for each image. The aesthetic is subjective. The distribution of the aesthetics score in AVA dataset is extreme and not balanced. In other word, the scores are concentrated on the relative high and low values. In this experiment, we explore the relation between evaluation performance and the distribution of aesthetics scores.

We select images from the second data group (as described in Sect. 4.1) randomly. And we use different fractions of images to train the classifiers. The trained classifiers are tested on the same test set. The experimental results on different data fractions are shown in Fig. 3.

It can be observed from Fig. 3, images in training set 3, i.e. the aesthetic scores fall in 4.0 to 4.5 and 6.7 to 7.0, can obtain promising results on aesthetic evaluation. On the other hand, a training set containing the most unambiguous images has a bad performance (i.e. training set 5 in Fig. 3). Then we choose images with aesthetic scores in the top and bottom 15 % scores as training set in the following experiments.

Comparison of Image Composition Features. In this experiment, we use the third group data in Sect. 4.1 as the training set and testing set. To speed up the computation, we sample part of the data from the the third group data.

We extract the features respectively and also fuse the features. The experimental results are shown in Fig. 4. It can be observed from the figure with the

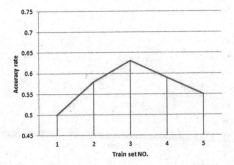

Fig. 3. Experimental result on influence of the distribution of scores.

increase of the training data, the performance is normally improved. On the other hand, DoF feature performs better when small number of training data is used. Also, the fused feature performs better than the separate feature.

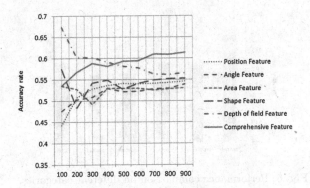

Fig. 4. Comparison of image composition features.

Selection of Parameters on Object Region Detection. As in Sect. 3.1, we introduce the method of object region detection. After BING method and k-means clustering, we select $\alpha\%$ proposal windows from the same cluster. In this section, we determine the parameter $\alpha\%$ by tuning on the validation set. In the experiment, 1000 images are used as validation set. 10-fold cross validation is performed. The parameter $\alpha\%$ is set to 60%, 65%, 70%, 75%, 80%, 85%, 90%, respectively. The experiment is performed 10 times by using 10 image sets as testing set separately.

Figure 5 shows the experimental results on the performance of the parameter α tuning. It can be observed from Fig. 5 the optimal performance can be obtained by setting $\alpha\%$ to 70% to 75%. And we set the $\alpha\%$ to 70%.

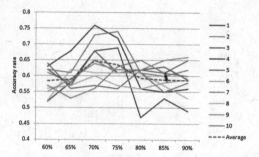

Fig. 5. Performance of parameter α tuning.

Performance on Different Categories. In this experiment, we evaluate the performance on different categories. Based on the experimental result in Sect. 4.2, we use the fused feature. The experimental data used is the first group as in Sect. 4.1. The experimental results are shown in Fig. 6.

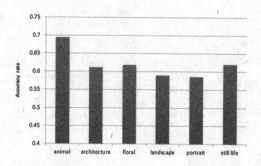

Fig. 6. Performance comparison on different categories.

It can be observed from Fig. 6 that the method performs better for animal and still life categories. On the other hand, the performance difference is not large for different categories.

5   Conclusions and Future Work

In this paper, we propose a method to evaluate the aesthetic quality of an image by extracting features from the salient object regions. The extracted features on the object composition can obtain promising results especially for object related categories such as animal, floral, etc. As for future work, we plan to explore the connections such as contrast and overlap of different object regions.

Acknowledgements. This work was supported in part by National Natural Science Foundation of China (No. 81373555), and Shanghai Committee of Science and Technology (14JC1402202, 14441904403).

References

1. Cheng, M.-M., Zhang, Z., Lin, W.-Y., Torr, P.: BING: binarized normed gradients for objectness estimation at 300fps. In: IEEE Conference on Computer Vision and Pattern Recognition, pp. 3286–3293 (2014)
2. Dhar, S., Ordonez, V., Berg, T.L.: High level describable attributes for predicting aesthetics and interestingness. In: IEEE Conference on Computer Vision and Pattern Recognition, pp. 1657–1664. IEEE (2011)
3. Guo, Y., Liu, M., Gu, T., Wang, W.: Improving photo composition elegantly: considering image similarity during composition optimization. Comput. Graph. Forum **31**, 2193–2202 (2012). Wiley Online Library
4. Hartigan, J.A., Wong, M.A.: Algorithm as 136: a k-means clustering algorithm. J. Roy. Stat. Soc. Ser. C (Applied Statistics) **28**(1), 100–108 (1979)
5. Khan, S.S., Vogel, D.: Evaluating visual aesthetics in photographic portraiture. In: Proceedings of the Eighth Annual Symposium on Computational Aesthetics in Graphics, Visualization, and Imaging, pp. 55–62. Eurographics Association (2012)
6. Li, C., Chen, T.: Aesthetic visual quality assessment of paintings. IEEE J. Sel. Top. Sign. Proces. **3**(2), 236–252 (2009)
7. Lu, H., Lin, J., Yang, B., Chang, Y., Guo, Y., Xue, X.: Leveraging color harmony and spatial context for aesthetic assessment of photographs. In: Ooi, W.T., Snoek, C.G.M., Tan, H.K., Ho, C.-K., Huet, B., Ngo, C.-W. (eds.) PCM 2014. LNCS, vol. 8879, pp. 323–332. Springer, Heidelberg (2014). doi:10.1007/978-3-319-13168-9_36
8. Murray, N., Marchesotti, L., Perronnin, F.: AVA: a large-scale database for aesthetic visual analysis. In: IEEE Conference on Computer Vision and Pattern Recognition, pp. 2408–2415 (2012)
9. Tang, X., Luo, W., Wang, X.: Content-based photo quality assessment. IEEE Trans. Multimedia **15**(8), 1930–1943 (2013)
10. Zhang, F.-L., Wang, M., Hu, S.-M.: Aesthetic image enhancement by dependence-aware object recomposition. IEEE Trans. Multimedia **15**(7), 1480–1490 (2013)
11. Zhang, L., Gao, Y., Zimmermann, R., Tian, Q., Li, X.: Fusion of multichannel local and global structural cues for photo aesthetics evaluation. IEEE Trans. Image Process. **23**(3), 1419–1429 (2014)

Video Affective Content Analysis Based on Protagonist via Convolutional Neural Network

Yingying Zhu[1,2], Zhengbo Jiang[1], Jianfeng Peng[1], and Sheng-hua Zhong[1(✉)]

[1] College of Computer Science and Software Engineering, Shenzhen University,
Shenzhen 518000, People's Republic of China
csshzhong@szu.edu.cn
[2] Department of Computer Science, The University of Texas at San Antonio,
San Antonio, TX 78249, USA

Abstract. Affective recognition is an important and challenging task for video content analysis. Affective information in videos is closely related to the viewer's feelings and emotions. Thus, video affective content analysis has a great potential value. However, most of the previous methods are focused on how to effectively extract features from videos for affective analysis. There are several issues are worth to be investigated. For example, what information is used to express emotions in videos, and which information is useful to affect audiences' emotions. Taking into account these issues, in this paper, we proposed a new video affective content analysis method based on protagonist information via Convolutional Neural Network (CNN). The proposed method is evaluated on the largest video emotion dataset and compared with some previous work. The experimental results show that our proposed affective analysis method based on protagonist information achieves best performance in emotion classification and prediction.

Keywords: Affective recognition · Video content analysis · Protagonist information · Convolutional neural network

1 Introduction

In the last decade, the number of videos takes on a trend of explosive increase. Automatic video content analysis plays an increasingly significant role in various applications, such as video retrieval [1] and summarization [2], video saliency detection [3] and quality assessment [4]. Therefore, automatic video content analysis is required to effectively organize videos and help users in quickly finding the meet mind collections. The traditional content-based video analysis focuses on common semantic contents, such as sports or news. As we known, while users were watching videos, their emotional states will be unavoidable influenced by the videos. More and more people select videos to satisfy some emotional needs, such as relieve stress or tediousness. It is therefore necessary to analyze the affective content of videos. Different from the common content-based video analysis, which usually concentrates on the main event happened in a video. The goal of video affective content analysis is to automatically recognize the emotions elicited by videos. It will benefit both the users and businesses, users could utilize the

© Springer International Publishing AG 2016
E. Chen et al. (Eds.): PCM 2016, Part I, LNCS 9916, pp. 170–180, 2016.
DOI: 10.1007/978-3-319-48890-5_17

emotional information to retrieve certain videos, filmmakers may change their editing to make a more stimulating movie that meet the emotional flow of audiences through the help of video affective content analysis [5]. The emotional analysis can be used for lots of applications, including mood-based personalized content distribute [6], video indexing and summarization [7].

The video affective content analysis mainly contains two steps: feature extraction and emotion classification or prediction. Audio and video features, such as MFCC [8], number of scene cuts and color [9] are often used for video affective content analysis. After the features are extracted, a classifier or regressor is used for mapping the features to the emotional spaces. For example, Wang et al. [9] employed a specially adapted variant of Support vector machine (SVM) to classify films into six basic emotions. Cui et al. [10] employed multiple linear regression and support vector regression (SVR) with different kernels for valence and arousal estimation.

Recent years, deep learning is widely used in computer vision, and it shows an appreciable performance. More and more work used Convolutional Neural Network (CNN) for video affective content analysis. In 2014, Acar et al. [8] proposed to use CNN, in order to learn mid-level representations from automatically extracted low-level features. Then the learned mid-level representations are given as input to multi-class SVM to classify affective music videos. Baveye et al. [11] conducted a serious of experiments using deep learning method. They used CNN as a feature extractor, then the features combined with the audio and video features are fed to the SVR to predict the emotions.

However, most of the previous methods are focused on how to effectively extract more features from videos for affective analysis. There are several issues are worth to be investigated, such as: what information is used to express emotions in videos, and which information is useful to affect audiences' emotions. In this paper, we try to explore what information is used to express emotions in videos, and which features are useful to detect and analyze emotions. Based on common sense, we believe the story line of the movie is alongside with the acts of the actors, especially the protagonists. And the construction and expression of emotions in videos are created by the acts of the actors on purpose. Furthermore, the audiences' emotions are mainly influenced by the actors especially the protagonists. Thus, in this paper, we propose a novel video affective content analysis method based on protagonist information. To the best of our knowledge, this work is the first paper do affective content analysis based on protagonist information.

The rest of this paper is organized as follows. Section 2 brief reviews the principle of CNN and the previous work used CNN for emotional analysis. In Sect. 3 we introduce our method for the affective analysis based on protagonist. Experimental results are presented in Sect. 4. Finally, conclusion and future work is provided in Sect. 5.

2 Relative Work

Convolutional neural network (CNN) is one type of feed-forward artificial neural networks. Four key ideas are behind CNN that take advantage of the properties of natural signals: local connections, shared weights, pooling and the use of many layers. The architecture of typical CNN is structured as a series of stages. The first few stages are composed of two types of layers: convolutional layers and pooling layers. The role of the convolutional layer is to detect local conjunctions of features from the previous layer, and the role of the pooling layer is to merge semantically similar features into one. Two or three stages of convolution, non-linearity and pooling are stacked, followed by more convolutional and fully-connected layers. Back-propagating gradients through Convolutional Neural Networks is as simple as through a regular deep network, allowing all the weights to be trained. The convolutional and pooling layers in CNN are directly inspired by the classic notions of simple cells and complex cells in visual neuroscience [12], and the overall architecture is reminiscent of the hierarchy in the visual cortex ventral pathway [13].

CNN achieved many practical successes during the period when neural networks were out of favor and it has recently been widely adopted by the computer-vision community, such as face verification, human action recognition [14], and object recognition [15]. In recent years, CNN is widely used in the affective computing field, such as facial expression recognition and video emotion analysis. In [16], Kahou et al. used a pre-trained CNN model based on ImageNet to recognize facial expressions in video frames. Acar et al. [8] tried to use a CNN to learn mid-level representations from automatically extracted low-level features. Then the learned mid-level representations are fed to multi-class SVM to classify the affective music videos. In 2014, Chen et al. [17] presents a visual sentiment concept classification model based on deep convolutional neural networks. Their experiments show that with the help of a pre-trained CNN model, the classification improved significantly. Baveye et al. [11] proposed several methods based on deep learning for video affective analysis. In their experiment, CNN was used as a feature extractor. The image features extracted from the key frames, coupled with the audio and video features, are then fed to a Support Vector Regression to predict the induced emotions of video clips. Above papers have already proved that CNN has a strong ability to extract features for video emotion analysis. Thus, we adopt the CNN as a feature extractor in our method. As we known, videos have a large amount of information, and features extracted from each video are extremely high dimensional. Therefore, it is necessary to discuss in the high-dimensional feature spaces, which features are more effectively to express emotions. Nevertheless, few work in history discuss about this issue. Considering of this, in our paper, we focus on the issue that what kind of representations are efficient for video affective analysis.

3 The Proposed Method

3.1 System Framework

The proposed system framework is illustrated in Fig. 1. For every video clip presented to the system, the audio features, video features and key frames with protagonist faces are extracted. Then, we use the sift detector to detect important patches in the key frames. After that, the patches are fed to a pre-trained CNN model to produce image features. Finally, we use these image features, audio and video features for affective analysis in valence and arousal spaces by a classifier or regressor.

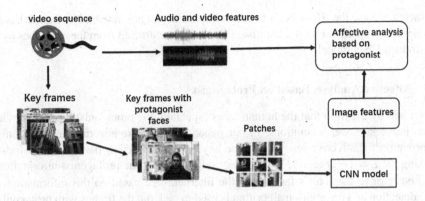

Fig. 1. The framework of our method.

3.2   Feature Extraction

In our method, we use three different features for affective analysis: audio, video, and image features. For affective analysis in arousal space, we extract audio and video features such as: 12 Mel-frequency Cepstral Coefficients (MFCCs), audio flatness, colorfulness, median lightness, normalized number of white frames, number of scene cuts per frame and cut Length. For affective analysis in the valence space, we extract 17 audio and video features which are commonly used, including zero-crossing rate, color-fulness, hue count, max saliency count, compositional balance, depth of field, entropy complexity, number of white frames, number of fades per frame and number of scene cuts per frame. After the audio and video features are extracted, we obtain the key frames to represent the emotional content of video clips.

Assume that a video clip V contains n frames, $V = \{F_1, F_2, \ldots, F_{n-1}, F_n\}$, where F_n is the n-th frame in video V. The RGB histogram of i-th frame is defined as $H(F_i)$. The Manhattan distance D between two frames F_i and F_j is calculated as follows:

$$D(F_i, F_j) = \left| H(F_i) - H(F_j) \right| \tag{1}$$

A key frame is the frame with the smallest distance to the mean RGB histogram of the whole excerpt as follows:

$$\underset{i}{\arg\min}\, D(F_i, \frac{1}{n} \sum_{i=1}^{n} H(F_i)) \tag{2}$$

where $\frac{1}{n} \sum_{i=1}^{n} H(F_i)$ compute the mean RGB histogram of the whole excerpt. We rank all the frames in accordance their Manhattan distance between the mean RGB histogram. Thus, we get a frames rank list $L = \{F'_1, F'_2, \ldots, F'_{n-1}, F'_n\}$, where F'_n is the frame have the maximum distance with the mean RGB histogram. Further, the first few frames in this list act as the key frames are used for affective analysis. After the key frames are extracted, we use the sift detector to detect important patches in these key frames based on the interest points. Finally, the image features are extracted from these patches by a pre-trained CNN model.

3.3 Affective Analysis Based on Protagonist

Motivated by the truth that the human faces especially the protagonist faces in movie, often induces viewer's emotions. In our paper, we take into account the protagonist information for affective analysis. In the key frames extraction part, we get a frame ranking list $L = \{F'_1, F'_2, \ldots, F'_{n-1}, F'_n\}$. Considering about the protagonist information, we first retrieve the actor's faces from the Internet, then based on this information, a face detection and recognition algorithm is used to pick out the frames with protagonist faces in L. This frames construct a frame ranking list L_a, the remaining frames in list L construct a frame ranking list L_b. All the frames in ranking list L_a and L_b retained their relative order in list L. Finally, a new frames list L' is obtained by L_a and L_b as follows:

$$L' = \{L_a, L_b\} \tag{3}$$

The front portion in list L' are frames with protagonist face, the remaining parts are frames without the corresponding protagonist face. Since one frame is poor to represent the emotional content of a video, we use the first few frames in list L' as the key frames are used for affective analysis. Considering that not all parts of the key frame are useful to express emotions. We use the sift detector to obtain patches from key frames based on the interest points. Assume that a video V, X as the audio and video features of video V. After the key frames extraction and patches detection steps, we get n patches, $V = \{P_1, P_2, \ldots, P_{n-1}, P_n\}$, where P_n is the n-th patches extracted from V. For patches P_i, using a pre-trained CNN model, we get a k-dimensional feature vector $p_i = [p_i^1, p_i^2, \ldots, p_i^k]$, where $k = 4096$. Then this image features together with the audio and video features acting as the features are used for affective analysis as follows:

$$f(P_i) = [p_i^1, p_i^2, \ldots, p_i^k, X] \tag{4}$$

where $f(P_i)$ is denoted as the features of the i-th patch which are used for affective analysis. To the video V, finally we get a feature matrix $f(V)$ as follows:

$$f(V) = \begin{bmatrix} f(P_1) \\ \vdots \\ f(P_n) \end{bmatrix} = \begin{bmatrix} p_1^1 & \cdots & p_1^k & X \\ \vdots & \ddots & \vdots & \vdots \\ p_n^1 & \cdots & p_n^k & X \end{bmatrix} \tag{5}$$

After these steps, video V is enlarged to n patches for affective analysis and the label of patches obtained from V is same. All the features are normalized using the standard score before being used for affective analysis. Finally, we use two independent SVR and SVM in our method for mapping the features to arousal and valence spaces separately.

4   Experiments

In the experiment, we explore whether our proposed method can effectively detect and analyze the emotions from video contents. Inspired by the fact that people's emotions are usually influenced by the actors in a movie, we believe that human face especially the protagonist face can efficiently convey the emotions in a movie. Meanwhile, the viewer is more likely to be infected by the protagonist face and generate corresponding emotions. Therefore, we conduct two experiments in this part. In the first experiment, we will explore the importance of human face in video emotion analysis. In the second experiment of this section, we will try to investigate the effect of protagonist face in video emotion analysis.

4.1   Experimental Setting

In the experiment section, we demonstrate the performance of the proposed method on LIRIS-ACCEDE dataset [18]. LIRIS-ACCEDE dataset is the largest video database currently in existence annotated by a broad and representative population using induced emotional labels. This dataset consists of 9,800 video clips, which are extracted from 160 movies, 1,517 annotators from 89 different countries participated in the rating-by-comparison experiments on crowdsourcing. Figure 2 shows the snapshots of samples from this dataset. From Fig. 2, we can find that LIRIS-ACCEDE dataset has a variety of video clips. The durations of video clips are from 8 to 12 s. Each video clip has a rank value of the induced valence and arousal axes respectively, and the ground truth is made up of these ranks, ranging from 0 to 9,799.

Fig. 2. Snapshots of video clips in LIRIS-ACCEDE dataset

In the experiment, we use the pre-trained CNN model in [19] to extract image features, the LIBSVM is used to implement the SVM and SVR, and the Radial Basis Function (RBF) is selected as the kernel function. As same as the setting in [18], we use a grid search to find the c, γ and p parameters. In the experiment part, we demonstrate the regression and classification results of different methods. We use mean squared error (MSE) to verify the performance of our method for regression. On the other hand, the accuracy is used to measure the effectiveness of our method for classification.

4.2   Experiment 1: Face Is Useful to Express Emotion

In this part, we explore the importance of human face in video emotion analysis. First, we compare the method using key frame with face detection (KFWF) or not (KF). Considering that not all parts of the key frame are useful to express emotions. We compare the method PWF (using patches which are detected from key frame with face detection) with method KFWF. In experimental part, we use one key frame, three key frames and five key frames for video affective content analysis respectively. We perform the experiments on valence and arousal dimension independently for Classifications and Regression. Two-thirds of video excerpts in the LIRIS-ACCEDE dataset are acted as the training set, and the rest form the testing set. Since the range of values of ground truth varies widely, for the experiment of regression, we uniformly rescale the ground truth rank values to a more common $[-1, 1]$ range, for the experiment of classification, we use K-means clustering the $[0$–$9, 799]$ values to six emotional classes.

Table 1 shows the prediction results of different methods in arousal space and valence space. From this table, we can find that the method PWF achieves the best results and method KFWF using key frames with faces as additional features is better than using key frame without face detection. Compared with method KF using three key frames without face detection, our method PWF reduces the MSE by 0.035 and 0.034 respectively in the arousal space and valence space. Figure 3 demonstrates the classification results of different methods in the two emotional spaces. From the figure, it can be seen that the method KFWF and PWF obtain a better performance for classification than the method KF in both emotional spaces.

Table 1.   Prediction mean square error (MSE) of different methods in arousal and valence spaces on the LIRIS-ACCEDE dataset

	Arousal			Valence		
	KF	KFWF	PWF	KF	KFWF	PWF
NF = 1	0.327	0.315	0.303	0.319	0.302	0.295
NF = 3	0.314	0.283	**0.279**	0.301	0.278	**0.267**
NF = 5	0.326	0.320	0.307	0.306	0.315	0.281

where NF denotes the number of frames used in the method.

Based on Table 1 and Fig. 3, we can find that the method PWF using patches from three key frames with face achieves the best results for predication and classification in both emotional spaces. It suggests that a key frame with face is indeed more efficient to induce emotions. Figure 4 shows two key frames extracted from the same video clip by the method with face detection and without. For this video clip, when we use Fig. 4(a) for affective classification, we could obtain a correct emotional label, while using Fig. 4(b) we get a wrong emotional label. From Fig. 4, it can be observed that, the use of a frame like Fig. 4(b) is very hard to extract any information to do the affective analysis. The experimental results demonstrate that the face information in key frames is useful to express emotions in video. Meanwhile, audiences are more easily to be induced by human face and generate corresponding emotions.

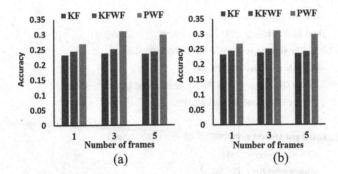

Fig. 3. Results on LIRIS-ACCEDE dataset. (a): Classification accuracy of different methods in arousal space, (b): Classification accuracy of different methods in valence space.

Fig. 4. Snapshots of the key frames extracted from a same video clip by two methods. (a): The key frame extracted by the method with face detection, (b): The key frame extracted by the method without face detection.

4.3 Experiment 2: Protagonist Face Is More Important

In this experiment, we try to investigate the effect of protagonist face in video emotion analysis. For this demand, we choose a subset from LIRIS-ACCEDE dataset for this experiment. Figure 5 shows the movies' name and the number of video clips selected from each movie. These movies are selected depending on whether the protagonist information is available or not. Finally, 1,514 video clips from the whole dataset are used to construct this subset database.

In this part, we compare the method PWF with the method using patches which are split from the key frame with protagonist face detection (PWPF). We adopt the protocol leave-one-video out cross-validations in our experiments. This protocol employs the whole excerpts of one movie is used for testing while the rest are used for training, this work is repeated until all the movies in database have been acted as the testing set, the final result is the average of these results.

Table 2 shows the predication results in arousal space and valence space. Compared with the method PWF using patches from three key frames without protagonist face detection, the method PWPF reduces the MSE by 0.014 in arousal space. In the valence space, the MSE is reduced by 0.009. Table 3 shows the results of different methods in two emotional spaces for classification. Compared to the method using patches from

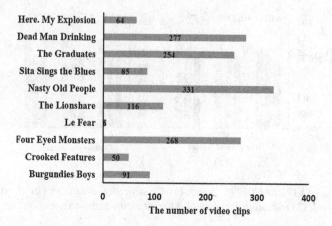

Fig. 5. Distribution of the sub dataset, the ordinate gives the movie name, the abscissa gives the number of video clips chosen from the corresponding movie.

key frames without protagonist face detection, the method PWPF achieves better performance in both emotional spaces.

Table 2. Prediction mean square error results in arousal and valence spaces on the subset

	Arousal		Valence	
	PWF	PWPF	PWF	PWPF
NF = 1	0.307	0.298	0.298	0.291
NF = 3	0.281	**0.267**	0.272	**0.263**

where NF denotes the number of frames used in the method.

Table 3. Classification results in the arousal and valence spaces on the subset

	Arousal		Valence	
	PWF	PWPF	PWF	PWPF
NF = 1	26.5 %	28.2 %	28.3 %	29.1 %
NF = 3	31.2 %	**32.4 %**	32.6 %	**33.9 %**

where NF denotes the number of frames used in the method.

The experiment results demonstrate that protagonist faces which are commonly used to communicate the emotions in a movie, are more efficient to attract the viewer's attention. Meanwhile, audiences are easily influenced by the protagonist and generate corresponding emotions. Of course, the popular protagonist to each viewer is not same. To the TV show "Friends", some viewers may concentrate on the sentimental Monica, some others may focus on the simple pure Joy. Hence, their mood will be affected by the happiness and sadness of actors they concerned. So we believe, if we able to prejudge the protagonist who is appreciated by a given audience, we can construct a customized video affective content analysis system to different audiences based on their favorite protagonist information.

5 Conclusion and Future Work

In this paper, we propose a novel video affective content analysis method based on protagonist information. In the experiments, we firstly investigate whether the key frame with human face could be used to predict the emotion of the video. Then, we explore the effect of protagonist face in video affective analysis. The experimental results indicate that key frames with human face, especially the protagonist face, are more efficient to transmit emotions in the video content.

In future work, we would like to construct a customized video affective content analysis system to different audiences based on their favorite protagonist information. We also want to utilize the context and prior knowledge such as gender difference for personalized video affective content analysis.

Acknowledgement. This work was supported by the National Natural Science Foundation of China (No. 61502311, No. 61373122), the Natural Science Foundation of Guangdong Province (No. 2016A030310053, No.2016A030313043), the Science and Technology Innovation Commission Foundation of Shenzhen (No. JCYJ20150324141711640, No. JCYJ20150324141711630), the Strategic Emerging Industry Research Foundation of Shenzhen (No. JCYJ20160226191842793), the Strategic Emerging Industry Development Foundation of Shenzhen (No. JCY20130326105637578), the Shenzhen University Research Funding (201535), NSFC-Guangdong Joint Fund for supercomputing application (Stage II), the National Supercomputing Center in Guangzhou (No. NSFC2015_275), and the Tencent Rhinoceros Birds Scientific Research Foundation (2015).

References

1. Zhu, Y., Huang, X., Huang, Q., Tian, Q.: Large-scale video copy retrieval with temporal-concentration sift. Neurocomputing **187**, 83–91 (2016)
2. Deng, C., Xu, J., Zhang, K., Tao, D., Gao, X., Li, X.: Similarity constraints-based structured output regression machine: an approach to image super-resolution. IEEE Trans. Neural Netw. Learn. Syst. **PP**, 1 (2015)
3. Zhong, S.h., Liu, Y., Ng, T.Y., Liu, Y.: Perception-oriented video saliency detection via spatio-temporal attention analysis. Neurocomputing **207**, 178–188 (2016)
4. Yuan, H., Kwong, S., Wang, X., Zhang, Y., Li, F.: A virtual view PSNR estimation method for 3-D videos. IEEE Trans. Broadcast. **62**(1), 134–140 (2016)
5. Wang, S., Ji, Q.: Video affective content analysis: a survey of state-of-the-art methods. IEEE Trans. Affect. Comput. **6**(4), 410–430 (2015)
6. Hanjalic, A.: Extracting moods from pictures and sounds: towards truly personalized TV. IEEE Sig. Process. Mag. **23**(2), 90–100 (2006)
7. Zhao, S., Yao, H., Sun, X., Xu, P., Liu, X., Ji, R.: Video indexing and recommendation based on affective analysis of viewers. In: Proceedings of the 19th ACM International Conference on Multimedia, pp. 1473–1476. ACM (2011)

8. Acar, E., Hopfgartner, F., Albayrak, S.: Understanding affective content of music videos through learned representations. In: Gurrin, C., Hopfgartner, F., Hurst, W., Johansen, H., Lee, H., O'Connor, N. (eds.) MMM 2014. LNCS, vol. 8325, pp. 303–314. Springer, Heidelberg (2014). doi:10.1007/978-3-319-04114-8_26

9. Wang, H.L., Cheong, L.F.: Affective understanding in film. IEEE Trans. Circuits Syst. Video Technol. **16**(6), 689–704 (2006)

10. Cui, Y., Luo, S., Tian, Q., Zhang, S., Peng, Y., Jiang, L., Jin, J.S.: Mutual information-based emotion recognition. In: The Era of Interactive Media, pp. 471–479. Springer, New York (2014)

11. Baveye, Y., Dellandrea, E., et al.: Deep learning vs. kernel methods: performance for emotion prediction in videos. In: Proceedings of the 2015 International Conference on Affective Computing and Intelligent Interaction (ACII), pp. 77–83. IEEE (2015)

12. Hubel, D.H., Wiesel, T.N.: Receptive fields, binocular interaction and functional architecture in the cat's visual cortex. J. Physiol. **160**(1), 106–154 (1962)

13. Felleman, D.J., Van Essen, D.C.: Distributed hierarchical processing in the primate cerebral cortex. Cereb. Cortex **1**(1), 1–47 (1991)

14. Jin, C.-B., Li, S., Do, T.D., Kim, H.: Real-Time human action recognition using CNN over temporal images for static video surveillance cameras. In: Ho, Y.-S., Sang, J., Ro, Y.M., Kim, J., Wu, F. (eds.) PCM 2015. LNCS, vol. 9315, pp. 330–339. Springer, Heidelberg (2015). doi: 10.1007/978-3-319-24078-7_33

15. He, K., Zhang, X., Ren, S., Sun, J.: Spatial pyramid pooling in deep convolutional networks for visual recognition. IEEE Trans. PAMI **37**(9), 1904–1916 (2015)

16. Kahou, S.E., Pal, C., Bouthillier, X., et al.: Combining modality specific deep neural networks for emotion recognition in video. In: Proceedings of the 15th ACM on International Conference on Multimodal Interaction, pp. 543–550. ACM (2013)

17. Chen, T., Borth, D., Darrell, T.: Deepsentibank: Visual sentiment concept classification with deep convolutional neural networks. arXiv preprint arXiv:1410.8586 (2014)

18. Baveye, Y., Dellandrea, E., Chamaret, C., Chen, L.: Liris-accede: a video database for affective content analysis. IEEE Trans. Affect. Comput. **6**(1), 43–55 (2015)

19. Krizhevsky, A., Sutskever, I.: Imagenet classification with deep convolutional neural networks. In: Advances in Neural Information Processing Systems, pp. 1097–1105 (2012)

Texture Description Using Dual Tree Complex Wavelet Packets

M. Liedlgruber[1], M. Häfner[2], J. Hämmerle-Uhl[1], and A. Uhl[1(✉)]

[1] Visual Computing and Security Lab (VISEL), Department of Computer Sciences,
University of Salzburg, Salzburg, Austria
andreas.uhl@sbg.ac.at
[2] Department for Internal Medicine, St. Elisabeth Hospital, Vienna, Austria

Abstract. In this work we extend several DWT-based wavelet and wavelet packet feature extraction methods to use the dual-tree complex wavelet transform. This way we aim at alleviating shortcomings of the different algorithms which stem from the use of the underlying DWT. We show that, while some methods benefit significantly from extending them to be based in the dual-tree complex wavelet transform domain (and also provide the best overall results), for other methods there is almost no impact of this extension.

1 Introduction

In the past, various different wavelet-based feature extraction methods have already been successfully applied to the problem of texture classification. However, since most of the approaches are based on the discrete wavelet transform (DWT) or the discrete wavelet packets transform (DWPT), they also inherit two major shortcomings inherent to the DWT when used for image processing and classification. First, the DWT is not able to capture directional information. Second, the DWT lacks shift-invariance.

An extension to the pyramidal DWT, which aims at coping with these problems, is the dual-tree complex wavelet transform (DT-CWT) [1]. In the past it has already been shown that features based on the DT-CWT are able to deliver superior classification results as compared to the pyramidal DWT and other feature extraction methods [2].

To exploit the benefits of the DT-CWT we extend a set of wavelet-packet-based feature extraction approaches originally defined to be used with the DWT to use the DT-CWT (resulting in a DT-CWPT). We then use these methods to extract features from two different image databases and investigate the classification performances as compared to the original (i.e. non-complex) version of the algorithms.

The remaining part of this work is organized as follows: in Sect. 2 we provide a rough overview of the DT-CWT and the complex wavelet packets transform (DT-CWPT). We then describe the methods evaluated and their extension to the complex domain in Sect. 3. Details on the experimental setup used are given in Sect. 4, followed by the results obtained in Sect. 5. We conclude this work in Sect. 6.

© Springer International Publishing AG 2016
E. Chen et al. (Eds.): PCM 2016, Part I, LNCS 9916, pp. 181–190, 2016.
DOI: 10.1007/978-3-319-48890-5_18

2   Background

2.1   Dual-Tree Complex Wavelet Transform

To overcome the limitations of the DWT the original DT-CWT uses 2^D pyramidal DWTs for a D-dimensional transform (i.e. for a 2-D DT-CWT four DWTs
are needed). The outcomes of these transforms are then combined to obtain
six complex-valued subbands in the 2-D case. These subbands capture image
details at $\pm 15°, \pm 45°$, and $\pm 75°$. In addition, the DT-CWT is approximately
shift-invariant.

The complex-valued wavelet, which forms the basis for the D-dimensional
DT-CWT, can be expressed as

$$\psi_c(t) = \psi_h(t) + j\psi_g(t), \tag{1}$$

where $\psi_h(t)$ and $j\psi_g(t)$ are the real and imaginary part of the complex wavelet,
respectively. The complex scaling function can be defined analogously as

$$\phi_c(t) = \phi_h(t) + j\phi_g(t). \tag{2}$$

Based on the separable implementation of the 2D-DWT the complex equivalent
can be written as:

$$\psi_{LH}^{(-)}(x,y) = \phi_c(x)\psi_c(y) \quad (3) \qquad \psi_{LH}^{(+)}(x,y) = \phi_c(x)\overline{\psi_c(y)} \quad (6)$$

$$\psi_{HL}^{(-)}(x,y) = \psi_c(x)\phi_c(y) \quad (4) \qquad \psi_{HL}^{(+)}(x,y) = \psi_c(x)\overline{\phi_c(y)} \quad (7)$$

$$\psi_{HH}^{(-)}(x,y) = \psi_c(x)\psi_c(y) \quad (5) \qquad \psi_{HH}^{(+)}(x,y) = \psi_c(x)\overline{\psi_c(y)}. \quad (8)$$

The four DWTs needed for the DT-CWT can now be easily developed by substituting Eqs. 1 and 2 into Eqs. 3 to 5 and computing the real and imaginary parts
of the results. This way we obtain the DWTs needed for the negative orientations (i.e. $-15°, -45°$, and $-75°$). To obtain the DWTs for the positive angles
(i.e. $+15°, +45°$, and $+75°$) the same computations must be carried out based
on Eqs. 6 to 8.

For the DT-CWT we need two filter banks for the first stage and two filter
banks for the the remaining stages. These filter banks are then combined in all
possible ways to obtain the filter banks for the four DWTs needed (i.e. different
filters are used for the row- and column-wise transform of the separable 2-D
transform).

We refer to the first stage real part filters as h_0 (low-pass) and h_1 (high-
pass). The imaginary part filters for the first stage are denoted by g_0 and g_1.
The remaining stages filters are denoted by $h_0^\bullet, h_1^\bullet, g_0^\bullet$, and $g_1^\bullet$. To get an analytic
wavelet (i.e. ability to capture directional information), h_1 and g_1 must form a
Hilbert transform pair (the same applies to $h_1^\bullet$ and $g_1^\bullet$). In addition, to obtain a
shift-invariant transform, h_0 and g_0 must meet the requirement of a one-sample
shift between them. The remaining stages low-pass filters $h_0^\bullet$ and $g_0^\bullet$ must have
a half-sample shift between them. Figure 1 shows the different 2-D frequency

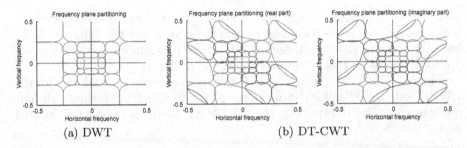

(a) DWT   (b) DT-CWT

Fig. 1. A comparison of the 2-D frequency plane partitioning between (a) the DWT and (b) the real and imaginary part of the DT-CWT. The plots show the 70 %-peak magnitude as contour lines for the first three levels of decomposition (different directions, i.e. positive and negative angles in case of the DT-CWT, are shown in red and blue, respectively). (Color figure online)

partitionings produced by the DWT and the DT-CWT. We notice that the DWT affects all four quadrants equally. Contrasting, the DT-CWT produces differently oriented parts which enables the DT-CWT to differentiate between more directions of details (i.e. two neighboring quadrants are colored differently).

2.2   Dual-Tree Complex Wavet Packets Transform

In order to extend methods which rely on a DWPT, we need a full wavelet packet transform based on the DT-CWT. Unfortunately, analyticity gets lost for deeper decomposition levels if the DT-CWT is just extended to decompose the high-frequency subbands too [3]. But it has already been shown that a solution to this problem can be obtained fairly easily [3,4]. We decided to use the method proposed in [3] due to its simplicity when it comes to integrate it into an existing DT-CWT implementation.

As already pointed out above, in the pyramidal case of the DT-CWT four different filter combinations are used among the four DWTs. The solution

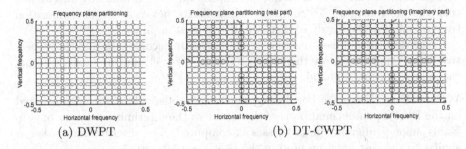

(a) DWPT   (b) DT-CWPT

Fig. 2. A comparison of the 2-D frequency plane partitioning between (a) the DWPT and (b) the real and imaginary part of the DT-CWPT. The plots show the 70 %-peak magnitude as contour lines for the first three levels of decomposition.

proposed in [3] is quite simple: to retain analyticity even for deeper levels of the transform, the filters used must remain the same across the different DWTs for most nodes in the decomposition tree for decomposition levels greater two. For more details on this extension we refer the reader to [3].

Figure 2 shows the different 2-D frequency partitionings produced by the DWPT and the DT-CWPT. Similar to the DWT, the DWPT affects all four quadrants equally. Contrasting, the DT-CWPT produces differently oriented parts.

3   Evaluated Feature Extraction Methods and Their Extensions

3.1   DWT-Based and DWPT-Based Methods

The following methods are either based on the real DWT or the real DWPT:

WPC: Each image is decomposed using the DWT. The features to be classified are then extracted based on coefficients in the resulting high-frequency subbands.

WT-BB [5]: Using the DWPT and the Best-basis algorithm [6], each image is decomposed into an optimal basis with respect to a cost function (based on the coefficients in the resulting subbands). The features are then extracted from all resulting subbands, ignoring the approximation subband.

Since it is very likely that the optimal bases differ among different images, the features would not be comparable directly in a meaningful way. As a consequence, a feature vector is filled with zeros at positions which correspond to subbands which are not present in that feature vector but which are present in at least one image decomposition structure in the remaining images from the image set. This way we end up with feature vectors which are comparable since each position in a feature vector then corresponds to a certain subband.

WT-BBCB [5]: This method also relies on the DWPT and the Best-basis algorithm. Hence, each image is decomposed into an optimal basis. Considering the decomposition trees for the resulting bases, the decomposition tree which on average is most similar to all other decomposition trees is searched for (we call this tree the centroid). To compute the similarity between two decomposition trees we employ the quadtree distance metric used in [5].

Once the centroid has been found, all images are decomposed into the respective basis. The features are then extracted from the resulting subbands, ignoring the approximation subband.

WT-LDB [7]: Using the Local discriminant bases algorithm [8], which is based on the DWPT, an optimal basis with respect to the discriminant power of subbands among different image classes is computed. The discriminant power is similar to the cost function used in the Best-basis algorithm.

Once the optimal basis has been found, all images are decomposed into the respective basis and the features are extracted from the resulting subbands, except for the approximation subband.

3.2 Extended Complex Methods

In case of WPC, extending the method to employ the DT-CWT is straight-forward, since the originally proposed DT-CWT yields a pyramidal transform already. There are just two differences:

- the DT-CWT yields complex coefficients. To extract features from the complex subbands we simply compute the coefficient magnitudes and compute the features from these.
- we obtain six high-frequency subbands instead of three, which doubles the feature vector lengths.

For methods, which rely on the DWPT, we can use the complex variant DT-CWPT, outlined in Sect. 2.2. Similar to WPC, we again extract the features based on the magnitudes of the complex coefficients. However, in the complex case we obtain subbands for features oriented at negative and positive angles, which can be considered to be two separate decomposition trees (these are the same in case of the DT-CWT). As a consequence we evaluate two different ways to extract features in the complex case when dealing with the DT-CWPT:

- **Symmetric case:** For the positive and negative directions the same decomposition structures are used. For each subband position considered for feature extraction features are extracted for both directions and stored in an inter-leaved fashion.
  In case an adaptive method is used to find an optimal basis, the pruning process inherent to the basis finding methods computes the cost for a decomposition tree node based on the sum of costs for the two directions.
- **Asymmetric case:** The decompositions for positive and negative directions are allowed to be different. As a consequence the two decomposition trees are pruned separately. The features are then extracted separately for both decomposition trees and concatenated to obtain the final feature vectors.
  Due to the fact that each subband in a complex decomposition depends on all four DWPTs involved, the trees must be kept synchronous to be able to perform an inverse transform. As a consequence we always perform a full DWPT on an image in the asymmetric case and keep the coefficients for all nodes at each decomposition stage. The pruning process is then not a traditional pruning based on an inverse transform but we merely mark nodes which should be included in the final basis for each direction (i.e. we end up with two different bases for the different directions).

Since in case of the WPC method the decomposition structures are always pyramidal ones, asymmetric trees are not used for this method. For all other methods hope is raised that using asymmetric decomposition trees allows the decomposition to adapt better to the characteristics of an image.

To extend the WT-LDB method to a complex one, the so-called time frequency energy map (TFEM) used in the Local discriminant bases algorithm must also be extended. Simply spoken the TFEM contains the mean energy at a certain coefficient position across all images of a class. Hence, we obtain

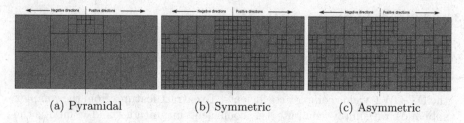

|(a) Pyramidal|(b) Symmetric|(c) Asymmetric|

Fig. 3. A comparison of the decomposition trees between (a) the pyramidal DT-CWT, (b) an example symmetric decomposition structure, and (c) an example asymmetric decomposition structure (in both cases a decomposition depth of 4 has been used).

one TFEM for each image class. To extend the TFEM for our needs, we simply compute two different TFEMs for each class, one for each direction. Then, depending on which decomposition tree is pruned, the right TFEM is used (in the symmetric case both TFEMs are used to compute the sum of discriminant powers for each node).

Figure 3 shows the difference between the pyramidal DT-CWT, the symmetric case, and the asymmetric case evaluated for feature extraction.

4   Experimental Setup

4.1   Image Databases Used

Kylberg Database (KB-DB [9]**):** The original Kylberg database consists of 28 image classes, each containing 160 grayscale images with a size of 576×576 pixels. The balanced nature of this database (i.e. same number of images in each class) and the high number of total images (4480) allowed us to split the database into two separate, equally-sized sets for training and validation (each containing 2240 images). The database split has been done by using 80 images from each class for training (Kylberg sample names c and d) and the remaining 80 images for validation (Kylberg sample names a and b). In order to reduce the computation time, especially in case of time-consuming feature extraction methods, we modified the image set by extracting center patches of size 128×128 pixels from the original images. The cropped images are then used for the experiments.

High-magnification Colonic Polyp Database (HM-DB) [2]**:** This image database is based on 327 endoscopic color images (either of size 624×533 pixels or 586×502 pixels) acquired between the years 2005 and 2009 at the Department of Gastroenterology and Hepatology (Medical University of Vienna) using a zoom-colonoscope (Olympus Evis Exera CF-Q160ZI/L) with a magnification factor of 150. In order to acquire the images 40 patients underwent colonoscopy. To obtain a larger set of images we manually extracted subimages (regions of interest) with a size of 256×256 pixels from the original images. This resulted in an extended image set containing 716 images in total.

Table 1. The detailed ground truth information for HM-DB.

Image Class	3 classes			2 classes		
	N_O	N_E	N_P	N_O	N_E	N_P
Normal	72	198	14	72	198	14
Non-invasive	212	420	27	255	518	32
Invasive	43	98	6			
Total	**327**	**716**	**47**	**327**	**716**	**46**

Lesions found during colonoscopy have been examined after application of dye-spraying with indigocarmine, as routinely performed in colonoscopy. Biopsies or mucosal resection have been performed in order to get a histopathological diagnosis.

Details on the endoscopic image database used are provided in Table 1. In these tables the columns N_O, N_E, and N_P denote the number of original images (i.e. the source images for patch extraction), the number of extracted patches, and the number of patients, respectively. From Table 1 we notice that the total number of patients given is slightly higher as compared to the number of patients who underwent endoscopy for the respective databases. The reason for this is that in case of some patients different types of pathologies showed up across the patient images. As a consequence a patient may be contained in more than one class.

In case of the colonic polyp database we distinguish between a 2-classes case and a 3-classes case. In the former we simply distinguish between normal mucosa (non-neoplastic) and mucosal changes which need a medical intervention (neoplastic). A more fine-grained classification was proposed in [10]. In this classification scheme the images are divided into three classes: normal lesions, non-invasive lesions, and invasive lesions. This classification scheme is of particular importance since normal mucosa needs not to be removed, non-invasive lesions must be removed endoscopically, and invasive lesions must not be removed endoscopically.

4.2 Wavelet-Transform Setup

In case of the complex methods we use Kingsbury's Q-Shift (14,14)-tap filters (for decomposition stages ≥ 2) in combination with (13,19)-tap near-orthogonal filters (for the first decomposition stage). For the DT-CWPT we use the Q-Shift filters for the decomposition nodes needing special treatment (using the methodology proposed in [3]). To make the real and complex methods more comparable, we use the Q-Shift filters also for the real methods (i.e. just one of the filter banks).

For methods which are based on the Best-basis algorithm we use the entropy as cost function. For the Local discriminant bases algorithm we use the l^2-norm as discriminant measure.

4.3 Feature Extraction and Classification

The feature we use for all methods is the entropy which is computed from the coefficients (magnitude) in the high-frequency subbands.

To reduce the dimensionality of the feature vectors and to improve the comparability of the techniques we perform a principal component analysis (PCA). Prior to applying the PCA to the features, we center the training feature vectors by subtracting the feature-wise mean from each feature. Then, after computing the eigenvalues and eigenvectors for a given set of training feature vectors, the eigenvalues and eigenvectors are sorted in descending manner with respect to the eigenvalues. This is followed by computing the number of components p to retain from the cumulative sum of the eigenvectors, such that the cumulative sum for the first p largest eigenvalues is above 0.99.

Once the validation features have been extracted and centered (using the means from the original training features), the feature projection computed from the training features is also applied to the validation features.

For the classification we use the k-Nearest neighbors (k-NN) classifier using the l^1-norm to compute the distances between feature vectors. This rather weak classifier has been chosen to emphasize more on the effect of extending the feature extraction methods to complex ones. We carried out experiments with different values for k (i.e. $k = 1, \ldots, 25$) and present the average results.

To estimate the classification accuracies in case of the colonic polyp database we use the leave-one-patient-out cross-validation (LOPO-CV).

5 Results

Figure 4 provides an overview of the overall classification rates we obtained in our experiments. The red, green, and blue bars denote the mean overall rates for real, complex, and complex asymmetric versions of the respective methods (over all choices for the k-value from the k-NN classifier). On top of each bar the we also indicate the range of classification rates over all choices for k.

As can be seen from Fig. 4(a), switching to the complex domain consistently improves the mean overall classification rates by up to 10 % in case of KB-DB. Only WT-BBCB is able to slightly benefit from switching from the complex

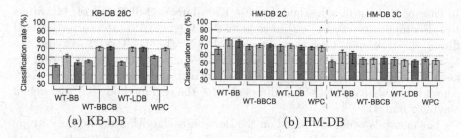

(a) KB-DB   (b) HM-DB

Fig. 4. An overview of the results from our experiments.

symmetric mode to the complex asymmetric mode. WT-BB delivers the lowest rates for KB-DB when compared to the other methods.

We notice from Fig. 4(b) that switching to the complex domain only improves the mean overall classification rates for WT-BB in case of HM-DB. In the 3-classes case we even observe a slight results drop slightly for WT-LDB and WPC. However, we also notice that, while the result range over all choices for k is rather small for all other methods, it is wider in case of WT-BB. When comparing the symmetric and asymmetric modes we again notice (similar to the results of the KB-DB) that only in case of WT-BBCB an improvement can be observed (although it is only a minor one). In all other cases switching to the asymmetric mode leads to a small result drop.

It is interesting to note that for the regular textures of the KB-DB the complex version of the WT-BBCB approach gives the best results (which employs a single decomposition structure to all images subject to classification – still this is adaptively chosen), while for the less regular (only texture-like) images of the endoscopical HM-DB the complex version of the WT-BB technique provides superior results, for which each image is potentially decomposed into a different decomposition structure. It seems that for the less homogeneous imagery the higher adaptivity potential of the WT-BB approach is beneficial.

6 Conclusion

The results obtained show that at least one method (WT-BB) is able to consistently improve the classification rates when using the complex version of it. For all other methods there is a dependency on the data set: For the KB-DB, the complex version improves the results for all considered feature extraction technique, partially significantly so. For the endoscopic HM-DB, we see improvements for WT-BB only, thus confirming results on earlier investigations on high-definition endoscopic data [11].

However, it also turned out that, at least for most of the methods evaluated, it is sufficient to use complex symmetric decomposition trees. Only WT-BBCB is able to consistently improve the classification rates when using the complex asymmetric version.

Acknowledgments. This work has been supported by the Austrian Science Fund (FWF) under Project No. TRP-206.

References

1. Selesnick, I.W., Baraniuk, R.G., Kingsbury, N.G.: The dual-tree complex wavelet transform - a coherent framework for multiscale signal and image processing. IEEE Sig. Process. Mag. **22**(6), 123–151 (2005)
2. Häfner, M., Kwitt, R., Uhl, A., Gangl, A., Wrba, F., Vécsei, A.: Feature-extraction from multi-directional multi-resolution image transformations for the classification of zoom-endoscopy images. Pattern Anal. Appl. **12**(4), 407–413 (2009)

3. Bayram, İ., Selesnick, I.W.: On the dual-tree complex wavelet packet and m-band transforms. IEEE Trans. Sig. Process. **56**(6), 2298 (2008)
4. Weickert, T., Kiencke, U.: Analytic wavelet packets - combining the dual-tree approach with wavelet packets for signal analysis and filtering. IEEE Trans. Sig. Process. **57**(2), 493 (2009)
5. Liedlgruber, M., Uhl, A.: Statistical and structural wavelet packet features for pit pattern classification in zoom-endoscopic colon images. In: Dondon, P., Mladenov, V., Impedovo, S., Cepisca, S. (eds.) Proceedings of the 7th WSEAS International Conference on Wavelet Analysis & Multirate Systems (WAMUS 2007), Arcachon, France, pp. 147–152, October 2007
6. Coifman, R.R., Wickerhauser, M.V.: Entropy based methods for best basis selection. IEEE Trans. Inf. Theor. **38**(2), 719–746 (1992)
7. Häfner, M., Liedlgruber, M., Wrba, F., Gangl, A., Vécsei, A., Uhl, A.: Pit pattern classification of zoom-endoscopic colon images using wavelet texture features. In: Sandham, W., Hamilton, D., James, C. (eds.) Proceedings of the International Conference on Advances in Medical Signal and Image Processing (MEDSIP 2006), Glasgow, Scotland, UK, pp. 1–4, July 2006
8. Saito, N., Coifman, R.R.: Local discriminant bases. In: SPIE's 1994 International Symposium on Optics, Imaging, and Instrumentation, International Society for Optics and Photonics, pp. 2–14 (1994)
9. Kylberg, G.: The Kylberg texture dataset v. 1.0. External report (Blue series) 35, Centre for Image Analysis, Swedish University of Agricultural Sciences and Uppsala University, Uppsala, Sweden, September 2011
10. Kato, S., Fu, K.I., Sano, Y., Fujii, T., Saito, Y., Matsuda, T., Koba, I., Yoshida, S., Fujimori, T.: Magnifying colonoscopy as a non-biopsy technique for differential diagnosis of non-neoplastic and neoplastic lesions. World J. Gastroenterol. **12**(9), 1416–1420 (2006)
11. Häfner, M., Liedlgruber, M., Uhl, A.: Colonic polyp classification in high- definition video using complex wavelet-packets. In: Proceedings of Bildverarbeitung für die Medizin 2015 (BVM 2015), pp. 365–370, March 2015

Fast and Accurate Image Denoising via a Deep Convolutional-Pairs Network

Lulu Sun[1,3(✉)], Yongbing Zhang[1], Wangpeng An[1,3], Jingtao Fan[3],
Jian Zhang[2], Haoqian Wang[1], and Qionghai Dai[1,3]

[1] Graduate School at Shenzhen, Tsinghua University, Beijing, China
`sunll15@mails.tsinghua.edu.cn`
[2] Institute of Digital Media, Peking University, Beijing, China
[3] Department of Automation, Tsinghua University, Beijing, China

Abstract. Most of popular image denoising approaches exploit either the internal priors or the priors learned from external clean images to reconstruct the latent image. However, it is hard for those algorithms to construct the perfect connections between the clean images and the noisy ones. To tackle this problem, we present a deep convolutional-pairs network (DCPN) for image denoising in this paper. With the observation that deeper networks improve denoising performance, we propose to use deeper networks than those employed previously for low-level image processing tasks. In our method, we attempt to build end-to-end mappings directly from a noisy image to its corresponding noise-free image by using deep convolutional layers in pair applied to image patches. Because of those mappings trained from large data, the process of denoising is much faster than other methods. DCPN is composed of three convolutional-pairs layers and one transitional layer. Two convolutional-pairs layers are used for encoding and the other one is used for decoding. Numerical experiments show that the proposed method outperforms many state-of-the-art denoising algorithms in both speed and performance.

Keywords: Convolutional Neural Networks · Deep Convolutional-Pairs Network · End-to-end · Image denoising

1 Introduction

Image denoising, a classic and fundamental problem in computer vision and image processing, aims at restoring the latent clean image x from its noise-corrupted version $y = x + v$, where v is commonly assumed to be additive white Gaussian noise. In order to obtain a visual pleasing image from its noisy counterpart, a variety of image denoising methods have been developed in the past decades, which can be classified into the traditional algorithms and the neural networks based methods. The traditional algorithms, which commonly use the engineered features to regularize the denoising process, include Wiener filter [18], median filter [1], bilateral filter [16], total variation [15], and sparse

© Springer International Publishing AG 2016
E. Chen et al. (Eds.): PCM 2016, Part I, LNCS 9916, pp. 191–200, 2016.
DOI: 10.1007/978-3-319-48890-5_19

representation methods [7,8]. However, these methods might degrade or remove the fine details and textures of the desired clean images.

On the other hand, in recent years, various kinds of neural networks have been used in image processing and computer vision tasks, especially for low level applications, showing their superior performance. The denoising auto-encoder (DAE) can be considered as the first successful try in image denoising, which received a corrupted data point as input and was trained to predict the original, uncorrupted data point as its output. Later, Vincent et al. [17] stacked these DAEs to form a deep network by feeding output of the previous layer to the current one as input. Moreover, Xie et al. [19] had success at combining sparse coding with SDAE for image denoising. Burger et al. [3] put up with a multi-layer perception (MLP) to exploit a training set of noisy and noise-free patches, which achieved the state-of-the-art performance. Though competing performances have been achieved by this type of algorithms, the neural network based methods still have some shortcomings. For example, they neglected the intrinsic features from natural images, which can be solved by adding network in network (NIN) [12] in our network.

Recently, with the rapid development of deep learning, an increasing number of new and deep networks have been perfectly used in computer vision, such as ImageNet classification [11], object detection [9], super-resolution [21], semantic segmentation [14] and so on. Among them, Dong et al. [6] has demonstrated that a convolutional neural network (CNN) can be used to learn a mapping from low-resolution to high-resolution image features in an end-to-end way. Their method, called SRCNN, does not demand any engineered features that are typically necessary in other methods and shows the state-of-the-art performance. From the network in network [12], we note that all the linear layers are actually implemented as convolutional layers applied on each patch with filter spatial size of 1×1. Inspired by SRCNN [6] and NIN [12], in this paper, we propose a deep convolutional-pairs network, named DCPN. Instead of using image priors, we learn end-to-end fully convolutional mappings from noisy images to the clean ones and apply the idea of pairs to our network. DCPN contains three convolutional-pairs layers and one transitional layer, of which, two convolutional-pairs layers are used for encoding and the other one is used for decoding. When training a CNN, some strategies on how to choose the optimization solvers (adam, stochastic gradient descent, adadelta, adaptive gradient, nesterovs accelerated gradient, et al.) are used. Moreover, We also consider if it is good to use dropout or weight decay. Meanwhile, the transitional layer eliminates the gap between encoder and decoder. Experiments demonstrate that our DCPN outperforms many state-of-the-art denoising algorithms.

Overall, the contributions of this work can be mainly summarized as follows. **First**, we propose a very deep convolutional-pairs network for image denoising. It builds end-to-end mappings directly from a noisy image to its corresponding noise-free image. To the best of our knowledge, it is the first time applying the idea of pairs to con-volutional neural networks for image denoising. **Second**, we verify that adam solver is more helpful in reducing the loss of the network for image denoising than others. Additionally, we find that it is useless to set dropout in our network. However, weight decay for regularizing denoising CNN is more efficient. **Third**, extensive experiments demonstrate the effectiveness of our method over state-of-the-art methods [3,4,10,13,20] both perceptually and quantitatively. More importantly, the running time of denoising one image by our method is far less than that of all the others.

2   Related Work

Image Denoising. Among the traditional methods, it is easy for us to find that nearly all the competitive algorithms are based on the image nonlocal self-similarity (NSS) [4,5,10,13,20]. Nonlocal means (NLM) [2], considered as the seminal work, brought the new era of denoising by finding nonlocal similar patches within a search window sliding across the image. NLM took it for granted that the similar patches are independent from each other, therefore the estimated value of a pixel is computed as a weighted average of all the pixels in the image. Another benchmark, called block-matching and 3D filtering (BM3D) [5], constructed 3D cubes of nonlocal similar patches and conducts collaborative filtering in the sparse 3D transform domain. Instead of modeling the image statistics in some transformed domain, weighted nuclear norm minimization (WNNM) [10] recovered the underlying low rank matrix from its degraded observation by exploiting the image NSS. However, WNNM neglected the NSS of clean natural images, which was the main consideration of the algorithm patch group prior based denoising (PGPD) [20]. PGPD contained the prior learning stage and the denoising stage. In the learning stage, it put nonlocal similar patches into groups to learn the NSS priors. In the denoising stage, based on the dictionaries provided by the learned Patch Group-Gaussian Mixture Model (PG-GMM), a simple weighted sparse coding model was developed for denoising. Lately, Chen et al. [4] proposed a new framework of patch clustering based low-rank regularization (PCLR) guided by a learned Gaussian mixture prior to obtain the latent patch subspaces with different structures. Liu et al. [13] presented a method using adaptive signal modeling and adaptive soft-thresholding (AST-NLS). It improved the image quality by regularizing all the patches in image based on distribution modeling in transform domain.

SRCNN. Super-Resolution Convolutional Neural Network [6], aiming at learning an end-to-end mappings, took the low-resolution image as input and directly outputs the high-resolution one. SRCNN was composed of three convolutional layers. The first layer performed patch extraction and representation, which extracted overlapping patches from the low-resolution image and represents each patch as a high-dimensional vector. The second layer mapped the high-dimensional vector of the first layer onto another high-dimensional vector. The last layer combined the predictions within a spatial neighborhood to produce the final high-resolution image.

Network-In-Network (NIN). It is an approach proposed by Lin et al. [12] aiming at increasing the representational power of neural networks. Actually,

NIN could be viewed as additional 1×1 convolutional layers followed by the rectified linear activation when applied to CNN. By adding NIN in our networks, computational bottlenecks have been removed, which made it helpful to increase both the depth and width of the networks without significant performance penalty.

Our network (DCPN) not only embeds three more 1×1 convolutional layers in SRCNN [6] after each layer respectively, but also alters the size of each convolutional filte, which is exceptionally effective in image denoising. Much more details of DCPN will be provided in the next section.

3   Deep Convolutional-Pairs Network (DCPN) for Image Denoising

This section presents our proposed DCPN, which is based on a lightweight architecture whose parameters are trained from scratch. To generate noise input, we add normal Gaussian distribution to the image. After the training is completed we can input a noisy image of any size, and the output is the denoised image. DCPN needs training different networks for different levels of noise variance. For a noisy image with a fixed variance noise, we will apply the corresponding DCPN to restore the clean one. It is an end-to-end mapping from the noisy images to the clean ones.

3.1   Architecture Overview

As shown in Fig. 1, the detailed description of the convolutional stages is given as follows:

The input volume has the size of 64×64, and the receptive field of the first 2D convolution is of size 11×11 (big kernel for reducing the computation resources), to define a convolutional layer with 64 neurons. This layer is followed by a rectified linear unit (ReLU) activation layer which applies an element wise non-linearly and leads a 1×1 convolution layer with 64 neurons (Network in Network). The output of the previous stage has a size of $54 \times 54 \times 64$. The size of the receptive field of second stage is 5×5. Then, it is followed by a ReLU layer and 1×1 convolutional layer, whose number is 32. Finally, the last convolutional layer is fed with an input of size $50 \times 50 \times 32$. The size of the receptive in this field is the same as before. A ReLU and 1×1 convolutional (the number is 16) layers are stacked to our network as well.

The last layer just has one 1×1 kernel to generate the final output. The network has a total of more than 150000 free parameters. Different strategies are considered to avoid overfitting. First, we use seven convolutional layers rather than the three as used in the classic SRCNN [6]. Second, the input images are designed to 64×64, and the initial 64×64 feature maps are set down to 64×46 by the convolutional layers. While having the above constraints, the network still overfits significantly. We fund that l_2 regularization is essential to mitigate the overfitting. We also try using dropout after the first convolutional layer with

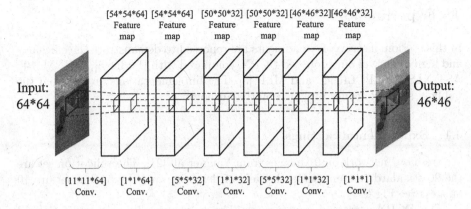

Fig. 1. Architecture of our DCPN.

a dropout ratio of 0.5. But this do not improve overfitting much, so the final model do not contain it.

3.2 Network In Network (NIN) as a Regularizer

Usually, convolutional neural networks consist of alternating convolutional layers and pooling layers. Convolutional layers take inner product of the linear filters and the underlying receptive fields followed by a nonlinear activation function at every local portion of the input. Also, convolutional networks almost always incorporate some forms of spatial pooling, it is usually an $a \times a$ max-pooling with $a = 2$. Max-pooling acts on the hidden layers of the network, to reduce their size by an integer multiplicative factor a. The amazing thing by product of discarding 75 % of the data is to let max pooling as a very strong regularizer. Therefore, it is unnecessary to use pooling in the field of image denoising.

3.3 Training

In this paper, we train our network on 91 images from Yang et al. [21]. We subtract the mean pixel value of the training set from the image pixels to zero center them and rescale the resulting values linearly to be in the interval $[-1, 1]$. We similarly preprocess the validation set by subtracting the mean and scaling it to $[-1, 1]$. Learning the end-to-end function F from noisy images to clean images needs to estimate the weights θ represented by the convolutional kernels. This is achieved by minimizing the Euclidean loss between the outputs of the network and the original image. More specifically, given a collection of n training image pairs $\boldsymbol{X}_i$, $\boldsymbol{Y}_i$, where $\boldsymbol{X}_i$ is a noisy image and $\boldsymbol{Y}_i$ is the clean version as the ground truth, we minimize the following Mean Squared Error (MSE):

$$L(\theta) = \frac{1}{n} \sum_{i=1}^{n} \|F(\boldsymbol{X}_i, \theta) - \boldsymbol{Y}_i\|_2^2. \tag{1}$$

4   Experiments

In this section, a series of experiments are reported to demonstrate the efficiency and high quality of our proposed DCPN, compared with BM3D [5], WNNM [10], AST-NLS [13], PCLR [4], and MLP [3]. The implementations are all from the publicly available codes provided by the authors[1].

4.1   Experimental Settings

We train our network on 91 images from Yang et al. [21]. The validation set are the 20 standard test images in the field of denoising and the testing set are 10 images. See Fig. 2.

This DCPN is trained from scratch. The weights in all layers are initialized from a normal Gaussian distribution with zero mean and a standard deviation of 0.0001, with biases initialized to 0.1. The network is trained with Adam optimization, whose advantages are that the magnitudes of parameter updates are invariant to rescaling of the gradient. Moreover, its stepsizes are approximately bounded by the stepsize hype parameter, which we find is greatly helpful for convergence. The learning rate changes over time, starting with a higher learning rate 0.01 and decreases to 0.000001 during training. We train the network for 300 thousand iterations. A data augmentation technique is used by mirroring all images. Our DCPN is implemented using the deep learning library Tensorflow. Processing is performed on an NVIDIA GTX TITAN X GPU with 3072 CUDA

Fig. 2. The 10 test images. From left to right: owl, rhino, view, snake, tiger, aquatic, deer, elephant, fawn, and leopards.

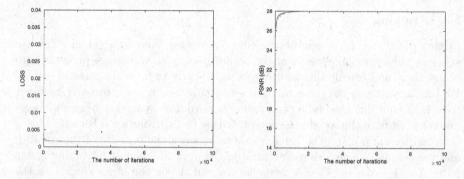

Fig. 3. Loss and PSNR (dB) values on the validation set during training.

---

[1] The source code of the proposed DCPN will be available after this paper is published.

cores and 12 GB of RAM. Compared to other deep learning framework, in Tensorflow, it is easy to visualize our TensorFlow graph. As illustrated in Fig. 3, we plot the process of validation loss and validation PSNR during training.

4.2   Complexity Analyses

Memory Requirements. The memory resources required by DCPN are dedicated to two different sides: the weights that define the network and the output tensor after weights that characterizes network response at the different processing stages. The convolution weights that define the network, are corresponding to the actual characterization of the network along with the architecture layout. These weights characterize the output of each neuron in the net, which can be defined as $f(wT(x) + b)$. Here w describes the filter parameters in the convolutional layers, b corresponds to the biases, and f is the non-linearity. Each neuron, therefore, has parameters w and b, which are fit during backpropagation. The data associated with the input image is the second source of memory requirements. The input image is hierarchically processed in the convolutional network, creating multiple intermediate feature maps (tensor) after each processing stage. It has significantly fewer parameters (because we do not have fully connect layers).

Running Time. By large amounts of experiments, we find that our method is much faster all the others. From Table 1, we can see that the running time of DCPN is almost 10000 times faster than PCLR, 42 times faster than MLP, and 6000 times faster than WNNM. Therefore, there are so many advantages learning the end-to-end mappings from a noisy image to its corresponding noise-free one. First of all, it could greatly speed up the running time, which is very suitable for those situations demanding for high real-time denoising. Secondly, our DCPN achieves better denoising performance than other methods. Much more details of the better denoising performance will be provided in the next section.

Table 1. Running time(s) of denoising a 321×481 image on average by different methods.

Methods	BM3D [5]	AST-NLS [13]	PCLR [4]	WNNM [10]	MLP [3]	DCPN
Time (s)	120.24	475.20	900.23	600.40	4.20	**0.10**

4.3   Evaluation on 10 Test Images

We evaluate the competing methods on 10 images. Zero mean additive white Gaussian noises with variance σ^2 are added to those test images to generate the noisy observations. Due to page limit, we show the results of 10 images on three noise levels, ranging from $\sigma = 30$ to $\sigma = 50$ to strong noise level $\sigma = 100$. It should be noted that the auther of MLP [3] does not provide the trained models with $\sigma = 30$ and $\sigma = 100$, so we use the models with $\sigma = 25$ and $\sigma = 75$ to replace them respectively to implement all the experiments. Table 2 presents the PSNR results of noise variation of $\sigma = 30$, 50, and 100. Some observations can be drawn from the results as follows. First of all, our DCPN achieved better results than the state-of-the-art methods, such as BM3D [5], AST-NLS [13], PCLR [4], WNNM [10] and MLP [3], which demonstrates that the idea of pairs and NIN in CNN for denoising works well. Moreover, our DCPN exceeds the secend best method PCLR [4] by 0.47 dB, 0.70 dB, and 0.09 dB on average at the noise level of $\sigma = 30$, $\sigma = 50$, and $\sigma = 100$ respectively, which shows the large improvement of our model. It is precisely because of the convolutional-pairs used in our network that DCPN can outperform these state-of-the-art denoising algorithms in PSNR.

Table 2. PSNR (dB) results with different σ on 10 images.

Methods	Rhino	Owl	View	Fawn	Elephant	Deer	Tiger	Leopards	Snake	Aquatic	Ave.
$\sigma = 30$											
BM3D [5]	31.75	32.26	28.25	25.92	28.20	27.82	28.05	26.55	25.18	28.75	28.27
WNNM [10]	31.63	32.29	28.25	25.82	28.09	27.74	27.93	26.46	22.96	28.73	27.99
AST-NLS [13]	31.29	31.87	28.18	25.79	27.98	27.61	27.84	26.44	25.15	28.62	28.07
PCLR [4]	31.81	32.58	28.27	25.93	28.15	27.80	28.01	26.51	25.16	28.74	28.29
MLP [3]	29.98	30.08	27.66	25.55	27.43	26.99	27.39	26.06	25.00	27.90	27.40
DCPN	**32.45**	**32.91**	**28.86**	**26.43**	**28.57**	**28.24**	**28.53**	**26.85**	**26.85**	**29.25**	**28.76**
$\sigma = 50$											
BM3D [5]	29.76	29.69	26.69	23.84	26.25	25.58	26.14	24.58	23.48	27.02	26.30
WNNM [10]	29.71	29.66	26.79	23.80	26.18	25.51	26.11	24.56	21.29	27.02	26.06
AST-NLS [13]	29.30	29.22	26.63	23.70	25.98	25.29	25.93	24.47	23.42	26.84	26.07
PCLR [4]	30.08	30.11	26.80	23.91	26.24	25.55	26.18	24.58	23.48	27.03	26.40
MLP [3]	30.12	29.98	26.94	24.04	26.34	25.68	25.36	24.74	23.63	27.20	26.40
DCPN	**30.80**	**30.72**	**27.38**	**24.68**	**27.12**	**26.40**	**26.95**	**25.19**	**24.09**	**27.67**	**27.10**
$\sigma = 100$											
BM3D [5]	26.54	25.87	24.39	21.59	23.78	22.68	23.66	22.31	21.60	24.69	23.71
WNNM [10]	27.21	26.06	24.91	21.53	24.00	22.73	23.99	22.40	19.14	24.93	23.69
AST-NLS [13]	26.92	25.56	24.76	21.27	23.83	22.32	23.76	22.16	21.55	24.75	23.69
PCLR [4]	**27.80**	**26.75**	**24.96**	21.64	24.11	22.91	24.16	22.49	21.76	**25.08**	24.17
MLP [3]	20.96	21.03	20.84	19.36	20.46	19.92	20.36	19.46	19.49	20.48	20.23
DCPN	27.67	26.31	23.92	**22.16**	**24.83**	**23.57**	**24.48**	**22.68**	**21.96**	25.00	**24.26**

4.4 Visual Comparisons

Figures 4 and 5 show some visual quality comparisons of our model and existing methods. At a lower noise level, e.g., $\sigma = 30$, besides that our model achieves higher PSNR, it shows visually closely to the original image from the view of the whole tones and perception. Compared with DCPN, methods BM3D, WNNM, AST-NLS and PCLR oversmooth more the textures in the lawn of image "view", and method MLP generate more artifacts. In particular, as can be seen in the

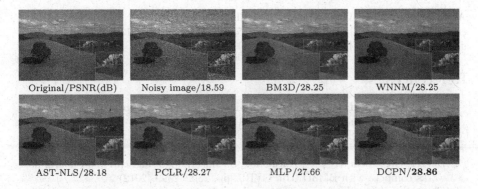

Fig. 4. Denoising results on "view" by different methods (noise level $\sigma = 30$).

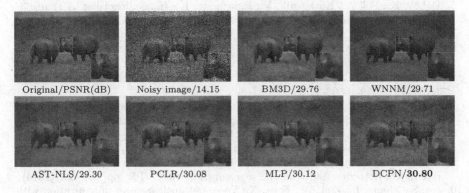

Fig. 5. Denoising results "rhino" by different methods (noise level $\sigma = 50$).

highlighted window, our DCPN can still reconstruct the steep rock and smooth water at the same time. In summary, DCPN generates less artifacts and preserves more image details than other methods.

5   Conclusion

In this paper, we have proposed a deep convolutional-pairs network (DCPN) for image denoising, which contains seven convolutional layers and each layer performs different function. We apply NIN to our network, which plays an important role in CNN for image denoising. Meanwhile, we verify that adam solver is more helpful in improving the loss of the network for image denoising than others and it is of no use setting dropout in our network.

Experimental results and our analysis show that our network (DCPN) achieves better denoising performance than the state-of-the-art methods. We plan to deepen our network and enlarge the training data to improve the visual denoising performance. Furthermore, we will apply this framework to other low-level image processing tasks, such as image super-resolution, deblurring, segmentation, and inpainting.

Acknowledgment. This work was partially supported by the National Natural Science Foundation of China under Grant 61571254, U1201255, U1301257, and Guangdong Natural Science Foundation 2014A030313751.

References

1. Arias-Castro, E., Donoho, D.L.: Does median filtering truly preserve edges better than linear filtering? Ann. Statist. **37**(3), 1172–1206 (2009)
2. Buades, A., Coll, B., Morel, J.M.: A non-local algorithm for image denoising. In: CVPR, pp. 60–65 (2005)
3. Burger, H.C., Schuler, C.J., Harmeling, S.: Image denoising: can plain neural networks compete with BM3D?. In: CVPR, pp. 2392–2399 (2012)
4. Chen, F., Zhang, L., Yu, H.: External patch prior guided internal clustering for image denoising. In: ICCV, pp. 603–611 (2015)
5. Dabov, K., Foi, A., Katkovnik, V., Egiazarian, K.: Image denoising by sparse 3-D transform-domain collaborative filtering. IEEE Trans. Image Process. **16**(8), 2080–2095 (2007)
6. Dong, C., Loy, C.C., He, K., Tang, X.: Learning a deep convolutional network for image super-resolution. In: Fleet, D., Pajdla, T., Schiele, B., Tuytelaars, T. (eds.) ECCV 2014. LNCS, vol. 8693, pp. 184–199. Springer, Heidelberg (2014). doi:10.1007/978-3-319-10593-2_13
7. Dong, W., Zhang, L., Shi, G., Li, X.: Nonlocally centralized sparse representation for image restoration. IEEE Trans. Image Process. **22**(4), 1620–1630 (2013)
8. Elad, M., Aharon, M.: Image denoising via sparse and redundant representations over learned dictionaries. IEEE Trans. Image Process. **15**(12), 3736–3745 (2006)
9. Girshick, R., Donahue, J., Darrell, T., Malik, J.: Rich feature hierarchies for accurate object detection and semantic segmentation. In: CVPR, pp. 580–587 (2014)
10. Gu, S., Zhang, L., Zuo, W., Feng, X.: Weighted nuclear norm minimization with application to image denoising. In: CVPR, pp. 2862–2869 (2014)
11. Krizhevsky, A., Sutskever, I., Hinton, G.E.: Imagenet classification with deep convolutional neural networks. In: NIPS, pp. 1097–1105 (2012)
12. Lin, M., Chen, Q., Yan, S.: Network in network. arXiv preprint arXiv:1312.4400 (2013)
13. Liu, H., Xiong, R., Zhang, J., Gao, W.: Image denoising via adaptive soft-thresholding based on non-local samples. In: CVPR, pp. 484–492 (2015)
14. Long, J., Shelhamer, E., Darrell, T.: Fully convolutional networks for semantic segmentation. In: CVPR, pp. 3431–3440 (2015)
15. Rudin, L.I., Osher, S., Fatemi, E.: Nonlinear total variation based noise removal algorithms. Phys. D Nonlinear Phenom. **60**(1), 259–268 (1992)
16. Tomasi, C., Manduchi, R.: Bilateral filtering for gray and color images. In: ICCV, pp. 839–846 (1998)
17. Vincent, P., Larochelle, H., Bengio, Y., Manzagol, P.A.: Extracting and composing robust features with denoising autoencoders. In: ICML, pp. 1096–1103 (2008)
18. Wiener, N.: Extrapolation, Interpolation, and Smoothing of Stationary Time Series, vol. 2. MIT Press, Cambridge (1949)
19. Xie, J., Xu, L., Chen, E.: Image denoising and inpainting with deep neural networks. In: NIPS, pp. 341–349 (2012)
20. Xu, J., Zhang, L., Zuo, W., Zhang, D., Feng, X.: Patch group based nonlocal self-similarity prior learning for image denoising. In: ICCV, pp. 244–252 (2015)
21. Yang, J., Wright, J., Huang, T.S., Ma, Y.: Image super-resolution via sparse representation. IEEE Trans. Image Process. **19**(11), 2861–2873 (2010)

Traffic Sign Recognition Based on Attribute-Refinement Cascaded Convolutional Neural Networks

Kaixuan Xie[1,2], Shiming Ge[1(✉)], Qiting Ye[1,2], and Zhao Luo[1,2]

[1] Beijing Key Laboratory of IOT Information Security,
Institute of Information Engineering, Chinese Academy of Sciences,
Beijing 100195, China
{xiekaixuan,geshiming,yeqiting}@iie.ac.cn, zhaoluo.lu@foxmail.com
[2] University of Chinese Academy of Sciences, Beijing, China

Abstract. Traffic sign recognition is a critical module of intelligent transportation system. Observing that a subtle difference may cause misclassification when the actual class and the predictive class share the same attributes such as shape, color, function and so on, we propose a two-stage cascaded convolutional neural networks (CNNs) framework, called attribute-refinement cascaded CNNs, to train the traffic sign classifier by taking full advantage of attribute-supervisory signals. The first stage CNN is trained with class label as supervised signals, while the second stage CNN is trained on super classes separately according to auxiliary attributes of traffic signs for further refinement. Experiments show that the proposed hierarchical cascaded framework can extract the deep information of similar categories, improve discrimination of the model and increase classification accuracy of traffic signs.

Keywords: Traffic sign recognition · Convolutional Neural Network · Attribute supervision · Deep learning

1 Introduction

Traffic signs play an important role in our daily life. They define a visual language providing useful information, which makes the driving safe and convenient. Traffic sign recognition (TSR) is a critical part of intelligent transportation system (ITS), such as advance driver assistance system (ADAS) and autonomous intelligent vehicles [1].

Traffic sign recognition belongs to image recognition in traffic sign domain. Generally, image recognition with traditional machine learning methods have three stages including image preprocessing, feature extraction and classification model learning. Image preprocessing includes extraction of the region of interest (ROI), affine transformations, histogram equalization, contrast normalization, etc. Feature extraction mostly refers to manual features, such as HoG, LBP,

© Springer International Publishing AG 2016
E. Chen et al. (Eds.): PCM 2016, Part I, LNCS 9916, pp. 201–210, 2016.
DOI: 10.1007/978-3-319-48890-5_20

Gabor filter feature and integral channel features, etc. Classification model learning includes machine learning algorithms, such as KNN [2], discriminative modeling methods [2,3], decision tree [4], random forest [5], support vector machine (SVM) [6–8], graph-based learning method [9,10], and extreme learning machine (ELM) [11]. These machine learning methods are trained on the manual features above independently or in combination.

Conventional machine learning techniques were limited to process natural data in their raw form. For decades, constructing a pattern recognition or machine learning system required careful engineering and considerable domain expertise to design a feature extractor that transformed the raw data into a suitable internal representation or feature vector from which the learning subsystem, often a classifier, could detect or classify patterns in the input. While deep learning requires very little engineering by hand and allows computational models that are composed of multiple processing layers to learn representations of data with multiple levels of abstraction. Convolutional neural networks (CNN) is one of the most widely used deep neural networks structures in images [12]. Supervised learning is the most common form of machine learning, especially in deep learning, which needs the supervision to construct object function and automatically adjust the weights in network [13–15]. CUHK proposed DeepID2 combined face identification and verification signals as supervision together when face recognition to increase inter-personal variations and reduce intra-personal variations [13]. Deeply-supervised nets (DSN) in [14] introduced companion objective function to the individual hidden layers, in addition to the overall objective at the output layer. This is a source of supervision that acts deep within the network at each layer and directly influence the hidden weights process to favor highly discriminative feature maps. In fast region-based CNN [15], the objective function is region bounding-box regression offsets and probability distribution of object categories, which means that it introduces region supervision in object detection besides category. We can see that CNN is increasingly introducing more supervisory signals.

In this paper, we propose a two-stage cascaded CNNs framework combined with multi-attribute supervision for traffic sign recognition, called attribute-refinement cascaded CNNs. In the following part, we first give the method including a brief description of basic CNN algorithm, the drawback of it and our modified cascaded CNN architecture based on this. Then we give the experiments including the data preprocessing, the creation of the training set and the procedures of the utilization of traffic sign attributes. At last we give the conclusion and the feature work.

2   Related Work

In recent years, traffic sign recognition has made much progress. Many researches focused on some pre-designed features. They usually used features included HoG, LBP, Gabor filter, Haar wavelets, Complementary features [16], etc. After extracting features, classifiers will be used. In addition, the popular codebook model showed excellent classification performance. Sparse representation has attracted considerable attention in traffic sign recognition [17,18]. On the other hand, traffic sign recognition with deep convolutional network methods has achieved satisfactory results. Compared with conventional methods, CNN needs less preprocessing and no independent designed feature extraction. In [19], Ciresan proposed a committee of CNNs and a multi-layer perceptron. They make many affine transformations on the training set and trained more than 30 CNNs, in which, each CNN gives a vote and the highest one is the final decision. In [20], multi-column CNN combines various deep neural networks trained on different preprocessed data into a multi-column DNN further boosts recognition performance, which makes the system insensitive both to variations in contrast and illumination. In [21], Yan proposed a CNN structure consisting of two blocks of weight layers and a classifier, in which each weights block contains a convolutional layer and a pooling layer. The output of the first stage is branched out and fed to the classifier together with the output of the second stage, compared with usual CNN that the output of one layer is fed only to the layer followed. In [22], Jin proposed a hinge-loss CNN of which cost function is hinge-loss instead of cross-entropy cost. It improves the model generalization and training speed.

Approaches above have their own superiorities and obtain different degrees of improvement in traffic sign recognition. They modify the object function, modify the structure, or train multiple CNNs. However, they share a common weakness that in the process of model learning, only the images and specific category labels have been utilized. Based on this, our paper has two contributions: first, we found that one single model for multi-category classification may be not sufficient. It will ignore the small differences among objects that share the same attributes. So we should take this into account. Second, based on the weakness, we proposed a cascaded convolutional neural networks with other attribute labels besides class labels.

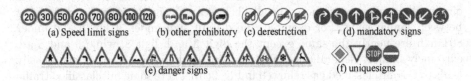

(a) Speed limit signs   (b) other prohibitory (c) derestriction   (d) mandatory signs

(e) danger signs   (f) uniquesigns

Fig. 1. Super categories in GTSRB.

3 Method

In this section, we first introduce our motivation of the proposed method based on the statistical regularity about traffic sign recognition results. Then we introduce the basic CNN structures and the proposed cascaded CNNs with attribute label, such as shape and function.

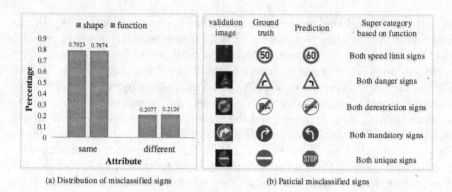

(a) Distribution of misclassified signs   (b) Paticial misclassified signs

Fig. 2. Analysis on the misclassified signs

3.1 Motivation

First we construct the conventional CNN model and analyse the recognition results on the training data of German Traffic Sign Recognition Benchmark (GTSRB), from which we discover the regulartions of the recognition results. In the data set, each specific traffic sign image corresponds to a specific class label.

The traffic signs in GTSRB are classified into 6 super categories according to the function attribute as shown in Fig. 1, including speed limit signs, other prohibitory signs, derestriction signs, mandatory signs, danger signs and unique signs. Signs in each super categories share the same function and usually have some same characteristics.

We are motivated by the following observation: nearly 80 % misclassified traffic in validation set have the same attributes (shape and function) as shown in Fig. 2(a). We think that only specific class labels will make the network focus on the whole differences among the all 43 classes while ignores the tiny differences between similar signs. For example, speed limit sign under 30 km/h and under 80 km/h are nearly the same except the digit 3 and digit 8, while 3 and 8 are extremely similar. Generally feeding these similar pairs with all other signs easily leads to the misclassified case showed in Fig. 2(b), where some misclassified traffic signs with the same function attribute. These mistakes are common but have serious consequences in advance driver assistance system. So we make our CNN structure focus on improving the discriminant between signs sharing the same attribute and have similar characteristics.

3.2 Baseline Method

The architecture of a basic convolutional neural network consists of a series of layers. Each layer consists of maps and parameters, while parameters are in the trained model, and maps of each layer are calculated according to this layers parameters and maps of the previous layers. The first layer is the input image and each layer's input is the previous layer's output. Usually, the first few layers are composed of two types of layers: convolutional layers and pooling layers, and the last few layers are fully connected convolutional layers.

Convolutional layer. The convolutional layer is to extract local pattern and detect conjunction of features from the previous layer and it performs a 2D convolution of its input feature maps $x_{i,j,k} \in R^{H \times W \times D}$ with the filter bank $w \in R^{H_k \times W_k \times D_k \times K}$ in the net model.

$$y_{i_y,j_y,k} = \sum_{i=1}^{H_k} \sum_{j=1}^{W_k} \sum_{d=1}^{D} w_{ijd} \times x_{i_y+i,j_y+j,d,k} + b_k. \tag{1}$$

Activation layer. Active layer contains a nonlinear activation function which can activate some neurons while suppress some others. It makes the CNN more sparse and more robust. The most common activation function is Rectified Linear Unit (ReLU), and softmax function:

$$ReLU : f(x) = max(0,x); \quad Softmax : f(x_i) = \frac{e^{x_i}}{\sum_{k=1}^{K} e^k} \tag{2}$$

Usually each convolutional layer is followed by a ReLU layer. Softmax function is used for multi-classification, so it is the very last layer in the network for requiring the probability distribution of the classification.

Max-pooling layer. The pooling layer is to merge semantically similar features into one. Because the relative positions of the features forming a motif can vary somewhat, reliably detecting the motif can be done by coarse-graining the position of each feature.

$$y_{i_y,j_y,k} = \max_{1 \leq i \leq H_p, 1 \leq j \leq W_p} x_{i_y+i,j_y+j,d}. \tag{3}$$

Baseline model. We applied AlexNet [23] in traffic sign recognition as the baseline CNN model in the later experiments as shown in Fig. 3. It contains 5 convolutional layers followed by ReLU activation layer, 3 max-pooling layer and 2 fully-connected convolutional layers.

3.3 Proposed Method

Based on the motivation above, we design a two-stage cascaded CNNs combined with attribute supervisory labels as shown in Fig. 4. First, we train a baseline C_0-way CNN with AlexNet, where C_0 is the number of the specific classes in addition to one negative-supervised class [24].

The cascaded CNNs contains two stages. The first stage is a baseline CNN based on class labels. We construct the network with alternative convolutional layer, ReLU activation layer, max-pooling layer, and at last followed softmax layer. With back-propagation modifying the weights in network, we get the probability distribution over all C_0 classes after the softmax layer.

$$P_0 = \left[p_0^1, p_0^2, ..., p_0^{C_0} \right]. \tag{4}$$

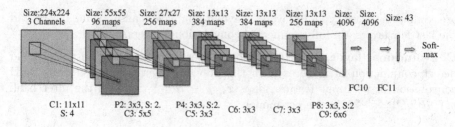

Fig. 3. Structure of AlexNet

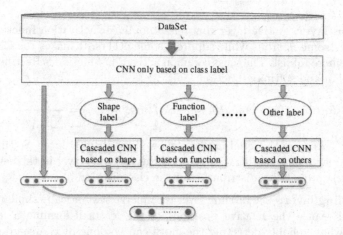

Fig. 4. Cascaded CNNs with Multi-attributes

Since C_0 classes traffic signs can be classified into 6 super categories. And most of the signs are recognized correctly into the super category even though the specifical is not, for example, one sign (30 km/h) belongs to speed limit sign category, or it is recognized as one another (eg. 80 km/h), it belongs to speed limit sign category.

So we design the second stage, which is the refine stage based on function attribute is shown in Fig. 5 concretely. In each super category, the signs in different classes are similar and easy to be misclassified. In this stage, we refine the distinction among signs in each one super category.

After the first stage, we do not make the signs into C_0 specifical classes while corresponding 6 super categories. This is because after first-stage CNN, signs are more likely to be recognized as the correct super category even though the specific class is not correct. We train a CNN on each super category for further refinement to make the misclassified signs in right super category correctly classified finally. In this stage, we get the probability distribution P_{kj} correspondingly.

$$P_{kj} = \left[p_{kj}^1, p_{kj}^2, ..., p_{kj}^{C_{kj}} \right].$$

$$(5)$$

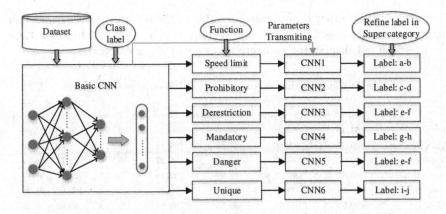

Fig. 5. The second stage based on Function Attribute-refinement.

P_{kj} is the probability of the j-th class based on k-th attribute and C_{kj} is the number of the super category. Specifically we need to translate P_{kj} to a 43-d vector corresponding to the 43 classes in GTSRB. So the final probability is:

$$P = P_0 + \alpha_k \cdot vector(P_{kj}), 0 < \alpha_k < 1. \tag{6}$$

The recognized class is the index of maximum of P.

4 Experiments

4.1 Data Preprocessing and Training

We conduct experiments on GTSRB, which was created from approximately 10 hours of video that was recorded while driving on different road types in Germany during daytime. It is a large lifelike data set of more than 50,000 traffic sign images in 43 classes and contains images of more than 1700 traffic sign instances. The size of the traffic signs varies from 15×15 to 222×193 pixels. We use our cascaded CNNs to recognize the traffic sign in GTSRB. In order to extend the dataset and improve the robustness of CNN, we need to do preprocessing on the date set. We do histogram equation on the images and affine transformations on the original images in training dataset, each image do eight rotation transformation with random angle between -15 and 15 Since images in GTSRB have 10% boundary, we cut the transformed image to get ROI. Then we feed the training set into the cascaded CNNs.

4.2 Results

In testing stage, we also do 8 affine transformations and cut the 10% boundary, by which for each single test we get 9 test images and 9 probability value to vote for the specific class and the class of most votes is the final decision.

The recognition accuracy is illustrated in Table 1. The separate accuracy of super categories of hinge-loss CNN and multi-column CNN were not shown in their papers, so we not display the concrete accuracy of super categories.

Table 1. Classification accuracy on GTSRB on super categories

	Speed limit	prohibitory	Derestriction	Mandatory	Danger	Unique	Overall
3-NN [2]	61.39	87.28	87.00	93.39	53.83	98.76	73.89
LDA [2]	95.37	96.80	85.83	97.18	93.73	98.63	95.68
Random forest [4]	95.95	99.13	87.50	99.27	92.08	98.73	96.14
Multi-Scale [21]	98.61	99.93	98.89	99.18	98.67	98.63	98.84
Committee [19]	99.14	99.57	100.00	97.89	98.83	100.00	98.98
ELM [11]	99.54	100.00	98.33	99.94	98.96	99.95	99.56
Our Method							
Basic CNN	97.46	98.93	86.94	90.91	93.80	96.37	95.19
Cascaded CNNs	99.15	99.01	97.03	94.95	96.22	99.85	97.94

From Table 1 we can see that even though the accuracy of our method is a little bit lower than the best few methods. Our cascaded CNNs improve the overall accuracy nearly 3 % and improve the accuracy of all super categories separately based on our basic single CNN. For further analysis, we illustrate the intra-class error and inter-class error of these 6 super categories. As shown in Table 2, we can see that the misclassified number of all category have been decreased. The cascaded refinement CNN can modify the errors in the same super category.

Table 2. The Intra-misclassification error of super categories

	Speed limit	prohibitory	Derestriction	Mandatory	Danger	Unique	Overall
Basic CNN	101	5	20	168	117	19	430
Cascaded-CNN	14	0	0	97	89	2	202

5   Conclusion

In this paper, we proposed a cascaded CNNs framework termed attribute-refinement cascaded CNN by combining multi-attributes with two stages. The first stage CNN is trained with class label while the second stage CNN is trained on super classes separately according to object attributes such as function and shape. Experiments on traffic sign recognition show that the proposed hierarchical cascaded framework can discover nuances between indistinguishable traffic signs, and improve the discrimination of the model and classification accuracy.

Acknowledgments. This work is supported in part by the National Key Research and Development Plan (Grant No.2016YFC0801005) and the National Natural Science Foundation of China (Grant No.61402463).

References

1. Fleyeh, H., Dougherty, M.: Road and traffic sign detection and recognition. In: Proceedings of the 16th Mini-EURO Conference and 10th Meeting of EWGT, pp. 644–653 (2005)
2. Stallkamp, J., Schlipsing, M., Salmen, J., Igel, C.: Man vs. computer: benchmarking machine learning algorithms for traffic sign recognition. Neural Netw. **32**, 323–332 (2012)
3. Wang, M., Gao, Y., Lu, K., Rui, Y.: View-based discriminative probabilistic modeling for 3D object retrieval and recognition. IEEE Trans. Image Process. **22**(4), 1395–1407 (2013)
4. Zaklouta, F., Stanciulescu, B., Hamdoun, O.: Traffic sign classification using k-d trees and random forests. In: IEEE Proceedings of International Joint Conference on Neural Networks (IJCNN), pp. 2151–2155 (2011)
5. Zaklouta, F., Stanciulescu, B.: Real-time traffic sign recognition using tree classifiers. IEEE Trans. Intell. Transp. Syst. **13**(4), 1507–1514 (2012)
6. Cortes, C., Vapnik, V.: Support-vector networks. Mach. Learn. **20**(3), 273–297 (1995)
7. Maldonado-Bascon, S., Lafuente-Arroyo, S., Gil-Jimenez, P., Gomez-Moreno, H., et al.: Road sign detection and recognition based on support vector machines. IEEE Trans. Intell. Transp. Syst. **8**(2), 264–278 (2007)
8. Shi, M., Wu, H., Fleyeh, H.: Support vector machines for traffic signs recognition. In: IEEE Proceedings of International Joint Conference on Neural Networks (IJCNN), pp. 3820–3827 (2008)
9. Wang, M., Fu, W., Hao, S., et al.: Scalable semi-supervised learning by efficient anchor graph regularization. IEEE Trans. Knowl. Data Eng. **28**(7), 1864–1877 (2016)
10. Wang, M., Liu, X., Wu, X.: Visual classification by ℓ1-hypergraph modeling. IEEE Trans. Knowl. Data Eng. **27**(9), 2564–2574 (2015)
11. Huang, Z., Yu, Y., Gu, J., et al.: An efficient method for traffic sign recognition based on extreme learning machine. IEEE Trans. Cybern. **99**, 1–14 (2016)
12. LeCun, Y., Bengio, Y., Hinton, G.: Deep learning. Nature **521**(7553), 436–444 (2015)
13. Sun, Y., Chen, Y., Wang, X., et al.: Deep learning face representation by joint identification-verification. In: Advances in Neural Information Processing Systems (NIPS), pp. 1988–1996 (2014)
14. Lee, C.Y., Xie, S., Gallagher, P., et al.: Deeply supervised nets. In: Proceedings of AISTATS (2015)
15. Girshick, R.: Fast RCNN. In: Proceedings of the IEEE International Conference on Computer Vision (ICCV), pp. 1440–1448 (2015)
16. Tang, S., Huang, L.L.: Traffic sign recognition using complementary features. In: IEEE Asian Conference on Pattern Recognition(ACPR), pp. 210–214 (2013)
17. Lu, K., Ding, Z., Ge, S.: Sparse-representation-based graph embedding for traffic sign recognition. IEEE Trans. Intell. Transp. Syst. **13**(4), 1515–1524 (2012)
18. Liu, H., Liu, Y., Sun, F.: Traffic sign recognition using group sparse coding. Inf. Sci. **266**, 75–89 (2014)
19. Ciresan, D., Meier, U., Masci, J., et al.: A committee of neural networks for traffic sign classification. In: IEEE International Joint Conference on Neural Networks (IJCNN), pp. 1918–1921 (2011)

20. Ciresan, D., Meier, U., Masci, J., et al.: Multi-column deep neural network for traffic sign classification. Neural Netw. **32**, 333–338 (2012)
21. Sermanet, P., LeCun, Y.: Traffic sign recognition with multi-scale convolutional networks. In: IEEE International Joint Conference on Neural Networks (IJCNN), pp. 2809–2813 (2011)
22. Jin, J., Fu, K., Zhang, C.: Traffic sign recognition with hinge loss trained convolutional neural networks. IEEE Trans. Intell. Transp. Syst. **15**(5), 1991–2000 (2014)
23. Krizhevsky, A., Sutskever, I., Hinton, G.E.: Imagenet classification with deep convolutional neural networks. In: Advances in Neural Information Processing Systems (NIPS), pp. 1097–1105 (2012)
24. Xie, K., Ge, S., Yang, R., et al.: Negative-supervised cascaded deep learning for traffic sign classification. In: Zha, H., Chen, X., Wang, L., Miao, Q. (eds.) CCCV 2015, Part I, vol. 546, pp. 249–257. Springer, Heidelberg (2015)

Building Locally Discriminative Classifier Ensemble Through Classifier Fusion Among Nearest Neighbors

Xiang-Jun Shen[1], Wen-Chao Zhang[1], Wei Cai[1], Ben-Bright B. Benuw[1], He-Ping Song[1], Qian Zhu[1(✉)], and Zheng-Jun Zha[2]

[1] School of Computer Science and Telecommunication Engineering, Jiangsu University, Zhenjiang, China
callmezq@ujs.edu.cn
[2] School of Information Science and Technology, University of Science and Technology of China, Hefei, China

Abstract. Many studies on ensemble learning that combines multiple classifiers have shown that, it is an effective technique to improve accuracy and stability of a single classifier. In this paper, we propose a novel discriminative classifier fusion method, which applies local classification results of classifiers among nearest neighbors to build a local classifier ensemble. From this dynamically selected process, discriminative classifiers are weighted heavily to build a locally discriminative ensemble. Experimental results on several UCI datasets have shown that, our proposed method achieves best classification performance among individual classifiers, majority voting and AdaBoost algorithms.

Keywords: Ensemble learning · Classifier ensemble · Classifier combination · Classifier fusion

1 Introduction

In the past few decades classification [1] has been a fundamental task in Pattern Recognition and Machine Learning. Prior methods proposed include Neural networks [2], Support Vector Machine (SVM) [3], Decision Tree [4], Naive Bayes [5] etc. These previous studies have shown that, it is somewhat not feasible to cover all the variability inherent to most pattern recognition problems for a monolithic classifier. Hence the recent active research in ensemble learning that combines multiple classifiers outputs to improve the accuracy and stability performance of a single classifier. Ensemble learning is also named as Multiple Classifier Systems (MCS) [6]. And in such a system, a classifier is called a base learner or individual classifier.

At present, many ensemble learning methods have been proposed, and two major issues are considered important in devising a classifiers ensemble method. The first issue is how to construct individual classifiers to obtain better classification performance. When constructing such classifiers, diversity is one of the

© Springer International Publishing AG 2016
E. Chen et al. (Eds.): PCM 2016, Part I, LNCS 9916, pp. 211–220, 2016.
DOI: 10.1007/978-3-319-48890-5_21

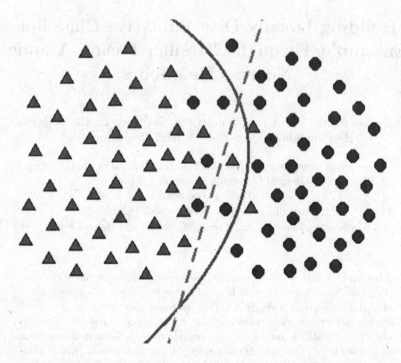

Fig. 1. Different classifiers have different impact on the final outputs.

most important strategies that could enhance the individual classifiers to produce uncorrelated errors. Classification errors can only propagate in few classifiers, and the classification performances are improved finally by combining
individual classifiers output. Diversity in classifiers could also be implemented
in several ways; one of which is to design directly diversity measure formulations
such as Disagreement [7], Double Fault [8] and Kappa [9]. Other researches
[10,11] have also shown that there is no clear correlation between accuracy and
diversity in ensembles. They stated that, the accuracy does not monotonically
increase with various diversity measures. Meanwhile another scheme is to design
classifier diversity implicitly [12–15]. The diversity is also achieved by varying the
information used to train individual classifiers. Bagging [12] and Boosting [13]
are the two most representative methods to train individual classifiers by using
different subsets of training data. While [14,15] are trained by using different
feature subspaces.

The other issue of concern however, is how a classifier ensemble can combine
the output of individual classifiers. This technique is considered as a research
hotspot of classifier ensemble in recent years. Many combination rules have been
proposed. And these methods can roughly be classified as voting weighted and
selective weighted rules. Weighted voting are the most frequent used rules [16–
18]. In such methods, the most popular used is simple vote strategy [16], which
combines all individual classifiers outputs with same weight. This strategy is

equivalent to majority vote [19]. Other methods proposed for weighted voting combination rule classifiers that have different contributions for improving the performance, and hence assign individual classifiers with different weights. Some weighted voting rules are based on regression settings [17,20]. And some others are based on classification settings [18,21]. Selective or pruning classifier ensemble is another type of combination rules, which assume that selecting a best subset of classifiers can produce better performance than selecting the whole classifiers [22]. Gurram and Kwon propose sparse kernel-based ensemble learning method [23], which optimizes kernel parameters for hyper-spectral classification problems. Yin et al. [24] propose a dynamic ensembles method that combines classifiers as an ensemble of all the interim ensembles dynamically from consecutive batches of non-stationary data.

Figure 1 above illustrates how different classifiers have impact on the final outputs. The figure shows that classification errors often happen near decision planes of individual classifiers. And data samples that are far away from the decision planes are always classified as correct. This gives us the motivation on building local classifier ensemble. This figure also illustrates that, if we evaluate a test sample, its nearest training samples have great impact on the final decision. This is very similar to K-NN algorithm [25], but different from the K-NN algorithm: the label information is not used in ensemble learning. However the generalization ability of classifiers is utilized when nearest neighbors of training samples are considered. Therefore different weights are applied in those classifiers. The less the local classifier error is, the heavier the weight of classifier.

The above observations motivate our research on building locally discriminative classifier ensemble. And our proposed method applies local classification results of classifiers among nearest neighbors. Based on those local classifier results, locally discriminative classifiers are selected and assigned heavy weights through a fusion method to form a locally classifier ensemble. Experimental results on several UCI datasets demonstrate that our proposed method achieves best classification performance among individual classifiers, majority voting [19] and AdaBoost algorithm [13].

This paper is organized as follows: Sect. 2 introduces our proposed method on building locally discriminative classifier ensemble. We present the experimental results in the real data sets in Sect. 3 and conclude in the last section.

2 Proposed Approach

Assuming that S=$\{d_1, d_2, ..., d_s\}$ is the training dataset, where $d_i \in R^n$ is one sample of training dataset, s is the number of training datasets and M=$\{\mu_1, \mu_2, ..., \mu_j\}$ is the set of class labels, where μ_j is one label of all labels and j is the number of labels. C=$\{c_1, c_2, ..., c_N\}$ denotes the set of N classifiers, which are trained separately with the datasets.

To build a locally discriminative classifier ensemble, we design a novel fusion method. For each test sample t, we choose its K nearest neighbors from the training dataset. These K nearest neighbors are chosen by calculating the Euclidean distance between the test sample t and each training sample. The K nearest neighbors of t compose a set KD=$\{d_i \mid d_i \in S\}$, where d_i is one sample of training datasets. Then, we classify the K nearest neighbors with the trained classifiers, and the weight for individual classifier was assigned.

Each individual classifier c_x in our local ensemble output support degrees of class labels with which a data sample is classified. For convenience, we assume that the degrees are of the interval $[0, 1]$. The class support degree of a training data sample d_i which is classified by individual classifiers c_x to class μ_k is denoted by $\rho_{x,k}(d_i)$. Apparently, the larger the value of $\rho_{x,k}(d_i)$, the more likely a data sample will belong to the class μ_k. The classifiers output a support degree matrix $BD(d_i)$ for each nearest neighbor d_i in the set of KD. And the matrix is as follows:

$$BD(d_i) = \begin{bmatrix} \rho_{1,1}(d_i) & \cdots & \rho_{1,k}(d_i) & \cdots & \rho_{1,j}(d_i) \\ \vdots & \cdots & \ddots & \cdots & \vdots \\ \rho_{N,1}(d_i) & \cdots & \rho_{N,k}(d_i) & \cdots & \rho_{N,j}(d_i) \end{bmatrix} \quad (1)$$

In the matrix above, each row represents a row vector of support degree of class labels that d_i is classified in the nth individual classifier. For example, $B_n(d_i) = (\rho_{n,1}(d_i), \cdots, \rho_{n,j}(d_i))$ denotes the support degree of class labels that d_i is classified to in n^{th} individual classifier.

We then calculate the means of all K nearest neighbors who actually belong to class μ_k, and is denoted by BT_k in Eq. 2 bellow:

$$BT_k = \frac{1}{M_k} \sum_{k \in \mu_k} BD(z) \quad (2)$$

where M_k is the number of K nearest neighbors that actually belong to μ_k, $BD(z)$ is the support degree matrix of training data sample z. BT_k is a support evidence matrix that shows how the data samples in KD whose class label is μ_k are trained. And BT_k^n is the nth row vector of BT_k. This row vector denotes the support evidence of class labels that data samples in KD are trained in the nth individual classifier.

For a test sample t, its class support degree matrix BD(t) is calculated, according to formula in Eq. 1. The similarity distance, $\|BT_k^n - B_n(t)\|$, between BT_k^n and $B_n(t)$ is calculated. The $\|.\|$ is the Euclidean distance which reflects the local errors that are collected in the nth classifier. The Smaller this distance, The better the nth individual classifier. This shows that the nth individual classifier could achieve a similar classification performance just like that of data samples in KD. Based on the training data samples in KD, the similarity distance that the nth classifier classifies the test sample t to the μ_k class label is defined as follows.

$$\psi_{k,n}(t) = \frac{(1 + \|BT_k^n - B_n(t)\|)^{-1}}{\sum_{k=1}^{j}(1 + \|BT_k^n - B_n(t)\|)^{-1}} \quad (3)$$

where $B_n(t)$ is the row vector of support degree of the test sample t which is classified by the nth individual classifier. BT_k^n is the vector of support evidence of class labels that data samples in KD are trained in n^{th} individual classifier. The numerator shows the similarity between test sample and training samples in KD, and the denominator is a normalized factor that make the formulation in interval $[0, 1]$. Obviously, the smaller the distance is, more support the testing sample t is classified to class label μ_k, through the nth individual classifier.

Now, based on the distance definition in Eq. 3 above, each individual classifier is weighted as follows.

$$w_k^n(t) = \frac{\psi_{k,n}(t) \prod_{m \neq k}(1 - \psi_{m,n}(t))}{\sum_{n=1}^{N} \psi_{k,n}(t) \prod_{m \neq k}(1 - \psi_{m,n}(t))} \tag{4}$$

where w_k^n is the weight of the nth individual classifier that classifies the test sample t to class label μ_k. The numerator is the individual classifiers support evidence for classifying the test sample t to class label μ_k, based on Eq. 3. And the denominator is a normalized factor to make the support evidence in the interval $[0, 1]$. Apparently, the bigger the weight is, the better contribution of the classifier is.

When this weight method is applied to individual classifiers, a local classifier ensemble is obtained by combining these weighted individual classifiers. For each test sample t, we calculate the weighted result from the local classifier ensemble for each class μ_k, and then output the maximum class label. Our proposed local classifier ensemble for classifying test sample t is as follows.

$$\underset{k}{argmax} : \sum_{n=1}^{N} w_k^n(t) B_n^k(t) \tag{5}$$

where w_k^n is the weight defined in Eq. 4 and $B_n^k(t)$ is the kth component of row vector $B_n(t)$. Formula 5 above gives the maximum output as the class label for the test sample t, upon which our proposed method is built. Our proposed method is summarized in Algorithm 1.

The experiments in Sect. 3 demonstrate the outperforming of our proposed method, compared with several ensemble methods and individual classifiers.

Algorithm 1. Our proposed method

Input: Test sample $t \in R^n$ with n dimension.
Output: Predicted Class label k of test sample t.
1: Select K nearest neighbors as a set of KD=$\{d_i | d_i \in S\}$ for test samples t.
2: Build the support degree matrix BD(d_i) for the K nearest neighbors, according to Eq. 1.
3: Calculate their support degree matrix BT_k of all K nearest neighbors, according to Eq. 2.
4: Get the support degree $B_n(t)$ of the test sample t which is classified by the nth individual classifier, and calculate their similarity distance by the Eq. 3.
5: Obtain the weight that the nth individual classifier classifies the test sample to class label μ_k, according to Eq. 4.
6: Output the class label k of test sample t, according to Eq. 5.

---

3   Experimental Results

3.1   Experimental Setup

Datasets: We performed our experiment on car license dataset and other published datasets, such as, Madelon and IJCNN1 from the UCI DB which is provided by the University of California Irvine to demonstrate the performance of our proposed methodLocally discriminative classifier ensemble through classifier fusion among nearest neighbors. Table 1 shows the detailed dimension, total number, train number and test number of the 3 training datasets.

Table 1. The detail of every dataset

Dataset	Dimension	Training samples	Test samples
Madelon	500	2,000	600
ICJNN1	22	49,990	91,701

Individual Classifiers: To implement diversity, two types of classifiers, Support Vector Machine (SVM) and Sparse Representation Classification (SRC), were selected because of their well-known strong theoretical foundations, and their parameters varied to obtain several individual classifiers. The parameters for SVM are shown in Table 2, where C and γ denote penalty and gamma coefficients respectively. Four kernel functions which constitute different classifiers were also chosen. They are RBF kernel, Liner kernel, Polynomial kernel, and sigmoid kernel.

With respect to SRC, we varied the number of train samples to obtain different sparse representation classifiers and the train samples are selected from the original dataset respectively occupying 90 %, 85 % and 70 % of all dataset. Besides, On the basis of the proportion we chose every proportion three times which resulted into 9 sparse models.

K nearest neighbors: The number of nearest neighbors in our proposed method is important to building our local ensembles. To find a best K and avoid accidental selection, we experimented on two different datasets. One dataset is our collected dataset of car license plate. We vary the values of K from 1 to 100 and observed the classification accuracy of our proposed method which changed in both datasets as shown in Fig. 2. It could be seen from the figure that, better clarification accuracy is achieved when K is about 9 hence the number of nearest neighbors were fixed at 9 and served as the precedence for experiments on other UCI datasets.

3.2   Experimental Results and Discussion

In this section, we first validate the performance of every single classifier and on that regard; we begin the comparison with Majority Voting [19], AdaBoost [13]

Table 2. Information of individual classifiers

Classifier A	C	G	Kernel
SVM1	0.5	0.0313	2(RBF)
VM2			0(Liner)
SVM3			1(Polynomial)
SVM4			3(Sigmoid)
SVM5	1.2	2.8	2(RBF)
SVM6			0(Liner)
SVM7			1(Polynomial)
SVM8			3(Sigmoid)
SVM9	0.354	0.0221	2(RBF)
SVM10			0(Liner)
SVM11			1(Polynomial)
SVM12			3(Sigmoid)

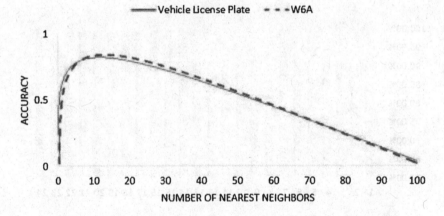

Fig. 2. Classification accuracy changes with the value of K varying

and our proposed method. More so, we would like to get significant results that could demonstrate that the locally discriminative classifier ensemble is more effective than the other two ensemble learning methods.

Figure 3 illustrates classification performances among individual classifiers, Majority Voting, AdaBoost and our proposed method. From the figure, individual classifiers achieved best classification performance of 64.50 % accuracy and worst performance of 50.00 % accuracy. In addition, the figure shows that the Polynomial kernel can achieve better performance than other kernel. Other ensemble methods such as Majority Voting and AdaBoost achieved 73.83 % and

Madelon

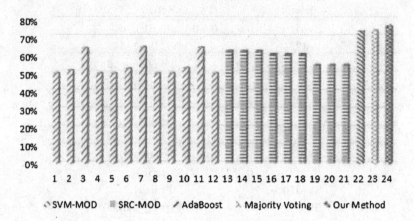

Fig. 3. Classification accuracies in the dataset Madelon on individual classifiers and ensemble methods

IJCNN1

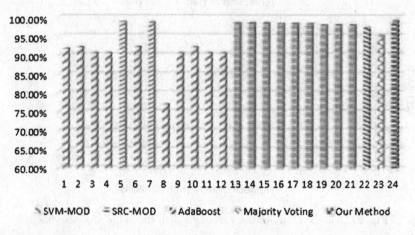

Fig. 4. Classification accuracies in the dataset Madelon on individual classifiers and ensemble methods

73.17 % classification accuracy respectively and that of our proposed method is 76.20 %. This figure demonstrates that, our proposed ensemble method outperforms other classifiers in the Madelon dataset.

Figure 4 shows the experiment results on the Ijcnn1 dataset. In this experiment individual classifiers like SRC obtained very similar results. As could be seen from the figure, the individual classifiers of SRC achieved 98.51 % best performance accuracy, and 97.93 % worst performance accuracy. On the other hand, SVM classifiers achieved best classification performance of 98.74 % accuracy and worst performance of 76.95 % accuracy. The figure also shows that the classification variance in individual classifiers is large, which illustrates that the accuracy of single individual classifiers depend on its parameters. Majority Voting and AdaBoost achieved 95.16 % and 97.22 % accuracy, respectively, and our proposed method achieved 98.97 % accuracy.

From the above experimental results, our proposed method can select locally discriminative classifiers and assign heavy weights through a fusion method to form a locally classifier ensemble. They demonstrate that our proposed method achieves best classification performance among individual classifiers, majority voting and AdaBoost algorithms.

4   Conclusions

In this paper, a locally discriminative classifier ensemble learning method is proposed. Based on the observations that local classification results of classifiers can help to build a locally discriminative classifier ensemble, our proposed method builds local ensembles through test samples and their nearest neighbors of training samples. The local classifier errors among nearest neighbors of testing samples are collected and used to assign weights to different classifiers through a fusion method. Thus less the local classifier error is, heavier the weight of classifier is. Experimental results on several UCI data sets demonstrate that our proposed method achieves best classification performance among individual classifiers, majority voting and AdaBoost algorithms.

Acknowledgments. This work was funded in part by the National Natural Science Foundation of China (No. 61572240,61502208), Natural Science Foundation of Jiangsu Province of China (No. BK20150522), and the Open Project Program of the National Laboratory of Pattern Recognition(NLPR) (No. 201600005).

References

1. Boucheron, S., Bousquet, O., Lugosi, G.: Theory of classification: a survey of some recent advances. ESAIM: Probab. Stat. **9**(1), 323–375 (2005)
2. Egmont-Petersen, M., de Ridder, D., Handels, H.: Image processing with neural networks C a review. Pattern Recogn. **35**(10), 2279–2301 (2002)
3. Wang, L.: The Support Vector Machines: Theory and Applications. Springer, Berlin (2005)
4. Quinlan, J.R.: Improved use of continuous attributes in C4.5. J. Artif. Intell. Res. **4**, 77–90 (1996)
5. Rennie, J., Shih, L., Teevan, J., Karger, D.: Spam filtering with Naive Bayes which Naive Bayes? In: Proceedings of the Twentieth International Conference on Machine Learning (ICML), pp. 285–295 (2003)
6. Britto Jr., A.S., sabourin, R., Oliveira, L.S.: Dynamic selection of classifiers - a comprehensive review. Pattern Recogn. **47**(11), 3665–3680 (2014)

7. Skalak, D.: The sources of increased accuracy for two proposed boosting algorithms. In: Proceedings of American Association for Artificial Intelligence, Integrating Multiple Learned Models Workshop, AAAI 1996, pp. 120–125 (1996)

8. Giacinto, G., Roli, F.: Design of effective neural network ensembles for image classification processes. J. Image Vis. Comput. **19**(9/10), 699–707 (2001)

9. Sim, J., Wright, C.C.: The Kappa statistic in reliability studies: use, interpretation, and sample size requirements. Phys. Therapy **85**(3), 257–268 (2005)

10. Kuncheva, L.I., Whitaker, C.J.: Measures of diversity in classifier ensembles. Mach. Learn. **51**(2), 181–207 (2003)

11. Saitta, L.: Hypothesis diversity in ensemble classification. In: Esposito, F., Pivert, O., Hacid, M.-S., Raś, Z.W., Ferilli, S. (eds.) ISMIS 2015. LNCS (LNAI), vol. 9384, pp. 662–670. Springer, Heidelberg (2006). doi:10.1007/11875604_73

12. Breiman, L.: Bagging predictors. Mach. Learn. **24**(2), 123–140 (1996)

13. Freund, Y., Schapire, R.E.: Experiments with a new boosting algorithm. In: Proceedings of the 13th International Conference on Machine Learning (ICML), pp. 148–156 (1996)

14. Ho, T.K.: The random subspace method for constructing decision forests. IEEE Trans. Pattern Anal. Mach. Intell. **20**(8), 832–844 (1998)

15. Rodrguez, J.J., Kuncheva, L.I., Alonso, C.J.: Rotation forest: a new classifier ensemble method. IEEE Trans. Pattern Anal. Mach. Intell. **28**(10), 1619–1630 (2006)

16. Zhang, L., Zhou, W.D.: Sparse ensembles using weighted combination methods based on linear programming. Pattern Recogn. **44**(1), 97–106 (2011)

17. Benediktsson, J.A., Sveinsson, J.R., Ersoy, O.K., Swain, P.H.: Parallel consensual neural networks. IEEE Trans. Neural Netw. **8**(1), 54–64 (1997)

18. Ueda, N.: Optimal linear combination of neural networks for improving classification performance. IEEE Trans. Pattern Anal. Mach. Intell. **22**(2), 207–215 (2000)

19. Kuncheva, L.I., Rodriguez, J.J.: A weighted voting framework for classifiers ensembles. Knowl. Inf. Syst. **38**(2), 259–275 (2014)

20. Breiman, L.: Stacked regressions. Mach. Learn. **24**(1), 49–64 (1996)

21. Yao, X., Liu, Y.: Making use of population information in evolutionary artificial neural networks. IEEE Trans. Syst. Man Cybern. Part B **28**(3), 417–425 (1998)

22. Zhou, Z.H., Wu, J., Tang, W.: Ensembling neural networks: many could be better than all. Artif. Intell. **137**(1–2), 239–263 (2002)

23. Gurram, P., Kwon, H.: Sparse kernel-based ensemble learning with fully optimized kernel parameters for hyperspectral classification problems. IEEE Trans. Geosci. Remote Sens. **51**(2), 787–802 (2013)

24. Yin, X.-C., Huang, K., Hao, H.-W.: De^2: dynamic ensemble of ensembles for learning nonstationary data. Neurocomputing **165**, 14–22 (2015)

25. Theodoridis, S., Koutroumbas, K.: Pattern Recognition, 4th edn. Academic Press, New York (2009)

Retrieving Images by Multiple Samples
via Fusing Deep Features

Kecai Wu[1]([✉]), Xueliang Liu[1], Jie Shao[2], Richang Hong[1], and Tao Yang[3]

[1] Hefei University of Technology, Hefei, China
kecai@mail.hfut.edu.cn
[2] University of Electronic Science and Technology of China, Chengdu, China
[3] The Third Research Institute of Ministry of Public Security, Beijing, China

Abstract. Most existing image retrieval systems search similar images on a given single input, while querying based on multiple images is not a trivial. In this paper, we describe a novel image retrieval paradigm that users could input two images as query to search the images that include the content of the two input images-synchronously. In our solution, the deep CNN feature is extracted from each single query image and then fused as the query feature. Due to the role of the two query images is different and changeable, we propose the FWC (Feature weighting by Clustering), a novel algorithm to weight the two query features. All the CNN features in the whole dataset are clustered and the weight of each query is obtained by the distance to the mutual nearest cluster. The effectiveness of our algorithm is evaluated in PASCAL VOC2007 and Microsoft COCO datasets.

Keywords: Image retrieval · Feature fusion · Convolutional neural network

1 Introduction

The goal of content-based image retrieval (CBIR) system is to search similar images from a large visual dataset on a given query. Moreover, most existing image retrieval systems only accept a single image as query and fail when the users want to search images containing the different concepts in the image. In recent few years, there are some existing work which address similar retrieval task [6, 15]. For example, Vaca-Castano et al. [15] presented a new search paradigm that utilizes multiple images as input to query the semantic behind these images. If you input milk, beef and ranch as query images, the system will return some images of cow. Ghodrati et al. [6] provided a swap retrieval framework that includes the visual and textual content as the query to search images with similar content but swapping the object class with another similar one. Such as, we input an image of dog with hat as query, then the system will return some images of cat with hat.

In this paper, we propose a novel retrieval framework which accepts two different images as the query and finds out the images containing the concepts in both inputs. For example, if you input one dog and one cat as queries, the retrieval system can search the

© Springer International Publishing AG 2016
E. Chen et al. (Eds.): PCM 2016, Part I, LNCS 9916, pp. 221–230, 2016.
DOI: 10.1007/978-3-319-48890-5_22

images that include dog and cat in the same image. The workflow of our framework is shown in Fig. 1.

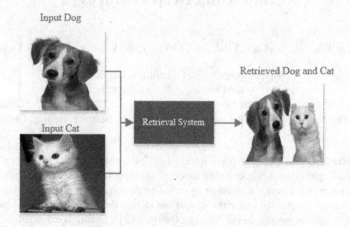

Fig. 1. Given a dog and a cat as query images, our work is to retrieve images with dog and cat.

There is some existing work which could accept multiple inputs in the image retrieval problem [1, 3, 4, 7]. However, it could be found out that extracting different features of the same image or multiple different perspective of the same object are used as the inputs in these work, which is completely different to our retrieval problem. The common characteristics of these methods is the multiple inputs that belongs to the same object. However, the content of two query images may be totally different object in our retrieval task, hence these existing methods cannot perform such a novel retrieval framework.

Therefore, we propose a novel algorithm for this challenge task by weighting and fusing the two query features. First of all, the Convolutional Neural Networks (CNN) [14] are employed to extract a compact representation feature due to their advantage on automatically learning compact features for recognition compared to hand-crafted features. Then, all the features of dataset are clustered by the K-means and the weights of two query features are generated by the distance to their mutual nearest cluster. Finally, we can search a joint latent semantic by fusing the two weighted features.

The remainder of this paper is structured as follows: in Sect. 2 we review some related work in the literatures of convolutional neural network and image retrieval. Then in Sect. 3 we will introduce our solution on the multiple inputs retrieval task. Several experimental and evaluated results will be discussed in the Sect. 4. Section 5 concludes this paper.

2   Related Work

2.1   Convolutional Neural Networks

In past few years, the Convolutional Neural Networks have made great performance in many multimedia directions. For example, Krizhevsky et al. [11] provided a deep

Convolutional Neural Networks framework to classify the 1.2 million images into the 1000 classes. Moreover, features based on convolutional networks also have led to the great performance on a range of vision tasks [8, 9, 14, 20, 21]. Razavian et al. [14] utilize the features extracted from the CNNs as a generic image representation to tackle the diverse range of recognition tasks of object image classification, scene recognition and image retrieval applied to a diverse set of public datasets. Inconceivably, they report consistent superior results compared to the highly tuned state-of-the-art visual systems in all the visual classification tasks on several public datasets. So, they strongly suggest that representation features obtained from deep learning with convolutional networks should be the primary candidate in most visual recognition tasks.

2.2 Multiple Query Image Retrieval

Most image retrieval algorithms are proposed for single query, which obtain good retrieval result [12, 13, 17–19]. However, multiple queries retrieving with multiple inputs can meet the special needs of users. In this problem, the key issue is to find a representation feature instead of multiple query features.

For example, Zhang et al. [16] provided an algorithm that fuses the different query features of the same image that making a good retrieval performance. Fernando et al. [3] provided a similar method to learn an object-specific mid-level representation, which can be used for merging several query images in different viewpoints or viewing conditions. A novel mobile visual searching algorithm is proposed by exploring saliency from multi-relevant photos in [17], and making a great performance by their method. However, the goal of these algorithms is to get a representation instead of all queries to performing the image retrieval.

We have discussed the general solution of multiple queries cannot solve our retrieval task. Our solution is inspired by the following methods, even though these methods cannot directly solve our retrieval problem. Gawande et al. [7] proposed a novel algorithm for feature level fusion utilizing Support Vector Machine (SVM) classifier that fuses the feature of two different modalities fingerprint and eye iris. The Mahalanobis distance is used for fusing the two query features. The Principal Component Analysis (PCA) approach is a commonly used method for satellite image fusing [1], since PCA keeps the principal information during the image fusion.

3 Our Methods

In this section, we introduce our solution on this special multiple queries retrieval task. Let A and B denote the query images that are selected from the different object classes. The CNN feature of two query images are extracted by Caffe [10] and denoted as F_A and F_B.

3.1   The Visual Feature Extraction

In our solution, the deep learning framework Caffe is utilized to extract the CNN feature of query and dataset. We know the network of ImageNet [11] has eight layers in total, containing five convolutional and three fully-connected layers. Since we are interested in high-level visual feature of the image instead of a classifier, we remove the eighth layer of the network. We use the pre-trained CNNs framework and the features are extracted by forward propagation of a mean subtracted 256 × 256 RGB color image over five convolutional and two fully-connected layers. Finally, we get a global feature descriptor that is a 4096d vector.

3.2   The Feature Weighting by Clustering

To weight the two query features, we cluster all the features in the dataset by the K-means and the weight of two query features are obtained by the distance to them mutual nearest cluster. Then the weighted feature of two queries can be used for searching them common latent semantic.

Firstly, we need to assign the CNN feature of dataset to K clusters. Secondly, calculating the Euclidean distance between the feature of image A and all of clusters. Finding the cluster K_A that the corresponding distance $dist_A$ is minimum all of the distances (1). We also can find the cluster K_B that the corresponding $dist_B$ is minimum all of the distances (2). The $dist_{Ai}$ means the Euclidean distance between the feature of image A and the ith cluster, and the $dist_{Bi}$ mean the distance between the feature of image B and the ith cluster. Finally, we need to determine whether the clusters K_A and K_B is the same cluster.

$$dist_A = \min_{i=1 \to k} \left\{ dist_{Ai} \right\} \tag{1}$$

$$dist_B = \min_{i=1 \to k} \left\{ dist_{Bi} \right\} \tag{2}$$

If the cluster K_A and the cluster K_B are the same cluster, we can get two parameters μ_A and μ_B as weighted for the CNN feature of two query images according the formulas (3) and (4).

$$\mu_A = \frac{dist_A}{dist_A + dist_B} \tag{3}$$

$$\mu_B = \frac{dist_B}{dist_A + dist_B} \tag{4}$$

If the cluster K_A and the cluster K_B are not the same cluster, we need to re-find a new cluster K_w from all clusters, the new cluster K_w should meet this condition that the sum of the distance between K_w, K_A and K_w, K_B is minimum (5). The $dist'_{Ai}$ mean the distance between the cluster K_A and the ith cluster, and the $dist'_{Bi}$ mean the distance between cluster K_B and the ith cluster.

$$K_w = \min_{i=1 \to k} \left\{ dist'_{Ai} + dist'_{Bi} \right\} \tag{5}$$

Once we find the cluster K_w, we calculate the distance between two query features and the cluster K_w, which are denoted as $dist'_A$ and $dist'_B$ respectively. The parameter μ_A and μ_B are calculated by the formulas (6) and (7). These parameters are also adopted as weights.

$$\mu_A = \frac{dist'_A}{dist'_A + dist'_B} \tag{6}$$

$$\mu_B = \frac{dist'_B}{dist'_A + dist'_B} \tag{7}$$

No matter whether the cluster K_A and K_B are the same cluster or not, we also get two parameters μ_A and μ_B as weights for the CNN feature of two query images. The weighted feature of two query images is generated by the formulas (8) and (9).

$$F'_A = \mu_A * F_A \tag{8}$$

$$F'_B = \mu_B * F_B \tag{9}$$

There are two images as query in our retrieval system, and we do not directly fuse the query features. We often apply different distance metrics and input a query image based on similarity features of which we can retrieve the output images in the traditional retrieval system. There are two query images in our retrieval system, so we proposed a new metric for this special retrieval task. Firstly, we denote the $dist_1$ and $dist_2$ as the Euclidean distance of feature F_A and F_B against to other items in the dataset respectively. Next, the sum of distance is $dist_1 + dist_2$ that will be used as the query metric. The result of sorting is the retrieval result by the proposed method.

4   Experiments

We evaluate the FWC algorithm on several public datasets, such as PASCAL VOC2007 and MS COCO datasets, then compare the retrieval results of the PCA and our method, and the mean average precision (mAP) and the precision at N of retrieval results are showed at Table 1 and Fig. 3.

Table 1. The mAP comparison to various indexing approaches in VOC2007 and COCO.

Methods and datasets	Top 5	Top 10	Top 15	Top 20	Top 25
PCA with raw feature (VOC)	0.3305	0.3281	0.3283	0.3235	0.3262
PCA with weighted feature (VOC)	0.6946	0.6662	0.6456	0.6289	0.6107
FWC with weighted SIFT (VOC)	0.5773	0.5569	0.5362	0.5260	0.5186
FWC with weighted CNN (VOC)	**0.9883**	**0.9431**	**0.8935**	**0.8479**	**0.8187**
PCA with raw feature (COCO)	0.6842	0.6849	0.6771	0.6709	0.6622
PCA with weighted feature (COCO)	0.8978	0.8651	0.8398	0.8157	0.7953
FWC with weighted SIFT (COCO)	0.5531	0.5403	0.5267	0.5191	0.5099
FWC with weighted CNN (COCO)	**0.9740**	**0.9219**	**0.8851**	**0.8563**	**0.8345**

4.1 Dataset and Implementation Details

For the evaluation purpose, we use the concept dog and cat in our experiments. We prepare two public datasets in which there are multiple objects per image. The first dataset is the PASCAL VOC2007[1], which contains about 10000 images and 20 different classes. The second dataset is the MS COCO[2], which is an image recognition dataset containing 80 object categories. Moreover, the MS COCO is too huge to our retrieval task. And a subset, we randomly select 10000 images from the MS COCO for the experiments. However, the two datasets have not enough images which contain dog and cat simultaneously. Hence we manually collect a subset with the images of dog and cat, and add them into these datasets. Finally, we collect 90 pairs of dog and cat respectively as query images from different categories.

We perform several experiments to evaluate the FWC method for 90 pairs of query images. For each pair of query images, we choose the top 25 or 50 retrieved images as the retrieved result. If the retrieved images were relevant to both queries, we denote the images as binary 1. Otherwise, the images were denoted as binary 0. We calculate the mAP and the precision at N of retrieved images from the 90 pairs of query images. The mAP is reported for the top 25 retrieved images, ranging from 5 to 25 in intervals of 5. The precision at N is reported the top 50 retrieved images, range from 5 to 50 in intervals of 5.

We know the K-means is an algorithm of vector quantization, which is popular for cluster analysis in data mining and computer vision. The K-means is performed in the proposed solution that need to partition all the feature of dataset to K clusters. So, we have to choose a suitable K for two different datasets. There are 20 different classes in the PASCAL VOC2007 and 80 different classes in the MS COCO. For simplicity, we choose the suitable K for two different datasets that the K of PASCAL VOC2007 is 21 and MS COCO is 81 in our experiments.

---

[1] http://pjreddie.com/projects/pascal-voc-dataset-mirror/.
[2] http://mscoco.org/home/.

4.2 Compared Approaches

To demonstrate the effectiveness of our proposed method by fusing the two query features, we compare our approach to following closely related methods. As aforementioned, the feature weighting and CNN feature are two crucial factors in our solution, but there is little work which addresses the multiple input query problems. And our compared approaches are designed with different fusing and visual features.

In order to demonstrate the benefit of the fusing method, we use the PCA to fuse the two inputs. First of all, the two query features F_A and F_B are 4096d vector, we can concatenate the two vectors into a new array. Secondly, the size of the new array is 2*4096, which is usually viewed as 2 observations and each observation is 4096 dimensions. However, we also think the new array containing 4096 observations and each observation is 2 dimensions by making a transpose operation. Thirdly, we utilize the extended algorithm of [1] to fusing the two query features by PCA. The dimension of each observation is reduced from 2 to 1, and the last array is a 4096d vector that is viewed as fusion feature containing the principal component about the image A and B. Finally, the fusion feature can be used to the ordinary retrieval system that measuring the similarity between the query feature and all the feature of dataset. The detail information of basic method is showed at Fig. 2.

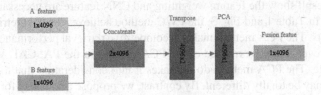

Fig. 2. The flow diagram of PCA fusing.

In order to illustrate the advantage of feature weighting, the raw CNN feature and the weighted CNN feature are used for performing our retrieval task. Moreover, we have introduced the state-of-the-art performance of CNNs in Sect. 2. As a contrast, we also extract the Scale Invariant Feature Transform (SIFT) [5] feature of two queries to implement our retrieval task by the FWC. Now, there are 4 retrieval solutions that PCA with raw feature, PCA with weighted feature, FWC with weighted SIFT feature and FWC with weighted CNN feature. These solutions will be used for performing our retrieval task in two public datasets.

4.3 Results and Discussion

These solutions are evaluated by the mAP and the precision at N in PASCAL VOC2007 and MS COCO datasets. Table 1 shows the evaluation result of the mAP in two datasets. Figure 3 reports the evaluation result of the Precision at N in two datasets respectively. Moreover, the *PCA−* means using the raw feature as query feature, and the *PCA+* means using the weighted feature. The PCA method with the weighted feature clearly outperforms the PCA method with the raw feature, and the CNN feature of two queries achieves better retrieval performance than the SIFT feature.

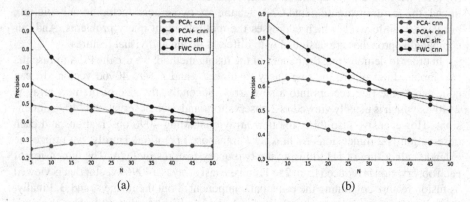

(a)   (b)

Fig. 3. The precision at N of in the VOC2007 (a) and COCO (b).

From the results, we can see that our approach outperforms other methods. The experiment result show the feature weighting and CNN feature are necessary factors in our solution. In Table 1 and Fig. 3, the FWC method achieves the best retrieval results in two datasets. The PCA method makes a competitive retrieval performance in the MS COCO. However, the performance of the PCA method in the PASCAL VOC2007 is not acceptable. The PCA method do not takes it into consideration that the objects in two queries may be totally different. By contrast, we propose a new way for solving the above problem by using the feature weighting as query. The weighted feature of two queries can match the latent semantic of the two queries. Hence the retrieval performance of the proposed method is more stable and effective in two different datasets.

5 Conclusion

In this paper, we propose a new retrieval framework, in which two input images are as query and we can retrieve the images that include the concepts in both queries. In our proposed solution, we present feature weighting method that search the mutual latent semantic of two queries. The weighted feature is obtained by calculating the metric distance between each query feature and their corresponding nearest cluster.

The proposed method is evaluated with the two different datasets. The experiment result indicates that proposed method make a promising retrieval performance, which suggests that the feature weighting can well model the latent semantic of the two different query features.

Acknowledgment. This work was partially supported by National High Technology Research and Development Program of China (Grant No. 2014AA015104), the Natural Science Foundation of China (NSFC) under Grant 61502139 and 61472116, The Natural Science Foundation of Anhui

Province under Grant 1608085MF128, and the program from the Key Lab of Information Network Security, Ministry of Public Security under Grant C14605.

References

1. Chiang, J.L.: Knowledge-based principal component analysis for image fusion. Appl. Math. **8**(1L), 223–230 (2014)
2. Elkan, C.: Using the triangle inequality to accelerate k-means. In: ICML, vol. 3, pp. 147–153 (2003)
3. Fernando, B., Tuytelaars, T.: Mining multiple queries for image retrieval: on-the-fly learning of an object-specific mid-level representation. In: Proceedings of the IEEE International Conference on Computer Vision, pp. 2544–2551 (2013)
4. Fu, Y., Cao, L., Guo, G., et al.: Multiple feature fusion by subspace learning. In: Proceedings of the 2008 International Conference on Content-Based Image and Video Retrieval, pp. 127–134. ACM (2008)
5. Lowe, D.G.: Distinctive image features from scale-invariant keypoints. Int. J. Comput. Vision **60**(2), 91–110 (2004)
6. Ghodrati, A., Jia, X., Pedersoli, M., et al.: Swap retrieval: retrieving images of cats when the query shows a dog. In: Proceedings of the 5th ACM on International Conference on Multimedia Retrieval, pp. 395–402. ACM (2015)
7. Gawande, U., Zaveri, M., Kapur, A.: A novel algorithm for feature level fusion using SVM classifier for multibiometrics-based person identification. Appl. Comput. Intell. Soft Comput. **2013**, 9 (2013)
8. Girshick, R., Donahue, J., Darrell, T., et al.: Rich feature hierarchies for accurate object detection and semantic segmentation. In: Proceedings of the IEEE conference on computer vision and pattern recognition, pp. 580–587 (2014)
9. Hariharan, B., Arbeláez, P., Girshick, R., et al.: Hypercolumns for object segmentation and fine-grained localization. In: Proceedings of the IEEE Conference on Computer Vision and Pattern Recognition, pp. 447–456 (2015)
10. Jia, Y., Shelhamer, E., Donahue, J., et al.: Caffe: Convolutional architecture for fast feature embedding. In: Proceedings of the 22nd ACM International Conference on Multimedia, pp. 675–678. ACM (2014)
11. Krizhevsky, A., Sutskever, I., Hinton, G.E.: ImageNet classification with deep convolutional neural networks. In: Advances in Neural Information Processing Systems, pp. 1097–1105 (2012)
12. Makadia, A.: Feature tracking for wide-baseline image retrieval. In: Daniilidis, K., Maragos, P., Paragios, N. (eds.) ECCV 2010, Part V. LNCS, vol. 6315, pp. 310–323. Springer, Heidelberg (2010). doi:10.1007/978-3-642-15555-0_23
13. Nister, D., Stewenius, H.: Scalable recognition with a vocabulary tree. In: 2006 IEEE Computer Society Conference on Computer Vision and Pattern Recognition (CVPR 2006), vol. 2, pp. 2161–2168. IEEE (2006)
14. Razavian, A.S., Azizpour, H., Sullivan, J., et al.: CNN features off-the-shelf: an astounding baseline for recognition. In: Proceedings of the IEEE Conference on Computer Vision and Pattern Recognition Workshops, pp. 806–813 (2014)
15. Vaca-Castano, G., Shah, M.: Semantic image search from multiple query images. In: Proceedings of the 23rd ACM International Conference on Multimedia, pp. 887–890. ACM (2015)

16. Zhang, S., Yang, M., Cour, T., Yu, K., Metaxas, D.N.: Query specific fusion for image retrieval. In: Fitzgibbon, A., Lazebnik, S., Perona, P., Sato, Y., Schmid, C. (eds.) ECCV 2012, Part II. LNCS, vol. 7573, pp. 660–673. Springer, Heidelberg (2012). doi: 10.1007/978-3-642-33709-3_47

17. Yang, X., Qian, X., Xue, Y.: Scalable mobile image retrieval by exploring contextual saliency. IEEE Trans. Image Proc. 24(6), 1709–1721 (2015)

18. Liu, X., Wang, M., Yin, B.-C., Huet, B., Li, X.: Event-based media enrichment using an adaptive probabilistic hypergraph model. IEEE Trans. Cybern. 45(11), 2461–2471 (2015)

19. Wang, M., Li, W., Liu, D., Ni, B., Shen, J., Yan, S.: Facilitating image search with a scalable and compact semantic mapping. IEEE Trans. Cybern. 45(8), 1561–1574 (2015)

20. Wang, M., Li, G., Lu, Z., Gao, Y., Chua, T.-S.: When Amazon meets Google: product visualization by exploring multiple information sources. ACM Trans. Internet Technol. 12(4), 1–17 (2013). Article 12

21. Wang, M., Gao, Y., Ke, L., Rui, Y.: View-based discriminative probabilistic modeling for 3D object retrieval and recognition. IEEE Trans. Image Proces. 22(4), 1395–1407 (2013)

A Part-Based and Feature Fusion Method for Clothing Classification

Pan Huo, Yunhong Wang, and Qingjie Liu$^{(\boxtimes)}$

State Key Laboratory of Virtual Reality Technology and System,
Beihang University, Beijing 100191, China
huopan0510@163.com, {yhwang,qingjie.liu}@buaa.edu.cn

Abstract. Clothing recognition and parsing have attracted substantial attention in computer vision community, which contribute to applications like scene recognition, event recognition, e-commerce, *etc*. In our work, a part-based and feature fusion method is proposed to classify clothing in natural scenes. Firstly, clothing is described with a part-based model, in which a Deformable Part based Model (DPM) and a key point regression method are used to locate the head-shoulder and human torso. Then, a novel Distinctive Efficient Robust Feature (DERF) and four other low-level features are extracted to represent human clothing. Finally, a feature fusion strategy is utilized to promote the classification performance. Experiments are conducted on a new and well labeled image dataset. The experimental results show the efficiency of our proposed method.

Keywords: Image analysis · Clothing classification · Part-based model · Feature fusion

1 Introduction

Clothing plays an important role in our daily life, which serves much more than covering and warmth. Generally, clothing is tightly associated with social status, wealth, hobby and occupation [1]. Given that, clothing classification can be useful in customer preference analysis, clothing design and fashion analysis. Furthermore, clothing can provide important cues to human identity as a kind of soft biometrics [2]. On this extent, it can contribute to person re-identification and person retrieval in video surveillance and it also provides an explicit clue that can be relevant in social network photo album labeling and specific movie character searching.

Clothing recognition is part of the scene classification task and it is closely tied to human description in images or videos. While there are relatively few attempts on it. Early clothing parsing focused on simply identifying the apparel layers and building a composition template [3] of upper body clothing. Later works started with a super pixel segmentation and features were extracted on the super pixels. The final goal lied in labeling every super pixel. Gallagher and Chen [4] utilized

© Springer International Publishing AG 2016
E. Chen et al. (Eds.): PCM 2016, Part I, LNCS 9916, pp. 231–241, 2016.
DOI: 10.1007/978-3-319-48890-5_23

Fig. 1. Some examples of national clothing images where face detection fails due to standing poses and camera viewpoints.

graph cuts to segment the clothing region and learned a global mask of clothing. Another strand of work [5] which employed segmentation focused on classifying clothing styles and items. More recently, Convolutional Neural Network (CNN) has gained growing interests and researchers make some attempts in clothing parsing. In [6], Zhu *et al.* propose a multi-label convolutional neural network (MLCNN) to predict multiple attributes together in a unified framework.

Most notably, clothing appearance characteristics are in strong correlation with human body parts. In some studies, part-based model has shown evident performance in clothing classification due to its efficiency and robustness to occlusion. The state-of-the-art object detector [7] and poselets detector [8] are frequently utilized to divide clothing region into some parts. Then typical shape, color and texture features are extracted to represent clothing information. The model has been used in clothing attributes recognition [9], clothing styles retrieval [10] and human occupation prediction [11].

In our work, a part-based and feature fusion method is proposed to address the problem. Firstly, we detect head-shoulder region, where a Deformable Part based Model(DPM) detector is utilized. Secondly, considering human body structure, a key points based regression method is employed to locate the torso. Then a new biologically inspired descriptor called DERF [12] is used and combined with other 4 low-level features to represent clothing part. Finally, a feature fusion strategy is utilized to promote the recognition accuracy. Note that we only focus on human upper body, because it contains more subtle clothing information and the lower body is easily to be occluded.

We test the method on a new collected national clothing dataset(NCD), which contains 12 representative specific categories. There are some available clothing datasets, however, the images are not taken naturally and they are collected aiming at specific problems. Some of the challenges on this dataset lie in: (1) In naturally captured pictures, the lack of face limits traditional face detection as is illustrated from Fig. 1. Furthermore, Human pose variations and body accessories like national headgear, kerchief make head or body detection extremely difficult. (2) Clothing in different classes can share similar characteristics like the headgear or haircut, while clothing in the same class display many different appearances on account of deformation, human pose variations and camera viewpoints. This strictly tests the clothing representation approach.

In summary, the contributions of our work are:

(1) An effective and robust part-based and feature fusion method for clothing classification is proposed and it shows good performance on naturally captured images.
(2) A new dataset is collected and annotated as benchmark for specific clothing recognition which will be released to encourage further research in this topic.

The remaining content of this paper is organized as follows. An overview of our method is given in Sect. 2. In Sect. 3, the benchmark dataset is given and our method is evaluated on it. The paper ends with conclusion in Sect. 4.

2 Proposed Method

2.1 Part-Based Body Detection

Locating the body parts is the first step to describe the clothing appearance. However, face detection fails in natural scene images and head detection is virtually impossible due to national head accessary variations. While human head-shoulder part displays a robust shape and structure, which appears to be effective in our problem. A state-of-the-art object detection called DPM [7] is used to train a head-shoulder detector.

To train the detector, we manually labelled 2260 images in the dataset as training samples. With the labeled head-shoulder region, an assumption is made that the training examples are given by positive bounding box P and a set of background images N. P is a set of pairs (I, B) where I is an image and B is a bounding box for an object of class c in I. We randomly sample 2000 images in PASCAL VOC dataset [13] as negative training examples. In addition, a mixture model of three detection components is designed to adapt different image viewpoints, human standing poses and head accessaries. Furthermore, five body key points are labeled, which are located on the top of the head, the left shoulder, the right shoulder, the centered connection points of neck and head and the centered connection points of upper body and lower body. Thus, after head-shoulder detection, an automatic linear regression method is applied to locate the latter two key points based on the first three points.

Some detection results are shown in Fig. 2. We can see, people with different standing poses all can be detected, which demonstrates the effectiveness of our detector in various viewpoints and gestures.

2.2 Distinctive Effective Robust Features

Thereafter, five low-level image descriptors are extracted from the image patches as representations to the mentioned human body parts. We adopt four widely-used image low-level features like HOG, LBP, SIFT, CIELAB color space to represent clothing color and texture feature. Furthermore, we use a novel feature descriptor called DERF, which is derived by modeling the response and distribution properties of the parvocellular-projecting ganglion cells (P-GCs) [14].

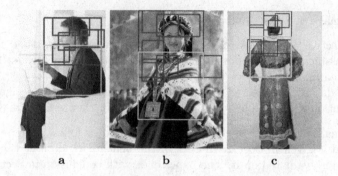

a   b   c

Fig. 2. The Head-shoulder and torso detection results by our detector. The larger red boundingboxes are head-shoulder regions, the smaller blue boxes are filter compositions and the yellow boxes are the torso regions. (Color figure online)

Firstly, The difference of Gaussian function (DoG) is used to convolve gradient maps at grid points close to the center and increases exponentially away from it. Then the grid points are arranged into concentric rings, and the radial distance between the grid points on neighboring rings also increases exponentially. Finally, convolution with a large Gaussian kernel can be obtained from several consecutive convolutions with smaller kernels. The four orientations DERF, eight orientations DERF and multi-scale DERF are shown in Fig. 3. In this paper, multi-scale DERF is employed. More details about DERF can be found in [12].

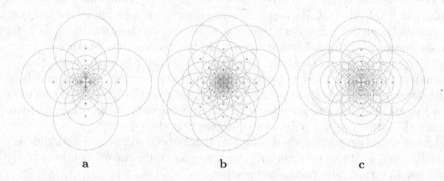

a   b   c

Fig. 3. DERF: Each circle represents a region in which the radius is proportional to the standard deviation of the DoG. By overlapping the regions, we can achieve smooth transition between the regions and obtain a degree of rotational robustness. (a) Four orientations. (b) Eight orientations. (c) Multi-scale DERF descriptor, two neighboring scales are added to each grid point. This structure is also circularly symmetrical and beneficial for tackling rotation [12].

2.3   Part Feature Encoding

Bag of features method has shown good performance in scene classification and image retrieval [15], while it disregards all information of spatial layout of the features. Hence, we use spatial pyramid matching. As introduced in [16], let X and Y be two sets of vectors in a d-dimension feature space. Specifically, if we construct a sequence of grids at resolution $0, ..., L$, such that the grid at level l has 2^l cells along each dimension, for a total of $D = 2^{dl}$ cells. Let H_X^l and H_Y^l denote the histograms of X and Y at l resolution. Then the number of matches at level l is given:

$$I(H_X^l, H_Y^l) = \sum_{i=1}^{D} \min(H_X^l(i), H_Y^l(i)). \tag{1}$$

In the following, $I(H_X^l, H_Y^l)$ is shorted for I^l. The number of new matches in level l is $I^l - I^{l+1}$ when $l = 0, \dots, L-1$. Therefore, the weight associated with level l is set as $\frac{1}{2^{L-l}}$. Thus, the pyramid match kernel is defined as follows:

$$k^L(X, Y) = I^L + \sum_{l=0}^{L-1} \frac{1}{2^{L-l}}(I^l - I^{l+1}) \tag{2}$$

$$= \frac{1}{2^L}I^0 + \sum_{l=1}^{L} \frac{1}{2^{L-l+1}}I^l. \tag{3}$$

However, the pyramid match kernel described above works with an orderless image representation. To solve the problem, all feature vectors are quantized into M discrete types. The final kernels is the sum of the separate channel kernels:

$$K^L(X, Y) = \sum_{m=1}^{M} k^L(X_m, Y_m). \tag{4}$$

2.4   Feature Fusion Based Classification

After feature encoding, five low-level features are extracted from each of the two parts. Thus, there are 10 feature vectors totally. In the classification method, we exploit a weight based feature fusion method. With each feature and a SVM classifier, a vector V is obtained, in which V_i denotes the probability that image I belongs to class i. The probability of each feature can be fused for comprehensive analysis in classification. In our study, a basic weighted sum rule is exploited for each image:

$$S = \sum w_i \cdot F_i \tag{5}$$

where F_i is a class-probability vector for each low-level feature of the two human part, which is normalized to the interval $[0, 1]$. The corresponding weight w_i is calculated dynamically during the online step using the scheme as follows:

$$w_i = \frac{A_i}{\sum_{i=1}^{10} A_i} \tag{6}$$

where A_i denotes the classification accuracy with single low-level feature of each human body part. An human body appearance probability vector is finally obtained in Eq. (5).

3   Experiments

3.1   National Clothing Dataset

To evaluate the proposed method, we collect a new National Clothing Dataset(NCD). NCD comprises of 11 representative national minorities in China. Note that normal clothing are also collected as a comparable clothing category. Two criterions are satisfied in our collected NCD. Firstly, the categories should be informative enough for recognition from images. Secondly, the clothing appearances are multiple for various poses and image viewpoints. A brief statistics of NCD is summarized in Table 1 and some image examples are given in Fig. 4. Note that some of the normal clothing images are borrowed from CCP dataset [17] and it consists of suits, skirts, pants, *etc.* In addition, 4 national minorities only have female clothing. Other images are collected from internet using image search engines of Google and Bing by typing corresponding key words, which contains 3391 images in total. We manually annotate peoples head-shoulder region with bounding box. Five key points are also annotated on human body.

Fig. 4. The collected National Clothing Dataset (NCD), including 12 representative nationalities.

Table 1. A summary of the National Clothing Dataset (NCD).

	Miao	Tibetan	Manchu	Zhuang	Uyghur	Bai	Mongol	Drung	Tu	Korea	Normal	Jino
Total	433	452	355	177	160	159	273	91	133	573	500	85
Male	145	205	135	0	75	0	140	40	0	136	240	0
Female	288	247	200	177	85	159	133	51	133	437	260	85

3.2   Nationality Classification

Experimental Setting. In the experiments, image patches are 16×16 for four features including HOG, SIFT, LBP and color. The overlapping is 8 pixels. Meanwhile the parameters of DERF are fixed as $R = 64, S = 6, T = 8, G = 8, D = 3$. In addition, we evaluate the number of k-means parameter M with each feature. Similarly to [16], it almost has no influence on SIFT and DERF in the range of $100 \sim 500$. While with other features, the best results are obtained when $M = 300$. So, we set $M = 100$ in SIFT and DERF and $M = 300$ for other features.

We also evaluate the pyramid levels L and the results are summarized in Table 2. As can be seen, when $L = 3$ the accuracy achieves the best. When L becomes larger, the runtime is high. Hence, we set $L = 3$.

Table 2. The clothing classification accuracy(%) with different pyramid level number L, features and body parts.

L	Head-Shoulder					Torso				
	DERF	SIFT	HOG	LBP	Color	DERF	SIFT	HOG	LBP	Color
1(1×1)	59.24	54.26	51.87	49.64	56.04	50.37	49.29	46.00	45.47	52.93
2(2×2)	68.76	65.54	61.28	60.83	61.55	58.24	57.46	54.44	56.39	56.04
3(3×3)	**74.38**	**72.56**	**68.12**	**65.81**	**67.50**	**64.36**	**62.97**	**60.48**	**61.46**	**60.12**

Improvement by Feature Fusion. The performance of each feature can be seen in Table 3. It can be found that head-shoulder part works better in classifying the national minority clothing, almost 5 % to 10 % higher than the torso part in classification accuracy. The fact indicates that head-shoulder part is more informative. Among the features, DERF performs the best and SIFT follows.

We also further investigate the feature fusion method. Two fusion strategies are exploited as shown in Table 3. The first fusion strategy (Fusion 1) is feature level fusion. The second fusion strategy (Fusion 2) is part level fusion. From the results, We can see:

(1) Fusion 1 achieves a better performance than any single feature for each part, indicating that each low-level feature extracted from the body is informative.
(2) Fusion 2 enhances the classification performance, demonstrating that both detected parts work in this problem, since the two parts contain effective and complementary information about clothing.

Table 3. The performance of the fusion strategy. The data is nationality classification accuracy of single feature and two fusion methods.

Feature	Head-shoulder	Torso	Fusion 2
Color	67.50 %	60.12 %	**70.34 %**
HOG	68.12 %	60.48 %	**70.43 %**
LBP	65.81 %	61.46 %	**71.58 %**
SIFT	72.56 %	62.97 %	**76.11 %**
DERF	74.38 %	64.36 %	**78.23 %**
Fusion 1	**79.98 %**	**73.94 %**	**83.30 %**

Comparison and Matrix Confusion. In the experiments, NCD is divided into training and testing sets (60 % for training and 40 % for testing). Our method reaches 83.30 % (See Table 4) about 2 % lower than experiments with manually labeled head-body. The fact indicates that head-shoulder detector and key points regression work. We use SPM [16] as baseline method. In regard to the performance, our proposed method surpasses the baseline method [18] more than 4.4 %, which verifies the effectiveness of the method.

Table 4. The classification results. "Auto-detection" means the upper body is detect automatically using the proposed detector. "Manually" means the body parts are labelled manually.

Method	Accuracy
Proposed Method (Auto-detection)	83.30 %
Proposed Method (Manually)	85.26 %
Method [18] (Auto-detection)	78.86 %

We further study the classification results and investigate what extent can different national clothing be separated from each other. The confusion matrix of clothing classification is shown in Fig. 5. From the results, Miao, Mongol, Drung and Uyghur nationalities are most likely to be mistaken as Tibetan nationality. It happens for the high similarity between the clothing styles. Similarly, Tu, Zhuang, Tibetan and Manchu are mostly missed recognized as Miao nationality.

3.3 Gender Classification

Feature Analysis and Fusion. In this subsection, we investigate the performance of five features in clothing classification between different genders. We conduct the experiment on 8 classes, for other classes contain only one gender. The experiment is conducted in a single class to avoid the nationality inter-class disturbance and parameter settings are the same with nationality classification. The results are shown in Table 5, we can see:

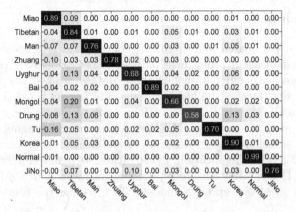

Fig. 5. The confusion matrix of nationality classification. The number of i-th row and j-th column denotes the false alarm rate to j-th class while predicting i-th class.

(1) The gender recognition of Tibetan and Uyghur are about 80 % with single feature, which is significantly inferior to other national minorities. A possible reason lies in that Tibetan and Uyghyr clothing have several different styles which are both suitable for male and female.

(2) The fusion method leads to a better performance than single feature gender classification. It indicates that different features are all informative.

Table 5. The gender classification accuracy(%) inside of 8 national minorities. Five different features are used and the feature fusion results are also shown.

	Miao	Tibetan	Normal	Korea	Manchu	Mongol	Uyghur	Drung
HOG	92.1	78.9	87.7	92.2	91.3	82.5	70.9	80.2
LBP	92.7	73.9	89.5	91.6	91.6	80.3	72.2	80.7
COLOR	92.3	75.1	85.2	91.4	90.1	81.6	74.3	81.3
SIFT	91.8	81.9	89.6	90.6	92.2	84.9	73.5	83.2
DERF	93.4	80.1	90.5	92.7	93.4	85.7	79.8	85.3
Fusion	94.6	82.6	91.2	93.5	94.1	87.2	83.9	87.6

Comparison Experiments. We also compare the proposed method with method [18] in clothing classification between male and female. Note that we compare the overall gender accuracy with in the 8 national minorities. From the results, our proposed method reaches **87.6 %** in classification accuracy which is superior to the method [18] (**82.2 %**) by **5.4 %**. This fact validates the efficiency of our proposed method in clothing recognition between different genders.

4   Conclusion

In this paper, a part-based and feature fusion method is proposed to address the clothing classification problem in natural scenes. Moreover, the method is tested on a new collected national clothing dataset and shows its efficiency. Our algorithm first locates the head-shoulder and human torso. Then multiple features such as DERF, SIFT, HOG, LBP and color features are extracted from the two body parts. Especially, DERF shows more encouraging results than others. Finally, a fusion strategy is employed and achieves a promising results in nationality and gender classification. In the future, we plan to further explore the possibility to (1) use other feature representation method to study the details of the clothing such as deep CNN models. (2) Consider the context and scene information.

Acknowledgments. The work is supported by the Hong Kong, Macao and Taiwan Science and Technology Cooperation Program of China (No. L2015TGA9004).

References

1. Yamaguchi, K., Hadi Kiapour, M., Ortiz, L.E., Berg, T.L.: Retrieving similar styles to parse clothing. TPAMI **37**(5), 1028–1040 (2015)
2. Moctezuma, D., Conde, C., Diego, I.M.D., Cabello, E.: Soft-biometrics evaluation for people re-identification in uncontrolled multi-camera environments. EURASIP J. Image Video Process. **2015**(1), 1–20 (2015)
3. Borràs, A., Tous, F., Lladós, J., Vanrell, M.: High-level clothes description based on colour-texture and structural features. In: Perales, F.J., Campilho, A.J.C., Blanca, N.P., Sanfeliu, A. (eds.) IbPRIA 2003. LNCS, vol. 2652, pp. 108–116. Springer, Heidelberg (2003). doi:10.1007/978-3-540-44871-6_13
4. Gallagher, A.C., Chen, T.: Clothing cosegmentation for recognizing people. In: CVPR, pp. 1–8. IEEE (2008)
5. Yamaguchi, K., Hadi Kiapour, M., Ortiz, L.E., Berg, T.L.: Parsing clothing in fashion photographs. In: CVPR, pp. 3570–3577. IEEE (2012)
6. Zhu, J., Liao, S., Yi, D., Lei, Z., Li, S.Z.: Multi-label cnn based pedestrian attribute learning for soft biometrics. In: ICB, pp. 535–540. IEEE (2015)
7. Felzenszwalb, P.F., Girshick, R.B., McAllester, D., Ramanan, D.: Object detection with discriminatively trained part-based models. TPAMI **32**(9), 1627–1645 (2010)
8. Bourdev, L., Malik, J.: Poselets: body part detectors trained using 3d human pose annotations. In: ICCV, pp. 1365–1372. IEEE (2009)
9. Bourdev, L., Maji, S., Malik, J.: Describing people: a poselet-based approach to attribute classification. In: ICCV, pp. 1543–1550. IEEE (2011)
10. Bossard, L., Dantone, M., Leistner, C., Wengert, C., Quack, T., Gool, L.: Apparel classification with style. In: Lee, K.M., Matsushita, Y., Rehg, J.M., Hu, Z. (eds.) ACCV 2012. LNCS, vol. 7727, pp. 321–335. Springer, Heidelberg (2013). doi:10.1007/978-3-642-37447-0_25
11. Song, Z., Wang, M., Hua, X., Yan, S.: Predicting occupation via human clothing and contexts. In: ICCV, pp. 1084–1091. IEEE (2011)
12. Weng, D., Wang, Y., Gong, M., Tao, D., Wei, H., Huang, D.: Derf: distinctive efficient robust features from the biological modeling of the p ganglion cells. TIP **24**(8), 2287–2302 (2015)

13. Everingham, M., Van Gool, L., Williams, C.K., Winn, J., Zisserman, A.: The pascal visual object classes (voc) challenge. IJCV **88**(2), 303–338 (2010)
14. Li, C.-Y., Zhou, Y.-X., Pei, X., Qiu, F.-T., Tang, C.-Q., Xu, X.-Z.: Extensive disinhibitory region beyond the classical receptive field of cat retinal ganglion cells. Vis. Res. **32**(2), 219–228 (1992)
15. Li, F.-F., Perona, P.: A bayesian hierarchical model for learning natural scene categories. In: CVPR, vol. 2, pp. 524–531. IEEE (2005)
16. Lazebnik, S., Schmid, C., Ponce, J.: Beyond bags of features: Spatial pyramid matching for recognizing natural scene categories. In: CVPR, vol. 2, pp. 2169–2178. IEEE (2006)
17. Yang, W., Luo, P., Lin, L.: Clothing co-parsing by joint image segmentation and labeling. In: CVPR, IEEE (2013)
18. Grauman, K., Darrell, T.: The pyramid match kernel: discriminative classification with sets of image features. In: ICCV, vol. 2, pp. 1458–1465. IEEE (2005)

Research on Perception Sensitivity of Elevation Angle in 3D Sound Field

Yafei Wu[1,3], Xiaochen Wang[4,5(✉)], Cheng Yang[2,3], Ge Gao[1,2], and Wei Chen[2]

[1] State Key Laboratory of Software Engineering, Wuhan University, Wuhan, China
yafee_wu@163.com, gaoge@whu.edu.cn
[2] National Engineering Research Center for Multimedia Software,
Computer School of Wuhan University, Wuhan, China
yangcheng41506@126.com, erhuchen@163.com
[3] Research Institute of Wuhan University in Shenzhen, Shenzhen, China
[4] Department of Electrical and Computer Engineering,
George Mason University, Fairfax, USA
clowang@163.com
[5] Collaborative Innovation Center of Geospatial Technology, Wuhan, China

Abstract. The development of virtual reality and three-dimensional (3D) video inspired the concern about 3D audio, 3D audio aims at reconstructing the spatial information of original signals, the spatial perception sensitivity and minimum audible angle (MAA) would help to improve the accuracy of reconstructing signals. The measurements and analysis of MAA thresholds are limited to the azimuth angle at present, lacking of elevation angles quantitative analyzing, it is unable to build the complete spatial perception model of 3D sound field, which could be used in accurate 3D sound field reconstruction. In order to study the perception sensitivity of elevation angle at different locations in 3D sound field, subjective listening tests were conducted, elevation minimum audible angle (EMAA) thresholds at 144 different locations in 3D sound field were tested. The tests were referred to the quantitative analysis of azimuth minimum audible angle (AMAA) thresholds of human ear, based on psychoacoustic model and manikin. The results show that the EMAA thresholds have obvious dependence on elevation angle, thresholds vary between 3° and 30°, reach the minimum value at the ear plane (elevation angle: 0°), increase proportional linearly as the elevation angle departs from the ear plane and reach a relative maximum value on both sides (elevation angle: −30° and 90°). Besides, the EMAA thresholds are dependent upon azimuth angle too, thresholds reach the minimum value around median plane (azimuth angle: 0°).

Keywords: Three-dimensional sound field · Minimum audible angle · Manikin · Elevation minimum audible angle · Elevation angle

The research was supported by National High Technology Research and Development Program of China (863 Program, No. 2015AA016306); National Nature Science Foundation of China (No. 61231015); National Nature Science Foundation of China (No. 61471271); Science and Technology Plan Projects of Shenzhen (No. ZDSYS2014050916575763).

© Springer International Publishing AG 2016
E. Chen et al. (Eds.): PCM 2016, Part I, LNCS 9916, pp. 242–249, 2016.
DOI: 10.1007/978-3-319-48890-5_24

1   Introduction

In the real acoustic environments, all signals perceived through human ears have their own locations (azimuth angle, elevation angle and distance). As a sound source changes its location in the three-dimensional (3D) sound field, humans are able to perceive the changes of location. The change could convert to the angle threshold which is called minimum audible angle (MAA) [1]. If the angle difference between virtual and original sound source is less than MAA, the reconstruction of the virtual sound source is considered to be accurate, because the difference is imperceptible. Here is a widely used way [2–5] for 3D sound field reconstruction: researchers collect signals at different locations in 3D sound field at first, explore the transfer functions between original and collected signals, and finally process other signals based on the functions.

The MAA has much dependence on locations, which should be taken into consideration when collecting and reconstructing signals in 3D sound field. For example, the widely used CIPIC head-related transfer functions (HRTF) database, which includes head-related impulse responses at 25 different azimuths and 50 different elevations at approximately 5 angular increments. There may exist errors in the CIPIC HRTF database because it ignored the fact that MAA varies with location.

The MAA-related work has begun for a long time, a large number of scholars measured and analyzed the MAA thresholds in the horizontal plane, and built the spatial perception model by reference to azimuth minimum audible angle (AMAA) thresholds, the model provided powerful data support for the reconstruction of two-dimensional (2D) sound field. Stevens [6] conducted objective listening tests about location sensitivity in 1936, and tested AMAA thresholds for different azimuth angles ($0°$, $15°$, $30°$, $45°$, $60°$, $75°$, $90°$), types, frequencies and intensities. The results showed that the ability to localize signals varies markedly with frequency, the relation between the azimuth angle of the signal and the error of localization is approximately the same for both high and low frequency, and it is the smallest near the median plane. Perrott [7] conducted listening tests for different orientations of the array of signals in 1990, tests were conducted with signals distributed on horizontal ($0°$), vertical ($90°$) and oblique planes ($10°$, $20°$, $30°$, $40°$, $50°$, $60°$, $70°$, $80°$) in the front region, and the results showed that the mean MAA thresholds are the smallest ($0.97°$) at the horizontal plane and the biggest ($3.65°$) at the vertical plane. In 2003, MAA thresholds and minimum audible movement angle (MAMA) were measured in horizontal, vertical and diagonal ($60°$) planes, Grantham [8] recorded signals through KEMARs ears and played them back to subjects through inserted earphones, and his results were similar in magnitude and pattern to those reported by Perrott. In 2009, Barreto [9] tested AMAA thresholds at different horizontal planes, the results showed that thresholds are related to the elevation angle and it nearly reaches the minimum value near the ear plane. On the basis of Barretos works, Wang [10] conducted further measurements in 2013, collected signals around the KEMARs manikin at 5 different horizontal planes and designed a program to test the AMAA thresholds. He suggested that the thresholds vary with both azimuth and elevation angle, and the drawn diagrams showed that the thresholds are the smallest at the front region (where azimuth and elevation angle are both 0°) and increase proportional linearly as the locations depart from this point.

Stereo-based 3D audio technology was used in the past to reconstruct spatial information, an important limitation was the spatial resolution, especially on elevation angle. A complete 3D spatial perception model (which includes EMAA and AMAA thresholds) could help to improve this situation, but few people are engaged in the EMAA-related measurement and analysis work at present. Here we proposed an experiment to measure EMAA thresholds at different locations in 3D sound field, draw the EMAA diagrams and surface, and analyze the changing rules of elevation angle perception sensitivity. Those results may be valuable to help to build the complete 3D spatial perception model, and could be used in virtual sound source processing as well.

2   Method

We conducted the experiments by reference to the widely used EMAA thresholds measurement method, collected signals with KEMAR's manikin at different locations in 3D sound field, implemented the testing program based on psychoacoustic model. The subjects were tested with headphones, and the results were analyzed with statistical analysis method.

17 graduates participated in our tests, 14 of them passed the primary tsets (8 mail and 6 female). All the subjects had repeatedly experiences in subjective listing tests, and their age ranged between 22 to 27.

2.1   Signals

We chose Gaussian white noise as the original signal, which doesn't have strict periodicity, this kind of property could effectively reduce the cone of confusion, and Grantham [8] chose it as testing signal in early studies. Signals were collected by microphones at the positions of manikin's ear canals, the intensity near the manikin's ear was about 70-dB, the collecting devices have been shown as Fig. 1. All signals were sampled at 48-kHz sampling rate, digitized at 16-bit, low-pass filtered at 20-kHz. Liang [11] suggested that signals with 640-ms duration are the most easy to be remembered, our testing signals lasts for 640-ms.

The collecting devices were built in an anechoic room, signals at different locations were collected in 3D sound field. The early studies have explained that sensitivity of human's left and right ears is approximately symmetrical, and it is more sensitive in the front area, so we selected 8 vertical planes heterogeneity (whose azimuth angles are 0°, 15°, 35°, 60°, 90°, 120°, 150°, 180°). The collecting signals heterogeneous located in edge of each vertical plane, the elevation angles ranged from −30° to 90°. We collected 831 points in the right part of the 3D sound field to build a testing signal database and took 144 points among them to be the testing signals. The locations of collecting and testing signals have been shown as Fig. 2.

Fig. 1. Signals collecting devices.

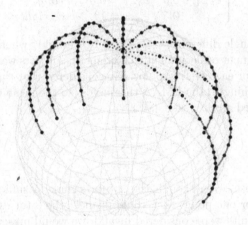

Fig. 2. Locations of collecting and testing signals, (Red) collecting points, (Blue) testing points. (Color figure online)

2.2   Procedure

The testing program was designed by reference to two-alternative forced-choice (TFAC) and 1 up/2 down method, subjects conducted listening tests with headphones. 144 testing points were divided into 24 groups, each group included 5 to 7 points and it took about 15 to 30 min to finish a set of tests. We found 17 subjects to take part in the tests, they are graduated student with age in 22 to 25, most of them engaged in audio research. 14 of them passed the listening screening and finally finished the tests.

During the tests, subjects would hear 2 signals (testing and reference signals) with 500-ms time difference, they were forced to make a choice about which signal's location sounds lower. The 2 signals were played in a random order, and the order changed randomly after every judgement. The default angle difference (ε_n) between the testing (α) and reference (β) points was 8°, which increases when subjects make the wrong choice, remains constant when subjects make 1 times right choice, and decreases when subjects make 2 times consecutive right choices.

$$\beta = \alpha + \varepsilon_n \tag{1}$$

$$\varepsilon_n = \begin{cases} 8° & n = 0 \\ \varepsilon_{n-1} & once\ right \\ \varepsilon_{n-1} + 2° & \varepsilon_{n-1} \geq 2°,\ wrong \\ \varepsilon_{n-1} - 2° & \varepsilon_{n-1} > 2°,\ twice\ right \\ \varepsilon_{n-1} + 1° & 2° > \varepsilon_{n-1} \geq 1°,\ wrong \\ \varepsilon_{n-1} - 1° & 2° \geq \varepsilon_{n-1} > 1°,\ twice\ right \\ \varepsilon_{n-1} + 0.5° & \varepsilon_{n-1} = 0.5°,\ wrong \\ 0.5° & \varepsilon_{n-1} = 1°,\ twice\ right \end{cases} \tag{2}$$

We called the angle difference ($\varepsilon^m{}_n$) "turn threshold" when it changed from increment to decrement or decrement to increment, subjects were forced to make 9 turn thresholds for each testing point. We considered that the previous 5 turn thresholds are reaching to the EMAA thresholds, so the mean of the last 4 turn thresholds was saved as the result ($\overline{\varepsilon^m}$).

$$\varepsilon^m{}_n = \frac{1}{4} \sum_{n=5}^{9} \varepsilon^m{}_n \tag{3}$$

In the worst case, even though the subjects make a sufficient number (70 times) of choices for one point, they couldn't meet the 9 turn thresholds. As to these cases, the results were considered invalid, we would present the processing method in next part.

2.3   Processing

All subjects conducted the listening tests with headphones, the inside-the-head effect and the cone of confusion [13] would impact the results during the tests. Take the errors into account, it is necessary to screen the obtained results. We got rid of the few outliers by observing the changing trend of adjacent points results, then interpolated the missing data through statistical analysis method. EMAA thresholds of several adjacent points on a vertical plane could be approximately represented as a curve, their intrinsic relations could be expressed as a mathematical function. We chose Lagrange Interpolation method (LIM) [14] to interpolate the missing data (Fig. 3).

As is shown above, points A, B, C, D are original results, it is obvious that point C was invalid. We used LIM to get the curve expression ($f(x)$) based on points A, B and D, and Point L ($f(x_3)$) was interpolated with its elevation angel (x_3). The formulas have been shown below.

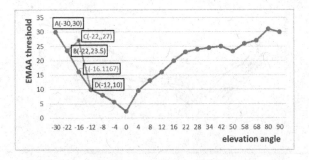

Fig. 3. Outlier screening and imputation example

$$A : (x_0, y_0) \ B : (x_1, y_1) \ C : (x_2, y_2) \ D : (x_3, y_3) \tag{4}$$

$$f(x) = \frac{(x - x_1)(x - x_2)}{(x_0 - x_1)(x_0 - x_2)} y_0 + \frac{(x - x_0)(x - x_2)}{(x_1 - x_0)(x_1 - x_2)} y_1 + \frac{(x - x_0)(x - x_1)}{(x_2 - x_1)(x_2 - x_0)} y_2 \tag{5}$$

$$y_3 = f(x_3) \tag{6}$$

3   Result

Different subjects have different audible perception sensitive areas, but the changing trends of the EMAA thresholds were nearly consistent. 14 groups results were processed and we took the mean values as the EMAA thresholds, EMAA diagrams and surface were drawn to help to analysis the rules.

3.1   EMAA Diagrams

As is shown in Fig. 4, EMAA thresholds have obvious dependence on elevation angle, the thresholds vary between 3° and 30°, reach the minimum value near the ear plane (elevation angle: 0°) and reach a relative maximum value on both sides (elevation angles: −30° and 90°). The thresholds proportional increase linearly as the elevation angles depart from the ear plane, they change dramatically between −30° and 30° and tend to be stable upper 30°. The 8 diagrams present that human ear is more sensitive when the signals locate near the ear plane, and the sensitivity would decrease as the signals leaving the ear plane.

For human ear, internal time difference (ITD) and internal level difference (ILD) are the main factors that affect the azimuth location [15], but these factors could not be used to analyze EMAA thresholds directly. As to the median plane (azimuth angle: 0°), it's obvious that the ITD and ILD of every point are nearly the same, but their EMAA thresholds are different with elevation angles. This phenomenon was interesting and we tried to explain it with visual characteristics and the internal structure of human head, the conjecture need further discussions.

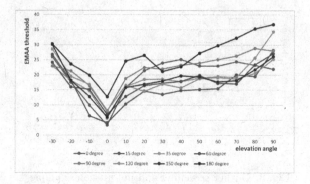

Fig. 4. EMAA diagrams in different vertical planes.

3.2 EMAA Surface

As is shown in Fig. 5, cubic spline interpolating function was used to draw the EMAA surface. EMAA thresholds have dependence on both elevation and azimuth angles, but the impact factor of azimuth angle is smaller than that of elevation angle. The changing trends of the thresholds change several times with azimuth angle. The thresholds reach the maximum values when the azimuth angle is about 90° and 180°. The surface presented that human ear is more sensitive when the signals locate in the front and posterolateral areas.

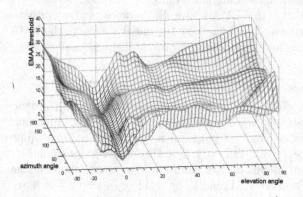

Fig. 5. EMAA surface.

4   Conclusion

We present the subjective listening tests for measuring and analyzing EMAA thresholds in 3D sound space, the tests were based on psychoacoustic model and manikin. The results show that EMAA thresholds have dependence on both azimuth and elevation angles, the thresholds vary between 3° and 30°. In the vertical plane, human ear is more sensitive when the signals locate near the ear plane, and the sensitivity decreases when signals depart from the ear plane. In the horizontal plane, human ear is more sensitive when the signals locate in the front and posterolateral area, and the sensitivity decreases when signals depart from these areas.

We cannot avoid errors during collecting signals and conducting subjective listening tests with headphones. For further study, we prepare to conduct listening tests that subjects sit in the center of the 3D sound space, and make choices directly. The tests would take much more time to avoid the unnecessary errors. The detailed measurements process and analyzed results will be presented in the future works.

References

1. Mills, A.W.: On the minimum audible angle. J. Acoust. Soc. Am. **30**(4), 237–246 (1958)
2. Gardner, W.G., Martin, K.D.: HRTF measurements of a KEMAR dummy-head microphone. J. Acoust. Soc. Am. **97**(6), 3907–3908 (1995)
3. Algazi, V.R., Duda, R.O., Thompson, D.M., et al.: The CIPIC HRTF database. In: IEEE Workshop on the Applications of Signal Processing to Audio and Acoustics, 2001, pp. 99–102. IEEE (2001)
4. Bertet, S., Daniel, J., Moreau, S.: 3D sound field recording with higher order ambisonics-objective measurements and validation of a 4th order spherical microphone. In: Audio Engineering Society Convention 120. Audio Engineering Society (2006)
5. Ward, D.B., Abhayapala, T.D.: Reproduction of a plane-wave sound field using an array of loudspeakers. IEEE Trans. Speech Audio Process. **9**(6), 697–707 (2001)
6. Stevens, S.S., Newman, E.B.: The localization of actual sources of sound. Am. J. Psychol. **48**, 297–306 (1936)
7. Perrott, D.R., Saberi, K.: Minimum audible angle thresholds for sources varying in both elevation and azimuth. J. Acoust. Soc. Am. **87**(4), 1728–1731 (1990)
8. Grantham, D.W., Hornsby, B.W.Y., Erpenbeck, E.A.: Auditory spatial resolution in horizontal, vertical and diagonal planes. J. Acoust. Soc. Am. **114**(2), 1009–1022 (2003)
9. Barreto, A., Faller, K.J., Adjouadi, M.: 3D sound for human-computer interaction: regions with different limitations in elevation localization. In: Proceedings of the 11th International ACMSIGACCESS Conference on Computers and Accessibility, pp. 211–212. ACM (2009)
10. Heng, W.: Research on perception characteristics of spatial cues in 3D audio. Wuhan University (2013)
11. Zhian, L., Qionghua, Y., Huaying, L.: Sound source location and discriminating threshold. Chin. J. Acoust. **3**(1), 27–34 (1966)
12. Shuixian, C., Ruimin, H., Yutian, L., et al.: Frequency dependence of spatial cues and its implication in spatial stereo coding. In: International Conference on Computer Science and Software Engineering, 2008, vol. 4, pp. 1066–1069. IEEE (2008)
13. Blauert, J.: Spatial Hearing: The Psychophysics of Human Sound Localization. MIT press, Cambridge (1997)
14. Little, R.J.A., Rubin, D.B.: Statistical Analysis with Missing Data. Wiley, New York (2014)
15. Pulkki, V., Karjalainen, M.: Localization of amplitude-panned virtual sources I: stereophonic panning. J. Audio Eng. Soc. **49**(9), 739–752 (2001)

Tri-level Combination for Image Representation

Ruiying Li[1], Chunjie Zhang[1,2(✉)], and Qingming Huang[1,2,3(✉)]

[1] School of Computer and Control Engineering,
University of Chinese Academy of Sciences, Beijing, China
{ruiying.li,chunjie.zhang,qingming.huang}@vipl.ict.ac.cn
[2] Key Laboratory of Big Data Mining and Knowledge Management,
Chinese Academy of Sciences, Beijing, China
[3] Key Laboratory of Intelligent Information Processing,
Institute of Computing Technology, Chinese Academy of Sciences, Beijing, China

Abstract. The context of objects can provide auxiliary discrimination beyond objects. However, this effective information has not been fully explored. In this paper, we propose Tri-level Combination for Image Representation (TriCoIR) to solve the problem at three different levels: object intrinsic, strongly-related context and weakly-related context. Object intrinsic excludes external disturbances and more focuses on the objects themselves. Strongly-related context is cropped from the input image with a more loose bound to contain surrounding context. Weakly-related one is recovered from the image other than object for global context. First, strongly and weakly-related context are constructed from input images. Second, we make cascade transformations for more intrinsical object information, which depends on the consistency between generated global context and input images in the regions other than object. Finally, a joint representation is acquired based on these three level features. The experiments on two benchmark datasets prove the effectiveness of TriCoIR.

Keywords: Image representation · Object categorization · Intrinsic and Context

1 Introduction

Object categorization has stimulated many researches in areas of feature extraction and image representation. Sometimes the information produced by objects themselves provides enough discrimination to unambiguously categorize the objects, which we call object-centered. Chai *et al.* [1] automatically segment out the most class-discriminative foregrounds for each image and ultimately use those foreground segmentations for the categorization system. They demonstrated that accurately segmenting objects from images could directly translate into an increase in accuracy of categorization task. These object-centered representations use exclusive object intrinsic features for performing visual tasks. Under such conditions, the visual categorization could relay exclusively on intrinsic object features and ignore any other information.

© Springer International Publishing AG 2016
E. Chen et al. (Eds.): PCM 2016, Part I, LNCS 9916, pp. 250–259, 2016.
DOI: 10.1007/978-3-319-48890-5_25

Fig. 1. Images from two different categories. Purely relaying on flowers themselves but ignoring the root and stem, the red/dashed could be classified as one class. But in fact, the left represents colts' foot and the right red/solid is dandelions. It is best viewed in color. (Color figure online)

However, sometimes purely object-centered representations are not enough for the reliable object categorization performance, as the Fig. 1 illustrates. Usually, the objects may only occupy a portion of the images, so context information introduced by the rest area of the image should be well utilized. Besides, there are strong relationships between the context and the objects themselves in the real world. For example, given the picture sky, what we think about is a bird rather than car; conversely, if we are given the road, the first flashed in our mind is the car instead of bird. Different parts of images should serve different roles for the categorization. The object intrinsic of course plays a key factor, while other information is also helpful for the categorization process. Even when objects can be identified via intrinsic information, context information can simplify the object discrimination based on the locations and features that need to be considered.

In the light of all these evidence, it is natural to investigate the combination of context information and the objects themselves for better categorization performance. Moreover, deep convolutional neural networks (CNNs) have gained tremendous attention due to powerful performance in 2012 Large Scale Visual Recognition Challenge (ILSVRC) [2]. The structure of CNNs simulates the human perception system, which can learn more discriminative features than hand-designed low-level features. There is no doubt that CNNs is the preferred feature extraction system.

In this paper, with the support of deep features, We propose a method called TriCoIR for Tri-level Combination for Image Representation, which respectively correspond to object intrinsic, strongly-related context and weakly-related

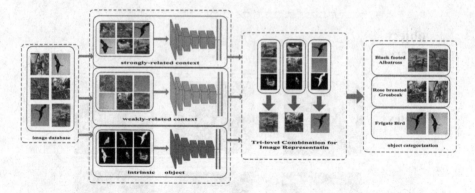

Fig. 2. An illustration of the modules for TriCoIR. With the effective combination of intrinsic object, strongly-related context and weakly-related context, the joint image representation is discriminative for categorization.

context. Our goal here is to use such a scheme to combine object intrinsic with sufficient context in object representations and to demonstrate their roles in facilitating individual object categorization. Figure 2 shows the framework of our method TriCoIR. First, we process the input image for strongly-related and weakly-related context. Second, a binary image is converted from the input based on the regions whether contain the object or not. In order to exclude external disturbances, we continue to translate the binary for a more discriminative object intrinsic. Finally, these three level features are combined for joint image representation. The effectiveness of TriCoIR is verified for high level object categorization. The accuracy results on various datasets are promising and outperform over many baseline methods.

2 Related Work

Categorizing objects in an image requires to combine many different signals from the raw image data. There are strong relationships between the context and the objects themselves in the real world. Visual system makes extensive use of these relationships for facilitating different visual tasks, suggesting that it usually first processes context information in order to index object properties. Sometimes the analysis of intrinsic object information alone cannot yield very reliable results. In such circumstances, available context appears to play a major role in enhancing the reliability of categorization.

The role of context in object categorization has become an important topic due to the psychological basis of context in the human visual system [3]. It is essential to make use of contextual information for visual categorization. Heitz and Koller [4] showed that spatial context information is useful for detecting objects. Galleguillos *et al.* [5] proposed an algorithm that uses spatial context information in image categorization. They pointed out that semantically important contexts, such as object co-occurrence, and particular object spatial relations are helpful for image categorization. Further, Nguyen *et al.* [6] and Bilen *et al.* [7] explicitly mentioned that some degree of context information(like road for cars) needs to be included into the detected object bounding box for better performance. The context information described in these papers is strongly-related context we proposed. Strongly-related context can provide more relevant information for the categorization of an object, particularly when there are strong similarities among different objects.

What we consider another is weakly-related context, which can be regarded as global information. It has been proved in [8] that the global context can often provide valuable discrimination for representation. Russakovsky *et al.* [9] first inferred that the location of the object of interest and then pooled low level features separately in the foreground and background to form the image-level representation. The background could be regarded as the weakly-related context. They proved that the foreground-background feature representation would provide more stronger performance than its foreground-only counterpart. So effective modeling to this weakly-related context is necessary for better categorization performance, which could contain important cues to support the discrimination.

Recently, the revival of interest has turned to CNNs, which is triggered by the theory of CNNs can learn rich mid-level image representations. A fundamental issue with these methods is how to generate an image representation from CNNs. Some methods [10,11] directly trained a convolutional network on input raw image data and extracted deep features from object level representation. We make cascade transformations to the input image in order to avoid the interference caused by disturbing factors. We hope to capture a more expressive representation from the translated object intrinsic.

3   Tri-level Combination for Image Representation

We have generated a full wish list of the joint representation between the intrinsic object and context information. In designing our approach, besides the objects themselves, we construct the strongly-related context and weakly-related one which could be reliably learned given the available image. Also, in order to get a more intrinsical object information, we make a translation to the input image. Based on these correlated and sufficient information, we can learn a discriminative image representation for various applications. Figure 2 clearly shows our modules for image representation.

Before we set forth our method, we make some definitions for the symbols that would be used later. I represents the input image and I_o is the object. I_c is the corresponding context, which consists of strongly-related one I_s and weakly-related one I_w. In addition, we use the I_i to denote the translated intrinsic object.

3.1   Context Extracting and Construction

Usually, the objects I_o may only occupy a portion of the images. In order to obtain better discrimination, context information in the rest area of images

Fig. 3. Example images in CUB 200.

Fig. 4. Example images in flower 17.

should be well utilized. We mainly consider two aspects: one is the strongly-related context I_s and the other is the weakly-related one I_w, as Figs. 3 and 4 show.

Strongly-related context can provide us with abundant semantic information. For example, a car drives on the road, a sofa is indoors, etc. This kind of co-occurrence is helpful for effectively recognizing objects. We try to retain the co-occurrence and represent it as one kind of image features.

We cut image with a loose bound to retain the object and contain correlated context information, which highlights the object itself, but reserves some strongly-related context information at the same time.

Weakly-related context and object often have strong relationships in the real word. Different objects often appear in different scenes. For example, a car could not appear in the sky or the sea. Capturing this specific global context can further improve the discrimination.

We cut image with a more tight bound to separate the object from background, but here the incomplete image without object is what we retain. Then we adopt a technique called "inpainting" to recover the weakly-related context from the damaged background image.

3.2   Intrinsic Modeling and Representation

Even though we emphasize that the context information I_c is helpful for object categorization, the object I_o still plays the key role. Considering we have extracted sufficient context in the Sect. 3.1; this section the focus is shifted to the object itself. Instead of discretely applying the input image I or the object image I_o, we make use of the previous I_s and I_w to translate another intrinsic image I_i.

Due to the influence of camera, shooting and other factors in the photographic process, there exists unpredictable noise in the image. What we need is the more expressive representation for identified image. In order to avoid disturbance and capture a more intrinsical object information, we make cascade transformations to the image I.

First, we construct a binary conversion to the original image I, which means translating I to a binary image, we call it I_b.

$$I_b^{ij} = \begin{cases} 255, & if \quad I^{ij} \in R_o \\ 0, & if \quad I^{ij} \notin R_o \end{cases} \tag{1}$$

R_o is the region that consists of the object. The result I_b removes all the background information, but it is so coarse that can just depict the outline of the object. Next we continue to translate for a more finer intrinsic information.

The second transformation is defined as Eq. 2 shows:

$$I_i = I_b + I_w - I \tag{2}$$

I_w is the recovered from the image I which cut out the region R_o. It should have the same disturbance as the image I other than R_o. I_b retains the outline region about the object. The difference avoids the interference outside and more focuses on the intrinsic of object itself.

3.3   Multiple Fusing and Categorization

So far, we have got both strongly and weakly-related context besides more intrinsical object information. We hope to learn discriminative representation for the input image.

CNNs have gained a huge success in a wide range of fields. It can extract more effective feature than hand-crafted descriptors. We apply the widely used Caffe [12] framework as our reference, copy the original parameter trained in tremendous databases, and separately retrain three more targeted networks for I_s, I_w and I_i. We use the combination of these three level deep features for our joint image representation.

In order to verify the effectiveness of our method, we apply TriCoIR on high-level visual categorization task. Given t labeled images $(x_i, y_i)_{i=1}^{t}$, where x_i denotes the ith image and $y_i \in \{1, 2, \ldots, t\}$ is its label. Each sample x_i is consisted of three kinds of deep features learned from I_s, I_w and I_i. We aim to learn a mapping model from x_i to y_i.

Support vector machine (SVM) is a classical classifier which is based on maximization of the margin around the hyperplane $w^T x + b$ that separates samples of the different classes. The maximization of the margin is defined as:

$$\{\omega^*, b^*, \xi^*\} = \arg\min_{\omega, b, \xi} \frac{1}{2}\|\omega\|^2 + C\sum_{i=1}^{m} \xi_i$$

$$s.t. \quad y_i(\omega^T x_i + b) \geq 1 - \xi_i, \xi_i \geq 0, \tag{3}$$

In this soft-margin SVM, ξ_i is a penalty for misclassification or classification within the margin. Parameter C sets the weight of this penalty. We classify the images to category with the highest probability.

4   Experiment

In this section, we construct experiments to verify the effectiveness of TriCoIR for object categorization. We apply the proposed approach for visual categorization on two datasets, *e.g.* Caltech-UCSD Birds 200 [13], *i.e.* CUB 200, and the Oxford Flowers 17 [14], *i.e.* Flower 17. We use the top fully connected layer of the retrained network as our feature vectors, which is 4096 dimensions. Three 4096-D feature vectors are extracted for I_s, I_w and I_i, and then are combined for the joint image representation.

4.1   CUB 200

CUB 200 is a dataset that contains 11,788 images of 200 bird subordinates. 5994 images are used for training and 5794 for testing. Many of the species in CUB 200 exhibit extremely subtle differences. It is sometimes even hard for humans to distinguish because of the large intra-class variance and small inter-class one. Figure 3 respectively shows the input image and the three level images on the CUB 200. Table 1 reports the result of TriCoIR compared to other performing baselines on this dataset.

Sift+Color+SVM in the Table 1 represents a combination of traditional feature extractor and classifier. Our accuracy is much better at a large margin by 61.43 % vs 17.30 %. This implies the effectiveness of our tri-level deep features. Another method BubbleBank [18] learns attributes, parts and object detectors, and then uses their responses for classification. Compared to BubbleBank, TriCoIR takes more consideration on the context information and intrinsic feature extraction. Random Forest proposed by Yao *et al.* [15] makes use of bounding box to let each tree node learn the location of the most discriminative features. Information of different locations is then pulled together for the final decision. They take into fully account the intrinsic of object but ignore the related context information, which results in a drop in performance.

TriCoIR makes full use of context information and further makes a reasonable modeling on intrinsic object. With the combination of tri-level deep features, we acquire a discriminative image representation and verify the effectiveness as Table 1 shows.

Table 1. Categorization result in CUB 200

Method	Mean accuracy (%)
Sift+Color+SVM [13]	17.30
Random Forest [15]	19.20
Hierarchical Matching [16]	19.20
Multi-cue [17]	22.40
TriCos [1]	26.70
BubbleBank [18]	32.80
Kernel Descriptors [19]	42.53
Template matching [20]	43.67
Deformable Part Descriptors [21]	51.00
TriCoIR	**61.43**

4.2 Flower 17

Flower 17 is a database of 17 categories with 80 flower images per category. The dataset is made of 3 predefined random splits and each split consists in 3 sets: training (40 images per class), validation (20 images per class) and test (20 images per class). There are both large intra-category variance owing to appearance variations and small inter-category variance owing to partial appearance similarities between categories. Figure 4 illustrates the different level images on this dataset.

Table 2 shows the results of different methods on the flower 17 dataset. It is worth mentioning that although using the representation in this paper leads to

Table 2. Categorization result in Flower 17

Method	Mean accuracy (%)
CG-Boost [22]	84.8
Multiple Kernel Learning (avg) [22]	84.9
Multiple Kernel Learning (SILP) [22]	85.2
Multiple Kernel Learning (Simple) [22]	85.2
Linear Programming-B [22]	85.4
Multiple Kernel Learning (prod) [22]	85.5
Augmented Kernel Matrix [23]	86.67
Multiple Kernel Learning (FDA) [24]	86.70
$Nonlinear Programming - \beta$ [25]	87.90
Nonlinear Programming-B [25]	87.80
$Nonlinear Programming - \nu MC$ [25]	87.80
TriCoIR	**94.68**

Test image

Misclassification

Fig. 5. Examples of misclassifications in Flower 17.

an improved performance compared with previous methods, there are still some declassification because of the similarities between categories. Figure 5 shows some examples of disclassification.

5   Conclusion

TriCoIR described in this paper provided a joint representation from three levels, *i.e.* object intrinsic, strongly-related context and weakly-related context. The aim is to leverage the object and context for effective image representations. First, we converted the input image for strongly-related and weakly-related context. Second, instead of directly extracting features from objects themselves, cascade transformations were made to exclude external disturbances. Third, these three level deep features were respectively extracted and then combined for joint representation. Last but not least, we verified the effectiveness of TriCoIR in conjunction with categorization system, improved performance was achieved over previously published results.

Acknowledgement. This work is supported by National Basic Research Program of China (973 Program): 2012CB316400 and 2015CB351802, National Natural Science Foundation of China: 61303154 and 61332016, the Open Project of Key Laboratory of Big Data Mining and Knowledge Management, Chinese Academy of Sciences.

References

1. Chai, Y., Rahtu, E., Lempitsky, V., Gool, L., Zisserman, A.: TriCoS: a tri-level class-discriminative co-segmentation method for image classification. In: Fitzgibbon, A., Lazebnik, S., Perona, P., Sato, Y., Schmid, C. (eds.) ECCV 2012. LNCS, vol. 7572, pp. 794–807. Springer, Heidelberg (2012). doi:10.1007/978-3-642-33718-5_57
2. Krizhevsky, A., Sutskever, I., Hinton, G.E.: Imagenet classification with deep convolutional neural networks. In: NIPS, pp. 1097–1105 (2012)
3. Oliva, A., Torralba, A.: The role of context in object recognition. Trends Cogn. Sci. **11**(12), 520–527 (2007)
4. Heitz, G., Koller, D.: Learning spatial context: using stuff to find things. In: Forsyth, D., Torr, P., Zisserman, A. (eds.) ECCV 2008. LNCS, vol. 5302, pp. 30–43. Springer, Heidelberg (2008). doi:10.1007/978-3-540-88682-2_4

5. Galleguillos, C., Rabinovich, A., Belongie, S.: Object categorization using co-occurrence, location and appearance. In: CVPR, pp. 1–8 (2008)
6. Nguyen, M.H., Torresani, L., de la Torre, F., Rother, C.: Weakly supervised discriminative localization, classification: a joint learning process. In: ICCV, pp. 1925–1932 (2009)
7. Bilen, H., Namboodiri, V.P., Van Gool, L.J.: Object and action classification with latent variables. In: BMVC, p. 3 (2011)
8. Divvala, S.K., Hoiem, D., Hays, J.H., Efros, A.A., Hebert, M.: An empirical study of context in object detection. In: CVPR, pp. 1271–1278 (2009)
9. Russakovsky, O., Lin, Y., Yu, K., Fei-Fei, L.: Object-centric spatial pooling for image classification. In: Fitzgibbon, A., Lazebnik, S., Perona, P., Sato, Y., Schmid, C. (eds.) ECCV 2012. LNCS, vol. 7578, pp. 1–15. Springer, Heidelberg (2012). doi:10.1007/978-3-642-33709-3_1
10. Gong, Y., Wang, L., Guo, R., Lazebnik, S.: Multi-scale orderless pooling of deep convolutional activation features. In: Fleet, D., Pajdla, T., Schiele, B., Tuytelaars, T. (eds.) ECCV 2014. LNCS, vol. 8693, pp. 392–407. Springer, Heidelberg (2014). doi:10.1007/978-3-319-10584-0_26
11. Zhou, B., Lapedriza, A., Xiao, J., Torralba, A., Oliva, A.: Learning deep features for scene recognition using places database. In: NIPS, pp. 487–495 (2014)
12. Jia, Y., Shelhamer, E., Donahue, J., Karayev, S., Long, J., Girshick, R.B., Guadarrama, S., Darrell, T.: Caffe: convolutional architecture for fast feature embedding. In: ACM Multimedia, p. 4 (2014)
13. Wah, C., Branson, S., Welinder, P., Perona, P., Belongie, S.: The Caltech-UCSD Birds-200-2011 Dataset, Technical report (2011)
14. Nilsback, M.-E., Zisserman, A.: A visual vocabulary for flower classification. In: CVPR, pp. 1447–1454 (2006)
15. Yao, B., Khosla, A., Li, F.: Combining randomization and discrimination for fine-grained image categorization. In: CVPR, pp. 1577–1584 (2011)
16. Chen, Q., Song, Z., Hua, Y., Huang, Z., Yan, S.: Hierarchical matching with side information for image classification. In: CVPR, pp. 3426–3433 (2012)
17. Khan, F.S., Weijer, J., Bagdanov, A.D., Vanrell, M.: Portmanteau vocabularies for multi-cue image representation. In: NIPS, pp. 1323–1331 (2011)
18. Deng, J., Krause, J., Fei-Fei, L.: Fine-grained crowdsourcing for fine-grained recognition. In: CVPR, pp. 580–587 (2013)
19. Bo, L., Ren, X., Fox, D.: Kernel descriptors for visual recognition. In: NIPS, pp. 244–252 (2010)
20. Yang, S., Bo, L., Wang, J., Shapiro, L.G.: Unsupervised template learning for fine-grained object recognition. In: NIPS, pp. 3122–3130 (2012)
21. Zhang, N., Farrell, R., Iandola, F., Darrell, T.: Deformable part descriptors for fine-grained recognition and attribute prediction. In: ICCV, pp. 729–736 (2013)
22. Gehler, P., Nowozin, S.: On feature combination for multiclass object classification. In: ICCV, pp. 221–228 (2009)
23. Awais, M., Yan, F., Mikolajczyk, K., Kittler, J.: Two-stage augmented kernel matrix for object recognition. In: Sansone, C., Kittler, J., Roli, F. (eds.) MCS 2011. LNCS, vol. 6713, pp. 137–146. Springer, Heidelberg (2011). doi:10.1007/978-3-642-21557-5_16
24. Yan, F., Mikolajczyk, K., Barnard, M., Cai, H., Kittler, J.: p norm multiple kernel Fisher discriminant analysis for object and image categorisation. In: CVPR, pp. 3626–3632 (2010)
25. Awais, M., Yan, F., Mikolajczyk, K., Kittler, J.: Augmented kernel matrix vs classifier fusion for object recognition. In: BMVC, p. 60.1 (2011)

Accurate Multi-view Stereopsis Fusing DAISY Descriptor and Scaled-Neighbourhood Patches

Fei Wang and Ning An[✉]

Institute of Artificial Intelligence and Robotics, Xi'an Jiaotong University,
Xi'an, Shaanxi Province, China
wfx@mail.xjtu.edu.cn, aning.393@stu.xjtu.edu.cn

Abstract. In this paper, we present an efficient patch-based multi-view stereo reconstruction approach, which is designed to reconstruct accurate, dense 3D models on high-resolution image sets. Wide-baseline matching becomes more challenging due to large perspective distortions, increased occluded areas and high curvature regions that are inevitable in MVS. Correlation window measurements, which are mainly used as photometric discrepancy function, are not appropriate for wide-baseline matching. We introduce DAISY descriptor for photo-consistency optimization of each new patch, which makes our algorithm robust on distortion, occlusion and edge regions against many other photometric constraints. Another key to the performance of Patch-based MVS is the estimation of patch normal. We estimate the initial normal of every seed patch via fitting quadrics with scaled-neighbourhood patches to handle the reconstruction of high local curvature regions. It demonstrates that our approach performs dramatically well on large-scale scene both in terms of accuracy and completeness.

Keywords: Multi-view stereo · Patch · DAISY descriptor · Normal estimation

1 Introduction

Multi-view stereopsis (MVS) is an algorithm can be described as: given a collection of images taken from an object or a scene, estimate the most likely 3D model that explains those images. It is a classic computer vision problem that occupied researchers for more than 30 years. Nowadays, more and more applications range from 3D mapping, 3D printing, virtual reality that enter our field of vision. It has seen a surge of interest that how to exploit diverse images collection ever assembled to reconstruct the 3D model about a scene [1].

We focus on the patch-based MVS algorithm and find that correlation window photometric measurements, such as NCC used in PMVS [3], are not appropriate for wide-baseline matching in MVS. Because they are not robust to perspective distortions and partial occlusions. We propose to replace NCC with DAISY descriptor [2], which let us take advantage of optimization to refine every generated patch. Another contribution is the estimation of patch normal via fitting quadrics with scaled-neighbourhood patches. It helps our approach reconstruct a scene despite the presence of occlusion or edge region. The improvement is shown on various datasets, including objects with fine

© Springer International Publishing AG 2016
E. Chen et al. (Eds.): PCM 2016, Part I, LNCS 9916, pp. 260–270, 2016.
DOI: 10.1007/978-3-319-48890-5_26

surface details, inclined planes, deep concavities, and thin structures, outdoor scenes observed from a restricted set of viewpoints.

The rest of this paper is organized as follows: we will first review related work (Sect. 2), and provide a more detailed overview of our method (Sect. 3). We then present the individual stages of our method, including a briefly description of DAISY descriptor (Sect. 4.1), DAISY-based photometric discrepancy function (Sect. 4.2) and the estimation of patch normal (Sect. 5). Experimental results and discussions are given in Sect. 6. We conclude with results in Sect. 7.

2 Related Work

Over the last decade, the MVS problem has achieved a great development, yielding a variety of reconstruction algorithms [6]. According to the taxonomy of Seitz et al. [4], MVS algorithms can be divided into four categories: (1) 3D volumetric approaches [5] extract the surface from a 3D volume by computing a cost function. These methods usually transform 3D modelling into finding the minimum graph cut algorithm; (2) surface evolution techniques [7] include algorithm based on voxels, level sets, and surface meshes. They always demand some initialization for further optimization process, which limits their applicability; (3) algorithms that compute and merge depth maps [8, 9] perform more flexible, however, the depth maps tend to be noisy and redundant that they need steps to clean up and merge the depth maps [9]; (4) techniques that grow regions or surfaces starting from a set of extracted features [3, 11]. Furukawa [3] presented a classic algorithm, PMVS, based on patch which generates a sparse set of patches corresponding to the salient image features, and then spreads the initial matches to nearby pixels and filters incorrect matches to maintain completeness and accuracy.

In Bleyer's [12] approach, a 3D scene is represented as a collection of visually distinct and spatially coherent objects. Inspired by Markov Random Field models of image segmentation, they employed object-level color models as a soft constraint, which can improve depth estimation in powerful ways. Hoang-Hiep [13] introduced a minimum s-t cut optimization over an adaptive domain that robustly and efficiently filters a quasi-dense point cloud from outliers and reconstructs an initial surface by integrating visibility constraints, followed by a mesh-based variational refinement that captures small details, smartly handling photo-consistency, regularization, and adaptive resolution. Qi Shan [14] leveraged occluding contours to improve the performance of multi-view stereo methods. This proposed approach outperforms state of the art MVS techniques for challenging Internet datasets, yielding dramatic quality improvements both around object contours and in surface detail.

3 Algorithm Overview

Ours patch-based multi-view stereo algorithm starts from a set of calibrated images. Methods about sparse multi-view stereo and how to obtain the camera poses and intrinsic parameters please refer to VisualSFM [10].

As shown in Fig. 1, similar to the framework of PMVS, the input images are detected corner features by Difference-of-Gaussian (DoG) and Harris operators. Features are first matched across multiple images, yielding a sparse set of patches associated with salient image regions. A patch is essentially a local tangent plane approximation of a surface. Its geometry is fully determined by its center $c(p)$, unit normal vector $n(p)$ orient toward the cameras observing it, and a reference image $R(p)$ in which p is visible.

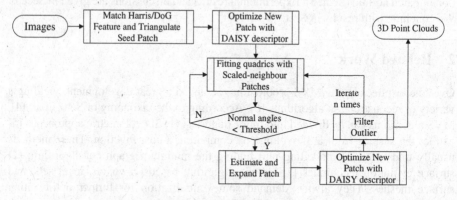

Fig. 1. Algorithm overview

Given a pair of features constrained to lie the corresponding epipolar lines across two images, a candidate patch p is triangulated with its center $c(p)$, normal vector $n(p)$, and reference image $R(p)$. Every new generated patch has its geometric parameters, $c(p)$ and $n(p)$, which are optimized by minimizing the discrepancy function score computed by DAISY descriptors. The patch center $c(p)$ is constrained to lie on a ray such that its image projection in one of the visible images. $n(p)$ is parameterized by Euler angles, yaw and pitch, yielding an optimization problem within three parameters only, which is solved by a conjugate-gradient method.

In the following step, we fuse neighbourhood information to initially estimate the patch normal. Multi-scale quadrics are fitted according to neighbourhood patches for acquiring their normals. Check if normal angles meet the threshold to determine the initial estimation of the patch normal. Expansion procedure is to spread the initial matches to nearby pixels and obtain a dense set of patches. The goal of the expansion step is to reconstruct at least one patch in every image cell. The final filter step eliminates incorrect matches and obstacles using visibility constrains. These three steps are repeated times to acquire a dense and smooth 3D point clouds.

4   Photometric Discrepancy Function

4.1   Brief Description of DAISY Descriptor

DAISY [2] is a local descriptor, inspired from SIFT and GLOH. It's combined convolved orientation maps and an isotropic Gaussian kernel that can be computed much faster. For an input image, H number of orientation maps is computed, G_i, $1 \leq i \leq H$, where $G_o(u, v)$ equals the image gradient norm at location (u, v) for direction o. Orientation maps are written as $G_o = \left(\dfrac{\partial I}{\partial o}\right)^{+} = max(\dfrac{\partial I}{\partial o}, 0)$, where I is the input image, o is the orientation of the derivative. Each orientation map is then convolved with Gaussian kernels of different $\sum$ values as $G_o^{\Sigma} = G_{\Sigma} * \left(\dfrac{\partial I}{\partial o}\right)^{+}$.

Let $h_{\Sigma}(u, v)$ represent the vector made of the values at location (u, v) in the orientation maps after convolution by a Gaussian kernel of standard deviation $\sum$.

$$h_{\Sigma}(u,v) = \left[G_1^{\Sigma}(u,v), \ldots, G_H^{\Sigma}(u,v)\right]^{T} \tag{1}$$

The full DAISY descriptor $D(u_0, v_0)$ for location (u_0, v_0) is defined Eq. (2), where $I_j(u, v, R)$ is the location with distance R from (u, v) in the direction given by j when the directions are quantized into T value.

$$
\begin{aligned}
D(u_0, v_0) = [&h_{\Sigma_1}^{T}(u_0, v_0), \\
&h_{\Sigma_1}^{T}(I_1(u_0, v_0, R_1)), \ldots, h_{\Sigma_1}^{T}(I_T(u_0, v_0, R_1)), \\
&\ldots, \\
&h_{\Sigma_Q}^{T}(I_1(u_0, v_0, R_Q)), \ldots, h_{\Sigma_Q}^{T}(I_T(u_0, v_0, R_Q))]^{T}
\end{aligned}
\tag{2}
$$

DAISY is parameterized with its radius R, number of rings Q, number of histograms in a ring T, and the number of bins in each histogram H. The total size of the descriptor vector is $(Q \times T + 1) \times H$.

4.2 DAISY-Based Photometric Discrepancy Function

Normalized cross correlation (NCC) is one of the most common photometric agreement measurements used in multi-view stereo algorithm. Considering it cannot work stably and robustly on the distortion, occlusion and edge region, we propose to utilize DAISY descriptor. Actually, in a worst-case scenario, DAISY will not perform any worse than a standard region-based metric like NCC. The photometric discrepancy function may not work well in the presence of specular highlights or obstacles, and we have so far assumed that the surface of a scene is nearly Lambertian as in most MVS algorithms.

Firstly, we need to determine the orientation of DAISY descriptor (Fig. 2). Given a feature, the orientation of its DAISY descriptor is defined as the vertical directions of corresponding epipolar line. It can be calculated easily. For the pair of features (f_i, f_j), the corresponding epipolar line on image i is $l_i = F^{T} * f_j$, where F is the fundamental matrix. The direction vector of epipolar line $\mathbf{e} = [u, v]^{T}$, rotation matrix $\boldsymbol{\theta} = \begin{bmatrix} 0 & -1 \\ 1 & 0 \end{bmatrix}$, the main direction of the DAISY descriptor can be computed as

$$
o = \begin{cases} \arccos(\langle \boldsymbol{\theta} \cdot \mathbf{e}\rangle / ||\mathbf{e}||), & \text{if } \boldsymbol{\theta} \cdot \mathbf{e} \cdot \mathbf{v} \geq 0 \\ \arccos(\langle \boldsymbol{\theta} \cdot \mathbf{e}\rangle / ||\mathbf{e}||) + \pi, & \text{else} \end{cases}
\tag{3}
$$

where **v** is a unit vector of the positive direction of vertical axis of the image.

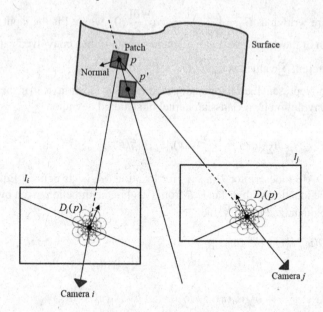

Fig. 2. Patch optimization

Now, we can get the DAISY descriptor vector $D(u, v, o)$ at the location (u, v) with the direction o. We define the dissimilarity function $d(p, I_i, I_j)$ as

$$d(p, I_i, I_j) = \frac{1}{S} \sum_{k=1}^{S} \left\| D_i^k(p) - D_j^k(p) \right\| \tag{4}$$

where $D_i(p)$ and $D_j(p)$ are the descriptors at locations obtained by projecting the patch p projected onto its visible image I_i and I_j. $D_i^k(p)$ is the kth histogram in $D_i(p)$, and S is the number of histograms used in the descriptor.

Let $V(p)$ denote a set of images in which p is visible. The photometric discrepancy function for the candidate patch p is defined as

$$c(p) = \frac{1}{|V(p)\backslash R(p)|} \sum_{I \in V(p)\backslash R(p)} d(p, I, R(p)) \tag{5}$$

We advocate replacing correlation window measurements with local region DAISY descriptor. In more complicated scenes, where images have varying resolutions and their location is non-uniformly, it becomes critical to adjust the size of the domain.

To improve the robustness of our approach, only images whose pairwise photometric discrepancy score with the reference image $R(p)$ is below a certain threshold α are used for further estimation. And we replace $V(p)$ in the photometric discrepancy function (5) with $V^*(p)$ to obtain the new formula (7). If the number of visible images of the candidate patch $|V^*(p)|$ is smaller than the threshold γ, it is failed and retry the next candidate patch ($\alpha = 0.6$, $\gamma = 3$). Otherwise, a new seed patch is generated successfully.

$$V * (p) = \{I | I \in V(p), d(p, I, R(p)) \le \alpha\} \tag{6}$$

$$c * (p) = \frac{1}{|V * (p) \backslash R(p)|} \sum_{I \in V*(p) \backslash R(p)} d(p, I, R(p)) \tag{7}$$

5   Normal Estimation

It is difficult to reconstruct a 3D model with PMVS where the local curvature is too high, including deep concavities and high convexities, because each new patch is constrained to lie on a ray for optimization such that its image projection in one of the visible images. From Fig. 3, the dashed lines are the initial estimation of candidate patch normal in PMVS. It can be assumed almost true when the reconstructed surface exactly faces towards cameras, while some high curvature regions are unavoidable. We propose to fuse the multi-scale neighbourhood information around the candidate patch to acquire a more accurate initial estimation of normal.

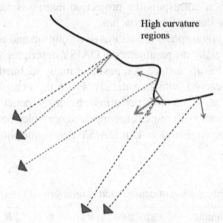

Fig. 3.   Cameras and the surface of a scene

We search $\sigma \times K$ neighbourhood patches to fit a quadric and search $\lambda \sigma \times K$ neighbourhood patches to fit another quadric in a lower scale ($K \in [30,60]$, $\sigma = 2$, $\lambda = 0.6$ in our experiment). Then we get two normals n_1, n_2. When the two normals satisfy the formula (8), the normals are regarded as the same direction, and the normal computed in higher scale is set to be the initial estimation of the new patch. Otherwise, $\lambda^2 \sigma \times K$ neighbourhood patches are searched to compute the normal n_3, checking whether n_2 and n_3 meet the threshold β ($\beta = \pi/9$). And repeat the above process. If the two normals still have comparatively large deviation, the normal computed in smaller scale is used to as the initial estimation of the new patch. With multi-scale neighbourhood information, the generated patch normal can be adjusted more effectively no matter on the plain regions or high curvature regions.

Right now the new seed patch already has a relatively accurate initial normal, and its geometric parameters, $c(p)$ and $n(p)$, can be refined by the further optimization of our DAISY-based photometric discrepancy function.

$$\cos^{-1}(normal_1, normal_2) < \beta \tag{8}$$

6   Results

Our algorithm is implemented by VC++ with the CGAL library. All experiments are conducted on a Windows PC with Intel i5 CPU @3.3 GHz, RAM 16 GB.

We compare and analyze our 3D reconstruction results with that of PMVS [3] method on four datasets. The datasets are acquired from the real-world scenes. We have one dataset taken from a sculpture by ourselves, and other three are the open datasets from Stecha et al. [15]. When we reconstruct a scene or an object, it is firstly captured form various viewpoints, then the structure-from-motion software [10] is used to reconstruct the pose of each camera and obtain the projection matrix for per visible image. We take images and their corresponding projection matrix as the input of the further patch-based multi-view stereopsis approaches.

The first dataset "*Typography-P9*", its image resolution and number of images are listed in Table 1, followed by the parameters of DAISY descriptor and K-neighbourhood numbers. This dataset has its surface composed of many inclined planes, and parts of them have characters carved with fine details. From the comparison of 3D models (Fig. 4), our DAISY-based method performs obviously better than PMVS on the completeness. The regions with red circles appear large holes because these areas are inclined and close to the edge region. Our DAISY descriptor photometric discrepancy

Table 1. Information of datasets and parameters set in experiments

Datasets	Resolution	Images	R	Q	H	T	K
Typography-P9	3264 × 2448	9	5	3	8	8	40
Castle-P10	3072 × 2048	10	5	3	8	8	50
Fountain-P11	3072 × 2048	11	5	3	8	8	50
Herz-Jesu-P8	3072 × 2048	8	5	3	8	8	50

Table 2. Experimental data

Method	Typography-P9	Castle-P10	Fountain-P11	Herz-Jesu-P8
PMVS	355142	1572701	1348187	1236046
DAISY-based	481073	1724573	1621941	1438512
Final method	486249	1849036	1644479	1537345
Percent	36.92 %	17.57 %	21.98 %	24.38 %

function performs robust against NCC used in PMVS. Table 2 gives the comparison of numbers of patches. And the denseness of our reconstructions improve a lot.

Fig. 4. *Typography-P9.* Top row: images from the dataset, the seed patches. Bottom row: from left to right, the 3D models reconstructed by PMVS, our DAISY-based and final method (Our MVS method with DAISY-based measurement and normal estimation).

On the datasets from Stecha et al. [15], our DAISY-based method and final method are proved to reconstruct more smooth 3D models (Fig. 5). *Castle-P10* has an obvious character of bending building wall, which is more apparently showed the limitation of PMVS. It is almost impossible to rebuild by PMVS on the region of bending building

Fig. 5. Datasets from Strecha et al. [15]. From top to bottom row, they are *Castle-P10, Fountain-P11, Herz-Jesu-P8.* And from left to right column, they are 3D models reconstructed by PMVS, our DAISY-based method and our final method.

wall, whereas our method has an estimation of patch normal fusing scale-neighbourhood information which helps perform well. There are building walls and some deep concavities, and thin structures on the dataset *Fountain-P11*. And our method produces more dense patches than that of PMVS with fine surface details (more clearly shown in Fig. 6). *Herz-Jesu-P8* has a large plain region, which leads to the fish-like scale of the 3D model reconstructed by PMVS with small correlation window. However, large size may lead to holes on the thin structure regions because unique local regions are weakly supported. It is necessary to replace correlation window measurements with stable local region descriptor for it's critical to adjust the size of the window.

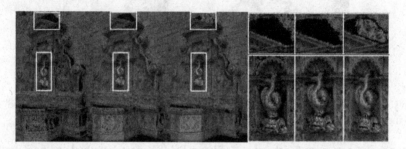

Fig. 6. Details of 3D models reconstructed by PMVS, our DAISY-based and final method.

Some details are given in Fig. 6, and it is obviously showed that our methods can produce better reconstructed results on the surface details, edge regions, deep concavities, occlusion areas, and thin structures. To measure quantitative evaluations of the reconstructed 3D models, we have two 3D point clouds comparing with their ground truths in Fig. 7. The correct rate is measured by changing the deviation of 3D point clouds from their corresponding actual depth value after 3D point clouds are aligned with their ground truth by iterative closest point (ICP).

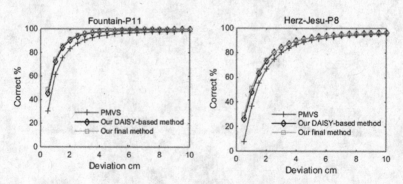

Fig. 7. Quantitative evaluation

7 Conclusion

In this paper, we introduced DAISY descriptor into patch-based MVS to be as photometric discrepancy function for wide-baseline matching, which performs robust than correlation window measurements. Especially on areas of different depths, edge regions or partial occlusions, PMVS cannot reconstruct for perspective distortions. Our estimation of patch normal via fusing scaled-neighbourhood information enhances the sensibility to the region of high curvature. It contributes to handle the areas of deep concavities and high convexities. The experiments are proved that the method proposed by us has a better performance on the high curvature regions, slanted surfaces and thin structures. In comparison to PMVS, the 3D models reconstructed by our algorithm have a great improvement on the accuracy and completeness.

Acknowledgment. National Natural Science Foundation of China (No. 61231018, No. 61273366), National Science and technology support program (2015BAH31F01), Program of introducing talents of discipline to university under grant B13043.

References

1. Snavely, N., Seitz, S.M., Szeliski, R.: Modeling the world from internet photo collections. Int. J. Comput. Vis. **80**(2), 189–210 (2008)
2. Tola, E., et al.: Daisy: an efficient dense descriptor applied to wide-baseline stereo. IEEE Trans. Pattern Anal. Mach. Intell. **32**(5), 815–830 (2010)
3. Furukawa, Y., Ponce, J.: Accurate, dense, and robust multiview stereopsis. IEEE Trans. Pattern Anal. Mach. Intell. **32**(8), 1362–1376 (2010)
4. Seitz, S.M., Curless, B., Diebel, J., et al.: A comparison and evaluation of multi-view stereo reconstruction algorithms. In: 2006 IEEE Computer Society Conference on Computer Vision and Pattern Recognition, vol. 1, pp. 519–528 (2006)
5. Sormann, M., Zach, C., Bauer, J., Karner, K., Bishof, H.: Watertight multi-view reconstruction based on volumetric graph-cuts. In: Ersbøll, B.K., Pedersen, K.S. (eds.) SCIA 2007. LNCS, vol. 4522, pp. 393–402. Springer, Heidelberg (2007). doi:10.1007/978-3-540-73040-8_40
6. Furukawa, Y., Hernández, C.: Multi-view stereo: a tutorial. Found. Trends Comput. Graph. Vis. **9**(1–2), 1–148 (2015)
7. Esteban, C.H., Schmitt, F.: Silhouette and stereo fusion for 3D object modeling. Comput. Vis. Image Underst. **96**(3), 367–392 (2004)
8. Xiao, X., et al.: Multi-view stereo matching based on self-adaptive patch and image grouping for multiple unmanned aerial vehicle imagery. Remote Sensing **8**, 89 (2016)
9. Shen, S., Hu, Z.: How to select good neighboring images in depth-map merging based 3D modeling. IEEE Trans. Image Process. **23**(1), 308–318 (2014)
10. Wu, C.: Towards linear-time incremental structure from motion. In: 2013, International Conference on 3D Vision-3DV, pp. 127–134. IEEE (2013)
11. Zhu, Z., Stamatopoulos, C., Fraser, C.S.: Accurate and occlusion-robust multi-view stereo. ISPRS J. Photogrammetry Remote Sens. **109**, 47–61 (2015)
12. Bleyer, M., Rother, C., Kohli, P., et al.: Object stereo - Joint stereo matching and object segmentation. In: IEEE Computer Society Conference on Computer Vision and Pattern Recognition, pp. 3081–3088 (2011)

13. Vu, H.H., Labatut, P., Pons, J.P., et al.: High accuracy and visibility-consistent dense multiview stereo. IEEE Trans. Pattern Anal. Mach. Intell. **34**(5), 889–901 (2011)
14. Qi, S., Curless, B., Furukawa, Y., et al.: Occluding contours for multi-view stereo. In: 2014 IEEE Conference on Computer Vision and Pattern Recognition, pp. 4002–4009 (2014)
15. Strecha, C., von Hansen, W., Gool, L.V., et al.: On benchmarking camera calibration and multi-view stereo for high resolution imagery. In: IEEE Conference on Computer Vision and Pattern Recognition, CVPR 2008, pp. 1–8 (2008)

Stereo Matching Based on CF-EM
Joint Algorithm

Baoping Li[1,2], Long Ye[1(✉)], Yun Tie[3], and Qin Zhang[1]

[1] Key Laboratory Media Audio and Video Ministry of Education,
Communication University of China, Beijing, China
Libaoping2003@126.com, yelong@cuc.edu.cn
[2] Henan Polytechnic University, Jiaozuo, China
[3] Zhengzhou University, Zhengzhou, China

Abstract. Cost Filtering (CF) and Energy Minimization (EM) are two main
cost aggregation methods in stereo matching. Due to global smoothness
assumption, EM methods can get higher matching accuracy. However, they tend
to fail in occluded areas, while locally adaptive support-weight CF method can
solve it well. This paper proposed a CF-EM joint stereo matching framework on
the basis of the proof that CF and EM methods can realize interconversion to
each other. In this joint framework, we firstly use CF method with fully connected Markov Random Field (F-MRF) model to yield a more robust unary
potential. And then, the output unary potential is used as the input to a standard
EM method to compute the final disparity in Local connected MRF (L-MRF)
model. Experiments results demonstrate that our method can improve the stereo
matching accuracy as the achievement of energy transferring from F-MRF to
L-MRF.

Keywords: Stereo-matching · Cost filtering · Energy minimization · Joint
algorithm · Belief propagation

1 Introduction

Depth estimation from stereo-images is a key technic for many applications such as 3D
reconstruction, robot navigation, virtual reality, etc. Through cameras calibration, focus
and axis-distance information of cameras can be obtained, thus depth estimation
problem is converted to stereo-matching problem.

According to the cost convergence way, stereo matching can be divided into two
categories: CF methods and EM methods [1]. CF methods is based on the smoothness
assumption that all pixels in the matching neighborhood have similar disparities [2, 3].
For a long time, because of the lack of global smoothness, CF methods were deemed
incapable of achieving the accuracy of EM methods. This is until, when the adaptive
support-weight is introduced into CF method [4]. Per-pixel is weighted by measuring

This work is supported by the Projects of NSFC (61371191, 61201236), and Research Project of
China SARFT (2015-53).

the space and color similarity between pixels. The use of the adaptive support weight greatly improved the accuracy of disparities nearby object boundaries. EM methods formulate the disparity labels assignment problem as an energy function, which is solved by energy optimization methods [5, 6]. CF and EM methods each have merits and faults. Local property of CFs, determine the efficiency of the algorithm, but also limit the transmission range of messages, affect the accuracy of stereo matching. EM methods by introducing smoothness term, optimize the disparities solution in the global scope, can improve the overall accuracy of matching, but in occluded regions have limitations. Although over-penalization of smoothness term can help to overcome the ambiguity in occluded regions but also damage the fine depth structure of other regions [1].

Because the two algorithms have their own limitations, many researchers try to use the combination of two methods. Dynamic Programming (DP) [8] algorithm limits the scope of energy optimization in the scan-lines, and achieves disparities smooth by filtering in scan-lines. Tree-Reweighted Message Passing (TRW) [7] algorithm limits the scope of energy optimization within the "trees", and by trees message propagation to achieve energy minimization. Also some methods based on cooperative optimization decompose the disparity assignment into a number of region-based sub-problems [12]. Recently, a similar method based on super-pixels patch matching [9], achieves good stereo matching results.

The above combined methods introduce the local CF methods into the global EM methods thorough different ways, which can improve matching accuracy and efficiency. Although some improvements have been made, even some methods have great ascension in performance, but none of them explain the cooperative relationship between the two methods in theory. Some control parameters are introduced into the cooperative algorithms, lead to high computational complexity, and lack of universal applicability. So in this paper, we will illustrate the relationships of the two methods by theoretical, and on this basis, design an effective CF-EM joint algorithm to compensate the drawbacks of each method, and improve the stereo-matching accuracy. The joint algorithm is based on the Two-Step EM method proposed by Mikhail and Joost in [1]. In the joint algorithm, $\rho_\sigma(n)$ function is introduced into cost measure function to reduce the affection of outliers. Sequential TRW (TRW-S) and Parallel TRW (TRW-P) energy minimization methods are used separately in our experiments. TRW-S can provide more accuracy results, while TRW-P has higher computation efficiency because it can eliminate the sequential data dependencies and can be parallelized computation compared with TRW-S.

The rest of the paper is organized as the following: In Sect. 2, the interconversion relationship between CF and EM is explained. In Sect. 3, the proposed CF-EM joint algorithm is introduced. Section 4 demonstrates the results of the tests and comparison with other methods. Finally, we conclude the paper in Sect. 5.

2   Interconversion of CF and EM

In the framework of EM methods, the global energy minimization problem can be expressed as:

$$\min_d\{E(d)\} = \min_d\left\{\sum_{p\in\mathcal{V}} C_p(d_p) + \sum_{(p,q)\in\mathcal{E}} V_{p,q}(d_p, d_q)\right\}, \tag{1}$$

where, $\mathcal{V}$ is the all points sets, and $\mathcal{E}$ is the all edge sets in image graph $\mathcal{G} = \langle\mathcal{V}, \mathcal{E}\rangle$. $C_p(\cdot)$ is a unary potential function, denotes to the conventional matching cost, $V_{p,q}(\cdot, \cdot)$ is a binary potential function denotes edge interaction between a pair of points. As shown in Fig. 1, if only relations between interest point and neighborhood points (4-neighborhood) are considered, called L-MRF model, if all points in image graph $\mathcal{G}$ with interest point relations are considered, called F-MRF.

The problem of energy minimization (1) can be solved in the framework of Belief Propagation (BP). The basic operation of BP is to pass message $m_{q,p}$ from node q to node p for directed edge $(q,p) \in \mathcal{E}$.

$$m^i_{q,p}(d) = \min_{d\in\mathcal{L}}\left(\widehat{C}_q(d) - m^{i-1}_{p,q}(d) + V_{q,p}(d, d_p)\right) \tag{2}$$

$$\widehat{C}^i_p(d) = C_p(d) + \sum_{p,q\in\mathcal{E}} m^{i-1}_{q,p}(d) \tag{3}$$

Where, i is the number of iterations, $\widehat{C}_p$ is a unary potential function. $\mathcal{L}$ denotes discrete disparity domain. After cost convergence, the disparity can be achieved by Winner Takes All (WTA) method.

$$d_p = \arg\min_d\left\{\widehat{C}_p(d)\right\} = \arg\min_d\left\{C_p(d) + \sum_{p,q\in\mathcal{E}} m^{i-1}_{q,p}(d)\right\} \tag{4}$$

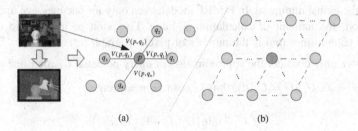

(a) (b)

Fig. 1. L-MRF (a) and F-MRF (b) models

2.1   EM Denotes CF

In CF methods, the disparity of the pixel p after cost aggregation can be denoted as:

$$\tilde{d}_p = \arg\min_d \left(\sum_{q \in \mathcal{N}_p} w(q,p)C_q(d) \right) \tag{5}$$

where, $\mathcal{N}_p$ is the neighborhood of the pixel p, $w(q,p)$ is the weight coefficients reflecting the mutual influence between the points p and q. The point p is separated from the summation formula, so Eq. (1) can be expressed as:

$$\tilde{d}_p = \arg\min_d \left(C_p(d) + \sum_{q \in \mathcal{N}p \backslash p} w(q,p)C_q(d) \right). \tag{6}$$

Set $w(q,p)C_q(d) = M_{q,p}(d)$, which denotes the confidence level from the point q to the point p. Thus,

$$\tilde{d}_p = \arg\min_d \left(C_p(d) + \sum_{q \in \mathcal{N}p \backslash p} M_{q,p}(d) \right). \tag{7}$$

From the comparison of formula (4) and (7), CF methods can be considered as an EM method with only one iteration cost aggregation. Below, we will show that EM problem can be denoted as CF form in F-MRF model.

2.2   CF Denotes EM

The energy minimization problem (1) is a NP-hard problem, and that is hard to rapidly compute the global minimum. In F-MRF model, even only for one message updating in BP method, the amount of calculation is huge. For point p, it needs to compute messages $|\mathcal{L}|mn$ times (mn is the number of pixels in graph set).

Here, we only consider the approximation of unary potential $\widehat{C}_P$ after one iteration. Set $m_{p,q}^0(d) = 0$, $\widehat{C}_q^0(d) = C_q(d)$, thus (2) can be rewritten as:

$$m_{q,p}^1(d) = \min_{d \in \mathcal{L}} \left(C_q(d) + V_{q,p}(d, d_p) \right). \tag{8}$$

Binary potential function $V_{q,p}$ in F-MRF can be expressed as below:

$$V_{q,p}(d_q, d_p) = w_{q,p}\varphi(d_q, d_p). \tag{9}$$

Here, $\varphi(\cdot, \cdot)$ is smoothness penalty term, Potts potential function is usually used.

Lemma 2.1. By setting the following constraints,

$$\begin{cases} C_q(d) \in \{0,1\} \\ \varphi(d,d_p) = 1 - \delta(d,d_p) \end{cases} \tag{10}$$

Equation (8) can be rewritten as:

$$m_{q,p}^1(d) = w_{q,p}(d,d_p)C_q(d) \tag{11}$$

Proof. See Appendix. Consequently, the disparity is calculated:

$$\tilde{d}_p = \arg\min_{d\in\mathcal{L}} \hat{C}_p^1(d) = \arg\min_{d\in\mathcal{L}} \left(C_p(d) + \sum_{p,q\in\mathcal{E}} m_{q,p}(d) \right)$$

$$= \arg\min_{d\in\mathcal{L}} \left(\sum_{q\in\mathcal{V}} w(p,q)C_q(d) \right) \tag{12}$$

By contrast Eq. (12) with (5), we found that the EM problem can be solved with CF method in F-MRF model. This provides us a new idea to solve the stereo matching problem. In F-MRF model, by using CF method to solve EM problem, yields a potential $\hat{C}_p$ with stronger robustness, and then it can be used as the input to a standard EM method to compute the convergence potential energy $\tilde{C}_p$ and the final disparity map in L-MRF model. By this approach, we can solve the energy transfer problem between F-MRF model and L-MRF model, and realize effective integration of CF and EM method.

3 CF-EM Joint Algorithm

The scheme of the proposed stereo matching algorithm is shown in Fig. 2. As traditional EM method, the first stage of algorithm is matching cost initialization, get the initial matching cost $C_p(d)$. In the cost convergence stage, standard traditional EM methods is directly solved in F-MRF model. Whereas in our method the cost

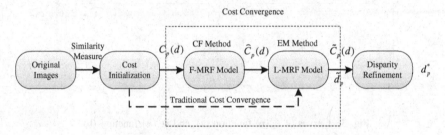

Fig. 2. The scheme of the CF-EM joint algorithm

convergence is divided into two steps, at first in F-MRF model, by using constraint conditions, convert EM problem to CF problem for solving, output a more robust unary potential energy $\hat{C}_p(d)$; Then in L-MRF model, through standard EM method to compute the final potential energy $\tilde{C}_p(d)$ and disparity $\tilde{d}_p$. At the last stage, we can get the final optimization disparity d_p^* by post refinement.

3.1 Cost Initialization

Similarity measure function selection is an important factor affecting stereo matching. Similarity measures can be divided into two categories: one is based on per-pixel, such as AD, Gradient, etc., The other is based on non-parametric transforms, such as Rank, Census, NCC, etc. Generally, measures based on non-parametric transform can achieve good stereo-matching while need high computing complexity. In F-MRF model, the affection of cost computation based on region transforms is similar to cost aggregation. So we use a linear combination of two per-pixel similarity measures: AD and Gradient.

AD's advantage is low calculation complexity, and high computational efficiency. Disadvantage is bad anti-noise performance. Gradient measure function can propagate edge information well, so it favors to improve the accuracy of stereo-matching in object edges. The AD-Gradient combined measure function is as below:

$$C(p,d) = (1 - \alpha) \cdot C_{AD}(p,d) + \alpha \cdot C_{GD}(p,d). \tag{13}$$

where, C_{AD}, C_{GD} denote AD and Gradient measure functions, respectively. Set $\alpha = \frac{2}{3}\frac{\mu_{C_{AD}}}{\mu_{C_{GD}}}$, and μ is the mean of matching costs.

To resolve the outlier problem and convenient to calculation, the $\rho_\sigma(n)$ function is introduced into cost function and forms a new cost function.

$$\rho_\sigma(n) = \log\left(1 + \frac{1}{2}\left(\frac{n^2}{\sigma}\right)\right) \tag{14}$$

$$C(p,d) = (1 - \alpha) \cdot \rho_\sigma(C_{AD}(p,d)) + \alpha \cdot \rho_\sigma(C_{GD}(p,d)) \tag{15}$$

The curves of $\rho_\sigma(n)$ and its derivative function $\psi_\sigma(n)$ are shown in Fig. 3. It can be seen from the analysis, that $\rho_\sigma(n)$ is growing fast in $[-\sqrt{2}\sigma, \sqrt{2}\sigma]$, and $\psi_\sigma(n)$ has a great

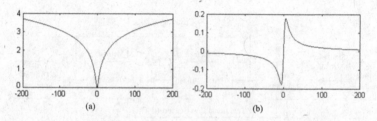

Fig. 3. Curves of $\rho_\sigma(n)$ function (a), and $\psi_\sigma(n)$ function (b)

value when $\rho_\sigma(n)$ is small, whereas the value is nearly zero when out of the region $[-\sqrt{2}\sigma, \sqrt{2}\sigma]$. Therefore the $\rho_\sigma(n)$ function can suppress the noise and outlier well.

3.2 F-MRF Model

In Sect. 2, it has been proved that the EM problem can be denoted as CF form within constraints in F-MRF model. Here we discuss how to achieve these constraints (10).

At first, the matching cost need to be discretized to $\{0, 1\}$. The constraint hypothesis has its rationality. If $C_q(d) = 0$, it means that the points q and p are at the same depth, while if $C_q(d) = 1$, the points q and p are not at the same depth. Discretization can be realized by simple threshold method. Due to the different probability distribution of matching cost in different images, that the constant threshold method is lack of generality and without strong robustness. Here we consider using exponential function, which has strong robustness.

$$C_p(d) = 1 - e^{-kC(p,d)} \tag{16}$$

Where, k is the stretched factor, here we set $k = 100$.

In constraint conditions, the scope of filter weight coefficient is $0 \leq w \leq 1$. Considering the confidence degree of the point p and q is relative to the space distance and the color similarity between two points, here we adopt bilateral filtering form:

$$w_{p,q} = e^{-\frac{|\mathbf{x}_p - \mathbf{x}_q|^2}{2\sigma_\mathbf{x}^2} - \frac{|I_p - I_q|^2}{2\sigma_I^2}}. \tag{17}$$

Where $\mathbf{x}_p$ is a coordinate of the pixel p, I_p defines the color vector value of the pixel p, $\sigma_\mathbf{x}$ and σ_I are intrinsic parameters of the bilateral kernel $w_{p,q}$, which equal to 8 and 1.4, respectively.

Using constraining conditions, the problem of EM in F-MRF model can be converted to the form of CF. In this process, due to the introduction of gradient measure function, and utilizing bilateral filtering form, the output potential function $\widehat{C}_p(d)$ has stronger robustness, especially in occulted regions, which can be used for further cost aggregation in L-MRF model.

3.3 L-MRF Model

In L-MRF model, we can do further cost aggregation for the potential function $\widehat{C}_p(d)$ passed from F-MRF, to realize energy minimization.

$$\min_d \{\tilde{E}(d)\} = \min_d \left\{ \sum_{p \in \mathcal{V}} \widehat{C}_p(d_p) + \sum_{\{p,q\} \in \mathcal{E}} V_{p,q}(d_p, d_q) \right\} \tag{18}$$

where the potential function $\widehat{C}_p(d)$ is the marginal potential function obtained in the previous step. $V(\cdot, \cdot)$ is smoothness function. In F-MRF model, we only consider four connected graph model as shown in Fig. 1. Here, we adopt commonly used Potts binary potential function.

$$V_{p,q}(d_p, d_q) = \lambda \cdot T = \begin{cases} \lambda_1 T & \text{if} & |I_p - I_q| \leq \theta_1 \\ \lambda_2 T & \text{if} & \theta_1 < |I_p - I_q| \leq \theta_2 \\ \lambda_3 T & \text{if} & \theta_2 \leq |I_p - I_q| \end{cases} \tag{19}$$

$$T = 1 - \delta(d_p, d_q) \tag{20}$$

In the experiment, we set $\lambda_1 = 2.5$, $\lambda_2 = 0.2$, $\lambda_3 = 0.1$; $\theta_1 = 8$, $\theta_2 = 20$.

Both BP and TRW-S [7] EM methods are based on the message passing pattern. Compared with BP, TRW-S has better convergence property and shows better accuracy of stereo-matching.

In TRW-S algorithm, unary potential function $\tilde{C}_p(\cdot)$ and message $m_{q,p}^i(d)$ can be expressed as:

$$\tilde{C}_p(d_p) = \widehat{C}_p(d_p) + \sum_{q \in \mathcal{N}_p} m_{q,p}(d_p) \tag{21}$$

$$m_{q,p}^i(d_p) = \min_{d \in \mathcal{L}} \left(\frac{1}{2} \tilde{C}_q(d) - m_{p,q}^{i-1}(d) + V_{q,p}(d, d_p) \right) \tag{22}$$

Using TRW-S EM method, we can get the output potential function $\tilde{C}_p(\cdot)$, and disparity $\tilde{d}_p$ with WTA method.

$$\tilde{d}_p = \arg \min_{d \in \mathcal{L}} \left(\tilde{C}_p(d) \right) \tag{23}$$

TRW-S always shows better accuracy than BP in experimental tests. However, it leads to a significantly higher cost in memory and the sequential message passing pattern makes it difficult to parallelize [10].To overcome the shortcomings, we introduce the TRW-P EM method.

```
Algorithm: TRW-P
1:   Initialize m^0_{q,p} = 0;
2:   for  Iteration i=1: N  do
3:       for Each node p∈V do
```
         compute and normalize the potential function as
$$\tilde{C}^i_p = \hat{C}_p + \sum_{(q,p)\in\varepsilon} m^{i-1}_{q,p}$$
```
     end for
4:       for Each edge (q,p)∈ε do
```
         update and normalize the messages as
$$m^i_{q,p}(d_p) = \min_{d_q}\left\{(\tilde{C}^i_q(d_q) - m^{i-1}_{p,q}(d_q)) + V_{q,p}(d_q,d_p)\right\}$$
```
     end for
5:       Check the stop criterion

6:   end for
```

Compared with TRW-S, TRW-P have the novel features as below [10]:

1. In each iteration i, nodes can be updated simultaneously by using messages from iteration $i - 1$, and there is no data dependency between neighboring nodes. So TRW-P can get high calculation efficiency by parallel computation.
2. Because TRW-P has not data reversing operations, so that memory accessing in TRW-P is very efficient.

3.4 Post Disparity Refinement

Disparity Refinement is one of the important steps in stereo matching. In order to deal with the missing disparities on object boundaries and occluded regions, a multi-step refinement is applied, including left-right cross check, weighted median filter and sub-pixel level correction.

4 Experiment

4.1 TRW-S and TRW-P Analysis

Stereo-matching accuracy and efficiency comparison of TRW-S with TRW-P are as shown in Fig. 4 and Table 1, respectively. Number of iterations is set 200. Through comparison we found: TRW-S algorithm can obtain better matching accuracy, average matching error rate is about 1.6 % lower than the TRW-P. But in terms of efficiency, TRW-P performs significantly better, an average of around 21.5 times faster than the TRW-S. Therefore, for the applications needed higher matching accuracy, we can use TRW-S. For the higher timeliness applications, TRW-S can be adopted.

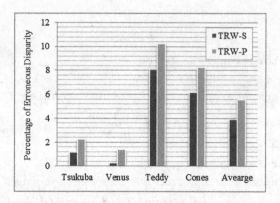

Fig. 4. Bad pixel ration of TRW-S and TRW-P

Table 1. Comparison of execution time for one iteration

	Tsukuba	Venus	Teddy	Cones
TRW-S	28.0495	723.0153	872.0639	107.0363
TRW-P	1.310722	39.24525	38.93142	4.535438
Speed Up	21.4×	18.4×	22.4×	23.6×

4.2 Compared with CF and EM

Here we compare the performance of the proposed CF-EM joint algorithm with the traditional CF, EM, and previous CF-EM combined methods. All these results are based on Middlebury datasets [11]. The comparison results are shown in Fig. 5 and Table 2.

First, we compared CF-EM joint algorithm with the traditional CF algorithms. Here we select adaptive weighting bilateral filtering algorithm [4] based on F-MRF model for comparison. From the results of comparison, the average error rate of CF-EM joint algorithm is 2.4 % lower than adaptive filtering method. The main reason is that in the joint algorithm, potential energy got from F-MRF model by bilateral CF method are sent to L-MRF model for further energy minimization. So we can get smaller energy, and better matching solution.

Traditional EM algorithm is based on L-MRF model. Here we choose classic graph-cuts algorithm [5] and BP algorithm [6] for comparison. According to the contrast results, CF-EM joint algorithm is better than BP in accuracy (average error rate low 3.15 %). This is because that a cost filtering module based on F-MRF model is added in joint algorithm. Compared with graph-cuts algorithm, joint algorithm matching accuracy in Venus and Teddy images is lower, whereas in Tsukuba and Cones is slightly better. From the point of average results, they are on the same level. These demonstrate that by setting the constraints, realizing energy transmission from F-MRF to L-MRF, can effectively improve the matching accuracy of BP, reach the level of the graph-cuts.

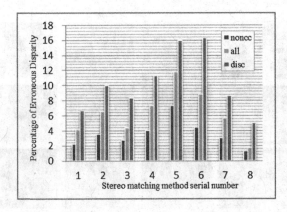

Fig. 5. Average bad pixels ration of stereo-matching

Table·2. Bad pixels percentage of stereo-matching.

No.	Methods	Tsukuba			Venus			Teddy			Cones		
		noncc	all	disc	noncc	all	disc	noncc	all	disc	noncc	all	disc
1	Proposed method	0.93	1.21	4.97	0.12	0.26	1.57	5.98	8.63	14.72	1.78	6.57	5.28
2	Adaptive Filtering[4]	1.38	1.85	6.90	0.71	1.19	6.13	7.88	13.30	18.60	3.97	9.79	8.26
3	Graph-Cuts[5]	1.28	1.57	6.79	0.09	0.17	1.24	5.28	6.64	13.90	4.23	9.06	11.40
4	Belief Propagation[6]	2.68	3.63	9.59	1.33	1.89	9.09	8.36	13.90	16.40	3.71	9.85	9.92
5	Dynamic Programming[8]	1.99	2.84	9.96	1.41	2.10	7.74	15.90	23.90	27.10	10.00	18.30	18.90
6	DP+Adaptive Filtering[13]	2.05	4.22	10.60	1.92	2.98	20.30	7.23	14.40	17.60	6.41	13.70	16.50
7	image segementaton+BP[12]	1.28	1.83	6.65	0.28	0.65	3.29	6.88	11.40	15.40	3.64	8.60	9.09
8	Superpixels Patch Matching[9]	1.63	2.17	8.71	0.15	0.19	2.13	1.91	2.29	5.47	1.32	2.02	3.69

4.3   Compared with Previous CF-EM Combined Methods

Finally, we compared CF-EM joint algorithm with Previous combined methods that have obtained better matching accuracy. DP [8] scatters energy minimization problem to each scan line, in order to reduce computational complexity. But it will produce stripes in disparity image. The adaptive filter combined with DP can improve the matching result. This can be proven by the comparison results of method 5 and 6 [8, 13]. Matching accuracy of CF-EM join algorithm is better than DP (compared with the algorithm 5 and 6, bad pixels ratio fell 7.62 % and 4.66 % respectively). The main reason is the joint algorithm energy minimization is based on "trees", which are smaller than scan-lines, so it can get a better matching accuracy.

Methods 7 is a BP algorithm based on image segmentation [12]. Compared with the traditional BP, belief messages are propagated in the segmentation regions, so matching results are more related to image segmentation, and image segmentation itself is not a trivial. Through the data contrast, CF-EM joint algorithm is slightly better than Method 7.

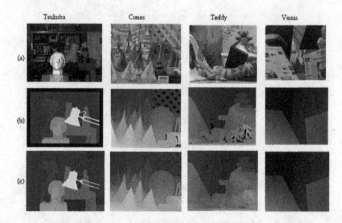

Fig. 6. Stereo-matching results of Middlebury datasets. (a) Original image; (b) ground truth disparity map; (c) Proposed method disparity map

Fig. 7. Results of stereo image pairs in real scenes.

Stereo matching method based on super-pixels patch [9] is thought the best accuracy matching method. The average matching error rate is around 2.5 % lower than CF-EM joint algorithm. But in Tsukuba and Venus images, two algorithms are with the same level accuracy. In the Teddy and Cones images, super-pixels patch matching method obviously has higher accuracy. One of the important reasons is that Teddy and Cones image texture is more abundant, with more super-pixels patch, which is more conducive to patch matching. Super-pixels segmentation now is a research hotspot in computer vision. Super-pixels segmentation is also a problem with high computational complexity. The computational complexity of super-pixels patch matching is $O(|\mathcal{L}| \times N \times P)$, $|\mathcal{L}|$ is the number of disparity tags, N is the number of pixels in images, and P is the number of super-pixels patch. CF-EM joint algorithm computing complexity is $O(|\mathcal{L}| \times N)$. So super-pixels patch matching algorithm is with higher computational complexity (Figs. 6 and 7).

5 Conclusion

In this paper, we give the proof that CF and EM stereo matching algorithm can interconversion with each other under the constraints. On this basis, a CF-EM joint stereo matching algorithm is proposed, which divides the energy minimization process into two stages. The first stage is in F-MRF model, by setting reasonable constraints, EM problem can be converted into CF form to solve, and get the optimization potential function $\hat{C}_p$ with strong robustness; The second stage is in L-MRF model, the output potential function $\hat{C}_p$ of the first stage is as the input of energy function in second stage, to realize further energy convergence with standard EM methods. Finally, optimization disparities are got by post refinement. We compared the performance of the proposed CF-EM joint algorithm with other classic stereo-matching methods. The experimental results demonstrate that the proposed method has good performance in stereo-matching.

Appendix

Proof of Lemma 2.1

Proof. If $d = d_p$, $\varphi(d, d_p) = 0$. We have $\left(C_q(d) + w_{q,p}\varphi(d, d_p)\right) = C_q(d_p)$.

If $d \neq d_p$, $\varphi(d, d_p) = 1$, thus, $\left(C_q(d) + w_{q,p}\varphi(d, d_p)\right) = C_q(d) + w_{q,p}$.
Therefore, $m_{q,p}^1(d) = \min_{d \in \mathcal{L}}\{C_q(d_p) | d = d_p, C_q(d) + w_{q,p} | d \neq d_p\}$.
When $C_q(d_p) = 1$, $C_q(d) = 1$, because $0 \leq \omega \leq 1$, thus

$$m_{q,p}^1(d) = C_q(d_p). \tag{24}$$

When $C_q(d_p) = 1$, $C_q(d) = 0$, thus,

$$m_{q,p}^1(d) = w_{q,p}C_q(d). \tag{25}$$

When $C_q(d_p) = 0$, $m_{q,p}^1(d) = C_q(d_p)$. Because $d = d_p$, $w_{q,p}(d, d_p) = 1$, thus,

$$C_q(d_p) = w_{p,q}C_q(d) | d = d_p \tag{26}$$

Synthesize (24–26), we can get: $m_{q,p}^1(d) = w_{q,p}(d, d_p)C_q(d)$, Eq. (11) is proved.

References

1. Mozerov, M.G., van de Weijer, J.: Accurate stereo matching by two-step energy minimization. IEEE Trans. Image Process. **24**(3), 1153–1163 (2015)
2. Veksler, O.: Stereo correspondence with compact windows via minimum ratio cycle. IEEE Trans. Pattern Anal. Mach. Intell. **24**, 1654–1660 (2002)
3. Xu, Y., Wang, D., Feng, T., Shum, H.-Y.: Stereo computation using radial adaptive windows. In: Proceedings of the 16th International Conference on Pattern Recognition, vol. 3, pp. 595–598 (2002)
4. Yoon, K.-J., Kweon, I.-S.: Locally adaptive support-weight approach for visual correspondence search. In: IEEE Computer Society Conference on Computer Vision and Pattern Recognition, CVPR 2005, vol. 2, pp. 924–931 (2005)
5. Altantawy, D., Obbaya, M., Kishk, S.: A fast non-local based stereo matching algorithm using graph cuts. In: 2014 9th International Conference on Computer Engineering & Systems (ICCES), pp. 130–135 (2014)
6. Yu, T., Lin, R.-S., Super, B., Tang, B.: Efficient message representations for belief propagation. In: IEEE 11th International Conference on Computer Vision, ICCV 2007, pp. 1–8 (2007)
7. Kolmogorov, V.: Convergent tree-reweighted message passing for energy minimization. IEEE Trans. Pattern Anal. Mach. Intell. **28**(10), 1568–1583 (2006)
8. Veksler, O.: Stereo correspondence by dynamic programming on a tree. In: IEEE Computer Society Conference on Computer Vision and Pattern Recognition, CVPR 2005, vol. 2, pp. 384–390 (2005)
9. Lu, J., Yang, H., Min, D., Do, M.: Patch match filter: efficient edge-aware filtering meets randomized search for fast correspondence field estimation. In: 2013 IEEE Conference on Computer Vision and Pattern Recognition (CVPR), pp. 1854–1861 (2013)
10. Zhao, W., Fu, H., Yang, G., Patra, L.W.: Parallel tree-reweighted message passing architecture. In: 2014 24th International Conference on Field Programmable Logic and Applications (FPL), pp. 1–6 (2014)
11. http://vision.middlebury.edu/stereo
12. Shi, C., Wang, G., Pei, X., He, B., Lin, X.: Stereo matching using local plane fitting in confidence-based support window. IEICE Trans. **95-D**(2), 699–702 (2012)
13. Wang, L., Liao, M., Gong, M., Yang, R., Nister, D.: High-quality real-time stereo using adaptive cost aggregation and dynamic programming. In: Third International Symposium on 3D Data Processing, Visualization, and Transmission, pp. 798–805, June 2006

Fine-Grained Vehicle Recognition in Traffic Surveillance

Qi Wang[1,2], Zhongyuan Wang[1,2,3(✉)], Jing Xiao[1,2,3], Jun Xiao[2], and Wenbin Li[2]

[1] State Key Laboratory of Software Engineering, Wuhan University, Wuhan, China
[2] National Engineering Research Center for Multimedia Software,
Computer School of Wuhan University, Wuhan, China
{wangqi1992,jing,junxiao}@whu.edu.cn,
wzy_hope@163.com, wenbin_li@outlook.com
[3] Hubei Provincial Key Laboratory of Multimedia and Network Communication Engineering,
Wuhan University, Wuhan, China

Abstract. Fine-grained vehicle recognition in traffic surveillance plays a crucial part in establishing intelligent transportation system. The major challenge lies in that differences among vehicle models are always subtle. In this paper, we propose a part-based method combining global and local feature for fine-grained vehicle recognition in traffic surveillance. We develop a novel voting mechanism to unify the preliminary recognition results, which are obtained by using Histograms of Oriented Gradients (HOG) and pre-trained convolutional neural networks (CNN), leading to fully exploiting the discriminative ability of different parts. Besides, we collect a comprehensive public database for 50 common vehicle models with manual annotation of parts, which is used to evaluate the proposed method and serves as supportive dataset for related work. The experiments show that the average recognition accuracy of our method can approach 92.3 %, which is 3.4 %–7.1 % higher than the state-of-art approaches.

Keywords: Fine-grained vehicle recognition · CNN feature · Discriminative parts · Fine-grained vehicle dataset

1 Introduction

Vehicle recognition in traffic surveillance is widely used in a variety of scenarios such as urban transportation management and public security administration. Traditional vehicle recognition mainly focuses on classifying vehicle into sedan, SUV, van, truck, etc. This coarse-grained recognition can only be used in certain scenes such as charging system in parking lot or highway entrances and exits. However, various applications, such as searching and controlling suspect vehicle in criminal investigation, require accurate identification of the vehicle model more than the basic type. Compared to coarse-grained recognition, fine-grained recognition is more applicable and significant to the establishment of the urban intelligent transportation system.

Fine-grained recognition refers to distinguishing subcategories, which has been well studied in many fields, such as bird species [1], cat or dog breeds [2]. In the task of fine-grained recognition, the major challenge lies in that the difference between subcategories

© Springer International Publishing AG 2016
E. Chen et al. (Eds.): PCM 2016, Part I, LNCS 9916, pp. 285–295, 2016.
DOI: 10.1007/978-3-319-48890-5_28

can be very subtle since their general appearances are highly similar. In vehicle fine-grained recognition, vehicles belonging to the same manufacture are likely to have similar designing styles but different appearance. Especially for the same series of different years, such as Chevrolet Cruze of 2011 and Chevrolet Cruze of 2013 in Fig. 1, have nearly the same appearance but can be distinguished by the details of specific parts (annotated in the red rectangles). This calls for a finer level appearance representation and focusing on the discriminative parts.

Fig. 1. Illustration of fine-grained vehicle recognition. Left: Chevrolet Cruze of 2011; Right: Chevrolet Cruze of 2013. The red boxes show the discriminative parts. (Color figure online)

Specifically, we try to address the effort to improve the performance of fine-grained recognition from these two aspects.

On the one hand, many researches focus on learning finer level feature to describe details. Descriptors such as SIFT [3] or HOG [4] have been proved effective for certain tasks such as key point detection or pedestrian detection, but they are far from enough to describe subtle details. Recently, the success of ImageNet Challenge [5] demonstrates that powerful features can be learned through CNN. Razavian et al. [6] used features extracted from OverFeat network, which is pre-trained on ImageNet classification task, to tackle a diverse range of recognition tasks and concluded that features obtained from CNN should be the primary candidate in most visual recognition tasks. Yang et al. [7] used the fine-tuned OverFeat model as a feature extractor to perform car model verification. [8] demonstrates the effectiveness of using either the first or second fully connected layers and provides competitive performance on plant classification. All these methods believe that CNN can explore feature information from pixel level and use the whole object as the input of CNN. However, it may lose lots of details when the input is high-resolution. Since generally the inputs of the network are required to be normalized to smaller fixed size. Also using the whole object as input may introduce redundant or even disturbing features for most of the parts of subcategories are highly-similar.

On the other hand, focusing on particular discriminative parts can make it easier to distinguish subordinate categories. Part-based representation that pays attention to detecting and describing certain parts is a common and effective method in fine-grained recognition. Zhang et al. [9] leveraged semantics inherent in strongly-supervised DPM parts and weak sematic annotation to develop deformable part descriptors for fine-grained recognition. Krause [10] proposed a method generating parts using co-segmentation and alignment to get over the great dependency on domain-specific annotation. Also there is another novel method leveraging the potential of crowdsourcing. [11] introduced a simple online game called "Bubbles" that reveals discriminative features human use to help computer to select the discriminative parts. All these method try to identify and select the discriminative parts in various ways. However, when using these parts in recognition, they are not treated discriminatively. That is, they just select the so called "discriminative parts" but make no distinction whether the part is highly-discriminative or averagely-discriminative in recognition.

In this paper, we improve fine-grained vehicle recognition by simultaneously boosting the performance of learning comprehensive feature and exploiting discriminative ability of parts. Firstly, we use strongly-supervised DPM (SSDPM) to detect and localize pre-defined parts. Then, we extract HOG feature of bounding box and CNN feature of each part individually to perform preliminary recognition. Finally a novel voting mechanism is utilized to weigh the results from last step, which leads to making the most of discriminative ability of different parts. Besides, considering there is no accessible and comprehensive dataset of vehicles, we build a database of 4584 high-resolution images for 50 common vehicle types from traffic surveillance, which contains at least 40 images of each type. Also we provide information of bounding boxes and part annotations in xml files.

The remainder of the paper is organized as follows: Details of our proposed method are showed in Sect. 2. We give a full description of our novel database in Sect. 3. Experimental results and analysis are presented in Sect. 4. Finally, we conclude our major contribution and future work in Sect. 5.

2 Proposed Method

2.1 Overview

Figure 2 depicts the framework of our proposed approach. Firstly, a trained SSDPM is used to localize the defined parts. Then we use HOG feature of bounding box to describe the global appearance and CNN feature of each part to represent the local details. Preliminary classification is performed using these features separately and a probability

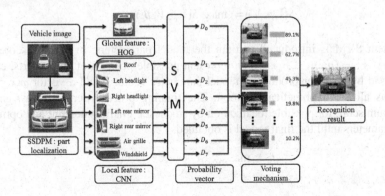

Fig. 2. Framework of proposed method

matrix can be obtained. Finally we leverage a voting mechanism based on the discriminative ability of parts to realize fine-level recognition.

2.2 Part Localization

Referring to related work, we define seven semantic parts of vehicle image: roof, left rearview mirror, windshield, right rearview mirror, left headlight, air grille, right headlight. As shown in Fig. 3, these parts can reveal almost all the information of vehicle image in traffic surveillance to identify particular make and model. To ensure no missing details, overlaps among parts are allowed.

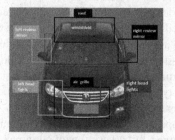

Fig. 3. Vehicle part definition

To localize certain parts, the current state-of-art approach is the Deformable Parts Model (DPM) proposed by Felzenszwalb [12]. The object is represented by a coarse root HOG filter and several higher resolution parts filters. SSDPM [13] employs part-level supervision to enhance the performance of DPM. Based on our annotated database and the symmetry of vehicle frontal image, we use SSDPM to handle precise part localization.

Firstly, we train a model $(F_0, P_1, \ldots, P_n, b)$ by maximizing the scoring function (1) to constrain model parts to be close to the manual part annotation on training images. F_0 denotes root filter, P_i is the ith part filter. The score of a model β in the image $\mathbf{I}$ is determined by given model parts locations p, and the visibility state V.

$$S(\mathbf{I}, p, V) = \max_{c \in \{1..C\}} S(\mathbf{I}, p, V, \beta_c) \tag{1}$$

Latent SVM is introduced to train the model parameters. In (2), the score of a hypothesis $z = (p_1, p_2 \ldots p_n)$, which represent possible position of target parts, can be expressed by an inner product of model parameter vector β and a vector $\varphi(x, z)$ that contains all the hypothetical position. The training process iteratively assigns the maximum score for possible localization by stochastic gradient descent and optimizes the parameters until the final model is obtained.

$$f_\beta = \max_{z \in Z(x)} \beta \cdot \varphi(x, z) \tag{2}$$

2.3 Feature Extraction

To describe detected parts, traditional hand-craft features are not discriminative enough. It works in object detection or coarse recognition representing the general appearance of object. But it usually fails in describing the subtle difference for highly similar subcategories. Section 1 shows trained CNNs can be regarded as a fine-level feature extractor for details of defined part. To recognize the basic and fine-grained categories, we combine global feature and local feature.

Global Feature Extraction. In last step for part localization, SSDPM use HOG template to find the defined part. Thus in our experiment we still use HOG feature to represent the general appearance of detected parts. We use the implementation from [4], which provides classical HOG descriptors with linear SVM classifiers on person detection. The R-HOG feature is calculated with the settings: 128×64 detecting window, 16×16 block size, 8×8 block stride, 8×8 cell size and 9 bins. The HOG feature of bounding box represents the global feature of the vehicle and describes the inter-class difference.

Local Feature Extraction. Caffe [14] developed by Berkeley Vision and Learning Venter (BVLC) provide a clean and modifiable framework for state-of-art deep learning algorithms and a collection of reference models. It provides a C++ library with Python and MATLAB bindings. We use Caffe code to extract the fc7 feature, that is the 7th fully connecter layer, with the default structure and parameter settings. The CNN feature of each part represents the local feature of the vehicle and describes the intra-class difference.

2.4 Voting Mechanism

According to our common sense, different parts are not equally important in recognition task. And features of different levels also reflect different characters. Here we propose a voting mechanism to make maximum use of discriminative ability of different parts and features. In last step, we use the feature of single part and general appearance to perform preliminary recognition and obtain the decision value in SVM classifier as the probability vector, which measures the probability that the target object belongs to certain category. Then we leverage a voting mechanism (3) to compute the final result.

$$\mathbf{P} = \mathbf{w} \cdot \mathbf{D} \tag{3}$$

$\mathbf{P} = (P_1, P_2, \dots, P_i)$ denotes the joint probability of all categories, P_i is the probability that the target vehicle belongs to the ith category. $\mathbf{D}$ is a $M \times N$ matrix, each column of which denotes the probability vector returned from a preliminary recognition using single feature of single part. $\mathbf{w} = (w_0, w_1, \dots, w_m)$ is learned by SVM to weight the importance of all the preliminary recognition results. The recognized label l is the index of the element that has the highest value in vector $\mathbf{P}$:

$$l = \arg \max_k P_k \tag{4}$$

3   Dataset

It is acknowledged that fine-grained recognition is highly domain-specific. Many works in various domains have established public dataset. For bird species recognition, [1] proposed a challenging dataset CUB-200-2011, which contains 200 bird species. This dataset enables related researches on fine-grained bird species [6, 15]. As for vehicle recognition, Krause [16] proposed the Cars Dataset, which is typically at the level of make, model and year. These images collected from the internet vary in background and viewpoints, which doesn't conform to our application. And the image number of each class is not balanced. To our knowledge, there are no such fine-grained vehicle dataset which can provide comprehensive and accessible data of vehicle models. Here we collect a vehicle dataset from traffic surveillance to evaluate our fine-grained method and provide supportive data for related research.

3.1   50 Vehicles Types in Traffic Surveillance

We choose several spots which pass across downtown of the city and have broad vision to ensure abundant traffic and avoid disturbing occlusion. We collect 4584 vehicle images belonging to 50 common vehicle models of 8 makers. There are 5–9 types belong to each maker, at least 40 images of each type. Here we regard the same vehicle model of different years as different vehicle types. Figure 4 shows examples of our 50 vehicle types. We name each model in the form of "manufacture-series-year". The general sketches of all these types seem similar. Especially for those belong to the same manufacture, differences among some types are very subtle.

Fig. 4. Examples of 50 vehicle models

3.2   Annotation Information

We annotate our pre-defined parts in our dataset. The annotation information of bounding boxes and each part are provided in xml files, which is convenient to import to MATLAB or C/C++ language. When we need information of certain parts, we just need to load the original image and the corresponding xml files.

4   Experiment

Our database provides a comprehensive vehicle dataset for our fine-grained task. In previous work [17] we have demonstrated that with increasing number of categories the results of recognition is quite stable. Thus we only present part of our experimental results on a representative portion of our data. Specifically, we choose five highly-similar types of BMW. Table 1 shows quantity distribution of our experiment data. We set the ratio of train samples and test samples as 1:1.

Table 1. Quantity distribution of experimental data

Vehicle model	Number of database	Number of training set	Number of testing set
BMW 3 Series 2010	65	33	32
BMW 3 Series 2013	42	21	21
BMW 5 Series 2013	101	50	51
BMW 7 Series 2011	45	23	22
BMW X5 Series 2011	55	27	28
Total	308	154	154

First of all, we test the precision of part localization using SSDPM. In Fig. 5, the horizontal axis is the overlap ratio of detected parts, which is defined as the percentage of the area of overlap and the area of annotated bounding box. The vertical axis is the average precision of detecting results that meet the corresponding threshold. As we can see, all the parts can reach more than 70 % precision when the threshold of overlap ratio is 50 %, which lays foundation for further recognition.

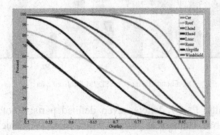

Fig. 5. Parts localization results using SSDPM

To eliminate the influence of part localization, we perform proposed method separately on annotated data and SSDPM localized data.

Firstly, we compute global and local feature of corresponding patches. For CNN feature of defined seven parts, we use pre-trained CNN to extract the fc7 feature, that is the 7th fully connecter layer, with the default structure and parameter settings. For HOG feature of vehicle bounding boxes, the R-HOG feature is calculated with the settings: 128×64 detecting window, 16×16 block size, 8×8 block stride, 8×8 cell size and 9 bins. Then we use computed feature from last step to perform preliminary recognition and calculate probability vector of each subcategory. The final recognition result is obtained using the voting mechanism.

Figure 6 shows the results of our method on annotated data and SSDPM localized data. Column 1–8 show the preliminary accuracy when using feature of each part or bounding box individually. The last column shows the final results after voting mechanism. Figure 7 shows the confusion matrix of recognition result using our proposed method. As we can see:

(1) The average precision of recognition on annotated data is apparently higher than the precision of recognition on SSDPM localized data, which is caused by the inevitable error in part localization. However, the accuracy of our proposed method can still reach 92.3 % in the case of SSDPM.
(2) The recognition accuracy varies when using different parts individually, which reflects different discriminative ability of different parts. Parts that contain rich texture, such as headlights and air grille, reflect much more information of vehicle type, leading to better performance in primary recognition. That is, the recognition based on highly-discriminative parts is more reliable. Thus it is reasonable that we use an adaptive weight to integrate the parts discriminatively.
(3) The performance is quite good for some relatively distinctive categories, e.g. the BMW X5 series of 2011 has accuracy of 100 % in both annotation data and SSDPM localized data. However, the accuracy of BMW 7 series of 2011 in SSDPM localized data is 76 % due to the similarity of models.

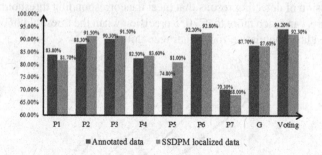

Fig. 6. Experiment results: P1-P7 denote seven defined parts: Roof, Left headlight, Right headlight, Left rear mirror, Right rear mirror, Air grille, Windshield; G denotes general appearance.

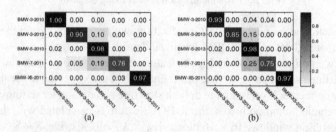

Fig. 7. Confusion matrix of experiment result on annotated dataset (a) and SSDPM localized dataset (b)

Also we use standard Caffe, which provides state-of-art results in fine-grained tasks, on the same train/test dataset as comparison. Besides, we also perform recognition by directly concatenating the feature of parts and bounding box. Here is the analysis of our results in Table 2:

(1) Our method outperforms the state-of-art Caffe method. The accuracy is 7.1 % higher in annotated dataset and 3.4 % higher in SSDPM localized dataset, which demonstrates the effectiveness of our part-based method. By combining the global and local feature, both the inter-class difference and intra-class difference can be presented. Besides, fine-tuning CNN can be time-consuming and needs plenty of samples. Our method based on pre-trained CNN is more efficient.

(2) Comparing to directly using the concatenated features, the accuracy of our method is 4.9 % higher in annotated data and 4.4 % higher in SSDPM localized data, which mainly due to our two-stage recognition and voting mechanism. In the preliminary recognition, probability vectors are computed to measure the discriminative ability of features and serve as the candidate recognition results. And the voting mechanism balances the weights of these results and computes the final results. Besides the dimension of concatenated features is quite high which puts higher requirement of computational capabilities.

Table 2. Comparison with Caffe and concatenated feature

	Caffe	Concatenated feature	Ours
Annotated data	87.1 %	89.3 %	**94.2 %**
SSDPM localized data	88.9 %	87.9 %	**92.3 %**

In conclusion, our experiment shows competitive results relative to previous work.

5 Conclusion

In fine-grained vehicle recognition in traffic surveillance, the major challenge lies in distinguishing highly-similar vehicle models by subtle differences. In this paper, we proposed a part-based method combining global and local features to improve the recognition results. There are two major contributions of our work: (1) We developed a part-based two-stage recognition method and adopted a novel voting mechanism to make the maximum use of discriminative ability of different parts; (2) We collected a comprehensive vehicle database from traffic surveillance with annotation information of parts to evaluate our method, which is also favorable to vehicle related work.

Experiments on our dataset show competitive results. The average precision can approach 92.3 %, which is 3.4 %–7.1 % higher than the state-of-art results.

Acknowledgements. This work was partly supported by the National Natural Science Foundation of China (61502348), the EU FP7 QUICK project under Grant Agreement No. PIRSES-GA-2013-612652, China Postdoctoral Science Foundation funded project (2014M562058), Scientific Research Foundation for the Returned Overseas Chinese Scholars,

State Education Ministry ([2014]1685), the Fundamental Research Funds for the Central Universities (2042016gf0033), Natural Science Fund of Hubei Province (2015CFB406).

References

1. Wah, C., Branson, S., Welinder, P., Perona, P., Belongie, S.: The caltech-UCSD birds-200-2011 dataset (2011)
2. Parkhi, O.M., Vedaldi, A., Zisserman, A., Jawahar, C.V.: Cats and dogs. In: IEEE Conference on Computer Vision and Pattern Recognition, pp. 3498–3505 (2012)
3. Lowe, D.G.: Distinctive image features from scale-invariant keypoints. Int. J. Comput. Vis. **60**(2), 91–110 (2004)
4. Dalal, N., Triggs, B.: Histograms of oriented gradients for human detection. In: IEEE Computer Society Conference on Computer Vision and Pattern Recognition, vol. 1, pp. 886–893 (2005)
5. Krizhevsky, A., Sutskever, I., Hinton, G.E.: ImageNet classification with deep convolutional neural networks. In: Advances in Neural Information Processing Systems, pp. 1097–1105 (2012)
6. Razavian, A., Azizpour, H., Sullivan, J., Carlsson, S.: CNN features off-the-shelf: an astounding baseline for recognition. In: Proceedings of the IEEE Conference on Computer Vision and Pattern Recognition Workshops, pp. 806–813 (2014)
7. Yang, L., Luo, P., Change Loy, C., Tang, X.: A large-scale car dataset for fine-grained categorization and verification. In: Proceedings of the IEEE Conference on Computer Vision and Pattern Recognition, pp. 3973–3981 (2015)
8. Sünderhauf, N., McCool, C., Upcroft, B., Perez, T.: Fine-grained plant classification using convolutional neural networks for feature extraction. In: CLEF (Working Notes), pp. 756–762 (2014)
9. Zhang, N., Farrell, R., Iandola, F., Darrell, T.: Deformable part descriptors for fine-grained recognition and attribute prediction. In: IEEE International Conference on Computer Vision, pp. 729–736 (2013)
10. Krause, J., Jin, H., Yang, J., Fei-Fei, L.: Fine-grained recognition without part annotations. In: Proceedings of the IEEE Conference on Computer Vision and Pattern Recognition, pp. 5546–5555 (2015)
11. Deng, J., Krause, J., Fei-Fei, L.: Fine-grained crowdsourcing for fine-grained recognition. In: Proceedings of the IEEE Conference on Computer Vision and Pattern Recognition, pp. 580–587 (2013)
12. Felzenszwalb, P.F., Girshick, R.B., McAllester, D., Ramanan, D.: Object detection with discriminatively trained part-based models. IEEE Trans. Pattern Anal. Mach. Intelle. **32**(9), 1627–1645 (2010)
13. Azizpour, H., Laptev, I.: Object detection using strongly-supervised deformable part models. In: Fitzgibbon, A., Lazebnik, S., Perona, P., Sato, Y., Schmid, C. (eds.) ECCV 2012. LNCS, vol. 7572, pp. 836–849. Springer, Heidelberg (2012). doi:10.1007/978-3-642-33718-5_60
14. Jia, Y., Shelhamer, E., Donahue, J., Karayev, S., Long, J., Girshick, R., Darrell, T.: Caffe: Convolutional architecture for fast feature embedding. In: Proceedings of the ACM International Conference on Multimedia, pp. 675–678 (2014)
15. Donahue, J., Jia, Y., Vinyals, O., Hoffman, J., Zhang, N., Tzeng, E., Darrell, T.: DeCAF: a deep convolutional activation feature for generic visual recognition. arXiv preprint arXiv: 1310.1531 (2013)

16. Krause, J., Stark, M., Deng, J., Fei-Fei, L.: 3D object representations for fine-grained categorization. In: Proceedings of the IEEE International Conference on Computer Vision Workshops, pp. 554–561 (2013)
17. Liao, L., Hu, R., Xiao, J., Wang, Q., Xiao, J., Chen, J.: Exploiting effects of parts in fine-grained categorization of vehicles. In: IEEE International Conference on Image Processing, pp. 745–749 (2015)

Transductive Classification by Robust Linear Neighborhood Propagation

Lei Jia[1,2], Zhao Zhang[1,2(✉)], and Weiming Jiang[1,2]

[1] School of Computer Science and Technology & Joint International Research
Laboratory of Machine Learning and Neuromorphic Computing,
Soochow University, Suzhou 215006, China
cszzhang@gmail.com
[2] Collaborative Innovation Center of Novel Software Technology and
Industrialization, Nanjing 210023, China

Abstract. We propose an enhanced label prediction method termed Transductive Classification Robust Linear Neighborhood Propagation (R-LNP). To encode the neighborhood reconstruction error more accurately, we apply the L2,1-norm that is proved to be very robust to noise for characterizing the manifold smoothing term. Since L2,1-norm can also enforce the neighborhood reconstruction error to be sparse in rows, i.e., entries of some rows are zeros. In addition, to enhance robustness in the process of modeling the difference between the initial labels and predicted ones, we also regularize the weighted L2,1-norm on the label fitting term, so the resulted measures would be more accurate. Compared with several transductive label propagation models, our proposed algorithm obtains state-of-the-art performance over extensive representation and classification experiments.

Keywords: Manifold smoothing term · L2,1-norm · Regularize · Classification

1 Introduction

Classification is a fundamental research topic in the fields of pattern recognition and data mining [5]. Existing classification methods can be categorized into supervised and semi-supervised [2] ones. Label propagation (LP) [1, 6, 10–12, 18–20], as a typical classification model by semi-supervised learning (SSL), has been arousing considerable research interests because of its efficiency and effectiveness. Typical transductive LP methods consist of *Gaussian Fields and Harmonic Function* (GFHF) [13], *Learning with Local and Global Consistency* (LLGC) [12] and *Linear Neighborhood Propagation* (LNP) [1], and *Special Label Propagation* [9]. LNP can not only detect the outliers in given data effectively, but also output the estimated unknown labels of data points as probabilistic values, by comparing with GFHF and LLGC. For label estimation, LNP propagates label information from labeled samples to the whole dataset by using linear neighborhoods with sufficient smoothness. In this study, we mainly discuss the issue of enhancing the LNP model by improving the robustness against noise and outliers in given data.

In this paper, we will propose a new robustness-promoting SSL algorithm for classification, called Robust Transductive Linear Neighborhood Propagation (R-LNP).

E. Chen et al. (Eds.): PCM 2016, Part I, LNCS 9916, pp. 296–305, 2016.
DOI: 10.1007/978-3-319-48890-5_29

R-LNP is built based on the idea of LNP but improves LNP from the following two aspects. First, we employ the L2,1-norm [4, 14] on the distance metric instead of the original Frobenius norm. The motivation behind employing the L2,1-norm [14] for measuring the neighborhood reconstruction error is that the distance metric resulted by L2,1-norm [14] is robust to noise and outliers in data, more importantly, it can enforce reconstruction error matrix to be sparse in each row, i.e., entries of some rows are zeros [4, 14, 15]. So, L2,1-norm regularization has the potential to reduce the reconstruction error. Second, similarly to enhance the robustness in the procedure of characterizing the difference between initial labels and predicted ones, we propose to use a weighted L2,1-norm regularization on the fitness error so that the resulted measurement would be more accurate as well in addition to make the results meet the terms of being robust to noise and being discriminatory. Simulations on data classification verified the superiority of our algorithm in performance and robustness over existing methods.

We outlined the paper as follows. Section 2 briefly reviews the formulation of LNP. In Sect. 3, we propose R-LNP. Section 4 describes the settings and evaluation results. Finally, the paper is concluded in Sect. 5.

2   Related Work

Given a collection of N samples in $X = [X_L, X_U] \in \mathbb{R}^{n \times (l+u)}$, where n is the original dimensionality of samples, $l + u = N$ is the number of samples, $X_L = [x_1, \cdots x_l] \in \mathbb{R}^{n \times l}$ represents a labeled set, $X_U = [x_{l+1}, \ldots, x_{l+u}] \in \mathbb{R}^{n \times u}$ is an unlabeled dataset and each column vector $x_i \in \mathbb{R}^n$ denotes a training sample. LNP assume that there are c classes in X_L, all classes are present in X_L and each sample has a unique label $l(x_i)$ belonging to $\{1, 2, \ldots, c\}$, where c is the number of classes. By propagating label information of labeled samples in X_L to the unlabeled points in X_U according their relationships based on the constructed weighted similarity graph. LNP first uses neighborhood information of each point to construct $G = (X, E)$ by assuming that each data point x_i can be optimally reconstructed with the linear combination of its neighbors [7], which can be formulated as

$$\underset{w_i}{Min} \left\| x_i - \sum_{j:x_j \in \mathbb{N}(x_i)} w_{i,j} x_j \right\|_2^2, Subj \sum_{j:x_j \in \mathbb{N}(x_i)} w_{i,j} = 1, w_{i,j} \geq 0, \tag{1}$$

where $\mathbb{N}(x_i)$ is the K-neighbor set of x_i, $\|\bullet\|_2$ is L2-norm, and $W_{i,j}$ measures the contribution of x_j for reconstructing x_i. Let $Y = [y_1, y_2, \ldots, y_{l+u}] \in \mathbb{R}^{c \times N}$ be the initial labels of all samples, where $y_{i,j} = 1$ if x_j is labeled as $i(1 \leq i \leq c)$ and else $y_{i,j} = 0$. Then the result of LNP can be solving the following problem:

$$J(F) = \arg \underset{F}{\min} \, tr\big(F(I^N - W)F^{\mathrm{T}}\big) + \mu \sum_{i=1}^{l+u} \|f_i - y_i\|_2^2, \tag{2}$$

where $F = [f_1, f_2, \ldots, f_{l+u}] \in \mathbb{R}^{c \times N}$ denotes the predicted soft label matrix. μ is a positive weighting parameter for trade-offing the involved two terms, I^N denotes an identity matrix in $\mathbb{R}^N$, and $I^N - W$ can be considered as the graph Laplacian of a graph. Let $\alpha = 1/\mu + 1$, the solution of LNP can be obtained as

$$F^* = (1 - \alpha)(I^N - \alpha W)^{-1} Y, \tag{3}$$

Then, the label of each point x_j can be assigned as $\arg\max_{i \leq c} F_{i,j}^*$, the position corresponding to the biggest element of each label vector decides label of x_j.

3   Robust Linear Neighborhood Propagation (R-LNP)

3.1   Proposed Formulation

We mainly present R-LNP for enhancing the performance of LNP for predicting the unknown labels of unlabeled samples by transductive label propagation. To measure the neighborhood reconstruction error more accurately, we include the L2,1-norm [4, 14, 15] on it. To make the distance metric for modeling the label fitness more accurately, we use a weighted L2,1-norm on the term. As a result, the robustness to noise and outliers can be enhanced. These lead to the following objective function for our R-LNP to represent and classify given samples:

$$\underset{F}{Min}\ \widehat{J} = \sum_{i=1}^{l+u} \left\| f_i^T - \sum_{j:x_j \in \mathrm{N}(x_i)} w_{i,j} f_j^T \right\|_2 + \sum_{i=1}^{l+u} \mu_i \left\| f_i^T - y_i^T \right\|_2, \tag{4}$$

where $f_i \in \mathbb{R}^c$ is the soft label of x_i, $\sum_{i=1}^{l+u} \left\| f_i^T - \sum_{j:x_j \in \mathrm{N}(x_i)} w_{i,j} f_j^T \right\|_2$ is the neighborhood reconstruction term for modeling the manifold smoothness, $\sum_{i=1}^{l+u} \mu_i \left\| f_i^T - y_i^T \right\|_2$ is the weighted L2,1-norm-based label fitting term that ensures the predicted soft labels of the labeled samples are similar to the initial ones. Besides, the measures on the manifold smoothing and label fitting terms will be more accurate and robustness will be enhanced since L2,1-norm regularization is used.

Based on using the matrix expressions, the above objective function (4) can be reformulated as

$$\underset{F}{Min}\ \widehat{J} = \left\| F^T - WF^T \right\|_{2,1} + tr\left((F^T - Y^T)^T UV (F^T - Y^T) \right), \tag{5}$$

when $\|h^i\|_2 \neq 0$, $i = 1, 2, \ldots, l+u$, where $F = [f_1, \cdots f_N] \in \mathbb{R}^{c \times N}$ is the predicted soft label matrix, U is a diagonal matrix with the adjustable parameter μ_i as its diagonal elements. As the labels of x_i is known, $\mu_i = 10^{10}$, and else $\mu_i = 0$. V denotes a diagonal matrix with elements being $v_{ii} = 1/2\|h^i\|_2$, $i = 1, 2, \ldots, l+u$, and h^i is the i-th row vector of $F^T - Y^T$. Clearly, since L2,1-norm is imposed on the manifold smoothing term, so the neighborhood reconstruction error matrix $F^T - \widetilde{W} F^T$ will be sparse in rows, i.e., entries of some rows are shrunk to zeros [3, 17]. Next, we will mainly describe its optimization procedures.

3.2 Optimization for Label Neighborhood Propagation

We describe the optimization procedure for the problem in (5). First, according to [14], we know that although $\|F^{\mathrm{T}} - WF^{\mathrm{T}}\|_{2,1}$ is convex, but it's derivative w.r.t. F does not exist when $(F^{\mathrm{T}} - WF^{\mathrm{T}})^j = 0, j = 1, 2, \cdots N$, where $(F^{\mathrm{T}} - WF^{\mathrm{T}})^j$ is the j-th row of the reconstruction error matrix $F^{\mathrm{T}} - WF^{\mathrm{T}}$, therefore when each $(F^{\mathrm{T}} - WF^{\mathrm{T}})^j \neq 0$. As seen from [14, 15], we can approximately represent the term $\|F^{\mathrm{T}} - WF^{\mathrm{T}}\|_{2,1}$ as

$$\|F^{\mathrm{T}} - WF^{\mathrm{T}}\|_{2,1} = tr\left((F^{\mathrm{T}} - WF^{\mathrm{T}})^{\mathrm{T}} Q (F^{\mathrm{T}} - WF^{\mathrm{T}}) \right), \tag{6}$$

where $Q \in \mathbb{R}^{N \times N}$ is a diagonal matrix with elements being $Q_{ii} = 1/(2\|T^i\|_2)$, $i = 1, 2, \ldots, N$, and T^i denotes the i-th row vector of $F^{\mathrm{T}} - WF^{\mathrm{T}}$. Note that the above approximation can hold when each $\|T^i\|_2 \neq 0$, $i = 1, 2, \ldots, N$.

By combining (5) with the formulation of $\|F^{\mathrm{T}} - WF^{\mathrm{T}}\|_{2,1}$, the optimization criterion for our presented R-LNP algorithm can be approximated written as

$$\underset{F,Q,V}{Min} \ tr\left(F(I - W^{\mathrm{T}}) Q (I - \widehat{W}) F^{\mathrm{T}} \right) + tr\left((F^{\mathrm{T}} - Y^{\mathrm{T}})^{\mathrm{T}} UV (F^{\mathrm{T}} - Y^{\mathrm{T}}) \right). \tag{7}$$

It's clearly that the involved problem has several variables (Q, F, V) to optimize and more importantly they are depend on each other, so it cannot be solved directly. By following the common procedure, we solve our problem by using an alternate optimization strategy. When both variables Q and V are known, we can update F_{k+1} at the $(k + 1)$-th iteration by solving (7), which produces the following soft label matrix:

$$F_{k+1} = YUV_k\left((I - W^{\mathrm{T}}) Q_k (I - W) + UV_k \right)^{-1}. \tag{8}$$

After F_{k+1} is computed, we focus on updating V and Q. where V is a diagonal matrix with the elements being $h^i_{k+1} = (F^{\mathrm{T}}_{k+1} - Y^{\mathrm{T}})^i$ and Q is a diagonal matrix with the elements being $T^i = (F^{\mathrm{T}}_{k+1} - WF^{\mathrm{T}}_{k+1})^i, i = 1, 2 \cdots N$.

After convergence of the algorithm, we can get the optimal F^*, where the position corresponding to the biggest element in label vector f_i decides the class assignment of each x_i. That is, the hard label of x_i can be assigned as $\arg \max_{i \leq c} (f_i)_i$, where $(f_i)_i$ is i-th entry of the estimated soft label vector f_i. For complete presentation of the approach, we summarize the procedures of R-LNP in Algorithm 1.

3.3 Approach for Including Outside Samples

We discuss the approach for our R-LNP to include the out-of-sample points using the similar method as LNP [1]. Given a new test sample x_{new}, first search its K-neighbors from the union of training samples and itself, and then compute the coefficient vector $w(x_{new}, x)$ that measures the contribution of its nearest neighbors for reconstructing the label of sample x_{new}.

For inductive classification, we use the smoothness criterion for x_{new} by solving the following optimization problem:

Algorithm 1. Proposed R-LNP framework

Inputs : Datasets $X = [x_1, x_2, ..., x_{l+u}] \in \mathbb{R}^{n \times N}$, Label set $Y = [y_1, y_2, ..., y_{l+u}] \in \mathbb{R}^{c \times N}$

Initialization : $tol=1e-5$; $V_0 = I^N$; $Q_0 = I^N$; $F=Y$; $max=1000$;

While not converged do

1. Fix Q and V, update the soft label matrix F by

$F_{k+1} = YUV_k \left((I - W^T)Q_k(I - W) + UV_k \right)^{-1}$;

2. Fix F and update V_{k+1} by $V_{k+1} = diag\left(1/2\|h^i\|_2\right)$, where

$h^i = \left(F^T - Y^T\right)^i$, $i = 1, 2 \cdots N$;

3. Fix F and update Q_{k+1} by $(Q_{i,i})_{k+1} = diag\left(1/2\|T^i\|_2\right)$, where

$T^i = \left(F^T - \hat{W}F^T\right)^i$, $i = 1, 2 \cdots N$;

4. Convergence check : if $\|F_{k+1} - F_k\|_F^2 \leq tol$, stop;

else $k = k + 1$.

End while

Outputs : The optimal predicted soft label matrix $F^* = F_{k+1}$

$$\vartheta(f(x_{new})) = \sum_{i: x_i \in X_L, x_i \in \mathbb{N}(x_{new})} w(x_{new}, x_i)(f(x_{new}) - f_i)^2. \tag{9}$$

Since $\vartheta(f)$ is convex in $f(x_{new})$, it is minimized when

$$f(x_{new}) = \sum_{i: x_i \in X_L, x_i \in \mathbb{N}(x_{new})} w(x_{new}, x_i)f_i, \tag{10}$$

where $\mathbb{N}(x_{new})$ is the K-neighborhood of x_{new}. Finally, the label of x_{new} can be optimally reconstructed from the labels of its neighbors in the training set, that is

$$f(x_{new}) = \min_{f(x_{new})} \left\| f(x_{new}) - \sum_{i: x_i \in X_L, x_i \in \mathbb{N}(x_{new})} w(x_{new}, x_i)f_i \right\|^2, \tag{11}$$

where the position corresponding to the biggest element in the label vector $f(x_{new})$ determines the class assignment of x_{new}. That is, the hard label of each test data x_{new} can be assigned as $\arg\max_{i \leq c}(f(x_{new}))$, where $f(x_{new})$ denotes the i-th entry of the estimated soft label vector f_{new}.

To illustrate the effective of using our R-LNP algorithm for including the out-of-sample points, provide the following experiment. We choose a dataset called Synthetic Control Chart Time Series from the UCI machine learning repository. It has 600 subjects. The number of K used in nearest neighbor search here is set to 3. We show the results in Fig. 1. When the size of training set is fixed, we divide training data

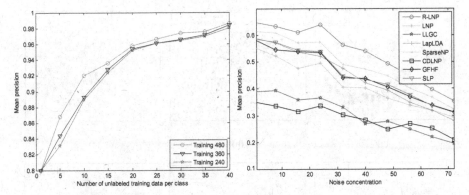

Fig. 1. Approach for out-of-sample data. We fix the size of the training set to be 240, 360 and 480, and remaining data points (outside samples) for testing.

Fig. 2. Classification accuracy of each model on the AR female face database.

into two subsets, including unlabeled and labeled training data. The horizontal axis is the number of unlabeled training samples from each class. It is clearly that the prediction performance can be effectively improved with the increasing number of training samples from each class.

4 Experiments

We evaluate our R-LNP for representation and classification, along with illustrating the comparison results with other related semi-supervised methods, including GFHF, LLGC, LNP, SLP, *Class Dissimilarity based LNP* (CD-LNP) [8], *Sparse Neighborhood Propagation* (SparseNP) [10] and Laplacian Linear Discriminant Analysis (LapLDA) [11]. The number of K used in nearest neighbor search is set to 7 for each method if without special remarks. We mainly evaluate the robustness property of our method to noise, we provide some numerical results of handing datasets with noise. Random Gaussian noise is manually added to given training data by $Data = Data + \sqrt{Var} \times randn(size(Data))$, where *var* is variance.

4.1 "Two-Moons" Dataset

We first perform an experiment on the artificial "two moons" dataset. This toy dataset contains two non-linearly separable two half-moon distributions, where each half-moon distribution corresponds to one class consisting of 400 data points. Figure 3(a) shows the original distribution of the "two moons" dataset. In this study, random Gaussian noise is added to each sample for evaluating the robustness property of each algorithm against corruptions, that is, we mainly examine the effectiveness of our R-LNP for predicting the labels of unlabeled data points in the noisy case, and the comparison results are shown in Fig. 3.

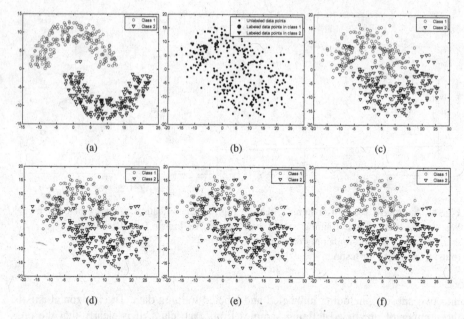

Fig. 3. Classification on the pattern of two noisy moons. (a) Original data set. (b) Original data set add with random noise. (c) LapLDA; (d) LLGC; (e) CD-LNP; (f) R-LNP.

We can observe easily from Fig. 3(c–e) that LapLDA, LLGC and CDLNP all deliver a worse performance for predicting the labels of unlabeled points than our R-LNP due to the negative effects of added noise, since the LapLDA, LLGC and CDLNP all measure the manifold smoothness degree or neighborhood reconstruction error by using the Frobenius norm regularization that which is proved to be very sensitive to noise and outliers [3]. On the contrary, our R-LNP can classify most unlabeled points accurately. Thus, our algorithm has the potential power to handle the case where some ambiguous are existed due to the positive effects brought by using L2,1-norm regularization to measure neighborhood reconstruction error and label fitness error.

4.2 Object Classification

We evaluate our proposed R-LNP for object recognition by using the COIL-20 database [16]. This object database contains 20 objects, each image is represented by using a 1024-dimensional vector. In this study, we prepare two experimental settings for evaluations. First, test each method on the original object images; Then, examine the performance on the noisy case. In noisy case, Gaussian noise with $\sqrt{Var} = 0.5$ is set here. Under each setting, we vary the number of labeled object images from 1 to 11 and observe the change trends. Comparable results are shown in Fig. 4. We can clearly see that the increasing number of training images from each class can significantly enhance classification results. More specifically, R-LNP also obtains better results than other

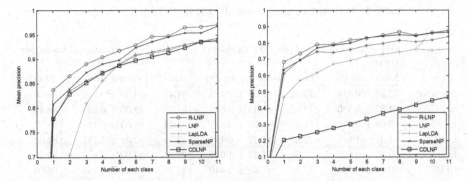

Fig. 4. Classification accuracy of each algorithm on the COIL-20 object database, where the left is the result on the original data points and the right is the result of adding noise.

methods on original images. For the results on noisy case, similar observations can be found. First, our proposed R-LNP achieves the better results in most cases due to the positive effects brought by using L2,1-norm for measuring the neighborhood reconstruction error and label fitness error, especially for cases that the number of training data is smaller.

4.3 Face Recognition

We evaluate the methods for representing and recognizing face images. Two face databases are used. The first one is Georgia Tech face database that includes 50 persons with each person having 15 face images, i.e., totally 750 face images. The second one is AR female face database that has 50 persons with 1300 face images as a whole, each image can be represented by using a 1024-dimensional vector. First examine our R-LNP on Georgia Tech face database. Table 1 describes the result of each approach. We report the mean accuracy (%) with standard deviation (STD) and highest accuracy (%) for each approach. We can see from the results that our proposed R-LNP can achieve higher accuracies than other algorithms in most cases due to the more reliable distance metric on the neighborhood reconstruction and label fitness errors. LLGC is the worst one over this database.

In addition, we also examine our R-LNP for recognizing the AR female face images under noisy case, and will focus on the problem of noise concentration. The evaluation results are shown in Fig. 2. Note that we include random noise to corrupt randomly chosen values of training images for evaluating the robustness property of each algorithm against corruptions. The number of training faces of each person is set to 20. We have the following observations. First, the overall performance of each algorithm is decreased when the level of noise is increased from low to high level. Second, we can see clearly that our proposed R-LNP method can always deliver a better performance than other methods, since its result goes down slower than other methods. It also can be found that the results of LLGC and CD-LNP [8] are comparable with each other, but both are inferior to the other algorithms. SparseNP can also obtain

Table 1. Performance comparison of on Georgia Tech face database.

Method	Result					
	GTF database (4 labeled per class)		GTF database (8 labeled per class)		GTF database (12 labeled per class)	
	Mean ± std (%)	Best (%)	Mean ± std (%)	Best (%)	Mean ± std (%)	Best (%)
SparseNP	72.27 ± 0.418	**75.45**	80.44 ± 0.495	81.43	84.00 ± 0.915	86.00
SLP	71.82 ± 0.650	73.82	80.43 ± 0.640	81.71	85.00 ± 0.855	**86.67**
LNP	69.09 ± 0.809	71.27	80.29 ± 0.425	81.14	85.00 ± 0.156	85.33
LLGC	45.37 ± 1.155	49.82	51.72 ± 0.495	52.71	62.49 ± 1.141	64.00
LapLDA	69.91 ± 0.865	71.64	75.57 ± 1.025	78.00	82.00 ± 0.656	83.33
GFHF	70.91 ± 0.820	72.55	80.43 ± 0.440	82.00	84.67 ± 0.734	86.00
CD-LNP	64.46 ± 0.405	65.27	74.57 ± 0.580	75.71	79.33±0.529	80.67
R-LNP	**73.00 ± 0.365**	74.73	**81.91 ± 0.295**	**82.50**	**85.34 ± 0.447**	**86.67**

the better results that are better than other remaining algorithms. The results of both GFHF and SLP are also comparative with each other in most cases.

5   Concluding Remarks

We proposed a robust transductive linear neighborhood propagation algorithm for enhanced SSL. The key idea is to improve the robust property of existing linear neighborhood propagation against noise by fully considering the robust and sparse properties of the L2,1-norm regularization. Technically, we regularize the L2,1-norm on the neighborhood reconstruction error so that the distance metric is more accurate and robust to noise. Besides, we apply a weighted L2,1-norm on the label fitness term so that the measured difference between predicted labels and the initial ones. The numerical results also demonstrate the superiority of the proposed method over other related transductive label propagation methods. In future work, we will extend the proposed algorithm to the out-of-sample extension for including the outside samples more efficiently. In addition, we will investigate other reliable distance metric for measuring both the neighborhood reconstruction error and label fitness term so that more accurate predictions can be obtained.

Acknowledgments. This work is partially supported by the National Natural Science Foundation of China (61402310, 61672365, 61672364 and 61373093), Major Program of Natural Science Foundation of Jiangsu Higher Education Institutions of China (15KJA520002), Special Funding of China Postdoctoral Science Foundation (2016T90494), Postdoctoral Science Foundation of China (2015M580462) and Postdoctoral Science Foundation of Jiangsu Province of China (1501091B), Natural Science Foundation of Jiangsu Province of China (BK20140008, BK20141195), and Graduate Student Innovation Project of Jiangsu Province of China (SJZZ15_0154, SJZZ16_0236).

References

1. Wang, F., Zhang, C.: Label propagation through linear neighborhoods. IEEE Trans. Knowl. Data Eng. **20**(1), 55–67 (2008)
2. Wang, Y., Chen, S., Zhou, Z.H.: New semi-supervised classification method based on modified cluster assumption. IEEE Trans. Neural Netw. Learn. Syst. **23**(5), 689–702 (2012)
3. Zhang, F., Yang, J., Qian, J.: Nuclear norm-based 2-DPCA for extracting features from images. IEEE Trans. Neural Netw. Learn. Syst. **26**(10), 2247–2260 (2015)
4. Yang, Y., Shen, H.T.: L2,1-norm regularized discriminative feature selection for unsupervised learning. In: Proceedings of the Twenty-Second International Joint Conference on Artificial Intelligence, vol. 2, pp. 1589–1594 (2011)
5. Data, C., Mining, D.: Concepts and techniques. San Franc. **29**(1), 1–18 (2010)
6. Zhang, F., Zhang, J.S.: Label propagation through sparse neighborhood and its applications. Neurocomputing **97**, 267–277 (2012)
7. Wang, J.: Locally Linear Embedding. Springer, Heidelberg (2012)
8. Zhang, C., Wang, S., Li, D.: Prior class dissimilarity based linear neighborhood propagation. Knowl. Based Syst. **83**, 58–65 (2015)
9. Nie, F., Xiang, S., Liu, Y.: A general graph-based semi-supervised learning with novel class discovery. Neural Comput. Appl. **19**(4), 549–555 (2010)
10. Zhang, Z., Zhang, L., Zhao, M.B., Jiang, W.M., Liang, Y.C., Li, F.Z.: Semi-supervised image classification by nonnegative sparse neighborhood propagation. In: Proceedings of the ACM International Conference on Multimedia Retrieval, Shanghai, pp. 139–146 (2015)
11. Tang, H., Fang, T., Shi, P.F.: Laplacian linear discriminant analysis. Pattern Recognit. **39**(1), 136–139 (2006)
12. Zhou, D., Bousquet, O., Lal, T.N., Weston, J., Scholkopf, B.: Learning with local and global consistency. Adv. Neural Inf. Proces. Syst. **17**(4), 321–328 (2004)
13. Zhu, X., Ghahramani, Z., Lafferty, J.: Semi-supervised learning using gaussian fields and harmonic functions. In: Proceedings of 20th International Conference on Machine Learning, pp. 912–919 (2003)
14. Hou, C.P., Nie, F.P., Li, X.L., Yi, D.Y., Wu, Y.: Joint embedding learning and sparse regression: a framework for unsupervised feature selection. IEEE Trans. Cybern. **44**(6), 793–804 (2014)
15. Nie, F., Huang, H., Cai, X., Ding, C.: Efficient and robust feature selection via joint L2,1-norms minimization. In: Advances in Neural Information Processing Systems, pp. 1813–121 (2010)
16. Nene, S.A., Nayar, S.K., Murase, H.: Columbia Object Image Library (COIL-20). Technical report CUCS-005-96 (1996)
17. Yang, S.Z., Hou, C.P., Nie, F.P., Wu, Y.: Unsupervised maximum margin feature selection via L2,1-norm minimization. Neural Comput. Appl. **21**(7), 1791–1799 (2012)
18. Zhang, Z., Jiang, W., Li, F., Zhang, L., Zhao, M., Jia, L.: Projective Label Propagation by Label Embedding. In: Azzopardi, G., Petkov, N. (eds.) CAIP 2015. LNCS, vol. 9257, pp. 470–481. Springer, Heidelberg (2015). doi:10.1007/978-3-319-23117-4_41
19. Zhao, M.B., Chow, T.W.S., Zhang, Z., Li, B.: Automatic image annotation via compact graph based semi-supervised learning. Know. Based Syst. **76**, 148–165 (2015)
20. Liang, Y.C., Zhang, Z., Jiang, W.M., Zhao, M.B., Li, F.Z.: Bilinear embedding label propagation: towards scalable prediction of image labels. IEEE Signal Process. Lett. **22**(12), 2411–2415 (2015)

Discriminative Sparse Coding by Nuclear Norm-Driven Semi-Supervised Dictionary Learning

Weiming Jiang[1,2], Zhao Zhang[1(✉)], Yan Zhang[1,2],
and Fanzhang Li[1,2]

[1] School of Computer Science and Technology & Joint International Research
Laboratory of Machine Learning and Neuromorphic Computing,
Soochow University, Suzhou 215006, China
cszzhang@gmail.com
[2] Collaborative Innovation Center of Novel Software Technology
and Industrialization, Nanjing 210023, China

Abstract. In this paper, we propose a Nuclear norm-driven Semi-Supervised Dictionary Learning (N-SSDL) approach for classification. N-SSDL incorporates the idea of the recent label consistent KSVD with the label propagation process that propagates label information from labeled data to unlabeled data via balancing the neighborhood reconstruction error and the label fitness error. To provide a more reliable distance metric for measuring the neighborhood reconstruction error, we apply the nuclear-norm that is proved to be suitable for modeling the reconstruction error, where the reconstruction coefficients are computed based on the sparsely reconstructed training data rather than original ones. Besides, we also use the robust $l_{2,1}$-norm regularization on the label fitness error so that the measurement is robust to noise and outliers. Extensive simulations on several datasets show that N-SSDL can deliver enhanced performance over other state-of-the-arts for classification.

Keywords: Semi-supervised learning · Discriminative sparse coding · Nuclear norm · $l_{2,1}$-norm regularization

1 Introduction

Sparse coding has been arousing considerable attention in the fields of pattern recognition and computer vision [1–4], etc. Sparse coding approximates each input signal x by a linear combination of a few items from a dictionary D. To learn a powerful dictionary D, some representative dictionary learning algorithms [6, 9, 11] were developed, among which *K-Singular Value Decomposition* (K-SVD) [6] is a very popular model that generalizes the K-means method [17], and can calculate an over-complete dictionary by an unsupervised way.

It is worth noting that several recent researches [9, 11] have demonstrated that dictionaries obtained by supervised learning are able to yield better representation performance. *Discriminative K-SVD* (D-KSVD) [9] incorporates a classification error into the problem of K-SVD, so that both the classification performance and the

© Springer International Publishing AG 2016
E. Chen et al. (Eds.): PCM 2016, Part I, LNCS 9916, pp. 306–317, 2016.
DOI: 10.1007/978-3-319-48890-5_30

representation power of dictionary can be enhanced at the same time. *Label Consistent K-SVD* (LC-KSVD) [11] improves K-SVD by further combining a label consistent constraint with the sparse reconstruction error and the classification error to form a joint problem. Note that enhanced results were obtained by both D-KSVD and LC-KSVD for image representation and classification [9, 11], but it should be noted that they are all fully supervised methods, i.e., needing the class labels of all training data for dictionary learning. However, the number of labeled samples is usually very limited in reality [13–16], which may restrict both D-KSVD and LC-KSVD in dealing with the real-world applications.

Recently, several efforts were made to incorporate the idea of semi-supervised learning into the sparse coding and dictionary learning formulations, such as semi-supervised sparse coding (SSSC) [18] and semi-supervised label consistent dictionary learning (SSDL) [19]. SSSC achieves the discriminative sparse codes by minimizing the reconstruction error, classification error and label approximation error over sparse codes, but it should be noticed that the inclusion approach of SSSC for involving the outside data is very costly due to the fact that it uses an alternate strategy to compute the class labels of data points. SSDL [19] is a semi-supervised extension of LC-KSVD by incorporating the adaptive label propagation process with the label consistent dictionary learning. Note that both SSSC and SSDL use the F-norm that is very sensitive to noise in data [12] to encode the reconstruction error and classification error, which may decrease the performance.

In this paper, we also discuss the semi-supervised dictionary learning approach for discriminant sparse coding and classification. Technically, a new *Nuclear norm-driven Semi-Supervised Dictionary Learning* (N-SSDL) approach is proposed. Our N-SSDL is built based on the idea of SSDL, i.e., incorporating the idea of recent label consistent KSVD with the label propagation process that propagates the labels from the labeled data to the unlabeled data via balancing the neighborhood reconstruction error and the label fitness error, but improves SSDL from three aspects. First, to provide a more reliable distance metric to measure the neighborhood reconstruction error, we replace the original F-norm by a nuclear-norm that has been proved to be more suitable for modeling the reconstruction error than both the l_1-norm and F-norm [12]. Second, we propose to apply a $l_{2,1}$-norm regularization on the label fitness error so that the resulted measurement would be robust to noise and outliers in the given data [7, 14]. Third, for the label propagation process, we compute the reconstruction coefficients over those sparsely reconstructed training data, inspired by SSSC [18]. But it is worth noting that the process of seeking the reconstruction weights in our N-SSDL offers certain advantages over that of SSSC, since we avoid the tricky issue of estimating the kernel width, which is one of the weakness of SSSC. The final solution of N-SSDL is achieved by an iterative manner. We first use Laplacian Linear Discriminant Analysis (Lap-LDA) [9] to label the unlabeled training samples initially. We can then use all the labeled training points for discriminative sparse coding by LC-KSVD. After that, we focus on updating the reconstruction weights with the sparsely reconstructed training data and then update predicted labels of unlabeled training data. Finally, a descriptive dictionary and a linear multiclass classifier can be alternately obtained from one objective function. The classification approach for involving outside samples is also discussed. More specifically, the classification process for a new test signal by applying our N-SSDL is very efficient, compared with those performing classification on the sparse codes, e.g., D-KSVD, LC-KSVD, SSSC, as can be observed from the simulations, since N-SSDL does not need to obtain the sparse codes of each outside signals by involving a separate reconstruction process with the trained dictionary D.

2   Nuclear Norm-Driven Semi-Supervised Dictionary Learning

2.1   Notation

For any matrix $M \in \mathbb{R}^{u \times v}$, its $l_{r,p}$-norm can be formulated as follows:

$$\|M\|_{r,p} = \left(\sum_{i=1}^{u} \left(\sum_{j=1}^{v} |M_{i,j}|^{r} \right)^{p/r} \right)^{1/p}. \tag{1}$$

When $p = r = 2$, it is the commonly used F-norm. Denote by $\|M\|_*$ the nuclear-norm of the matrix M. According to [8], for the matrix M, one can have

$$\|M\|_* = tr\left(\left(MM^{T} \right)^{-1/2} MM^{T} \right) = \left\| \left(MM^{T} \right)^{-1/4} M \right\|_{F}^{2}, \tag{2}$$

which represents the nuclear norm in the form of F-norm.

2.2   The Objective Function

We present the problem formulation of N-SSDL. Let $X = [X_L, X_U] \in \mathbb{R}^{n \times (l+u)}$ be a set of n-dimensional $N = l + u$ input signals, where $X_L = [x_1, x_2, \cdots, x_l] \in \mathbb{R}^{n \times l}$ is a labeled dataset, $X_U = [x_{l+1}, x_{l+2}, \ldots, x_{l+u}] \in \mathbb{R}^{n \times u}$ is an unlabeled dataset, each column vector x_i is a training signal, each signal in X_L is associated with a class label c_i from $\{1, 2, \cdots, c\}$, and c is the number of classes. By introducing a reliable Nuclear-norm based distance metric for measuring the manifold smoothness degree defined over the neighborhood reconstruction error and a robust $l_{2,1}$-norm for measuring the label fitness error, our N-SSDL solves the following optimization problem:

$$\langle D, S, A, P \rangle = \arg \min_{D, S, A, P} \|X - DS\|_{F}^{2} + \alpha \left\| \hat{Q} - AS \right\|_{F}^{2} + \beta \sum_{i=1}^{l+u} \left\| x_i^{T} P - \sum_{j: x_j \in \mathbb{N}(x_i)} \widetilde{w}_{i,j} x_j^{T} P \right\|_{*}$$

$$+ \sum_{i=1}^{l+u} \mu_i \left\| x_i^{T} P - y_i^{T} \right\|_{2}, \text{ Subj } \|s_i\|_{0} \leq T_1, \ i \in \{j | j = 1, 2, \ldots, N\}, \tag{3}$$

where $\mathbb{N}(x_i)$ is the K-nearest neighbor set, $\widetilde{w}_{i,j}$ is the reconstruction coefficient for measuring the contribution of $x_j \in \mathbb{N}(x_i)$ to reconstruct x_i, $\|X - DS\|_{F}^{2}$ is the reconstruction error, $D = [d_1, \cdots d_K] \in \mathbb{R}^{n \times K}$ is the dictionary, $S = [s_1, \cdots s_N] \in \mathbb{R}^{K \times N}$ are the sparse codes of input signals, T_1 is a sparsity constraint factor to ensure each signal has fewer than T_1 nonzero items in its decomposition. $\left\|\widehat{Q} - AS\right\|_F^2$ denotes a discriminative sparse-code error, where $\widehat{Q} = [q_1, q_2, \ldots, q_N] \in \mathbb{R}^{K \times N}$ are "discriminative" sparse codes of original signals X, and are similarly defined as [19]. A is a linear transformation matrix. $\sum_{i=1}^{l+u} \left\|x_i^T P - \sum_{j:x_j \in \mathbb{N}(x_i)} \widetilde{w}_{i,j} x_j^T P\right\|_*$ is an accumulated nuclear norm-based neighborhood reconstruction error that defines the manifold smoothness term used in label propagation to help decide the class labels of points. $\sum_{i=1}^{l+u} \mu_i \left\|x_i^T P - y_i^T\right\|_2$ is the $l_{2,1}$-norm based label fitness term to support learning an optimal classifier $P \in \mathbb{R}^{n \times c}$, and $x_i^T P$ is the estimated soft label vector of x_i with the position associated with the biggest entry in $x_i^T P$ deciding the class assignment of x_i. μ_i is a parameter for x_i. As the labels of x_i is known, $\mu_i = 10^{10}$, and else $\mu_i = 0$. $y_i \in \mathbb{R}^{c \times 1}$ is a pre-defined class indicator vector:

$$y_{ji} = \begin{cases} 1/\sqrt{\phi_j} - \sqrt{\phi_j}/N, & \text{if } x_i \text{ belongs to the } j\text{ - th class} \\ -\sqrt{\phi_j}/N, & \text{if } x_i \text{ does not belong to the } j\text{ - th class} \end{cases} \tag{4}$$

where ϕ_j is the number of points in the j-th class. Note that the reconstruction coefficients $\widetilde{w}_{i,j}$ are shown in (9). Let $W = [\widetilde{w}_{i,j}] \in \mathbb{R}^{N \times N}$ and $Y = [y_1, \cdots, y_{l+u}] \in \mathbb{R}^{c \times N}$. According to the property of $l_{2,1}$-norm [7, 14] and the relationship between the Nuclear-norm and F-norm given in (2), we can approximate the problem in (3) as

$$\langle D, S, A, P, \mathfrak{S}, G \rangle = \arg \min_{D, S, A, P, \mathfrak{S}, G} \|X - DS\|_F^2 + \alpha \left\|\widehat{Q} - AS\right\|_F^2 + \beta \left\|G(X^T P - W X^T P)\right\|_F^2$$
$$+ tr\left((X^T P - Y^T)^T U \mathfrak{S}(X^T P - Y^T)\right), \quad \text{Subj } \|s_i\|_0 \leq T_1, \ i \in \{j | j = 1, 2, \ldots, N\} \tag{5}$$

Where $G = \left((X^T P - W X^T P)(X^T P - W X^T P)^T\right)^{-1/4}$. $U \in \mathbb{R}^{N \times N}$ and $\mathfrak{S} \in \mathbb{R}^{N \times N}$ are diagonal matrixes with the entries being $U_{ii} = \mu_i$ and $\mathfrak{S}_{ii} = 1/\left(2\|x_i^T P - y_i\|_2\right)$, $\mathfrak{S}_{ii} \neq 0$.

2.3   Optimization for Solution

Since the optimization involves several variables (i.e. D, S, A, P) that depend on each other, so we choose an alternate optimization strategy to solve (5).

Discriminative sparse coding by dictionary learning. As the projection P, $\mathfrak{S}$, G are known, by removing terms that are independent of D, A, and S from the objective function in (5), we can have the following simplified formulation:

$$\langle D, S, A \rangle = \arg\min_{D,S,A} \left\| \widehat{X} - DS \right\|_F^2 + \alpha \left\| \widehat{Q} - AS \right\|_F^2, \quad \text{Subj } \|s_i\|_0 \leq T_1, \ i$$
$$\in \{j | j = 1, 2, \ldots, N\}, \tag{6}$$

where $\widehat{X} = \left[\widehat{X_1}, \widehat{X_2}, \cdots \widehat{X_c} \right] \in \mathbb{R}^{n \times N}$ is the set of training points sorted according to their class information and $\widehat{X_i}$ is the labeled subset of class i. Note that the above equation can be expressed equivalently as

$$\langle D, S, A \rangle = \arg\min_{D,S,A} \left\| \begin{pmatrix} \widehat{X} \\ \sqrt{\alpha}\widehat{Q} \end{pmatrix} - \begin{pmatrix} D \\ \sqrt{\alpha}A \end{pmatrix} S \right\|_F^2, \quad \text{Subj } \|s_i\|_0 \leq T_1, \ i$$
$$\in \{j | j = 1, 2, \ldots, N\}. \tag{7}$$

Let $X_{new} = \left(\widehat{X}^T, \sqrt{\alpha}\widehat{Q}^T \right)^T$ and $D_{new} = (D^T, \sqrt{\alpha}A^T)^T$. Suppose D_{new} is l_2-normalized columnwise, then the above optimization problem can be rewritten as

$$(D_{new}, S) = \arg\min_{D_{new}, S} \|X_{new} - D_{new}S\|_F^2, \quad \text{Subj} \|s_i\|_0 \leq T_1, i = \{j | j = 1, 2, \cdots, N\}. \tag{8}$$

This is exactly the problem that K-SVD [6] solves.

Update the labels of training signals and the projection classifier P. After the variables D, A and S are updated at each iteration, we can use the reconstructed training data (i.e., DS) to update the reconstruction weights in a similar way as *Locally Linear Embedding (LLE)* [20] by minimizing the reconstruction error:

$$\widetilde{w}_{i,j} = \underset{w_i}{Min} \left\| Ds_i - \sum_{j:x_j \in N(x_i)} \widetilde{w}_{i,j}(Ds_j) \right\|_2^2, \quad \text{Subj} \sum_{j:x_j \in N(x_i)} \widetilde{w}_{i,j} = 1, \ \widetilde{w}_{i,j} \geq 0. \tag{9}$$

By repeating the above process for each sample, we can obtain the weight matrix $W = \left[\widetilde{w}_{i,j} \right] \in \mathbb{R}^{N \times N}$. Then, we can update the projection P by the label propagation process to re-estimate the labels of unlabeled training data to boost performance. Let $Z = \widehat{X}^T P - W\widehat{X}^T P$ be an auxiliary matrix, it is noted that the computation of G will be ill-conditioned if some of the singular values of Z is small [8]. To solve the problem, we fix a parameter $\varepsilon > 0$, and increase the smaller singular values of Z according to $\sigma_i(Z) \to \max\{\sigma_i(Z), \varepsilon\}$ before computing G at each iteration. In other words, we replace Z by its ε-stabilization, $Z_\varepsilon = U \sum_\varepsilon V^T$, where $\sum_\varepsilon = diag(\max\{\sigma_i, \varepsilon\})$. The idea behind is Z_ε is well-conditioned. Besides, if Z is well-approximated by a k-rank matrix, then Z_ε is also well-approximated by the same k-rank matrix [8]. But for a fixed ε, the nuclear norm solution cannot converge. Therefore, we select $\varepsilon^{(t)} = \min\{\varepsilon^{(t-1)}, \sigma_f(Z^{(t)})\}$ at the t-th iteration. As a result, given $P^{(t)}$, we can update G by

$$G^{(t)} = \left((Z)_{\varepsilon^{(t)}} (Z)_{\varepsilon^{(t)}}^T \right)^{-1/4}. \tag{10}$$

And then, by removing the terms that are independent of P from (5), we can obtain the following formulation:

$$P = \arg\min_{P} \beta\|GZ\|_F^2 + tr\left((X^TP - Y^T)^T U\Im(X^TP - Y^T)\right), \tag{11}$$

which produces the following projection classifier $P^{(t+1)}$:

$$P = \left(\beta\widehat{X}(I - W^T)G^TG(I - W)\widehat{X}^T + XU\Im X^T\right)^{\dagger} XU\Im Y^T, \tag{12}$$

With computed projection classifier P, we can estimate the labels of each unlabeled training signal x_i by Sect. 2.5. Based on computed P, we can update the diagonal matrix $\Im$ as

$$\Im^{(t+1)} = diag\left(\Im_{ii}^{(t+1)}\right), \quad \Im_{ii}^{(t+1)} = 1/\left(2\|x_i^TP^{(t+1)} - y_i\|_2\right), \tag{13}$$

where $i = 1,\ldots,N$. After that, we can use the re-estimated labels of all training signals to update the entries of $\widehat{Q}$ and $\widehat{X}$ at each iteration and re-conduct the label consistent dictionary learning for updating the dictionary D and sparse codes S.

2.4   Initialization

In this section, we show the procedure of initializing $P^{(0)}$, $\widehat{Q}^{(0)}$, $\widehat{X}^{(0)}$, $D^{(0)}$ and $A^{(0)}$ for our N-SSDL. We first use Lap-LDA to initialize $P^{(0)}$ and estimate the labels of unlabeled training data by solving

$$J(P) = \min_{P} \sum_{i=1}^{l} \|y_i^T - x_i^TP\|_F^2 + \lambda_m \sum_{i,j=1}^{l} \|P^Tx_i - P^Tx_j\|(E_m)_{ij}, \tag{14}$$

where E_m is a weight matrix defined by Gaussian function, for measuring pairwise similarities between samples. Then, we can use the labels of all training signals to initialize $\widehat{X}^{(0)}$. Next, we can utilize the "supervised" information of training signals (including labeled and unlabeled data whose labels have already been estimated) to initialize the dictionary $D^{(0)}$ by performing K-SVD for several times within each class and then combining outputted dictionary items from each class by each K-SVD, similarly as [11]. The label of each dictionary item is then initialized based on its corresponding class. With initialized $D^{(0)}$, we use the original K-SVD method to compute the sparse codes $S^{(0)}$ of training signals $\widehat{X}^{(0)}$. By using supervised information of training signals, we initialize $\widehat{Q}^{(0)}$ according to [19]. With initialized $\widehat{Q}^{(0)}$, we can initialize the transformation $A^{(0)}$ according to [11].

2.5   Classification Approach

For a new test signal x_{new}, we embed it onto the subspace spanned by the columns of P by using the form of $P^T x_{new}$ to achieve its soft label. i.e., the soft label vector $f_{new} \in \mathbb{R}^{c \times 1}$ of each test signal x_{new} can be computed as

$$f_{new} = P^T x_{new} \in \mathbb{R}^{c \times 1}, \tag{15}$$

where the position corresponding to biggest element in the label vector f_{new} determines the class assignment of x_{new}. That is, the hard label of each signal x_{new} can be assigned as $\arg\max_{i \le c}(f_{new})_i$, where $(f_{new})_i$ represents the i-th entry of the estimated soft label vector f_{new}.

3   Simulation Results and Analysis

We evaluate our proposed N-SSDL for semi-supervised classification, along with describing the comparison results with SRC [2], D-KSVD, LC-KSVD, SSSC and SSDL which are closely related to our N-SSDL. Since we mainly focus on semi-supervised learning, we set the dictionary size K to the number of training points simply in each dictionary learning algorithm. Notice that D-KSVD, LC-KSVD1 and LC-KSVD2 are all supervised methods, so they can only use labeled training samples for dictionary learning. In contrast, SRC is an unsupervised method, and both SSSC and SSDL are semi-supervised algorithms, so they all can employ both labeled and unlabeled training data for learning dictionaries. In our simulations, the number of iterations is set to 20 and the sparsity constraint factor T_1 is fixed to 15 for each model for coding. The model parameters of each method are carefully selected for fair comparison. We conduct the simulations over 15 times random splits of training set and testing set on each dataset. We perform all simulations on a PC with Intel(R) Core(TM) i3-4130 CPU @ 3.4 GHz 3.4 GHz 4G.

3.1   Machine Fault Datasets

In this subsection, we use two machine fault datasets, i.e., rolling element bearing datasets (i.e., 2HP and 3HP), to test the performance our proposed N-SSDL. The test bearings were SKF 6205 JEM, a type of deep groove ball bearing. Vibration signals were collected for different conditions under different motor loading [21]. The two datasets contains 10 types of 800 samples, each instance has 15 features.

In this simulation, we randomly choose 3 samples from each class as labeled and the same number of unlabeled samples to form the training set, the rest is applied for testing. We give the comparison results on the rolling bearing datasets in Table 1. The testing time is also described. We see clearly that the mean and best results of our N-SSDL are superior to other approaches. Considering the runtime performance, we

Table 1. Performance comparison based on the rolling bearing dataset (2HP and 3HP)

Result	2 HP (3 labeled, 3 unlabeled)			3HP (3 labeled, 3 unlabeled)		
Method	Mean ± STD (%)	Best (%)	Time (s)	Mean ± STD (%)	Best (%)	Time (s)
SRC	91.59 ± 4.82	97.03	1.325	88.60 ± 2.96	95.13	1.342
D-KSVD	92.85 ± 3.07	95.41	1.043	91.69 ± 4.98	98.19	1.059
LC-KSVD1	93.60 ± 2.75	96.46	1.050	92.03 ± 3.77	98.25	1.059
LC-KSVD2	93.68 ± 2.35	96.49	1.050	92.31 ± 3.62	98.32	1.059
SSSC	95.19 ± 2.82	97.01	14.791	93.11 ± 2.49	97.18	15.098
SSDL	95.35 ± 2.31	97.88	**0.004**	94.13 ± 2.61	98.91	**0.004**
N-SSDL	**96.12 ± 2.24**	**98.10**	**0.004**	**94.78 ± 3.71**	**100**	**0.004**

can observe that our N-SSDL spend very short time for testing, compared with those of others that need to involve the time-consuming sparse reconstruction process for each test sample.

We also provide some numerical results to illustrate the robustness of N-SSDL for handing the above datasets with noise. Random Gaussian noise is manually added to each signal by $Data = Data + \sqrt{Var} \times randn(size(Data))$, where Var is the variance, and $randn$ is a function of Matlab used to normally distribute pseudorandom numbers. The experiment results are illustrated in Figs. 1 and 2. We see that the increasing value of Var can decrease the performance of each method, and our N-SSDL deliver higher accuracy than other method in most cases. For 3HP dataset, we see that SSSC can obtain higher accuracy with varying Var.

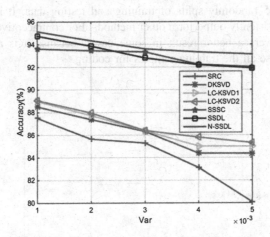

Fig. 1. Classification performance with varying Var on 2HP dataset

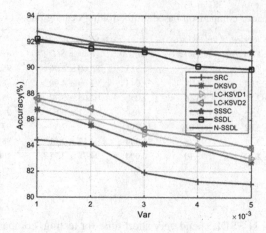

Fig. 2. Classification performance with varying *Var* on 3HP dataset

3.2   Real-Word Datasets

We use two real-world UCI datasets to evaluate these methods. These datasets are as follows: (1) Abalone dataset: This dataset contains 3 types of 1473 samples, each instance contains 8 features [10]; (2) Contraceptive method choice dataset: This set contains 3 types of 1473 samples and each instance has 9 features [5].

For the above two datasets, we create the training set by selecting 50 samples from each category as labeled and the same amount of unlabeled ones. The experimental results on the datasets are given in Figs. 3 and 4, which illustrates the best, average and worst results of 15 randomly splits of training and testing data. It is clear that our algorithm can consistently outperform other methods. For contraceptive method choice dataset, SRC delivers a better result in some cases, because it is an unsupervised method and can use all the training samples for coding.

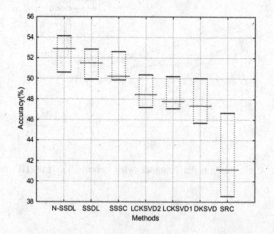

Fig. 3. Classification performance on the abalone dataset

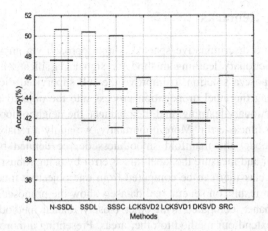

Fig. 4. Classification performance on the contraceptive method choice dataset

3.3 Investigation of Parameter Selections

We mainly investigate the effects of different parameter selections on the performance of our method. We use the rolling bearing datasets as examples, because similar findings can be found from the other datasets. We illustrate the results by exploring the effects of the two parameters using the approach of grid search. For each pair of parameters, we average the results over 10 random splits of training and test data with the varied parameters from $\{10^{-8}, 10^{-6}, \cdots, 10^{8}\}$. For rolling bearing datasets (i.e., 2HP), we choose 6 samples per class as the training set including 3 labeled and 3 unlabeled samples and test on the rest. Two parameter selection results are shown in Fig. 5. We can observe that our N-SSDL is able to perform well in a wide range of the parameters for each dataset.

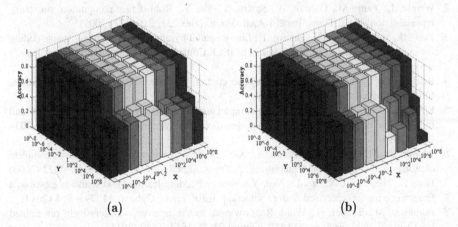

(a)   (b)

Fig. 5. Parameter sensitivity analysis under different parameter selections on (a) Rolling bearing dataset (2HP); (b) Rolling bearing dataset (3HP). Where, X represents $\sqrt{\alpha}$, Y denotes $\sqrt{\beta}$.

4 Concluding Remarks

We have proposed a discriminative sparse coding approach via nuclear norm-driven semi-supervised dictionary learning method for signal classification. The main contribution is to propose a solution to improve the full supervised dictionary learning method by including the label propagation process into the objective function of the label consistent dictionary learning, and then balance the neighborhood reconstruction error and the label fitness error. More importantly, we apply a reliable Nuclear-norm based metric to model the manifold smoothness degree defined by neighborhood reconstruction error and measure the label fitness error by using robust $l_{2,1}$-norm. Thus, a dictionary and a classifier can be computed from one objective function.

The experiment results on several real datasets show the proposed approach yields promising performance compared with other closely related methods. One possible future work is to extend our method to other areas. Presenting a more efficient way to improve the scalability of training phase is also worth exploring.

Acknowledgements. This work is partially supported by the National Natural Science Foundation of China (61402310, 61672365, 61672364 and 61373093), Major Program of Natural Science Foundation of Jiangsu Higher Education Institutions of China (15KJA520002), Special Funding of China Postdoctoral Science Foundation (2016T90494), Postdoctoral Science Foundation of China (2015M580462) and Postdoctoral Science Foundation of Jiangsu Province of China (1501091B), Natural Science Foundation of Jiangsu Province of China (BK20140008, BK20141195), and Graduate Student Innovation Project of Jiangsu Province of China (SJZZ15_0154).

References

1. Elad, M., Aharon, M.: Image denosing via sparse and redundant representations over learned dictionaries. IEEE Trans. Image Proces. **54**(12), 3736–3745 (2006)
2. Wright, J., Yang, M., Ganesh, A., Sastry, S., Ma, Y.: Robust face recognition via sparse representation. IEEE Trans. Pattern Anal. Mach. Intell. **31**, 210–227 (2009)
3. Yang, J., Yu, K., Gong, Y., Huang, T.: Linear spatial pyramid matching using sparse coding for image classification. In: Proceedings of IEEE Conference on Computer Vision & Pattern Recognition (2009)
4. Bradley, D., Bagnell, J.: Differential sparse coding. In: Proceedings Conference on Neural Information Processing System (2008)
5. Lim, T.S., Loh, W.Y., Shih, Y.S.: A comparison of prediction accuracy, complexity, and training time of thirty-three old and new classification algorithms. Mach. Learn. **40**(3), 203–228 (1999)
6. Aharon, M., Elad, M., Bruckstein, A.: K-SVD: an algorithm for designing overcomplete dictionaries for sparse representation. IEEE Trans. Signal Process. **54**(1), 4311–4322 (2006)
7. Hou, C., Nie, F., Li, X., Yi, D., Wu, Y.: Joint embedding learning and sparse regression: a framework for unsupervised feature selection. IEEE Trans. Cybern. **44**, 793–804 (2014)
8. Fornasier, M., Rauhut, H., Ward, R.: Low-rank matrix recovery via iteratively reweighted least squares minimization. SIAM J. Optim. **21**(4), 1614–1640 (2011)

9. Zhang, Q., Li, B.: Discriminative K-SVD for dictionary learning in face recognition. In: Proceedings of IEEE Conference on Computer Vision and Pattern Recognition (2010)

10. Chen, J., Ye, J., Li, Q.: Integrating global and local structures: a least squares framework for dimensionality reduction. In: Proceedings of IEEE Conference on Computer Vision and Pattern Recognition (2007)

11. Jiang, Z., Lin, Z., Davis, L.: Label consistent K-SVD: learning a discriminative dictionary for recognition. IEEE Trans. Pattern Anal. Mach. Intell. **35**, 2651–2664 (2013)

12. Zhang, F., Yang, J., Qian, J., Xu, Y.: Nuclear norm-based 2-DPCA for extracting features from images. IEEE Trans. Neural Netw. Learn. Syst. **26**(10), 2247–2260 (2015)

13. Chapelle, O., Scholkopf, B., Zien, A.: Semi-Supervised Learning. MIT Press, Cambridge (2006)

14. Zhang, Z., Zhang, L., Zhao, M., Jiang, W., Liang, Y., Li, F.: Semi-supervised image classification by nonnegative sparse neighborhood prediction. In: Proceedings of ACM International Conference on Multimedia Retrieval, Shanghai, pp. 139–146 (2015)

15. Zhu X.: Semi-supervised learning literature survey. Technical report 1530, University of Wisconsin-Madison (2005)

16. Zhang, Z., Chow, T.W.S., Zhao, M.B.: Trace ratio optimization based semi-supervised nonlinear dimensionality reduction for marginal manifold visualization. IEEE Trans. Knowl. Data Eng. **25**(5), 1148–1161 (2013)

17. Kanungo, T., Mount, D.M., Netanyahu, N.S., Piatko, C.D., Silverman, R.: An efficient K-means clustering algorithm: analysis and implementation. IEEE Trans. Pattern Anal. Mach. Intell. **24**, 881–892 (2002)

18. Jing, J., Wang, Y., Gao, X.: Semi-supervised sparse coding. arXiv:1311.6834 (2015)

19. Jiang, W., Zhang, Z., Li, F., Zhang, L., Zhao, M., Jin, X.: Joint label consistent dictionary learning and adaptive label prediction for semi-supervised machine fault classification. IEEE Trans. Ind. Inform. **12**(1), 248–256 (2016)

20. Roweis, S.T., Saul, L.K.: Nonlinear dimensionality reduction by locally linear embedding. Science **290**(5500), 2323–2326 (2000)

21. Zhao, M., Jin, X., Zhang, Z., Li, B.: Fault diagnosis of rolling element bearings via discriminative subspace learning: visualization and classification. Expert Syst. Appl. **41**, 3391–3401 (2014)

Semantically Smoothed Refinement
for Everyday Concept Indexing

Peng Wang[1]($\boxtimes$), Lifeng Sun[1], Shiqiang Yang[1], and Alan F. Smeaton[2]

[1] National Laboratory for Information Science and Technology,
Department of Computer Science and Technology, Tsinghua University,
Beijing, People's Republic of China
{pwang,sunlf,yangshq}@tsinghua.edu.cn

[2] Insight Centre for Data Analytics, Dublin City University,
Glasnevin, Dublin 9, Ireland
alan.smeaton@dcu.ie

Abstract. Instead of occurring independently, semantic concepts pairs tend to co-occur within a single image and it is intuitive that concept detection accuracy for visual concepts can be enhanced if concept correlation can be leveraged in some way. In everyday concept detection for visual lifelogging using wearable cameras to automatically record everyday activities, the captured images usually have a diversity of concepts which challenges the performance of concept detection. In this paper a semantically smoothed refinement algorithm is proposed using concept correlations which exploit topic-related concept relationships, modeled externally in a user experiment rather than extracted from training data. Results for initial concept detection are factorized based on semantic smoothness and adjusted in compliance with the extracted concept correlations. Refinement performance is demonstrated in experiments to show the effectiveness of our algorithm and the extracted correlations.

Keywords: Semantic indexing · Concept refinement · Detection refinement · Semantic smoothness · Lifelogging

1 Introduction

Measuring human behavior can be carried out by utilizing sensors embedded in smartphones or wearable devices. This has enabled high-resolution insights into human behavior for quantified-self applications. Lifelogging [2] is the term used to describe the process of automatically, and ambiently, digitally recording human behavior using a variety of sensor types. The richness of contextual sensor information makes it practical to characterise and measure occurrences of human behavior [15] and in so doing to observe behavior patterns.

This work was part-funded by 973 Program under Grant No. 2011CB302206, National Natural Science Foundation of China under Grant No. 61272231, 61472204, 61502264, Beijing Key Laboratory of Networked Multimedia and by Science Foundation Ireland under grant SFI/12/RC/2289.

E. Chen et al. (Eds.): PCM 2016, Part I, LNCS 9916, pp. 318–327, 2016.
DOI: 10.1007/978-3-319-48890-5_31

Visual media in digital format is now widespread and *visual lifelogging* which employs wearable cameras to capture image or video of everyday activities, has become popular in quantified-self applications. As a new form of multimedia content, the visual lifelog presents many challenges if its content is to be managed in a way that helps maximize benefit for the eventual applications. This requires searching through lifelogs based on content, and for this the automatic detection of semantic concepts is needed. The conventional approach to content-based indexing, as taken in the annual TRECVid benchmarking [11,12], is to annotate a collection covering both positive and negative examples of the presence of each concept and then to train a machine learning classifier to recognize the presence of the concept. This typically requires a classifier for each concept without considering inter-concept relationships or dependencies yet in reality, many concept pairs will co-occur rather than occur independently.

In contrast to isolated concept detectors, *multi-label training* tries to classify and model correlations between concepts simultaneously. A typical multi-label training method is presented in [10], in which concept correlations are modeled in the classification model using Gibbs random fields. Similar multi-label training methods can be found in [20]. Since all concepts are learned from one integrated model, one shortcoming is the lack of flexibility, which means that the learning stage needs to be repeated when the concept lexicon is changed. Another disadvantage is the high complexity when modeling pairwise correlations in the learning stage. This also hampers the ability to scale up to large-scale sets of concepts and to complex concept inter-relationships.

As an alternative, *detection refinement or adjustment* methods post-process detection scores obtained from individual detectors, allowing independent and specialized classification techniques to be leveraged for each concept. Context-Based Concept Fusion (CBCF) is an approach to refining the detection results for independent concepts by modeling relationships between them [3]. Concept correlations are either learned from annotation sets [4] or in earlier work, inferred from pre-constructed knowledge bases [5,19] such as WordNet. However, annotation sets are almost always inadequate for learning correlations due to their limited sizes and the annotation having being done with independent concepts rather than correlations in mind. The use of external knowledge networks also limits the flexibility of CBCF because they use a static lexicon which is costly to create. When concepts do not exist in an ontology, these methods cannot adapt to such situations.

To deal with such challenges, a training-free refinement method was proposed in [18] to post-process the outputs of individual concept detectors, independent of training corpora. While ontological relations can be employed in this method, the concept graph cannot be integrated for joint refinement in terms of semantic smoothness.

In this paper we propose a semantically smoothed refinement algorithm which extends our previous work and exploits concept relationships modeled externally in a user experiment rather than extracted from training data. As a training-free method, this algorithm can exploit inherent co-occurrence patterns for concepts which exist in the detection results, exempt from the restrictions of correlation learning from a training corpus. Results for initial concept detection are factorized and adjusted in compliance with the concept correlations.

The contribution of our work is three-fold. First, we present an algorithm based on weighted non-negative matrix factorization to improve concept detection accuracy and we then semantically smooth the factorization procedure to constrain the results to comply with the concept correlations. Second, in contrast to training-dependent methods which learn concept correlations from training corpora, this paper tries to deal with concept refinement problem in a training-free way. Our concept correlations are inferred from a simple user experiment to exploit topic-related concept semantics. Finally, we compare our approach with various methods on different concept detection accuracy levels and we demonstrate our method to be advantageous in different ways.

2   Semantically Smoothed Everyday Concept Refinement

2.1   Motivation and Problem Statement

Our work is based on concept detection results from a series of images taken from lifelog events which have been automatically segmented based on the technique introduced in [8]. A lifelog event corresponds to a single activity in the wearer's day such as watching TV, commuting, or eating a meal, with an average stream of 20 or more events of varying duration in a typical day.

Let $\{E_1, E_2, ..., E_n\}$ be a set of event streams, event E_i is represented by successive images $I^{(i)} = \{Im_1^{(i)}, Im_2^{(i)}, ..., Im_k^{(i)}\}$. We assume a universe of concepts, C. Each image $Im_j^{(i)}$ might have several concepts detected, we assume the concepts appearing in image $Im_j^{(i)}$ are represented as a vector $C_j^{(i)} = \{c_{j1}^{(i)}, c_{j2}^{(i)} ... c_{jM}^{(i)}\}$ for M concepts. The set of passively captured images in a lifelog is denoted as $I = \{I^{(1)}, I^{(1)}, ..., I^{(n)}\}$ which has dimensionality $N = \sum_{i=1}^{n} k_i$, where k_i is the number of images in each event E_i. Concept detection for these N images for M concepts can be described as a confidence matrix $C_{N \times M}$.

The semantic refinement task is to modify the $N \times M$ dimensional matrix C in order to keep consistency with the underlying contextual pattern of concepts. According to [7], matrix C can be represented as $C \approx WH$, in which W and H represent image-specific and concept-specific latent features respectively. The intuition behind this is to form the confidence matrix by simply combining partial information (columns in W) with an additive operator since all elements in H are non-negative. That is to say, various concepts can be mapped to combinations of semantic units and concept-concept contextual semantics can be evaluated through this new encoding. If we constrain the factorization with these inferred concept-concept correlations to comply with the external concept graph, the factorized results can better reflect this contextual information which leads to improved refinement.

2.2   Refinement Specification

Let the dimensions of component matrix W and H be $N \times r$ and $r \times M$. The approximation factorization defined above can be solved by optimizing the cost function defined to qualify the quality of the approximation. In factorizing the confidence matrix, the weighted measure cost function is used. To distinguish the contribution of different concept detectors to the cost function, the weighted Frobenius norm [9,18] can employed as:

$$G(W, H) = \frac{1}{2} \sum_{ij} w_{ij}(c_{ij} - W_{i\cdot}H_{\cdot j})^2 + \frac{\lambda}{2}(\|W\|_F^2 + \|H\|_F^2) \qquad (1)$$

such that $W \geq 0, H \geq 0$ and where $\|\cdot\|_F^2$ denotes the Frobenius norm. The role of the quadratic regularization term $\lambda(\|W\|_F^2 + \|H\|_F^2)$ is to prevent overfitting.

Because each value c_{ij} in C denotes the probability of the occurrence of concept v_j in sample c_i, the estimation of the existence of v_j is more likely to be correct when c_{ij} is high, which is also adopted by [18] under the same assumption that the initial detectors are reasonably reliable if the returned confidences are larger than a threshold *thres*. To distinguish contributions of different concept detectors to the cost function, we employ a weighted matrix $W = (w_{ij})_{N \times M}$ whose elements are larger for reliable and lower for less reliable detections. After factorization, refinement can be expressed as a fusion of confidence matrices:

$$C' = \alpha C + (1 - \alpha)\tilde{C} = \alpha C + (1 - \alpha)WH \qquad (2)$$

2.3   Semantic Smoothness

According to the factorization described in Sect. 2.2, matrix $H_{r \times M}$ represents a low rank latent feature matrix for M concepts. Therefore, concept correlations can be formalized based on this new form of concept representation. We also denote a smooth function S in weighted form to constrain two concepts with high correlation to have coordinates which are close to each other. Under this rationale, function S can be calculated as

$$\begin{aligned} S(H) &= \frac{1}{2} \sum_{ij} \|H_{\cdot i} - H_{\cdot j}\|_F^2 Correl(c_i, c_j) \\ &= \sum_{ij} H_{\cdot i}^T Correl(c_i, c_j)H_{\cdot i} - \sum_{ij} H_{\cdot i}^T Correl(c_i, c_j)H_{\cdot j} \\ &= \sum_{ij} H_{\cdot i}^T D_{ii}H_{\cdot i} - \sum_{ij} H_{\cdot i}^T Correl(c_i, c_j)H_{\cdot j} \\ &= tr(H(D - Correl)H^T) = tr(HL_{Correl}H^T) \end{aligned} \qquad (3)$$

where $Correl$ is a concept correlation matrix whose element $Correl(c_i, c_j)$ stands for the quantitative relationship between two concepts c_i and c_j, $D_{ii} = \sum_j Correl(c_i, c_j)$ stands for a diagonal matrix, $L_{Correl} = D - Correl$

represents the Laplacian of the concept correlation matrix. By assembling the above defined functions, we can achieve the following semantically smoothed factorization problem:

$$min_{W,H} F(W, H) = G(W, H) + \tfrac{\beta}{2} S(H) \qquad \text{s.t. } W, H \geq 0 \qquad (4)$$

where β is a nonnegative scalar to weight the penalty of concept correlations in the optimization of $F(W, H)$. In Eq. (4), $G(W, H)$ interacts with $S(H)$ by sharing the concept feature matrix H, through which the factorization is optimized in compliance with concept correlation $Correl$. In this way, $Correl$ influences concept feature matrix H in terms of its Laplacian matrix L_{Correl}.

Because there is no close-form solution for optimizing Eq. (4), we employed the classical gradient descent method to find a local optimization, implemented by updating W and H in the opposite direction to the gradient at each iteration. Note that the gradient of $S(H)$ with respect to H is $\nabla_H S(H) = 2HL_{Correl}$. Based on the above formalization, the partial derivations of F with respect to W and H can be calculated respectively by

$$\frac{\partial F}{\partial W} = [(WH - C \circ W]H^T + \lambda L \qquad (5)$$

$$\frac{\partial F}{\partial H} = W^T[(WH - C) \circ W] + \beta H L_{Correl} + \lambda H \qquad (6)$$

where $\circ$ denotes Hadamard multiplication. The semantically smoothed factorization solution of W and H is further applied to Eq. (2) to calculate C' which can then be further enhanced by neighborhood-based propagation, shown in [18].

3   Inferring External Concept Correlations

In domains where context is very important, such as lifelogging, concepts are more contextually correlated within single event topics such as "talking", "cooking", etc. Concepts can play different roles in representing event semantics, and some will interact with each other through their relationships. This means that if we plot the concepts in a vector space, the dimensions in a concept vector are not independent because of their relationships to each other which are intermediated by event topic semantics. As shown in Fig. 1, the event semantic space can be defined as a linear space with a set of concepts as the bases. Since concepts are highly connected through event topics, we infer concept correlations through a topic-related method.

To investigate quantitative correlations among a set of candidate concepts related to everyday activities, we carried out user experiments on concept rating where candidate concepts related to each of the activity topics were pooled based on user input. Although individual wearers may have different contexts and personal characteristics, there is a common understanding of concepts that is already socially agreed and allows people to communicate about these according to [6,17]. This makes it reliable for users to choose suitable concepts relevant

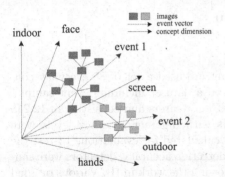
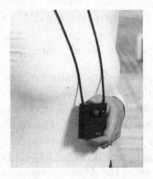

Fig. 1. Topic-related concept correlations in concept space.   **Fig. 2.** SenseCam worn by a participant

to activities. User experiments were carried out to discover candidate concepts which potentially have high correlation with activity semantics.

A group of 13 participants were chosen from among researchers within our own group, some of whom log their own everyday lives with the SenseCam wearable camera [13], shown in Fig. 2. In the experiment, target activities were first described to the participants to familiarise them. They were then shown Sense-Cam images for selected activity examples and surveyed by questionnaire about their interpretation of the SenseCam activity images as well as of the concepts occurring regularly in those SenseCam images. The aim of the user experiment was to determine candidate semantic concepts which have high correlation with various human activities. After several iterations and refinements we selected 85 base concepts [15, 17] which have highest agreement among participants, i.e. more than half of respondents think each are relevant to the activity.

Using rating results from the user experiment, concept correlation can be calculated based on the intuition that the higher the number of subjects who thought a concept pair was relevant to a given activity, the implication of a stronger concept correlation. By summation across all target activity categories, the aggregated correlation score can be quantified. The correlation score of a concept pair c_i and c_j is calculated by

$$Correl(c_i, c_j) = \frac{\sum_{act \in A} min(v_{act}(c_i), v_{act}(c_j))}{\sum_{act \in A} v_{act}(c_i) * \sum_{act \in A} v_{act}(c_i)}), i \neq j \qquad (7)$$

where A denotes the set of activities investigated in the user experiment. $v_{act}(c_i)$ is the number of votes concept c_i gets with regard to a specific activity type act, and $min(v_{act}(c_i), v_{act}(c_j))$ reflects the number of overlapping votes for a concept pair in activity type act. Since higher overlapping votes implies stronger agreement among all subjects on the relevance of two concepts within the context of a specific activity, the correlation of two concepts should be higher if the sum of overlapping votes are higher across all activity types. $\sum_{act \in A} v_{act}(c_i)$ and $\sum_{act \in A} v_{act}(c_j)$ denote the total vote numbers of c_i and c_j in all activities, which are used to normalize the correlation values.

4   Experiments and Evaluation

4.1   Experimental Dataset

To assess the performance of our algorithm, we used a set of 85 everyday concepts [15,17] introduced in Sect. 3. We used a dataset including event samples of 23 activity types collected from 4 SenseCam wearers and consisting of 12,248 SenseCam images [15]. Concept detectors with different accuracy levels were used and mean average precision (MAP) calculated for evaluation. To test the performance on different levels of concept detection accuracy, detectors were simulated using the *Monte Carlo* method following the work in [1]. Various original concept detection accuracies were provided by varying the controlling parameter μ_1 in the range [0.5...10.0]. For each setting we executed 20 repeated runs and the averaged concept MAP was calculated. Fig. 3 shows the improvement in concept MAP with increasing μ_1. Near-perfect detection performances are achieved when $\mu_1 \geq 5.5$.

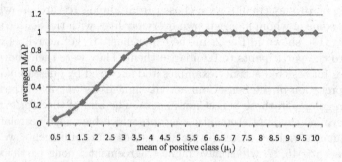

Fig. 3. Averaged concept MAP with different controlling parameter μ_1.

4.2   Evaluation and Discussion

In Table 1, our semantically smoothed refinement (SSR) method is compared with a variety of concept detection refinement methods including ontological refinement [19], a Random Walk-based method [14], Tensor-based refinement for wearable sensing [16], training-free refinement (TFR) [18], as well as domain adaptive semantic diffusion (DASD) [4]. We applied the same ontological structure of 85 concepts with *subsumption* and *disjointness* concept relationships as used in [18] and applied to ontological refinement. Motivated by [18], we implement the SSR in a training-free manner followed with neighbourhood-based propagation as introduced by [18] after semantically smoothed factorization. That is, applying a propagation algorithm to C' to further refine the results based on neighbors connected to each samples. In DASD, the concept correlation $Correl$ as generated in Sect. 3 is employed as the semantic graph used in the diffusion. In this experiment, we employ the same parameter settings as reported in TFR method [18] during the factorization procedure. That is, we choose the

Table 1. MAP of SSR, TFR, Ontological, Random Walk, Tensor and DASD (mean over 20 runs).

Method	$\mu_1 = 1.0$	$\mu_1 = 1.5$	$\mu_1 = 2.0$	$\mu_1 = 2.5$	$\mu_1 = 3.0$	$\mu_1 = 3.5$	$\mu_1 = 4.0$
Onto	0.159	0.273	0.421	0.586	0.735	0.850	0.926
RW	0.156	0.267	0.426	0.603	0.752	0.857	0.924
Tens	0.164	0.287	0.456	0.624	0.774	0.877	0.941
TFR	0.165	0.295	0.477	0.658	0.800	**0.893**	**0.947**
DASD	**0.176**	0.300	0.454	0.602	0.719	0.805	0.869
SSR	0.168	**0.302**	**0.480**	**0.662**	**0.802**	**0.893**	0.944

number of latent features as $r = 10$ and we threshold the detection results with $thres = 0.3$. The fusion parameter in Eq. (2) is simply set to $\alpha = 0.5$, assigning equal importance to the two matrices. We use 30 nearest neighbours in the propagation step.

From Table 1, we find that SSR outperforms the other methods at most levels of original detection MAP from $0.15@\mu_1 = 1.0$ to $0.92@\mu_1 = 4.0$. At $\mu_1 = 1.0$, SSR is outperformed by DASD. This makes sense as initial detection accuracy is low. In this case, very few correctly detected concepts are selected by thresholding for further refinement which is impractical in real world applications. Though DASD performs well at $\mu_1 = 1.0$, it is significantly outperformed by TFR and SSR methods at $\mu_1 \geq 2.0$. This is probably because the concept correlation graph is inferred from the user experiment rather than from the training dataset. Thus the knowledge-driven correlation graph only reflects the co-occurrence tendency which is difficult to precisely incorporate in DASD refinement. When the original concept detection accuracy is low such as at $\mu_1 = 1.0$, the overfitting of DASD to semantic graph $Correl$ can enhance the results but this can not be generalized to other concept detection accuracy levels. However, SSR can adapt to various levels of concept detections and make full use of external knowledge graph $Correl$. Compared to the TFR method, SSR incorporates the imprecisely constructed concept graph but outperforms TFR in most cases. This demonstrates the potential of SSR in everyday concept refinement through semantic smoothness. Recall that we employed a flexible but imprecisely constructed concept correlation graph for smoothness. We believe that if the correlation can be inferred more precisely from data annotations, the improvement will be more significant with the semantic smoothness.

To further demonstrate the effects of concept correlations on indexing refinement, we compared the semantically smoothed refinement results to non-smoothed results ($\beta = 0$) by varying parameter β which controls the influence of concept correlations. As we can see from Eq. (4), the SSR method degenerates to TFR at $\beta = 0$. In Figs. 4 and 5, comparisons at detection accuracy controlled by $\mu_1 = 2.0$ are shown for refinement results without and with neighborhood propagation respectively. In Fig. 4, the blue dashed line represents the refinement results evaluated on the intermediate results of C' calculated by optimizing

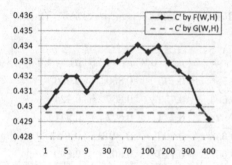
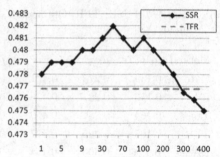

Fig. 4. Effects of concept correlations without propagation ($@\mu_1 = 2.0$)

Fig. 5. Effects of concept correlations with propagation ($@\mu_1 = 2.0$)

non-smoothed function $G(W, H)$. As we can see from Fig. 4, the results obtained from smoothed function $F(W, H)$ surpasses $G(W, H)$ in a wide range of β. While β increases, the performance using a smoothed function $F(W, H)$ climbs first, and then declines when the contribution of concept correlations dominate the factorization with very large β. This can interpret the overfitting of the DASD method in which the cost function is defined on the concept graph [4] for semantic diffusion, similar to the function $G(W, H)$ we used. When further applying neighborhood-based propagation to C', both smoothed and non-smoothed methods can be boosted, as shown in Fig. 5 in which the final enhanced results of SSR and TFR are compared. As in Fig. 4, SSR still surpasses TFR in most cases in Fig. 5 showing the advantages of semantic smoothness even if neighborhood-based propagation is applied.

5 Conclusions and Future Work

We tackle the multi-concept refinement task in quantified-self like visual lifelogging where activity engagements of users usually dominate the contextual evolution of concept appearance. We propose a semantically smoothed refinement algorithm to exploit topic-related concept relationships to further improve semantic indexing performance. Instead of extracting concept correlations from annotated training data, which is usually employed in other research but might be constrained by the labeling quality of a training corpus, we investigated a simple method of externally generating concept graphs in a user experiment. Though loosely constructed, the concept correlation graph has been demonstrated as effective when incorporated into the smoothed refinement algorithm. Incorporating automatic generation of concept graphs from a knowledge base or other sources is future work to extend the algorithm.

References

1. Aly, R., Hiemstra, D., de Jong, F., Apers, P.: Simulating the future of concept-based video retrieval under improved detector performance. Multimed. Tools Appl. **60**(1), 1–29 (2011)

2. Gurrin, C., Smeaton, A., Doherty, A.: Lifelogging: personal big data. Found. Trends Inf. Retr. **8**(1), 1–127 (2014)
3. Jiang, W., Chang, S.F., Loui, A.: Context-based concept fusion with boosted conditional random fields. In: ICASSP 2007, vol. 1, pp. I-949–I-952, April 2007
4. Jiang, Y.G., Dai, Q., Wang, J., Ngo, C.W., Xue, X., Chang, S.F.: Fast semantic diffusion for large-scale context-based image and video annotation. IEEE Trans. Image Proces. **21**(6), 3080–3091 (2012)
5. Jin, Y., Khan, L., Wang, L., Awad, M.: Image annotations by combining multiple evidence & WordNet. In: ACM MULTIMEDIA 2005, pp. 706–715 (2005)
6. Lakoff, G.: Women, fire, and dangerous things. University of Chicago Press, April 1990
7. Lee, D., Seung, H.: Learning the parts of objects by nonnegative matrix factorization. Nature **401**, 788–791 (1999)
8. Lee, H., Smeaton, A., O'Connor, N., Jones, G., Blighe, M., Byrne, D., Doherty, A., Gurrin, C.: Constructing a SenseCam visual diary as a media process. Multimed. Syst. **14**(6), 341–349 (2008)
9. Pan, R., Zhou, Y., Cao, B., Liu, N.N., Lukose, R., Scholz, M., Yang, Q.: One-class collaborative filtering. In: ICDM 2008, pp. 502–511. IEEE (2008)
10. Qi, G.J., Hua, X.S., Rui, Y., Tang, J., Mei, T., Zhang, H.J.: Correlative multi-label video annotation. In: ACM MULTIMEDIA 2007, pp. 17–26 (2007)
11. Smeaton, A.F., Over, P., Kraaij, W.: Evaluation campaigns and trecvid. In: Proceedings of the ACM International Workshop on Multimedia Information Retrieval, pp. 321–330. ACM (2006)
12. Smeaton, A.F., Over, P., Kraaij, W.: High-level feature detection from video in TRECVid: a 5-year retrospective of achievements. In: Divakaran, A. (ed.) Multimedia Content Analysis, Theory and Applications, pp. 1–24. Springer, Boston (2009). http://dx.doi.org/10.1007/978-0-387-76569-3_6
13. Steve, H., Emma, B., Ken, W.: Sensecam: a wearable camera that stimulates and rehabilitates autobiographical memory. Memory **19**(7), 685–96 (2011)
14. Wang, C., Jing, F., Zhang, L., Zhang, H.J.: Image annotation refinement using random walk with restarts. In: ACM MULTIMEDIA 2006, pp. 647–650 (2006)
15. Wang, P., Smeaton, A.: Using visual lifelogs to automatically characterise everyday activities. Inf. Sci. **230**, 147–161 (2013)
16. Wang, P., Smeaton, A.F., Gurrin, C.: Factorizing time-aware multi-way tensors for enhancing semantic wearable sensing. In: He, X., Luo, S., Tao, D., Xu, C., Yang, J., Hasan, M.A. (eds.) MMM 2015. LNCS, vol. 8935, pp. 571–582. Springer, Switzerland (2015). doi:10.1007/978-3-319-14445-0_49
17. Wang, P., Smeaton, A.F.: Semantics-based selection of everyday concepts in visual lifelogging. Int. J. Multimed. Inf. Retr. **1**(2), 87–101 (2012)
18. Wang, P., Sun, L., Yang, S., Smeaton, A.F.: Towards training-free refinement for semantic indexing of visual media. In: Tian, Q., Sebe, N., Qi, G.-J., Huet, B., Hong, R., Liu, X. (eds.) MMM 2016. LNCS, vol. 9516, pp. 251–263. Springer, Heidelberg (2016). doi:10.1007/978-3-319-27671-7_21
19. Wu, Y., Tseng, B., Smith, J.: Ontology-based multi-classification learning for video concept detection. In: ICME 2004, vol. 2, pp. 1003–1006 (2004)
20. Xue, X., Zhang, W., Zhang, J., Wu, B., Fan, J., Lu, Y.: Correlative multi-label multi-instance image annotation. In: ICCV 2011, pp. 651–658 (2011)

A Deep Two-Stream Network for Bidirectional Cross-Media Information Retrieval

Tianyuan Yu[✉], Liang Bai, Jinlin Guo, Zheng Yang, and Yuxiang Xie

College of Information System and Management, National University of Defense Technology,
Changsha 410073, China
{yutianyuan92,xabpz}@163.com, gjlin99@gmail.com,
yz_nudt@hotmail.com, yxxie@nudt.edu.cn

Abstract. The recent development in deep learning techniques has showed its wide applications in traditional vision tasks like image classification and object detection. However, as a fundamental problem in artificial intelligence that connects computer vision and natural language processing, bidirectional retrieval of images and sentences is not as popular as the traditional problems, and the results are far from satisfying. In this paper, we consider learning a cross-media representation model with a deep two-stream network. Previous models generally use image label information to train the dataset or strictly correspond the local features in images and texts. Unlike those models, we learn globalized local features, which can reflect the salient objects as well as the details in the images and sentences. After mapping the cross-media data into a common feature space, we use max-margin as the criterion function to update the network. The experiment on the dataset of Flickr8k shows that our approach achieves superior performance compared with the state-of-the-art methods.

Keywords: Cross-media · Deep learning · Two-stream network

1 Introduction

Nowadays, cross-media information exists in many real-world applications, especially those in the Internet. As a result, there is a great value in the ability to retrieve cross-media information (such as images and texts). It is also imperative for many practical applications to associate natural language descriptions with images, and vice versa. Besides, the relative approaches can be applied to image/text search engines. Furthermore, it is a fundamental work for automatically generating image descriptions.

However, the task is difficult. The main reason is the inevitable phenomenon of heterogeneity-gap between cross-media information, which is widely considered as a basic barrier to multi-model information retrieval. The general method to bridge the gap is to map cross-media data into a common feature space, where the relevant data would be closer to each other so that the queries are conducted and expected to get satisfying results. What is more, the task requires the machine to understand the details in the images, texts, and their connections rather than just the saliency in the images or the verbs and nouns in the texts. As shown in Fig. 1, to retrieve relevant images and texts,

© Springer International Publishing AG 2016
E. Chen et al. (Eds.): PCM 2016, Part I, LNCS 9916, pp. 328–337, 2016.
DOI: 10.1007/978-3-319-48890-5_32

machine has to identity all the detailed objects and entities, and neglect the unimportant information to map them each other.

Fig. 1. Representation of the mapped segments of an image and a relevant sentence. The noisy input is also showed. The difficult is to encourage computer to learn the useful correlations and neglect the unimportant visual and textual information.

Recently, deep learning has been successfully applied to various fields as a major breakthrough in artificial intelligence. In terms of the task of bidirectional cross-media information retrieval, a large number of researches use the classified labels of images as the targets in their networks [1, 2]. However, the label information cannot represent the whole image. There must be loads of details neglected during the training process, which would definitely affect the final ranking results.

In this work, we introduce a two-stream model, illustrated in Fig. 2, which learns globalized local features in a common feature space from visual and textual representations respectively so that we can consider the mapped features as relevant or irrelevant. In each epoch during training, we forward propagate the two-stream network to map the textual and visual information into a common space respectively, and then use max margin as the criterion function to backward propagate the network.

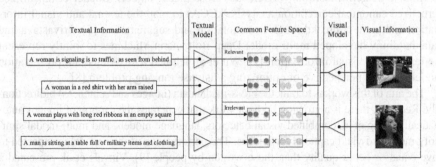

Fig. 2. The textual modal learns globalized local feature vectors for sentences based on tri-letters. The visual model maps the images into the same feature space. Then the max margin would be used as criterion function to back propagate the network.

Our model for mapping textual data into the common space is based on Deep Structured Semantic Models (DSSM) [3]. DSSM is used to search textual results given a textual query. It contains a convolutional layer and a max-pooling layer to extract local and global features. Unlike DSSM model, we improve the convolutional layer in order to strengthen the affection of local features to get a globalized local feature.

Our contributions are three-fold: the primary one is that we introduce a two-stream deep network to map the cross-media data into a common feature space. Unlike previous works, we extract globalized local features via the network. Second, we use the CNN-like model to analyze the textual information and extract features. Third, the extensive empirical evaluation validates our approach. In particular, the two-stream deep network achieves convincing performance on Flickr8K dataset [4] to bidirectional cross-media information retrieval.

2   Related Work

The proposed method is relevant to several fields in natural language processing and visual information research. As a result, large quantities of works are related to this work. In this sector, we just list the latest and profound papers.

The first step in the proposed method is to extract textual and visual features from cross-media data. In terms of computer vision, CNN method and its extensive models are undoubtedly the first choice to extract visual features. The features extracted by CNN have been widely used in realistic applications, such as image classification [5], object detection [6] and so on. In textual domain, Recurrent Neural Networks (RNN) is much more popular because they can handle sequences of flexible length. Besides, a particular extension Long Short Term Memory (LSTM) [1] gradually becomes the mainstream on natural language tasks and pattern recognition such as machine translation [2], scene analyzing [3] and so on. Recently, Convolutional Latent Semantic Model (CLSM) is considered as the first successful attempt in applying the CNN-like methods to textual information retrieval [4].

Multi-modal embedding methods map cross-media data into a common feature space in order to search the similar or relevant cross-media objects. Socher et al. utilized kernelized canonical correlation analysis (kCCA) to map the textual and visual information and made a breakthrough in annotation and segmentation [5]. Srivastava and Salakhutdinov developed multi-model Deep Boltzmann Machines to jointly represent the textual and visual information [7]. Wu et al. learned a cross-media representation model from the perspective of optimizing a listwise ranking problem [8].

The aim of this work is to rank the cross-media data (images and sentences) bidirectionally. Recently, there is a growing body of work that generates the caption of images automatically. Feng et al. combined visual detectors, language models, and multi-modal similarity models to yield captions for images. The performance of their modal is expected to have equal or better quality than those written by people [9]. Vinyals et al. presented a generative model based on a deep recurrent architecture that combined advances in computer vision and machine translation [10]. More closely related to our motivation are methods that allow bidirectional embedding between textual and visual information. In

2013, a deep visual-semantic embedding model was introduced to identify visual objects using labeled image data as well as semantic information gleaned from unannotated text [11]. Similarly, Socher et al. proposed a Dependency Tree Recursive Neural Network (DT-RNN) to process textual information [1]. Recently, Karpathy et al. proposed a model which embeds fragments of images and sentences into a common space [12]. Among the methods above, they all used Recurrent Neural Network or Recursive Neural Network to process textual information and utilized the inner products or strict correspondence between cross-media data features to describe the similarity or relevance. Except Karpathy's method, other models only extract global features. For images, the background usually takes up a large proportion while it may be not even important. When it comes to the sentences, the extracted keywords hardly match the saliency in the image. As a result, the inner product with global features would cause an inevitable mistake. For Karpathy's model, they use the fragments of cross-media data, which has achieved the state-of-the-art. However, as they mentioned in [12], sentence fragments are not always appropriate, especially when it comes to multiple adjectives for one noun. Furthermore, it is hard to correspond each fragment in one image with each word or phrase in the relevant sentence. In contrast, our model focuses on the local and global features in images and sentences. The extracted globalized local features make better performance compared with that of the previous global features.

3   Two-Stream Deep Network

Our aim is to learn a common feature space for textual and visual data, and make the semantic similar pair of images and sentences get closer in the common space. As a result, we train our model on a set of images and sentences, and their relationship is labeled as relevant or irrelevant. During the training process in the common space, we use max-margin function to force the semantic similar cross-media information to get closer (have a higher inner product). Once the training process is complete, all the training data is discarded and the network is validated on another set of images and sentences. The validation process scores and sorts the image-sentence pair in the testing dataset. In the meantime, the locations of ground truth results are recorded.

The proposed two-stream network can be separated as three parts. The first one is responsible for training textual data with CNN and extracting the globalized local features. The second part is expected to map the images into a common space where textual information has been embedded. The combination part includes a criterion function in order to encourage the relevant pair to have a high inner product. Finally, we back propagate the whole network with SGD method. These three phases and optimization process are showed as follows.

3.1   Textual Model

Deep semantic similarity model (DSSM) [3] has been proved to lead significant improvement on automatic highlighting and contextual entity search. The convolutional layer in DSSM sets a fixed number of words as a group of input, which limits its function because there would always be descriptions containing multiple adjective and a noun.

For example, for the phrase "a black and white cat", it is hard to link the adjective "black" and the noun "cat" unless considering the number equal or more than 4 as the group number. As a result, we improve the model to extract globalized local features. The overview of the textual model is showed in Fig. 3.

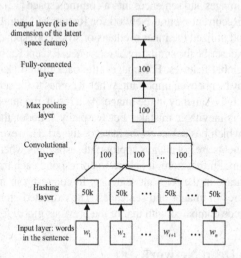

Fig. 3. Illustration of the network architecture and information flow of the textual model

The input of the textual model is each word in the sentence. In the hashing layer, we build a vector of letter 3-grams (tri-letter vector) for each word. For example, given the word "man", we first add boundary symbol "#" to the word, and then the word is separated as "#ma", "man", "an#". Then the word is represented by the tri-letter vector. The prominent advantage of tri-letter vectors is that the number of them is always limited though the English words is numerous. According to [13], a set of 500K-word vocabulary only contains 30621 tri-letters. Finally, all the words in the textual data are converted to tri-letter vectors.

Then, the vectors are considered as the input of the convolutional layer, in which the local features in the sentence are extracted. In this layer, we set a window to concatenate words to generate a new vector as the input to a linear function and *tanh* activation. The size of window is varied from 1 to the number of words in the sentence. It is necessary to change the size of window rather than using a fixed-size window because the length of phrase in not certain. Each word has chance to be relevant to any other word in the sentence. Such as the caption "a group of people stand in the back of a truck filled with cotton", which contains three two important objects "a group of people stand" and "truck filled with cotton". Any word is not only relevant to the nearby words. Another best illustrated example is the caption "two men look up while hiking", in which the single word "hiking" is a significant object in the sentence. What is more, the duplicated appearance of words will weight the important words and phrases so that we can extract more representative local features. As a result, the number of neurons in this layer depends on the number of words (n) in the sentence. It would not take up too much memory because most of captions are very short and the dimension of output is far fewer than that of tri-letter vectors.

The following layer is a max-pooling layer. Its aim is to globalize the local features extracted from the convolutional layer. We set the ith value of output vector of max-pooling layer as the maximum value of all the ith values in the input vectors. The step is to encourage the network to keep the most useful local features and form the globalized local feature for each sentence. The features extracted by convolutional and max-pooling layers mainly represent the keywords and important phrases in the sentence. They also keep useful details and remove meaningless items.

At the end of textual model, there are two fully-connected layers to reduce the dimension of the extracted features. The nonlinear activation function we use is *tanh*. Finally, the textual data is converted vectors in a fixed-dimensional space.

3.2 Visual Model

The visual model architecture used in this paper is based on the network described in [14]. The network is the winning model for the 1000-class ImageNet Large Scale Visual Recognition Challenge (ILSVRC) in 2012. The deep neural network consists of several convolutional filters, local contrast normalization, and max-pooling layers, followed by several fully-connected layers and nonlinear activation function. We remove the softmax prediction layer from this core visual model and add a linear layer that projects the 4096-D representation at the top of the model into the feature space where textual information has been embedded. Finally, we fine-tune the entire ImageNet model with the experimental dataset.

3.3 Multi-modal Embedding

In this sector, we define the multi-modal objective function for learning joint image-sentence representations with these models. The aim of the objective function is to force the corresponding pairs of images and sentences to have a higher inner product. Although it can be considered as a simple linear classification problem, the traditional approaches such as logistic function cannot be used because it cannot train the ranking information. As a result, we take the measure of max-margin objective function to force the difference between the inner products of correct pairs and other pairs to reach a fixed margin, which is showed as follows:

$$loss = \sum_{(i,j)\in P}\sum_{(i,k)\notin P} \max(0, margin - v_i^T t_j + v_i^T t_k) + \sum_{(i,j)\in P}\sum_{(k,j)\notin P} \max(0, margin - v_i^T t_j + v_k^T t_j) \qquad (1)$$

where v_i is a column vector denoting the visual feature for the given image, t_j is a column vector representing the textual feature for the given sentence. We also define P as the set of all the corresponding image-sentence pairs (i, j). It is obviously time consuming if all the irrelevant cross-media information is used. As a result, we randomly select 9 false samples for one true sample to restrict the scale of the training dataset. The hyper-parameter *margin* is usually set around 1. However, the range of the variable is wide. For example, it is set to 3 in [1] while 0.1 in [11]. In this paper, the margin is 0.5.

We use Stochastic Gradient Descent (SGD) with mini-batches of 10, momentum of 0.9 and make 15 epochs through the training data. The learning rates are varied in different parts of the network. The initial learning rates are 0.1, 0.01, and 0.01 for textual model, visual model, and the multi-model embedding. They are annealed by a fixed value which is also varied for each epoch. After 10 epochs, we set the learning rate a fixed value (0.0001) to continue training.

4   Experiments

We use the dataset of Flickr8K [4] which consists of 8000 images, each with 5 sentences. The examples are showed in Fig. 4.

1. A blonde horse and a blonde girl in a black sweatshirt are staring at a fire in a barrel .
2. A girl and her horse stand by a fire .
3. A girl holding a horse 's lead behind a fire .
4. A man , and girl and two horses are near a contained fire .
5. Two people and two horses watching a fire

1. A young couple inspect merchandise from a street vendor .
2. People are gathering around a table of food and outside a taxi wisks by .
3. Three people prepare a table full of food with a police car in the background .
4. two people look at a street vendor .
5. Two women and a man at a food counter in dim lights

Fig. 4. Two examples in the dataset of Flickr8K.

In terms to other methods, we choose several outstanding results so far to compare. In 2013, Hodosh et al. introduced the dataset of Flickr8K and proposed a method to bidirectionally rank the cross-media information [4]. Later, Google made state-of-the-art performance on the 1000-class ImageNet using a deep visual-semantic embedding model [11]. Although they focused on potential image labels and zero-shot predictions, their model laid the foundation for latter models. Then, Socher et al. embedded a full-frame neural network with the sentence representation from a Semantic Dependency Tree Recursive Neural Network (SDT-RNN) [1], which has made prominent progress in the indices such as Mean Rank and Recall@k compared with kCCA.

In our experiments, we split the data into 6000 training, 1000 validating, and 1000 testing images. Since there are 5 labeled description for each image, we get 30000 training sentences and 5000 testing sentences. We set the number of pairs in a batch as 10, and use the 10 corresponding pairs and 90 irrelevant pairs. Before each epoch, we shuffle the dataset in order to force the network to adapt to more irrelevant image-sentence pairs. In the textual model, we directly use the existing tri-letters dictionary prepared by the open source demo "sent2vec"[1]. The dictionary includes about 50 thousand tri-letters. After removing the punctuation mark, we map the captions into the tri-letter vectors. If there are new tri-letters vector appearing, we add them in the dictionary. For images in Flickr8K, color channels (YUV) are normalized globally in the entire dataset. We set the dimension of the common feature space as 20.

We use the popular indices recall and median rank scores. R@k is the percentage of ground truth among the first k results, which is a useful index of performance especially for search engines and ranking systems. The median rank indicates the location k at which a system has a recall of 50 %.

4.1 Feature Extracted by Textual Model

In this section, we focus on the globalized local feature of textual model. After mapping all the sentences in the test dataset into the multi-modal space, we can find which words or phrases are considered important by the network. A simple result is showed in Fig. 5. In the textual model, we extract a 100-D globalized local feature for each sentence through convolutional and max-pooling layers, and some of words or phrases would keep more information in the global feature while others only keep a very low proportion of their own features. From the figure, we can find that the global feature repeat the keywords in order to keep their features.

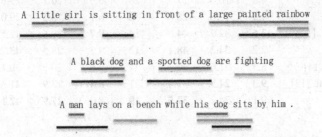

Fig. 5. Some words are repeated in the extracted features, which is considered as the keywords. The first underlined words (blue) are the main features, followed by the second underlined words (green), then the third lines (red). There are still other words existing in the final global feature, but only take up a low proportion. (Color figure online)

Then, we try to find the nearest sentences by the means of inner product for each sentence. It is expected that the sentences describing the same image should have higher inner products. We sort the inner products and record the location of the first ground truth. If the given sentences use unique words for different images, the rank value should be very low (good). However, the words for different images are similar, especially the words like "boy", "dog", and so on.

---

[1] http://research.microsoft.com/en-us/downloads/731572aa-98e4-4c50-b99d-ae3f0c9562b9/default.aspx.

4.2 Image Annotation and Image Search

This experiment evaluates how well we can find textual or visual information that describes the content of the given image or sentence. The results are showed in the Table 1. Because of the lack of source code of these papers, the experiments cannot be made again. In the paper, most results listed are based on the results in [12]. When comparing with Hodosh et al. [4], we only use a subset of N sentences out of total $5N$. From the table, we can find that our model outperform the state-of-the-art, especially in the index of R@10. The main reason is that [12] requires the fragments of images and sentences to be matched exactly to each other, which is a very hard task especially when the sentences may only focus on a part of contents in the images. At that time, it would lead a wrong match in the test dataset. However, in our model, the globalized local features are extracted according to the information in the sentence, and it is more likely to match the local and global feature of the corresponding image.

Table 1. Result comparison on Flickr8K data

Flickr8K Model	Image annotation				Image search			
	R@1	R@5	R@10	Med r	R@1	R@5	R@10	Med r
Random Ranking	0.1	0.5	1.0	635	0.1	0.5	1.0	537
DeViSE [11]	4.8	16.5	27.3	28	5.9	20.1	29.6	29
SDT-RNN [1]	4.5	18.0	28.6	32	6.1	18.5	29.0	29
Karpathy et al. [12]	**12.6**	32.9	44.0	14	**9.7**	**29.6**	42.5	**15**
Our model	12.2	**34.2**	**48.1**	**12**	9.1	28.5	**43.2**	**15**
*Hodosh et al. [4]	8.3	21.6	30.3	34	7.6	20.7	30.1	38
*Karpathy et al. [12]	**9.3**	**24.9**	37.4	21	**8.8**	**27.9**	41.3	**17**
Our model	9.1	24.7	**37.5**	**19**	8.0	**27.9**	**42.1**	**17**

5 Conclusion

In this paper, we introduced a novel two-stream network model to solve the task of bidirectional cross-media information retrieval. For details, we mapped the textual and visual data into a common feature space and evaluated whether cross-media pair is relevant by the means of inner product. Our model outperforms baselines and other commonly used models that carry out the same task. The extracted globalized local features are also proved to be robust to process different images and sentences.

References

1. Hochreiter, S., Schmidhuber, J.: Long short-term memory. Neural Comput. **9**(8), 1735–1780 (1997)
2. Sutskever, I., Vinyals, O., Le, Q.V.: Sequence to sequence learning with neural networks. In: Advances in Neural Information Processing Systems, pp. 3104–3112 (2014)

3. Byeon, W., Breuel, T.M., Raue, F., et al.: Scene labeling with LSTM recurrent neural networks. In: Proceedings of the IEEE Conference on Computer Vision and Pattern Recognition, pp. 3547–3555 (2015)
4. Shen, Y., He, X., Gao, J., et al.: A latent semantic model with convolutional-pooling structure for information retrieval. In: Proceedings of the 23rd ACM International Conference on Conference on Information and Knowledge Management, pp. 101–110. ACM (2014)
5. Socher, R., Fei-Fei, L.: Connecting modalities: Semi-supervised segmentation and annotation of images using unaligned text corpora. In: 2010 IEEE Conference on Computer Vision and Pattern Recognition (CVPR), pp. 966–973. IEEE (2010)
6. Girshick, R., Donahue, J., Darrell, T., et al.: Rich feature hierarchies for accurate object detection and semantic segmentation. In: Proceedings of the IEEE Conference on Computer Vision and Pattern Recognition, pp. 580–587 (2014)
7. Srivastava, N., Salakhutdinov, R.R.: Multimodal learning with deep Boltzmann machines. In: Advances in Neural Information Processing Systems, pp. 2222–2230 (2012)
8. Wu, F., Lu, X., Zhang, Z., et al.: Cross-media semantic representation via bi-directional learning to rank. In: Proceedings of the 21st ACM International Conference on Multimedia, pp. 877–886. ACM (2013)
9. Fang, H., Gupta, S., Iandola, F., et al.: From captions to visual concepts and back. In: Proceedings of the IEEE Conference on Computer Vision and Pattern Recognition, pp. 1473–1482 (2015)
10. Vinyals, O., Toshev, A., Bengio, S., et al.: Show and tell: a neural image caption generator. In: Proceedings of the IEEE Conference on Computer Vision and Pattern Recognition, pp. 3156–3164 (2015)
11. Frome, A., Corrado, G.S., Shlens, J., et al.: Devise: a deep visual-semantic embedding model. In: Advances in Neural Information Processing Systems, pp. 2121–2129 (2013)
12. Karpathy, A., Joulin, A., Li, F.F.F.: Deep fragment embeddings for bidirectional image sentence mapping. In: Advances in Neural Information Processing Systems, pp. 1889–1897 (2014)
13. Huang, P.S., He, X., Gao, J., et al.: Learning deep structured semantic models for web search using clickthrough data. In: Proceedings of the 22nd ACM International Conference on Conference on Information & Knowledge Management, pp. 2333–2338. ACM (2013)
14. Krizhevsky, A., Sutskever, I., Hinton, G.E.: Imagenet classification with deep convolutional neural networks. In: Advances in Neural Information Processing Systems, pp. 1097–1105 (2012)

Prototyping Methodology with Motion Estimation Algorithm

Jinglin Zhang[1], Jian Shang[1], and Cong Bai[2(✉)]

[1] School of Atmospheric Science,
Nanjing University of Information Science and Technology, Nanjing, China
`jinglin.zhang@nuist.edu.cn`
[2] The College of Computer Science, Zhejiang University of Technology,
Hangzhou, China
`congbai@zjut.edu.cn`

Abstract. With CPU, GPU and other hardware accelerators, heterogeneous systems can increase the computing performance in many domains of general purpose computing. Open Computing Language (OpenCL) is the first open and free standard for heterogeneous computing on multi hardware platforms. In this paper, a parallelized *Full Search* Motion Estimation (FSME) approach exploits the parallelism available in OpenCL-supported devices and algorithm. Different from existing GPU-based ME approach, the proposed approach is implemented on the heterogeneous computing system which contains CPU and GPU. In the meantime, we propose the prototyping framework directly generates the executable code for target hardware from the high level description of applications, and balances the workload distribution in the heterogeneous system. It greatly reduces the development period of parallel programming and easily access the parallel computing without concentrating on the complex kernel code.

1 Introduction

General-Purpose computing on Graphics Processing Units (GPGPU) is the technique of using a GPU, which typically handles computation only for computer graphics, to perform computation across a variety of applications traditionally handled by the CPU. Compute Unified Device Architecture (CUDA) is a parallel computing platform and programming model created by NVIDIA and implemented by the GPUs that they produce. Open Computing Language (OpenCL) is a framework executing programs on heterogeneous platforms consisting of CPUs, GPUs and other dedicated processors. It is also a good candidate in comparison with the CUDA approach specifically developed for GPU platforms of NVIDIA.

Generally speaking, programming with GPU is one complex, error-prone and time-consuming procedure comparing with sequential dataflow and programming. For computer vision algorithms, there are various programming environments and languages of different platforms. So it is very hard to make one rapid

E. Chen et al. (Eds.): PCM 2016, Part I, LNCS 9916, pp. 338–344, 2016.
DOI: 10.1007/978-3-319-48890-5_33

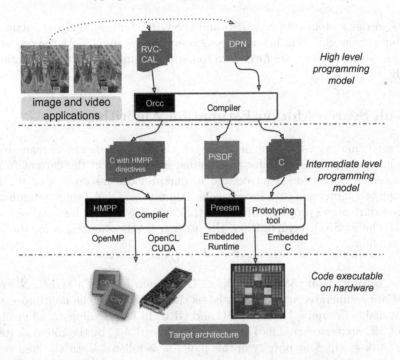

Fig. 1. The flowchart of proposed prototyping framework

development on various hardware accelerators like GPU. In general, there are two ways to perform the code porting from sequential code to the code executable on GPU. One is to manually write the kernel code of CUDA or OpenCL, which redesigns and compiles the kernel code with the specified compiler. Another way is to automatically generate code executable for hardware accelerators from the high-level description of application with the aid of the prototyping framework. Proposed prototyping framework consists of such three tools: Open Reconfigurable Video Coding Compiler (Orcc) [1], Parallel and Real-time Embedded Executives Scheduling Method (Preesm) [2], and Hybrid Multicore Parallel Programming (HMPP) [3] as shown in Fig. 1. As the high level programming model, Orcc contains an Reconfigurable Video Coding(RVC)-CAL textual editor, a compilation infrastructure, a simulator and a debugger which is proposed by IETR of INSA-Rennes. Lots of works have been proposed with Orcc and many backends are supported in Orcc like *C, C++, VHDL, HMPP* and so on [6–8,11]. As the intermediate level programming model, Preesm offers a fast prototyping tool for parallel implementations used in many applications like LTE RACH-PD algorithm. HMPP directive-based programming model is such a tool that offers a powerful syntax to efficiently offload computations on hardware accelerators and keeps the original C/C++ or Fortran codes [3–5,9,10].

In this paper, we evaluate the prototyping framework with the previous *Full Search* ME method. We not only implement the ME method on the heterogeneous system with one CPU and one GPU, but also find the balance to distribute the workload in heterogeneous computing system. With the prototyping framework, we can generate code automatically and evaluate the performance rapidly.

2   Full Search Motion Estimation Algorithm

Full Search motion estimation is to search the best candidate of macroblock (MB) in the reference frame for the original macroblock in the current frame. The detailed illustration is introduced in our previous research work [4]. The following two subsection with Pseudo code: Algorithms 1 and 2 simply summarize the procedure of the proposed ME algorithm, which is divided into two OpenCL kernels. One is SADs computation; the other is SADs comparison for the best SAD candidate.

SAD Computation. When an OpenCL program invokes a kernel, N work-groups are enumerated and distributed as thread blocks to the multiprocessors with available Compute Units of CPU and GPU. In $kernel\_compute$, all pixels of current MB are transferred into local memory ($local[256]$) by the 256 work-items in one work-group. One novelty of this paper is as follows. Until all these work-items in the same work-group reach the synchronous point using $barrier()$ function, all the 256 work-items continue transferring the 2304 pixels of search region concerned of reference image into local memory ($local\_ref[2304]$). This differentiates our approach from previous approaches of [12,13] and obtains better time efficiency (speed-up). In their work, current MB is stored in local memory, but the search region of reference frame still locates in the global memory, which results in inevitable re-fetching from global memory with performance loss. At the end, we adopt *Full Search* strategies to calculate the 1024 SAD candidates in local memory, in order to avoid re-fetching from the global memory as presented in Algorithm 1. All these 1024 SAD candidates are transferred back to global memory ($cost[1024]$) for SAD comparison.

SAD Comparison. In $kernel\_compare$, we search the best candidate with the minimum SAD from $cost[1024]$ using 256 work-items as presented in Algorithm 2. First, we transfer the $cost[1024]$ into the local memory. Then, each work-item compares 4 candidates with a *stride* to find the minimum value. We employ the parallel reduction method [14] which adopts x times iterations ($2^x = 256, x = 8$) to find the candidate with the minimum SAD value from the remaining 256 candidates, also to obtain the final MV.

2.1   Experiments Discussion

We evaluate the performance of the proposed ME algorithm with manual OpenCL kernels in such hardware HASEE environment: Intel I7 2630qm

---

Algorithm 1. *kernel_compute()*

---

   input   : Current and reference frames
   output: SAD costs candidates with offset in the x and y axis
1 Initialize the local memory space for macroblocks and search window;
2 **for** $n = 0; n <$ *number of macroblocks/number of CUs*$; n + +$ **do**
3   **for** $m = 0; m < 4; m + +$ **do**
4   256 work-items in one work-group calculate 256 SAD candidates simultaneously;
5   **end**
6 **end**
7 **return** (SAD, MV)

Algorithm 2. *kernel_compare()*

---

   input   : SAD costs candidates with offset in the x and y axis
   output: motion vector with the minimum SAD cost
1 Initialize the local memory for 1024 costs candidates of each blocks;
2 Each work-items compares 4 SAD candidates and return the minimum;
3 **for** $n = 0; n < \log_2 256; n + +$ **do**
4   Parallel reduction for the minimum SAD, half number of work-items compare the adjacent data and return the minimum data to next iteration;
5 **end**
6 **return** MV with the minimum SAD

(2.8 GHz), NVIDIA GT540m. We compare the performance of GPU-based FSME implementation and available state-of-the-art fast ME algorithms. To the best of our knowledge, there are two criterions of evaluation: *time efficiency, and matching accuracy.* Our experimental results mainly focus on PSNR.

The PSNR is defined as:

$$psnr = 10 \cdot log10(width \times height \times 255 \times 255/sse) \tag{1}$$

$$sse = \sum_{n=0}^{sum} \sum_{i=0}^{blocksize} \sum_{j=0}^{blocksize} (current_{frame}(i,j) - ref_{frame}(i + dx, j + dy))^2 \tag{2}$$

where sse is the error sum of square, *sum* is the total number of macroblocks in one frame, and (dx, dy) is the calculated motion vector. Proposed approach has faster speed and better accuracy than the state-of-the-art fast ME methods.

3 Heterogeneous Parallel Computing with OpenCL

Besides of manually writing the kernel code of OpenCL, we target to parallel computing with the aid of prototyping framework. Based on our previous research on motion estimation, we describe the proposed motion estimation approach with one high level description (RVC-CAL). There are two branches in our

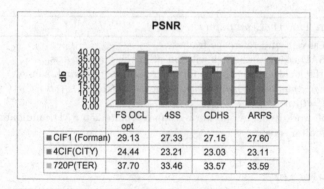

Fig. 2. PSNR comparison of specified state-of-the-art fast ME algorithms

---

Algorithm 3. *HMPP_Transformation()*

---

1 #pragma hmpp motion_estimation *codelet*, target=CUDA;
2 Definition of function motion_estimation();
3 ...;
4 Main(argc, argv);
5 #pragma hmpp motion_estimation *callsite*;
6 Function call of motion_estimation();

---

rapid prototyping framework, one branch is $RVC-CAL \to Orcc \to HMPP \to GPU(OpenCL/CUDA)$, and another one is $RVC-CAL \to Orcc \to Preesm \to DSP/ARM(EmbeddedC)$ as shown in Fig. 1: rapid prototyping framework. In this paper, we choose the first branch to generate and verify C/OpenCL/CUDA implementation on heterogeneous platforms such as multi-core CPU and GPU platforms respectively. With the HMPP-backend of Orcc, we obtain the C code with HMPP directives from the high level description. Then the HMPP compiler will automatically generate the OpenCL/CUDA kernel code. Our prototyping methodology framework can greatly simplify the procedure of implementation target to hardware devices (Fig. 2).

In the aforementioned discussion, there are paired directives of HMPP: *Codelet* and *Callsite*. Algorithm 3 presents the pseudo-code of default HMPP Transformation. Using simple paired directives, HMPP can replace the complex procedure of manually writing the CUDA/OpenCL kernel code. As shown in the above sample code, the *codelet* is the routine implementation for hardware accelerator and the *callsite* is the routine invocation of ME function on hardware. When we compile the sample code with HMPP, we can obtain the .cu or .cl kernel of proposed method which targets to GPUs. Instead of manually designing the CUDA/OpenCL kernel, HMPP greatly reduces the development period with GPU and CPU device.

The Reconfigurable Video Coding (RVC) [15] defines a set of standard coding techniques called Functional Units (FUs). A FU is described with a portable,

/

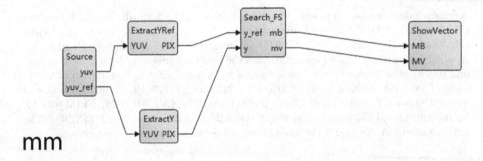

mm

Fig. 3. The dataflow diagram of proposed ME approach

platform-independent language called RVC-CAL. It is one high level language of description which is designed to describe the reconfigure video coding standard. Now RVC-CAL is not only used in video coding, but also in some image and video processing algorithms, like motion estimation and stereo matching [4]. RVC defines a XML-based format called FU Network Language (FNL) that is used for the description of networks, also named the XML Dataflow Format (XDF). The Model of Computation defines the behavior of *Full Search* ME as a dataflow graph shown in Fig. 3.

In the block diagram of the motion estimation, the block "source" indicates the function of *load_frame*, a FU that loads video frames; the block "ExtractYRef" and "ExtactY" indicate the function of *extractY*, a FU that extracts Y channel from the current and reference frames of YUV format video sequence; the block "Search_FS" indicates the function of *fullSearchME*, a FU that does the *Full Search* motion estimation; the block "ShowVector" indicates the function of *display*, a FU that shows the calculated motion vectors. With the high level description of applications, the prototyping framework can directly and rapidly generate the target code like OpenCL/CUDA for heterogeneous systems, which greatly reduces the development period of parallel programming and easily accesses the parallel computing without concentrating on the complex kernel code.

4   Conclusion

We introduce one prototyping framework to implement the proposed ME method, and evaluate the prototyping methodology. Experimental results show that, our implementation has better performance than other GPU-based FSME implementations. One basic method is introduced to find the balance of workload on the heterogeneous parallel system with OpenCL. Additionally, we have found the accurate method to distribute the workload in video applications based on the heterogeneous system. It is also the first prototyping methodology generating target code for OpenCL-supported device from the high level description (different with other code generator like OpenACC), which greatly reduces the development period of parallel programming and easily accesses the parallel computing without concentrating on the complex kernel code.

Acknowledgements. This work was carried out with the Scientific Research Foundation (s8113055001) of Nanjing University of Information Science & Technology, Scientific Research Foundation (BK20150931) of JiangSu Province and Special Program for Applied Research on Super Computation of the NSFC-Guangdong Joint Fund (the second phase). The work of Cong Bai is funded by Natural Science Foundation of China under Grant No. 61502424, 61402415, U1509207 and 61325019, Zhejiang Provincial Natural Science Foundation of China under Grant No. LY15F020028, LY15F030014, LY16F020033 and Zhejiang University of Technology under Grant No. 2014XZ006. The authors would like to thank the anonymous reviewers and the associate editor.

References

1. IETR, Orcc. http://orcc.sourceforge.net/
2. IETR, Preesm. http://preesm.sourceforge.net/website/
3. CAPS, Hybrid multicore parallel programming (HMPP). http://www.caps-entreprise.com/technology/hmpp/
4. Zhang, J., Nezan, J.-F., Cousin, J.-G.: Implementation of stereo matching using a high level compiler for parallel computing acceleration. In: 27th Image and Vision Computing New Zealand, pp. 279–283 (2012)
5. Grauer-Gray, S., Xu, L., Searles, R., Ayalasomayajula, S., Cavazos, J.: Auto-tuning a high-level language targeted to GPU codes. In: Proceedings of Innovative Parallel Computing, pp. 1–10 (2012)
6. Gorin, J., Wipliez, M., Prêteux, F., Raulet, M.: LLVM-based and scalable MPEG-RVC decoder. J. Real-Time Image Process **6**(1), 59–70 (2011)
7. Gu, R., Janneck, J.W., Bhattacharyya, S.S., Raulet, M., Wipliez, M., Plishker, W.: Exploring the concurrency of an MPEG RVC decoder based on dataflow program analysis. IEEE Trans. Circuits Syst. Video Technol. **19**(11), 1646–1657 (2009)
8. Zhang, J., Bai, C., Nezan, J.F.: Joint motion model for local stereo video-matching method. Opt. Eng. **54**(12), 123108.1–123108.10 (2015)
9. Wang, M., Hong, R., Yuan, X.-T., Yan, S., Chua, T.-S.: Movie2Comics: towards a lively video content presentation. IEEE Trans. Multimedia **14**(3), 858–870 (2012)
10. Wang, M., Hong, R., Li, G., Zha, Z.-J., Yan, S., Chua, T.-S.: Event driven web video summarization by tag localization and key-shot identification. IEEE Trans. Multimedia **14**(4), 975–985 (2012)
11. Janneck, J.W., Miller, I.D., Parlour, D.B., Roquier, G., Wipliez, M., Raulet, M.: Synthesizing hardware from dataflow programs. J. Signal Process. Syst. **63**(2), 241–249 (2011)
12. Lee, C.-Y.: Multi-pass, frame parallel algorithms of motion estimation in H.264/AVC for generic GPU. In: IEEE International Conference on Multimedia and Expo, pp. 1603–1606 (2007)
13. Chen, W.-N.: H.264/AVC motion estimation implementation on compute unified device architecture (CUDA). In: IEEE International Conference on Multimedia and Expo, pp. 697–700 (2008)
14. NVIDIA, OpenCL Programming for the CUDA Architecture, v2.3
15. Mattavelli, M., Amer, I., Raulet, M.: The reconfigurable video coding standard [standards in a nutshell]. IEEE Signal Process. Mag. **27**(3), 159–167 (2010)

Automatic Image Annotation Using Adaptive Weighted Distance in Improved K Nearest Neighbors Framework

Jiancheng Li[1,2] and Chun Yuan[2(✉)]

[1] Department of Computer Science, Tsinghua University, Beijing, China
lijc15@mails.tsinghua.edu.cn
[2] Graduate School at Shenzhen, Tsinghua University, Shenzhen, China
yuanc@sz.tsinghua.edu.cn

Abstract. Automatic image annotation is a challenging problem due to the label-image-matching, label-imbalance and label-missing problems. Some research tried to address part of these problems but didn't integrate them. In this paper, an adaptive weighted distance method which incorporates the CNN (convolutional neural network) feature and multiple handcrafted features is proposed to handle the label-image-matching and label-imbalance issues, while the K nearest neighbors framework is improved by using the neighborhood with all labels which can reduce the effects of the label-missing problem. Finally, experiments on three benchmark datasets (Corel-5k, ESP-Game and IAPRTC-12) for image annotation are performed, and the results show that our approach is competitive to the state-of-the-art methods.

Keywords: Image annotation · Adaptive weighted distance · K nearest neighbors

1 Introduction

Automatic image annotation is to annotate a few relevant textual labels for each given image based on the visual contents. It is still a challenging problem because of the label-image-matching problem, i.e., matching textual labels to image contents is hard. Most of the approaches in the past extracted distinguishable visual features from the images and tried to model the image-to-label similarity to overcome the label-image-matching problem. So multiple handcrafted features are extracted from the images. As deep learning is becoming popular, CNN have demonstrated promising results for single-label image classification and it can extract useful visual features from images. Some approaches tried to incorporate CNN to automatic image annotation. [5] trained a multi-label CNN to map image visual contents to label space. In [12], only the CNN feature instead of the multiple handcrafted features was adopted while [8] used both of them. Besides using more complex visual features, some researchers also extracted textual features [8,12] and model image-to-image [4,7,11] and label-to-label [1,11]

© Springer International Publishing AG 2016
E. Chen et al. (Eds.): PCM 2016, Part I, LNCS 9916, pp. 345–354, 2016.
DOI: 10.1007/978-3-319-48890-5_34

(a) leaf, flowers, close-up, plants   (b) leaf, flowers, petals   (c) tree, beach, people, palm

(d) grass, bear, meadow, grizzly   (e) leaf, flowers, tulip, petals   (f) field, horses, mare, foals

Fig. 1. Some images with ground-truth annotations from Corel-5k dataset. (Color figure online)

similarities. However, all these methods used the same combination of image features to calculate the similarities when sharing labels. In fact, the annotations of different labels are determined by different types of image features. Sometimes some visual features are similar between two images but they do not share the same labels. For example, both *leaf* (Fig. 1(a)) and *grass* (Fig. 1(d)) are green and the color features are similar, but their labels are totally not the same. In this example, the color features cannot be used as the evidence for distinguishing these two labels. What's more, one label can match very different visual feature vector for the same type of visual feature, e.g. pink flowers (Fig. 1(b)) and yellow flowers (Fig. 1(e)) are annotated by *flowers* in the dataset, but the color feature vectors are obviously not close which means the color features cannot determine whether the *flowers* label is annotated or not. Some research [6,10] assigned different weights of the features to solve the problem, i.e., features with large weights play more important roles when annotating labels.

Besides the label-image-matching problem, the label-imbalance and label-missing issues are often shown in the datasets and also happen in the real world [19]. The label-imbalance issue means some labels don't occur frequently in the dataset which leads these labels are not so easy to determine whether they should be annotated or not. The label-missing issue means some images in the training set are not annotated all relevant labels, i.e., some relevant labels are missing in the ground-truth annotations, e.g. people sometimes forget to annotate *sky*, *water* after annotating *beach*, *palm* and *people* (Fig. 1(c)), and it is also easy to forget to annotate *tree* in Fig. 1(f). Apparently, this increases the difficulty of matching labels and images. Recent research tried to handle the label-imbalance and label-missing issues by using semantic neighborhoods in K Nearest Neighbors (KNN)

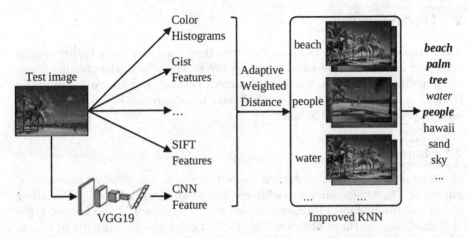

Fig. 2. Schematic of our approach. The labels in **bold** and *italics* means the labels are in ground-truth and prediction

framework [16,19]. The KNN model is one of the nearest neighbor based models which are the most popular and successful methods, and many KNN based models achieved great performance, such as TagProp [7], 2PKNN [19], NMF-KNN [9], CCA-KNN [12]. Specifically, these models select K similar images from the training set based on visual features as the nearest neighbors and then annotate the labels based on the annotations of the neighbors. The label-imbalance and label-missing issues can be addressed if K similar images are selected for each label which can be named as semantic neighborhoods, because all labels including the infrequent and easy-to-forget labels are considered.

In this paper, an adaptive weighted distance method based on improved K nearest neighbors framework (AWD-IKNN) is proposed. The proposed approach is summarized in Fig. 2. Given a test image, multiple handcrafted features are extracted from the image while the CNN feature is the output of a VGG19 network. To combine all features, an adaptive weighted distance is calculated based on each label's trained weight vector. The improved KNN framework selects K training images with minimum distances for each label and transfers the most probable labels. After evaluating on three benchmark datasets (Corel-5k, ESP-Game and IAPRTC-12) for image annotation, it turns out that AWD-IKNN achieves a promising performance compared to the state-of-the-art methods.

Our contributions are:

1. **Handle different types of features**. The CNN feature and multiple handcrafted features are combined by the adaptive weighted distance, which handles the label-image-matching problem.
2. **Adapt to all labels**. The weight vector is adaptive and specially designed for each label, so that the label-imbalance issue can be addressed.
3. **Improve KNN**. The traditional KNN is improved by using a neighborhood with all labels to tackle the label-missing situation.

2 Our Approach

The approach first extracts image features, then optimizes the adaptive weight vector for each label based on the triplet loss function using the training image set. Finally, the adaptive weighted distances between test image features and training image features are calculated, and the improved KNN framework is used to predict the suitable labels.

2.1 Image Features

Given an image, different visual feature vectors can be extracted to represent it. Similar to [7], some common traditional handcrafted image features including global features and local features are used in our approach. There are two types of global image features: Gist features [13] and color histograms with 16 bins in each color channel for RGB, LAB, and HSV representations. The local features comprise SIFT features and hue descriptors that are extracted densely on a multi-scale grid and Harris-Laplacian interest points [18].

However, these features are not enough. Though they consider the colors, points or shapes, it is still not so easy to employ them to annotate labels. So the VGG19 model [15] pre-trained on the ImageNet dataset is employed and a 4096-dimensional feature vector is extracted as the CNN visual feature. According to [21], as the layer goes deeper, the output of the neural network has more complex and useful invariance. The output of the last layer reveals the entire objects with significant pose variation which is more distinguishable and close to the human cognition.

2.2 Adaptive Weighted Distance

In Fig. 1(b) and (e), it is clear that the color feature of flowers is less important than the shape feature and other features. So we propose to use different weights of different image features for each label when combining all the features to calculate the distance. Specifically, the weights of the corresponding features are bigger than the others. In this way, each label is matched to a specific combination of image features and the distance calculation is hardly affected by label-imbalance problem.

Let $X = \{x_1, \cdots, x_m\}$ denotes the training set of m images and each element $x_i \in R^{f \times F_j}$ denotes feature vectors set: the j-th row represent the j-th feature vector of length F_j. Similarly, let $Y = \{y_1, \cdots, y_m\}$ denotes the annotations of these m images, and each element $y_i \in R^c$ is a binary vector represent the annotation vector, i.e., $y_{ij} = 1$ means the i-th image is annotated by the j-th label and $y_{ij} = 0$ means otherwise. Thus, the visual feature distance between two images x_i, x_j for a pre-defined weight matrix $W = \{w_1, \cdots, w_f\}$ can be calculated like this:

$$D(i,j) = \sum_{k=1}^{f} \frac{\sum_{l \in \Omega_1} W(l,k) + \sum_{l \in \Omega_2} W(l,k) + 1}{|\Omega_1| + |\Omega_2| + 1} \cdot d_k\left(x_{ik}, x_{jk}\right) \tag{1}$$

where Ω_1 and Ω_2 represent the annotation sets of the image x_i and x_j. So the first term in the equation means the average weight between two image feature vectors for their annotations. If there are some common annotations between two images, then the weights for these labels will be calculated twice which means the corresponding features for these labels play important roles in the distance between these two images. Obviously, this is reasonable and fit the facts. The $d_k(x_{ik}, x_{jk})$ function means the distance between k-th feature vectors of the image x_i and x_j. The distance function varies on different features. Here we follow [7] and use cosine similarity for the CNN feature, L_1 distance for color histograms, L_2 distance for Gist feature, and χ^2 measure for SIFT feature and hue descriptors. In the equation, each row of W is a weight vector for a label, and an adaptive weight vector is designed for each label to represent the correlation between the corresponding images and the label. So the distance can be named as adaptive weighted distance. All labels are treated equally even though some labels did not occur frequently and the distance between two images will be shorter if two images share the same annotations. Thus, the label-imbalance issue will not affect the final results.

Now the aim is to find a good weight matrix W to make the distance be useful for KNN. In order to measure the usefulness of the distance, the triplet loss function [14] is used to determine whether the algorithm should continue optimizing the weight matrix or stop. The philosophy of triplet loss function is to minimize the distance between an anchor and a positive and maximize the distance between the anchor and a negative, which meets the same goal of ours: the positive means the images that share the same annotations with the anchor, while the negative means the otherwise. Thus, for an anchor x_i, its positive sets x_i^p and its negative sets x_i^n, the triplet loss function can be represented as below:

$$L = \sum_{i=1}^{m} \left[D(i,j)^2 - D(i,k)^2 + \alpha \right]_+, x_j \in x_i^p, x_k \in x_i^n \tag{2}$$

where α is a margin that is enforced between positive and negative pairs and $[x]_+ = \max(0, x)$. Apparently, the goal is to minimize the loss function L, and we can simply employ the stochastic gradient descent algorithm to get the weight matrix W.

A brief description of the algorithm is given in Algorithm 1.

Algorithm 1. Optimize the distance weight matrix

Initialize W
while do not converge **do**
    Select a random image x_i in the training set
    for each label $l \in \{l \mid y_{il} = 1\}$ **do**
        $X^p \leftarrow \{x_j \mid y_{jl} = 1, j \neq i\}$, $X^n \leftarrow \{x_j \mid y_{jl} = 0\}$
        $W \leftarrow argmin\, L$
    end for
end while

2.3   K Nearest Neighbors

The traditional K Nearest Neighbors algorithm is to find the K closest training samples in the feature space of the input sample and determine the output using the K samples' outputs. To get the K closest training samples, i.e., the nearest neighbors, the mentioned adaptive weighted distances between the test image and the training images can be used as the key to rank, the images with top K minimum distances will be the nearest neighbors. Considering the label-missing issue, we find K neighbors for each label and combine them into a neighborhood. Though some relevant labels are not annotated in some training images, the relevant labels can be annotated in the test image because all labels are present in the neighborhood and the distances between the test image and the images that annotated by the missing labels are short enough.

After getting the neighborhood, all the distances between the test image and the neighbors are normalized and then used to calculate the scores for each label in order to transfer the labels from the neighborhood to test image. The score function for a test image x_i, its neighborhood N and label l is

$$Score(l) = \sum_{x_j \in N, y_{jl}=1} e^{-\theta \cdot D_{norm}(i,j)} \tag{3}$$

The $D_{norm}(i,j)$ means the normalized adaptive weighted distance between x_i and its neighbor x_j, and θ is a parameter to control the margin between high score and low score. Finally, like the other approaches, a fixed number of labels are selected as the annotations, so the labels with top scores are selected. The overview of the algorithm is given in Algorithm 2.

Algorithm 2. Improved K Nearest Neighbors

---
for each test image x_i **do**
  for each label l **do**
    $N_l \leftarrow \{x_j \mid D(i,j) \leq D(i,k)\}, x_k \in training\ set, |N_l| = K$
  end for
  $N \leftarrow \bigcap_l N_l$
  $D_{norm} \leftarrow normalize\ D$
  predicted annotations $A \leftarrow \{l \mid Score(l) \leq Score(l')\}, |A| = K'$
end for

---

3   Experiments

3.1   Datasets

Three standard publicly available image annotation datasets are used to evaluate our approach: Corel-5k, ESP-Game and IAPRTC-12. The separation of dataset

Table 1. Details of the datasets. The entries in last two columns are given in the format mean/maximum.

Dataset	No. of images	No. of labels	No. of training images	No. of test images	Labels per image	Images per label
Corel-5k	4999	260	4500	499	3.4/5	58.6/1004
ESP-Game	19627	291	17665	1962	5.7/23	347.7/4999
IAPRTC-12	20770	268	18689	2081	4.7/15	326.7/4553

is identical to those used in the previous works. The statistics of the datasets are shown in Table 1.

Corel-5k dataset was first used by [3], and is the most common dataset for image annotation. This dataset contains 4500 training images and 499 test images with 260 labels. Each image is manually annotated with 1 to 5 different labels, and 3.4 labels on average.

ESP-Game dataset contains a wide variety of images including logos, drawings and personal photos annotated through an on-line game [20] in which the players annotated images with communication. Only common labels are accepted. Thus the players are encouraged to annotate meaningful and important labels. The dataset is divided into 18689 training images and 2081 testing images. The number of labels is 268 and each image is annotated 4.7 labels on average.

IAPRTC-12 dataset is a collection of images of natural scenes, including different sports, actions, animals and many other aspects of contemporary life [11]. The training set and test set consist of 17665 and 1962 images. Each image has 5.7 labels on average from a vocabulary of 291 labels.

3.2   Results and Performances

We perform our approach on the three benchmark datasets and follow the evaluation measure metrics used in other approaches: 5 labels are annotated for each test image and the average precision (P), average recall (R) and F1-score across all labels are computed. The non-zero recall (N+) is also reported. Some well-performed approaches are listed besides the traditional methods and compare the performance between these methods and our approach. Our approach is named as AWD-IKNN which is short for Adaptive Weighted Distance with Improved K Nearest Neighbors. The results are shown in Table 2.

From the result, it is obvious that on all the three datasets, our approach performs competitive to the previous methods. Specifically, for Corel-5k and IAPRTC-12 dataset, our approach outperforms the state-of-the-art methods in F1 term, the recall and the N+ score are the best results in IAPRTC-12 dataset. Though the F1 score is slightly worse than CCA-KNN in ESP-Game dataset, it is still comparable. The CCA-KNN also used the CNN feature, but our approach gets better results on Corel-5k and IAPRTC-12 datasets, and have comparable

Table 2. Comparison of annotation performance among different methods on three benchmark datasets. P for average precision, R for average recall, F1 for F1 score, N+ for number of labels with non-zero recall value.

Method	Corel-5k				ESP-Game				IAPRTC-12			
	P	R	F1	N+	P	R	F1	N+	P	R	F1	N+
MBRM [4]	24	25	24.5	122	18	19	18.5	209	24	23	23.5	223
JEC [11]	27	32	29.3	139	22	25	23.4	224	28	29	28.5	250
FastTag [2]	32	43	36.7	166	46	22	29.8	247	47	26	33.5	**280**
TagProp(ML)[7]	33	42	37.0	160	39	27	31.9	239	46	35	39.8	266
GLKNN [16]	36	47	40.8	184	41	**36**	38.3	**282**	34	31	32.4	255
2PKNN+ML [19]	**44**	46	45.0	191	53	27	35.8	252	54	**37**	**43.9**	278
NMF-KNN [9]	38	**56**	45.3	150	33	26	29.1	238	-	-	-	-
CCA-KNN [12]	42	52	**46.5**	**201**	46	**36**	**40.4**	260	45	38	41.2	278
context-RM-B [17]	-	-	-	-	**61**	24	34.4	242	**61**	20	30.1	234
IKNN	39	44	41.7	181	46	23	31.0	251	50	31	38.5	275
AWD-IKNN	42	55	**47.7**	198	48	34	40.2	257	50	**40**	**44.5**	**282**

	Corel-5k	ESP-Game	IAPRTC-12
Image	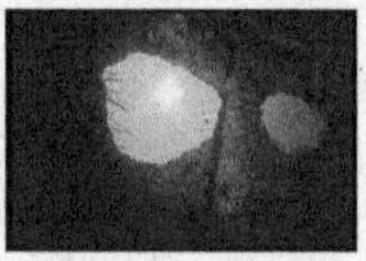		
Ground-truth	coral, ocean, reefs, cave	airplane, fly, plane, wing	chair, landscape, mountain, cloud, sky
IKNN	*basket*, *fish*, **coral**, *anemone*, **ocean**	*truck*, **fly**, *red*, **plane**, *anime*	**chair**, **mountain**, **landscape**, *net*, **sky**
AWD-IKNN	**coral**, **ocean**, *fish*, **reefs**, **cave**	*truck*, **fly**, **wing**, **plane**, **airplane**	**chair**, **landscape**, **mountain**, **cloud**, **sky**
Image			
Ground-truth	wall, cars, tracks, formula	man, show, tie, tv	house, roof, sky, tree
IKNN	**cars**, **tracks**, **formula**, *terrace*, *pots*	**tie**, **man**, *picture*, **tv**, *anime*	**tree**, **sky**, *hill*, *bush*, **house**
AWD-IKNN	**wall**, **formula**, **cars**, **tracks**, *turn*	**tie**, **show**, **man**, **tv**, *suit*	**house**, **tree**, **sky**, *hut*, **roof**

Fig. 3. Example images from three datasets and the corresponding top 5 predicted labels. The labels in **bold** are same with ground-truth while the labels in *italics* do not appear in ground-truth.

results on ESP-Game dataset. Comparing to the KNN based methods, the performance of our approach is promising because the traditional KNN framework is improved and the performance is hardly affected by the label-missing situation in the training set.

The results of our approach without using the adaptive weighted distance method (IKNN) is also reported. In that approach, the distance is averaged among all feature vectors. It is easy to notice that the F1 score improves a lot on three datasets if the adaptive weighted distance is incorporated. Figure 3 illustrates the predicted annotations using IKNN and AWD-IKNN. Apparently, the AWD-IKNN approach predicted more ground-truth labels than the IKNN approach because the AWD-IKNN can handle different types of features and find the correlation between images and labels which tackles the label-image-matching and label-imbalance problems. For example, there are only 4 training images annotated by *cave* and a small number of images annotated by *reefs* in Corel-5k dataset, but the AWD-IKNN can annotate the right ground-truth labels while IKNN cannot. Therefore, the adaptive weighted distance is significant.

4   Conclusions

In this paper, an adaptive weighted distance method based on improved K nearest neighbors framework (AWD-IKNN) is proposed to handle the label-image-matching, label-imbalance and label-missing problems. The CNN feature and multiple hand-crafted features are incorporated by using an adaptive weighted distance method which addresses the label-image-matching and label-imbalance issues. The traditional KNN algorithm is improved by using the neighborhood with all labels to tackle the label-missing problem. The performance of experiments on three benchmark datasets (Corel-5k, ESP-Game and IAPRTC-12) for image annotation is promising and competitive to the state-of-art methods.

References

1. Carneiro, G., Chan, A.B., Moreno, P.J., Vasconcelos, N.: Supervised learning of semantic classes for image annotation and retrieval. IEEE Trans. Pattern Anal. Mach. Intell. **29**(3), 394–410 (2007)
2. Chen, M., Zheng, A., Weinberger, K.: Fast image tagging. In: Proceedings of the 30th International Conference on Machine Learning, pp. 1274–1282 (2013)
3. Duygulu, P., Barnard, K., Freitas, J.F.G., Forsyth, D.A.: Object recognition as machine translation: learning a lexicon for a fixed image vocabulary. In: Heyden, A., Sparr, G., Nielsen, M., Johansen, P. (eds.) ECCV 2002. LNCS, vol. 2353, pp. 97–112. Springer, Heidelberg (2002). doi:10.1007/3-540-47979-1_7
4. Feng, S., Manmatha, R., Lavrenko, V.: Multiple Bernoulli relevance models for image and video annotation. In: Proceedings of the 2004 IEEE Computer Society Conference on Computer Vision and Pattern Recognition, CVPR 2004, vol. 2, pp. II:1002–II:1009. IEEE (2004)
5. Gong, Y., Jia, Y., Leung, T., Toshev, A., Ioffe, S.: Deep convolutional ranking for multilabel image annotation. arXiv:1312.4894 (2013)

6. Gu, Y., Qian, X., Li, Q., Wang, M., Hong, R., Tian, Q.: Image annotation by latent community detection and multikernel learning. IEEE Trans. Image Process. **24**(11), 3450–3463 (2015)
7. Guillaumin, M., Mensink, T., Verbeek, J., Schmid, C.: TagProp: discriminative metric learning in nearest neighbor models for image auto-annotation. In: 2009 IEEE 12th International Conference on Computer Vision, pp. 309–316. IEEE (2009)
8. He, Y., Wang, J., Kang, C., Xiang, S., Pan, C.: Large scale image annotation via deep representation learning and tag embedding learning. In: Proceedings of the 5th ACM on International Conference on Multimedia Retrieval, pp. 523–526. ACM (2015)
9. Kalayeh, M.M., Idrees, H., Shah, M.: NMF-KNN: Image annotation using weighted multi-view non-negative matrix factorization. In: 2014 IEEE Conference on Computer Vision and Pattern Recognition (CVPR), pp. 184–191. IEEE (2014)
10. Liu, W., Tao, D.: Multiview Hessian regularization for image annotation. IEEE Trans. Image Process. **22**(7), 2676–2687 (2013)
11. Makadia, A., Pavlovic, V., Kumar, S.: A new baseline for image annotation. In: Forsyth, D., Torr, P., Zisserman, A. (eds.) ECCV 2008. LNCS, vol. 5305, pp. 316–329. Springer, Heidelberg (2008). doi:10.1007/978-3-540-88690-7_24
12. Murthy, V.N., Maji, S., Manmatha, R.: Automatic image annotation using deep learning representations. In: Proceedings of the 5th ACM on International Conference on Multimedia Retrieval, pp. 603–606. ACM (2015)
13. Oliva, A., Torralba, A.: Modeling the shape of the scene: a holistic representation of the spatial envelope. Int. J. Comput. Vis. **42**(3), 145–175 (2001)
14. Schroff, F., Kalenichenko, D., Philbin, J.: FaceNet: a unified embedding for face recognition and clustering. In: Proceedings of the IEEE Conference on Computer Vision and Pattern Recognition, pp. 815–823 (2015)
15. Simonyan, K., Zisserman, A.: Very deep convolutional networks for large-scale image recognition. arXiv:1409.1556 (2014)
16. Su, F., Xue, L.: Graph learning on k nearest neighbours for automatic image annotation. In: Proceedings of the 5th ACM on International Conference on Multimedia Retrieval, pp. 403–410. ACM (2015)
17. Tariq, A., Foroosh, H.: Feature-independent context estimation for automatic image annotation. In: Proceedings of the IEEE Conference on Computer Vision and Pattern Recognition, pp. 1958–1965 (2015)
18. de Weijer, J., Schmid, C.: Coloring local feature extraction. In: Leonardis, A., Bischof, H., Pinz, A. (eds.) ECCV 2006. LNCS, vol. 3954, pp. 334–348. Springer, Heidelberg (2006). doi:10.1007/11744047_26
19. Verma, Y., Jawahar, C.V.: Image annotation using metric learning in semantic neighbourhoods. In: Fitzgibbon, A., Lazebnik, S., Perona, P., Sato, Y., Schmid, C. (eds.) ECCV 2012. LNCS, vol. 7578, pp. 836–849. Springer, Heidelberg (2012). doi:10.1007/978-3-642-33712-3_60
20. Von Ahn, L., Dabbish, L.: Labeling images with a computer game. In: Proceedings of the SIGCHI Conference on Human Factors in Computing Systems, pp. 319–326. ACM (2004)
21. Zeiler, M.D., Fergus, R.: Visualizing and understanding convolutional networks. In: Fleet, D., Pajdla, T., Schiele, B., Tuytelaars, T. (eds.) ECCV 2014. LNCS, vol. 8693, pp. 818–833. Springer, Heidelberg (2014). doi:10.1007/978-3-319-10590-1_53

One-Shot-Learning Gesture Segmentation and Recognition Using Frame-Based PDV Features

Tao Rong$^{(\boxtimes)}$ and Ruoyu Yang$^{(\boxtimes)}$

State Key Laboratory for Novel Software Technology,
Nanjing University, Nanjing, China
raymond_rong@163.com, yangry@nju.edu.cn

Abstract. This paper proposes one novel on-line gesture segmentation and recognition method for one-shot-learning on depth video. In each depth image, we take several random points from the motion region and select a group of relevant points for each random point. Depth difference between each random point and its relevant points is calculated in Motion History Images. The results are used to generate the random point's feature. Then we use Random Decision Forest to assign gesture label to each random point and work out the probability distribution vector (PDV) for each frame in the video. Finally, we gain a probability distribution matrix (PDM) using PDVs of sequential frames and do on-line segmentation and recognition for one-shot-learning. Experimental results show our method is competitive to the state-of-the- art methods.

Keywords: On-line segmentation · Gesture recognition · One-shot-learning · Motion History Image

1 Introduction

On-line gesture recognition and segmentation can be widely used in games, sign language recognition and human-computer interaction, etc. The related research work has been popular topics in computer vision.

Gesture recognition has been studied extensively in the past decades. The early works were mainly based on RGB images and have obtained good results. Despite many inspiring research achievements, gesture recognition is still a challenge task. In recent years, depth images on gestures could be easily obtained with depth sensors like the Kinect camera. With RGB-D information, there are many good research results such as [1–4].

In On-line gesture recognition, recognition result should be generated timely when performer begins gesturing. So, sliding window [5, 6] is widely used for on-line action recognition, but the computation cost is high because of its iterative calculation.

The study on segmentation for continuous gestures has also brought some nice algorithms [7], although it doesn't get as much attention as gesture recognition. They mainly include bound detection [8–10], DTW segmentation [3, 4], and so on. Some methods [8–10] tried to find the frames similar to the beginning or ending frame in

© Springer International Publishing AG 2016
E. Chen et al. (Eds.): PCM 2016, Part I, LNCS 9916, pp. 355–365, 2016.
DOI: 10.1007/978-3-319-48890-5_35

gesture sequence. These frames are likely to be the segmentation point of two neighboring gestures. Obviously, these methods have demanding requirement on gesture sequences. DTW segmentation [3, 4] could achieve good results. In fact, the high accuracy of DTW segmentation method partly depends on the information that performer's hands will return to the resting position after one gesture.

In this paper, we propose a novel on-line gesture segmentation and recognition method for one-shot-learning (only one training example for each class).

In gesture recognition, effective spatio-temporal features are important. There are many appearance and motion descriptors, such as HOG, HOF, HOG3D and 3D EMoSOFT. In [11], simple depth comparison features are employed to predict position of body joints. Inspired by the work, we propose one novel spatio-temporal feature based on depth difference between selected points and aim to generate a recognition result for each depth frame once the gesture begins. In addition, we propose an on-line gesture segmentation method which does not have special requirement on gesture sequences.

The dataset we use is Chalearn gesture dataset (CGD2011) [12] which includes depth gesture videos we need. The experimental results reveal that our method is competitive to the state-of-the-art methods.

The remainder of this paper is organized as follows. In Sect. 2, we present the proposed on-line gesture recognition and segmentation method. In Sect. 3, the experimental results for Chalearn gesture dataset (CGD2011) are reported. Finally, we conclude our paper in Sect. 4.

2 Proposed Method

The framework of our method is shown in Fig. 1. First, we should do preprocessing to reduce noise and gain the motion region in depth images. Otsu's method is used to separate the foreground from the background. Then, we regard the first frame in the video as background. Frame difference algorithm is used between the first frame and later frames. After noise reduction, we gain the motion region, as well as the rest region of human body. The process is shown in Fig. 1(A–D).

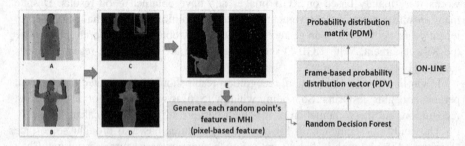

Fig. 1. The framework of our method. (A) The first frame in the depth video; (B) Another frame in the depth video; (C) The region of motion; (D) The rest region of human body; (E) Take random points from the motion region.

Then, we randomly select several points from the motion region (Fig. 1(E)) and select a group of relevant points for each random point. Depth difference between each random point and its relevant points is calculated in Motion History Images (MHI). The results are used to generate the random point's feature (pixel-based feature). Then we use Random Decision Forest to assign gesture label to each random point and work out the probability distribution vector (PDV) for each frame in the video. Finally, we could gain a probability distribution matrix (PDM) using PDVs of sequential frames and do on-line recognition and segmentation for one-shot-learning.

2.1   Pixel-Based Feature

In depth image, the adjacent points may have similar depth information. That is, to some extent, a point's depth information can represent the depth information of the point's adjacent region.

Our idea is as follows. For each depth image, we take some random points and select a group of relevant points for each of them. Let RP denotes random point and let VP denotes relevant point. Then, we could get pixel-based feature from the depth difference between one RP and its VPs. Finally, if we select sufficient VPs from suitable location, by using the pixel-based feature, we could take the random point as the center and outline the shape of the gesture. With these pixel-based features, Random Decision Forest is adopted to do learning or classification for each RP.

But how to select sufficient VPs from suitable location for each RP?

2.1.1   Select Relevant Points

For each RP, the collection of its VPs should meets the following conditions:

- Cover the region of motion and involve the rest region of human body.
- Easy to obtain and the computation cost is low.
- The closer to the RP, the greater the density of VPs is, and vice versa.

First, we take the RP as the center and generate a plurality of concentric circles with different radii. Second, we set horizontal right direction as 0° angle and along the direction of 0°–330° (30° as interval, such as 30° 60°, 12 directions in total) angle to construct the offset vector. Finally, the intersections between concentric circles and offset vectors are selected as the RP's VPs.

Then how to determine the radii of concentric circles?

Suppose there are S frames in the training video and let Frame[i] denotes the ith frame. After preprocessing on Frame[i], we get the motion regions. First, we add bounding boxes to the moving regions. Then, we calculate the lengths of the bounding boxes' diagonals. Let L_i and L_j denote the lengths. If there is only one moving region, we set L_j to 0. The sizes of different frames' motion regions tend to be different, so we take the maximum value of L_i and L_j ($1 \leqslant i \leqslant S, 1 \leqslant j \leqslant S$):

$$L = \underset{1 \leq i \leq S, 1 \leq j \leq S}{Max} \{L_i, L_j\} \tag{1}$$

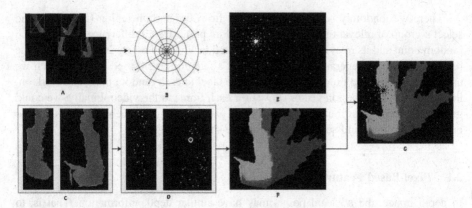

Fig. 2. The flowchart to generate pixel-based feature. (A) Calculate the value of L; (B) Generate concentric circles with the center of random point; (C) The region of motion (D) Random points in motion region; (E) Relevant points of the random point which is surrounded by the yellow circle in D; (F) MHI (we only show a part of MHI in F); (G) Relevant points and the random point on MHI. (Color figure online)

For any frame in videos, when we set any RP as the center, with L as the radius of circle, the circle can contain the motion region. Because the value of L tends to be a little larger, the circle often covers a part of the body not moving.

In fact, L is threshold of all concentric circles' radii. We use Fibonacci number to gain the radii. In Fibonacci number, the elements less than L are used as the radii of the concentric circles. That is to say, if the value of L is 150, the radii will be 1, 2, 3, 5, 8, 21, 34, 55, 89 and 144. The process is shown in Fig. 2(A–E).

2.1.2   Features on the MHI

After choosing VPs, we calculate depth difference between the RP and its VPs and generate pixel-based feature. However, if we calculate the depth difference only on the current one frame, the obtained feature only describes the shape information of the motion region in this current frame. Therefore, we get the depth difference from Motion History Images (MHI).

Motion History Images (MHI) is an effective method used to identify movements within continuous frames.

As mentioned above, we take some RPs and choose VPs for each RP. Then, the motion area in the current frame will be grouped together with several previous frames' motion areas. In order to avoid confusion, in MHI, all points' values are set to different constants. Suppose the current frame is Frame[α], if a point is in the motion area of Frame[α], the value of related point at the same position in MHI is assigned to X. Then, in MHI, the values of points at the same position with those in the motion area of Frame [$\alpha-1$] are assigned to X–Y and the values of points at the same position with those in the motion area of Frame[$\alpha-2$] are assigned to X–2*Y, and so on. The values of points in the background and rest region of body are assigned to the same value as in Frame[α]. In addition, if there is an overlap in the motion areas of different frames, the MHI will save the motion region of the latter frame. An example is shown in Fig. 2(F–G).

According to the values on MHI, we can know whether RPs and VPs are in the motion region of a certain frame or not. Then we come back to the real depth image of each frame. The range of each point's depth value is: 0–255. Suppose there are N RPs and each RP has M VPs. So, the depth difference Dif_{ij} between RP_i (denotes the ith RP, $i \in [1,N]$) and VP_{ij} (denotes the jth VP of the RP_i, $j \in [1,M]$) is calculated by the following steps:

1. In order to reflect the shape information, if VP_{ij} is located in the motion region of Frame[α], using depth value of VP_{ij} in Frame[α] and RP_i in Frame[α], we can calculate Dif_{ij} as follows:

$$Dif_{ij} = (Depth_{VP_{ij}} - Depth_{RP_i}) * 0.001 \qquad (2)$$

2. In order to reflect the motion information, if VP_{ij} is in the motion region of Frame[α−k], using depth value of VP_{ij} in Frame[α−k] and RP_i in Frame[α], we can calculate Dif_{ij} as follows:

$$Dif_{ij} = (Depth_{VP_{ij}} - Depth_{RP_i}) * 0.001 + k \qquad (3)$$

3. In order to reflect the location of VP_{ij}, Dif_{ij} is assigned to different constants corresponding to the different location of VP_{ij}, i.e. ε, ζ, η respectively when VP_{ij} is located in the rest region of human body, in the background and out of the image.

$$Dif_{ij} = \begin{cases} \varepsilon & \varepsilon > 255 \\ \zeta & \zeta > 255 \&\& \zeta \neq \varepsilon \\ \eta & \eta > 255 \&\& \eta \neq \zeta \&\& \eta \neq \varepsilon \end{cases} \qquad (4)$$

4. We also need reflect the position information of RP_i in the moving region. Let (x, y) denotes position of the centroid point of the moving region. And let (u, v) denotes position of RP_i. We calculate the polar coordinates of RP_i to the centroid point:

$$\begin{cases} \theta = \arctan((y - v)/(x - u)) \\ \rho = \sqrt{(x - u)^2 + (y - v)^2} \end{cases} \qquad (5)$$

Now, we use a 1*(M+2) feature vector to record the pixel-based feature of RP_i:

$$(\theta, \rho, Dif_{i1}, Dif_{i2}, Dif_{i3}...Dif_{iM})$$

After generating pixel-based feature vector for all the RPs in Frame[α], Random Decision Forest is adopted to do learning or classification for each RP.

Random Decision Forest (RDF) is a classifier which contains multiple decision trees. It is an ensemble learning method for classification, regression and other tasks.

Suppose the collection of gesture labels is {$Label_i$ | $1 \leqslant i \leqslant$ TotalNum}. TotalNum is the amount of gestures.

After classification, each RP has a label representing a gesture type which the RP's feature vector implies. For example, if classification result of a RP is Label$_2$, that is, considering the RP and its VPs, the gesture in Frame[α] is most likely to be Label$_2$.

2.2 Frame-Based Probability Distribution Vector (PDV)

In Sect. 2.1, we take N RPs in each frame and assign a label for each RP. However, for various reasons, these labels are not always the same. We cannot determine directly which label is the true label of this frame.

Let Sum$_i$ denotes the amount of RPs assigned with Label$_i$. First, we count the N labels and gain a vector: (Sum$_1$, Sum$_2$, Sum$_3$...Sum$_{TotalNum}$), $N = \sum_{i=1}^{TotalNum} Sum_i$. We normalize the vector and gain P$_α$:

$$(Sum_1/N, \ Sum_2/N, \ Sum_3/N...Sum_{TotalNum}/N)$$

P$_α$ is the probability distribution vector of Frame[α]. In P$_α$, P$_{αi}$ is the ith element of the vector and represents the possibility that the gesture in Frame[α] is Label$_i$.

Combine all frames' PDVs, we have a probability distribution matrix (PDM) M. For a video from CGD2011, the M is shown as follows:

$$
\begin{bmatrix}
0 & 0 & 0 & 0 & 0 & 0 & 0 & 0 & 0 & 0 \\
\vdots & \vdots & \vdots & \vdots & \vdots & \vdots & \vdots & \vdots & \vdots & \vdots \\
0 & 93.3\% & 0 & 0 & 0 & 3.3\% & 0 & 0 & 0 & 3.3\% \\
0 & 93.3\% & 0 & 0 & 0 & 1.7\% & 0 & 0 & 0 & 5.0\% \\
\vdots & \vdots & \vdots & \vdots & \vdots & \vdots & \vdots & \vdots & \vdots & \vdots \\
0 & 30.0\% & 0 & 0 & 0 & 1.7\% & 3.3\% & 0 & 0 & 65.5\% \\
0 & 28.3\% & 0 & 0 & 0 & 3.3\% & 8.3\% & 0 & 0 & 60.0\% \\
\vdots & \vdots & \vdots & \vdots & \vdots & \vdots & \vdots & \vdots & \vdots & \vdots \\
0 & 0 & 0 & 0 & 0 & 0 & 0 & 0 & 0 & 0
\end{bmatrix}
$$

Each row in M represents a frame's PDV. For example, the element in M [i, j] represents the possibility that the gesture in Frame[i] is Label$_j$.

2.3 Recognition

PDM can be converted to a line graph as shown in Fig. 3. From Fig. 3, humans can easily recognize where and which gestures are present, but it is a bit more challenging task for a computer in on-line recognition.

2.3.1 On-line Gesture Recognition with Candidate Cuts Information in CGD2011 (First)

In the video from Chalearn gesture dataset (CGD2011), performer's hands return to a resting position between each pair of neighboring gestures. The dataset provides

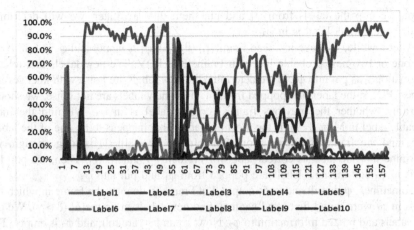

Fig. 3. The line chart transformed from the probability distribution matrix M.

candidate cuts based on similarities with the resting position. With these information, we know when gestures begin or end.

We read the video frame by frame and generate each Frame's PDV which is added into PDM M. Let Frame[β] denotes the frame which we have just read. Let Frame[α] denotes the frame when the gesture begins. Let M[α] denotes the αth row in M, i.e. Frame[α]'s PDV. Let M[$\alpha : \beta$] denotes the αth–β^{th} rows in M. By calculating the sum of αth–β^{th} rows in M, we can get the label with the largest cumulative probability in Frame [α]–Frame[β]. Then we regard this label as Frame[β]'s recognition result. If we have just read the frame when the gesture ends, we regard this frame's label as the final recognition result of the gesture.

2.3.2 On-line Gesture Recognition with Our Segmentation Method (Second)

In this section we perform on-line recognition simultaneously with segmentation with our segmentation method. On-line gesture segmentation is a challenging task. We should not only deal with a variety of noise, but also to identify when a gesture begins or ends in a timely manner. For example, if we have found a probable label in Frame[α] and then detect another likely label in Frame[β], the reason may be that a new gesture begins, or we encounter noise. It is challenging to solve these problems effectively.

Three buffers (φ_1, φ_2 and φ_3) are used in our algorithm. All buffers' capacities are set to 1. For reducing computation cost, at the same time, there are at most two non-empty buffers.

We read the video frame by frame and do recognition for each frame. Let Frame[α] denotes the frame which we have just read. We generate Frame[α]'s PDV which is added into the PDM M.

If we find one or two probable labels in Frame[α]'s PDV and three buffers are empty, the labels and related information is put into φ_1. According to the labels' tendencies in later several frames, we will determine whether the labels are noise or not.

If not, we pop the labels from φ_1 and put them into φ_3. Later, we will determine whether the correct label is in φ_3.

After a while, we have just read Frame[β] ($\beta > \alpha$). φ_1 is empty and φ_3 is full. If we find one or two new probable labels in Frame[β]'s PDV. The new labels and related information was put into φ_1. If we determine the new labels are noise with later several frames' PDVs, the labels are popped from φ_1. If the new labels are not noise, we should determine whether the previous frames' correct label is in φ_3. We find the most probable label in M[α: β−1]. If the most probable label happens to be one of the labels in φ_3 and the frames sequence from Frame[α] to Frame[β−1] is long enough, we determine that the label is correct label for Frame[α]–Frame[β−1]. Then, we pop the labels in φ_3 and the new labels are popped from φ_1 and put into φ_3.

Sometimes, φ_1 is full and φ_3 is empty. Let Frame[γ] denotes the frame in which the labels in φ_1 were found first. And we may find new labels in Frame[δ] ($\delta > \gamma$). We put new labels and related information to φ_2. Now, φ_1 and φ_2 are full, and φ_3 is empty. The Algorithm 1 mainly describes the method for this situation. In the pseudo code there are several variables as follows: depth gesture video V = {Frame}^{FrameNum}, PDV P, PDM M (only δ rows in M now), Labels$_i$ denote the labels in φ_1, Labels$_j$ denote the labels in φ_2 and R denotes the video's labels sequence. Besides, λ means the number of successive frames in which the Labels$_j$ are most likely.

Algorithm 1. Online Gesture Segmentation and Recognition When φ_1 and φ_2 Are Full

Input: V, M, Labels$_i$, Labels$_j$, R
Initialization: $\lambda \leftarrow 1$, S $\leftarrow 0$
1: **for** T = δ + 1: FrameNum
2:     Read Frame[T], generate P$_T$. M $\leftarrow$ M $\cup$ P$_T$, S $\leftarrow$ T.
3:     **for** K = S: T
4:        Update λ if needed.
5:        Judge tendencies of Labels$_j$ from M[δ : K].
6:        **if** we have gain enough information, **then**
7:           **if** Labels$_j$ are noise, **then**
8:              Pop Labels$_j$ from φ_2.
9:           **else, then**
10:             Pop Labels$_j$ from φ_2 and push Labels$_j$ into φ_3.
11:             Determine Labels$_i$ from M[γ : δ-1].
12:             Update R if the correct label is in Labels$_i$. Pop Labels$_i$ from φ_1.
13:          **end if**
14:          S $\leftarrow$ δ + λ − 1, K $\leftarrow$ S, λ $\leftarrow$ 0. Return R.
15:       **end if**
16:    **end for**
17: **end for**
Output: labels sequence R

3   Experimental Results

In Chalearn gesture dataset (CGD2011), we choose the first 20 batches of the development dataset to test our system. Each batch consists of 47 gestures sequences including depth and RGB videos, which are divided into a training set and a testing set.

In the training set, only one training example is available for each gesture. In the testing set, each video sequence contains one or more gestures. Besides, the actor will return to the rest position after performing a gesture.

In order to evaluate the performance of the proposed method, the Levenshtein Distance (LD) measure is employed. By counting the minimum number of operations required to transform one string into the other, Levenshtein Distance can quantify how dissimilar two strings are to each other.

The experimental result is shown in Fig. 4. We have also added some of the experimental results in other papers: SM [3] and BoVDW [2].

SM method [3] uses both HOG and HOF and perform temporal segmentation simultaneously with recognition. The segmentation method in SM partly relies on the information that performer's hands return to a resting position between each pair of neighboring gestures. BoVDW [2] is A Bag-of-Visual-and-Depth-Words model. In BoVDW, state-of-the-art RGB and depth features, including a newly depth descriptor proposed in [2], are combined in a late fusion form. The method is integrated in a Human Gesture Recognition pipeline, together with a novel probability-based Dynamic Time Warping (PDTW) algorithm which is used to perform prior segmentation of idle gestures.

According to Fig. 4, First method (proposed in Sect. 2.3.1) achieved good effect. This is because our pixel-based feature is effective in reflect gestures' shape and motion information. Besides, each RP's label can be considered as a preliminary recognition

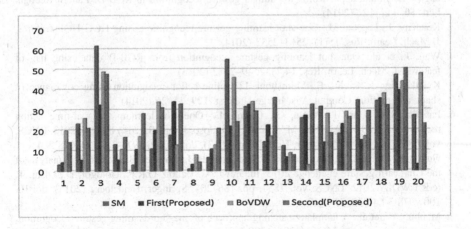

Fig. 4. The performance of each batch (devel01–devel20) on Chalearn dataset. The mean Levenshtein Distance of the methods above are as follows: SM: 23.78; First (Proposed in Sect. 2.3.1): 18.47; BoVDW: 26.62; Second (Proposed in Sect. 2.3.2): 26.39.

result. After generating PDV for each frame and do on-line recognition as in Sect. 2.3.1, we can gain the final recognition result effectively.

For Second method (proposed in Sect. 2.3.2), 26.39 (Second) is lower than 26.62 (BoVDW) and higher than First (18.47). In fact, On-line segmentation is a more challenging task for various reasons. After inspecting the video, we find that there is much noise in depth images after preprocessing sometimes and it causes a reduction in the accuracy of Second method. This is because a simple frame differencing is used in pre-processing stage for motion estimation. We will do more research with a more refined motion estimation scheme. From another perspective, our segmentation method does not have special requirement on gesture sequences. Besides, the baseline of the dataset is 62.32. So 26.39 (Second) is acceptable.

4 Conclusion

In this paper, a novel on-line gesture recognition and segmentation method based on the depth difference information between selected pixels is proposed. We design a novel spatio-temporal feature and generate the probability distribution vector (PDV) for each frame in the video. PDVs of sequential frames help us implement online gesture recognition and segmentation. Furthermore, we will consider more elegant features aiming at lower LD and higher training speed.

References

1. Fanello, S.R., et al.: Keep it simple and sparse: real-time action recognition. J. Mach. Learn. Res. **14**(1), 2617–2640 (2013)
2. Hernández-Vela, A., et al.: Probability-based dynamic time warping and bag-of-visual-and-depth-words for human gesture recognition in RGB-D. Pattern Recogn. Lett. **50**, 112–121 (2014)
3. Konečný, J., Hagara, M.: One-shot-learning gesture recognition using HOG-HOF features. J. Mach. Learn. Res. **15**(1), 2513–2532 (2014)
4. Wan, J., et al.: One-shot learning gesture recognition from RGB-D data using bag of features. J. Mach. Learn. Res. **14**(1), 2549–2582 (2013)
5. Kviatkovsky, I., Rivlin, E., Shimshoni, I.: Online action recognition using covariance of shape and motion. Comput. Vis. Image Underst. **129**, 15–26 (2014)
6. Fanello, S.R., Gori, I., Metta, G., Odone, F.: One-shot learning for real-time action recognition. In: Sanches, João, M., Micó, L., Cardoso, Jaime, S. (eds.) IbPRIA 2013. LNCS, vol. 7887, pp. 31–40. Springer, Heidelberg (2013). doi:10.1007/978-3-642-38628-2_4
7. Guyon, I., Athitsos, V., Jangyodsuk, P., Escalante, H.,J., Hamner, B.: Results and analysis of the ChaLearn gesture challenge 2012. In: Jiang, X., Bellon, O.R.P., Goldgof, D., Oishi, T. (eds.) WDIA 2012. LNCS, vol. 7854, pp. 186–204. Springer, Heidelberg (2013). doi:10.1007/978-3-642-40303-3_19
8. Mahbub, U., et al.: A template matching approach of one-shot-learning gesture recognition. Pattern Recogn. Lett. **34**(15), 1780–1788 (2013)

9. Wu, D., Fan Z., Ling S.: One shot learning gesture recognition from RGBD images. In: 2012 IEEE Computer Society Conference on Computer Vision and Pattern Recognition Workshops (CVPRW). IEEE (2012)
10. Lui, Y.M.: A least squares regression framework on manifolds and its application to gesture recognition. In: 2012 IEEE Computer Society Conference on Computer Vision and Pattern Recognition Workshops (CVPRW). IEEE (2012)
11. Shotton, J., et al.: Real-time human pose recognition in parts from single depth images. Commun. ACM **56**(1), 116–124 (2013)
12. ChaLearn Gesture Dataset (CGD2011), ChaLearn, California (2011)

Multi-scale Point Set Saliency Detection Based on Site Entropy Rate

Yu Guo[✉], Fei Wang, Pengyu Liu, Jingmin Xin, and Nanning Zheng

Institute of Artificial Intelligence and Robotics,
Xi'an Jiaotong University, Xi'an 710049, China
cvyuguo@gmail.com, {wfx,jxin,nnzheng}@mail.xjtu.edu.cn,
liu.pengyu@stu.xjtu.edu.cn

Abstract. Visual saliency in images has been studied extensively in many literatures, but there is no much work on point sets. In this paper, we propose an approach based on pointwise site entropy rate to detect the saliency distribution in unorganized point sets and range data, which are lack of topological information. In our model, a point set is first transformed to a sparsely-connected graph. Then the model runs random walks on the graphs to simulate the signal/information transmission. We evaluate point saliency using site entropy rate (SER), which reflects average information transmitted from a point to its neighbors. By simulating the diffusion process on each point, multi-scale saliency maps are obtained. We combine the multi-scale saliency maps to generate the final result. The effectiveness of the proposed approach is demonstrated by comparisons to other approaches on a range of test models. The experiment shows our model achieves good performance, without using any connectivity information.

1 Introduction

Visual saliency is an important and fundamental research topic in psychology and neuroscience, since visual attention plays an important role in the human visual system. In last decade years, saliency detection is an attractive topic in computer vision for applying it to many applications, e.g. object recognition, matching and downsampling. Most of works focus on images [4,5,12,22,30], videos [8,11,26]. Less work for detecting saliency on 3D surfaces [13,21,23,29] is explored and a few addressed on unorganized point sets [1,20,24].

In computer graphics, most tasks of shape processing are taken on polygonal meshes. So mesh saliency [21,23,27] has been mostly studied on such surface representation in recent years. Some work extending the existing techniques of image saliency detection to 3D meshes. These mesh-based methods depend on spectral properties [21] or shape descriptors [14] are not trivial to extend to unorganized point sets, since it lacks topological information and surface reconstruction is also a challenging problem with noisy point sets. Furthermore, when the size of the point data is large, much extending methods of images are computationally expensive.

© Springer International Publishing AG 2016
E. Chen et al. (Eds.): PCM 2016, Part I, LNCS 9916, pp. 366–375, 2016.
DOI: 10.1007/978-3-319-48890-5_36

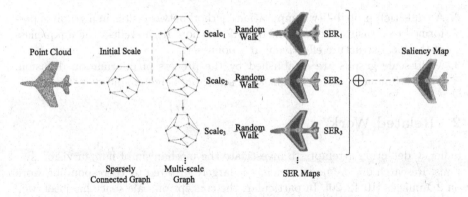

Fig. 1. Framework of our proposed method

Due to the fast development of 3D data acquisition techniques and increase of 3D point sets, it is important to handle this type of data. Our work is inspired by recent methods in image saliency detection [28]. In this paper, we propose a novel, simple and computationally efficient method for detecting points saliency on point sets. This computational model of human attention is biology-imitated. Different from visual saliency detection commonly based on center-surround mechanism, our model is derived from the principle of information maximization, which suggests that the human vision system tends to focus on the most informative points. The proposed framework is presented in Fig. 1, which shows the procedure of generating a saliency map of a point set. First, we transform the input point set to a sparsely connected graph. For each point, it connects with its k nearest neighbors. This graph is called 0-scale graph, and it is able to capture the short range relation between two sites in a point set. We assign the transition probabilities to each pair of connected sites. The values of transition probabilities are computed based on a diffusion tensor. Secondly, a diffusion process on the 0-scale graph is performed for capturing different scale saliency structures. The diffusion step is discretized for establishing multi-scale graphs. Then a random walk is operate on each scale graph in order to model the signal transmission among the sites in the graph. As the entropy rate (ER) of the random walk is the average information of one step move, we use it to compute the total transmitted information of all the graph nodes. By distributing the entropy rate onto each sites, we use Site Entropy Rate (SER) to measure the average information from a node to all the others. In this way, we obtain a SER map for each scale graph. Finally, the saliency maps is computed by integrating over SER maps of all the scales.

Our proposed saliency algorithm does not use topological information. Experiments demonstrate that our multi-scale pointwise method has better performance compared with state-of-art methods [20,21,23,24], especially some methods on 3D meshes. The main contributions of our method are as follows:

1. A biology-mimic framework is introduced to model the human visual system for point sets saliency detection. It is easy to compute.

2. A transition probability computation method between sites in a graph is performed to measure the transmitted information. It can reflect the uniqueness of the local structure effectively in a point set.
3. Multi-scale graphs are established by the process of information diffusion. This technique is more efficient than searching neighbors at every scale.

2   Related Work

Saliency detection attempts to investigate the mechanism of human vision systems. Research on 3D model saliency is largely inspired by corresponding work on 2D images [10,12,20]. In particular, the concept of scale space has been well developed in 2D domains. In 2D image processing, scale spaces are usually established by manipulating downsampled images with different scales for saliency detection [12]. Early work on 3D data saliency detection are addressed on 3D mesh model, which computes mesh saliency by projecting the data to 2D space [7]. Recently, some works compute saliency on meshes directly. Galand Cohen-Or [19] approximate a mesh by a sparse set of local patches represented by descriptors. Gelfand et al. [6] design the Integral Volume Descriptor for each point on a mesh, and saliency of a point is based on the uniqueness of its associated descriptor. Many mesh saliency methods are typically based on saliency techniques for images [13,21,29]. For example, several 3D saliency methods based on the Difference of Gaussian scale space [2,18] are inspired from method of image saliency detection.

Relatively few saliency models support point clouds [1,15,20,24]. The approach of [20] extends context-aware method [22] to pointwise saliency detection of point sets. A cluster based approach proposed by Flora Ponjou Tasse [24] for efficient computation of saliency on point sets, which is inspired from image region based method. Our work is inspired by the idea of [28] and we generalize it to saliency detection of point sets.

3   Our Model

In this section, we introduce our framework of saliency detection on point sets without connective information. In this framework, we first transform the input point set to an initial indirected graph, which is sparsely connected between each point with its neighbors in a small neighborhood. The weights of edges in this graph are decided by a normal tensor reflecting local structures. Then a class of multi-scale graphs is generated based on the initial graph by diffusion process. Finally Site entropy rate is computed in each graphs and a saliency map is generated.

3.1   Tensor Based Similarity Measurement

The normal voting tensor $T(p_i)$ of a vertex p_i can be computed by the sum of the weighted covariance matrices, which is called tensor voting [16,17].

$$T(p_i) = \sum_{p_j \in N(p_i)} \mu_j \mathbf{n}_{p_j} \mathbf{n}_{p_j}^T \qquad (1)$$

where $N(p_i)$ denotes the set of neighboring points of p_i, $\mathbf{n}_{p_i}$ is the normal vector of point p_i, and μ_j is the weight. To eliminate the effect of different densities of points distribution, the μ_j is defined as

$$\mu_j = exp\left(-\frac{\|p_j - c_i\|}{\|N(p_i) - c_i\|_{max}}\right) \qquad (2)$$

where c_i is the barycenter of neighbor points of p_i, and $\|N(p_i) - c_i\|_{max}$ is the maximum value between c_i and points in $N(p_i)$. Then we define the similarity measurement between two points as

$$Q(i,j) = exp\left(-\frac{(p_i - p_j)^T (T(p_i) + T(p_j))(p_i - p_j)}{\sigma_i + \sigma_j}\right) \qquad (3)$$

where σ_i is the average distance of point p_i to its neighbors, and $\sigma_i + \sigma_j$ is taken as normalization parameter here. In such definition, the geometric similarity measurement between neighboring points can be well characterized. We define a matrix Q whose entry is $Q(i,j)$ as similarity matrix.

3.2   Multi-scale Graphs Representation

Now we model the information flow from one point to another as a random walk process from one site to another on an initial scale sparsely connected graph of the input point set. Each point in point sets is taken as a node in this graph. Edges are only connected points with k nearest neighbors. In the initial scale graph, k is a small number for searching efficiency. So the similarity matrix of initial scale graph is sparse. The transition probability of the random walk between two sites in terms of the normalized edge weights of them.

$$w(i,j) = \frac{Q(i,j)}{\sum_j Q(i,j)} \qquad (4)$$

It is known that if the finite-state Markov chain is irreducible and aperiodic, the stationary distribution π is unique and $\pi = W\pi$. Where W is the transition matrix. And the element of π at node i can be computed as

$$\pi(i,j) = \frac{Q_i}{2Q_{sum}} \qquad (5)$$

where $Q_i = \sum_j Q(i,j)$ is the sum of row i of similarity matrix Q, and $Q_{sum} = \sum_{i,j}$ is the total sum of all entries of matrix Q.

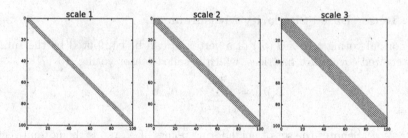

Fig. 2. Corresponding transition matrices of three scale graphs of 1D signal

Here we denote similarity matrix and transition matrix of the initial scale graph Q^1 and P^1. Inspired from [9], then we adopt a bottom-up approach to establish multi-scale graphs, which is different from the traditional method by downsampling the image. The transition matrix P^1 of initial scale graph is considered as a basis matrix to represent a random walk process. The next level of similarity matrix Q^2 and transition matrix P^2 can be computed as

$$Q^2 = P^1 * P^1$$
$$P^2 = [Q^2]_r \qquad (6)$$

where $[\cdot]_r$ denote the row based normalization. Following the above paradigm, the relative matrix of next scale can be established as

$$Q^m = P^{m-1} * P^{m-1}$$
$$P^m = [Q^m]_r \qquad (7)$$

The established scaling graphs are locally supported and their corresponding transition matrix is sparse. The multi-scale graphs can capture different scale feature or special information of the random walk process. In Fig. 2, a schematic visually depicts transition matrices corresponding to three scale graphs of a 1D signal. The matrices are sparser for point clouds with much more points.

3.3   Site Entropy Rate

In information theory, the entropy rate $H(\chi)$ is defined to measure the average entropy of a sequence with n random variables. It stands the average information obtained along with the time as $n- > \infty$. Entropy rate is defined as

$$H(\chi) = -\sum_{ij} \pi_i P(i,j) \log P(i,j) \qquad (8)$$

where $\{X_i\}$ is a Markov chain with stationary distribution $\pi = \{\pi_i\}$ and transition matrix $P = \{p(i,j) : P(X_n = j | X_{n-1} = i)\}$. we follow the definition of Site Entropy Rate (SER) in literature [28], it can be denoted as

$$SER_i = \pi_i \sum_j -P(i,j) \log P(i,j) \qquad (9)$$

SER can measure the average information between node i and its neighbors. From Eq. 9, it can be found that SER has two aspects for measuring the information. The stationary distribution term π reflects the frequency at which a random walker visits node i. The entropy term $\sum_j -P(i,j)\log P(i,j)$ tells the the uncertainty of node i jumping to the other nodes in one step. It is related to the amount of information transmitted from node i to the others in one step. SER is the product of the two terms and it reflects the average total information transmitted from node i to the others of next step. The higher value of a node in a graph, the more salient is the points corresponding to this node. For multi-scale graph representation of a point set, geometric structures with different scale can be measured. In the set of scale graphs, next scale graph of the current scale graph stands a walker go forward with on step. Node i transmits its local information to more neighbors, so it connects more nodes in the graph and a smoother value of SER is assigned. As expected, if the walker moves forward on this graph with enough number of steps, SER of each node will achieve a balance status. This status is no more changed as steps increased.

3.4   Saliency Map

We obtain the SER map for each scale graph. According to the Feature-Integrated Theory [25], the final saliency map is the sum of all the SER maps. The saliency is computed as

$$S_i = \sum_m SER_{m,i} \tag{10}$$

where m is the scale script of graphs.

4   Experiments

In this section, we compare our method against previous point-based and mesh-based saliency methods, followed by a discussion on the influence of the scale selection. We show the final results of saliency distribution by coloring each point with heat map.

4.1   Compared with Point-Based Method

In Fig. 3, we compare our results with state of art salient detection approach based on point sets, which are proposed by Shtrom et al. [20] and Tasse et al. [24]. It is shown that our method can capture the saliency region such as facial feature in Max Planck model. Shtrom's method tries to propagate the high value of saliency to the entire model. Because our method is based on pointwise manner, we did not highlight the whole region of eyes as Tasse's method. Also it can be found in the dragon model, the proposed method capture different scale feature region such as the left front foot, which is not completely detected by the previous approaches.

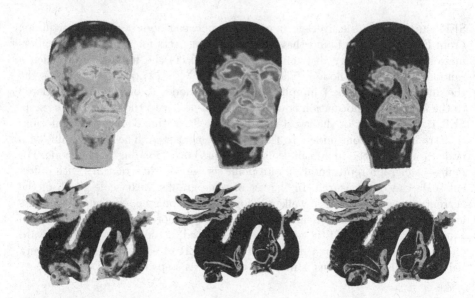

Fig. 3. Comparison with point-based method of saliency detection. From left to right: [20,24] and our method.

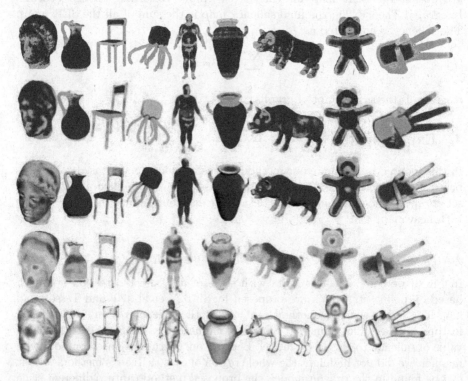

Fig. 4. Comparison with mesh-based method of saliency detection. From top to down: Our method, Tasse et al. [24], Tao et al. [23], Song et al. [21] and ground-truth [3].

4.2 Compared with Mesh-Based Method

In Fig. 4, our results are compared with mesh based approach developed by Song et al. [21], Tao et al. [23], and Tasse et al. [24]. The bottom in Fig. 4 is the ground truth data in literature [3]. Spectral mesh saliency produces correct saliency maps but some unsalient regions are also highlighted. Method of [23] does not produce all correct maps in the test models, such as Igea and the chair. The point based method [24] fails for saliency detection on hand model. It can be found our results are more close to the ground truth.

4.3 Complexity Analysis

For an input point set with N points, the complexity of our approach depends on three aspects. First, establishing initial graph for representation has complexity $O(mN)$, where m is the number of neighbors of each point. In second of constructing multi-scale graphs, it is $O(sN^2)$, where s is the number of scales. Third, the complexity of saliency computation is $O(mN)$. For computation efficiency, we select 3 scales in second step in our experiment.

5 Conclusion and Future Work

We present a novel approach to detect multi-scale saliency of 3D point sets without using any connective information. According to transforming point set to multi-scale undirected graphs, we measure site entropy rate of each point in different scales. The SER is based on the principle of information maximization. SER reflects the average total information that can be transmitted of each point. We also propose a bottom-up method to construct the scale graphs, which can capture geometrical structures of surfaces with different scales. This method is computation efficient and implementing easy, so it can be performed on huge point sets. In our experiment, it is shown that the proposed approach is competitive. It even often outperforms the approaches for 3D mesh saliency, which take advantage of the connective information.

In the future, we will incorporate our method into solving problem of shape analysis, i.e., to guide the segmentation or simplification of 3D point sets. It will also be interesting to explore further novel applications of mesh saliency such as range image scene analysis and shape from shading.

Acknowledgments. This work was partially supported by National Natural Science Foundation of China under Grant No. 61231018 and No. 61273366; National Science and technology support program under Grant 2015BAH31F01; Program of introducing talents of discipline to university under grant B13043.

References

1. Akman, O., Jonker, P.: Computing saliency map from spatial information in point cloud data. In: Blanc-Talon, J., Bone, D., Philips, W., Popescu, D., Scheunders, P. (eds.) ACIVS 2010. LNCS, vol. 6474, pp. 290–299. Springer, Heidelberg (2010). doi:10.1007/978-3-642-17688-3_28
2. Castellani, U., Cristani, M., Fantoni, S., Murino, V.: Sparse points matching by combining 3D mesh saliency with statistical descriptors. Comput. Graph. Forum **27**(2), 643–652 (2008)
3. Chen, X., Saparov, A., Pang, B., Funkhouser, T.: Schelling points on 3D surface meshes. ACM Trans. Graph. **31**(4), 13–15 (2012)
4. Cheng, M.M., Zhang, G.X., Mitra, N.J., Huang, X., Hu, S.M.: Global contrast based salient region detection. IEEE Trans. Pattern Anal. Mach. Intell. **37**(3), 409–416 (2015)
5. Gao, D., Mahadevan, V., Vasconcelos, N.: The discriminant center-surround hypothesis for bottom-up saliency. Adv. Neural Inf. Process. Syst. **20**, 497–504 (2007)
6. Gelfand, N., Mitra, N.J., Guibas, L.J., Pottmann, H.: Robust global registration. In: Proceedings of Eurographics Symposium on Geometry Processing, p. 197 (2005)
7. Guy, G., Medioni, G.: Inference of surfaces, 3D curves, and junctions from sparse, noisy, 3D data. IEEE Trans. Pattern Anal. Mach. Intell. **19**(11), 1265–1277 (1997). http://dx.doi.org/10.1109/34.632985
8. Jong, S.H., Peyman, M.: Static and space-time visual saliency detection by self-resemblance. J. Vis. **9**(12), 1–27 (2009)
9. Hou, T., Qin, H.: Admissible diffusion wavelets and their applications in space-frequency processing. IEEE Trans. Visual Comput. Graph. **19**(1), 3–15 (2013)
10. Hou, X., Zhang, L., Saliency detection: a spectral residual approach. In: 2013 IEEE Conference on Computer Vision and Pattern Recognition, pp. 1–8 (2007)
11. Hou, X., Zhang, L.: Dynamic visual attention: searching for coding length increments. In: Conference on Neural Information Processing Systems, Vancouver, British Columbia, Canada, December, pp. 681–688 (2008)
12. Itti, L., Koch, C., Niebur, E.: A model of saliency-based visual attention for rapid scene analysis. IEEE Trans. Pattern Anal. Mach. Intell. **20**(11), 1254–1259 (1998)
13. Lee, C.H., Varshney, A., Jacobs, D.W.: Mesh saliency. ACM Trans. Graph. **24**(3), 659–666 (2005)
14. Leifman, G., Shtrom, E., Tal, A.: Surface regions of interest for viewpoint selection. In: IEEE Conference on Computer Vision and Pattern Recognition, pp. 414–421 (2012)
15. Li, X., Guskov, I.: Multiscale features for approximate alignment of point-based surfaces. In: Eurographics Symposium on Geometry Processing, pp. 217–226 (2005)
16. Medioni, G., Tang, C.K., Lee, M.S.: Tensor voting: theory and applications. Proc. Rfia **34**(8), 1482–1495 (2000)
17. Min, K.P., Lee, S.J., Lee, K.W.: Multi-scale tensor voting for feature extraction from unstructured point clouds. Graph. Models **74**(4), 197–208 (2012)
18. Pauly, M., Keiser, R., Gross, M.: Multi-scale feature extraction on point-sampled surfaces. Comput. Graph. Forum **22**, 281–289 (2003)
19. Ran, G., Cohen-Or, D.: Salient geometric features for partial shape matching and similarity. ACM Trans. Graph. **25**(1), 130–150 (2006)
20. Shtrom, E., Leifman, G., Tal, A.: Saliency detection in large point sets. In: 2013 IEEE International Conference on Computer Vision, pp. 3591–3598, December 2013

21. Song, R., Liu, Y., Martin, R.R., Rosin, P.L.: Mesh saliency via spectral processing. ACM Trans. Graph. **33**(1), 57–76 (2014)
22. Stas, G., Stas, G., Lihi, Z.M., Ayellet, T.: Context-aware saliency detection. IEEE Trans. Pattern Anal. Mach. Intell. **34**(10), 1915–1926 (2012)
23. Tao, P., Cao, J., Li, S., Liu, L., Liu, X.: Mesh saliency via ranking unsalient patches in a descriptor space. Comput. Graph. **46**, 264–274 (2014)
24. Tasse, F.P., Kosinka, J., Dodgson, N.: Cluster-based point set saliency. In: IEEE International Conference on Computer Vision, pp. 637–639 (2015)
25. Treisman, A.M., Gelade, G.: A feature-integration theory of attention. Cogn. Psychol. **12**(1), 97–136 (1980)
26. Vijay, M., Nuno, V.: Spatiotemporal saliency in dynamic scenes. IEEE Trans. Pattern Anal. Mach. Intell. **32**(1), 171–177 (2010)
27. Wang, S., Li, N., Li, S., Luo, Z., Zhixun, S., Qin, H.: Multi-scale mesh saliency based on low-rank, sparse analysis in shape feature space. Comput. Aided Geom. Des. **35-36**, 206–214 (2015)
28. Wang, W., Wang, Y., Huang, O., Gao, W.: Measuring visual saliency by site entropy rate. In: IEEE Conference on Computer Vision and Pattern Recognition, pp. 2368–2375 (2010)
29. Jinliang, W., Shen, X., Zhu, W., Liu, L.: Mesh saliency with global rarity. Graph. Models **75**(5), 255–264 (2013)
30. Wu, Y., Shen, X.: A unified approach to salient object detection via low rank matrix recovery. In: IEEE Conference on Computer Vision and Pattern Recognition, pp. 853–860 (2012)

Facial Expression Recognition with Multi-scale Convolution Neural Network

Jieru Wang and Chun Yuan[✉]

Graduate School at Shenzhen, Tsinghua University, Shenzhen, China
wangjr14@mails.tsinghua.edu.cn, yuanc@sz.tsinghua.edu.cn

Abstract. We present a deep convolutional neural network (CNN) architecture for facial expression recognition. Inspired by the fact that regions located around certain facial parts (e.g. mouth, nose, eyes, and brows) contain the most representative information of expressions, an architecture extracts features at different scale from intermediate layers is designed to combine both local and global information. In addition, noticing that in specific to facial expression recognition, traditional face alignment would distort the images and lose expression information. To avoid this side effect, we apply batch normalization to the architecture instead of face alignment and feed the network with original images. Moreover, considering the tiny differences between classes caused by the same facial movements, a triplet-loss learning method is used to train the architecture, which improves the discrimination of deep features. Experiments show that the proposed architecture achieves superior performance to other state-of-the-art methods on the FER2013 dataset.

Keywords: Facial expression recognition · Multi-scale convolution neural network · Triplet network

1 Introduction

Facial expressions provide rich information about one's personality and play an important role in human's communication. Ekman *et al.* laid the foundation for facial expressions research in [12], they identified six facial expressions (anger, disgust, fear, happiness, sadness, and surprise) as basic emotional expressions that are universal among human beings. Being able to understand one's facial expression is a key factor of effective human-computer interaction.

Traditional methods for facial expression recognition often extract features manually, which make the features have little tolerances to face images containing extreme poses, illumination, and occlusion variations. The datasets used for these methods are mostly collected in a specific environment (e.g. in a lab) with only frontal facial images, and some of the expressions are unnatural and exaggerated (Fig. 1), which then result in many methods subject to database. If these methods generalize to other datasets or reality, the probability of get a good performance would be very small.

© Springer International Publishing AG 2016
E. Chen et al. (Eds.): PCM 2016, Part I, LNCS 9916, pp. 376–385, 2016.
DOI: 10.1007/978-3-319-48890-5_37

Fig. 1. The datasets used by traditional methods (first line) only contain frontal facial images and are collected in conditional environment. The dataset we used (second line, FER2013) contains more variations in pose, illumination, and occlusion.

To get more generalization ability, recent advances in facial expression recognition focus more on spontaneous facial expressions. Deep learning has achieved remarkable performance on many face recognition tasks (e.g. face detection, face verification), but it is still difficult to learn discriminative representation of facial expression. The reason for this problem, on the one hand, is that the training data for facial expression recognition is quite small compare with the other tasks. For example, training data for face verification task tends to be millions [1–4], while it is only thousands for expression recognition. On the other hand, it is difficult to classify with large intra-class variations. In an expression dataset, images of one expression class contain many diverse people. There will lead to large intra-class variations due to the appearance, gender and race difference.

As demonstrated in [17], layers contain information hierarchically throughout the network. Lower layers contain more edges and corners features, which are local information. On the other hand, features in higher layers are more global and class-specific. Based on this, we design a new concatenated CNN architecture to extracts features at different scale for expression recognition. It achieves state-of-the-art result on FER2013 dataset. The main contributions of this paper are as follows:

(a) An architecture extracts features from different intermediate layers is proposed. The features contain both local and global information, and become more representative.

(b) We apply batch normalization to the architecture instead of face alignment. Batch normalization allows the network focus on original images by distorting them less. It also can reduce the large intra-class variations (e.g. appearance, gender, and race) in a sense.

(c) To avoid some different expressions share similar facial movements may cause ambiguous understanding for the network, a triplet-loss learning method is used to improve the discrimination of learned features.

2 Related Work

Several works based on deep learning have been done for facial expression recognition problem.

Burkert *et al.* proposed a much shallow CNN architecture [11] based on the Inception layer proposed by [13]. Google introduced the inception layer during the Image Net Large Scale Visual Recognition Challenge (ILSVRC) 2014. It applied differently sized filters to one convolution layer, with an architecture ensemble by several Inception layers achieved better results on CKP and MMI than the earlier proposed CNN based approaches. The performance of the proposed architecture endorses the efficacy and reliable use for real world application. Another deep neural network architecture was proposed in [9] to address the facial expression recognition problem across multiple well-known standard face dataset. The proposed architecture consists of two convolution layers each followed by max pooling and then four Inception layers. It took registered facial images as input to classify them into either of the six basic or neutral expressions, and achieved results comparable to or better than the state-of-the-art methods on MutiPIE, MMI, CKP, FER2013.

For classification tasks, most of the deep learning models employ the softmax activation function for prediction and minimize cross-entropy loss. Tang reported a deep CNN jointly learned with a linear support vector machine output [18]. They replaced the softmax layer with a linear support vector machine. Learning minimizes a margin-based loss instead of the cross-entropy loss. Their method achieved 71.2 % accuracy on the FER2013 dataset. It is the winner of the Facial Expression Recognition 2013 Challenge. Yu *et al.* proposed a CNN based pipeline on expression recognition challenge [8]. The proposed method contains a face detection module based on the ensemble of three state-of-the-art face detectors, followed by a classification module with the ensemble of multiple deep convolutional neural networks. To combine multiple CNN models, they presented two schemes for learning the ensemble weights of the network response: by minimizing the log likelihood loss, and by minimizing the hinge loss. They initialized each CNN model randomly and pre-trained them on FER2013 dataset. Then the pre-trained models are fine-tuned on the training set of SFEW 2.0. The proposed method generates state-of-the-art result on the FER2013 dataset and surpassing the challenge baseline of SFEW with significant gains.

All the methods mentioned above paid more attention to the improvement of architecture, but ignored the internal property of facial expression recognition problem—large intra-class variation and tiny difference between classes. In this paper, we proposed our method based on the specific analysis of facial expression recognition.

3   The Proposed Architecture

This section we describe the details of the proposed CNN architecture. We propose a CNN model that concatenates the features that extracted from low layers and high layers as the representation of facial expression.

3.1   Multi-scale CNN

The architecture we designed is inspired by the 16 layers VGG Net [6], which achieves the first and second places in the localization and classification tasks during the Image Net Large Scale Visual Recognition Challenge (ILSVRC) 2014. It consists of five convolution modules with each contains two or three convolution layers. The size of

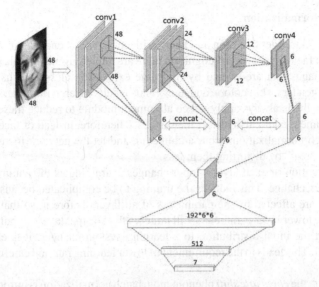

Fig. 2. The proposed architecture consists of four modules (conv1, conv2, conv3 and conv4) with each module contains two or three convolution layers, and between each module is a max pooling layer. After conv4 module, we concatenate three layers extracted from different convolution layers. Then add another convolution layer to reduce dimension (1 × 1 filters), and two full connect layers are added to get classification results.

filters between two convolution layers is 3 × 3, with padding one added around the image and the stride is one. Then we extract features from multiple intermediate layers at different scale and thus our architecture is called Multi-scale CNN (Fig. 2). We do this based on two facts:

(a) Each layer in a CNN contains information, i.e. features distribute hierarchically in the network. Lower layers respond to texture and corner features, and hence contain more local information. Higher layers are class-specific and more suitable for complex tasks that need global features. The visualized feature maps in Fig. 3 indicate that the features get more complex and global as the layers get deeper.

Fig. 3. Feature maps of intermediate layers in a CNN

(b) Facial expressions have natural connection with local features. Studies in physiology and psychology indicate that the regions located around certain facial parts (e.g. mouth, nose, eyes, and brows) contain the most representative information of expressions. For example, lip corners pull up if one is happy and pull down if sad. Facial expression recognition is a classification task, so if use both local features and global features, it would get more discriminative representation for facial expression.

3.2   Batch Normalization

Unlike tasks of face identification and face verification, which one class represents just one person, in facial expression recognition there are numerous individuals in one class. Therefore, images that are owned by the same expression class may have different appearances, genders, skin colors, and ages. Thus results in large intra-class variations. Traditional methods always apply a face alignment module to reduce these variations, but face alignment could also distort the images. Therefore, instead of face alignment, we apply batch normalization to our architecture and let the network focus on images that are more "real" by distorting them less.

The distribution of each layer's input changes in training as the parameters of the previous layers change. This induces the training to be complicated because the inputs of each layer are affected by the parameters of all layers before it, so that even small changes in the lower layer parameters will largely affect deeper layers' input. According to [19], when the input distribution to a learning system changes, it is experiencing *covariate shift*. This leads to the requirement of lower learning rate and careful parameter initialization.

To alleviate the *covariate shift* phenomenon, batch normalization is introduced in [7]. During SGD training, each activation of the mini-batch is centered to zero-mean and unit variance. For a layer with d-dimensional input x $= \left(x^{(1)} \ldots x^{(d)} \right)$, the normalization for each dimension would be

$$\hat{x}^{(k)} = \frac{x^{(k)} - E[x^{(k)}]}{\sqrt{\mathrm{Var}[x^{(k)}]}}$$

The input for a layer in CNN has four dimensions (batch size, channels, width and height), so the normalization would be applied to each dimension.

By using batch normalization, not only the internal covariant shift reduces but the dependence of gradients on the scale of the parameters or their initials reduces too. Batch Normalization also decreases the need for dropout, local response normalization and image distortions. It allows using higher learning rates and makes the network convergence sooner.

In our multi-scale CNN network, batch normalization is used after each layer (except pooling layer and the last layer). However, in consideration of the over-fitting caused by small dataset, dropout is still added after convolution layer and full connect layer.

3.3   Triplet Loss

How to increase the discrimination between classes' representations is one of the main challenges of classification tasks. For facial expression recognition, it is easy to confuse two expressions when they have similar facial movements (e.g. angry and disgust both with frowns, surprise and fear both with big open eyes). The large intra-class variations also increase difficulty in classification. To avoid this confusion, we pre-train our multi-scale CNN model with softmax loss, and then fine-tune the network with triplet loss.

Triplet loss is first used for face verification task in [4]. Hoffer *et al.* [5] extended it to multi-classification. A triplet network takes three images (x, x^+, x^-) as its input. Based on the L_2 distance between two images' representations, the purpose of triplet loss is ensure that x (the anchor) of a specific expression is closer to the same expression x^+ than it is to any image x^- of any other expressions. If the embedded representation of the network were denoted as $f(x)$, the loss function would be

$$\| f(x) - f(x^+) \|_2^2 + \alpha \ < \| f(x) - f(x^-) \|_2^2,$$

where α is a margin between the same and different face pairs. An architecture uses triplet loss would be like Fig. 4. The triplet net can reduce intra-class variations and increase discrimination between classes' representation.

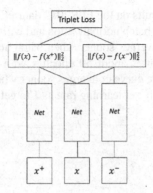

Fig. 4. Triplet network pipeline

4 Experiments

4.1 Dataset

We evaluate our proposed method on the large dataset provided by the Facial Expression Recognition (FER) Challenge 2013. It is a representative dataset for spontaneous facial expressions. There are 28,709 training images and 3,589 test images with seven labels: angry, disgust, fear, happy, neutral, sad, and surprise.

4.2 Data Augmentation

We believe data augmentation is necessary and can improve the performance significantly because FER dataset is quite small compared with most datasets used in deep learning tasks. First images are flipped horizontally to get simple data augmentation. Then each image is rotated in three degrees $(-\pi/18, 0, \pi/18)$. We reported the network performances before and after data augmentation.

4.3   Training

We first train the multi-scale CNN network on the FER dataset with softmax loss. A large learning rate is initialized around 0.8~1.2, with batch normalization added after each convolution layer and full connect layer. The batch size is set as 256. We pick out the model gets the best classification accuracy after 300 epoches. Then based on this pre-trained model, the network is fine-tuned with triplet loss. Each epoch we randomly select 640,000 triplets as training data. When the loss stops descending we stop fine-tuning. Then we use the triplet network to extract features of the full dataset, and train a simple 1-layer model to do the classification task.

4.4   Results

We report our experiment results on the FER2013 dataset. Figure 5 shows the training and test accuracy curves with batch normalization and without it on a single model. We can see that the network converges sooner when batch normalization is applied. The proposed model converges after about 50 epoches with using batch normalization. Moreover, we observe that the curve converges sooner when the learning rate is larger in a specified range. We finally set learning rate as 1 to get the best performance.

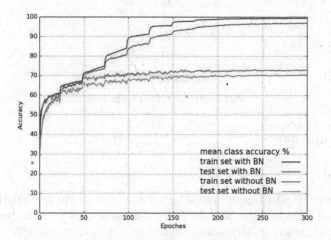

Fig. 5.   Training and test accuracy curves on FER2013 dataset

Table 1 shows that the pre-trained multi-scale model with softmax loss achieves comparable accuracy with the FER-2013 winner. The increase of accuracy from single conventional CNN to multi-scale CNN proves that the features extracted by multi-scale CNN are more representative. After data augmentation, the model gets result comparable to the state-of-the-art method. Triplet fine-tune helps to improve the performance further and achieves the best result. It indicates that data augmentation and triplet fine-tune both can get about 1 % performance gains.

Table 1. Classification accuracy on FER2013 dataset

Method	Accuracy
FER2013 winner	71.2 %
Yu *et al.*	72.0 %
Single CNN	69.18 %
Multi-scale CNN	70.71 %
Multi-scale CNN + data augmentation	71.57 %
Multi-scale CNN + data augmentation + triplet fine-tune	**72.82 %**

Figure 6 shows the confusion matrices of the proposed networks. (a) is for softmax network and (b) is for triplet network. Obviously, the margin between two classes enlarged (e.g. angry and fear, sad and neutral) after triplet fine-tuning process. This reduces the variations between classes and improves the performance.

	Angry	Disgust	Fear	Happy	Sad	Surprise	Neutral
Angry	56.82%	1.43%	11.00%	4.68%	15.07%	1.63%	9.37%
Disgust	20.00%	70.91%	3.64%	1.82%	0.00%	1.82%	1.82%
Fear	8.52%	0.19%	50.19%	5.11%	18.94%	7.58%	9.47%
Happy	1.14%	0.00%	1.02%	88.17%	4.44%	1.37%	3.87%
Sad	5.56%	0.17%	8.92%	4.55%	59.93%	1.18%	19.70%
Surprise	1.20%	0.24%	4.09%	4.81%	2.64%	83.17%	3.85%
Neutral	3.67%	0.32%	5.27%	4.63%	16.45%	1.12%	68.53%

(a) confusion matrix of softmax network

	Angry	Disgust	Fear	Happy	Sad	Surprise	Neutral
Angry	61.30%	1.02%	8.76%	3.67%	13.24%	2.04%	9.98%
Disgust	21.82%	65.45%	7.27%	1.82%	0.00%	1.82%	1.82%
Fear	11.55%	0.38%	52.27%	1.89%	15.34%	7.95%	10.61%
Happy	1.71%	0.00%	1.48%	89.53%	2.39%	1.25%	3.64%
Sad	7.58%	0.00%	12.29%	3.70%	57.58%	1.52%	17.34%
Surprise	1.92%	0.24%	4.81%	2.64%	1.68%	85.58%	3.13%
Neutral	4.47%	0.32%	3.04%	6.23%	14.70%	1.28%	69.97%

(b) confusion matrix of triplet network

Fig. 6. Confusion matrices of the proposed network with different criteria.

5 Conclusion

In this paper, we proposed a convolution neural network extracts multi-scale features from different layers to combine local and global information. In order to feed the network with original images, we apply batch normalization to the architecture and pre-train the model on the FER2013 dataset using softmax loss. To increase the discrimination of the learned representations, we fine-tune the pre-trained model with triplet loss. The proposed method achieves state-of-the-art result on the FER2013 dataset.

Acknowledgements. This work is supported by the High Technology Development Program of China (863 Program), under Grant No. 2011AA01A205, National Significant Science and Technology Projects of China, under Grant No. 2013ZX01039001-002-003; by the NSFC project under Grant Nos. U1433112 and 61170253.

References

1. Parkhi, O.M., Vedaldi, A., Zisserman, A.: Deep face recognition. In: Proceedings of the British Machine Vision, vol. 1(3), p. 6 (2015)
2. Yi, D., Lei, Z., Liao, S., et al.: Learning face representation from scratch. Eprint Arxiv (2014)
3. Sun, Y., Wang, X., Tang, X.: Deep learning face representation from predicting 10,000 classes. In: 2014 IEEE Conference on Computer Vision and Pattern Recognition (CVPR), pp. 1891–1898. IEEE (2014)
4. Schroff, F., Kalenichenko, D., Philbin, J.: FaceNet: a unified embedding for face recognition and clustering. In: 2015 IEEE Conference on Computer Vision and Pattern Recognition (CVPR), pp. 815–823. IEEE (2015)
5. Hoffer, E., Ailon, N.: Deep metric learning using triplet network. In: Feragen, A., Pelillo, M., Loog, M. (eds.) SIMBAD 2015. LNCS, vol. 9370, pp. 84–92. Springer, Heidelberg (2015). doi:10.1007/978-3-319-24261-3_7
6. Simonyan, K., Zisserman, A.: Very deep convolutional networks for large-scale image recognition. arXiv preprint arXiv:1409.1556 (2014)
7. Ioffe, S., Szegedy, C.: Batch normalization: accelerating deep network training by reducing internal covariate shift. arXiv preprint arXiv:1502.03167 (2015)
8. Yu, Z., Zhang, C.: Image based static facial expression recognition with multiple deep network learning. In: Proceedings of the 2015 ACM on International Conference on Multimodal Interaction, pp. 435–442. ACM (2015)
9. Mollahosseini, A., Chan, D., Mahoor, M.H.: Going deeper in facial expression recognition using deep neural networks. arXiv preprint arXiv:1511.04110 (2015)
10. Khatri, N.N., Shah, Z.H., Patel, S.A.: Facial expression recognition: a survey. IJCSIT Int. J. Comput. Sci. Inf. Technol. **5**(1), 149–152 (2014)
11. Burkert, P., Trier, F., Afzal, M.Z., et al.: DeXpression: deep convolutional neural network for expression recognition. arXiv preprint arXiv:1509.05371 (2015)
12. Ekman, P., Friesen, W.V.: Constants across cultures in the face and emotion. J. Pers. Soc. Psychol. **17**(2), 124 (1971)
13. Szegedy, C., Liu, W., Jia, Y., et al.: Going deeper with convolutions. In: Proceedings of the IEEE Conference on Computer Vision and Pattern Recognition, pp. 1–9 (2015)
14. Liu, Z., Luo, P., Wang, X., et al.: Deep learning face attributes in the wild. In: Proceedings of the IEEE International Conference on Computer Vision, pp. 3730–3738 (2015)
15. Liu, M., Li, S., Shan, S., et al.: Au-aware deep networks for facial expression recognition. In: 2013 10th IEEE International Conference and Workshops on Automatic Face and Gesture Recognition (FG), pp. 1–6. IEEE (2013)

16. Ranjan, R., Patel, V.M., Chellappa, R.: HyperFace: a deep multi-task learning framework for face detection, landmark localization, pose estimation, and gender recognition. arXiv preprint arXiv:1603.01249 (2016)
17. Zeiler, M.D., Fergus, R.: Visualizing and understanding convolutional networks. CoRR, abs/1311.2901 (2013)
18. Tang, Y.: Deep learning using linear support vector machines. arXiv preprint arXiv:1306.0239 (2013)
19. Shimodaira, H.: Improving predictive inference under covariate shift by weighting the log-likelihood function. J. Stat. Planning Infer. **90**(2), 227–244 (2000)

Deep Similarity Feature Learning
for Person Re-identification

Yanan Guo[1], Dapeng Tao[1(✉)], Jun Yu[2], and Yaotang Li[1]

[1] Yunnan University, Kunming, China
YananGuo.YNU@qq.com, dapeng.tao@gmail.com,
liyaotang@ynu.edu.cn
[2] Hangzhou Dianzi University, Hangzhou, China
yujun@hdu.edu.cn

Abstract. Person re-identification aims to match the same pedestrians across different camera views and has been applied to many important applications such as intelligent video surveillance. Due to the spatiotemporal uncertainty and visual ambiguity of pedestrian image pairs, person re-identification remains a difficult and challenging problem. The huge success of deep learning has focused attention on the use of deep features for person re-identification. However, for person re-identification, most deep learning methods minimize cross-entropy or triplet-based losses, thereby neglecting the fact that the similarities and differences between image pairs can be considered simultaneously to increase discrimination. In this paper, we propose a novel deep learning method called deep similarity feature learning (DSFL) to extract more effective deep features for image pairs. Extensive experiments on two representative person re-identification datasets (CUHK-03 and GRID) demonstrate the effectiveness and robustness of DSFL.

Keywords: Person re-identification · Deep learning · Video surveillance · Deep features

1 Introduction

Person re-identification has attracted attention due to its successful application to camera tracking and pedestrian retrieval in video surveillance [1]. Person re-identification aims to identify individual pedestrians from videos or images captured by different cameras, but the approach is inherently challenging because video sequences tend to be highly variable in terms of pose, visual appearance, illumination, background clutter, and occlusions.

Most person re-identification approaches involve two main steps: feature representation and metric learning. Deriving a robust and discriminative feature representation from pedestrian images that is robust to viewpoint changes and illumination is extremely important for person re-identification. In general, robust feature representations [28] can be grouped into two categories: handcrafted features and learned features. Most handcrafted features are heuristic, in that they extract various kinds of low-level global and local features from pedestrian images. Global features are body-region or

© Springer International Publishing AG 2016
E. Chen et al. (Eds.): PCM 2016, Part I, LNCS 9916, pp. 386–396, 2016.
DOI: 10.1007/978-3-319-48890-5_38

whole-image characteristics, with the global color histogram the most widely used global feature [4]. Color histograms are generally robust to partial occlusions and are scale-invariant, but they suffer from sensitivity to brightness. In contrast, local features refer to the characterization of a small section of the image, and the extracted regions can be chosen in various ways including by dense sampling, an interest operator, or at random. Typical local features [17, 18, 24] such as Maximally Stable Color Regions (MSCR) [6], Recurrent Highly-Structured Patches (RHSP) [5], and Local Binary Patterns (LBP) [19] are frequently used for person re-identification and have achieved good performance on several accepted person re-identification benchmarks. However, when tackling the misalignment problem [14, 25, 26], these local features are less useful for matching patches in two different (misaligned) camera views.

The huge success of deep learning has focused attention on learned features, especially deep features, for person re-identification. Deep features extracted from deep learning methods can capture global and local information simultaneously and are generalizable to novel data. However, for person re-identification, most deep learning methods minimize cross-entropy loss or triplet-based loss and neglect the fact that the similarities and differences between image pairs can be considered simultaneously to increase discrimination.

Unlike existing deep learning methods, here we propose a deep learning method termed Deep Similarity Feature Learning (DSFL) for person re-identification. DSFL directly learns a non-linear mapping from an original image space to a Euclidean space, where the relative distance corresponds to a measure of pedestrian similarity. Specifically, DSFL measures similarity by considering the similarities and differences between image pairs. Further, due to the different ways features are extracted, the deep features extracted by DSFL and handcrafted features are complementary and can be combined to boost person re-identification accuracy. We conduct extensive experiments on the CUHK-03 [12] and GRID [16] datasets to demonstrate the effectiveness and robustness of DSFL.

The remainder of the paper is organized as follows. In Sect. 2, we briefly review related works on feature representation using deep learning methods and the typical methods used for person re-identification. We detail the newly proposed DSFL in Sect. 3. The experimental results on the two representative datasets are described in Sect. 4, and we conclude in Sect. 5.

2 Related Works

Typical person re-identification methods include Large-margin Nearest-Neighbor Learning (LMNN) [27], Information-Theoretic Metric Learning (ITML) [3], Probabilistic Relative Distance Comparison (RRDC) [31], and Keep It Simple and Straightforward Metric Learning (KISSME) [10, 22, 23]. LMNN, one of the most widely used Mahalanobis distance learning methods, was defined in a local way such that the k-nearest neighbors of any training sample should belong to the correct class while samples of other classes are kept further away. From the information theory perspective, ITML is an important work that combined LogDet divergence regularization and the Mahalanobis distance. RRDC maximized the probability that distances corresponding to incorrect matches were larger than those corresponding to correct matches. KISSME learned the Mahalanobis metric from equivalence constraints and does not rely on complex optimization.

Deep learning has recently delivered state-of-the-art performance for person re-identification as a feature representation or classifier. Li *et al.* [12] proposed a novel deep learning method termed Filter Pairing Neural Network (FPNN), which was the first work to use deep learning for person re-identification by jointly handling photometric and geometric transforms, misalignment, occlusions, and background clutter. Ahmed *et al.* [1] presented a novel deep architecture for person re-identification by designing a novel layer to compute cross-input neighborhood differences between mid-level features.

3   Deep Similarity Feature Learning

Unlike existing deep learning methods, we present a novel deep feature learning method - DSFL - which measures image similarity by considering the similarities and differences between image pairs.

3.1   The Network Architecture

The network architecture is shown in Fig. 1. It consists of two convolutional layers, three pooling layers, one inception module, and one fully connected layer. Specifically, the first layer is a convolutional layer, and each convolutional layer is followed by a max pooling layer with dropout [9]. The two convolutional layers include 32 kernels each, and the dropout ratio is set at 0.5. Following these layers, an inception module is added followed by an average pooling layer, the inception module consisting of 1×1,

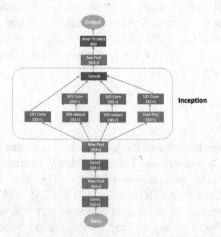

Fig. 1. The network architecture. The red blocks refer to the convolution layer, the green blocks refer to the pooling layer, the purple block refers to the fully connected layer, and the gray blocks refer to the input and output. (Color figure online)

3×3, and 5×5 convolution layers in parallel including 64, 96, and 32 kernels respectively. The final layer is a fully connected layer with dropout [9] and normalization [11]; the dropout ratio is set at 0.2. The non-linear activation functions, rectified linear units (ReLUs) [11], are used for all convolutional layers, and using ReLUs helps to avoid the vanishing gradient problem. The inception layer improves computing resource utilization inside the network. Dropout can reduce the risk of network overfitting, and normalization ensures that the feature norm is 1; that is, all features are in a unit of one.

3.2 Loss Function and Optimization

Triplet loss [21] training aims to learn an optimal feature representation that maximizes the relative distance. However, image similarity is only measured through the difference between an image pair. Here we measure image similarity by considering both the similarities and the differences between image pairs.

Let $f(x)$ and $f(y)$ be the network output of pedestrian images x and y. Since $\|f(x) - f(y)\|^2$ measures the difference between image pair (x, y) and $\|f(x) + f(y)\|^2$ measures the similarity between (x, y) [29], the similarity of (x, y) can be calculated as

$$Sim(x, y) = \frac{\|f(x) - f(y)\|^2}{\|f(x) + f(y)\|^2 + \|f(x) - f(y)\|^2} \tag{1}$$

From (1), we observe that $Sim(x, y) \in [0, 1]$; that is, the similarity of (x, y) has a bound. Furthermore, similar image pairs have small values, because the value of $\|f(x) - f(y)\|^2$ is small but that of $\|f(x) + f(y)\|^2$ is large, but dissimilar image pairs have large values, because the value of $\|f(x) - f(y)\|^2$ is large but that of $\|f(x) + f(y)\|^2$ is small.

Take a set of triplets $X = \{x_i\} = \{(x_i^a, x_i^p, x_i^n)\}$, where x_i^a and x_i^p are images containing the same pedestrian, and x_i^a and x_i^p are images containing different pedestrians. We want to learn effective features $f(x_i^a)$, $f(x_i^p)$, and $f(x_i^n)$ to ensure that $Sim(f(x_i^a), f(x_i^p))$ has a relatively large value while $Sim(f(x_i^a), f(x_i^n))$ has a relatively small value. Thus, the loss function is

$$
\begin{aligned}
L &= \sum_{(x_i^a, x_i^p, x_i^n) \in X} L_i \\
&= \sum_{(x_i^a, x_i^p, x_i^n) \in X} \max\{\gamma + Sim(f(x_i), f(x_i^p)) - Sim(f(x_i), f(x_i^n)), 0\} \\
&= \sum_{(x_i^a, x_i^p, x_i^n) \in X} \max\left\{\gamma + \frac{\|f(x_i^a) - f(x_i^p)\|^2}{\|f(x_i^a) - f(x_i^p)\|^2 + \|f(x_i^a) + f(x_i^p)\|^2} \right. \\
&\qquad\qquad\qquad\left. - \frac{\|f(x_i^a) - f(x_i^n)\|^2}{\|f(x_i^a) - f(x_i^n)\|^2 + \|f(x_i^a) + f(x_i^n)\|^2}, 0\right\}
\end{aligned}
\tag{2}
$$

where the fixed scalar $\gamma \geq 0$ is a learning margin.

The gradients with respect to $f(x_i^a)$, $f(x_i^p)$, and $f(x_i^n)$ are

$$\frac{\partial L_i}{\partial f(x_i^a)} = \begin{cases} \dfrac{2\left(\Delta_{ap}\left(f(x_i^a)-f(x_i^p)\right)-2f(x_i^a)\left\|f(x_i^a)-f(x_i^p)\right\|^2\right)}{\Delta_{ap}^2} \\ -\dfrac{2\left(\Delta_{an}\left(f(x_i^a)-f(x_i^n)\right)-2f(x_i^a)\left\|f(x_i^a)-f(x_i^n)\right\|^2\right)}{\Delta_{an}^2}, \\ \quad Sim\left(f(x_i),f(x_i^n)\right) - Sim(f(x_i),f(x_i^p)) < \gamma \\ \quad 0, Sim\left(f(x_i),f(x_i^n)\right) - Sim(f(x_i),f(x_i^p)) \geq \gamma \end{cases}$$

$$\frac{\partial L_i}{\partial f(x_i^p)} = \begin{cases} -\dfrac{2\left(\Delta_{ap}\left(f(x_i^a)-f(x_i^p)\right)+2f(x_i^p)\left\|f(x_i^a)-f(x_i^p)\right\|^2\right)}{\Delta_{ap}^2}, \\ \quad Sim\left(f(x_i),f(x_i^n)\right) - Sim(f(x_i),f(x_i^p)) < \gamma \\ \quad 0, Sim\left(f(x_i),f(x_i^n)\right) - Sim(f(x_i),f(x_i^p)) \geq \gamma \end{cases}$$

$$\frac{\partial L_i}{\partial f(x_i^n)} = \begin{cases} \dfrac{2\left(\Delta_{an}\left(f(x_i^a)-f(x_i^n)\right)+2f(x_i^n)\left\|f(x_i^a)-f(x_i^n)\right\|^2\right)}{\Delta_{an}^2}, \\ \quad Sim\left(f(x_i),f(x_i^n)\right) - Sim(f(x_i),f(x_i^p)) < \gamma \\ \quad 0, Sim\left(f(x_i),f(x_i^n)\right) - Sim(f(x_i),f(x_i^p)) \geq \gamma \end{cases}$$

where Δ_{ap} and Δ_{an} denote $\left\|f(x_i^a)-f(x_i^p)\right\|^2 + \left\|f(x_i^a)+f(x_i^p)\right\|^2$ and $\left\|f(x_i^a)-f(x_i^n)\right\|^2 + \left\|f(x_i^a)+f(x_i^n)\right\|^2$ respectively. Hence, the loss function in (2) can easily be integrated by network back-propagation.

4 Experimental Results

We conducted person re-identification experiments on the CUHK-03 [12] and the GRID [16] datasets to demonstrate the effectiveness of DSFL. The CUHK-03 dataset contains 13,164 pedestrian images collected from 1,360 individuals; each individual has roughly 9.6 images captured from two disjointed camera views. These images were taken from six surveillance cameras over several months. In addition to manually cropped pedestrian images, samples detected using a state-of-the-art pedestrian detector are also provided. This represents a more realistic setting considering misalignment, occlusions, and missing parts. Compared to existing datasets, CUHK-03 is much larger and therefore suited to training deep neural networks. The GRID dataset contains 1275 pedestrian images collected from 1025 individuals. The probe set contains 250 individuals represented by one image each. The gallery set contains 1025 individuals represented by one image each and 775 individuals not matching any person in the probe set. The dataset contains snapshots of people captured from eight disjointed camera views in an underground station, with example pedestrian images selected to produce the final dataset. GRID is another challenging dataset due to variations in resolution and image quality. Example images from GRID are shown in Fig. 2.

The widely used cumulative match curve (CMC) approach [7] was adopted to quantify performance. The CMC provides a ranking for every example in the gallery

Fig. 2. Typical images from the GRID dataset. Each column corresponds to the same pedestrian captured by different cameras.

set with respect to the probe set. The images of both datasets were normalized to 230×80, and a single-shot evaluation approach was used. After obtaining deep features by DSFL, we employed the cosine metric to calculate the similarity of the deep features.

The learning rate was set between 0.01 and 0.0001, and the learning rate was reduced by one-tenth after each 15,000 iterations. Each training epoch had $[N/100]$ batches, where N was the size of the training set, with the training images randomly selected from the training set. At each iteration, we randomly selected 50 individuals and generated 100 triplets for each individual. The learning margin γ was set to 0.2. For CUHK-03, the termination criterion for the training model was the new highest value for the validation set after 30 iterations. Since GRID is relatively small and prone to overfitting when trained on DSFL, we pre-trained the model on CUHK-03 and then fine-tuned on GRID. Furthermore, we terminated GRID training after 600 iterations.

4.1 Performance on CUHK-03

The CUHK-03 dataset was partitioned into a training set of 1,160 persons, a validation set of 100 persons, and a test set of 100 persons. The validation set was used to judge the termination criterion and design the network parameters. Experiments were conducted with 20 random splits, which is the same as in [12].

The performance of DSFL on CUHK-03 was compared to other state-of-the-art methods including SDALF [2], ITML [3], LMNN [27], eSDC [30], LDML [8], KISSME [10], DeepReID [12], and XQDA [13]. To further show that deep features extracted from DSFL were complimentary to the handcrafted features, we combined the handcrafted feature LOMO [13] with the deep features extracted by DSFL. Specifically, the two features were used with the cosine metric to calculate their respective distances and then combined to obtain the final distance. The CMC curves of the various methods are shown in Figs. 3 and 4. The top 1 ranking results are shown in Table 1. "LOMO+cos" refers to the accuracy of LOMO used with the cosine metric. "DSFL+cos" refers to the accuracy of deep features extracted by DSFL used with the cosine metric. "Confused" refers to the accuracy of the final combined distance. Except for the "Confused" and XQDA method, DSFL obtains the highest recognition rate with

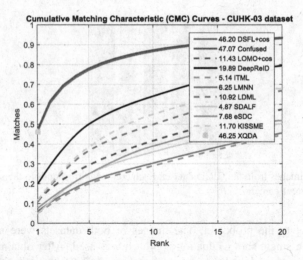

Fig. 3. CMC curves comparing method performance on CUHK-03 dataset using automatically detected pedestrian bounding boxes.

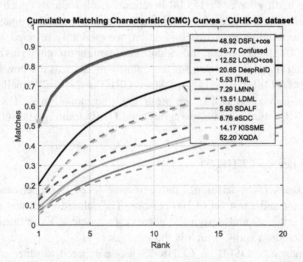

Fig. 4. CMC curves comparing method performance on CUHK-03 dataset using manually labeled bounding boxes.

the detected setting, demonstrating its effectiveness and robustness for person re-identification. "Confused" obtains the highest recognition rate with the detected and the second highest recognition rate with the labeled settings, demonstrating that the deep features extracted by DSFL and the LOMO handcrafted features are indeed complementary. Because the detected setting represents a more realistic setting considering misalignment, occlusions, and missing parts, experiment results with detected setting is more valuable.

Table 1. Person re-identification matching rates on the CUHK-03 dataset compared to other state-of-the-art-methods with both detected and labeled setting. Some results are from [13].

Rank	Detected	Labeled
	1	1
DSFL+cos	46.20	48.92
Confused	47.07	49.77
LOMO+cos	11.43	12.52
SDALF	4.87	5.60
ITML	5.14	5.53
LMNN	6.25	7.29
eSDC	7.68	8.76
LDML	10.92	13.51
KISSME	11.70	14.17
DeepReID	19.89	20.65
XQDA	46.25	52.20

4.2 Performance on GRID

125 image pairs were randomly selected from GRID for training, and the remaining 125 image pairs and the 775 additional background images were used for testing. The procedure was repeated 10 times to report the CMC.

DSFL performance was compared to other state-of-the-art methods including L1-norm [15], PRDC [31], RankSVM [20], MRank-PRDC [15], MRank-RankSVM [15], MtMCML [30], and XQDA [13]. The CMC curves of the various methods are shown in Fig. 5, and the top 1, 5, 10, and 20 ranking results are shown in Table 2. Similar to Sect. 4.1, "LOMO+cos" and "confused" were also evaluated. Except for the

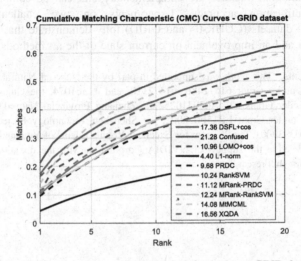

Fig. 5. CMC curves comparing method performance on GRID dataset.

Table 2. Person re-identification matching rates on the GRID dataset compared to other state-of-the-art-methods. Some results are from [13].

Rank	$p = 125$		
	1	10	20
DSFL+cos	17.36	43.12	55.28
Confused	21.28	49.76	62.32
LOMO+cos	10.96	36.88	45.36
L1-norm	4.40	16.24	24.80
PRDC	9.68	32.96	44.32
RankSVM	10.24	33.28	43.68
MRank-PRDC	11.12	35.76	46.56
MRank-RankSVM	12.24	36.32	46.56
MtMCML	14.08	45.84	59.84
XQDA	16.56	41.84	52.40

"Confused" method, it can be seen that DSFL obtains highest performance to the other methods, demonstrating its generalizability for person re-identification.

5   Conclusion

This work introduces a novel deep learning method termed DSFL for person re-identification. DSFL consists of two convolutional layers, three pooling layers, one inception module, and one fully connected layer. Furthermore, DSFL can directly learn a non-linear mapping from the original image space to a Euclidean space, where image similarity is measured by considering the similarities and differences between image pairs. Due to the different ways features are extracted, the deep features extracted by DSFL and handcrafted features are complementary and can be combined to boost person re-identification accuracy. Experiments on two challenging person re-identification datasets (CUHK-03 and GRID) fully demonstrate that our proposed DSFL is robust and an improvement on current state-of-the-art methods.

Acknowledgements. This work was supported in part by the National Natural Science Foundation of China under Grant 61572486, 61472110, and 11361074, the Guangdong Natural Science Funds under Grant 2014A030310252,the Zhejiang Provincial Natural Science Foundation of China under Grant LR15F020002, the Shenzhen Technology Project under Grant JCYJ20140901003939001, the Program for Excellent Young Talents of Yunnan University. We gratefully acknowledge the support of NVIDIA Corporation with the donation of the Tesla K40 GPU used for this research.

References

1. Ahmed, E., Jones, M., Marks, T.K.: An improved deep learning architecture for person re-identification. In: Proceedings of the Conference on Computer Vision and Pattern Recognition (CVPR), pp. 3908–3916 (2015)
2. Bazzani, L., Cristani, M., Murino, V.: Symmetry-driven accumulation of local features for human characterization and re-identification. Comput. Vis. Image Underst. 117(2), 130–144 (2013)
3. Davis, J.V., Kulis, B., Jain, P., Sra, S., Dhillon, I.S.: Information-theoretic metric learning. In: Proceedings of the International Conference on Machine Learning (ICML), New York, pp. 209–216 (2007)
4. Elgammal, A.M., Harwood, D., Davis, L.S.: Non-parametric model for background subtraction. In: Proceedings of the European Conference on Computer Vision (ECCV), pp. 751–767 (2000)
5. Farenzena, M., Bazzani, L., Perina, A., Murino, V., Cristani, M.: Person re-identification by symmetry-driven accumulation of local features. In: Proceedings of the IEEE Conference on Computer Vision and Pattern Recognition (CVPR), pp. 2360–2367 (2010)
6. Forssen, P.: Maximally stable colour regions for recognition and matching. In: Proceedings of the IEEE Conference on Computer Vision and Pattern Recognition (CVPR), pp. 1–8 (2007)
7. Gray, D., Brennan, S., Tao, H.: Evaluating appearance models for recognition, reacquisition and tracking. In: Proceedings of the International Workshop on Performance Evaluation of Tracking and Surveillance (PETS) (2007)
8. Guillaumin, M., Verbeek, J., Schmid, C.: Is that you? Metric learning approaches for face identification. In: Proceedings of the IEEE Conference on Computer Vision and Pattern Recognition (CVPR), pp. 498–505 (2009)
9. Hinton, G.E., Srivastava, N., Krizhevsky, A., Sutskever, I., Salakhutdinov, R.R.: Improving neural networks by preventing coadaptation of feature detectors. arxiv preprint arXiv:1207.0580 (2012)
10. Kostinger, M., Hirzer, M., Wohlhart, P., Roth, P.M., Bischof, H.: Large scale metric learning from equivalence constraints. In: Proceedings of the Computer Society Conference on Computer Vision and Pattern Recognition (CVPR), pp. 2288–2295 (2012)
11. Krizhevsky, A., Sutskever, I., Hinton, G.E.: Imagenet classification with deep convolutional neural networks. In: Proceedings of the Conference on Neural Information Processing Systems(NIPS), pp. 1097–1105 (2012)
12. Li, W., Zhao, R., Xiao, T., Wang, X.: DeepReID: deep filter pairing neural network for person re-identification. In: Proceedings of the Computer Society Conference on Computer Vision and Pattern Recognition (CVPR), pp. 152–159 (2014)
13. Liao, S., Hu, Y., Zhu, X., Li, S.Z.: Person Re-identification by local maximal occurrence representation and metric learning. In: Proceedings of the Computer Society Conference on Computer Vision and Pattern Recognition (CVPR), pp. 2197–2206 (2015)
14. Liu, T., Tao, D.: Classification with noisy labels by importance reweighting. IEEE Trans. Pattern Anal. Mach. Intell. 38(3), 447–461 (2016)
15. Loy, C.C., Liu, C., Gong, S.: Person re-identification by manifold ranking. In: Proceedings of the International Conference on Image Processing (ICIP), pp. 3567–3571 (2013)
16. Loy, C.C., Xiang, T., Gong, S.: Multi-camera activity correlation analysis. In: Proceedings of the Computer Society Conference on Computer Vision and Pattern Recognition (CVPR), pp. 1988–1995 (2009)

17. Lu, X., Gong, T., Yan, P., Yuan, Y., Li, X.: Robust alternative minimization for matrix completion. IEEE Trans. Syst. Man Cybern. Part B (Cybern.) **42**(3), 939–949 (2012)
18. Lu, X., Wang, Y., Yuan, Y.: Sparse coding from a Bayesian perspective. IEEE Trans. Neural Netw. Learn. Syst. **24**(6), 929–939 (2013)
19. Ojala, T., Pietikainen, M., Maenpaa, T.: Multiresolution gray-scale and rotation invariant texture classification with local binary patterns. IEEE Trans. Pattern Anal. Mach. Intell. **24**(7), 971–987 (2002)
20. Prosser, B., Zheng, W.-S., Gong, S., Xiang, T., Mary, Q.: Person re-identification by support vector ranking. In: BMVC (2010)
21. Schroff, F., Dmitry, K., James, P.: Facenet: a unified embedding for face recognition and clustering. In: Proceedings of the IEEE Conference on Computer Vision and Pattern Recognition (CVPR), pp. 815–823 (2015)
22. Tao, D., Jin, L., Wang, Y., Li, X.: Person re-identification by minimum classification error-based KISS metric learning. IEEE Trans. Cybern. **45**(2), 242–252 (2015)
23. Tao, D., Jin, L., Wang, Y., Yuan, Y., Li, X.: Person re-identification by regularized smoothing KISS metric learning. IEEE Trans. Circ. Syst. Video Technol. **23**(10), 1675–1685 (2013)
24. Wang, M., Hong, R., Li, G., Zha, Z., Yan, S., Chua, T.-S.: Event driven web video summarization by tag localization and key-shot identification. IEEE Trans. Multimedia **14**(4), 975–985 (2012)
25. Wang, M., Li, W., Liu, D., Ni, B., Shen, J., Yan, S.: Facilitating image search with a scalable and compact semantic mapping. IEEE Trans. Cybern. **45**(8), 1561–1574 (2015)
26. Wang, M., Liu, X., Wu, X.: Visual classification by l1-hypergraph modeling. IEEE Trans. Knowl. Data Eng. **27**(9), 2564–2574 (2015)
27. Weinberger, K.Q., Blitzer, J., Saul, L.K.: Distance metric learning for large margin nearest neighbor classification. J. Mach. Learn. Res. **10**, 207–244 (2009)
28. Xu, C., Tao, D., Xu, C.: Multi-view intact space learning. IEEE Trans. Pattern Anal. Mach. Intell. **37**(12), 2531–2544 (2015)
29. Yang, Y., Liao, S., Lei, Z., Li, S.Z.: Large scale similarity learning using similar pairs for person verification. In: Proceedings of Association for the Advancement of Artificial Intelligence (AAAI) (2016)
30. Zhao, R., Ouyang, W., Wang, X.: Unsupervised salience learning for person re-identification. In: Proceedings of the IEEE Conference on Computer Vision and Pattern Recognition, pp. 3586–3593 (2013)
31. Zheng, W.S., Gong, S., Xiang, T.: Re-identification by relative distance comparison. IEEE Trans. Pattern Anal. Mach. Intell. **35**(3), 653–668 (2012)

Object Detection Based on Scene Understanding and Enhanced Proposals

Zhicheng Wang[(✉)] and Chun Yuan[(✉)]

Graduate School at Shenzhen, Tsinghua University, Beijing, China
wang-zcl4@mails.tsinghua.edu.cn,
yuanc@sz.tsinghua.edu.cn

Abstract. This paper studies the role of scene understanding in object detection by proposing a two-stream pipeline model called Scene-Object Network for Detection (SOND). Specifically, SOND is based on scene-like info and object detection method, which are separately implemented by two deep ConvNets and merged at the end of the pipeline. Moreover, we raise a novel approach to proportionally combine proposals generated by Selective Search and Edge Box to reduce the high localization error when only Selective Search is used. The enhanced combined proposals are used in the training and testing process of our method. Proving that scene info and enhanced proposals are indeed of great help to improve object detection, we achieve competitive results on PASCAL VOC 2007 (mAP 74.2 %) and 2012 (mAP 71.8 %), which surpass the baseline of Fast-RCNN by 4.2 % on VOC 2007 and 3.4 % on VOC 2012.

Keywords: Object detection · Scene understanding · SOND · Selective Search · Edge Box

1 Introduction

Techniques of image recognition [1, 2, 19], such as object detection have got a significant rise thanks to the extensive use of deep learning and of massive image datasets. Image classification aims to classify which category the image belongs to while object detection additionally gives the location of objects in the image. Therefore, object detection requires more labels and more complex information of images.

In recent years, object detection has undergone much development. DPM [15] method using pyramid-like deformable features leads the way for many years. However, the performance of DPM has been largely improved by RCNN [2] taking use of deep learning. RCNN employed Selective Search [7] to generate candidate proposals, which is subsequently pushed through a CNN to extract its features and followed by a non-maximum suppression (NMS) process and bounding box regression. It boosts the accuracy of object detection by a large extent in contrast with DPM [15]. However, drawbacks such as extracting the feature of the proposal straightforward from the raw input image one by one results in tremendous time consumption. Fast-RCNN [1] then is presented to handle this problem.

Fast-RCNN [1] (FRCN) which incorporates the merits of SPP-net [4] and RCNN [2] greatly shortens the time of object detection process. It obtains excellence via an

© Springer International Publishing AG 2016
E. Chen et al. (Eds.): PCM 2016, Part I, LNCS 9916, pp. 397–406, 2016.
DOI: 10.1007/978-3-319-48890-5_39

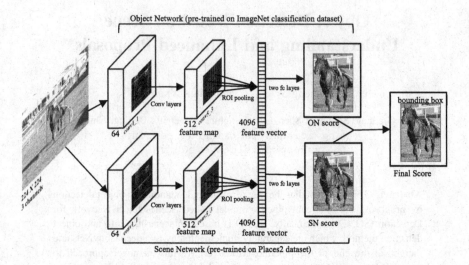

Fig. 1. The demonstration of SOND: the top stream of the flow chart describes the Object Network, and the bottom one depicts the Scene Network.

implementation of Regions of Interest (ROI) strategy with the form of a pooling layer. ROI pooling layer pools feature vectors from feature map which is outputted by the last convolutional layer in the network. It wisely circumvents a huge amount of time cost by convolutional layers. In addition, FRCN uses a multi-class classifier softmax instead of multiple bi-level classifier SVMs. This implementation further decreases the consumption time in test period. FRCN does a great job in speed, however, it stays on the mechanism established by RCNN and does not make distinct progress in accuracy.

Afterward, there emerges improved object detection methods based on FRCN [1]. The most representative one is Faster-RCNN (FFRCN) [5]. It mainly contributes at replacing the selective search generating proposal process with a deep network called Region Proposal Network (RPN). Some other methods improve or combine with FRCN from various aspects. You Look Only Once (YOLO) [16] proposes a single deep network to replace the three-step conventional detection pipeline: generating candidate proposal first, extracting features of the proposals and then classifying them to certain categories. It tends to preserve more global features and ought to be complementary with object-based detection method. However, YOLO itself could not obtain a satisfactory performance unless combines with FRCN.

Limin Wang in the paper Object-. [12] proposes a model which takes in scene-like information is called Object-Scene Convolutional Neural Network (OS-CNN). OS-CNN is used to boost the accuracy in the domain of event recognition and gains the 1st place in the ChaLearn Looking at People (LAP) challenge 2015. Inspired by Wang, we have good reason to deem scene-like information also of use to object detection. However, few methods related to object detection have taken scene-like information into consideration.

In this paper, we mainly explore the role of scene understanding in object detection. Referring to the two-stream pipeline architecture of OS-CNN, a Scene-Object Network

Fig. 2. Detected images of our proposed method. (a). It is an outdoor scene, and the car is an object in big size. (b). It is an indoor scene, and objects in the image are relatively small.

for Detection (SOND) is presented in this paper. Quite different from OS-CNN, the interior structure of the two sub-networks of SOND is designed for object detection. What is more, the scene network part of SOND is fine-tuned using a more powerful dataset Places2 [9] while OS-CNN uses the dataset Places [18]. Places2 which contains 10 + million images belonging to 400 + unique scene categories is chosen to be the canonical dataset of scene classification task in Large Scale Visual Recognition Challenge (ILSVRC) [10] 2015, also known as ImageNet 2015. We also extend the process of fine-tuning by increasing iterations and employing more stages of learning than FRCN in the object network part.

In RCNN, localization error is the most significant factor to lead false positive results. As localization error is directly related to proposals, Selective Search as the proposal generating approach of RCNN should be responsible for it. Therefore, it is reasonable to infer that methods using Selective Search all have this property. Edge Box [8] locating object proposals from edges is quite different from Selective Search in principle, which generates proposals by merging tiny regions to larger ones using features like texture, color, size and fill. These two approaches share relatively equal performance in accuracy while in totally diverse implementation procedure. So, their combination is in prospect by nature. This paper combines Selective Search with Edge Box resulting in enhanced proposals. The sample detected images are displayed in Fig. 2, from which it is shown that we get a remarkable performance in both outdoor big sized objects and indoor small sized objects.

Our contributions are two aspects as follows:

(1) A new model named Scene-Object Network for Detection (SOND) integrating scene-like information into the process of object detection is proposed. It is fine-tuned using a more comprehensive dataset Places2 [9] instead of Places [18] used by OS-CNN. Moreover, the Object Network part of SOND is improved on FRCN by occupying more stages of learning in the training process.
(2) Considering the limitation of Selective Search and the complementarity between Selective Search [7] and Edge Box [8], we combine the proposals generated by Selective Search and Edge Box in a proportional way to integrate the two methods' strengths.

2   Proposed Methods

2.1   Scene-Object Network for Detection

Scene conveys comprehensive message in an image. Hopefully, scene will make a great contribution to image recognition as it makes the image easy to understand. However, it is quite difficult to take advantage of the scene information because it is always full of ambiguity to assign the image to a certain scene category. For instance, an image contains mountains, sea and sand beach is inappropriate to be assigned to any of these three scene categories. There have been some datasets describing image as composed of multiple scenes such as SUN [20], Places [18]. However, these datasets are far less satisfactory in comparison to Places2 [9]. Therefore, we make use of Places2 and propose a novel model named Scene-Object Network for Detection (SOND), the Scene Network of which is pre-trained by it. Following the two-stream pipeline of OS-CNN, SOND incorporates both the merits of OS-CNN and Fast-RCNN, aiming at improving object detection. Moreover, we improve FRCN by taking more steps of learning in training process.

SOND comprises an Object Network (ON) and a Scene Network (SN). ON is designed to output the original object detection score, which is an implementation of VGG-Net [6] modified to the FRCN [1] style. It is pre-trained by ImageNet Classification data afterward fine-tuned by the dataset of PASCAL VOC [3, 13] object detection task. SN takes the same architecture as ON, however, is pre-trained by Places2 [9] and further fine-tuned by PASCAL VOC [3, 13] dataset. Figure 1 illustrates the demonstration of SOND. The top part of the figure describes the process of ON while the bottom part depicts the procedure of SN.

Indicated by Fig. 1, each stream of SOND outputs a score of the input bounding box which is detected by the corresponding network. As two scores of the same bounding box predicted by ON and SN individually combine at the end of the flow, an enhanced score is eventually obtained. Regarding the combination approach, we adopt the simple linear combination, that is, multiply the two scores with two different coefficients then add them up. The mathematical illustrations are described in Equation

$$Score = \alpha Score_{object} + \beta Score_{scene} \tag{1}$$

1, where α, β respectively stands for the coefficients of the object score and scene score. To keep the ultimate score ranging in a reasonable scope, we make a constraint that the summation of α and β be 1. By experiments, we find out that the best score is obtained when α is 0.7 and β equals 0.3.

2.2   Enhanced Proposals

General object detection approach is supposed to include two main steps: feature extraction and classification. Feature extraction is always accompanied by proposal generation method. As a proposal approach, Selective Search (SS) [7] is widely used owing to its short time-consuming character. However, SS has many limitations, as it only considers the color, texture, size and fill information while lacks of some significant features like contours of an image. Conversely, Edge Box (EB) [8] generating proposals via analyzing edge information of objects incorporates contours of the image meanwhile lacks the color or texture information. These two methods, therefore, have inborn merits to be combined to reach excellence. NoC [11] proposed by Sun. tries to employ the SS + EB strategy while in a stiff way, which combines the top-ranked 2 k proposals generated by EB with 2 k Selective Search proposals. The number of proposals generated by EB for an individual image ranges from several hundred to 6 k + . From experiments, we find that it is not the case that more proposals the better results. Based on our further analysis, it can be figured out that proposals with low confidence could confuse the training procedure leading to inferior results. Therefore, we take the strategy of combining the top-ranked 1/3 proposals generated by EB [8] with those 2 k proposals proposed by SS [7].

3 Experimental Results

3.1 Training Set

Our experiments use VGG16 [6], which is pre-trained by ImageNet classification task data set, as the initial weights of ON and use VGG16 pre-trained by Places2 [9] scene category dataset as the initial weights of SN. Both ON and SN are fine-tuned in the PASCAL VOC [3, 13] detection datasets. We respectively do the pre-training process in VOC 07trainval, VOC 12trainval, VOC 07trainval +12trainval and VOC 07trainval merged by 07test + 12trainval. There is no doubt that the last one will do best. Upon training, both ON and SN use 0.001 as their initial learning rate, and will decrease to one-tenth of the current learning rate after on step of 100 k iterations. ON experiences three steps fine-tuning, which is superior to the default two steps' strategy of Fast-RCNN [1]. The first two steps change the learning rate at the iteration of 100 k while the last step changes at 50 k iterations. The SN is fine-tuned by two-step strategy with the step being 100 k.

Regarding the combination of Selective Search and Edge Box, we set α to 0.7 and β to 0.3 by adaptive trials. We use the default setting (threshold 0.75) of Edge Box [8]. The combined boxes are used to make a contribution in the training process of ON as well as in the test process. Notably, the whole process of SN does not take in the combined boxes. The whole training process is implemented using Caffe [14].

3.2 Results and Analysis

We evaluate our proposed methods on PASCAL VOC2007 [3] and PASCAL VOC 2012 [13]. As Object Network (ON) and Scene Network (SN) in SOND are implemented in VGG16 [6] with the last convolutional layer followed by ROI pooling as FRCN does, FRCN is therefore used as our baseline and some methods improved on the basis of FRCN such as Faster-RCNN used as our comparable methods. To the best of our knowledge, NoC [11] is the first and only one method that incorporates the strategy of combining SS and EB to improve object detection. Therefore, NoC [11] is also included as our comparable method. The results of our method and comparable methods are displayed in Tables 1 and 2.

Table 1. Results on PASCAL VOC 2007 [3] test set. SOND* stands for SOND + SS unions by EB. 07 + 12 means that training data on VOC 07trainval + 12trainval is used.

Method	Data	mAP	Areo	Bike	Bird	Boat	Bottle	Bus	Car	Cat	Chair	Cow	Table	Dog	Horse	Mbike	Person	Plant	Sheep	Sofa	Train	TV
Fast-RCNN	07 + 12	70.0	77.0	78.1	69.3	59.4	38.3	81.6	78.6	86.7	42.8	78.8	68.9	84.7	82.0	76.6	69.9	31.8	70.1	74.8	80.4	70.4
Faster-RCNN	07 + 12	73.2	76.5	79.0	70.9	65.5	52.1	83.1	84.7	86.4	52.0	81.9	65.7	84.8	84.6	77.5	76.7	38.8	73.6	73.9	83.0	72.6
NoC	07 + 12	73.3	76.3	81.4	74.4	61.7	60.8	84.7	78.2	82.9	53.0	79.2	69.2	83.2	83.2	78.5	68.0	45.0	71.6	76.7	82.2	75.7
SOND (ours)	07 + 12	72.6	78.1	79.1	69.7	61.9	42.4	84.9	81.7	87.5	51.4	82.4	73.1	84	83.9	77.7	72.7	36.5	71.8	76	84.9	72.7
SOND* (ours)	07 + 12	74.2	78.9	80.4	71.3	67.1	48.5	87.6	82.9	87.8	53.5	77.1	71.9	85.2	84.6	79.5	76.8	39.7	74	76.9	86.7	73.5

Table 2. Results on PASCAL VOC 2012 [13] test set. 07 ++12 signifys that VOC 07trainval + 12trainval + 07test is used.

Method	Data	mAP	Areo	Bike	Bird	Boat	Bottle	Bus	Car	Cat	Chair	Cow	Table	Dog	Horse	Mbike	Person	Plant	Sheep	Sofa	Train	TV
Fast-RCNN	07 + 12	68.4	82.3	78.4	70.8	52.3	38.7	77.8	71.6	89.3	44.2	73.0	55.0	87.5	80.5	80.8	72.0	35.1	68.3	65.7	80.4	64.2
NoC	07 + 12	68.8	82.8	79.0	71.6	52.3	53.7	74.1	69.0	84.9	46.9	74.3	53.1	85.0	81.3	79.5	72.2	38.9	72.4	59.5	76.7	68.1
Faster-RCNN	07 ++12	70.4	84.9	79.8	74.3	53.9	49.8	77.5	75.9	88.5	45.6	77.1	55.3	86.9	81.7	80.9	79.6	40.1	72.6	60.9	81.2	61.5
FRCNN&YOLO	07 ++12	70.4	83.0	78.5	73.7	55.8	43.1	78.3	73.0	89.2	49.1	74.3	56.6	87.2	80.5	80.5	74.7	42.1	70.8	68.3	81.5	81.5
SOND[a](ours)	07 ++12	70.9	84.0	81.0	70.6	55.6	42.7	79.7	74.8	89.8	48.6	74.7	62.1	88.3	82.4	82.3	74.6	40.6	68.5	69.6	83.5	65.3
SOND*[b](ours)	07 ++12	71.8	84.1	81.1	73.1	57.8	47.9	80.1	76.3	89.7	48.6	75.5	60.9	87.7	82.9	81.5	77.6	41.9	71.4	68.2	83.3	66.7

[a]http://host.robots.ox.ac.uk:8080/anonymous/LUBXVT.html
[b]http://host.robots.ox.ac.uk:8080/anonymous/NFGHN2.html

In Fig. 3, we analyze the results on the classes of bottle and potted plant which are relatively small in size and hard to detect in the 20 classes of VOC. Figure 3(a) shows that all kinds of errors drop in our method compared with FRCN owing to the good effect of SOND. In addition, Fig. 3(b) illustrates that the proportion of localization error in total false positives of our method drops by a large extent in contrast with that of FRCN thanks to the combination of the proposals. The results of other 18 classes in VOC are similar with that illustrated in Fig. 3.

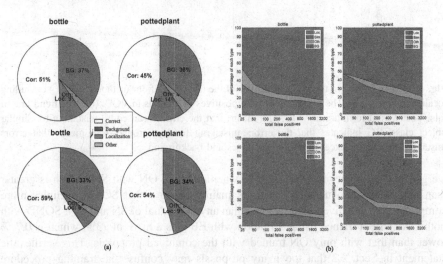

Fig. 3. (a): The distribution of overall true positives and false positives of results in bottle and potted plants on VOC 2007 [3] test. (b): Analysis of the top ranked false positive predictions of bottle and potted plants on VOC 2007 test. Loc signifies that the error is caused by poor localization. Sim denotes that the error is caused by similar classes. BG indicates that the prediction is fired on background. Oth means that the prediction mistakes for dissimilar category. For both (a) and (b): Top row: the results of Fast-RCNN. Bottom row: the results of SOND*. This analysis is done with the help of the diagnosing tool of [17].

Figure 4 demonstrates the trend line of false positives of two general classes in VOC, excluding localization error which is analyzed in the above paragraph. Seeing from Fig. 4(a), the primary types of false positives of animals are similar-class caused error and background error. The low trend line of Oth in Fig. 4(a) indicates animals are not likely to be recognized as other classes. However, low trend line of Oth in Figure (b) has a comparative distribution with other two types of errors, which implies furniture is more likely to be mistaken for other classes than animals. This leads to the fact that furniture is relatively harder to be detected than animals.

Ablation experiments are done according to the several elements that contribute to the improvement of object detection in this paper. All experiments in Table 3 are fine-tuned on VOC 07trainval + 12trainval. Scene Net pre-trained on Places2 dataset obtains a relatively low accuracy of 68.3, which indicates that SN cannot do a great job in detection on its own. Object Net which incorporates a three-step fine-tune strategy alone gets an accuracy of 71.4 %, which is 1.4 % higher than 70.0 % of FRCN. Therefore, it is essential to incorporate three-stage fine-tuning. However, dramatically

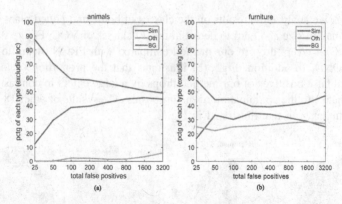

Fig. 4. The trend line of total false positives of the detection of our method (SOND*) excluding localization error. (a): The trend line of false positives of animals in VOC. (b): The trend line of false positives of furniture in VOC. Sim means that the error is caused by mistaking for similar object class. BG indicates that the errors mistaking for background. Oth means that errors mistaking for classes except for similar classes and background.

we get an even higher mAP of 72.6 % when combine ON with SN, which is greater than any of the two networks. This is mainly because that SOND occupies more comprehensive and diversified features than any individual of SN and ON. SOND with both ON and SN trained using SS union with EB gets a mAP of 73.5, which is 0.7 % lower than that with only ON trained with the combined proposals. This verifies the statement in Sect. 2.2 that too many proposals may confuse the training procedure leading to inferior results. Moreover, the number of scenes in an image is far less than that of objects, therefore, the upper limit of the number of the proposals of SN resulting in good result is lower than that of ON. This results in total opposite performances when SN and ON incorporate the combined proposals. Eventually, we get a competitive mAP of 74.2 %, which integrates the strengths of scene-like information and enhanced combined proposals.

Table 3. Ablation experiments on VOC 2007 test

Method	mAP
Fast-RCNN	70.0
Scene Net (SN)	68.3
Object Net (ON)	71.4
SOND (ON + SN)	72.6
SOND + (ON with EB + SN with EB)	73.5
SOND + (ON with EB + SN)	74.2

4   Conclusion

In this paper, we propose a novel model named Scene-Object Network for Detection (SOND) for object detection. SOND consists of two sub deep ConvNets [19], one of which is Object Net (ON) responsible for extracting object features and the other one is

Scene Net (SN) aiming to extract scene features. Eventually, ON and SN are combined to obtain the final score of the proposal. Also, we propose a novel method to merge proposals generated by Selective Search (SS) and Edge Box (EB) and use the merged proposals to augment training and testing data. Extensive experiments on VOC 2007 [3] and VOC 2012 [13] show that the proposed SOND and SS [7] + EB [8] combination method can make a significant improvement by exploiting scene information and the diversity of proposals. Regarding future work, we find that the presence of objects in a real normal image is highly correlated with the scene it belongs to. For example, a real image of an indoor scene is much more likely to have a cat in it than a horse and objects with aeroplane annotations are much more related to the scene of airfield or airport_terminal than any other scene categories. Therefore, we can probe the inner correlation of objects and scenes. We may statistically analyze the correlation between objects and scenes and get an overall demonstration of the correlation of scenes and objects, which will be likely to make great contributions to object detection as well as even more fields.

References

1. Girshick, R.: Fast R-CNN. arXiv:1504.08083 (2015)
2. Girshick, R., Donahue, J., Darrell, T., Malik, J.: Rich feature hierarchies for accurate object detection and semantic segmentation. In: 2014 IEEE Conference on Computer Vision and Pattern Recognition (CVPR), pp. 580–587. IEEE (2014)
3. Everingham, M., Van Gool, L., Williams, C.K.I., Winn, J., Zisserman, A.: The PASCAL Visual Object Classes Challenge 2007 (VOC2007) Results (2007)
4. He, K., Zhang, X., Ren, S., Sun, J.: Spatial pyramid pooling in deep convolutional networks for visual recognition. In: Fleet, D., Pajdla, T., Schiele, B., Tuytelaars, T. (eds.) ECCV 2014. LNCS, vol. 8691, pp. 346–361. Springer, Heidelberg (2014). doi:10.1007/978-3-319-10578-9_23
5. Ren, S., He, K., Girshick, R., Sun, J.: Faster r-cnn: towards real-time object detection with region proposal networks. arXiv preprint arXiv:1506.01497 (2015)
6. Simonyan, K., Zisserman, A.: Very deep convolutional networks for large-scale image recognition. arXiv preprint arXiv:1409.1556 (2014)
7. Uijlings, J.R., van de Sande, K.E., Gevers, T., Smeulders, A.W.: Selective search for object recognition. IJCV **104**, 154–171 (2013)
8. Zitnick, C.L., Dollár, P.: Edge boxes: locating object proposals from edges. In: Fleet, D., Pajdla, T., Schiele, B., Tuytelaars, T. (eds.) ECCV 2014. LNCS, vol. 8693, pp. 391–405. Springer, Heidelberg (2014). doi:10.1007/978-3-319-10602-1_26
9. Zhou, B., Khosla, A., Lapedriza, A., Torralba, A., Oliva, A.: Places2: A Large-Scale Database for Scene Understanding (2015)
10. Fei-Fei, L.: ImageNet: crowdsourcing, benchmarking & other cool things, CMU VASC Seminar, March 2010
11. Ren, S., He, K., Girshick, R., Zhang, X., Sun, J.: Object detection networks on convolutional feature maps. arXiv:1504.06066 (2015)
12. Wang, L., Wang, Z., Du, W., Qiao, Y.: Object-Scene Convolutional Neural Networks for event recognition in images. In: 2015 IEEE Conference on Computer Vision and Pattern Recognition Workshops (CVPRW), pp. 30–35. doi:10.1109/CVPRW.2015.7301333
13. Everingham, M., Van Gool, L., Williams, C.K.I., Winn, J., Zisserman, A.: The PASCAL visual object classes (VOC) challenge. Int. J. Comput. Vis. **88**(2), 303–338 (2010)
14. Jia, Y., Shelhamer, E., Donahue, J., Karayev, S., Long, J., Girshick, R., Guadarrama, S., Darrell, T.: Caffe: convolutional architecture for fast feature embedding, arXiv:1408.5093 (2014)

15. Felzenszwalb, P.F., Girshick, R.B., McAllester, D., Ramanan, D.: Object detection with discriminatively trained partbased models. TPAMI **32**, 1627–1645 (2010)
16. Redmon, J., Divvala, S., Girshick, R., Farhadi, A.: You Only Look Once: Unified, Real-Time Object Detection. arXiv:1506.02640 (2015)
17. Hoiem, D., Chodpathumwan, Y., Dai, Q.: Diagnosing error in object detectors. In: Fitzgibbon, A., Lazebnik, S., Perona, P., Sato, Y., Schmid, C. (eds.) ECCV 2012. LNCS, vol. 7574, pp. 340–353. Springer, Heidelberg (2012). doi:10.1007/978-3-642-33712-3_25
18. Zhou, B., Lapedriza, A., Xiao, J., Torralba, A., Oliva, A.: Learning deep features for scene recognition using places database. In: NIPS, pp. 487–495 (2014)
19. Krizhevsky, A., Sutskever, I., Hinton, G.E.: Image classification with deep neural networks. In: NIPS, pp. 1106–1114 (2012)
20. Xiao, J., Hays, J., Ehinger, K., Oliva, A., Torralba, A.: SUN database: large-scale scene recognition from Abbey to Zoo. In: IEEE Conference on Computer Vision and Pattern Recognition (2010). Some images deteced by our method are listed below

Video Inpainting Based on Joint Gradient and Noise Minimization

Yiqi Jiang, Xin Jin$^{(\boxtimes)}$, and Zhiyong Wu

Shenzhen Key Lab of Broadband Network and Multimedia,
Graduate School at Shenzhen, Tsinghua University, Shenzhen, China
yq-ji14@mails.tsinghua.edu.cn, {jin.xin,zywu}@sz.tsinghua.edu.cn

Abstract. Video inpainting is a process of filling in missing pixels or replacing undesirable pixels in a video. State-of-the-art approaches show limited efficiency to the videos in which the regions to be filled are large and irregular or the occlusions move slowly. Inpainted results on these videos are coarse and have small noise remained or have mosaic appearance. In this paper, we propose a new inpainting method to fix the problem. We rarefy the gradient fields of recovered frames along the horizontal and vertical direction and minimize noise remained after the initial inpainting while still considering the rank minimization of to-be-inpainted matrix. An algorithm which uses partial updates for the dual variables and approximates gradient fields based on Alternating Direction Minimizing strategy is designed to efficiently and effectively optimize the formulation. The experimental results on both simulated and real video data demonstrate the superior performance of the proposed method over state-of-the-arts in terms of preserving details as well as guaranteeing piecewise smoothness of recovered frames.

Keywords: Inpainting · Gradient and noise minimization · Joint optimization

1 Introduction

Video inpainting is a process of filling in missing pixels or replacing undesirable pixels in a video. It has been extensively explored in recent years and various kinds of approaches have been proposed.

The primary study in video inpainting is analogous to image inpainting [1], which applied image inpainting methods frame by frame. This method neglected the temporal continuity and the results may be inconsistent and fluctuant. Then a motion layer video completion method which split the video sequence into different motion layers and completed each motion layer separately with different methods or priorities was proposed [2]. Some other researchers filled holes using fragments in other frames. For example, Shih *et al.* [3] and Patwardhan *et al.* [4] inpainted subregions separately with different methods or priorities. Mounira *et al.* [5] and Miguel *et al.* [6] utilized the spatial and temporal consistency explicitly. They applied motion composition and conducted block matching

© Springer International Publishing AG 2016
E. Chen et al. (Eds.): PCM 2016, Part I, LNCS 9916, pp. 407–417, 2016.
DOI: 10.1007/978-3-319-48890-5_40

(a)   (b)

Fig. 1. (a) is the original frame with to-be-removed region labeled, (b) is the inpainted result by rank-minimization method

across frames to estimate the unknown regions. Jia *et al.* [7] repaired static background with motion layers and repaired moving foreground using model alignment. Although the inter-frame block matching helps in obtaining reasonable results, the exploration of the temporal consistency is limited to several frames out of the whole sequence and artifacts exist widely. Wexler *et al.* [8] extended the image inpainting approach by belief propagation along temporal dimension to build a spatio-temporal 3D graph model. His results proved that temporal information can improve the video completion results. However, his algorithm is very time consuming. Based on the algorithm of Wexler *et al.*, Newson *et al.* [9] proposed a new patch-based video inpainting method which considered texture feature matching as well as realignment. It worked better than Wexler *et al.* while using less time. Ebdelli *et al.* [10] used region-based registration approach to align a group of neighboring frames and inpainted missing areas of one frame by minimizing an energy function formed according to the consistency of neighboring frames.

Recently, the matrix completion approach has been studied and some methods have been proposed. In these methods, the rank minimization is used as a powerful tool to utilize the global information. However, direct solving the rank minimization problem is difficult because it is an NP-hard problem. Fazel *et al.* [11] proved that trace norm function is the convex envelop of rank function over the unit ball of matrices. Candes and Recht *et al.* [12] had shown that under mild conditions, the minimization of trace norm is equivalent to the minimization of rank. So, many researchers tried to fix the matrix completion problem by minimizing the trace norm of a matrix. Applying rank minimization to video inpainting, Liu *et al.* [13] estimated the missing data in video via tensor completion which is generalized from matrix completion methods. Xiao *et al.* [14] aligned the video frames based on the RASL model [15] in advance and perform inpainting based on matrix completion.

Although the existing approaches can partially solve video inpainting problems, they still have many difficulties in inpainting large and irregular occlusions or slowly moving occlusions. The inpainted results are coarse and have remained noises as well as mosaic appearance. Figure 1 gives a result by a rank-minimization method. We can see that the inpainted area is not piece-wise smooth and neat. In order to fix these problems, in this paper, a novel video inpainting method which provides visually pleasing results is proposed. The proposed approach extends the rank-minimization methods by bringing following main contributions: (1) An inpainting model which rarefied the gradient fields, minimized remained noises and guaranteed low rankness of to-be-inpainted matrix is established; (2) An optimizing algorithm which uses partial updates for the dual variables and approximates gradient fields based on Alternating Direction Minimizing strategy is designed to efficiently and effectively solve inpainting model; (3) Providing visually pleasing results in removing large and irregular objects compared with other existing inpainting methods.

The paper is organized as follows. In Sect. 2, the proposed method is described starting by an overview of the complete algorithm followed by a detailed description of each updating step. The performance of the algorithm and experimental results are shown in Sect. 3. Finally, Sect. 4 concludes the paper.

2 Proposed Method

2.1 Inpainting Model

In the spatio-temporal consistent videos, the scenes can be rotated and translated because of camera pose changes, but the adjacent video frames are generally related. We assume the size of processing window is n, which corresponds to processing n frames in the video. For each frame, we firstly label an interesting region which includes the occlusion and name this region as f. A to-be-inpainted region f in frame i can be modeled by a linear combination of the background a and the occlusion r as $\forall i \in [1, ..., n], f_i = a_i + r_i$. We let $vec : \mathbb{R}^{w \times h} \to \mathbb{R}^m$ denotes the operator that selects an m-pixels interesting region from a frame and stacks it as a column-vector. Then, as a matrix, $F = [vec(f_1) \mid ... \mid vec(f_n)] \in \mathbb{R}^{m \times n}$ are the vectorized interesting regions, where m is the number of pixels in the interesting region and n is the number of frames. So the above relationship $f = a + r$ can be rewritten in a matrix form $F = A + R$. A represents the inpainted regions matrix and R represents the occlusion matrix. In this paper, we suppose that the to-be-inpainted occlusions include not only the mask, but also the noises remained after initial inpainting. We model minimizing noise level as minimizing its $\|N\|_2$ where $\|\cdot\|_2$ denotes the l_2 norm so that we can eliminate these noises and get neat results. Then the occlusion term, named by R, can be split into the mask term E and a noise term N.

By the observations of natural images, we find that most images are largely piecewise smoothness and their gradient fields are typically sparse [16]. So for getting a better inpainting result and eliminating mosaic effect, we introduce a gradient fields sparse prior: the responses of inpainted region A to derivative-like filters $(d_1, d_2, ..., d_J)$, which is $\sum_{j=1}^{J} \|d_j * a_j\|_0$ are sparse. $\|\cdot\|_0$ denotes the l_0 norm and $*$ is the operator of convolution. In this paper, we consider about the filters in horizontal direction d_1 and in vertical direction d_2 for simplicity, which means $\|DA\|_0 = \sum_{i=1}^{n} \sum_{j=1}^{2} \|d_j * A_i\|_0$. So we can model rarefying gradient fields as minimizing $\|DA\|_0$.

Based on the priors and the modeling above, we formulated the desired inpainting process as a mathematical model as follow:

$$min \; rank(A) + \gamma_1 \|R\|_0 + \gamma_2 \|N\|_2^2 + \gamma_3 \|DA\|_0 ,$$
$$s.t. F \circ \tau = A + R; R = E + N; \tag{1}$$

where $\gamma_1, \gamma_2, \gamma_3$ are the coefficients controlling the weights of different terms; $\tau \equiv [\tau_1, \tau_2, ..., \tau_n]$ is the collection of all transformations; $rank(*)$ is the process of solving the rank of a matrix, which is minimized to enforce the aligned inpainted regions to be highly correlated; R represents the occlusion term, which is the linear combination of mask term E and noise term N as mentioned above. Since E occupies most part of R, We minimize $\|R\|_0$ to make R and E be sparse. N is the remained noises, which can be eliminated by minimizing its l_2 norm. DA is the gradient of A along the horizontal direction and vertical direction. We minimize its l_0 norm to enforce the inpainted region to be piece-wise smoothness.

2.2 Optimization

To optimize the objective function (1) and linearize the constraints, we adopt convex surrogates strategy. With this strategy, above optimization problem can be formulated as follow:

$$\begin{cases} min \, \|A\|_* + \gamma_1 \|R\|_1 + \gamma_2 \|N\|_2^2 + \gamma_3 \|DA\|_1 \\ s.t. \; F \circ \tau + \sum_{i=1}^{n} J_i \Delta \tau \epsilon_i \epsilon_i^T = A + R; R = E + N. \end{cases} \tag{2}$$

τ should be initialized properly so that (2) can converge to an optimal solution with an iterative fashion. In this paper we firstly adopt SIFT algorithm [17] which is proved to be resist from the change of scale and rotation when finding feature points to extract hundreds of marker points for each frame and select three feature points that match best among all the frames to fit a global transformation in terms of Mean Square Error (MSE). Then three basic canonical coordinate points are set according to the feature points. Finally, Using the affine operation, we can get the initial transformation τ.

Based on the Augmented Lagrange Multiplier (ALM) and Alternating Direction Minimizing (ADM) strategy, we propose an efficient algorithm which uses partial updates for the dual variables as well as approximates gradient fields to solve the optimizing problem of formulation (2). Firstly, two auxiliary variables L, G are introduced to replace A and DA in the objective function, respectively, so that our objective function is separable. The augmented Lagrangian function of (2) turns to be:

$$\begin{cases} \pounds \left(L, R, N, G, E, A, \Delta \tau \right) \\ = \|L\|_* + \gamma_1 \|R\|_1 + \gamma_2 \|N\|_2^2 + \gamma_3 \|G\|_1 \\ + \phi \left(X_1, F \circ \tau + \sum_{i=1}^{n} J_i \Delta \tau \epsilon_i \epsilon_i^n - A - R \right) \\ + \phi \left(X_2, R - E - N \right) + \phi \left(X_3, L - A \right) + \phi \left(X_4, G - DA \right) . \end{cases} \tag{3}$$

In formulation (3), $\phi(X, P) \equiv \langle X, P \rangle + \frac{\mu}{2} \|P\|_2^2$, where $\langle \cdot, \cdot \rangle$ represents matrix inner product and μ is a positive penalty scalar. X_1, X_2, X_3, X_4 are the Lagrangian multipliers. Then we iteratively updates one variable at a time while fixing the items irrelevant to the variable.

Update L: We remove the items irrelevant to L in (3) and get:

$$L^{t+1} = \underset{L}{argmin} \; \|L\|_* + \phi\left(X_3^t, L - A^t\right) = U S_{\frac{1}{\mu^t}} [\Sigma] V^T. \tag{4}$$

Here $U\Sigma V^T$ denotes the Singular Value Decomposition (SVD) of $\left(A^t - \frac{X_3^t}{\mu^t}\right)$. $\{\mu^t\}$ is a monotonically increasing positive sequence; $S_{\epsilon>0}[\cdot]$ represents the shrinkage operator; the definition of which on scalars is: $S_{\epsilon>0}[x] = sgn(x) \, max(|x| - \epsilon, 0)$.

Update R: We reserve the items related to R and get the convex optimization function as follow:

$$
\begin{aligned}
R^{t+1} &= \underset{R}{argmin} \; \gamma_1 \|R\|_1 + \phi\left(X_1^t, P^t - A^t - R\right) + \phi\left(X_2^t, R - E^t - N^t\right) \\
&= S_{\frac{2\gamma_1}{\mu^t}}\left[P^t - A^t + E^t + N^t + \frac{X_1^t - X_2^t}{\mu^t}\right].
\end{aligned}
\tag{5}
$$

In the formulation above, $P^t \equiv F \circ \tau^t + \sum_{i=1}^{n} J_i \Delta \tau^t \epsilon_i \epsilon_i^T$.

Update N: Like the approach as above, we remove the items irrelevant to N and get this formulation:

$$N^{t+1} = \underset{N}{argmin} \; \gamma_2 \|N\|_2^2 + \phi\left(X_2^t, R^{t+1} - E^t - N\right) = \frac{X_2^t + \mu^t\left(R^{t+1} - E^t\right)}{2\gamma_2 + \mu^t}. \tag{6}$$

Update G: G is the gradient of aligned matrix A along the horizontal direction and vertical direction, we also keep the items related to G and get that:

$$G^{t+1} = \underset{G}{argmin} \; \gamma_3 \|G\|_1 + \phi\left(X_4^t, G - DA^t\right) = \hat{S}_{\frac{\gamma_3}{\mu^t}}\left[\frac{\mu^t DA^t/2 - X_4^t/2}{\mu^t/2}\right]. \tag{7}$$

Here $\hat{S}_E[X]$ denotes the shrinkage on the elements of X with thresholds given by corresponding entries of E.

Update A: We remove the items irrelevant to A in (3) and get:

$$A^{t+1} = \underset{A}{argmin} \; \phi\left(X_1^t, P^t - R^{t+1} - A\right) + \phi\left(X_3^t, L^{t+1} - A\right) + \phi\left(X_4^t, G^{t+1} - DA\right). \tag{8}$$

Update E: We keep the items related to E and get optimizing formulation as follow:

$$E^{t+1} = \underset{E}{argmin} \; \phi\left(X_2^t, R^{t+1} - E - N^{t+1}\right). \tag{9}$$

Update $\Delta\tau$: In terms of MSE we mentioned above, we calculate the energy terms with respect to τ by follow formulation:

$$\Delta\tau^{t+1} = \underset{\Delta\tau}{argmin}\ \phi\left(X_1, F\circ\tau + \sum_{i=1}^{n} J_i\Delta\tau\epsilon_i\epsilon_i^T - A - R\right)$$
$$= \sum_{i=1}^{n} J_i^\dagger\left(A^{t+1} + R^{t+1} - F\circ\tau - \frac{X_1^t}{\mu^t}\right)\epsilon_i\epsilon_i^T \tag{10}$$

where $J_i^\dagger$ denotes the Moore-Penrose pseudoinverse of J.

Update Lagrangian Multipliers: Finally, we update the Lagrangian Multipliers X_1, X_2, X_3, X_4 according to the ALM algorithm, the formulations are as follow:

$$X_1^{t+1} = X_1^t + \mu^t\left(P^{t+1} - A^{t+1} - R^{t+1}\right);$$
$$X_2^{t+1} = X_2^t + \mu^t\left(R^{t+1} - E^{t+1} - N^{t+1}\right);$$
$$X_3^{t+1} = X_3^t + \mu^t\left(L^{t+1} - A^{t+1}\right);$$
$$X_4^{t+1} = X_4^t + \mu^t\left(G^{t+1} - DA^{t+1}\right); \tag{11}$$

Where $P^{t+1} \equiv F\circ\tau^{t+1} + \sum_{i=1}^{n} J_i\Delta\tau^t\epsilon_i\epsilon_i^T$.

Algorithm 1. Optimizing algorithm

Input: $\gamma_1 > 0, \gamma_2 > 0, \gamma_3 > 0$. The original video F, the initial transformation τ.
1: **while** not converged **do**
2:     $L^0 = R^0 = N^0 = A^0 = E^0 = X_1^0 = X_2^0 = X_3^0 = \mathbf{0} \in \mathbb{R}^{m*n}, \Delta\tau = 0, t = 0, \mu^0 > 0, \rho > 1, G^0 = X_4^0 = \mathbf{0} \in \mathbb{R}^{2m*n}$;
3:     compute the Jacobian matrix $\{J_{1...i...n}\}$, $J_i = \frac{\partial}{\partial\tau_i}F_i\circ\tau_i$;
4:     compute the initial aligned areas $O \leftarrow F\circ\tau$;
5:     **while** not converged **do**
6:         Update L^{t+1} via Eq. (4);
7:         Update R^{t+1} via Eq. (5);
8:         Update N^{t+1} via Eq. (6);
9:         Update G^{t+1} via Eq. (7);
10:         **for** i from 1 to n **do**
11:             Update A_i^{t+1} via Eq. (8);
12:         **end for**
13:         Update E^{t+1} via Eq. (9);
14:         $A^{t+1}\left(A^{t+1} < 0\right) = 0;\ E^{t+1}\left(E^{t+1} < 0\right) = 0$;
15:         Update $\Delta\tau^{t+1}$ via Eq. (10);
16:         Update the multipliers via Eq. (11);
17:         $\mu^{t+1} = \mu^t\rho;\ t = t + 1$;
18:     **end while**
19:     update transformation $\tau = \tau + \Delta\tau^t$;
20: **end while**
Output: Aligned inpainted video A, sparse occlusion E, final transformation τ, small Gaussian noise N.

The entire algorithm of solving Eq. (1) is summarized in Algorithm 1. After one iteration of inner loop, we set the negative elements in A and E to be 0, respectively. The outer loop terminates when the change of objective function value between two neighboring iterations is sufficiently small or the maximum number of iterations is reached. The inner loop is stopped when $\left\| F \circ \tau^{t+1} + \sum_{i=1}^{n} J_i \Delta \tau^t \epsilon_i \epsilon_i^T - A^{t+1} - R^{t+1} \right\|_F \leq \delta \left\| F \circ \tau^t \right\|_F$ with $\delta = 10^{-6}$ or the maximum number of inner iterations is reached.

3 Experimental Results

In order to demonstrate the effectiveness of the proposed algorithm, we compared the processing results provided by the proposed algorithm with those provided by Wexler et al. [8], Xiao et al. [14] as well as Newson et al. [9] in terms of visual quality. For more general, we do the comparisons on both simulated and real data. We conduct the experiments on a PC running Windows 10 64bit operating system with Intel Core i5 3.4 GHz CPU and 4.0 GB RAM. The parameters are determined empirically as: $\gamma_1 = 100\omega, \gamma_2 = 5\omega, \gamma_3 = 10\omega$ with $\omega = \frac{1}{\sqrt{m*n}}$. For simplicity, we apply our algorithm to one color channel first and utilize the transformation parameter τ obtained in the first channel to optimize other two channels for reduced complexity. Finally we concatenate the three channels' results as the final result.

Firstly, we synthesize an occluded video by adding a mask we generate in advance into a video clip. The compared results are shown in the first column of Fig. 2. we can see that results by Wexler et al. and Newson et al. shown on the second row and the fourth row, respectively, have the problem of mosaic appearance, i. e. the edges of right pillar cannot be inpainted smoothly. Since their methods try to fill the missing area with similar patches in and around the hole from the available parts of frames, they will fail when the occlusion is very big and no enough available patch can be found. Similarly, Xiao et al. cannot get clear result because they didn't minimize remained noise and gradient fields. Compared to the three results above, our method, shown on the last row, achieves the best performance which not only preserves the edges and shadows, but also eliminates the noises remained.

Then, we try to remove the car from a video clip. The results are compared in the middle column of Fig. 2. As we can see, the shape of the car is irregular and there are no exact mask to cover the car. So it is more difficult to inpaint this video than the synthesized videos. The second row is the inpainted result by Wexler et al.. We can see that Wexler et al.'s result have mosaic appearance in large area. The third row is the inpainted result by Xiao et al.. Although Xiao et al. doesn't have the mosaic appearance, their inpainted results still have the noises and the recovered region is not piecewise smoothness. The fourth row is the inpainted results by Newson et al.. Newson et al. improve Wexler et al.'s work and they achieve a better performance than Wexler et al.. But their result still has the mosaic appearance and the details of leaves cannot be recovered.

(a) original frames

(b) By Wexler *et al.* [8]

(c) By Xiao *et al.* [14]

(d) By Newson *et al.* [9]

(e) Our results

Fig. 2. Visual comparison with state-of-the-arts on synthesized video and real video. **Top row** is original frames captured from three different video clips; **second row** is the inpainted results by Wexler *et al.* [8], respectively; **third row** is the inpainted results by Xiao *et al.* [14], respectively; **fourth row** is the inpainted results by Newson *et al.* [9], respectively; **fifth row** is the inpainted result by our method, respectively.

The fifth row is the inpainted result generated by our method. Result shows that our method outperforms the others in terms of visual quality of the inpainted frames.

The last column of Fig. 2 compares the processing results on removing larger occlusion like a helicopter. We can easily see that Wexler *et al.* and Newson *et al.*, shown on the second row and the fourth row, respectively, cannot recover

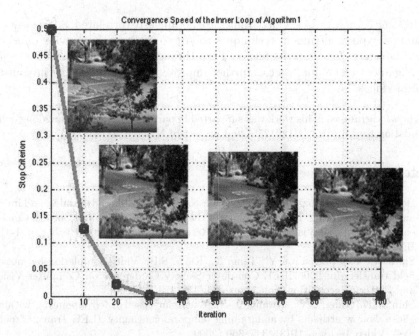

Fig. 3. The convergence speed of the inner loop of Algorithm 1

the building's details behind the helicopter perfectly. Xiao *et al.* can recover the building's details, but their result shown on the third row are not piecewise smoothness. Compared to the three results above, result provided by our method shown on the last row recovers the building's details behind the helicopter and enhance the piecewise smoothness for the inpainted regions. All the experiments demonstrate that the proposed approach is able to inpaint various occlusion successfully.

Figure 3 displays the convergence speed of the inner loop of Algorithm 1, without loss of generality, on the R channel of the car clips sequence, in which the stop criterion sharply drop to the level of 10^{-4} with about 30–40 iterations. We also show four layers compares at 10, 20, 40 and 100 iterations. We see that the results at 40 iterations is very close to those at 100.

4   Conclusion and Future Work

This paper proposes a new video inpainting method which keeps the sparsity of gradient fields and the minimality of noise while still considering the correlation within adjacent frames. We formulate the problem in a unified optimization framework and propose an efficient algorithm to find the optimal solution. The experimental results, compared to the state-of-the-arts, have demonstrated the advantages in terms of preserving details and keeping piecewise smoothness of the recovered frames.

In some complex cases, video frames are not linearly correlated. So, we will try to find an explicit alignment techniques robust to the irregular moving of occlusions and shots change in the future. Then through combining our method with the alignment technique, we can further improve the performance of inpainting general videos.

Acknowledgments. This work was supported in part by the NSFC-Guangdong Joint Foundation Key Project (U1201255) and project of NSFC 61371138, China.

References

1. Bertalmio, M., Bertozzi, A.L., Sapiro, G.: Navier-stokes, fluid dynamics, and image and video inpainting. In: Proceedings of the 2001 IEEE Computer Society Conference on Computer Vision and Pattern Recognition, CVPR 2001, vol. 1, p. I-355. IEEE (2001)
2. Shiratori, T., Matsushita, Y., Tang, X., Kang, S.B.: Video completion by motion field transfer. In: 2006 IEEE Computer Society Conference on Computer Vision and Pattern Recognition, vol. 1, pp. 411–418. IEEE (2006)
3. Shih, T.K., Tang, N.C., Hwang, J.-N.: Exemplar-based video inpainting without ghost shadow artifacts by maintaining temporal continuity. IEEE Trans. Circuits Syst. Video Technol. **19**(3), 347–360 (2009)
4. Patwardhan, K., Sapiro, G., Bertalmío, M., et al.: Video inpainting under constrained camera motion. IEEE Trans. Image Process. **16**(2), 545–553 (2007)
5. Ebdelli, M., Guillemot, C., Le Meur, O.: Examplar-based video inpainting with motion-compensated neighbor embedding. In: 2012 19th IEEE International Conference on Image Processing (ICIP), pp. 1737–1740. IEEE (2012)
6. Granados, M., Kim, K.I., Tompkin, J., Kautz, J., Theobalt, C.: Background inpainting for videos with dynamic objects and a free-moving camera. In: Fitzgibbon, A., Lazebnik, S., Perona, P., Sato, Y., Schmid, C. (eds.) ECCV 2012. LNCS, vol. 7578, pp. 682–695. Springer, Heidelberg (2012). doi:10.1007/978-3-642-33718-5_49
7. Jia, J., Tai-Pang, W., Tai, Y.-W., Tang, C.-K.: Video repairing: inference of foreground and background under severe occlusion. In: Proceedings of the 2004 IEEE Computer Society Conference on Computer Vision and Pattern Recognition, CVPR 2004, vol. 1, p. I-364. IEEE (2004)
8. Wexler, Y., Shechtman, E., Irani, M.: Space-time completion of video. IEEE Trans. Pattern Anal. Mach. Intell. **29**(3), 463–476 (2007)
9. Newson, A., Almansa, A., Fradet, M., Gousseau, Y., Pérez, P.: Video inpainting of complex scenes (2015). CoRR, abs/1503.05528
10. Ebdelli, M., Meur, O.L., Guillemot, C.: Video inpainting with short-term windows: application to object removal and error concealment. IEEE Trans. Image Process. **24**(10), 3034–3047 (2015). http://dx.doi.org/10.1109/TIP.2015.2437193
11. Fazel, M.: Matrix rank minimization with applications. Ph.D. dissertation, Ph.D. thesis, Stanford University (2002)
12. Candès, E.J., Recht, B.: Exact matrix completion via convex optimization. Found. Comput. Math. **9**(6), 717–772 (2009)
13. Liu, M., Chen, S., Liu, J., Tang, X.: Video completion via motion guided spatial-temporal global optimization. In: Proceedings of the 17th ACM International Conference on Multimedia, pp. 537–540. ACM (2009)

14. Xiao, Y., Suo, J., Bian, L., Zhang, L., Dai, Q.: Automatic inpainting of linearly related video frames. In: 2014 IEEE International Conference on Image Processing (ICIP), pp. 4692–4696. IEEE (2014)
15. Peng, Y., Ganesh, A., Wright, J., Xu, W., Ma, Y.: Rasl: robust alignment by sparse and low-rank decomposition for linearly correlated images. IEEE Trans. Pattern Anal. Mach. Intell. **34**(11), 2233–2246 (2012)
16. Guo, X., Ma, Y.: Generalized tensor total variation minimization for visual data recovery? In: IEEE Conference on Computer Vision and Pattern Recognition, CVPR 2015, 7–12 June 2015, Boston, MA, USA, pp. 3603–3611 (2015). http://dx.doi.org/10.1109/CVPR.2015.7298983
17. Lowe, D.G.: Object recognition from local scale-invariant features. In: 1999 The Proceedings of the Seventh IEEE International Conference on Computer Vision, vol. 2, pp. 1150–1157. IEEE (1999)

Head Related Transfer Function Interpolation Based on Aligning Operation

Tingzhao Wu[2,4], Ruimin Hu[1,2,3]([✉]), Xiaochen Wang[2,4], Li Gao[2],
and Shanfa Ke[2]

[1] State Key Laboratory of Software Engineering, Wuhan University, Wuhan, China
[2] National Engineering Research Center for Multimedia Software,
Computer School of Wuhan University, Wuhan, China
{Tingzhao_Wu,gllynnie}@126.com, hrm@whu.edu.cn, {clowang,kimmyfa}@163.com
[3] Hubei Provincial Key Laboratory of Multimedia
and Network Communication Engineering, Wuhan University, Wuhan, China
[4] Research Institute of Wuhan University in Shenzhen, Shenzhen, China

Abstract. Head related transfer function (HRTF) is the main technique
of binaural synthesis, which is used to reconstruct spatial sound image,
and the HRTF data only can be obtained by measurement. A high resolution HRTF database contains too many HRTFs, the workload of measurement is too huge to be finished. As a solution, in order to calculate new
HRTF by measured HRTFs, many researchers concentrate on the interpolation of HRTF. But, before interpolating, HRTFs should be aligned
because there is time delay between different HRTFs. Some researchers
try to implement aligning operation based on phase, but the method is not
appropriate since the periodicity of phase. Another idea to align HRTFs
is by detecting method, however, the time difference is too tiny to detect
exactly. None of the methods can provide a good and stable performance.
In this paper, we propose a new method to align HRTFs based on correlation. And the experiments show that the proposed aligning method
improves the accuracy index SDR 18.5 dB for the most, furthermore, the
proposed method could improve the accuracy for all positions.

Keywords: HRTF interpolation · Spatial sound image · Binaural synthesis · Aligning operation

1   Introduction

In 3D audio reconstruction techniques [1], binaural synthesis [2] technique based
on HRTF is applied in the headphone playback environment, as well as multichannel rendering technique [3] is applied in the multiple speakers playback
environment. Binaural synthesis technique attracts more attention because it

The research was supported by National High Technology Research and Development
Program of China (863 Program) (No. 2015AA016306); National Nature Science
Foundation of China (No. 61231015); National Nature Science Foundation of China
(No. 61471271).

E. Chen et al. (Eds.): PCM 2016, Part I, LNCS 9916, pp. 418–427, 2016.
DOI: 10.1007/978-3-319-48890-5_41

is able to reconstruct spatial sound images through mobile terminal, such as mobile phone. Based on it, 3D audio reconstruction becomes more convenient and portable. HRTF is the main technique used in binaural synthesis, it describes the transmission process of sound from source to the ears in free field. Each position in spatial sphere corresponds a unique HRTF, so reconstructing a sound image in a certain position requires the corresponding HRTF [4].

There are many HRTF databases have been established by measurement [5], such as CIPIC HRTF database [6], PKU&IOA HRTF database [7], MIT HRTF database [8], etc. If the resolution of HRTF database is high enough, we can reconstruct a sound image in high quality, especially, when reconstructing a moving sound image, the advantage of high resolution HRTF database is more remarkable. But high resolution HRTF database is hard to establish by measurement because the number of positions needed to cover the whole sphere is too large. As a result, in order to improve the quality of recovered sound images, HRTF interpolation is applied to calculate the HRTF of new position with low resolution HRTF database.

There are many research work about HRTF interpolation have been carried out. Wenzel applied simple linear interpolation method to HRTF [9], Begault and Savioja applied bilinear interpolation method to HRTF [10,11], and Jenison adopted the pole-zero model for interpolation [12]. But the methods mentioned here ignored the time difference between HRTFs. The subsequent scholars took notice of the time difference. For example, Hartung pointed out that the time delay difference should be eliminated before interpolation [13]. And Christensen also stated that interpolation should operate on aligned HRTFs [14]. However, none of them proposed a specific method to implement aligning operation of HRTFs. Refer to HRTF could be modeled with modified phase spectra [15], some research work tried to aligning HRTFs based on phase in frequency domain. But phase is a periodic variable, it is hard to determine the time difference by phase. While in time domain, Matsumoto attempted to correct the arrival time by detecting the time difference [16]. But the time difference is microsecond level, it is too tiny to be detected. And the experiment results in his work were not satisfactory, in some directions, for example, from 95° to 115°, the interpolation accuracy was decreased after aligning operation.

Hence, an effective aligning method is required to be investigated. In this paper we proposed a new aligning method based on correlation, marked as AMBC, and the method could eliminate the time difference, and more details are described in Sect. 3.

This paper is organized as follows. Section 2 reviews the classical methods, such as linear and bilinear method. Section 3 discusses the proposed aligning method in detail, and we also try to combine different methods to further improve interpolation accuracy. Experiments and some discussions about the results are provided in Sect. 4. The conclusion is drawn in Sect. 5.

2   Related Work

Linear method and bilinear method are widely used methods to interpolation. Linear method calculates the HRTF of target position by the HRTFs of two

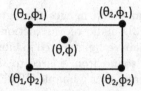

(θ_1,ϕ_1) (θ_2,ϕ_1)

(θ,ϕ)

(θ_1,ϕ_2) (θ_2,ϕ_2)

Fig. 1. Bilinear method sketch map.

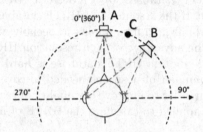

Fig. 2. Distance from source to ears. The distances from A and B to left ear are different, so the sound from A and B arrival at left ear in different time. HRTF of position C can be calculated with HRTFs of A and B.

linear adjacent positions, refer to [17], it can be expressed by formula as:

$$HRTF(\theta,\phi) = \frac{\theta_2 - \theta}{\theta_2 - \theta_1}HRTF(\theta_1,\phi) + \frac{\theta - \theta_1}{\theta_2 - \theta_1}HRTF(\theta_2,\phi) \qquad (1)$$

Where θ, ϕ represent the azimuth angle and elevation angle of target position respectively, $HRTF(\theta,\phi)$ represents the HRTF data of position (θ,ϕ), and $\theta_1 < \theta < \theta_2$.

Bilinear method is similar to linear method, the target position is inside a rectangle, and its HRTF can be calculated by the HRTFs of four vertexes, as shown in Fig. 1.
The $HRTF(\theta,\phi)$ can be calculated by [11]:

$$HRTF(\theta,\phi) = \alpha\beta HRTF(\theta_2,\phi_1) + (1-\alpha)(1-\beta)HRTF(\theta_1,\phi_2) \\ + (1-\alpha)\beta HRTF(\theta_1,\phi_1) + \alpha(1-\beta)HRTF(\theta_2,\phi_2) \qquad (2)$$

Where $\alpha = \frac{\theta_2 - \theta}{\theta_2 - \theta_1}$ and $\beta = \frac{\phi_1 - \phi}{\phi_1 - \phi_2}, \theta_1 < \theta < \theta_2$ and $\phi_2 < \phi < \phi_1$.

The time difference is an important feature of HRTF, and relates to azimuth angles. For example, as shown in Fig. 2, the distances from position A and B to left ear are different, so the arrival time of sound from A and B would be different. So simple interpolation cant calculate the right arrival time of target HRTF, and wrong arrival time would lead to an inaccurate interpolation result. In order to get a better interpolation result, Matsumoto thought up an idea to eliminate the time difference by detecting it [16], but the time difference was difficult to detect exactly. And the experiment results showed the performance of detecting method was unstable, because in some positions, his method even leaded to a worse interpolation result.

So a steady and easily accomplished method to align HRTFs needs to be proposed. And by this we can ensure a better interpolation result, so that we can reconstruct a moving sound image more smoothly.

3   Proposed Method

First in this chapter, we illuminate the proposed AMBC method refer to Fig. 2. It is known to all, HRTF data contains two channels, one is the HRTF data of left ear and the other is of right ear. If we want to obtain the left ear HRTF data of the position C, we should eliminate the arrival time difference between left ear HRTF data of position A and B. Assuming that if we modify the arrival time exactly, the left ear HRTF data of position A and B would have the highest correlation, so we proposed the aligning method based on correlation.

The framework of AMBC is described in Fig. 3.

From the Fig. 3, we can divide AMBC method into three steps. First is to panning the operation HRTF, and the process is marked as:

$$pan\_HRTF[m] = pan\_Function\{Operation\_HRTF, m\} \tag{3}$$

Where *pan_HRTF* represents the operation HRTF after panning, *pan_Function*$\{\cdot\}$ means panning the HRTF by m samplepoints, and $0 \leq m \leq N$, N is specified by user. The second step is to calculate the correlation of reference HRTF and panned operation HRTF, it can be expressed as:

$$array[m] = corCal\{Reference\_HRTF, pan\_HRTF[m]\} \tag{4}$$

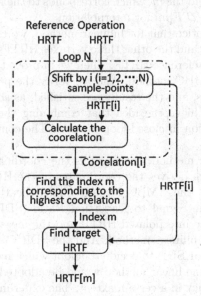

Fig. 3. The flow chart of AMBC method. Input of the AMBC method are the reference HRTF and operation HRTF. It should be noticed that the reference HRTF is the HRTF data of position A (or B), while the operation HRTF is the HRTF data of position B (or A).

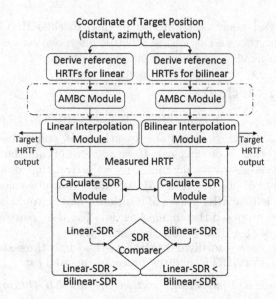

Fig. 4. The flow chart of proposed framework.

Where $corCal\{\cdot\}$ is used to calculate the correlation value of $Reference\_HRTF$ and pan_HRTF, and $array$ stores the value.

The last step is to find the m, which corresponds to the maximum correlation, and output the $pan\_HRTF[m]$ for interpolation.

It is necessary to notice that for bilinear method, we choose a vertex HRTF as the reference HRTF, and the other three vertexes HRTFs are operated to keep aligned with the same reference HRTF. Then we improve the linear method and bilinear method by AMBC method. And we verify the performance of AMBC method by experiments, and the results are satisfied, as shown in Sect. 4.

Besides, we also achieve the idea that combining the linear interpolation and bilinear interpolation in closed-loop manner. The combination process was described in Fig. 4.

In the combination method, the input is the coordinate of target position HRTF, then the system derives the coordinates of the HRTFs which are used to interpolation. Next, the AMBC Module aligns the HRTFs to prepare for interpolation. Then the Signal to Distortion Ratio (SDR) Module calculates the SDR value with the interpolated HRTF and the measured HRTF of target position for linear and bilinear method. And the SDR Comparer compares the Linear_SDR and Bilinear_SDR to decide to adopt which method, for example, if Linear_SDR is larger, the linear method would be adopted. By this method, we can improve the accuracy in a certain extent. The experiment results are shown in Sect. 4.

It should be noticed that after interpolating, the arrival time of target position HRTF is ought to be recovered. A direct method is to calculate the time difference between the reference HRTF and the operation HRTF by the number of m, and half of the time difference adds the arrival time of reference HRTF is the arrival time of the target position HRTF. We also verify the performance through experiments in next chapter.

4   Experiments and Results

In this chapter, we carry out three experiments to verify the performance of our work. First experiment verifies the aligning effect of AMBC method, and second experiment is about to observe the improvement of accuracy after applying AMBC method to interpolate, the last experiment aims to ensure the combination of different method can further increase the accuracy.

The experiments are carried out on the PKU&IOA HRTF database [7], which is measured on Chinese people and sorted by five distances, seventy-three azimuth angles and fourteen elevation angles. We choose one distance, twenty five azimuth angles and three elevation angles to be interpolated, which is displayed in Table 1. And the interpolation experiments are carried out on the left channel of HRTF, since the HRTF data of two channels are processed individually by the same steps when interpolating. And the interpolation experiments are carried out on the left channel of HRTF, since the HRTF data of two channels are processed individually by the same steps when interpolating.

The first experiment is carried out to verify the precision of AMBC method. In the experiment we choose three HRTFs of azimuths $(20°, 30°, 40°)$ on horizontal plan as test HRTFs, the original data is shown in Fig. 5. While after operated by AMBC method, the result is shown in Fig. 6.

As shown in Fig. 5, the response of HRTFs started at different samplepoints, for example, the responses of azimuth angle $20°$, $30°$ and $40°$ respectively started

Table 1. The list of target positions

Distance:cm	Azimuth:°	Elevation:°
75	300, 305, ..., 355, 0,5, ... 55, 60	−10
75	300, 305, ..., 355, 0,5, ... 55, 60	0
75	300, 305, ..., 355, 0,5, ... 55, 60	10

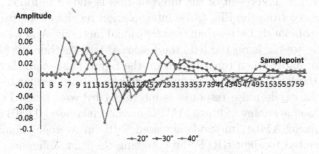

Fig. 5. The waveform of HRTFs before aligned operation (elevation angle is $0°$).

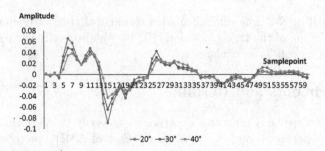

Fig. 6. The waveform of HRTFs after aligned operation (elevation angle is 0°).

at the fourth point, the seventh point and the tenth point. That means the sound from different azimuths arrive at our left ear on different time. While, as shown in Fig. 6, the three waveforms are aligned exactly. So the AMBC method could eliminated the time difference.

The second experiment intends to test the performance of interpolation method enhanced by AMBC method. In this experiment, we select the second row in Table 1 as the target positions.

We use the parameter Signal to Distortion Ratio (SDR) to evaluate the accuracy of interpolation method [16]. The SDR can be derived by:

$$SDR = 10lg \frac{HRTF(\theta,\phi)}{HRTF(\theta,\phi) - I\_HRTF(\theta,\phi)} \tag{5}$$

Where $HRTF(\theta,\phi)$ represents the measured HRTF of target position, while $I\_HRTF(\theta,\phi)$ is the interpolated result.

In linear interpolation, we choose two reference HRTFs to calculate the target HRTF. For example, we define the distance is 75, we interpolate the HRTF of the point (azimuth 305, elevation 0) by the two HRTFs of point (azimuth 300, elevation 0) and point (azimuth 310, elevation 0). In bilinear interpolation, we use the HRTFs of four vertexes to calculate the HRTF of the position inside. For instance, we derive the HRTF (azimuth 305, elevation 0) by four vertexes HRTFs (azimuth 300, elevation −10; azimuth 300, elevation 10; azimuth 310, elevation −10; azimuth 310, elevation 10). Then we use the measured HRTF of the point (azimuth 305, elevation 0) and the result of interpolation to calculate the SDR by Eq. 5. The result of the interpolation is shown in follow picture.

As we can see from the Fig. 7, the interpolation results of the two enhanced methods were obviously better than the traditional methods. And we also learned that when the source is on the left, the linear_AMBC method performs better than its performance when the source is on the right. That might because when source is on the left, the left ear impulse response is more similar to the reality while the right ear impulse response is interfered by your head. Furthermore, the interpolation accuracy of linear_AMBC method increased 9.6 dB on average, while the bilinear_AMBC method increased 7 dB on average. Similarly, Matsumoto attempted to align HRTFs by detecting the time difference, but experiment results showed his method might have a worse interpolation result after

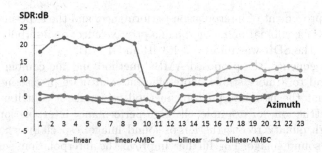

Fig. 7. The accuracy of different interpolation methods when distance is 75. Where linear_AMBC means the interpolation result of linear method enhanced by AMBC method, and so is bilinear_AMBC.

Table 2. The average SDR of three methods

Method	Distance:cm	SDR:dB
Linear_method	75	13.6
Bilinear_method	75	10.8
Combination method	75	14.9

aligning operation in some positions [16]. While as shown in Fig. 7, the AMBC method is more sable since it can improve the interpolation accuracy for each position.

The third experiment plans to verify the combination method could further improve the accuracy of interpolation. We also choose the target positions as the same as the second experiment. And we derive the SDR of linear_AMBC method, bilinear_AMBC method and combination method (Table 2).

From the table we can learn that the combination method even has a better performance than enhanced single method. Compared with linear_AMBC and bilinear_AMBC method, combination method, respectively, increases the SDR 1.3 dB and 4.1 dB on average. The reason is the combination method selects the better method from above two enhanced methods. For example, in Fig. 7, when the source is on the left, the combination method would choose the linear_AMBC method. In other words, the combination method could take the advantage of different methods and improve the interpolation accuracy for each position.

5   Conclusion

The method proposed in this paper has two innovations. First is also the major innovation, AMBC method is based on correlation, so it is more exactly than the aligned method based on phase, and it is more easily to accomplish compared with detecting method. And the AMBC method could bring a great progress to HRTF interpolation, the experiments showed that it could increase SDR 11.1 dB and 10.3 dB respectively. Second, we combined the two enhanced methods to get a further improvement of interpolation performance, and the experiment results proved that the combination method had a positive effect on interpolation. After combination, the SDR was improved 1.3 dB and 4.1 dB.

As a consequence, the proposed AMBC method and the combination manner could lead to a more stable, more efficient, and more precise interpolation result. So that the new interpolation method can make a contribution to 3D audio reconstruction, for example, the high performance interpolation of HRTF supports high quality reconstruction of sound image, especially when recovering moving sound image. For further improve the interpolation performance, we need to focus on how to recover the arrival time of target HRTF. At last, the continuous work may even promote the development of moving 3D audio technology.

References

1. Begault, D.R.: 3-D Sound for Virtual Reality and Multimedia. AP Professional, Boston (1994)
2. Freeland, F.P., Biscainho, L.W.P, Diniz, P.S.R.: Efficient HRTF interpolation in 3D moving sound. In: Audio Engineering Society Conference: 22nd International Conference on Virtual, Synthetic, and Entertainment Audio. Audio Engineering Society (2002)
3. Herre, J., Kjörling, K., Breebaart, J., et al.: MPEG surround-the ISO/MPEG standard for efficient and compatible multichannel audio coding. J. Audio Eng. Soc. 56(11), 932–955 (2008)
4. Carlile, S., Jin, C., Van Raad, V.: Continuous virtual auditory space using HRTF interpolation: acoustic and psychophysical errors. In: Proceedings of the First IEEE Pacific-Rim Conference on Multimedia, pp. 220–223 (2000)
5. Gardner, W.G., Martin, K.D.: HRTF measurements of a KEMAR. J. Acoust. Soc. Am. 97(6), 3907–3908 (1995)
6. Algazi, V.R., Duda, R.O., Thompson, D.M. et al.: The CIPIC HRTF database. In: 2001 IEEE Workshop on the Applications of Signal Processing to Audio and Acoustics, pp. 99–102. IEEE (2001)
7. Qu, T., Xiao, Z., Gong, M., et al.: Distance-dependent head-related transfer functions measured with high spatial resolution using a spark gap. IEEE Trans. Audio Speech Lang. Process. 17(6), 1124–1132 (2009)
8. Gardner, B., Martin, K.: HRFT measurements of a KEMAR dummy head microphone (1994)
9. Wenzel, E.M., Foster, S.H.: Perceptual consequences of interpolating head-related transfer functions during spatial synthesis. In: 1993 IEEE Workshop on Applications of Signal Processing to Audio and Acoustics, Final Program and Paper Summaries, pp. 102–105. IEEE (1993)
10. Begault, D.R.: 3D Sound for Virtual Reality and Multimedia. Academic Press, Cambridge (1994)
11. Savioja, L., Huopaniemi, J., Lokki, T., et al.: Creating interactive virtual acoustic environments. J. Audio Eng. Soc. 47(9), 675–705 (1999)
12. Jenison, R.L.: A spherical basis function neural network for pole-zero modeling of head-related transfer functions. In: 1995 IEEE ASSP Workshop on Applications of Signal Processing to Audio and Acoustics, pp. 92–95. IEEE (1995)

13. Hartung, K., Braasch, J., Sterbing, S.J.: Comparison of different methods for the interpolation of head-related transfer functions. In: Audio Engineering Society Conference: 16th International Conference: Spatial Sound Reproduction. Audio Engineering Society (1999)
14. Christensen, F., Møller, H., Minnaar, P., et al.: Interpolating between head-related transfer functions measured with low-directional resolution. In: Audio Engineering Society Convention 107. Audio Engineering Society (1999)
15. Kulkarni, A., Isabelle, S.K., Colburn, H.S.: On the minimum-phase approximation of head-related transfer functions. In: 1995 IEEE ASSP Workshop on Applications of Signal Processing to Audio and Acoustics, pp. 84–87. IEEE (1995)
16. Matsumoto, M., Yamanaka, S., Toyama, M., et al.: Effect of arrival time correction on the accuracy of binaural impulse response interpolation-interpolation methods of binaural response. J. Audio Eng. Soc. **52**(1/2), 56–61 (2004)
17. Dyn, N., Levin, D., Rippa, S.: Data dependent triangulations for piecewise linear interpolation. IMA J. Numer. Anal. **10**(1), 137–154 (1990)

Adaptive Multi-window Matching Method for Depth Sensing SoC and Its VLSI Implementation

Huimin Yao, Chenyang Ge[✉], Liuqing Yang, Yichuan Fu, and Jianru Xue

Institute of Artificial Intelligence and Robotics,
Shaanxi Digital Technology and Intelligent System,
Xi'an Jiaotong University, Xi'an, China
huimin.yao@stu.xjtu.edu.cn,
{cyge,jrxue}@mail.xjtu.edu.cn

Abstract. This paper presents the full VLSI implementation of adaptive multi-window matching method for depth sensing system on a chip (SoC) based on active infrared structured light, which estimates the 3D scene depth by matching randomized speckle patterns, akin to the Microsoft Kinect. We present a simple and efficient hardware structure for the adaptive multi-window block-matching-disparity estimation algorithm, which facilitates rapid generation of disparity maps in real-time. Then the disparity map is calculated to the depth value according to the triangulation principle. We have implemented these ideas in an end-to-end SoC using FPGA and demonstrate that our depth sensing SoC can ensure the matching accuracy and improve the details of depth maps, such as, small objects and the edge of objects.

Keywords: Multi-window matching · Depth sensing SoC · VLSI

1 Introduction

Vision is the most direct and important way for human to observe and understand the world. Human vision not only can perceive the surface brightness, color, texture, shape, motion of the objects, but also can distinguish its spatial position and distance to the viewer. If high precision 3D depth information can be acquired in real-time in machine vision systems, it will facilitate building higher intelligence in a machine vision system. "Virtual world is infinitely close to the real world; human-computer interaction model will become more natural, intuitive and immersive". As "gateway device" between a physical reality world and virtual online world, 3D depth sensing technology achieve the interaction among human, machine, and the virtual networks. Recent advances in 3D depth sensors such as Microsoft Kinect [1] have meanwhile created many opportunities for many application fields, such as industrial, medical, consumer electronics and other areas, such as driver assistance, industrial designing, 3D printing, medical imaging, and 3D vision for internet of things [2–5]. The 3D depth sensors can also facilitate a wide variety of applications applied on electronic devices, such as smart

E. Chen et al. (Eds.): PCM 2016, Part I, LNCS 9916, pp. 428–437, 2016.
DOI: 10.1007/978-3-319-48890-5_42

TVs, smart phones, smart home appliances, and tablets and PCs, to make the devices more intelligent. That is, it builds human-machine interfaces that allow human to interact and control the devices more naturally with facial expressions, gestures, or body actions for users.

The fully studied methods for acquiring depth information can be classified into two categories: passive methods and active methods. In the active depth sensing method, Time of Flight (ToF) and structured light are mainly used. Based on these methods, several international giant companies, such as, Apple, Google, Microsoft, Intel, Samsung and so on, have invested considerable human and material resources into depth perception technologies. In 2010, Microsoft first released the somatosensory equipment-Kinect, the principle of which is based on structured light. While the Kinect One issued in 2013 also by Microsoft Co. is based on ToF principle [6]. And Microsoft holographic visor "Hololens" has appeared on the market in 2015. In 2013, Apple purchase Primesense Co. and claim an invention Patent "Depth Perception Device and System (application number: 20130027548)", intends to employ it as input devices of human-machine interfaces for their product. In the early 2014, Intel announced a three-dimensional depth imaging device "RealSense 3D Camera" [7]. In February 2014, Google announced a new project "Tango" [8], intends to make a smart phone with 3D visual recognition capabilities.

In this paper, We present a multi-window adaptive matching method for depth sensing SoC. The system is based on infrared structured light coding and can generate real-time three-dimensional depth information with high-resolution, high-precision. The rest of this paper is organized as follows. Section 2 describes the depth sensing system and the over-all architecture of depth sensing SoC. Section 3 gives some experiment results. Section 4 summarizes and concludes this paper.

2 Depth Sensing System

This section will describe the detail of the whole depth sensing method.

2.1 Principle of Depth Sensing Based on Active Structured Light

The principle of the structured light depth sensing has been an active area of research for decades. Typically, the system is composed of a pattern projector and one or more cameras. Figure 1 is the schematic diagram of depth sensing system we used in this paper. Our system contains one camera. The designed speckle pattern formed by the interference of certain wavelength light is projected onto an object in the scene, and deformed by the geometric shape of the surface of the object. The camera captures the deformed pattern. By analyzing the distortion of the observed pattern to get the disparity from the original projected pattern, then the depth information can be extracted. The projector used in our system is originally designed and developed by PrimeSense Co. Since the light source is near-infrared laser, it is less sensitive to the ambient light within a certain distance range compared with visible light sources.

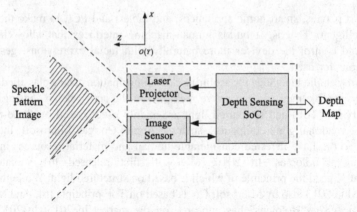

Fig. 1. The schematic diagram of depth sensing system based on active structured light

2.2   Architecture of Depth Sensing SoC

In this section, we present the architecture of depth sensing SoC. Figure 2 is the block diagram of the system pipeline, which includes modules for speckle pattern pre-processing, adaptive block-matching-based disparity estimation, depth calculation, depth mapping to grayscale, video scaling and so on. The details of the signal processing: firstly, the speckle pattern sequence (depth is unknown) is input from the external image sensor and then sent to the pre-processing module by consistency enhancement [9] in order to remove noise and improve the contrast of the speckle spots. Secondly, the disparity between the input speckle image and reference speckle image (depth is known as the benchmark) is calculated by the multi-window adaptive disparity estimation in the block-matching-disparity estimation module. Thirdly, the function of the depth calculation module calculates the depth information according to the triangle ranging formula. Finally, the depth value is one-to-one mapped to the gray value which is utilized to indicate the distance from the scene or object to the image sensor and then the gray image is output through the video scaling module to adapt to the different video formats. In our depth sensing SoC, the reference speckle pattern is first processed by the speckle pattern preprocessing module, and then fixed and stored in memory. In all other operations, the SoC only needs to read the reference speckle pattern from memory and matched with the captured speckle pattern image.

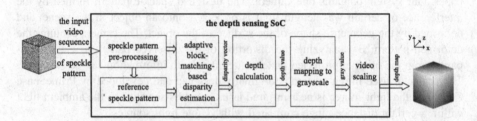

Fig. 2. Architecture of depth sensing SoC

2.3   Adaptive Multi-window Block-Matching-Disparity Estimation

The key problem of depth sensing we proposed is to exactly find the optimal disparity of image block extracted form input speckle video relative to the reference speckle image. In the matching process, the block matching accuracy and the spatial resolution of the depth map is directly affected by the selected size of the support window. The bigger size is conducive to the elimination of mismatch noise and well fit for the father distance in vertical direction from the reference position. But it make the spatial resolution of the X-Y direction reduce, furthermore, some details of the depth information are lost. Though smaller size is easily interfered by mismatch, the accuracy of the closer distance in depth direction can be ensured. So we employ the smaller size for the support window in the closer distance relative to the reference image to maintain the details and the X-Y direction's resolution of the depth map.

In this paper, we present a multi-window adaptive block-matching-disparity estimation method to find the optimal disparity. Fist, find the optimal matching block for image blocks of different sizes and get the corresponding disparity. Then, under certain constraints adaptively select the optimal disparity used to depth calculation. The detailed structure of the Multi-window adaptive matching algorithm module is shown in Fig. 3. The process is described as follows.

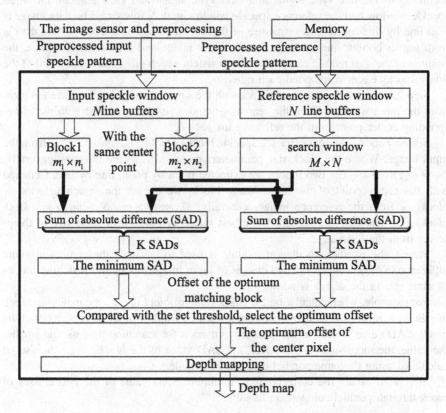

Fig. 3. The structure of the multi-window adaptive matching algorithm module

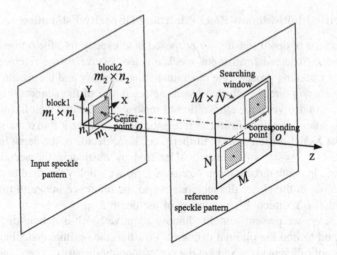

Fig. 4. The schematic representation of image block and search window

Step 1, the input image and the reference speckle image are read in N line buffers according to the line sync signal and field sync signal and then generate the input speckle window and the reference speckle window with N row size. The data image is read line by line forming the structure of the line buffers. The latency of line data is from top to bottom line by line. For the input image and the reference image, the position of the start read-in row is mutual consistent which make the center point of the image blocks easier correspond each other.

Step 2, we extract two image blocks with the same center point, but different sizes from the input window. Then the searching window is also extracted with the corresponding center point from the reference image.

Figure 4 shows the two extracted speckle blocks $block1_{m_1 \times n_1}$, $block2_{m_2 \times n_2}$ from the input image. Where the block size parameters m_1, m_2, n_1, n_2 are integers, generally, $m_1 > m_2, n_1 > n_2$. The two blocks are extracted point by point, line by line. Centered with the center point of the input image block, we extract the searching window $block_{M \times N}$ from the reference image, generally, $M > m_1 > m_2$, $N > m_1 > m_2$. Both $block1_{m_1 \times n_1}$ and $block2_{m_2 \times n_2}$ search the best matching block with same size of themselves from the $block_{M \times N}$.

Step 3, the parallel calculation module is used to calculate the sum of absolute difference (SAD) between the two classes of input image blocks and matching blocks of same size in the search window.

For example, when calculating the SAD value of $block1_{m_1 \times n_1}$, the matching block of size $m_1 \times n_1$ need to be extracted from the search window of the same size out of the block. SAD value is used as the similarity criterion for searching process, the smaller the value, the more similar. Moreover, the SAD value of the $block2_{m_2 \times n_2}$ can also be calculated using the same parallel calculation module.

Step 4, to obtain the corresponding minimum SAD value of the two classes of block through parallel comparison module.

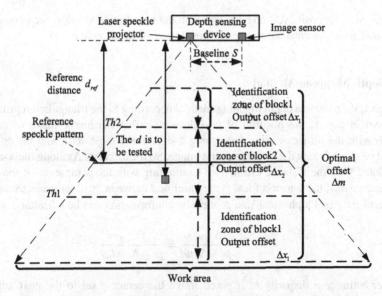

Fig. 5. The schematic representation for selecting the optimal disparity

After obtaining the all SAD values of the $block1_{m_1 \times n_1}$, we find the minimum SAD relative to the optimal matching block through the parallel comparison module. The disparity of the center of the $block1_{m_1 \times n_1}$ and the optimal matching block is the disparity vector $(\Delta x_1, \Delta y_1)$. The larger disparity represents the vertical distance of the center of the $block1_{m_1 \times n_1}$ is father from the reference plane. Similarly, the corresponding optimum disparity $(\Delta x_2, \Delta y_2)$ of the image block $block2_{m_2 \times n_2}$ is also obtained by the similar parallel structure.

Step 5, according to the threshold $Th1$ and $Th2$ experimentally set, we select the disparity vector from the calculated optimum disparity $(\Delta x_1, \Delta y_1)$, $(\Delta x_2, \Delta y_2)$ as the disparity of the center pixel of the corresponding image block.

As shown in Fig. 5, take the selection of the X-direction disparity as an example. Relative to the reference speckle image (depth is known), the disparity of the father distance is negative, the disparity of the nearer is positive. Compare the Horizontal disparity Δx_1, Δx_2 with the two threshold value $Th1$, $Th2(Th1 > Th2 > 0)$. Then the final disparity can be selected as:

$$\Delta m = \begin{cases} \Delta x_1, & \text{if } \Delta x_1 < 0, \text{ and } |\Delta x_1| > Th1 \\ \Delta x_2, & \text{if } \Delta x_1 < 0, \text{ and } |\Delta x_1| \leq Th1 \\ \Delta x_2, & \text{if } \Delta x_1 > 0, \text{ and } \Delta x_1 \leq Th2 \\ \Delta x_1, & \text{if } \Delta x_1 > 0, \text{ and } \Delta x_1 > Th2 \end{cases} \quad (1)$$

Compare the disparity Δx_1 of the bigger image block with $Th1$, $Th2$. If $|\Delta x_1|$ is greater than the two threshold value, that is, the distance from the reference plane is father. In order to eliminate noise caused by the mismatch problem, we choose Δx_1 as the final result. Oppositely, if $|\Delta x_1|$ is less than the two threshold value, we choose Δx_2 as the final result to enhance the spatial resolution of depth image.

2.4 Depth Mapping Method

In this part, we present a depth mapping method according to the triangulation principle. As shown in Fig. 1, the position of two devices is that the image plane of camera overlaps with the projector after performing a shift along the X-axis, and the epipolar line will be aligned with the scanline of the image. So the disparity Δx along the X-axis is only related with the distance estimation. Combining with the parameters of the reference distance d_{ref}, the sensor's focal f, the baseline s between the laser projector and the sensor and the pixel's physical size μ, the depth information can be calculated as

$$d = d_{ref} - \frac{\Delta x \mu d^2}{fs + \Delta x \mu d} = \frac{fsd_{ref}}{fs + \Delta x \mu d_{ref}} \tag{2}$$

After estimate a disparity of a pixel, move the center pixel to the next adjacent pixel, repeat the steps from 1 to 5 in Sect. 2.3, and map the depth according to formula (2), then we can get the depth map point by point, line by line.

3 Experimental Results

Figure 6 is the test platform of the depth sensing device using FPGA. It is composed of a near-infrared laser speckle projector, infrared image sensor and depth sensing SoC (FPGA). The depth sensing method proposed in this paper is designed by VLSI, and verified correctly on the platform. The platform can also be used as the collection device of speckle pattern.

First, we perform the feasibility analysis about the proposed method. Specifically, we test the matching error rate of vertical planes with different distance under the block

Fig. 6. The depth perception chip

Table 1. The error rate (%) of the test planes at different distance

Distance(m)	0.7	0.9	1.1	1.3	1.5	1.7
25 × 25	0	0	0	0	0	0
15 × 15	0	0	0.0015	0	0	0
Distance(m)	1.9	2.1	2.3	2.5	2.7	2.9
25 × 25	0	0	0	0	0	0
15 × 15	0.0045	0	0.0035	0.008	0.0250	0.0495
Distance(m)	3.1	3.3	3.5	3.7	3.9	4.1
25 × 25	0	0	0	0	0	0
15 × 15	0.0495	0.1	0.0505	0.12	0.33	0.72

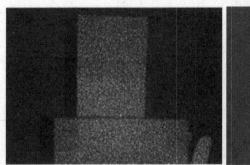 

    (a) the speckle image   (b) our method's depth map

Fig. 7. The real-time output from the depth sensing module

size $m_1 \times n_1$ and $m_2 \times n_2$, where $m_1 = n_1 = 25$, $m_2 = n_2 = 15$. The test range is from 0.7 m to 4.1 m. The Table 1 lists the experimental results. It can conclude that the error rate is mainly greater with the father distance, so we use the bigger block size for the father objects or scenes. While for the location that are much close with the depth sensor, the speckle pattern formed on the surface of objects or scenes are more deformed, so we also use the bigger block size. After testing, we prove that the optimum distance for using the smaller block size $m_2 \times n_2$ is 1.0 m to 2.5 m. The distance is optimal for interaction between users and the characters in the games.

Figure 7 is the real-time output video sequence of the depth sensing device, and (a) is a speckle image collected by the test platform, and (b) is the corresponding depth map, the distance is represented with the gray level, the greater gray value indicates the nearer distance from the laser projector, and vice versa.

In Fig. 8, we test the adaptive multi-window matching method in different scenarios. The first and third column is the color images, following is the corresponding depth maps generated by the multi-window method. Figure 9 shows the 3D reconstruction results of the plaster model. Compared with the Kinect's, the result of our method is more outstanding and the details of face are stereoscopic, especially, the eye part.

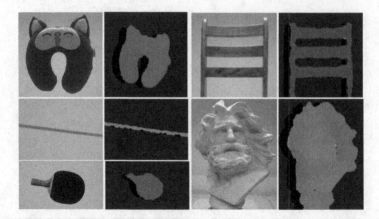

Fig. 8. The test results for different scenarios

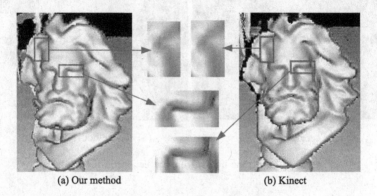

(a) Our method   (b) Kinect

Fig. 9. The results of 3D reconstruction

From the above results, we can conclude that through the adaptive multi-window matching, mismatch noise caused by the wide range block-matching can be reduced under smaller block size, some depth details can be maintained and the resolution of the X-Y direction is also improved.

4 Conclusions

In this paper, based on the active depth sensing method, we propose and implement an adaptive multi-window matching method for disparity estimation and depth perception calculation method based on image block. Through FPGA validation, this method can reduce the mismatching noise caused by the large range search based on block matching, while maintain some depth mapping details, enhance the ability to identify the depth of small objects in the X-Y direction, and finally output the depth video sequence in real time. The depth video is stable and reliable and the interference from ambient light is very small. The real-time depth video can be used for the real-time 3D image recognition, motion capture or scene perception and has broad application prospects in the field of consumer electronics, e-commerce, 3D printing.

Acknowledgment. Supposed by the project of National Natural Science Foundation of China under Grant Nos. 61571358.

References

1. Zhang, Z.: Microsoft kinect sensor and its effect. IEEE Multimedia **19**(2), 4–10 (2012)
2. Harvent, J., Coudrin, B., Brèthes, L., Orteu, J.J., et al.: Multi-view dense 3D modelling of untextured objects from a moving projector-cameras system. Mach. Vis. Appl. **24**(8), 1645–1659 (2013)
3. Rengier, F., Mehndiratta, A., Tengg-Kobligk, H.V., Zechmann, C.M., et al.: 3D printing based on imaging data: review of medical applications. Int. J. Comput. Assist. Radiol. Surg. **5**(4), 335–341 (2010)
4. Nguyen, D.V., Kuhnert, L., Jiang, T., Kuhnert, K.D.: A novel approach of terrain classification for outdoor automobile navigation. In: 2011 IEEE International Conference on Computer Science and Automation Engineering (CSAE), pp. 609–616 (2011)
5. Goesele, M., Curless, B., Seitz, S.M.: Multi-view stereo revisited. In: IEEE Computer Society Conference on Computer Vision & Pattern Recognition, pp. 2402–2409 (2006)
6. Sarbolandi, H., Lefloch, D., Kolb, A.: Kinect range sensing: structured-light versus time-of-flight kinect. Comput. Vis. Image Underst. **139**, 1–20 (2015)
7. http://www.intel.com/content/www/us/en/architecture-and-technology/realsense-overview.html##intel-realsense
8. https://www.google.com/atap/projecttango/
9. Yao, H., Ge, C., Hua, G., Zheng, N.: The VLSI implementation of a high-resolution depth-sensing SoC based on active structured light. Mach. Vis. Appl. **26**(4), 533–548 (2015)

A Cross-Domain Lifelong Learning Model for Visual Understanding

Chunmei Qing, Zhuobin Huang, and Xiangmin Xu[✉]

School of Electronic and Information Engineering,
South China University of Technology, Guangzhou, China
{qchm,xmxu}@scut.edu.cn, huang-zhuobin@qq.com

Abstract. In the study of media machine perception on image and video, people expect the machine to have the ability of lifelong learning like human. This paper, starting from anthropomorphic media perception, researches the multi-media perception which is based on lifelong machine learning. An ideal lifelong machine learning system for visual understanding is expected to learn relevant tasks from one or more domains continuously. However, most existing lifelong learning algorithms do not focus on the domain shift among tasks. In this work, we propose a novel cross-domain lifelong learning model (CD-LLM) to address the domain shift problem on visual understanding. The main idea is to generate a low-dimensional common subspace which captures domain invariable properties by embedding Grassmann manifold into tasks subspaces. With the low-dimensional common subspace, tasks can be projected and then model learning is performed. Extensive experiments are conducted on competitive cross-domain dataset. The results show the effectiveness and efficiency of the proposed algorithm on competitive cross-domain visual tasks.

Keywords: Lifelong machine learning · Visual understanding · Domain shift · CD-LLM

1 Introduction

As we know, we human are capable of continually and efficiently learning new knowledge, holding the lifelong learning capability. In the study of media perception on image and video, people expect the machine system to be capable of learning continually like human. When a new visual task comes, the learning system can leverage previous knowledge to help solve the current task. If the current task is related to one of the previous tasks, valuable knowledge may be shared among these relevant tasks to improve their performances, as studied on transfer learning and multi-task learning [1].

This work is supported in part by the National Natural Science Founding of China under Grant 61171142 and Grant 61401163, Science and Technology Planning Project of Guangdong Province, China under Grant 2011A0108005, Grant 2014B010111003, Grant 2014B010111006 and Grant 2016B010108008, Guangzhou Key Lab of Body Data Science under Grant 201605030011, the Young Innovative Talent in High Education of Guangdong Province under Grant 2014KQNCX015 and the Fundamental Research Funds for the Central Universities under Grant 2015ZZ032.

© Springer International Publishing AG 2016
E. Chen et al. (Eds.): PCM 2016, Part I, LNCS 9916, pp. 438–448, 2016.
DOI: 10.1007/978-3-319-48890-5_43

Lifelong machine learning is such an agent that considers learning tasks sequentially and retaining knowledge from previous tasks for better learning new tasks.

Lifelong machine learning is similar to multi-task learning. Multi-task learning tries to improve the performance of all the tasks at high computational cost. When the number of tasks is very large, multi-task learning may be inefficient. On the contrast, lifelong machine learning focuses on generalizing new samples and new tasks with the knowledge learnt from existing tasks. Some early papers on lifelong machine learning emphasized on learning distance metric [2] and sharing structure in neural network [3]. Silver et al. presented a theory of task knowledge consolidation that uses two multi-task learning networks [4–6], one for long-term consolidation using task rehearsal to overcome the stability-plasticity problem and a second for using task rehearsal to selectively transfer prior knowledge. Otherwise, Silver presented a survey on lifelong machine learning system [7]. Some recent work has explored task cluster [8], creating online multi-task learners [1, 9] and feature learner [10]. In particular, Ruvolo and Eaton proposed an efficient lifelong learning algorithm (ELLA) that incorporated aspects of both transfer and multi-task learning together [1]. The authors took parametric approach and the task-specific parameter vector is assumed to be represented by the linear combination of shared model component. Their method showed identical accuracy of batching multi-task learning with short runtime on synthetic data and three multi-task problems. However, ELLA runs slowly when faced with high-dimensionality data and it doesn't consider the domain shift problem. We know that our brain is capable of transferring cross-domain knowledge and dealing with various tasks from different domains. For example, after we learn how to distinguish dog and cat, we can also distinguish them in any other places.

In order to simulate human brain, addressing the domain shift is essential for creating an ideal machine learning system on visual understanding which is expected to handle problems from various domains. In this paper, we present a cross-domain lifelong learning model (CD-LLM) for visual understanding to deal with the domain shift between visual tasks on a lifelong learning setting. Firstly, the subspaces of each visual task are viewed as a point of Grassmann manifold and then intermediate subspaces are generated with the geodesic flow between the subspaces. Secondly, each task is projected into the intermediate space. Lastly, model learning is performed, which is similar to ELLA. We test the proposed CD-LLM on cross-domain image datasets. Extensive experiment results show that the proposed CD-LLM outperforms the ELLA on a cross-domain lifelong learning setting with short runtime.

2 The Cross-Domain Lifelong Learning Model for Visual Understanding

Our main idea is to introduce cross-domain transfer into the lifelong learning framework for visual understanding. Specifically, we project visual tasks from different domains into a common space and perform an existing lifelong machine algorithm.

2.1 Problem Description

A cross-domain lifelong machine learning system for visual understanding deals with a collection of visual tasks $(Z^{(1)}, Z^{(2)}, \ldots, Z^{(t)}, \ldots)$. The samples of each task are generated from the corresponding instance space. In the collection of tasks $Z^{(t)} = \{D^{(t)}, f^{(t)}, X^{(t)}, Y^{(t)}\}$, $f^{(t)}$ is the mapping function of $X^{(t)} - > Y^{(t)}$, $D^{(t)}$ is the data distribution of task t, $X^{(t)}$ is the instance space of task t and $Y^{(t)}$ is the label space of task t. When a new task arrives, the system uses the training samples of the new task and the knowledge learnt from previous task to train a model $f^{(t)}$ for the new task. After training the model, the knowledge system is updated, and the knowledge from new task is integrated into the system. In this process, the distribution of new task is unknown to the system and it may be the same with or different from previous tasks.

Most existing lifelong learning algorithms suppose that the new task has the same data distribution with previous tasks, such as the state-of-art lifelong learning algorithm ELLA [1]. In ELLA, a repository of k latent model components $L \in R^{d \times k}$ is learnt and maintained, which forms a basis for all task models and serves as the mechanism for knowledge transfer between tasks. For each task t, ELLA learns a model $f(x; \theta) = \theta^T x$ which is parameterized by a d-dimensional task-specific vector $\theta^{(t)} = Ls^{(t)}$ represented as a sparse linear combination of the columns of L using the weight vector $s^{(t)} \in \mathbb{R}^K$. The specific form of $f^{(t)}(x)$ is dependent on the base learning algorithm, as described below. With the training data, ELLA optimizes the predictive loss of each model. At the same time, the existence of L forces each model to share structure. The objective function is formulated as following:

$$e_T(L) = \frac{1}{T} \sum_{t=1}^{T} \min_{s^{(t)}} \{ \frac{1}{n_t} \sum_{i=1}^{n_t} \ell(f(x_i^{(t)}; Ls^{(t)}), y_i^{(t)}) + \mu \|s^{(t)}\|_1 \} + \lambda \|L\|_F^2, \tag{1}$$

where ℓ is a known loss function for fitting the model (e.g. squared loss or log loss). This optimization problem is closely related to a number of batch MTL algorithms, such as GO-MTL [11]. Equation (1) is not jointly convex in L and $s^{(t)}$, and so most batch MTL methods yield a local optimum using an alternating optimization procedure which is prohibitively expensive for lifelong learning.

ELLA achieves good results on multi-task datasets with promising time cost. However, the speed of original ELLA progressively slows as the dimensionality become high. More important, ELLA proposed to optimal $s^{(t)}$ only on task t and if task t is from different domain negative transfer is probably brought in, which hurts the performance of lifelong learning system. To address the domain shift and dimensionality problem, we propose a novel cross-domain efficient lifelong learning algorithm.

2.2 Proposed CD-LLM

Domain adaption algorithms try to characterize and address domain shift problem. One of the mainstream ideas is to fix a befitting common space to capture domain invariable properties. To address the dimensionality problem, based on the above discussion, a nature idea is to capture a lower dimensional subspace for projection. Gopalan et al.

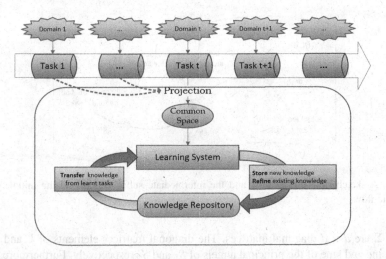

Fig. 1. The block diagram of our cross domain efficient lifelong learning system.

[12] presented to create intermediate subspaces between two domains by embedding Grassmann manifold into two domains and integrating the meaningful subspaces along geodesic between them. Different domains are then projected into those intermediate subspaces. Their method does not make any assumption on feature distribution and the experiment results validate the effectiveness of the proposed algorithm. In this paper, we use a similar method for obtaining meaningful subspaces. The framework of the proposed CD-LLM is shown in Fig. 1. The proposed approach consists of three main steps.

Step I: Generate geodesic flow. Given two subspaces, our goal is to generate useful intermediate for projection. Considering requirement of the consistence of geometry, Gopalan's work identified the space of d-dimensional subspaces in R^N with the Grassmann manifold. Then they defined the subspaces as the points of the Grassmann manifold. They work out the geodesic flow through the properties and statistical analysis methods of Grassmann manifold [13].

Next, we present how to construct the geodesic flow by formula (2). Let S_1, S_2 denote two sets of basic of the subspaces for the first and the second tasks, $R_1 \in R^{D \times (D-d)}$ denotes the orthogonal complement to S_1. The geodesic flow is parameterized as $\Psi : q \in [0, 1] \to \Psi(q) \in G(d, D)$ under the constraints $\Psi(0) = S_1$ and $\Psi(1) = S_2$. For other q,

$$\Psi(q) = S_1 U_1 \Gamma(q) - R_1 U_2 \Sigma(q) \tag{2}$$

where $U_1 \in R^{d \times d}$ and $U_2 \in R^{(D-d) \times d}$ are orthonormal matrices, which are given by the following SVDs,

$$S_1^T S_2 = U_1 \Gamma V^T, R_1^T S_2 = -U_2 \Sigma V^T \tag{3}$$

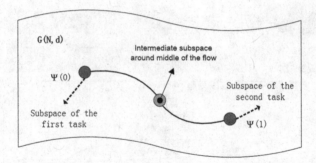

Fig. 2. A sketch of geodesic flow and the intermediate subspaces around the middle of the geodesic flow.

Γ and Σ are $d \times d$ diagonal matrices. The diagonal matrices elements of Γ and Σ are the cosine and sine of the principal angels of S_1 and S_2 respectively. Furthermore, $\Gamma(q)$ and $\Sigma(q)$ are also diagonal matrices whose diagonal matrices elements are the cosine and sine of the principal angels multiply by q. At this point, we obtain the geodesic flow $\Psi(q)$ and we could get an infinite number of subspaces by plugging different $q\,(0 < q < 1)$ into $\Psi(q)$.

Step II: Select optimal subspace for projection to common space. In the previous step, we get a collection of intermediate subspaces $\Psi(q)$, in reference [12], the authors proposed to sample a definite number of intermediate subspaces and then concatenated them to form super-vectors of feature. There are two limitations of this approach. On one hand, the dimensionality of super-vectors is usually high. On the other hand, using too much intermediate subspaces may hurt the generalization performance when the feature spaces of other tasks are different from the ones of the first two tasks.

To this end, we propose to use only one intermediate subspace of the geodesic flow $\Psi(q)$ (in our experiment, set $q = 0.4$). Figure 2 shows the geodesic flow and the middle intermediate subspace. Intuitively, as Fig. 2 shown, the subspaces around the middle of the geodesic flow capture more desirable domain invariant properties than the ones of the endpoint. That is to say, the "middle" subspaces are more suitable for our cross-domain tasks because it has better generalization. The experiment results demonstrate that projection on the "middle" subspaces performs better.

Step III: Model learning. Similarly to ELLA, for the lifelong-long learning objective function (1), we use a second-order Taylor expansion around to replace the inner summation to avoid high computational cost, then the objective function can be rewritten as follows:

$$g_T(L) = \frac{1}{T} \sum_{t=1}^{T} \min_{s^{(t)}} \{ \frac{1}{n_t} ||\theta^{(t)} - L s^{(t)}||_{D^{(t)}}^2 + \mu ||s^{(t)}||_1 \} + \lambda ||L||_F^2, \tag{4}$$

where

$$D^{(t)} = \frac{1}{2}\nabla^2_{\theta,\theta}\frac{1}{n_t}\sum_{i=1}^{n_t}\ell(f(x_i^{(t)};\theta),y_i^{(t)})|_{\theta=\theta^{(t)}}, \tag{5}$$

$$\theta^{(t)} = \arg_\theta \min \frac{1}{n_t}\sum_{i=1}^{n_t}\ell(f(x_{P_i}^{(t)};\theta),y_i^{(t)}). \tag{6}$$

$x_{P_i}^{(t)}$ denotes the i-th sample of task t after projection, n_t denotes the number of training samples of tasks t. When new task arrives, we first perform subspace projection according to step I, II. After projection, to update our model, we have to compute $s^{(t)}$ and update L. We use a single task learner to obtain model parameter $\theta^{(t)}$ and with $\theta^{(t)}$, $D^{(t)}$ can be computed. Next, we use the bias L_m to compute $s^{(t)}$. Finally, we update knowledge L as Eq. (9).

The optimization of $s^{(t)}$ is shown in Eq. (7).

$$s^{(t)} \leftarrow \arg\min_{s^{(t)}} l(L_m, s^{(t)}, \theta^{(t)}, D^{(t)}) \tag{7}$$

$$L_{m+1} \leftarrow \arg\min_L \hat{g}_m(L), \tag{8}$$

$$\hat{g}_m(L) = \lambda||L||_F^2 + \frac{1}{T}\sum_{t=1}^{T}l(L, s^{(t)}, \theta^{(t)}, D^{(t)}), \tag{9}$$

where

$$l(L, s, \theta, D) = \mu||s||_1 + ||\theta - Ls||_D^2. \tag{10}$$

For function (9), we null its gradient and solve L. Then the updated L can be represented as $A^{-1}b$, where

$$A = \lambda I_{d\times k, d\times k} + \frac{1}{T}\sum_{t=1}^{T}(s^{(t)}s^{(t)T})\otimes D^{(t)} \tag{11}$$

$$b = \frac{1}{T}\sum_{t=1}^{T}vec(s^{(t)T}\otimes(\theta^{(t)T}D^{(t)})) \tag{12}$$

For binary classification, we can use logistic regression as the single task learner. Then, $f(x;\theta) = 1/(1+e^{-\theta^T x})$. When new task arrives, we compute $\theta^{(t)}$ and with $\theta^{(t)}$, we compute $D^{(t)}$ as follows:

$$D^{(t)} = \frac{1}{2n_t}\sum_{i=1}^{n_t}\sigma_i^{(t)}(1-\sigma_i^{(t)})x_i^{(t)}x_i^{(t)T}, \text{ where } \sigma_i^{(t)} = \frac{1}{1+e^{-\theta^{(t)T}x_i^{(t)}}}. \tag{13}$$

At this point we have computed $s^{(t)}$ and updated L, and regression or classification can be performed. The optimization of CD-LLM is summaried in Algorithm 1.

Algorithm 1.CD-LLM

Input: $Z^{(t)} = \{X^{(t)}, Y^{(t)}\}$

Algorithm parameters: k, d, λ, μ, q

Output: bias L and weight $s^{(t)}$

Initialize: $T \leftarrow 0$, $A \leftarrow zeros_{k \times d, k \times d}$, $b \leftarrow zeros_{k \times d, 1}$, $L \leftarrow zeros_{d,k}$ $\Psi \leftarrow$ **Equation (2)**

   While New Tasks ($X^{(t)}, y^{(t)}$) arrives, do

   $X_p^{(t)} \leftarrow X^{(t)} \times \Psi(q)$

   $T \leftarrow T + 1$

   $(\theta^{(t)}, D^{(t)}) \leftarrow$ **singleTaskLearner($X_p^{(t)}, y^{(t)}$)**

   $L \leftarrow zeros_{d,k}$

   $s^{(t)} \leftarrow \arg\min_{s^{(t)}} l(L_m, s^{(t)}, \theta^{(t)}, D^{(t)})$

   $A \leftarrow A + (s^{(t)} s^{(t)T}) \otimes D^{(t)}$

   $b \leftarrow b + vec(s^{(t)T} \otimes (\theta^{(t)T} D^{(t)}))$

   $L \leftarrow mat((\frac{1}{T}A + \lambda I_{k \times d, k \times d})^{-1} \frac{1}{T} b)$

   End while

It is worth mentioning that the original ELLA is designed for binary classification or regression. We extend ELLA to multi-category classification by training ELLA model for each category.

3 Experiment

The experimental settings are listed as follows.

Datasets: Amazon, DSLR, Webcam and Caltech: We use three datasets (Amazon, DSLR, Webcam) of [14] and one dataset (Caltech-256) of [15]. The four datasets are regarded as four tasks respectively. Since the classes of the four dataset make some difference, we select ten common classes out of them, including BACKPACK, TOURINGBIKE, CALCULATOR, HEADPHONES, COMPUTER-KEYBOARD, LAPTOP101, COMPUTER-MONITOR, COMPUTER-MOUSE, COFFEE-MUG and VIDEO-PROJECTOR. Figure 3(a) shows some example images of the four datasets. We could obviously observe that the four datasets come from different domains, which is challenging for existing lifelong learning system. We use SURF for feature extraction [16], and follow the feature extraction setting suggested by [14]. The codebook size is set to 800. And, each image is represented as a 800d histogram vector.

COIL20: COIL20 is an object dataset which consists of twenty objects with 1440 images. The size of each image is 32×32 pixels with grey level. The feature we use is

Amazon   Caltech-256   Dslr   Webcam

(a)   Example images in Amazon, Caltech-256, Dslr and Webcam dataset.

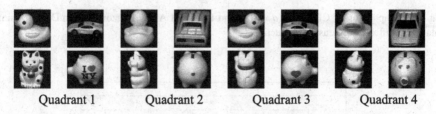

Quadrant 1   Quadrant 2   Quadrant 3   Quadrant 4

(b)   Example images in COIL20 dataset.

Fig. 3. Example images of two datasets used in our experiments.

the original image and thus the dimension is 32×32. For each of the objects, the images are taken every 5 degree on a turntable and there are 72 images of each object. We divide the dataset into 4 part according to 4 quadrants ($[0–85°]$, $[90–175°]$, $[180–265°]$, $[270–355°]$) as in the paper [17]. Each part is regarded as a task to form a cross-view multi-task dataset. Figure 3 (b) shows some example tasks images on COIL20.

Baseline: In [1], the author introduced using PCA to reduce the dimension of the facial expression image, then apply ELLA for classification. For comparision, we use the PCA-ELLA as the baseline.

Setting: We test CD-LLM and the baseline PCA-ELLA by different reduction dimensionality. The maximum of reduction dimensionality is half of feature dimensionality ($800/2 = 400$) due to the SVD decomposition limitation. For each trial, we randomly shuffle the task order. For each task, we randomly chose 20 percent as training samples and the rest 80 percent for test. In our experiments, the parameters of ELLA are all set to default on CD-LLM and PCA-ELLA. Furthermore, we carry out 50 replication tests and report the average results.

Performance: Figures 4 and 5 show the detail accuracy results of CD-LLM ($q = 0.4$) and PCA-ELLA at each dimensionality on two datasets. Compared to PCA-ELLA, our proposed CD-LLM achieves promising performance. In the respect of time cost, as shown in Table 1, our proposed CD-LLM is almost as fast as PCA-ELLA.

In Sect. 2, we discussed how to select the optimal subspace along the geodesic flow. We suggest that the intermediate subspaces around the middle of the geodesic flow has better generationality ability than the ones near the endpoint. Figure 6 shows

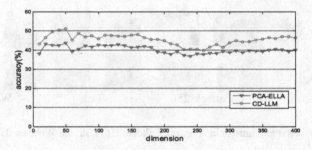

Fig. 4. Comparision of CD-LLM ($q = 0.4$) and PCA-ELLA on Amazon/Caltech/Dslr/webcam dataset by different dimensionalreduction.

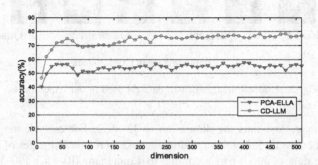

Fig. 5. Comparision of CD-LLM ($q = 0.4$) and PCA-ELLA on COIL20 by different dimensional.

Table 1. Runtime comparision onAmazon/Caltech/Dslr/Webcam and COIL20 datasets

Runtime (s)	Amazon/Caltech/Dslr/Webcam	COIL20
CD-LLM	1.17	11.12
PCA-ELLA	1.11	9.10

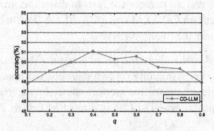

Fig. 6. Performance of CD-LLM with q from 0.1 to 0.9 on Amazon/Caltech/Dslr/webcam.

the results of the proposed CD-LLM with q from 0.1 to 0.9. It is obvious that when q nears the middle, our proposed CD-LLM achieves better performance.

4 Conclusion

To address the domain shift and dimensionality problem, we propose a novel cross-domain lifelong learning model (CD-LLM) for visual understanding. CD-LLM embeds Grassmann manifold into visual tasks subspaces, generates a low-dimensional projection subspace which captures domain invariable properties and performs task projection before model learning. We carry out extensive experiments and the results show that the proposed method gains significant improvement on accuracy against the original ELLA on cross-domain datasets. For future, we will explore more models to address the domain shift of the lifelong learning system for visual understanding.

References

1. Eaton, E., Ruvolo, P.L.: Ella: an efficient lifelong learning algorithm. In: ICML, pp. 507–515 (2013)
2. Thrun, S., O'Sullivan, J.: Discovering structure in multiple learning tasks: the TC algorithm. In: ICML, pp. 489–497 (1996)
3. Thrun, S.: Explanation-Based Neural Network Learning. Springer, New York (1996)
4. Silver, D.L., Alisch, R.: A measure of relatedness for selecting consolidated task knowledge. In: FLAIRS, pp. 399–404 (2005)
5. Silver, D.L., Mercer, R.E.: The parallel transfer of task knowledge using dynamic learning rates based on a measure of relatedness. Connect. Sci. Special Issue: Transf. Inductive Syst. 8(2), 277–294 (1996)
6. Silver, D.L., Mercer, R.E.: The task rehearsal method of life-long learning: overcoming impoverished data. In: Cohen, R., Spencer, B. (eds.) AI 2002. LNCS (LNAI), vol. 2338, pp. 90–101. Springer, Heidelberg (2002). doi:10.1007/3-540-47922-8_8
7. Silver, D.L., Yang, Q., Li, L.: Lifelong machine learning systems: beyond learning algorithms. In: AAAI Spring Symposium: Lifelong Machine Learning, pp. 49–55 (2013)
8. Mishra, M., Huan, J.: Learning task grouping using supervised task space partitioning in lifelong multitask learning. In: ACM CIKM, pp. 1091–1100 (2015)
9. Eaton, E., Ruvolo, P.L.: Active task selection for lifelong machine learning. In: AAAI (2013)
10. Alsharif, O., Bachman, P., Pineau, J.: Lifelong learning of discriminative representations. In: AAAI (2014)
11. Kumar, A., Daume III, H.: Learning task grouping and overlap in multi-task learning. arXiv preprint arXiv:1206.6417 (2012)
12. Gopalan, R., Li, R., Chellappa, R.: Domain adaptation for object recognition: an unsupervised approach. In: IEEE ICCV, pp. 999–1006 (2011)
13. Chikuse, Y.: Procrustes analysis on the special manifolds. In: Springer Statistics on Special Manifolds. Lecture Notes in Statistics, vol. 174, pp. 231–246. Springer, New York (2003)

14. Saenko, K., Kulis, B., Fritz, M., Darrell, T.: Adapting visual category models to new domains. In: Daniilidis, K., Maragos, P., Paragios, N. (eds.) ECCV 2010. LNCS, vol. 6314, pp. 213–226. Springer, Heidelberg (2010). doi:10.1007/978-3-642-15561-1_16
15. Griffin, G., Holub, A., Perona, P.: Caltech-256 object category dataset (2007)
16. Bay, H., Tuytelaars, T., Gool, L.: SURF: speeded up robust features. In: Leonardis, A., Bischof, H., Pinz, A. (eds.) ECCV 2006. LNCS, vol. 3951, pp. 404–417. Springer, Heidelberg (2006). doi:10.1007/11744023_32
17. Long, M., Wang, J., Ding, G., Sun, J., Yu, P.: Transfer feature learning with joint distribution adaptation. In: IEEE ICCV, pp. 2200–2207 (2013)

On the Quantitative Analysis of Sparse RBMs

Yanxia Zhang[1,2], Lu Yang[3], Binghao Meng[3], Hong Cheng[3(✉)], Yong Zhang[1], Qian Wang[4], and Jiadan Zhu[4]

[1] School of Mathematical Sciences, University of Electronic Science and Technology of China, Chengdu 611731, China
mathzy@uestc.edu.cn
[2] Department of Mathematics and Information Engineering, Chongqing University of Education, Chongqing 400067, China
[3] School of Automation Engineering, Center for Robotics, University of Electronic Science and Technology of China, Chengdu 611731, China
{yanglu,hcheng}@uestc.edu.cn
[4] Ricoh Software Research Center of Beijing, Beijing 100044, China
http://jp.linkedin.com/pub/lu-yang/36/a94/5b2

Abstract. With the development of deep neural networks, the model of restricted Boltzmann machine(RBM) has gradually become one of the essential aspects in deep learning researches. Because of the presence of the partition function, it is intractable to get the model selection, control the complexity, and learn an exact maximum likelihood in RBM model. A kind of effective measure is approximate inference that adopts annealing importance sampling(AIS) scheme only to evaluate a RBM's performance. At present, there is little quantitative analysis on discrepancies generated by different RBM models. So we focus on the innovation research on some quantitative evaluation of the generalization performance of all kinds of sparse RBM models, including the classical sparse RBM(SpRBM) and the log sum sparse RBM(LogSumRBM). We discuss the influence and efficiency of the AIS strategy for these sparse RBMs' estimations. Particularly, we confirm that the LogSumRBM is the optimal model in RBM and sparse RBMs for its smaller deviations in the assessment results regardless of the training MNIST data and the test, which provides a guarantee on some theories and experience in the choice of the deep learning models in the future.

Keywords: Restricted Boltzmann Machine · Sparse Restricted Boltzmann Machine · Contrastive Divergence · Reconstruction Error · Annealed importance sampling

1 Introduction

As a kind of random neural network based on statistical mechanics, the restricted Boltzmann machine(RBM) can effectively extract features from original input data. Deep Belief networks (DBN) stacking by the multiple RBMs has been

© Springer International Publishing AG 2016
E. Chen et al. (Eds.): PCM 2016, Part I, LNCS 9916, pp. 449–458, 2016.
DOI: 10.1007/978-3-319-48890-5_44

used to extract more abstract features after contrastive divergence(CD) algorithm proposed by Hinton [4]. In the part of theories, Bengio [10] and Fischer [1] studied the residual term in CD estimation of RBM's log likelihood gradient and justified truncation's loose and tight bounds. Some quantitative analysis are achieved to directly assess the performance of RBM and DBN as geneative models [8]. So far a RBM has been successfully applied in different machine learning problems, such as classification and recognition, dimension reduction, text presentation, machine transliteration and so on [2,3,9]. Recently some researchers have generated several sparse RBMs [5–7,9]. Lee [5] suggested that we should control the expected activations at a fixed level in RBM's hidden layer by adding norm regularizer to the sparse term in 2007. Nair [9] promoted a cross entropy regularizer in 2012 to represent sparse penalty term and achieved effective results in 3D object recognition. In 2014, another sparse model called as log and sum sparse RBM(LogSumRBM) is proposed by Ji [7]. Besides, Jakub [6] advised a symmetric cross entropy(or Symmetric Kullback Leibler) rule to represent the sparse term that is on the basis of the relative entropy and a promotion of cross entropy sparse RBM.

In generally, we use reconstruction error method to evaluate a learned RBM's advantages·and disadvantages. This case is very simple and can reflect a RBM's likelihood function to training data while it is not completely reliable to some extent. At present, the annealing importance sampling(AIS) [8] has been effectively applied to estimate the likelihood function of RBM. Moreover, the LogSumRBM enhancing performance of RBM via Log-Sum regularization is carried out some experiments by Ji on several data sets (the nature image, the MNIST data, the NORB data and the Caltech101 Silhouettes) to investigate its effectiveness and superiority [7]. But so far without any evaluations about the case, so we firstly apply the assessment strategies (the reconstruction error and the AIS) to the classical SpRBM and the LogSumRBM model, which provides important guarantees for kinds of models in engineer applications.

2   RBM Model

A RBM model contains a visible layer and a hidden layer in which neuronal units satisfy there are fully connections in interlayer's and none of connections in each other layer's. Supposing a binary RBM: $v_i, h_j \in \{0, 1\}, i = 1, 2, \cdots, n, j = 1, 2, \cdots, m$, its energy function is defined as:

$$E_\theta(v, h) = -b^T v - c^T h - h^T W v \tag{1}$$

where $\theta = (W, b, c)$, b and c respectively present visible layer and hidden layer bias, W is the connection weight matrix. Its objective function is to maximizing logarithmic likelihood in all training set(assuming that it contains T samples):

$$\theta^* = \max_\theta L(\theta) = \max_\theta \sum_{t=1}^{T} log P_\theta(v^{(t)}) \tag{2}$$

where the likelihood function $P_\theta(v^{(t)})$ (shorted as $P_\theta(v)$) is given by:

$$P_\theta(v) = \frac{P_\theta^*(v)}{Z(\theta)} = \frac{1}{Z(\theta)} \sum_h e^{-E_\theta(v,h)} \tag{3}$$

with $Z(\theta) = \sum_{v,h} e^{-E_\theta(v,h)}$ is the normalizing factor (or partition function), $P_\theta^*(v)$ is considered as a probability without normalization processing. The optimal parameter is usually obtained by the stochastic gradient ascent(SGA):

$$\frac{\partial L(\theta)}{\partial w_{i,j}} = E_{p_0}[v_i h_j] - E_{p_{model}}[v_i h_j] \tag{4}$$

$$\frac{\partial L(\theta)}{\partial b_i} = E_{p_0}[v_i] - E_{p_{model}}[v_i] \tag{5}$$

$$\frac{\partial L(\theta)}{\partial c_j} = E_{p_0}[h_j] - E_{p_{model}}[h_j] \tag{6}$$

where $E_{p_0}[\cdot]$ denotes a expectation under data distribution, $E_{p_{model}}[\cdot]$ is a expectation under model distribution. The RBM's learning process based on k steps CD(CDk) is given in the first step algorithm1 which ε is a learning rate, $E_{p_{recon}}[\cdot]$ is a distribution after performing CDk process.

3   The Sparse RBM Model

The sparse RBM model is a kind of promotion of RBM including an extra term in the basis of original logarithmic likelihood, which makes the hidden layer units activation sparse. The objective function is defined as:

$$\theta^* = \min_\theta - L(\theta) + \lambda L_{s*} \tag{7}$$

where L_{s*} is a sparse punishment term, λ is a regularization coefficient. As shown in algorithm1, the iterations of gradient decent on sparse regularization are added in learning sparse RBMs based on the CDk.

3.1   The SpRBM Model

The classical sparse model proposed by LEE, et al. [5] constrains the expected activation of every hidden unit to the same sparsity level. In other words, It achieves sparse activity or sparse representation by punishing each hidden layer unit's average deviation level from the given activation probability caused by the loss. In this paper, we call it SpRBM model whose penalty term is as follows:

$$L_{s1} = \sum_{j=1}^m |p - \frac{1}{T} \sum_{t=1}^T E[h_j^{(t)}|v^{(t)}]|^2 \tag{8}$$

where p is a constant to control the hidden unit sparse degree. The parameters' gradient calculations of penalty term L_{s1} have the following formats:

$$\frac{\partial L_{s1}}{\partial w_{ij}} = 2 \left(\sum_{j=1}^{m} |p - \frac{1}{T} \sum_{t=1}^{T} \sigma| \right) \cdot \left(\frac{1}{T} \sum_{t=1}^{T} \sigma(1 - \sigma)v_i^{(t)} \right) \tag{9}$$

$$\frac{\partial L_{s1}}{\partial c_j} = 2 \left(\sum_{j=1}^{m} |p - \frac{1}{T} \sum_{t=1}^{T} \sigma| \right) \cdot \left(\frac{1}{T} \sum_{t=1}^{T} \sigma(1 - \sigma) \right) \tag{10}$$

where $\sigma = S(\sum_i w_{ij}v_i^{(t)} + c_j)$, $S(x) = \frac{1}{(1+e^{-x})}$ is an activation function.

Algorithm1.   Sparse RBM learning algorithm

---

1. Using CD Algorithm to update the parameters:
   $w_{i,j} := w_{i,j} + \varepsilon(E_{p0}[v_i h_j] - E_{precon}[v_i h_j])$
   $b_i := b_i + \varepsilon(E_{p0}[v_i] - E_{precon}[v_i])$
   $c_j := c_j + \varepsilon(E_{p0}[h_j] - E_{precon}[h_j])$
2. Using gradient format of the penalty term to update parameter again:
   $w_{i,j} := w_{i,j} + \frac{\partial L_{s*}}{\partial w_{i,j}}$
   $c_j := c_j + \frac{\partial L_{s*}}{\partial c_j}$
3. Repeat steps 1 and 2 until converge

3.2   The LogSumRBM Model

The SpRBM's sparse degree is controlled by a "firing rate" that leads to its limitation. This is another sparse RBM model based on log sum rule claimed as LogSumRBM [7] with the penalty term:

$$L_{s2} = \sum_{t=1}^{T} \sum_{j=1}^{m} log \left(1 + \frac{E[h_j^{(t)}|v^{(t)}]}{\eta} \right) \tag{11}$$

where η is used to control the similarity between L_0 norm and logarithmic norm. Its gradient calculation formats of punishment item L_{S2} are given by:

$$\frac{\partial L_{s2}}{\partial w_{ij}} = \frac{1}{\eta} \sum_{t=1}^{T} \frac{1}{1 + \frac{\sigma}{\eta}} \sigma(1 - \sigma)v_i^{(t)} \tag{12}$$

$$\frac{\partial L_{s2}}{\partial c_j} = \frac{1}{\eta} \sum_{t=1}^{T} \frac{1}{1 + \frac{\sigma}{\eta}} \sigma(1 - \sigma) \tag{13}$$

where σ is the same as the SpRBM's. Ji indicated that the LogSumRBM model can learn sparser and more discriminative representations compared with the RBM and SpBM model. Moreover, a lot of experiments showed that deep hierarchy network stacked by the LogSumRBM can learn more significant features such as corners, angles, surface boundaries in the higher layers and achieve better performance of classifications.

4   Assessment Methods

4.1   Reconstruction Error

The reconstruction error(RE) is a simple measure used to describe the difference of two distributions between the original data and the approximate generation by a RBM model. In general, the reconstruction error(the algorithm2) is very practical in engineering as it can reflect the likelihood degree under a RBM's distribution and the real training data. Nevertheless, it is not absolutely reliable.

Algorithm2.   Reconstruction Error Algorithm

---

1. Intialize: $error = 0$
2. For each sample $v^{(t)}(t = 1, 2, \cdots, T)$, calculate:
   sample the hidden layer $h \sim p(h|v^{(t)})$
   sample the visible layer $v \sim p(v|h)$
   the current error
      $error = error + \|v - v^{(t)}\|$
3. return $error$

4.2   Annealing Importance Sampling

The AIS algorithm can be used to assess a RBM, that is indirectly to approximately calculate the partition function, in turn to estimate its likelihood function. Suppose there are two RBMs(as shown in Fig. 1) with parameter respectively $\theta_A(W^A, b^A, c^A), \theta_B(W^B, b^B, c^B)$ that are used to define probability distributions p_A and p_B. Each model has a different number of hidden layer units: $h_A \in \{0, 1\}^{M_A}$, $h_B \in \{0, 1\}^{M_B}$. If we can draw some independent samples $v^{(i)}$ from p_A in accordance with $v^{(i)} \sim p_A, i = 1, \cdots, M$, the following ratio of partition function in Eq. 14 is obtained via the simple MCMC approximation and its variance is defined as Eq. 15:

$$\frac{Z_B}{Z_A} \approx \frac{1}{M} \sum_{i=1}^{M} \frac{P_B^*(v^{(i)})}{P_A^*(v^{(i)})} = \frac{1}{M} \sum_{i=1}^{M} w^{(i)} = \hat{r}_{AIS} \tag{14}$$

$$var(\hat{r}_{AIS}) = \frac{1}{M} var(\omega^i) = \hat{\sigma}^2 \tag{15}$$

Then we introduce the following sequence of intermediate probability distributions for $k = 0, 1, \cdots, K$ with similarities each other:

$$p_k(v) = \frac{p_k^*(v)}{Z_k} = \frac{1}{Z_k} \sum_h e^{-E_k(v,h)} \tag{16}$$

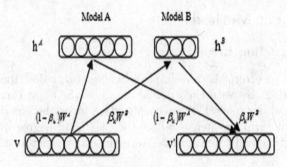

Fig. 1. The relationship between two RBMs.

Algorithm3.   Annealing Importance Sampling Algoithm (AIS)

---

for $k = 1, \cdots, M$

1. According to the following to produced $v_1, v_2, \cdots, v_k$:
   Sampling v_1 from $p_A = P_0$
   Sampling v_2 given v_1 using state transition operator $T_{K-1}(v_K, v_{K-1})$

   $\vdots$

   Sampling v_K given v_{K-1} using state transition operator $T_{K-1}(v_K, v_{K-1})$
2. calculate:
   $$w^i = \frac{p_1^*(v^{(1)})}{p_0^*(v^{(1)})} \frac{p_2^*(v^{(2)})}{p_1^*(v^{(2)})} \cdots \frac{p_K^*(v^{(K)})}{p_{K-1}^*(v^{(K-1)})}$$
end for
3. Estimate the ratio of partition function:
   $\frac{Z_B}{Z_A} \approx \frac{1}{M} \sum_{i=1}^{M} w^{(i)} = \hat{r}_{AIS}$

---

where $E_k(v, h) = (1 - \beta_k)E_A + \beta_k E_B, 0 = \beta_0 < \beta_1 < \beta_2 < \cdots < \beta_{K-1} < \beta_K = 1$, $E_A = E(v, h^A; \theta^A), E_B = E(v, h^B; \theta^B)$, $p_0(v) = p_A(v), p_K(v) = p_B(v)$. The AIS process is shown in algorithm3.

As above algorithm3, the Markov chain transition operator $T_k(v', v)$ can directly derive from the Gibbs sampling :

$$p(h_j^A = 1|v) = S((1 - \beta_k)u_h^A) \tag{17}$$

$$p(h_j^B = 1|v) = S(\beta_k)u_h^B \tag{18}$$

$$p(v_i' = 1|h) = S((1 - \beta_k)u_h^A + \beta_k u_v^B) \tag{19}$$

where $u_v^A = \sum_j w_{ij}^A h_j^A + b_i^A, u_v^B = \sum_j w_{ij}^B h_j^B + b_i^B, u_1 = \sum_i b_i^A v_i, u_2 = \sum_i b_i^B v_i$.

There is a simple "Base Rate" RBM model with parameter $\theta_A(0, b^A, c^A)$ whose partition and likelihood are easy to calculate: $Z_A = 2^{M_A} \prod_i (1 + e^{b_i})$, $p_A(v) = \prod_i (\frac{1}{1+e^{-b_i}})$. Therefore, we can collect some precision independent samples from the distribution of $p_A(v)$ and the "Base rate" model. This method is very close to the stochastic simulated annealing process since a sequence of intermediate probability distributions are achieved by Eq. 20. When these β_k changing from 0 to 1, the model will gradually change from the simple "Base Rate" model to a complex model.

$$P_k(v) = \frac{e^{(1-\beta_k)v^T b^A}}{Z_K} \sum_{h^B} e^{-\beta_k E(v,h^B;\theta_B)} \tag{20}$$

5   Experiments

The data set in our experiment is MNIST, including 60000 training images and 10000 test images. Based on experience, the weight decay, learning rate and sparsity rate are successively set to 0.0002, 0.05, 0.2. We limit that the number units of hidden layers is 15 and the CD step is 1,3,20(We call these models CD1,CD3 and CD20 respectively). The training cycle of all three models is 20.

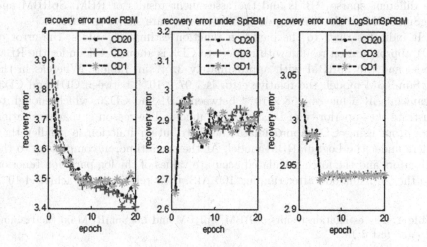

Fig. 2. The reconstruction error results under three models.

5.1   Evaluating the RBM, SpRBM and LogSumRBM Using RE

In our first experiment we evaluate RBM, SpRBM and LogSumRBM by using reconstruction error provided algorithm2. Figure 2 shows that the assessment results of reconstruction error for all three models. With the gradually increasing of the iteration, the reconstruction error of the RBM and LogSumRBM will decrease, and the effect of LogSumRBM is obviously superior to the RBM, while the error under the SpRBM will appear relatively large concussion. Considering the total complex, the CD1 algorithm is more popular in the engineering application, which is also illustrated in the results of reconstruction error.

5.2 Evaluating the RBM, SpRBM and LogSumRBM Using AIS

According to the "base rate" model and AIS algorithm, the main goal of our second experiment is to calculate:

(1) the partition function term Z_B from Eq. 19 in which the ratio $\hat{r}_{IS}$ has been estimated by AIS algorithm and the Z_A also has been obtained through the "base rate" model.
(2) the likelihood function term $p_B(v)$.

In AIS, we also set the value β_k according to Salakhutdinov's design in conference11 that there are 14,500 β_k in total among 500 β_k spaced uniformly from 0 to 0.5, 4,000 β_k spaced uniformly from 0.5 to 0.9, and 10,000 500 β_k spaced uniformly from 0.9 to 1.0. 100. The training sessions are set 100. Salakhutdinov indicated that with the increase of number of the simulated annealing in AIS, the RBM's estimated values of the distribution function gradually will be stable without violent shock. In this paper, we extend the method to estimate the different sparse RBMs and the assessment results of RBM, SpRBM and LogSumRBM on the training data and test data are shown in Table 1.

It indicates that, to the partition function estimation values, the error of CD1 approximation results with respect to CD3 is about 2.4 % under the RBM model and the SpRBM with approximately 3.7 % in Table 1. Whereas in the LogSumRBM model, the relative error is 7.97×10^{-5} between CD1 and CD3. Meanwhile, It achieves 5.58×10^{-4} between CD1 and CD20, which enough to illustrate the superiority of LogSumRBM model. The reason is that truncation error from using CD1 approximate the distribution function is smaller than others under the LogSumRBM model. At the same time, in comparison to the estimators and the force calculated accurate values of the log partition function and the log likelihood after running 100 AIS, their relative error achieved 10^{-4}

Table 1. The estimation results of RBM, SpRBM and LogSumRBM on the training data and test data

Type		Log partition			Avg. Log likelihood			
		LogZ		$Log(Z \pm \hat{\delta})$	Train data		Test data	
		True	Est		True	Est	True	Est
RBM	CD1	210.68	10.73	210.60, 210.89	−175.81	−175.86	−175.31	−175.37
	CD3	215.97	215.93	215.82, 216.05	−173.40	−173.37	−172.99	−172.96
	CD20	207.78	207.73	207.64, 207.83	−158.83	−158.77	−158.33	−158.27
SpRBM	CD1	141.98	142.08	141.83, 142.15	−479.35	−479.44	−484.08	−484.18
	CD3	136.82	136.81	136.80, 136.86	−498.65	−498.65	−503.88	−503.87
	CD20	137.38	137.38	137.32, 137.44	−492.43	−492.42	−497.45	−497.44
LSRBM	CD1	125.57	125.48	125.39, 125.67	−483.39	−483.30	−488.73	−488.63
	CD3	125.55	125.49	125.39, 125.65	−468.76	−468.71	−473.33	−473.28
	CD20	125.53	125.55	125.43, 125,64	−474.48	−474.50	−479.24	−479.27

magnitude. It is AIS that is very effective regardless of assessment models. Due to the presence of a sparse penalty term, it is reasonable that the results of RBM and sparse RBM assessment are not consistent in the table.

5.3 Compute the Important Weights

In the process AIS, the parameters β_k are consistent in number with the intermediate distributions, whose size and scale have impacts on ratio of the two RBMs partition functions. When these β_k changing from 0 to 1, the model anneals from a simple "base rate" one to the final complex one. As show in Fig. 3, their relationship diagrams between the parameters β_k and the logarithmic weights under the model of RBM, SpRBM and LogSumRBM are given respectively. The left shows that log weights are random distribution under RBM model. However the variance of log weights under the classical SpRBM model is higher than LogSumRBM's. Moreover the SpRBM's variance of log weights is almost increasing as β_k changing from 0 to 1. Adversely, it keeps decreasing under LogSumRBM model. The phenomenon presents the LogSumRBM model is more stable as its parameters will not have impact on important weights.

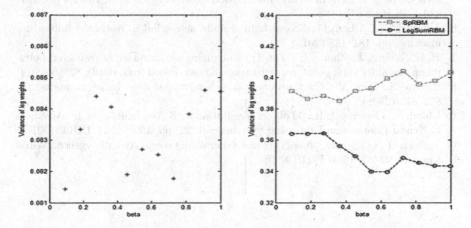

Fig. 3. The relationship between parameters β_k and important weights(the left: RBM model, the right: two sparse RBM models).

6 Conclusion

We present in this paper the feasibility of assessment methods for two sparse RBMs. Unlike the simple reconstruction error that only characterized two distributions' difference between the original data and the approximates of models, our research focuses on how to use AIS procedure to evaluate sparse RBMs more effectively. So we provide a good assessment of the log partition function and likelihood function that are difficult calculate directly in sparse RBMs. From the result of the estimates, we can confirm that the LogSumRBM model is the optimal model compared with the models of RBM and SpRBM, which also explains its advantage with more discriminative performance. At the same time, it further provides a reliable theoretical basis for sparse RBM models in engineering application.

References

1. Asja, F., Christian, I.: Bounding the bias of contrastive diverence learning. Neural Comput. **23**(3), 664–673 (2011)
2. Athanasios, K.N., Ben, J.A.K.: Deep belief networks for dimensionality reduction, vol. 20, pp. 185–191 (2008)
3. Geoffrey, E.H., Ruslan, S.: Reducing the dimensionality of data with nerual networks. Science **313**, 504–507 (2006). American Association for the Advancement of Science
4. Geoffrey, E.H., Simon, O., Yee-Whye, T.: A fast learning algorithm for deep belief nets. Neural Comput. **18**, 1527–1554 (2006). Massachusetts Institute of Technology Press
5. Honglak, L., Chaitanya, E., Andrew, Y.N.: Sparse deep belief net model for visual area v2. In: Advances in Neural Information Processing Systems, vol. 20, pp. 873–880. DBLP (2007)
6. Jakub, M.T., Adam, G.: Sparse hidden units activation in restricted boltzmann machine, pp. 181–185 (2015)
7. Ji, N., Zhang, J., Zhang, C., Yin, Q.: Enhancing performance of restricted boltzmann machines via log-sum regularization. Knowl. Based Syst. **63**(3), 82–96 (2014)
8. Ruslan, S., Iain, M.: On the quantitative analysis of deep belief networks, pp. 872–879 (2008)
9. Vinod, N., Geoffrey, E.H.: 3d object recognition with deep belief nets. In: Advances in Neural Information Processing Systems, vol. 22, pp. 1527–1554. DBLP (2012)
10. Yoshua, B., Olivier, D.: Justifying and generalizing contrastive divergence. Neural Comput. **21**(6), 1601–1621 (2009)

An Efficient Solution for Extrinsic Calibration of a Vision System with Simple Laser

Ya-Nan Chen[✉], Fei Wang, Hang Dong, Xuetao Zhang,
and Haiwei Yang

Xi'an Jiaotong University, Xi'an, Shaanxi, China
{chenyanan,dhunter,yanghw.2005}@stu.xjtu.edu.cn,
{wfx,xuetaozh}@mail.xjtu.edu.cn

Abstract. Strong demands for accurate reconstruction of non-cooperative target have been arising recent years. The existing methods which combine cameras and laser range finders (LRF) are inconvenient and cost much. We replace the widely used laser range finder with a simple laser, and find that the combination of a camera and a simple calibrated laser is also enough to reconstruct the highly accurate 3-D position of the laser spot. In this paper, we propose a method to calibrate the extrinsic parameters between a camera and a simple laser, and show how to use it to reconstruct a laser spot's 3-D position. The experiments show that our proposed method can obtain a result which is comparable to the state-of-the-art LRF-based methods.

Keywords: Extrinsic calibration · Simple laser · Reconstruction · Non-cooperative

1 Introduction

In recent years, there are many systems and applications which combine cameras and laser range finders (LRF) for non-cooperative target reconstruction. This camera-LRF fusion system can be widely applied in city model acquisition [7], object mapping [8–10], object tracking [11–13], augmented reality [14], and mobile robotics [8–13]. The reconstruction methods based on this setup require to get the relative pose between the camera and the laser in advance. Therefore the calibration of such setups has attracted more and more attention from the researchers. In our method, we replace the widely used laser range finder with a simple laser. A simple laser is much cheaper and lower power-consuming than an accurate laser range finder. Meanwhile, it can still provide an accurate reconstruction result.

The extrinsic calibration process of camera-LRF fusion system has been discussed in published works [1–4, 6]. The most well-known calibration method is proposed by Zhang and Pless in [2]. They calibrated the extrinsic parameters with a planar calibration pattern which can be viewed simultaneously by camera and laser range finder. Soon, Unnikrishnan and Hebert developed an easy-to-use software to calibrate the relative pose of 3-D LRF [3]. [6] proposed a self-calibration method used in rotation platform. In [4], a minimal solution for extrinsic calibration is proposed by Vasconcelos and Barreto,

E. Chen et al. (Eds.): PCM 2016, Part I, LNCS 9916, pp. 459–468, 2016.
DOI: 10.1007/978-3-319-48890-5_45

which requires as least as five planes. Most Recently, Nguyen and Reitmayr [1] proposed two methods to calibrate a camera-LRF fusion system.

In this paper, we propose an efficient method to calibrate the extrinsic parameters of a camera and a simple laser, and show how to use the calibrated laser and camera to reconstruct the 3-D position of a laser spot. Our calibration method assumes that the accurate intrinsic matrix of camera is obtained by Zhang's algorithm [5], and all the unknowns are extrinsic parameters. During the calibration process, we only need a checkerboard plane. The checkerboard plane will be moved for several times to get an accurate calibration result. Then, we use the calibration result to reconstruct the 3-D position of the laser spot. Our experiments show that this method can give an accurate calibration and reconstruction result. Compared to Nguyen and Reitmayr's calibration result in [1], our method achieves a better result when using synthetic data. And our method is validated in field experiment.

The remainder of our paper is organized as follows. The Sect. 2 describes our proposed calibration method and shows how to reconstruct the laser spot with a calibrated laser-camera system in application. We evaluate the method on synthetic data in the Sect. 3, and the experimental results are also shown. And we conclude our work in the final section.

2   Method Description

The laser-based measurement system is as shown in the Fig. 1. This system is formed by two parts: a camera and a simple laser. A checkboard is used in our proposed method and 4 checkboard settings captured in field experiment are also shown in Fig. 1. The aim of our calibration method is to acquire the laser's direction D_L and position P_{XOY} with respect to the camera coordinate frame.

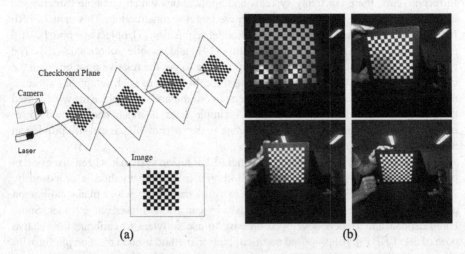

Fig. 1. Figure (a) shows the design of the proposed calibration method. Figure (b) shows 4 checkboard settings captured by the camera.

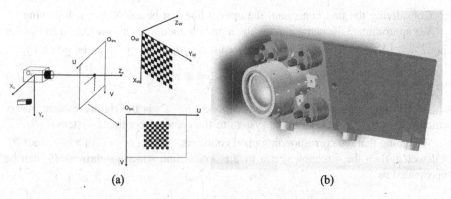

Fig. 2. Figure (a) shows the diagram of reference coordinate frames and labels. Figure (b) shows the designed 3-D model of our laser-camera system used in our filed experiment.

The calibration system has three different coordinate frames: the world coordinate frame with its origin at the upper-left corner of the checkboard; the camera coordinate frame with its origin at the optical center of the camera; the image coordinate frame with its origin at the top left corner of the image plane. A diagram of coordinate frames is shown in Fig. 2(a). Figure 2(b) shows the designed 3-D model of our laser-camera system, and it has already validated in field experiment.

2.1 Calibration Algorithm

This section shows our proposed calibration method for extrinsic calibration of a camera and a simple laser. We assume that the intrinsic matrix A of camera is known and the radial distortion has already been wrapped. The laser beam's extrinsic parameter can be represented as the function of laser beam with respect to the camera coordinate system:

$$[x \quad y \quad z]^T = k * D_L + P_{XOY} \tag{1}$$

where k is an positive scale factor, D_L is the direction vector of the laser beam, P_{XOY} is the intersection point of laser beam and image plane.

We place the checkboard at n different poses. At each pose, the laser falls on the checkboard plane and forms a spot. This laser spot's coordinate is represented as $P_{Li} = [X \quad Y \quad Z]^T, i = 1, 2, \cdots, n$ in the camera coordinate system. The function of laser beam can be calculated if we get all these laser spots' coordinates. In order to get the coordinate of each laser spot, we utilize these two constraints at each different checkboard pose:

- The laser spot is on the line which go through the camera optical center and the laser spot. We call it the optical line for convenience.
- The laser spot is on the plane of checkboard.

Considering the first constraint, the optical line can be calculated as following.

We approximate the camera model by a pinhole model, then a projection from laser spot $P_{Li} = [X \quad Y \quad Z]^T$ to 2D image coordinates $p_{Li} = [u \quad v]^T$ can be given by

$$p_{Li} \sim A * (R * P_{Li} + T) \tag{2}$$

where A is the intrinsic matrix of camera, and $[R \quad T]$ is the rigidly motion matrix which relates the world coordinate system to the camera coordinate system.

Assuming that the corresponding pixel coordinate $p_{Li} = [u \quad v]^T$ of a laser spot P_{Li} is detected, then the direction vector of the optical line which go through P_{Li} can be represented as

$$D_O = A^{-1} * \begin{bmatrix} p_{Li} \\ 1 \end{bmatrix} \tag{3}$$

Then the optical line's function can be given by

$$[x \quad y \quad z]^T = k * D_O \tag{4}$$

Where k is a scale factor, D_O is the direction vector of optical line.

By substituting (3) into (4), we can derive

$$P_{Li} = k * D_O = k * A^{-1} * \begin{bmatrix} p_{Li} \\ 1 \end{bmatrix} \tag{5}$$

Consider the second constraint. The checkboard plane's function can be calculated as following.

The transformation matrix $[R \quad T]$ which relates the world coordinate system to the camera coordinate system can be calculated by Zhang's method [10]. Then the normal vector of this plane can be represented as

$$N = -R_3 * (R_3^T * T) \tag{6}$$

Where R_3 is the third column of R. Therefore the function of this plane is

$$[N^T \quad \|N\|_2] * \begin{bmatrix} P_{Li} \\ 1 \end{bmatrix} = 0 \tag{7}$$

By substituting (6) into (7), the checkboard plane's function can be represented as

$$[N^T \quad \|N\|_2] * \begin{bmatrix} P_{Li} \\ 1 \end{bmatrix} = \left[-R_3 * (R_3^T * T) \quad \|-R_3 * (R_3^T * T)\|_2 \right]^T * \begin{bmatrix} P_{Li} \\ 1 \end{bmatrix} = 0 \tag{8}$$

Utilizing the two constraints mentioned above, we can get the coordinate of P_{Li} combining (5) and (8).

Since we move the checkboard plane for several times, a series of 3-D coordinates of laser spots $\tilde{P}_L = \{P_{L1}, P_{L1}, \cdots, P_{Ln}\}$ can be acquired. Assuming that the laser is fixed, these spots should be on the same line. Then the function of laser beam can be determined using these points. In order to get the optimal parameters of laser beam, we use PCA to minimize the projection error of all these spots. The steps is as follows:

- First, calculate the center point of all the laser spots $\bar{P}_L = \frac{sum(\tilde{P}_L)}{n}$.
- Second, normalize all the laser spots $\breve{P}_L = \frac{\tilde{P}_L - \bar{P}_L}{\max(\tilde{P}_L)}$.
- Third, compute the covariance matrix $\Sigma = \frac{\breve{P}_L^T * \breve{P}_L}{n}$ and compute the eigenvectors of covariance matrix $[U \quad S \quad V] = svd(\Sigma)$.
- Then, the direction vector of laser beam is $D_L = U(:, 1)$.

So the laser beam's function is

$$[x \quad y \quad z]^T = k * D_L + \bar{P}_L \tag{9}$$

But this function's parameters are not unique. In order to disambiguate, we transform this function to another equivalence form. The direction vector D_L will be replaced by $\frac{D_L}{\|D_L\|}$, and point $\bar{P}_L$ will be replaced by $P_{XOY} = [x_0 \quad y_0 \quad 0]^T$ which is the intersection point of laser beam and image plane. And this transformed function is the final result.

2.2 Reconstruction Method

Once the extrinsic parameters of a simple laser are calibrated, we can reconstruct the laser spot's coordinate P_L. The laser spot should satisfy the following two constraints:

- The laser spot is on the optical line.
- The laser spot is on the laser beam which has been calibrated in the prior section.

Considering the first constraint, we firstly detect the laser spot's coordinate $p_L = [u \quad v]^T$ in the image. Then, the function of optical line can be calculated by the approach described in last section. We represent this line as

$$[x \quad y \quad z]^T = k_1 * D_O \tag{10}$$

Considering the second constraint, the function of laser beam can be calibrated using our proposed method, which can be represented as

$$[x \quad y \quad z]^T = k_2 * D_L + P_{XOY} \tag{11}$$

Then we can reconstruct the laser spot's coordinate utilizing these two constraints. The laser spot is the intersection of these two lines. Taken (10) and (11) together, the laser spot's coordinate can be calculated using the least square method. It is equivalent to minimize

$$\|k_1 * D_O - (k_2 * D_L + P_{XOY})\|_2 \tag{12}$$

k_1, k_2 can be given by

$$\begin{bmatrix} k_1 \\ k_2 \end{bmatrix} = -\left(\begin{bmatrix} D_O^T \\ D_L^T \end{bmatrix} * \begin{bmatrix} D_O & D_L \end{bmatrix} \right)^{-1} * \begin{bmatrix} D_O^T \\ D_L^T \end{bmatrix} * P_{XOY} \tag{13}$$

So, the reconstruction result of laser spot can be given by

$$P_L = \frac{1}{2} * (k_1 * D_O + k_2 * D_L + P_{XOY}) \tag{14}$$

3   Experiments

In this section, we design a series of simulation experiments to validate the performance of our proposed method. First we evaluate the robustness of our calibration algorithm. Then we evaluate the accuracy of our reconstruct method. In order to simulate a realistic measuring environment, the measurement scenario is designed as follows: (1) The extrinsic parameters of laser beam are defined by direction $D_L = \begin{bmatrix} -5 & -5 & 100 \end{bmatrix}$ and intersection point $P_{XOY} = \begin{bmatrix} 40\,mm & 40\,mm & 0 \end{bmatrix}$. (2) The checkboard and target are placed in front of camera in the range [200 mm, 1200 mm]. (3) The camera's intrinsic matrix is generated according to a real camera with resolution 512 × 512, and the radial distortion is set to 0.

3.1   Calibration Result

The ground truth is generated with the following rules. The checkboard plane is defined as 12 × 12 square grids, and the length of every square is 20 mm. It is placed in a limited distance from 200 mm to 1200 mm. At each distance, we produce a random angle in the range [−10 degree, 10 degree] and translation in the range [−20 mm, 20 mm]. Then, we calculate the intersection point of laser beam and checkboard plane at each place. Finally, we calculate the re-projection point of checkboard grid and laser spot according to the generated angle and translation.

To check the robustness of our proposed calibration method, Gaussian noises, with mean 0 and standard deviation 1 pixel, is added to each re-projection of checkboard corner and laser spot. For different magnitude of noises validation, we scale the default standard deviations by a factor in the range [0.25, 3.0].

The calibration result is calculated by the method we proposed. We compare the result with the ground truth. The direction error is measured by the absolute angle error between our result and ground truth in degree. The intersection point error is measured

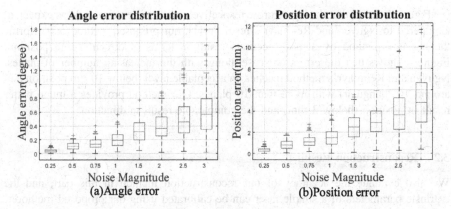

Fig. 3. Error distribution under noise levels in the range of [0.25, 3.0] simulated on synthetic data. The boxes illustrate the angular error of the direction and position error where the box shows the 25 %–75 % quantiles, and the whiskers to 0.993.

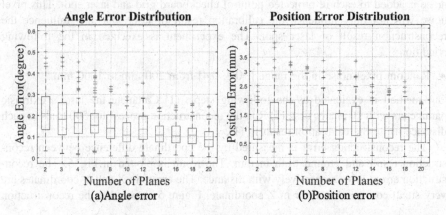

Fig. 4. Error distribution under different numbers of poses in the range of [2, 20] simulated on synthetic data. The boxes illustrate the angular error of the direction and position error where the box shows the 25 %–75 % quantiles, and the whiskers to 0.993.

by the Euclidean distance between our result and ground truth. We evaluate the proposed method in two different conditions:

- Different magnitude re-projection noise with the same amount poses.
- Different number of poses with the same magnitude re-projection noise.

We run 100 trials for every different magnitude noise and every different number poses. First, we evaluate the first condition with 3 poses. The standard deviation of Gaussian noises is 1 pixel and it's scaled by a factor in the range [0.25, 3.0] in our experiments. The result is shown in Fig. 3. Then, our method is evaluated under the second condition and the number of poses is in the range of [2, 20]. The result is displayed in Fig. 4.

Figure 3 shows that the errors grow respectively with noise magnitude as expected. Compared to Nguyen and Reitmayr's result in [1], our proposed method outperforms the baseline method by a more accurate result in terms of direction and position. Figure 4 shows that the errors decrease along with the increasing number of planes. Nguyen and Reitmayr's method reaches an acceptable level (below 10^{-2}m position and around 10^{-1} angular) with more than 10 planes. Our method provides a much better result in position (below 3 mm) and the comparable result in direction.

3.2 Reconstruction Result

We also evaluate the accuracy of our reconstruction method in this part, and the extrinsic parameters of a simple laser can be calibrated using our proposed method.

The ground truth is generated with the following rules. In each distance in the range [200 mm, 1000 mm], we calculate the laser spot's coordinate in the camera coordinate frame. Then we calculate the re-projection of laser spot in the image coordinate frame.

To check the robustness of our proposed reconstruction method, random pixel noise is added to each re-projected point of checkboard grid and laser spot. This pixel noise will not only influence the calibration result of laser, but also influence the reconstruction result of laser spot. The experiment is executed in the following condition:

- Random pixel noise in the range [−0.4, 0.4] from 200 mm to 1000 mm.

Our method is evaluated as the following steps: (1) Calculate the laser's extrinsic parameters with 20 planes first. (2) Run the reconstruction process for 500 trials in each distance using the calibration result in (1).

The reconstruction error is measured by the coordinate difference between reconstruction result and ground truth in mm. The result is plotted in Fig. 5. The reconstruction errors grow respectively with distance. The errors in X and Y coordinates are very small compared to error in Z coordinate. Figure 5 shows that the reconstruction

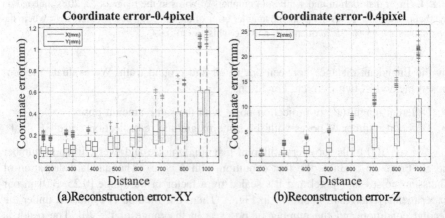

Fig. 5. Error distribution under different distance. The boxes illustrate the position error where the box shows the 25 %–75 % quantiles, and the whiskers to 0.993.

result is very sensitive to distance. We can get an accurate result in a close distance. The maximum error of reconstruction is less than 20 mm when the distance is less than 1000 mm. It can provide a sufficient accuracy in many application scenarios.

4 Conclusion

In this paper, an efficient method is proposed to calibrate the extrinsic parameters between a camera and a simple laser. Besides, a reconstruction method is proposed. Compared to camera-LRF systems, camera-laser system proposed in this paper is more economical. The proposed calibration method only requires a few poses of checkboard to get an accurate result. Our experiment shows that our method can provide both an accurate calibration and reconstruction result. The accuracy of proposed camera-laser system makes sure that it can be broadly used in many application scenarios.

Acknowledgements. This research was supported by National Natural Science Foundation of China (No.61231018, No.61273366), National Science and technology support program (2015BAH31F01), Program of introducing talents of discipline to university under grant B13043.

References

1. Nguyen, T., Reitmayr, G.: Calibrating setups with a single-point laser range finder and a camera. In: IEEE/RSJ International Conference on Intelligent Robots & Systems, pp. 1801–1806 (2013)
2. Zhang, Q., Pless, R.: Extrinsic calibration of a camera and laser range finder (improves camera calibration). In: Proceedings. 2004 IEEE/RSJ International Conference on Intelligent Robots and Systems, (IROS 2004), vol.3, pp. 2301–2306. IEEE (2004)
3. Unnikrishnan, R., Hebert, M.: Fast Extrinsic Calibration of a Laser Rangefinder to a Camera. Carnegie Mellon University, Pittsburgh (2005)
4. Francisco, V., Barreto, J.P., Urbano, N.: A minimal solution for the extrinsic calibration of a camera and a laser-rangefinder. IEEE Trans. Pattern Anal. Mach. Intell. **34**(11), 2097–3107 (2012)
5. Zhang, Z.: Flexible camera calibration by viewing a plane from unknown orientations. In: Iccv, p. 666 (1999)
6. Scaramuzza, D., Harati, A., Siegwart, R.: Extrinsic self calibration of a camera and a 3D laser range finder from natural scenes. In: IEEE/RSJ International Conference on Intelligent Robots and Systems, IROS 2007, pp. 4164–4169. IEEE (2007)
7. Früh, C., Zakhor, A.: An automated method for large-scale, ground-based city model acquisition. Int. J. Comput. Vis. **60**(1), 5–24 (2004)
8. Chou, Y.S., Liu, J.S.: A robotic indoor 3D mapping system using a 2D laser range finder mounted on a rotating four-bar linkage of a mobile platform. Int. J. Adv. Robot. Syst. **10** 257–271 (2013)
9. Droeschel, D., Stuckler, J., Behnke, S.: Local multi-resolution representation for 6D motion estimation and mapping with a continuously rotating 3D laser scanner. In: IEEE International Conference on Robotics and Automation, pp. 5221–5226. IEEE (2014)

10. Sheng, J., Tano, S., Jia, S.: Mobile robot localization and map building based on laser ranging and PTAM. In: International Conference on Mechatronics & Automation, pp. 1015–1020. IEEE (2011)

11. Jung, E.J., Lee, J.H., Yi, B.J., et al.: Development of a laser-range-finder-based human tracking and control algorithm for a marathoner service robot. IEEE/ASME Trans. Mechatron. **19**(6), 1963–1976 (2014)

12. Aguirre, E., Garcia-Silvente, M., Plata, J.: Leg detection and tracking for a mobile robot and based on a laser device, supervised learning and particle filtering. In: Armada, M.A., Sanfeliu, A., Ferre, M. (eds.) ROBOT2013 First Iberian Robotics Conference, pp. 433–440. Springer, New York (2014)

13. Chen, T.C., Li, J.Y., Chang, M.F., et al.: Multi-robot cooperation based human tracking system using Laser Range Finder. In: Proceedings - IEEE International Conference on Robotics and Automation, pp. 532–537 (2011)

14. Nguyen, T., Grasset, R., Schmalstieg, D., et al.: Interactive syntactic modeling with a single-point laser range finder and camera. In: 2013 IEEE International Symposium on Mixed and Augmented Reality (ISMAR), pp. 107-116. IEEE (2013)

A Stepped-RAM Reading and Multiplierless VLSI Architecture for Intra Prediction in HEVC

Wei Zhou[1](✉), Yue Niu[1], Xiaocong Lian[1], Xin Zhou[2], and Jiamin Yang[1]

[1] School of Electronics and Information,
Northwestern Polytechnical University, Xi'an, China
zhouwei@nwpu.edu.cn
[2] School of Automation, Northwestern Polytechnical University, Xi'an, China

Abstract. An efficient hardware architecture for intra prediction in High Efficiency Video Coding is proposed in this paper. The architecture supports all prediction modes and units. First, stepped-RAM reading method is proposed to realize reading RAM pixels in one pipeline period. Second, a new reference pixel-mapping method is also presented to solve hardware-consumed reference mapping process in angle prediction. A universal address arbitration and multiplierless prediction calculation unit which integrates angle, planar and DC prediction are also included in the design, which efficiently reduce hardware cost. Experimental results show that, with TSMC 65 nm CMOS technology, the proposed architecture reach a high operating clock frequency of 695 MHz with and meet the real time requirement for 2560 × 1440 video at 35 fps. The hardware cost of our proposed architecture is only 42 K gates. Compared with previous architectures, the proposed architecture can greatly increase working throughput and reduce hardware cost.

Keywords: HEVC · Intra prediction · VLSI architecture

1 Introduction

High Efficiency Video Coding (HEVC) [1, 2] is a new video coding standard developed by Joint Collaborative Team on Video Coding (JCT-VC). It aims to double the compression rates in comparison with H.264/AVC under the same visual quality.

In HEVC intra prediction, frames are divided in Coding Units (CU) and each CU can be recursively divided into smaller CUs. The CU can be partitioned into Prediction Units (PU) which range from 4 × 4 to 64 × 64. Intra prediction in HEVC is an efficient method to reduce the spatial data redundancy by using the coded sample as reference. HEVC increases the computational complexity compared with H.264/AVC in order to achieve gains in the coding efficiency. Therefore, an efficient VLSI architecture for intra prediction is required.

Extensive high-throughput intra prediction VLSI architectures have been proposed for HEVC [3–9]. Work [3] proposed a VLSI architecture only for 4 × 4 PU intra prediction. In [4], high throughput design was proposed, which costs large gate area. The architecture proposed in Work [5] supports all modes and PU sizes with high working

© Springer International Publishing AG 2016
E. Chen et al. (Eds.): PCM 2016, Part I, LNCS 9916, pp. 469–478, 2016.
DOI: 10.1007/978-3-319-48890-5_46

frequency. Work [6] proposed a novel design with low power consumption for intra prediction. In [7], a combined angle and planar prediction logic was proposed to meet low hardware demand. However, it has a relative low working frequency. Although a low-area design is proposed in [8], its throughput is low and it can only process 2 samples per cycle. Work [9] consumes 4 cycles for one 4 × 4 PU prediction and full-modes prediction is not supported in the design.

To overcome the above problems, a novel VLSI architecture is proposed for the real-time high-throughput implementation of intra prediction in HEVC in this paper. The novel architecture consists of three parts. First, LUT method is used to obtain address for SRAM which can save hardware resource. Second, the Stepped-RAM reading design is proposed to read necessary reference pixels in one pipeline clock and save internal registers for reference pixels. Finally, a universal multiplier less prediction architecture for angle, planar and DC instead of parallel prediction architecture is proposed to reduce hardware cost.

The rest of the paper is organized as follows: Sect. 2 briefly introduces the intra prediction in HEVC. The proposed intra prediction architecture is described in Sect. 3. Section 4 illustrates the experimental results and conclusions are drawn in Sect. 5.

2   Intra Prediction in HEVC

Intra prediction in HEVC is employed to reduce the redundancy within a frame, using the adjacent pixels of the decoded frames as references. The intra prediction module of HEVC follows the same paradigm as the one used in H.264/AVC, but offers more options. These include a planar and a DC mode to estimate smooth image content, as well as 33 angular modes (Fig. 1).

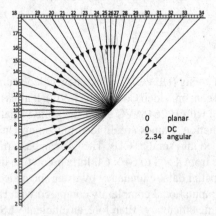

Fig. 1. Intra prediction modes in HEVC

For angle prediction, each predicted samples is calculated according to the Eq. (1):

$$p[x][y] = ((32 - f) * ref[a] + f * ref[b] + 16) >> 5 \tag{1}$$

For planar prediction, each predicted samples is calculated as:

$$p[x][y] = (p_h[x][y] + p_v[x][y] + N) >> (\log_2(N) + 1) \tag{2}$$

$$p_h[x][y] = (N - 1 - x) * p[-1][y] + (x + 1) * n[N][-1] \tag{3}$$

$$p_v[x][y] = (N - 1 - y) * p[x][-1] + (y + 1) * p[-1][N] \tag{4}$$

Where $p_h[x][y]$ is horizontal planar prediction, $p_v[x][y]$ is vertical planar prediction and N is the size of PU, with =0, 1...N-1.

For DC prediction, each prediction samples is the DC value of the top and left reference pixels. Additionally, predicted pixels in top row and left column are filtered when PU size is less than 32.

3   Proposed VLSI Architecture

Based on feature of the intra prediction in HEVC, a universal architecture is design to support all the prediction modes for angle, planar and DC prediction and prediction units. In order to save the hardware costs and internal registers for reference pixels, LUT method is used to obtain address for SRAM and Stepped-RAM reading design is proposed to read necessary reference pixels in one pipeline clock.

3.1   System Level

In this paper, an efficient prediction engine is designed based on 4×4 prediction block since 4×4 prediction blocks are the smallest prediction unit (PU). The top architecture is shown in Fig. 2. Three LUT modules in Fig. 2 are used to obtain offset and weight for angle prediction. Address transform module in 2nd stage is used to transform the offset to real SRAM address in angle prediction and reference filter module is used to filter necessary reference pixels. In last stage, universal prediction unit is used to calculate predicted pixels for angle, planar and DC prediction.

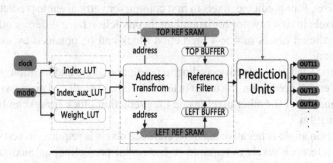

Fig. 2. Top architecture

As shown in Fig. 2, at the 1st stage, offset for certain prediction angle is obtained by two LUTs. For positive angle prediction, only one LUT is used to generate offset and another auxiliary LUT is used if prediction angle is negative. The detailed will be explained in the following sections. At the 2nd stage, offset output from LUT is transformed to corresponding address for SRAM. The SRAM is well designed to read all needed reference pixels in one pipeline period. At the 3rd stage, prediction calculation unit is implemented to calculate prediction pixels. The registering stage is used to guarantee stability of the prediction output data.

A three-stage pipeline architecture of intra prediction is presented to increase the throughput. Figure 3 illustrates the proposed pipeline mechanism. As shown in Fig. 3, block A is used to represent obtaining RAM-reading address according to current prediction mode and PU. Similarly, block B is used to represent obtaining corresponding reference pixels from SRAM according to available address. Symbol C is used to represent calculating predicted pixels.

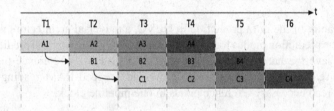

Fig. 3. Pipeline mechanism in intra prediction

3.2 LUT Design for Address Offset and Re-mapping Design

It is very hardware-consuming to process address offset calculation by using combinational logic circuit. As shown in Fig. 4, different prediction modes have different address offset and left (top) reference pixels are required to map to top (left) side if prediction angle is negative. Difference negative angle has different mapping direction. Therefore, LUT method is applied to address offset. Since certain prediction mode have a corresponding offset, four predicted pixels in first column for vertical angle prediction or four predicted pixels in first row for horizontal angle prediction have different offset. Offset for other predicted pixels in 4 × 4 prediction block can be obtained by using simple transformation.

Data in the LUT is obtained according to prediction angle and location of predicted pixels. For vertical prediction, the offset in left side (black) predicted pixels will be stored into LUT, and offset for other pixel inside the prediction block (gray) can be obtained by transformation.

If prediction angle is negative and left reference pixels is required in vertical prediction or top reference pixels is required in horizontal prediction, an auxiliary LUT is available instead of using combinational logic units to realize reference pixel-mapping. The detailed design is shown in Fig. 5.

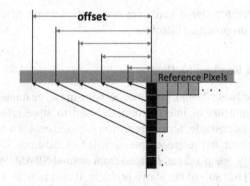

Fig. 4. LUT Data

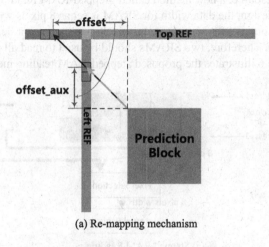

(a) Re-mapping mechanism

(b) Re-mapping circuit design

Fig. 5. Re-mapping design in negative prediction

As show in Fig. 5(a), if prediction angle is negative and reference pixels is located in the negative top side, left reference pixels may be mapped to negative top side. In normal designs like literature [4], hardware-consuming combinational logic circuit was used to obtain the negative top offset, which has been avoided in this work. As show in Fig. 5(b), the proposed auxiliary LUT is used to obtain another offset in left side in negative vertical angle prediction according to the prediction angle. Data stored in the auxiliary LUT is obtained according to prediction angle, which is similar to the normal LUT in Fig. 4. The auxiliary offset is transformed into address for left SRAM to obtain reference pixels. Therefore large hardware cost for reference pixel-mapping can be avoided through the proposed architecture.

3.3 Stepped-RAM Reading Method

In intra prediction hardware design, pipeline mechanism can guarantee high throughput. However, the requirements of internal register used to store reference pixels have become a more serious obstacle. Since prediction is based on 4×4 block in this paper, top 8 reference pixels or left reference pixels will be read from SRAM in one clock period. However, only one pixel can be read from normal SRAM. Although a method proposed in paper [7] has solved the above problem, it also introduces redundant pixels and costs large RAM resources. In order to reduce the number of redundant pixels and the cost of RAM resource, a new method called Stepped-RAM Reading is proposed in this paper. In our design, the data width for SRAM is set as 8 pixels width. Although 8 pixels can be read out of SRAM, continuous pixels reading cannot be realized if only one SRAM is used. Therefore, two SRAMs should be used to read all necessary reference pixels. Figure 6 illustrates the proposed stepped-RAM reading method.

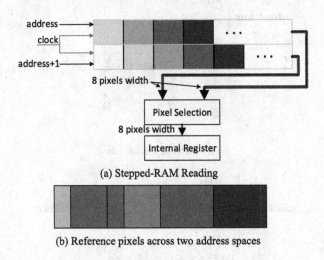

(a) Stepped-RAM Reading

(b) Reference pixels across two address spaces

Fig. 6. Stepped-RAM (Color figure online)

With the design of the proposed architecture, several necessary reference pixels can be read in one pipeline period when setting the output data width to 8 pixels. Furthermore, continuous RAM-reading can be realized. As shown in Fig. 6(b), RAM-reading may be discontinuous in one RAM in the case that the blue reference pixels cross two address spaces in one pipeline period. For this case, a redundant SRAM is introduced, and two addresses lines are connected to two SRAMs separately. Consequently, two 8-pixles width is obtained, and necessary reference pixels are multiplexed to remove redundant useless pixels. As shown in Fig. 6(a), any arbitrary continuous reading can be realized by introducing a redundant RAM and setting the addresses appropriately.

3.4 Universal Multiplierless Prediction Unit for Intra Prediction

To improve the throughput, a parallel hardware architecture for angle, planar and DC prediction was proposed in work [4] which also causes high hardware costs. Therefore a universal architecture is proposed to implement the three prediction modes. Due to the similarity (weighted mean) between angle and planar prediction calculation, angle and planar prediction can be combined by using a few of multiplexers. In the similar way, DC prediction can also be embedded into angle and planar prediction unit.

Universal prediction architecture consists of universal address arbitration and universal calculation unit. Universal address arbitration is realized by using several multiplexers among angle, planar and DC address arbitration circuits. The proposed universal calculation architecture for one prediction pixel is shown in Fig. 7. N is a variable decided by prediction mode and prediction unit. Shifter and multiplexer are used in universal prediction unit which replace multiplier in calculation equations. For angle and planar prediction, 16×4 multipliers are saved in 4×4 block-based prediction units by using shifters and multiplexers. Furthermore for DC prediction, first row and first column are filtered selectively based on the position of 4×4 block in the prediction unit (PU).

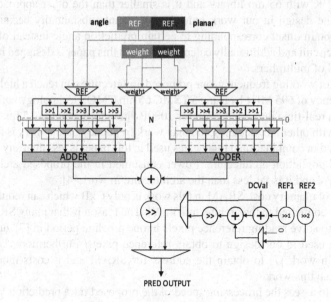

Fig. 7. Universal calculation unit

4   Implement Result

The proposed architecture is implemented in Verilog-HDL at RTL level and synthesized with TSMC 65 nm library. To assess the performance of the proposed intra prediction VLSI architecture, Table 1 compares the performance of the proposed architecture with the state-of-arts in literatures in terms of hardware cost, speed, memory and consumed power.

Table 1. Comparison of HEVC intra prediction architecture

	This work	[4]	[5]	[7]
Technological process	65 nm TSMC	90 nm TSMC	65 nm TSMC	90 nm TSMC
Processing object	4×4	8×8	4×4	4×4
Gates	42 K	700 K	77 K	89 K
SRAM	6 kB	N/A	N/A	21 kB
Modes	All	All	All	All
PU sizes	All	All	All	All
Max working frequency	695 MHz	353 MHz	600 MHz	222 MHz
Power	11.2 mW	114 mW	N/A	N/A

In terms of hardware cost, the gate account of our proposed intra prediction architecture is 42 K with 65 nm library and it is smaller than the other approaches in the literature. The design in our work reduces gate count substantially because LUT is applied to obtain offset corresponding to certain prediction angle instead of combinational logic circuit and additionally calculation unit in this paper is designed in universal form instead of multipliers.

In terms of working frequency, our proposed architecture can reach a high operating clock frequency of 695 MHz by using a TSMC 65 nm CMOS technology which enables to perform a real-time intra prediction for 1080P video format at the 35 fps frame rate. Compared with other architectures, the max work frequency in this work is highest and the reason is that combinational logic gates used in this paper is less than any other 4×4 block-based prediction architecture. Power consumed in the proposed architecture is only 11.2 mW and it is far less than the architecture in work [4].

In terms of memory cost, SRAM in this work is only 6 kB which can reduce memory cost by 70% compared to the architecture in [7]. The reason is that many SRAM arrays are applied to solve reading reference pixels in one pipeline period in [7] and only two SRAMs are used in our design to obtain reference pixels. Furthermore, LUT is also introduced in work [7] to obtain the address for SRAM and it costs more memory resources than this work.

In order to assess the processing speed of the proposed intra prediction VLSI architecture, Table 2 compares the throughput of the proposed architecture with work [8] and work [9]. As we can see from Table 2, the proposed architecture is faster than the other approaches in the literature in terms of processing speed and it allows achieving higher throughput. The throughput in this work is 16 pixels /cycle, and consumes only 1 clock cycles per 4×4 PU. In work [8], only 2 pixels can be predicted in one cycle and a 4×4 PU prediction will be performed in 8 cycles. In work [9], a 4×4 PU prediction will take 4 cycles. As a result, the proposed intra prediction architecture can greatly reduce the processing cycles and improve the system throughput, which reduces the number of clock cycles per 4×4 PU by 75 % ~ 87.5 % compared to the methods in [8, 9].

Table 2. Comparison of throughput of the proposed architecture with work [8] and work [9]

	This work	[8]	[9]
Technological process	65 nm TSMC	40 nm TSMC	65 nm TSMC
Pixels /cycle	16 pixels	2 pixels	4 pixels
Cycles /4 × 4 PU	1 cycle	8 cycles	4 cycles

5 Conclusion

A stepped-RAM reading and multiplierless VLSI architecture for intra prediction in HEVC is proposed in this paper. In order to increase the throughput, stepped-RAM reading method is proposed to realize reading RAM pixels in one pipeline period. A new reference pixel-mapping method, universal address arbitration and multiplierless prediction calculation unit are proposed to reduce hardware cost. Experimental results show that, the proposed architecture can reach a high operating clock frequency of 695 MHz by using a TSMC 65 nm CMOS technology which enables to perform a real-time intra prediction for 2560 × 1440 video at the 35 fps frame rate. Compared with previous architectures, the proposed architecture can greatly increase working frequency and reduce hardware cost.

Acknowledgment. This work was supported in part by the Fundamental Research Funds for the Central Universities (3102016ZY024), Fundamental Natural Science Research Funds of Shaanxi Province (2016JM6077), Innovation Foundation for Dissertation of Northwestern Polytechnical University (CX201616) and Graduate Starting Seed Fund of Northwestern Polytechnical University (Z2016119).

References

1. Kim, I.-K., McCann, K., Sugimoto, K., Bross, B., Han, W.-J., Sullivan, G.: High efficiency video coding (HEVC) test model 12 (HM12) encoder description. In: ITUT/ISO/IEC Joint Collaborative Team on Video Coding (JCTVC) document JCTVC-N1002 (2013)
2. Sullivan, G.J., Ohm, J.-R., Han, W.-J., Wiegand, T.: Overview of the high efficiency video coding (HEVC) standard. IEEE Trans. Circ. Syst. Video Technol. **22**(12), 1649–1668 (2012)
3. Li, F., Shi, G., Wu, F.: An efficient VLSI architecture for 4x4 intra prediction in the high efficiency video coding (HEVC) standard. In: 18th IEEE International Conference on Image Process, pp. 373–376 (2011)
4. Liu, Z., Wang, D., Zhu, H., et al.: 41.7BN-pixels/s reconfigurable intra prediction architecture for HEVC 2560×1600 encoder. In: 38th International Conference on Acoustics, Speech, and Signal Processing, pp. 2634–2638 (2013)
5. Liu, C., Shen, W., Ma, T., Fan, Y., Zeng, X.: A highly pipelined VLSI architecture for all modes and block sizes intra prediction in HEVC encoder. In: 19th IEEE International Conference on ASIC, pp. 201–204 (2013)
6. Kalali, E., Adibelli, Y., Hamzaoglu, I.: A high performance and low energy intra prediction hardware for High Efficiency Video Coding. J. Real-Time Image Process. 719–722 (2012)

7. Zhou, J., Zhou, D., Sun, H., et al.: VLSI architecture of HEVC intra prediction for 8 K UHDTV applications. In: 21th IEEE International Conference on Image Processing, pp. 1273–1277 (2014)
8. Huang, C.T., Tikekar, M., Chandrakasan, A.P.: Memory-hierarchical and mode-adaptive HEVC intra prediction architecture for quad full HD video decoding. IEEE Trans. Very Large Scale Integr. Syst. **22**(7), 1515–1525 (2014)
9. Palomino, D., Sampaio, F., Agostini, L., et al.: A memory aware and multiplierless VLSI architecture for the complete Intra Prediction of the HEVC emerging standard. In: 19th IEEE International Conference on Image Processing, pp. 201–204 (2012)

A Sea-Land Segmentation Algorithm
Based on Sea Surface Analysis

Guichi Liu[✉], Enqing Chen, Lin Qi, Yun Tie, and Deyin Liu

School of Information Engineering, Zhengzhou University, Zhengzhou, China
iegcliu@gs.zzu.edu.cn,
{ieeqchen,ielqi,ieytie}@zzu.edu.cn

Abstract. Ship detection from optical remote sensing imagery is an important and challenging task. Sea-land segmentation is a key step for ship detection. Due to the complex and various sea surfaces caused by waves, illumination and shadows, traditional sea-land segmentation algorithms often misjudge between land and sea. Thus, a new segmentation scheme based on sea surface analysis is proposed in this paper. Then the adaptive threshold can be determined according to statistical analysis to different types of patches from the optical remote sensing images. Experimental results show that our algorithm has better performance compared to the traditional algorithms.

Keywords: Sea-land segmentation · Optical remote sensing imagery · Sea surface analysis

1 Introduction

Ship detection from optical remote sensing imagery is of vital importance due to its wide range of applications such as oceanic traffic surveillance, vessel traffic services, fishery management, and so forth. Many existing algorithms used to detect ships in the ocean suffer from different weather conditions like clouds, mists and ocean waves. Besides, the disturbance from land area results in more pseudotargets for ship detection. All these factors lead to a higher false alarm rate for ship detection. If sea and land areas can be separated correctly, then all false targets in land area can be removed to improve the detection accuracy. Therefore, sea-land segmentation becomes a key issue for ship detection from optical remote sensing imagery.

There are three categories of sea-land segmentation methods: prior geographical information based, gray value histogram based and texture based methods. The methods based on prior geographical information utilize the normalized difference water index (NDWI) [1] to generate a very precise sea-land mask [2]. For the gray value histogram based algorithms, sea-land segmentation is implemented according to a threshold. The threshold is determined based on some specific criteria, such as OTSU

This work is supported in part by "the National Natural Science Foundation of China under Grant, 61331021".

E. Chen et al. (Eds.): PCM 2016, Part I, LNCS 9916, pp. 479–486, 2016.
DOI: 10.1007/978-3-319-48890-5_47

[3] based on the optimal principle of maximum between-class variance and minimum within-class variance, Bayesian segmentation [4] based on maximum likelihood, minimum error based method [5, 6] and maximum entropy [7, 8]. However, these traditional algorithms may not applicable to the images with even-distributed gray level. For optical remote sensing imagery with sea waves, noises and shadows, there always exists misjudgment between land and sea among these algorithms.

Another category of sea-land segmentation methods are based on texture analysis. Zhu [9] combined gray value and texture to form a new mixed image and then implement segmentation for the new mixed image. Xia [10] integrated the original gray-level remote sensing image with texture features extracted by local binary patterns for sea-land segmentation. Li [11] proposed that the sea area in optical remote sensing image meets the Gaussian distribution. Parameters of the Gaussian statistical model of sea are applied for sea-land segmentation. You [12] presented a new sea-land segmentation scheme based on the adaptively established statistical model of sea. This solution can work well for harbor background with docked ships, but it may be less successful for optical remote sensing images in open oceans, especially in cluttered sea surfaces.

This paper proposes a new sea-land segmentation algorithm based on sea surface analysis. First, the sea surface of the input image is analyzed, and the sea regions are blocked out. Then, the statistical parameters of sea area are calculated from the pre-determined sea area. Finally, the adaptive threshold according to the difference of variance of sea area and other regions can be used to do segmentation. The experiments validate the effectiveness and robustness of our segmentation algorithm.

The remainder of this paper is organized as follows. Section 2 explains the sea surface analysis in detail. Section 3 presents our sea-land segmentation algorithm. Section 4 gives the simulation results carried on the optical remote sensing images and finally conclusions are drawn in Sect. 5.

2   Sea Surface Analysis

The complex sea surface usually leads to misjudgment between land and sea, therefore, sea surface analysis can improve performance of sea-land segmentation. Besides, appropriate sea surface analysis can make the segmentation results less easily influenced by the variation of illumination and sea surface conditions. Two novel features are proposed in [13] to describe the image intensity distribution on the majority and the effective pixels. Clearly, sea water is the major component of the sea surface, hence, local intensity similarity and local texture similarity exist in sea surfaces from optical remote sensing images. However, this similarity can be ruined by land areas, ships and their wakes, as well as clouds and islands, so these areas become abnormal regions relative to the sea surfaces. It is obvious that sea water is the main region of the image, so the majority intensity number can be defined as follows:

$$C_m = Min\left\{ arg\left(\sum_{i=1}^{2^b} X(i) > P_1 N_I \right) \right\} \tag{1}$$

Where X is the descending array of the image grey-level histogram, b is the digitization bit of the gray image, P_1 is the percentage which describes the proportion of majority pixels in the image, and N_I is the number of whole image pixels. Therefore, the majority intensity number C_m can be used to count the intensity number of P_1 majority pixels.

The effective component of the image is made up of sea water and abnormal regions. Obviously, besides the effective component, sea surfaces comprise some random noises. If the proportion of random noises in the image is defined as P_2, then the proportion of effective pixels in the image is $1 - P_2$. Similarly, the effective intensity number can be defined as follows:

$$C_e = Min\left\{ arg\left(\sum\nolimits_{i=1}^{2^b} X(i) > (1 - P_2)N_I \right) \right\} \qquad (2)$$

From the definition of these two features, we can conclude that the number of majority or effective intensities on complex sea surfaces is usually larger than that on sea water. Namely, the heterogeneous sea surfaces have larger C_m or C_e values than the homogeneous ones. Therefore, when $C_m < m$ or $C_e < e$ (thresholds m and e are set according to the image to be analyzed), the corresponding P_1 or $1 - P_2$ pixels are connected for sea region extraction from homogeneous sea surfaces or heterogeneous ones. As shown in Fig. 1, compared with (a), (d) is more heterogeneous with various abnormal regions, such as land, ships and man-made places, so (d) should have larger C_m or C_e values. After analyzing, we find that $C_m = 12$, $C_e = 120$ for the first image

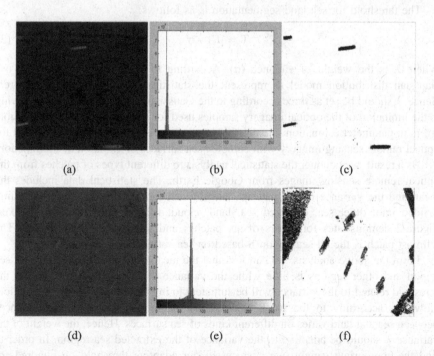

Fig. 1. Examples of sea region extraction: (a) and (d) are sample images from Google Earth;(b) and (e) are their gray value histograms;(c) and (f): the white pixels illustrate the sea water regions, while the black pixels represent the abnormal regions.

in (a) and $C_m = 16$, $C_e = 98$ for the second image in (d). Therefore, the small value for C_m or C_e can be adopted to locate the sea regions, which can be seen from (c) and (f), the white pixels correspond to sea regions.

3   Sea-Land Segmentation with Adaptive Threshold

From the above sea surface analysis, sea regions can be extracted from the image, in which sea regions are marked as 1 s and abnormal regions are marked as 0 s. Our sea-land segmentation algorithm is based on the adaptive threshold according to statistical parameters of the sea region. Here, a statistical Gaussian model [11] is adopted to adaptively estimate the statistical parameters of the sea regions and the algorithm is as follows.

1. Sea regions extraction based on sea surface analysis.
2. The largest connective sea region can be obtained based on the previous result, and then locate its geometric center P.
3. Point P is adopted as the starting point; then traverse the sea region to find a set of points P' satisfying that all pixels in the $N \times N$ (empirically set as 50 in our experiments) neighboring regions are marked as sea. Then we can label points P' as all sea regions S.
4. The mean μ and variance σ are calculated from the all sea region S, and they are adopted as the statistical parameters of the Gaussian model.

The threshold for sea-land segmentation is as follows:

$$T = \mu + \lambda\sigma \tag{3}$$

Where λ is the weight of variance (σ). According to [11], it is acceptable to use Gaussian distribution model to represent the statistical characteristics of sea area. Hence, λ should be set as three according to the Gaussian distribution. However, owing to the limitation of the optical imagery samples used for statistical test and the possible errors in parameter estimation, the threshold with λ set as three cannot work well for optical remote sensing imagery with complex sea surfaces or variation of illumination.

As a result, we conduct the statistical analysis to different types of patches from the optical remote sensing images from Google Earth. The statistical data includes the mean and the variance of the patches, and the categories of patches can be mainly divided into: quiet sea, cluttered sea, land, cloud, islands, ships and their wakes. Figure 2 demonstrates four pairs of six patches and their mean and variance. The leftmost patch is the all sea region S based on sea surface analysis.

From the above analysis, we can find that the mean difference between the all sea region and other regions is little while the variance difference is significant, so the threshold related to the variance will be sufficient to implement sea-land segmentation. However, according to the patch analysis, the degree of the variance differences between sea and land varies on different kinds of sea surfaces. Hence, the weight of the variance λ should be adaptive to the variance of the extracted sea region. In order to find the appropriate weight, we have tested our adaptive threshold on hundreds of

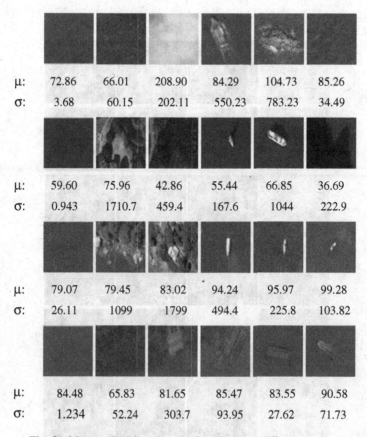

Fig. 2. Mean and variance comparison between different patches

optical sensing images. Finally, the empirical formulas used to calculate the threshold
are concluded as follows.

$$T = \begin{cases} \mu_R + 20 * \sigma_R (0 < \sigma_R \ll 1) \\ \mu_R + 10 * \sigma_R (1 < \sigma_R \ll 3) \\ \mu_R + 5 * \sigma_R (\sigma_R > 3) \end{cases} \tag{4}$$

Where μ_R and σ_R are the mean and variance of the extracted all sea region S
respectively. Simultaneously, we find that the threshold is the same as that proposed in
[12] when the variance of the all sea region is bigger than three.

4 Experimental Results

In experiments, we apply the optical remote sensing images from Google Earth to test
the performance of the proposed sea-land segmentation algorithm. To compare the
performance of the proposed method, another two approaches are also performed on

484   G. Liu et al.

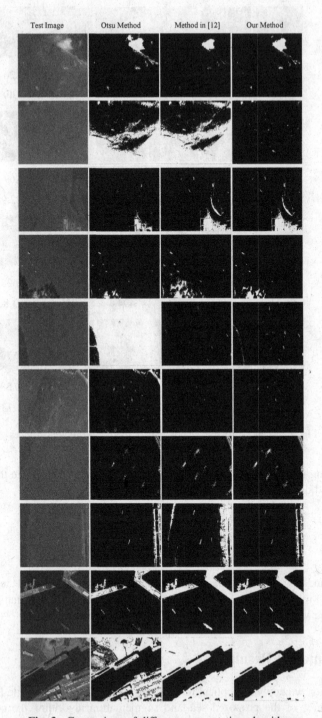

Fig. 3. Comparison of different segmentation algorithms

these test images. One is Otsu method and the other is the method based on statistical model of sea [12]. Figure 3 gives some segmentation examples and comparative results on test images.

From the results in Fig. 3, we can see that Otsu method cannot always implement rough sea-land segmentation correctly. If the segmentation scheme is based on Otsu method, the final segmentation result may be unsatisfactory. While our method is based on sea surface analysis, this can avoid the negative segmentation such as the segmentation results presented in the second row. Besides, if the threshold is inappropriate, then the segmentation result cannot maintain the integrity for suspected targets. As sea-land segmentation is the key step in ship detection, the inappropriate threshold may lead to an increase in the false alarm rate in the subsequent ship detection. Taking the 5th and 6th images as examples, we can see that the suspected targets using other methods are not so obvious or complete as using our method. From the comparative results of last three inshore images, we can see both our method and the method in [12] are much better than Otsu method, for some land area are marked as sea area in Otsu method, while in our method sea area and land area can be separated clearly.

5 Conclusion

In this paper, we present a sea-land segmentation algorithm based on sea surface analysis. Sea surface is firstly analyzed to extract sea regions, and the sea regions are then used to locate the all sea region which is used to compute statistical parameters of the sea model. Finally, the adaptive threshold is obtained based on the significant variance difference between sea region and other regions.

Our algorithm avoids the unsatisfactory segmentation caused by Otsu method or segmentation scheme based on Otsu method, while our method can correctly classify the land and sea. Furthermore, the adaptive threshold based on the variance difference analysis is more efficient and conducive to the subsequent ship detection for its ability to maintain the integrity of suspected targets, as demonstrated in the experiments. In conclusion, our solution can not only deal with the segmentation for harbor background with docked ships, but also work well for optical remote sensing images in open oceans.

References

1. Gao, B.C.: Ndwi - a normalized difference water index for remote sensing of vegetation liquid water from space. Remote Sens. Environ. **58**(3), 257–266 (1996)
2. Besbinar, B., Alatan, A.A.: Inshore ship detection in high resolution satellite images: approximation of harbours using sea-land segmentation. In: Proceedings of SPIE Image and Signal Processing for Remote Sensing XXI, vol. 9643 (2015)
3. Otsu, N.: A threshold selection method from gray level histogram. IEEE Trans. Syst. Man Cybern. **1**(1), 62–66 (1979)
4. Zhaoliang, C., Qinghua, W., Hailin, C., Shoushi, X.: Ship auto detection method based on minimum error threshold segmentation. Comput. Eng. **33**(11), 239–241 (2007)
5. Kittler, J., Illingworth, J.: Minimum error thresholding. Pattern Recogn. **19**, 41–47 (1986)

6. Cho, S., Haralick, R., Yi, S.: Improvement of kittler and illingworth's minimum error thresholding. Pattern Recogn. **22**, 609–617 (1989)
7. Kapur, J.N., Sahoo, P.K., Wong, A.K.C.: A new method of gray-level picture thresholding using the entropy of the hisgram. Comput. Vis. Graph. Image Process. **29**(2), 273–285 (1985)
8. Wang, S., Schuurmans, D., Peng, F., Zhao, Y.: Learning mixture models with the regularized latent maximum entropy principle. IEEE Trans. Neural Netw. **15**(4), 903–916 (2004)
9. Zhu, C., Zhou, H., Wang, R., Guo, J.: A novel hierarchical method of ship detection from spaceborne optical image based on shape and texture features. IEEE Trans. Geosci. Remote Sens. **48**(9), 3446–3456 (2010)
10. Xia, Y., Wan, S., Jin, P., Yue, L.: A novel sea-land segmentation algorithm based on local binary patterns for ship detection. Int. J. Sig. Process. Image Process. Pattern Recogn. **7**(3), 237–246 (2014)
11. Wenwu, L., Yi, L.: Detection of ship in optical remote sensing image of median-low resolution. Master's thesis of national university of defense technology (2008)
12. You, X., Li, W.: A sea-land segmentation scheme based on statistical model of sea. In: 4th International Congress on Image and Signal Processing, vol. 3, pp. 1155–1159. IEEE Press (2011)
13. Yang, G., Li, B., Ji, S., Gao, F., Xu, Q.: Ship detection from optical satellite images based on sea surface analysis. IEEE Geosci. Remote Sens. Lett. **11**(3), 641–645 (2014)

Criminal Investigation Oriented Saliency Detection for Surveillance Videos

Yu Chen[1], Ruimin Hu[2,3(✉)], Jing Xiao[3,4], Liang Liao[2], Jun Xiao[2], and Gen Zhan[2]

[1] State Key Laboratory of Software Engineering, Wuhan University, Wuhan, China
cynercms@whu.edu.cn
[2] National Engineering Research Center for Multimedia Software,
Computer School of Wuhan University, Wuhan, China
{hrm,liaoliangwhu,zhangen}@whu.edu.cn
[3] Hubei Provincial Key Laboratory of Multimedia and Network Communication Engineering,
Wuhan University, Wuhan, China
junxiao@whu.edu.cn
[4] Research Institute of Wuhan University in Shenzhen, Shenzhen, China

Abstract. Detecting the salient regions, namely locating the key regions that contain rich clues, is of great significance for better mining and analyzing the crucial information in surveillance videos. Yet, to date, the existed saliency detection methods are mainly designed to fit human perception. Nevertheless, what we value most during in surveillance videos, i.e. criminal investigation attentive objects (CIAOs) such as pedestrians, human faces, vehicles and license plates, is often different from those sensitive to human vision in general situations. In this paper, we proposed criminal investigation oriented saliency detection method for surveillance videos. A criminal investigation attentive model (CIAM) is constructed to score the occurrence probabilities of CIAOs in spatial domain and novelly utilize score to represent saliency, thus making CIAO regions more salient than non-CIAO regions. In addition, we refine the spatial domain saliency map with the motion information in temporal domain to obtain the spatio-temporal saliency map that has high distinctiveness for regions of moving CIAOs, static CIAOs, moving non-CIAOs and static non-CIAOs. Experimental results on surveillance video datasets demonstrate that the proposed method outperforms the state-of-art saliency detection methods.

Keywords: Surveillance videos · Saliency detection · CIAO · CIAM

1 Introduction

Surveillance videos have been widely utilized in various applications among which criminal investigation is the most common one. Different from traditional videos, they are captured not for better viewing experience but for analysis and recognition of special objects or events. As a consequence, detecting the salient regions, namely locating the key regions that contain rich clues, is of great significance for better mining and analyzing the crucial information in surveillance videos.

E. Chen et al. (Eds.): PCM 2016, Part I, LNCS 9916, pp. 487–496, 2016.
DOI: 10.1007/978-3-319-48890-5_48

Existing saliency models are based on multiple disciplines including cognitive psychology, neuroscience and computer vision and can be generally classified into two categories: block/pixel based methods and region based methods according to the shapes of visual subsets [1].

Most of early approaches [2, 3] are block/pixel based where pixel-wise center-surround contrast is commonly used. Valenti et al. [4] made an assumption that salient objects in the visual field have specific structural properties, being edges, colors or shapes that make them different than their surroundings. Based on this assumption, global important structures are inferred by utilizing these properties and saliency map is generated by weighing the structural information. Achanta et al. [5] proposed an efficient saliency detection method by simply calculating the pixel-wise difference of image feature vectors which contain color information and illumination information as well. Other than measuring distance in Euclidean space, Klein et al. [6] defined the center-surround contrast in an information-theoretic way as the Kullback-Leibler Divergence on difference features such as intensity, color and orientation.

With the development of image segmentation methods, especially superpixel segmentation [7], region based saliency detection emerges. Different from block based methods, global regional contrast [8, 9] is widely adopted in regional based methods [10–13]. Generally speaking, the input images are first segment into regions aligned with intensity edges and then compute a regional saliency map. For each region, saliency score is defined as the average saliency scores of its contained pixels. Perazzi et al. [14] decomposed a given image into perceptually homogeneous elements then saliency measurement in terms of color and spatial distribution is consistently formulated as high dimensional Gaussian filters. Jiang et al. [15] proposed an iterative method which combines both bottom-up salient stimuli and object-level shape prior. Fang et al. [16, 17] proposed a novel saliency detection model incorporating spatio-temporal cues in compressed domain.

Both kinds of methods are developed on the basis of the human perception theory. Nevertheless, what we value most during in surveillance videos, i.e. criminal investigation attentive objects (CIAOs) such as pedestrians, human faces, vehicles and license plates, is often different from those sensitive to human vision in general situations. It is inappropriate to directly apply the abovementioned methods to determine where is salient in surveillance videos.

In this paper, we proposed a saliency detection method for surveillance videos based on the criminal investigation attentive model (CIAM), which highlights regions that contribute most in criminal investigation (typically pedestrians, human faces, vehicles and license plates) rather than that of where human eyes are drawn. This model scores the occurrence probability for CIAOs, and the output score is then innovatively utilized to represent the saliency in spatial domain and obtain a spatial domain saliency map. Then, motion information in temporal domain is introduced to refine the spatial domain saliency map hence the moving CIAOs are better distinguished from the static CIAOs and make regions of moving CIAOs more salient, which is in accord with the criminal investigation attention.

The rest of this paper is organized as follows. Section 2 details our proposed saliency detection method for surveillance videos. Section 3 presents the experimental results. Conclusion and future work of this paper are described in Sect. 4.

2   Proposed Method

2.1   The Overall Framework

The proposed criminal investigation oriented saliency detection framework is shown in Fig. 1. First, a feature based CIAM is constructed to score the occurrence probability for each kind of CIAOs (i.e. pedestrians, faces, vehicles, license plates) separately. Spatial domain saliency map for each kind of CIAOs is calculated by utilizing the score. We then fuse these maps to obtain the final spatial domain saliency map. Incorporated with temporal saliency map, the final spatio-temporal saliency map is generated.

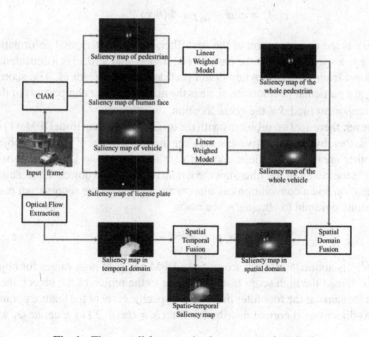

Fig. 1. The overall framework of our proposed method

2.2   Saliency Calculation in Spatial Domain

The saliency map in spatial domain indicates the occurrence probability of CIAO. To measure the occurrence probability in each picture, CIAM is built to detect the CIAO-like features and return the score maps. By employing some post-processing (i.e. non-linear transformation, normalization and so on), we can then obtain the spatial saliency map.

- The Criminal Investigation Attentive Model

– Pedestrian and vehicle score generation

In order to get the score maps of pedestrian and vehicle, we employ deformable part-based models (DPM) [18, 19]. Since the approaches for calculating the score map are the same for pedestrians and vehicles, we use object to refer to them in general in the description of the approaches.

To obtain the score of an image from DPM, a HOG feature pyramid is extracted, and we use the trained DPM to calculate the score on each level of the pyramid. For better understanding of the approach, we briefly introduce the DPM model first. It is a combined filter on histogram of oriented gradient (HOG) features to represent an object category, consisting of a root filter with a set of parts filters and associated deformation models. The example ϑ at a certain position and scale is scored by a function of the following form:

$$f_\gamma = max_{c \in C(x)} \gamma \cdot \Phi(\vartheta, c) \tag{1}$$

Here, γ is the concatenation of the root filter, the part filters, and deformation cost weights, c is a specification of the parts configuration, and $\Phi(\vartheta, c)$ is a concatenation of subwindows from a feature pyramid and part deformation features. The score of the model f_γ at a particular position and scale is the maximum over components of the score of that component model at the given location.

However, there are two problems with the original score map from DPM: (1) it suffer from noise thereby the distinctiveness between the score values of interested objects and that of other area is not obvious enough; (2) the scores from DPM only show high response at the center of the filter, not the whole region of the object. Thus a non-linear transformation and a convolution calculation are applied on the scores from each level of the feature pyramid to obtain a score map:

$$score_L(x, y) = e^{f_r(x,y)} * \psi_L \tag{2}$$

where $e^{f_r(x,y)}$ is applied to stretch scores from DPM and give high values for objects. ψ_L is used to spread the high score from the center to the region of the object, the size of which is the same as the root filter in DPM at a specific level of the feature pyramid. We use a two-dimensional normal distribution filter $h = f(x, \mu, \Sigma)$ to generate ψ_L with

$$\mu = \left[\frac{m+1}{2} \quad \frac{n+1}{2} \right]^T, \quad \Sigma = \begin{bmatrix} m & 0 \\ 0 & n \end{bmatrix} \tag{3}$$

where m, n denote the size of the filter in the specific level L of the feature pyramid. Then the filter is formed as follows:

$$\psi_{L_{ij}} = \frac{h(i,j)}{min(h)} \quad L = 1, 2 \dots p, i = 1, 2 \dots m, j = 1, 2 \dots n \tag{4}$$

After the score map of each level is obtained, a bilinear interpolation is employed to ensure the size of the score map equals to that of the origin image. The final score map is:

$$score_{p/v}(x, y) = max_{L=1,2...p} \frac{score_L(x, y) - s_{min}}{s_{max} - s_{min}} \tag{5}$$

where s_{max} and s_{min} denote the maximum and minimum value of the score map.

The score map of pedestrian $score_p$ and vehicle $score_v$ are obtained by using the DPM templates of pedestrian γ_p and vehicle γ_v respectively.

- Human face saliency score generation

In surveillance videos, the human faces are usually quite small, so we consider the whole face as a salient region. Furthermore, the human face in surveillance videos is difficult to detect due to pose variations, illumination changes, blurring artifacts and low resolution. To solve these problems, we use a new type of feature proposed by Liao et al. [20], called Normalized Pixel Difference (NPD). This feature is efficient to compute and has several desirable properties, including scale invariance, boundedness, and the capability of reconstructing the original image. The NPD feature between two pixels in an image is defined as:

$$D(x, y) = \frac{x - y}{x + y} \tag{6}$$

where $x, y \geq 0$ are intensity values of the two pixels, and $D(0, 0)$ is defined as 0 when $x = y = 0$.

A deep quadratic tree learner is used to learn and combine an optimal subset of NPD features to boost their discriminative power. The faces are then scored by only a single soft-cascade AdaBoost classifier, without pose labeling or clustering in the training stage. The scores of AdaBoost classifiers in all stages of the cascade are used to generate the final score of the human face:

$$score_f = G(x) = G(D(x, y)) \tag{7}$$

- License plate saliency score generation

The features used for license plate detection are usually low level features and they are designed for specific scenes. Due to the lack of generality, we only treat the possibility of license plates in surveillance video as a two-value problem, namely the license plate exists or not. We detect the license plate using an open source code EasyPR [21] which performs well in our datasets. The score map of the license plate is:

$$score_l = \begin{cases} 1 & where\ license\ plate\ exist \\ 0 & otherwise \end{cases} \tag{8}$$

- The saliency map in spatial domain

Once the score map is obtained, we normalize it to a grey-scale map values from 0 to 255 according to the score value:

$$S = 255 \times \frac{score(x, y) - s_{min}}{s_{max} - s_{min}} \tag{9}$$

where s_{max} and s_{min} denote the maximum and minimum value of the score map.

The saliency maps of pedestrian S_p, vehicle S_v, human face S_f and license plate S_l are generated by the score maps computed from Eq. (5) for pedestrians and vehicle, Eq. (7) for faces and Eq. (8) for license plates respectively.

2.3 Saliency Calculation in Temporal Domain

In criminal investigation, moving objects also contain rich information which may be valuable clues. Therefore, motion information is introduced to refine saliency detected in spatial domain. Different from common videos, the background of surveillance videos are usually static. In such condition, noise caused by the motion of background is significantly reduced, thus making it much easier to obtain clean saliency map in temporal domain. Employing the optical flow estimation method proposed by Brox [22], the motion vector field MVF of each frame is produced. As most of the motion vectors of background regions are null, we can simply utilize the length of the motion vector to measure the saliency in temporal domain for the sake of low computational complexity. We denote U, V as the motion in horizontal and vertical orientations respectively, then the saliency at the coordinate (x, y) in temporal domain is formulated as:

$$S_T(x, y) = \sqrt{U(x, y)^2 + V(x, y)^2} \tag{10}$$

Then, we normalize S_T into [0 255] to generate the saliency map in temporal domain.

2.4 Saliency Map Fusion

- Fusion of spatial domain saliency maps

For the reason that face/license plate is a part of pedestrian/vehicle, we propose to fuse maps of pedestrians and faces as well as that of vehicles and license plates to obtain the pedestrian-face saliency map S_{pf} and the vehicle-license plate saliency map $S_{v,l}$ first. Linear weighed model is employed to perform the saliency map fusion, which is expressed in Eqs. (13) and (14):

$$S_{pf} = \alpha_{pf} \cdot S_f + (1 - \alpha_{pf}) \cdot S_p \tag{13}$$

$$S_{v,l} = \alpha_{v,l} \cdot S_l + (1 - \alpha_{v,l}) \cdot S_v \tag{14}$$

where α_{pf} and $\alpha_{v,l}$ denote the weights for pedestrian-face saliency map fusion and vehicle-license plate saliency map fusion respectively, in the range of [0 1]. According to our knowledge, face/license plate is more informative and valuable than other parts of pedestrian/vehicle. Therefore, a higher weight is given for regions of faces and license plates during the fusion. In Eqs. (13) and (14) the weight for face or license plate regions approximates to 1 for the reason that face/license plate is a part of pedestrian/vehicle and the saliency values for regions of faces or license plates in S_p or S_v are positive. By forcing the saliency values of face/license plate in S_f/S_l higher than the maximum value in S_p/S_v and adding the saliency values of the face/license plate regions in both S_f and S_p/S_l and S_v, we guarantee that the regions of face/license plate are more salient.

After obtaining the pedestrian-face saliency map $S_{p,f}$ and the vehicle-license plate saliency map $S_{v,l}$, the final spatial domain saliency map S_S is generated by fusing them. For saliency value of S_S at the coordinate (x, y), we take the max value between $S_{p,f}$ and $S_{v,l}$. Then, the final saliency map in spatial domain is formulated as:

$$S_S(x, y) = max(S_{p,f}(x, y), S_{v,l}(x, y)) \tag{15}$$

From probabilistic aspect, we choose the one between face/pedestrian and license plate/vehicle that is more likely to appear in the frame for the reason that there can't be a region belonging to both pedestrian and vehicle. Hence, max value is more reasonable than average or linear weighted value to represent the probability based saliency.

• Generation of spatial-temporal saliency map

For the purpose of distinguishing the saliency of moving objects and static objects, motion information in temporal domain is incorporated. The final saliency map $S_{S,T}$ is generated by linear combination of the saliency maps in spatial domain and temporal domain, which is defined as:

$$S_{S,T} = \alpha_{S,T} \cdot S_S + (1 - \alpha_{S,T}) \cdot S_T \tag{16}$$

where $\alpha_{S,T}$ denotes the fusion coefficient that weighs the influence of spatial domain saliency and temporal domain saliency. By introducing motion information, we highlight the moving CIAOs over static CIAOs, which is in accord with our knowledge to criminal investigation that moving objects are usually more informative and valuable.

3   Experimental Results

3.1   Test Video Sequences

As there is a high-definition trend of surveillance videos, we carried out the experiments on eight HD surveillance video clips from both public and private datasets to better illustrate the effectiveness of our proposed method: Gate of resolution 720p HD (1280×720) from the public PKU-SVD [23] dataset, Road of resolution 1080p HD (1920×1080) from the public PKU-HUMANID [24] dataset, Crossroad of resolution 720p HD from a street surveillance, and Playground, Park and Community of resolution 1080p HD from campus surveillance. Examples of the eight videos are shown in Fig. 2.

Fig. 2. Example frames of the test videos.

3.2   Visual Comparison

We measure the performance of our spatio-temporal saliency approach, and compare our method with two image saliency methods: region based contrast (RC) [8], spectral residual saliency (SR) [2], and two video saliency works: cluster-based co-saliency (CS) [9], self-resemblance based saliency detection (SD) [3]. Figure 3 gives a visual comparison of different methods.

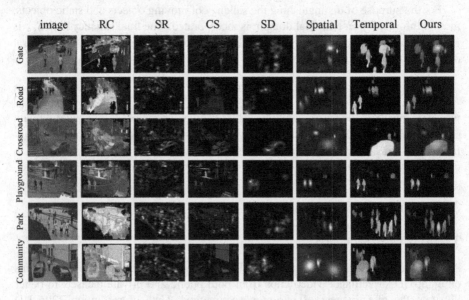

Fig. 3.   Saliency detection results on the test sequences

From the results, we can clearly observe that all the comparison methods detect the background and non-CIAOs more or less while our proposed approach only emphasizes the CIAO regions. This is mainly because that the comparison methods are developed based on human perception, which emphasize the regions by the rule of HVS other than according to the classification of CIAOs and non-CIAOs. Moreover, our method further highlights the faces and license plates among CIAOs, which can be seen more obviously in the spatial domain saliency map. In addition, the proposed spatial-temporal saliency map can distinguish the moving CIAOs and static CIAOs and highlight the former ones (e.g. the vehicles at the center in Crossroad and the vehicle on the right in Community are static). In our method, the saliency maps in feature and temporal domain improve each other, mutually completing the missing information, thus achieving better results. Taking Community as an example, we cannot detect the car on the right in temporal domain because it is static. However, it is detected in spatial domain. For another instance, the region of the car in Villa is missing in spatial domain saliency map due to the miss detection of DPM method, while it is well detected in temporal domain.

The saliency map in temporal domain may seem noisy, thereby affecting the overall result. This is because the background is not exactly static. We can further improve the performance by employing more complex but accurate temporal saliency detection methods.

4 Conclusion

Different from the human perception model widely used in saliency detection, we propose a criminal investigation attentive model oriented to surveillance video analysis to score the occurrence probability of CIAOs. Based on it, we develop a spatial domain saliency detection method, which highlights the CIAO regions over non-CIAO regions in accord with the criminal investigation attention. By integrating the score information in spatial domain with the motion information in temporal domain, we divide each frame into regions of moving CIAOs, static CIAOs, moving non-CIAOs and static non-CIAOs whose saliency values progressively decrease. In this way, the saliency map is further refined. Experimental results on surveillance video datasets demonstrate that the proposed method outperforms the state-of-art saliency detection methods.

Acknowledgements. This work was partly supported by the National Natural Science Foundation of China (61231015), the National High Technology Research and Development Program of China (2015AA016306), the National Natural Science Foundation of China (61502348), the EU FP7 QUICK project under Grant Agreement (PIRSES-GA-2013-612652) and the Natural Science Fund of Hubei Province (2015CFB406).

References

1. Borji, A., Cheng, M.M., Jiang, H., et al.: Salient object detection: a survey. arXiv preprint arXiv:1411.5878 (2014)
2. Hou, X., Zhang, L.: Saliency detection: a spectral residual approach. In: IEEE International Conference on Computer Vision and Pattern Recognition, pp. 1–8 (2007)
3. Seo, H.J., Milanfar, P.: Static and space-time visual saliency detection by self-resemblance. J. Vis. **9**(12), 15 (2009)
4. Valenti, R., Sebe, N., Gevers, T.: Image saliency by isocentric curvedness and color. In: IEEE International Conference on Computer Vision, pp. 2185–2192 (2009)

5. Achanta, R., Hemami, S., Estrada, F., et al.: Frequency-tuned salient region detection. In: IEEE International Conference on Computer Vision and Pattern Recognition, pp. 1597–1604 (2009)
6. Klein, D.A., Frintrop, S.: Center-surround divergence of feature statistics for salient object detection. In: IEEE International Conference on Computer Vision, pp. 2214–2219 (2011)
7. Achanta, R., Shaji, A., Smith, K., et al.: SLIC superpixels compared to state-of-the-art superpixel methods. IEEE Trans. Pattern Anal. Mach. Intell. **34**(11), 2274–2282 (2012)
8. Cheng, M., Mitra, N.J., Huang, X., et al.: Global contrast based salient region detection. IEEE Trans. Pattern Anal. Mach. Intell. **37**(3), 569–582 (2015)
9. Fu, H., Cao, X., Tu, Z.: Cluster-based co-saliency detection. IEEE Trans. Image Proc. **22**(10), 3766–3778 (2013)
10. Zhang, J., Wang, M., Zhang, S., et al.: Spatio-chromatic context modeling for color saliency analysis. IEEE Trans. Neural Netw. Learn. Syst. **27**(6), 1177–1189 (2016)
11. Chen, Y., Nguyen, T., Harish, K., et al.: Audio Matters in Visual Saliency. IEEE Trans. Circuits Syst. Video Technol. **24**(11), 1992–2003 (2014)
12. Wang, M., Hong, R., Yuan, X., et al.: Movie2Comics: towards a lively video content presentation. IEEE Trans. Multimedia **14**(3), 858–870 (2012)
13. Zhang, J., Wang, M., Gao, J., et al.: Saliency Detection with a deeper investigation of light field. In: International Joint Conference on Artificial Intelligence, pp. 2212–2218 (2015)
14. Perazzi, F., Krähenbühl, P., Pritch, Y., et al.: Saliency filters: contrast based filtering for salient region detection. In: IEEE International Conference on Computer Vision and Pattern Recognition, pp. 733–740 (2012)
15. Jiang, Z., Davis, L.: Submodular salient region detection. In: Proceedings of the IEEE Conference on Computer Vision and Pattern Recognition, pp. 2043–2050 (2013)
16. Fang, Y., Lin, W., Chen, Z., et al.: A video saliency detection model in compressed domain. IEEE Trans. Circuits Syst. Video Technol. **24**(1), 27–38 (2014)
17. Fang, Y., Wang, Z., Lin, W., et al.: Video saliency incorporating spatiotemporal cues and uncertainty weighting. IEEE Trans. Image Process. **23**(9), 3910–3921 (2014)
18. Felzenszwalb, P.F., Girshick, R.B., McAllester, D., et al.: Object detection with discriminatively trained part-based models. IEEE Trans. Pattern Anal. Mach. Intell. **32**(9), 1627–1645 (2010)
19. Zhu, L., Chen, Y., Yuille, A., et al.: Latent hierarchical structural learning for object detection. In: IEEE International Conference on Computer Vision and Pattern Recognition, pp. 1062–1069 (2010)
20. Liao, S., Jain, A., Li, S.: A fast and accurate unconstrained face detector. IEEE Trans. Pattern Anal. Mach. Intell. **38**(2), 211–223 (2016)
21. EasyPR. https://github.com/liuruoze/EasyPR. 14 Jan 2016
22. Brox, T., Malik, J.: Large displacement optical flow: descriptor matching in variational motion estimation. IEEE Trans. Pattern Anal. Mach. Intell. **33**(3), 500–513 (2011)
23. Gao, W., Tian, Y., Huang, T., et al.: The IEEE 1857 standard: empowering smart video surveillance systems. Intell. Syst. **29**(5), 30–39 (2014)
24. Wei, L., Tian, Y., Wang, Y., et al.: Swiss-system based cascade ranking for gait-based person re-identification. In: AAAI Conference on Artificial Intelligence, pp. 1882–1888 (2015)

Deep Metric Learning with Improved Triplet Loss for Face Clustering in Videos

Shun Zhang, Yihong Gong$^{(\boxtimes)}$, and Jinjun Wang

Institute of Artificial Intelligence and Robotics, Xi'an Jiaotong University,
Xi'an 710049, Shaanxi, China
zhangshun876@stu.xjtu.edu.cn, {ygong,jinjun}@mail.xjtu.edu.cn

Abstract. Face clustering in videos is to partition a large amount of faces into a given number of clusters, such that some measure of distance is minimized within clusters and maximized between clusters. In real-world videos, head pose, facial expression, scale, illumination, occlusion and some uncontrolled factors may dramatically change the appearance variations of faces. In this paper, we tackle this problem by learning non-linear metric function with a deep convolutional neural network from the input image to a low-dimensional feature embedding with the visual constraints among face tracks. Our network directly optimizes the embedding space so that the Euclidean distances correspond to a measure of semantic face similarity. This is technically realized by minimizing an improved triplet loss function, which pushes the negative face away from the positive pairs, and requires the distance of the positive pair to be less than a margin. We extensively evaluate the proposed algorithm on a set of challenging videos and demonstrate significant performance improvement over existing techniques.

Keywords: Face clustering in videos · Deep metric learning · Improved triple loss

1 Introduction

Face clustering in real-world videos has attracted increased attention in recent years due to the fast growing popularity of the videos on the Internet, such as movies, TV sitcoms, music videos. Given the faces automatically extracted from target videos, the face clustering task is to partition these faces into a given number of clusters, such that some measure of distance is minimized within clusters and maximized between clusters. A successful solution to face clustering can be applied to many related applications, including automatic annotation of large-scale face dataset, content based video retrieval, video organization, video segmentation, just to name a few.

The video face clustering problem is challenging. In real-world videos, the faces of people have large appearance variations due to changes in head pose,

© Springer International Publishing AG 2016
E. Chen et al. (Eds.): PCM 2016, Part I, LNCS 9916, pp. 497–508, 2016.
DOI: 10.1007/978-3-319-48890-5_49

facial expression, scale and illumination in different shots. There may exist partial occlusions caused by other objects such as hands, glasses and hair. In addition, many uncontrolled factors raise the difficulty, such as low resolution, motion blurring, nonrigid deformation and complex background.

To address these issues, many existing approaches [2,5,12,15–17] explore two kinds of visual constraints based on face tracks: (1) the must-link constraints: all pairs of faces in one face track are from the same person; (2) the must-not-link constraints: two face tracks that appear in the same frame contain faces of different persons. In [2,5], a cast-specific distance metric is learned with the logistic discriminant metric (LDML), such that similar input faces are mapped to nearby points on a manifold and dissimilar faces are mapped apart from each other. Besides, some methods use these constraints explicitly for constrained clustering [16], for joint tracklets linking and clustering [15], or for subspace clustering [17]. However, these methods usually rely on hand-crafted features and then learn a linear transformation over the extracted features, and thus are limited in capturing variety of image appearance and handling complicated nonlinear manifold.

With the remarkable success from the state-of-the-art convolutional neural networks (CNNs), most existing works [1,4,10,13] discriminatively train neural networks to directly learn the non-linear metric function from the input image to a low-dimensional feature embedding given the input label annotations. Among these approaches, the triplet-based network [4,10,13] usually applies a kind of triplet loss function to learn discriminative feature embedding, such that the embedded distance of the positive pair (images of the same class) is closer than that of the negative pair (images of different classes) by a distance margin. For example, FaceNet [10] applies this triplet framework to the face and achieve state-of-the-art performance on the face recognition and verification tasks.

However, the triplet-based methods merely use offline *annotated* images and need to perform hard negative/positive mining [10] for training, while the annotated images are not available in our face clustering problem. In addition, the existing triplet loss function pushes the negative face away from only one positive face, and it does not specify how close the positive pair should be (see details in Sect. 3.2). Faces belonging to the same person may form a large cluster with a relatively large intra-class distance in the learned feature space. In this paper, we explore the visual constraints among face tracks to generate online training samples and then apply the triplet-based network to address large face appearance variations and capture the complicated nonlinear manifold. Moreover, we design an improved triplet loss function which pushes the negative face away from the positive pairs simultaneously, and requires the distance of the positive pair to be less than a margin. Our experiments show that the proposed method of learning the non-linear metric with the improved triplet loss outperforms other existing methods on a set of challenging videos.

2   Related Work

There are several existing works [2,5,15,16] for face clustering in videos. Specifically, based on the visual constraints among face tracks, the unsupervised logistic discriminative metric learning (ULDML) method [2] learns a distance metric, so that faces in the same track are pulled closer, while faces in any face track are pushed away from the ones in another face track with the must-not-link constraints. More recently, based on the Hidden Markov Random Fields (HMRF) model, a probabilistic constrained clustering method [16] is proposed for face clustering in videos. The method exploits the prior knowledge in the neighborhood system of HMRF, and has shown competitive clustering performance. An extension work of [16] is for joint tracklets linking and face clustering in videos [15]. Besides, [17] treats the problem of face clustering in video as the subspace clustering problem and presents a method of weighted block-sparse low rank representation (WBSLRR) to learn a low rank data representation. However, existing approaches often rely on hand-crafted features and then learn a linear transformation over the extracted features, which may not be effective to capture the nonlinear manifold where face samples lie on. In this work, we apply a deep nonlinear metric learning method by adapting all layers of the CNN to learn discriminative face feature representations.

With advances in deep learning [4,13], some face recognition and verification methods [1,10] focus on learning the non-linear metric function from the input image to a low-dimensional feature embedding in a fully supervised way. For example, Chopra et al. [1] discriminatively train the Siamese network with contrastive loss to learn deep metric for face verification. The recently proposed FaceNet [10] directly optimize the compact feature embedding based on the triplet-based loss in [14], using large amount of training data (about tens of millions face images). In contrast, our problem is basically a clustering problem, where labeled data (i.e., the faces with groundtruth names) are not available. Moreover, we analyze the weakness in the original triplet loss, and introduce a new triplet loss function and demonstrate its effectiveness over the commonly used contrastive loss and triplet loss.

3   The Proposed Method

3.1   Problem Statement

Given a set of face tracks $\mathscr{T} = \{T_1, \cdots, T_M\}$ in videos, let $T_i = \{r_1^{(i)}, \ldots, r_{n_i}^{(i)}\}$ denote the ith face track that contains n_i face detections. Let us define a matrix $\mathbf{H} \in \mathbb{R}^{M \times M}$, where $H_{i,j} = 1$ if one face from the face track T_i and one face from the face track T_j appear in one frame, and $H_{i,j} = 0$ otherwise. We can generate a set of positive pairs $\mathscr{P}^+$ with must-link constraints: $\mathscr{P}^+ = \{(r_q^{(i)}, r_u^{(i)})\}$, s.t. $\forall i = 1, \ldots, M$, $\forall q, u = 1, \ldots, n_i$, $q \neq u$. Similarly, if $H_{i,j} = 1$ for T_i and T_j, we can generate a set of negative pairs $\mathscr{N}^-$ with the must-not-link constraints: $\mathscr{N}^- = \{(r_q^{(i)}, r_v^{(j)})\}$, s.t. $\forall i, j = 1, \ldots, M$, $i \neq j$, $\forall H_{i,j} = 1$, $\forall q = 1, \ldots, n_i$, $\forall u = 1, \ldots, n_j$. The goal of our task is to cluster all faces into K groups, where each group contains the faces from one subject.

For a training pair r_1 and r_2, we aim to minimize the distance between a pair of faces from the same person and maximize the distance between a pair

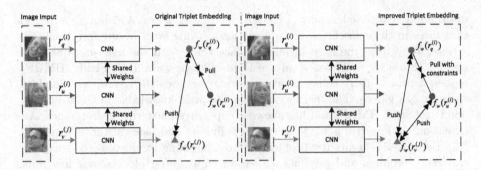

Fig. 1. Illustration of the triplet-based network with the original triplet loss (left) and the improved triplet loss (right) for deep metric learning. The Triplet network consists of three CNNs that share the same architectures and parameters. The circles denote faces from the same person while the triangle denotes a different person.

of faces from different persons. The affinity between r_1 and r_2 is determined by their squared Euclidean distance $D(r_1, r_2)$ in the feature embedding space:

$$D(r_1, r_2) = \|f_w(r_1) - f_w(r_2)\|_2^2 \tag{1}$$

where $f_w(\cdot)$ is the feature embedding output from a CNN that embeds an image into a space where Euclidean distance is appropriate. The smaller the distance $D(f_w(r_1), f_w(r_2))$ is, the more similar the two face patches r_1 and r_2 are.

In the rest of this section, we first briefly introduce the original triplet loss function of the Triplet network. Then, we present a new loss function to improve deep metric learning for face clustering in videos.

3.2   Deep Metric Learning

The triplet-based network consists of three identical CNNs that share the same architectures and parameters. Each triplet consists of two face images of the same person and one face image from another person. The existing triplet-based methods [4,10,13] merely use offline *annotated* images and need to perform hard negative/positive mining for training, and achieve state-of-the-art performance on the face recognition and verification tasks (*e.g.* FaceNet [10]). Although the labeled data (*i.e.*, the faces with groundtruth names) are not available in our problem, we can generate a set of triplets $\mathscr{S}$ using must-link constraints and must-not-link constraints among face tracks: $\mathscr{S} = \{(r_q^{(i)}, r_u^{(i)}, r_v^{(j)})\}$, s.t. $\forall i, j = 1, ..., M$, $i \neq j$, $H_{i,j} = 1$, $\forall q, u = 1, ..., n_i$, $q \neq u$, $\forall v = 1, ..., n_j$. Here, the faces $r_q^{(i)}$ and $r_u^{(i)}$ are from the same face track T_i, while $r_v^{(j)}$ is from the face track T_j which overlaps with T_i in some frames.

In the conventional triplet embedding [10], the face $r_q^{(i)}$ is referred to as an *anchor* of a triplet, $r_u^{(i)}$ is the positive face and $r_v^{(j)}$ is the negative face. The training process encourages the CNN to find an embedding where the embedded distance of the positive pair $(r_q^{(i)}, r_u^{(i)})$ is closer than that of the negative pair

$(r_u^{(i)}, r_v^{(j)})$ by a distance margin α ($\alpha = 1$ in our experiments) as shown in Fig. 1(left). For one triplet, the original triplet loss function is defined as:

$$L_o = \frac{1}{2} \max \left\{ 0, D(r_q^{(i)}, r_u^{(i)}) - D(r_q^{(i)}, r_v^{(j)}) + \alpha \right\}. \tag{2}$$

However, the conventional triplet embedding pushes the negative face $r_v^{(j)}$ away from the anchor $r_q^{(i)}$, not both the faces $r_q^{(i)}$ and $r_u^{(i)}$. Moreover, it does not specify how close the positive pair $r_q^{(i)}$ and $r_u^{(i)}$ should be. Hence, faces belonging to the same person may form a large cluster with a relatively large intra-class distance in the learned feature space.

We illustrate the problem of the original triplet embedding by analyzing the gradients of the loss in (2). We first define three difference vectors $\Delta_{u,q}$, $\Delta_{v,q}$ and $\Delta_{v,u}$:

$$\Delta_{u,q} = f_w(r_u^{(i)}) - f_w(r_q^{(i)}), \quad \Delta_{v,q} = f_w(r_v^{(j)}) - f_w(r_q^{(i)}), \quad \Delta_{v,u} = f_w(r_v^{(j)}) - f_w(r_u^{(i)}). \tag{3}$$

We use a parameter $\beta_0 \in \{0,1\}$ to indicate if the triplet loss in (2) is non-zero, i.e., if $L_o > 0$, $\beta_0 = 1$, and otherwise $\beta_0 = 0$. We can compute the gradients $\frac{\partial L_o}{\partial f_w(r_q^{(i)})}$, $\frac{\partial L_o}{\partial f_w(r_u^{(i)})}$ and $\frac{\partial L_o}{\partial f_w(r_v^{(j)})}$ as:

$$\frac{\partial L_o}{\partial f_w(r_q^{(i)})} = -\beta_0(\Delta_{u,q} - \Delta_{v,q}), \quad \frac{\partial L_o}{\partial f_w(r_u^{(i)})} = \beta_0 \Delta_{u,q}, \quad \frac{\partial L_o}{\partial f_w(r_v^{(j)})} = -\beta_0 \Delta_{v,q}. \tag{4}$$

Based on the above gradients, the triplet embedding encourages the feature points to move in negative gradient directions during the training process with back propagation. Figure 2(a) visualizes the negative gradient directions for each feature point in the embedding space. We can see three issues from the figure of the original triplet loss. First, the negative point $r_v^{(j)}$ is only pushed away from the anchor $r_q^{(i)}$, not both of faces $r_q^{(i)}$ and $r_u^{(i)}$. Second, the original triplet embedding does not specify how close the positive pair $(r_q^{(i)}, r_u^{(i)})$ should be. Finally, the positive pair $(r_q^{(i)}, r_u^{(i)})$ do not move consistently. For example, $r_u^{(i)}$ only move in the direction between $r_q^{(i)}$ and $r_u^{(i)}$, while $r_q^{(i)}$ would move in the direction with a certain angle.

To address these issues, we propose an improved triplet loss function (referred as ImpTriplet) by pushing the negative face $r_v^{(j)}$ away from both the faces $r_q^{(i)}$ and $r_u^{(i)}$, and requiring the distance of the positive pair $(r_q^{(i)}, r_u^{(i)})$ to be less than a threshold $\hat{\alpha}$ ($\hat{\alpha} = 0.1$) as shown in Fig. 2(b). We define the ImpTriplet loss as:

$$L_s = \underbrace{\max \left\{ 0, \ \Phi(r_q^{(i)}, r_u^{(i)}, r_v^{(j)}) \right\}}_{inter-class \ constraints} + \lambda \underbrace{\max \left\{ 0, \Psi(r_q^{(i)}, r_u^{(i)}) \right\}}_{intra-class \ constraints}, \tag{5}$$

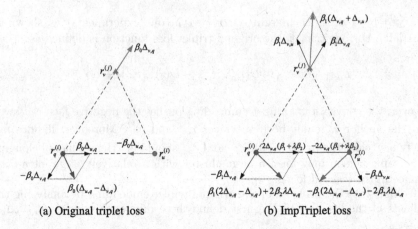

(a) Original triplet loss   (b) ImpTriplet loss

Fig. 2. Illustration of the negative partial gradient direction to the triplet sample. (a) the original triplet loss; (b) the ImpTriplet loss. The triplet samples $r_q^{(i)}$, $r_u^{(i)}$ and $r_v^{(j)}$ are highlighted with blue, red and green, relatively. The circles denote faces from the same person whereas the triangle denotes a different person. The gradient directions are color-coded. (Color figure online)

where $\Phi(r_q^{(i)}, r_u^{(i)}, r_v^{(j)})$ and $\Psi(r_q^{(i)}, r_u^{(i)})$ are defined as:

$$\Phi(r_q^{(i)}, r_u^{(i)}, r_v^{(j)}) = D(r_q^{(i)}, r_u^{(i)}) - \frac{1}{2}\left(D(r_q^{(i)}, r_v^{(j)})) + D(r_u^{(i)}, r_v^{(j)}) \right) + \alpha,$$

$$\Psi(r_q^{(i)}, r_u^{(i)}) = D(r_q^{(i)}), r_u^{(i)})) - \hat{\alpha}. \tag{6}$$

The parameter $\lambda\,(\lambda = 0.02)$ in (5) is a weight to balance the inter-class and intra-class constraints. We also introduce the parameters $\beta_1 \in \{0, 1\}$ and $\beta_2 \in \{0, 1\}$ to indicate if $\Phi(r_q^{(i)}, r_u^{(i)}, r_v^{(j)})$ and $\Psi(r_q^{(i)}, r_u^{(i)})$ are non-zero, respectively. If $\Phi(r_q^{(i)}, r_u^{(i)}, r_v^{(j)}) > 0$, $\beta_1 = 1$, and otherwise $\beta_1 = 0$. Similarly, if $\Psi(r_q^{(i)}, r_u^{(i)}) > 0$, $\beta_2 = 1$, and otherwise $\beta_2 = 0$. We can compute the gradients of the ImpTriplet loss in (5) as:

$$\frac{\partial L_s}{\partial f_w(r_q^{(i)})} = -\beta_1(2\Delta_{u,q} - \Delta_{v,q}) - 2\beta_2\lambda\Delta_{v,q},$$

$$\frac{\partial L_s}{\partial f_w(r_u^{(i)})} = \beta_1(2\Delta_{u,q} + \Delta_{v,u}) + 2\beta_2\lambda\Delta_{u,q}, \quad \frac{\partial L_s}{\partial f_w(r_v^{(j)})} = -\beta_1(\Delta_{v,q} + \Delta_{v,u}). \tag{7}$$

We visualize the negative gradient directions in Fig. 2(b). We show that the proposed ImpTriplet loss directly optimize the embedding space, so that the negative sample $r_v^{(j)}$ is pulled away from the two positive samples $(r_q^{(i)}, r_u^{(i)})$ simultaneously and the positive pair $(r_q^{(i)}, r_u^{(i)})$ are pulled closer to each other until their distance is less than the margin $\hat{\alpha}$. This property allows us to improve the discriminative ability of the learned features.

We train the triplet-based network model with the ImpTriplet loss function by the stochastic gradient decent with momentum. We compute the derivatives of (5) as follows:

$$\frac{\partial L_s}{\partial w} = \beta_1 \frac{\partial \widetilde{L_s}}{\partial w} + \beta_2 \lambda \frac{\partial \hat{L}_s}{\partial w}, \tag{8}$$

where $\frac{\partial \widetilde{L_s}}{\partial w}$ and $\frac{\partial \hat{L}_s}{\partial w}$ are:

$$\begin{cases} \dfrac{\partial \widetilde{L_s}}{\partial w} = 2(f_w(r_q^{(i)}) - f_w(r_u^{(i)}))\dfrac{\partial f_w(r_q^{(i)}) - \partial f_w(r_u^{(i)})}{\partial w} \\[2mm] \qquad - (f_w(r_q^{(i)}) - f_w(r_v^{(j)}))\dfrac{\partial f_w(r_q^{(i)}) - \partial f_w(r_v^{(j)})}{\partial w} \\[2mm] \qquad - (f_w(r_u^{(i)}) - f_w(r_v^{(j)}))\dfrac{\partial f_w(r_u^{(i)}) - \partial f_w(r_v^{(j)})}{\partial w} \\[2mm] \dfrac{\partial \hat{L}_s}{\partial w} = 2(f_w(r_q^{(i)}) - f_w(r_u^{(i)}))\dfrac{\partial f_w(r_q^{(i)}) - \partial f_w(r_u^{(i)})}{\partial w} \end{cases}$$

For the above derivations, we can compute the gradients from each input triplet examples given the values of $f_w(r_q^{(i)})$, $f_w(r_u^{(i)})$, $f_w(r_v^{(j)})$ and $\frac{\partial f_w(r_q^{(i)})}{\partial w}$, $\frac{\partial f_w(r_u^{(i)})}{\partial w}$, $\frac{\partial f_w(r_v^{(j)})}{\partial w}$, which can be obtained by running the standard forward and backward propagations separately for each image in the triplet examples.

4   Experimental Results

4.1   Implementation Details

We first adopt the AlexNet [7] network architecture to pre-train a face CNN (referred as AlexNet-Face) on an external face recognition dataset. The difference is that the number of nodes in the output layer is equal to the number of persons in the training dataset. We use the open source Caffe library [6] to train the network on an external CASIA-WebFace dataset [18] (494,414 images of 10,575 subjects available for the public) for face recognition task in a fully supervised manner. We select 9,427 persons that each person contains more than 15 face images and select 80 % of the images (431,300 images) as our training set and the rest 20 % (47,140 images) as the validation set. All face images are resized to $227 \times 227 \times 3$ pixels.

We compare our proposed method to two state-of-the-art deep metric learning methods with contrastive loss [1] and original triplet loss [10]. The convolutional layers and fully connected layers of the network are initialized from the pre-trained face CNN. We replace the classification layer in the pre-trained CNN with 64 output nodes for feature embedding. Maximum training iteration was set to 10,000 for all the experiments. The learning rate for fine-tuning is set to 0.0001 and keep fixed during the training process.

After extracting 64-D learned features, we use the bottom-up hierarchical agglomerative clustering algorithm [2,11] to merge pairs of face tracks until all face tracks have been merged into the ideal number of clusters (*i.e.* the actual number of people in the video).

4.2   Dataset Information

We evaluate the proposed deep metric learning algorithm on three publicly available videos: *Frontal* video in [15], the first episode from Season 1 of the Bing Bang Theory TV Sitcom (referred as BBT01) in [9,15], and 4 videos from the music dataset[1]. The *Frontal* video is a short video in a constrained scene taken in an indoor environment with a fixed camera. Four persons facing the camera move around and occlude each other in the scene. The BBT01 video is significantly longer (23 min) with the main cast of 5 persons and mostly indoors. The main difficulty in the BBT videos lies in the frequent changes of camera view and scenes. It often includes many full-view shots which contain multiple people at a time. Furthermore, the faces are rather small with averaged size around 75×75 pixels.

We evaluate our method on 4 challenging music videos from YouTube. The sequence of *T-ara* is recorded in live vocal concerts from multiple cameras with different views. The other three sequences of *Darling*, *Bruno Mars* and *Girls Aloud* are MTV videos and they contain multiple shots captured in different scenes. All these videos contain many challenging aspects for multi-object tracking. All music videos contain large face appearance variations across different shots due to changes in pose, view angle, scale, makeup, illumination, camera motion, and heavy occlusions. Moreover, similar faces raise the difficulty due to the challenging inter-class variations. We summarize the statistics of these datatsets in Table 1.

4.3   Evaluation Metrics

We use two measures to evaluate the quality of clustering. The primary measure is the weighted purity as we want to perform clustering with no errors: $W =$

Table 1. Statistics of the video datasets used in our experiments.

Video	Duration (sec)	Frame	Person	Track	Face detection
Frontal	51	1,277	4	43	4,267
BBT01	1,373	32,976	7	689	51,981
T-ara	152	4,547	6	280	12,595
Bruno Mars	270	6,483	11	507	14,837
Darling	197	4,729	8	637	11,522
Girls Aloud	221	5,531	5	984	22,798

---

[1] http://shunzhang.me.pn/papers/eccv2016/.

$\frac{1}{M} \sum_c m_c \cdot p_c$, where each cluster c contains m_c elements and its purity p_c is measured as a fraction of the largest number of faces from the same person to m_c, and M denotes the total number of face tracks in the video. Along with the weighted purity, we also report the clustering accuracy which is referred as the trace of the confusion matrix between the predicted clusters and the ground-truth classes. We evaluate the clustering accuracy at two levels: (1) face detections and (2) tracklets.

4.4 Evaluation Results

We compare our deep metric learning method with four recent state-of-the-art face clustering algorithms [2,15–17] on the Frontal and BBT01 videos using the same face tracklets input and metric as in [15,16]. These algorithms all exploit the visual constraints from face tracks, extract hand-crafted features and learn linear transformations. However, we apply a deep nonlinear metric learning method by adapting all layers of the CNN to learn discriminative face feature embedding. Table 2 shows the clustering accuracy results over faces and tracklets. The results show that our deep metric leaning method with the improved triplet loss achieve higher clustering accuracy than the other four competing methods on both videos.

We quantitatively evaluate the proposed deep metric learning algorithm with several alternatives: AlexNet, a generic feature with 4,096 dimensions learned from the AlexNet on the ImageNet dataset [3]; AlexNet-Face, a 4,096-D face feature trained on the WebFace dataset with the AlexNet architecture; VGG-Face [8], a publicly available face descriptor with 4,096 dimensions. Contrastive: a 64-D face feature trained on the training pairs $\mathscr{P}^+$ and $\mathscr{N}^-$ with the contrastive loss [1]; and Triplet, a 64-D face feature trained on the training triplets $\mathscr{T}$ with the original triplet loss [10]. Table 3 shows the weighted purity of three identity-preserving features (AlexNet, AlexNet-Face and VGG-Face) and three online learned features (Contrastive, Triplet and Ours-ImpTriplet) on 4 music videos. We show that the deep features trained with contrastive and triplet loss functions achieve superior performance to the identity-preserving features trained

Table 2. We compare our deep metric learning method with four recent state-of-the-art face clustering algorithms [2,15–17] on the Frontal and BBT01 videos using the same face tracklets input and metric as in [15,16].

Method	Frontal		BBT01	
	Faces	Tracklets	Faces	Tracklets
ULDML [2]	0.84	0.86	0.58	0.57
HMRF-1 [16]	0.95	0.91	0.63	0.60
HMRF-2 [15]	0.95	0.91	0.67	0.67
WBSLRR [17]	0.96	0.94	0.69	0.72
Ours-ImpTriplet	**1.00**	**1.00**	**0.95**	**0.96**

Table 3. The weighted purity measured on the ideal clusters of each music video.

Videos	T-ara	Bruno Mars	Darling	Girls Aloud
#Face tracks	280	507	236	984
#Ideal	6	11	8	5
AlexNet	0.25	0.36	0.18	0.30
AlexNet-Face	0.31	0.50	0.24	0.33
VGG-Face	0.23	0.44	0.20	0.31
Contrastive	0.69	0.88	0.46	0.67
Triplet	0.51	0.83	0.49	0.67
Ours-ImpTriplet	**0.83**	**0.90**	**0.57**	**0.69**

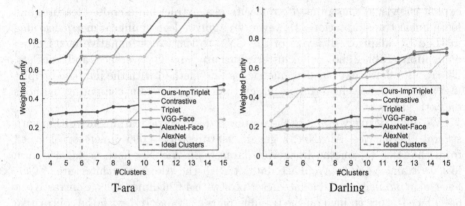

Fig. 3. Quantitative comparison of different deep features with the weighted purity versus the number of clusters on the *T-ara* and *Darling* music videos. The ideal line (dash line) means that all faces are correctly grouped into ideal clusters.

offline (AlexNet, AlexNet-Face and VGG-Face), highlighting the importance of online metric learning. Using the proposed new triplet loss function, Ours-ImpTriplet achieves the best performance. For example, in the *T-ara* sequence, Ours-ImpTriplet achieves the highest weighted purity of 0.83, significantly outperforming other metrics, *e.g.* Contrastive: 0.69 and Triplet: 0.51.

In Fig. 3, we plot the weighted purity measures obtained at different numbers of clusters for different deep features on *T-ara* and *Darling* music videos. The ideal line (dash line) means that all faces are correctly grouped into ideal clusters. The more effective feature can aggregate all faces with higher purity at a smaller number of clusters. The figures show that Ours-ImpTriplet outperforms all other deep features, and is effective to identify persons with large face appearance variations.

5   Conclusions

In this paper, we propose a deep metric learning algorithm in the deep CNN model to learn a low-dimensional feature embedding from the input image with the visual constraints among face tracks. We minimize an improved triplet loss function, which pushes the negative face away from the positive pairs simultaneously, and requires the distance of the positive pair to be less than a margin, such that the Euclidean distances correspond to a measure of semantic face similarity. The experimental results show that the proposed algorithm performs favorably against the state-of-the-art methods on the clustering performance on a set of challenging videos.

Acknowledgement. This work is supported by National Basic Research Program of China (973 Program) under Grant No. 2015CB351705, and the National Natural Science Foundation of China (NSFC) under Grant No. 61332018.

References

1. Chopra, S., Hadsell, R., LeCun, Y.: Learning a similarity metric discriminatively, with application to face verification. In: CVPR (2005)
2. Cinbis, R.G., Verbeek, J., Schmid, C.: Unsupervised metric learning for face identification in TV video. In: ICCV (2011)
3. Deng, J., Dong, W., Socher, R., Li, L.J., Li, K., Fei-Fei, L.: Imagenet: a large-scale hierarchical image database. In: CVPR (2009)
4. Ding, S., Lin, L., Wang, G., Chao, H.: Deep feature learning with relative distance comparison for person re-identification. PR **48**(10), 2993–3003 (2015)
5. Guillaumin, M., Verbeek, J., Schmid, C.: Is that you? metric learning approaches for face identification. In: CVPR (2009)
6. Jia, Y., Shelhamer, E., Donahue, J., Karayev, S., Long, J., Girshick, R., Guadarrama, S., Darrell, T.: Caffe: convolutional architecture for fast feature embedding. arXiv (2014)
7. Krizhevsky, A., Sutskever, I., Hinton, G.E.: Imagenet classification with deep convolutional neural networks. In: NIPS (2012)
8. Parkhi, O.M., Vedaldi, A., Zisserman, A.: Deep face recognition. In: BMVC (2015)
9. Roth, M., Bauml, M., Nevatia, R., Stiefelhagen, R.: Robust multi-pose face tracking by multi-stage tracklet association. In: ICPR (2012)
10. Schroff, F., Kalenichenko, D., Philbin, J.: FaceNet: a unified embedding for face recognition and clustering. In: CVPR (2015)
11. See, J., Eswaran, C.: Exemplar extraction using spatio-temporal hierarchical agglomerative clustering for face recognition in video. In: ICCV, pp. 1481–1486 (2011)
12. Tapaswi, M., Parkhi, O.M., Rahtu, E., Sommerlade, E., Stiefelhagen, R., Zisserman, A.: Total cluster: a person agnostic clustering method for broadcast videos. In: ICVGIP (2014)
13. Wang, J., Song, Y., Leung, T., Rosenberg, C., Wang, J., Philbin, J., Chen, B., Wu, Y.: Learning fine-grained image similarity with deep ranking. In: CVPR, pp. 1386–1393 (2014)

14. Weinberger, K.Q., Blitzer, J., Saul, L.K.: Distance metric learning for large margin nearest neighbor classification. In: NIPS (2005)
15. Wu, B., Lyu, S., Hu, B.G., Ji, Q.: Simultaneous clustering and tracklet linking for multi-face tracking in videos. In: ICCV (2013)
16. Wu, B., Zhang, Y., Hu, B.G., Ji, Q.: Constrained clustering and its application to face clustering in videos. In: CVPR (2013)
17. Xiao, S., Tan, M., Xu, D.: Weighted block-sparse low rank representation for face clustering in videos. In: Fleet, D., Pajdla, T., Schiele, B., Tuytelaars, T. (eds.) ECCV 2014, Part VI. LNCS, vol. 8693, pp. 123–138. Springer, Heidelberg (2014). doi:10.1007/978-3-319-10599-4_9
18. Yi, D., Lei, Z., Liao, S., Li, S.Z.: Learning face representation from scratch. arXiv (2014)

Characterizing TCP Performance for Chunk Delivery in DASH

Wen Hu[1(✉)], Zhi Wang[2], and Lifeng Sun[1]

[1] Tsinghua National Laboratory for Information Science and Technology,
Department of Computer Science and Technology,
Tsinghua University, Beijing, China
hu-w12@mails.tsinghua.edu.cn, sunlf@tsinghua.edu.cn
[2] Graduate School at Shenzhen, Tsinghua University, Shenzhen, China
wangzhi@sz.tsinghua.edu.cn

Abstract. Dynamic Adaptive Streaming over HTTP (DASH) has emerged as an increasingly popular paradigm for video streaming [12], in which a video is segmented into many chunks delivered to users by HTTP request/response over Transmission Control Protocol (TCP) connections. Therefore, it is intriguing to study the performance of strategies implemented in conventional TCPs, which are not dedicated for video streaming, e.g., whether chunks are efficiently delivered when users perform interactions with the video players. In this paper, we conduct measurement studies on users chunk requesting traces in DASH from a representative video streaming provider, to investigate users behaviors in DASH, and TCP-connection-level traces from CDN servers, to investigate the performance of TCP for DASH. By studying how video chunks are delivered in both the *slow start* and *congestion avoidance* phases, our observations have revealed the performance characteristics of TCP for DASH as follows: (1) Request patterns in DASH have a great impact on the performance of TCP variations including *cubic*; (2) Strategies in conventional TCPs may cause user perceived quality degradation in DASH streaming; (3) Potential improvement to TCP strategies for better delivery in DASH can be further explored.

1 Introduction

Recent years have witnessed the increasing popularity of DASH [13], which allows users with heterogeneous networks and devices to receive video streaming with satisfactory quality-of-experience (QoE). Powered by the infrastructure of Content Delivery Networks (CDN), DASH uses standard HTTP requests for chunk delivery. Since such HTTP requests and responses are based on TCP, it is intriguing to study whether the strategies in conventional TCP variations (e.g., cubic) are effective and efficient for chunk delivery in DASH [4].

Generally, DASH videos in the CDN servers requested by users will firstly be segmented into different sizes of chunks, and chunks are then delivered over TCP which goes through two phases, *slow start* and *congestion avoidance* [15], in a video session. Finally, the chunks are parsed by DASH clients, as illustrated

© Springer International Publishing AG 2016
E. Chen et al. (Eds.): PCM 2016, Part I, LNCS 9916, pp. 509–519, 2016.
DOI: 10.1007/978-3-319-48890-5_50

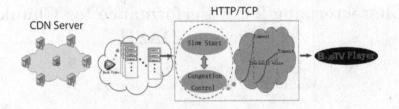

Fig. 1. A demonstration of TCP activity in DASH.

in Fig. 1. To deliver a video chunk, a TCP connection is established between the CDN server and the client. By maintaining the size of the sending window, the server will not over-send packets that can not be received by the client. For quick access to network resources at the beginning, the window size generally grows faster in the slow start phase than in the congestion avoidance phase. In DASH, there are many typical patterns for users to download video chunks, e.g., a user can download chunks intermittently, instead of downloading continuously in large file transmission; and the download intervals change over time, due to the bitrate switch and the dynamic network environment.

On one hand, such chunk request patterns may affect the effectiveness of TCP strategies significantly and on the other hand, one-size-fits-all strategies in conventional TCPs also affect the quality of user experience in DASH. Based on extensive traces on how users request chunks in a large DASH system, and connection-level traces on how CDN servers serve clients, we are able to investigate users behaviors in DASH and measure the performance of TCP for DASH. Our observations reveal not only the mutual effect between TCP strategies and chunk request patterns in DASH, but also the potential improvement that can be conducted to both phases for a better streaming video quality. In particular, our contributions can be summarized as follows.

- *Download behaviors in DASH affect TCP performance.* In our measurement study, we observe that chunk request strategies are designed independently without the awareness of the TCP strategies. (1) Many small flows are generated by todays DASH players, which request the meta files (e.g., a .m3u8 file) and chunks with very small bitrates frequently, and such small flows affect the overall performance of TCP strategies in both phases; (2) Download patterns are changing over time. Due to the users interactions and the dynamic bitrate selection, the TCP performance is far from expected.
- *Possible performance degradation of TCP for chunk delivery in DASH.* Strategies in TCP are not dedicated for DASH streaming either, leading to the user perceived quality degradation. (1) Slow resource allocation. When users perform a sudden player interaction, e.g., seeking, a new TCP connection is established to download the demanded chunks which usually encounters a slow download speed; (2) Bitrate fluctuation. In DASH, bitrate is assigned according to the download speed dynamically. Since the player is not able to predict the download speed of the next TCP connection accurately, the bitrate

changes frequently; (3) Flow competition. Since TCP does not guarantee QoS, a DASH connection needs to compete against other flows, leading to quality degradation including bitrate fluctuation and unfair bandwidth sharing at the user side.

- *Insights on improving TCP strategies for DASH.* Based on the observations in the extensive measurement study, we further discuss the possible improvement that we can do to enhance the performance of DASH videos transmission in the two phases of TCP.

The rest of the paper is structured as follows. We present the background and our measurement results in Sect. 2. We present the lessons learnt from the measurement studies in Sect. 3. We survey related works in Sect. 4. Finally, we conclude the paper with a discussion on the potential improvement for DASH in Sect. 5.

2   Chunk Download Patterns in DASH

Before we present the measurement results, we illustrate the framework of our measurement study in Fig. 2. To begin with, we study the chunk download patterns in a representative DASH system, including the small flows, discontinuous download, and varying download patterns. Then we study the strategies in TCP and focus on the slow start and congestion avoidance phases, which have the major impact on the performance of chunk delivery for DASH. Finally, we present that such chunk download patterns over TCP strategies lead to chunk delivery issues, including the slow resource allocation and inefficient resource competition.

In this section, we study the chunk download patterns in DASH, which will eventually affect the delivery performance over TCP. We have collected session traces from BesTV [6], one of the largest online video providers in China. It is worth noting that the traces consist of the logs recording how users request the video chunks in DASH.

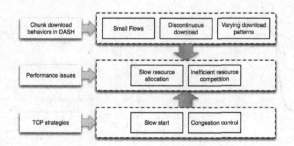

Fig. 2. Framework of our measurement study.

2.1 Data Collection

In order to provide a real and in-depth understanding of relationship between chunk download patterns and delivery performance over TCP, we have collected video session traces from BesTV over 5 month from Jan. 2013 to May 2013. This dataset contains about 1, 390 thousand video sessions and 104 million items. Each item of the BesTV traces recorded how a DASH video chunk was delivered, including the timestamp when the connection was established, the size of the chunk, the time taken to download the chunk, the device information (e.g., OS type) and the bitrate of the chunk, indicated by S1 (avg. 700 kbps), S2 (avg. 1300 kbps), S3 (avg. 2300 kbps), and S4 (avg. 4000 kbps).

We also have collected real world TCP-connection-level traces of DASH video delivery from Tencent [16] from Jun. 2013 to Aug. 2013. These traces are collected from two servers, which are dedicated for video delivery, of Tencent in Shenzhen, China. Note that the two servers are deployed by Tencent for DASH video delivery and under our control. We adopt different strategies to adjust congestion window (CWND) sizes for the servers. One server is under default TCP and another adopts an intelligent and adaptive algorithm proposed in [18] to adjust CWND size according to network status and chunk size.

2.2 Small Flows

We study the size of flows in chunk delivery in DASH sessions. Chunk size is statistically related to the bitrate because playback time is almost the same according to the traces. As illustrated in Fig. 3, each curve is the cumulative distribution function (CDF) of the flow size for a particular DASH bitrate version. We observe that the size of all the chunks delivered is smaller than 2 MB. In particular, for the bitrate version S1, the size of flows is smaller than 400 KB mostly. Besides, DASH meta files (i.e., .m3u8 file in BesTV) are frequently requested by DASH players, and the size of the .m3u8 files is much smaller than video chunks. As illustrated in Fig. 4, over 53 % (resp. 99.5 %) of .m3u8 files have a size smaller than 1 KB (resp. 30 KB). In summary, TCP has to handle small flows for DASH.

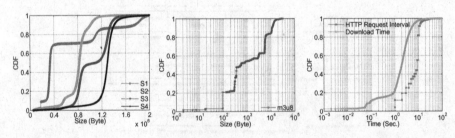

Fig. 3. CDF of chunk files size.

Fig. 4. CDF of .m3u8 files size.

Fig. 5. CDF of HTTP request interval and download time.

Those small flows can affect the performance of TCP strategies greatly in the slow start and congestion avoidance phases, since the network resource has to be allocated in a very instantaneous manner for the delivery of such small flows.

2.3 Discontinuous Chunk Download

In our study, we also observe that DASH video chunks are downloaded discontinuously. As illustrated in Fig. 5, the curves denote the CDF of chunk request interval (i.e., the average time elapse between two consecutive chunk requests), and the CDF of the download time (i.e., the time used to download a chunk) respectively. (1) We observe that over 98 % (resp. 20 %) of the video chunks are downloaded within 10 s (resp. 1 s). (2) We observe that nearly 50 % of the chunk request interval is around 10 s and the download time is much smaller than the chunk request interval, indicating that the downloads take place discontinuously. (3) Furthermore, for more detailed analysis, we decompose the chunk request intervals into different bitrate versions, as illustrated in Fig. 6. We observe that such discontinuous downloads exist in both the meta files (.m3u8) and chunks with different bitrates, and chunks with higher bitrate tend to have a relative concentration interval, which is consistent with users' watching experience. Users expect to obtain high speed and stable network when they watch high quality DASH videos, and that network in turn ensures a higher proportion of request interval concentrates on a small scale (around 10 s) as shown in Fig. 6.

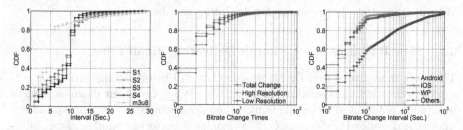

Fig. 6. CDF of download intervals of chunks and metafiles.   **Fig. 7.** CDF of bitrate change times.   **Fig. 8.** CDF of bitrate change interval.

2.4 Changing Request Patterns over Time

Due to both the users' interactions and the dynamic bitrate selection, DASH video chunks' download patterns are changing over time, which also makes the TCP performance far from expected. Before diving into the details, we define several bitrate "changes" as follows. (1) *High resolution change* indicates that the client requests to download a chunk with a higher bitrate than the previous chunk request. (2) *Low resolution change* indicates that the client requests to download a chunk with a lower bitrate than the previous chunk request.

First, we study the changes in bitrates when users download chunks in DASH sessions. As illustrated in Fig. 7, each curve is the CDF of the number of bitrate changes in a session. We observe that over 80 % of the sessions have a change number smaller than 4, which is largely caused by short video playback time, while there is still a certain fraction of sessions with frequent bitrate changes.

Second, we investigate the intervals between consecutive bitrate changes. As illustrated in Fig. 8, the curves represent the CDF of intervals between consecutive bitrate changes in DASH sessions for different types of operating system (OS) devices. We have the following observations: (1) It is consistent with the previous result, that requesting patterns are changing over time; (2) For different OS devices, it seems that the distribution of bitrate change interval is different. The reason may be that DASH players in different OS devices are designed with different strategies to change the bitrate selection, but this is not our focus. We do observe that nearly 90 % of conversion interval of three different OSes (Android, iOS, and others) and 60 % of WP (Windows Phone) is within 10 s, which further indicates that bitrate changes happen in a short time and frequently.

3   Performance of Chunk Delivery over TCP

In this section, we study the performance of TCP strategies, when chunks are delivered according to the request patterns studied in the previous section. As illustrated in Fig. 1, when a chunk is delivered over TCP, the initial CWND size and congestion avoidance affect the transmission of DASH videos. In particular, We will study their performance for delivering chunks.

3.1   Slow Resource Allocation in Delivering Small Files

There are many cases in a DASH session that will cause a competition for network resource in the slow start phase, e.g., (1) When the client downloads meta files (e.g., .m3u8 files) or small chunks, the initial congestion window size determines the download performance. (2) When users perform a sudden player interaction, a new TCP connection is established to download the demanded chunks which usually encounters a slow download speed. Since CWND determines the performance of TCP in the slow start phase, we study the impact of CWND on the chunk/meta file delivery in DASH.

Results in the wild. Based on the TCP traces, we have got the average delivery time for video chunks in DASH. Figure 9 compares the average delivery time of a chunk with different sizes, under different initial CWND sizes in the real-world network environment. In this figure, each sample represents the average delivery time versus the initial CWND size. We have made the following observations: (1) There is a general trend that a larger initial CWND leads to less delivery time, i.e., the average delivery time has been reduced by 50 % when the initial CWND grows from 1 to 10. (2) The initial CWND tends to have a larger

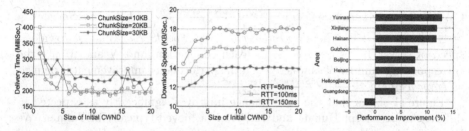

Fig. 9. Delivery time versus initial CWND.

Fig. 10. Download speed versus initial CWND.

Fig. 11. Performance improvement of different areas.

impact on smaller chunks, e.g., for the chunk size of 10 KB, the delivery time is reduced by about 50 %, while for the chunk size of 30 KB, the same initial CWND increment reduces the delivery time by only about 25 %. (3) We observe that when the initial CWND is large enough, increasing it continuously will not reduce the delivery time any more. The reason is that the DASH chunk transmission goes to the other phase, the congestion avoidance phase. And we conduct another experiment that we download two group files from Beijing to Shenzhen respectively. One group is one thousand chunks with 1 MB, and another is two thousands chunks with 500 KB. Transmission of those files must go through congestion avoidance phase and we find that average download speed of files with 500 KB is 23.08 % improved compared to that of files with 1 MB. The results above can confirm the conclusion that request patterns of DASH players have a significant impact on the performance of the TCP congestion controls.

Results in the controlled experiments. In order to eliminate the impact of changing round-trip time (RTT) on the download speed, we also run experiments in a controlled platform (i.e., PlanetLab) to demonstrate the correlation between download speed and the initial CWND. The results are illustrated in Fig. 10. All samples are with the same chunk size and RTT, under different initial CWND sizes. We observe similar results, i.e., the download speed is increasing along with the initial CWND size. In particular, an improvement of download speed by 25.6 % is observed, when the initial window size improves by $3 \sim 4$, and RTT is 50 ms. However, when the initial CWND size is larger than 6, the download speed tends to level off.

Performance improvement. Based on the results in the wild and controlled experiment, we conduct real measurements by configuring two servers with the same setting except the CWND size strategies adopted according to the results as mentioned in Sect. 2. We assume that the connections between clients and servers are independent and random, and TCP performance and delivery speed of DASH video are positive correlated. Then we can study the download speed simply to investigate the TCP performance for DASH. Let us define the average download speed of the server with default TCP and the server with adaptive

CWND size as $AverageServer1 = \frac{\sum_{n=1}^{N} SpeedServer1(n)}{N}$ and $AverageServer2 = \frac{\sum_{m=1}^{M} SpeedServer2(m)}{M}$, where $SpeedServer1$ (resp. $SpeedServer2$) is the download speed of server 1 (resp. server 2) for each connection, and N and M are the corresponding number of samples. Then the performance improvement is defined as $Improvement = \frac{AverageServer2 - AverageServer1}{AverageServer1}$.

Figure 11 shows that the performance improves significantly as expected in different areas except Hunan, and 12.75 % is achieved typically in Yunnan. We then investigate the reason why negative results happened in Hunan and find that the samples is only 2 % of the total number in nine provinces, which is too small to have statistical significance.

3.2 Resource Competition in Chunk Delivery

First, we study the resource competition in TCP when users download via a bottleneck. Two users competed for a bottleneck with each other are selected from our traces. As illustrated in Fig. 12, we set the start time to 0 and the curves represent the download speed of two users. We have made the following observations: (1) Download speed jitter is very intense, e.g., the download speed of user1 changes in a range of 50 KBps to 1 MBps. (2) There is a obvious negative correlation between two users' download speed. We observe that the download speed of user1 increases rapidly after user2 experiences the first speed peak. The results indicate that TCP is not designed with QoS guarantee. Let users compete bandwidth resource at the bottlenecks may have a great impact on the streaming quality in DASH. TCP should adjust the bandwidth allocation to improve QoE for users based on the dynamic characteristics of the video and the current bitrate, although bottleneck link bandwidth competition is a general problem for all types of traffic.

Since TCP does not guarantee QoS, a DASH connection needs to compete against other flows, resulting in a changing quality of streaming at the users. In our traces, we have collected multiple users with the same IP address (e.g.,

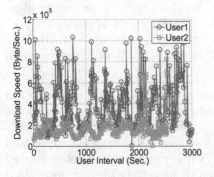

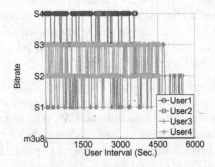

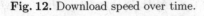

Fig. 12. Download speed over time.   **Fig. 13.** Bitrate fluctuation over time.

in a NAT) requesting chunks during the same period. As illustrated in Fig. 13, such users are competing resource at the bottleneck close to them, e.g., the local downlink capacity. We observe that user3 and user4 are intensively competing for bandwidth, resulting in frequent bitrate changes, e.g., user3 encounters frequent changes between S1 and S2. Our results indicate that as TCP strategies are not streaming aware fundamentally, especially for streaming in DASH with adaptive bitrates, it is hard for users to take full advantage of the dynamic bitrate adaptation.

4   Related Work

4.1   DASH Streaming and Its Chunk Delivery

Sodagar et al. [14] defined the MPEG-DASH standard for multimedia streaming over internet and further defined five specific profiles, each of which addressed a different class of applications, and a set of constraints, limiting the MPD and segment formats to a subset of the entire specification. Apple [5] presented an overview for HTTP Live Streaming, and introduced the architecture of HTTP streaming and how to use the HTTP Live Streaming in details. Adobe [1] introduced Adobe HTTP Dynamic Streaming and even shared a user guide to tell us how to use the DASH system. Joseph et al. [11] presented a simple asymptotically optimal online algorithm, NOVA, to optimize video delivery for a network supporting video clients streaming stored video and maximize the QoE of video clients. Akhshabi et al. [2] studied the performance problems when two adaptive streaming players shared the same network bottleneck and competed for the available bandwidth. However, these works either did not consider the TCP performance for DASH or did not design strategies based on the unique characteristics of DASH, e.g., small flows, discontinuous download, and varying download patterns.

4.2   TCP for Video Chunk Delivery

Hacker et al. [10] proposed an approach to improve the throughput effectively on an uncongested network and maintain fairness using parallel TCP when the network was congested. Esteban et al. [7] investigated the interplay between HTTP adaptive streaming and TCP, and the impact of network delay on achievable throughput. Allman et al. [3] studied the advantages and disadvantages if we raised the initial window size and how TCP should begin transmission after a relatively long idle period. However, none of them took the size of chunk to be delivered and network status into consideration. On the other hand, congestion control algorithm has been explored in [8,9,18,19], and a variety of algorithms have been proposed to improve the performance of congestion avoidance. Wang et al. [17] proposed a new congestion control algorithm, which was more efficient for data delivery in the case of long distance and wireless network than other algorithms such as TCP CUBIC [9] and Veno [8]. However, few of them have been particularly designed for DASH.

5   Concluding Remarks

We conduct a measurement study on the performance of TCP for chunk delivery in DASH. Our observations and results not only reveal that the chunk request patterns in DASH have a great impact on the performance of TCP strategies, but also identify that conventional TCP strategies may cause user perceived quality degradation in DASH streaming. To improve the streaming quality in DASH according to our measurement studies, we discuss the potential improvement to both DASH request strategies and TCP strategies in slow start and congestion avoidance phases.

Increasing CWND in Slow Start. The problem in the slow resource allocation when small files are delivered in DASH over TCP, is that for most cases the size of CWND is small in the existing TCPs – the size of CWND becomes a bottleneck for chunks transmission. Potential improvement can be summarized as follows.

- First, the intuition for us to improve it is to increase the CWND size to an appropriate value, so as to reduce the time for the CWND size increase at the slow start phase. Such strategies have already been adopted by industrial implementation (e.g., Google TCP improvement).
- Second, especially in DASH, we need to study the impact of chunk size, videos' bitrate, network status and the mobile device status (e.g., the remaining energy), and design a new adaptive CWND optimization scheme taking such information into consideration, instead of just simply mapping chunk size to CWND size. The basic idea is to use cross-layer information in DASH to help CWND fast adapt to an optimal size for later chunks delivery.

DASH-Awareness in Congestion Avoidance. In our measurement studies, we also observe that all of the different types of resource competitions result in degraded quality of streaming in DASH. To enhance the streaming quality, on the other hand, chunk request strategies in DASH also need to be TCP-aware, in a way that a proper time elapse is allowed for TCP to eventually gain resources.

Acknowledgement. This work is supported in part by the National Natural Science Foundation of China under Grant No. 61210008, 61272231 and 61402247.

References

1. Adobe: HTTP Dynamic Streaming (2011)
2. Akhshabi, S., Anantakrishnan, L., Begen, A.C., Dovrolis, C.: What happens when HTTP adaptive streaming players compete for bandwidth? In: ACM NOSSDAV (2012)
3. Allman, M., Paxson, V., Stevens, W., et al.: TCP congestion control (1999)
4. Alvarez-Horine, R., Moh, M.: Experimental evaluation of Linux TCP for adaptive video streaming over the cloud. In: IEEE Globecom WKSHPS (2012)
5. Apple: HTTP Live Streaming Overview (2011)

6. Bestv: http://www.bestv.com.cn/
7. Esteban, J., Benno, S.A., Beck, A., Guo, Y., Hilt, V., Rimac, I.: Interactions between HTTP adaptive streaming and TCP. In: ACM NOSSDAV (2012)
8. Fu, C.P., Liew, S.C.: TCP Veno: TCP enhancement for transmission over wireless access networks. IEEE JSAC **21**, 216–228 (2003)
9. Ha, S., Rhee, I., Xu, L.: Cubic: a new TCP-friendly high-speed TCP variant. ACM SIGOPS Operating Syst. Rev. **42**, 64–74 (2008)
10. Hacker, T.J., Noble, B.D., Athey, B.D.: Improving throughput and maintaining fairness using parallel TCP. In: IEEE INFOCOM (2004)
11. Joseph, V., de Veciana, G.: NOVA: QoE-driven optimization of dash-based video delivery in networks. In: IEEE INFOCOM (2014)
12. Li, B., Wang, Z., Liu, J., Zhu, W.: Two decades of internet video streaming: a retrospective view. ACM TOMM **9** (2013)
13. (MPEG), I.J.S.W.: Dynamic adaptive streaming over HTTP (2010)
14. Sodagar, I.: The MPEG-DASH standard for multimedia streaming over the internet. IEEE MultiMedia **18**, 62–67 (2011)
15. Stevens, W,R.: TCP slow start, congestion avoidance, fast retransmit, and fast recovery algorithms (1997)
16. Tencent: Tencent Video (2013)
17. Wang, J., Wen, J., Han, Y., Zhang, J., Li, C., Xiong, Z.: CUBIC-FIT: a high performance and TCP cubic friendly congestion control algorithm. IEEE Commun. Lett. **17**, 1664–1667 (2013)
18. Wang, J., Wen, J., Zhang, J., Han, Y.: TCP-FIT: an improved TCP congestion control algorithm and its performance. In: IEEE INFOCOM (2011)
19. Wei, D.X., Jin, C., Low, S.H., Hegde, S.: FAST TCP: motivation, architecture, algorithms, performance. IEEE/ACM ToN **14**, 1246–1259 (2006)

Where and What to Eat: Simultaneous Restaurant and Dish Recognition from Food Image

Huayang Wang, Weiqing Min, Xiangyang Li, and Shuqiang Jiang[✉]

Key Laboratory of Intelligent Information Processing, Institute of Computing Technology, Chinese Academy of Sciences, Beijing 100190, China
{huayang.wang,weiqing.min,xiangyang.li}@vipl.ict.ac.cn, sqjiang@ict.ac.cn

Abstract. This paper considers the problem of simultaneous restaurant and dish recognition from food images. Since the restaurants are known because of their some special dishes (e.g., the dish "hamburger" in the restaurant "KFC"), the dish semantics from the food image provides partial evidence for the restaurant identity. Therefore, instead of exploiting the binary correlation between food images and dish labels by existing work, we model food images, their dish names and restaurant information jointly, which is expected to enable novel applications, such as food image based restaurant visualization and recommendation. For solution, we propose a model, namely Partially Asymmetric Multi-Task Convolutional Neural Network (PAMT-CNN), which includes the dish pathway and the restaurant pathway to learn the dish semantics and the restaurant identity, respectively. Considering the dependence of the restaurant identity on the dish semantics, PAMT-CNN is capable of learning the restaurant's identity under the guidance of the dish pathway using partially asymmetric shared network architecture. To evaluate our model, we construct one food image dataset with 24,690 food images, 100 classes of restaurants and 100 classes of dishes. The evaluation results on this dataset have validated the effectiveness of the proposed approach.

Keywords: Dish recognition · Restaurant recognition · Multi-Task CNN

1 Introduction

Food tourism is to explore the food as the purpose of the tourism and has become one important part of tourism[1]. In food tourism, where (i.e., the restaurant) and what (i.e., the dish) to eat is a basic need among tourists. In addition, the visual appearance of meals is one of the most important factors in assisting people's food choices [5,17]. Therefore, effectively modeling the visual information and multi-attribute information (e.g., the dish and restaurant information) plays an important role in novel applications like food image based restaurant visualization and recommendation [6,9]. The proliferation of online food image sharing

---

[1] https://en.wikipedia.org/wiki/Culinary_tourism#cite_note-lucy-long-2.

© Springer International Publishing AG 2016
E. Chen et al. (Eds.): PCM 2016, Part I, LNCS 9916, pp. 520–528, 2016.
DOI: 10.1007/978-3-319-48890-5_51

websites (e.g., Yelp and Dianping[2]) has provided rich food data, such as the food images and different attribute information (e.g., the dish labels and the restaurant information) for this research.

Existing methods mainly focus on visual information for food recognition. For example, Yang *et al.* [18] proposed a visual representation for food items that calculates pairwise statistics between local features. Such approach is bound to standardized meals. Lukas *et al.* [4] mined discriminative parts of food images using random forests for dish recognition. Compared with these shallow models, Kagaya *et al.* [10] applied the CNN for food detection and recognition. In addition, some work [1,3,7,16] developed restaurant-specific dish recognition. Based on the food image recognition, Meyers *et al.* [14] further proposed a system which can recognize the contents of the meal from one image, and then predicted its nutritional contents. However, little work has investigated the problem of modeling the correlation among visual content and rich attribute information, especially for simultaneous restaurant and dish recognition from food images.

It is non-trivial to model the visual content, the dish label and the restaurant identity for simultaneous restaurant and dish recognition. Firstly, although the context information such as GPS information enables the restaurant recognition, we do not always obtain this kind of information, especially in the food-related websites. Secondly, simply recognizing the restaurant identity and dishes separately is not reasonable. Each restaurant has its own special dishes with similar visual patterns, which are different from other restaurants, and thus the dish semantics provides the evidence for recognizing the restaurant identity. For example, if we have recognized the dish "hamburger", we can infer that the food image is from the restaurant "KFC" or "McDonald" with larger probability. Therefore, how to design a model to consider the dependence of the restaurant identity on the dish semantics is challenging.

In order to address these problems, after constructing a food image dataset from Dianping including the food images, the dish labels and the restaurant identity, we propose a model called Partially Asymmetric Multi-Task Convolutional Neural Network (PAMT-CNN) to capture both the dish semantics and the restaurant identity (Fig. 1). Considering the dependence of the restaurant

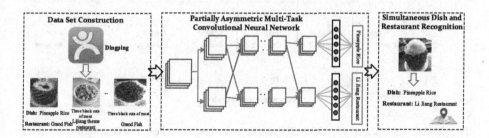

Fig. 1. The proposed framework

---

[2] The largest venue review website in China, similar to Yelp.

identity on the dish semantics, PAMT-CNN makes the lower layer from the restaurant pathway guided by the dish layer to constitute partially asymmetric network architecture. Based on the PAMT-CNN, we can recognize both the dish and restaurant identity from one food image. The right of Fig. 1 shows an example: PAMT-CNN can not only recognize the dish "Pineapple Rice", but also the restaurant identity "Li Jiang Theme Restaurant".

2 PAMT-CNN

2.1 Network Architecture

The designed PAMT-CNN is illustrated in Fig. 2. Two pathways are designed for classification. "Conv", "Pool" and "Fc" represent the convolutional layer, the pooling layer, and the fully connected layer respectively. In addition, the dish pathway is considered as the first pathway and the restaurant pathway as the second pathway. For instance, "Conv5_2" indicates that it is the fifth convolutional layer in the second pathway.

Two key ideas are exploited in PAMT-CNN. (1) The dish semantics and the restaurant identity describe different aspects of the food image and thus need different learning pathways from the raw data to the supervised information. In order to realize it, PAMT-CNN consists of the dish pathway and the restaurant pathway to learn the dish semantics and the restaurant identity, respectively. (2) As discussed before, the restaurant identity should also be influenced by the dish semantics of the food image. To realize this, PAMT-CNN adopts the partially asymmetric network architecture to make the higher layer of the restaurant pathway determined by both the lower layer of the restaurant pathway and

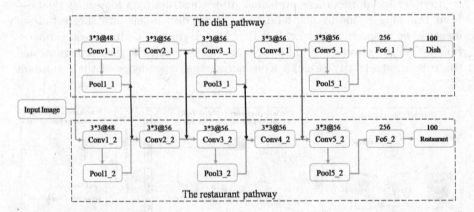

Fig. 2. An illustration of PAMT-CNN. The top imaginary line box is designed for dish classification task and the bottom one is for restaurant classification task. The black double arrow line between two layers denotes that these two layers interact with each other. The red arrow line indicates that the fifth layer from the restaurant pathway is guided by the fourth layer from the dish pathway. (Color figure online)

the dish pathway [8]. Specifically, the fifth convolutional layer of the restaurant pathway is also guided by the fourth convolutional layer of the dish pathway. This is because the higher layers learn not only generic patterns, but also semantically meaningful dish features in the dish pathway [13].

Now we describe the proposed model in details. In the dish pathway, there are five convolutional layers and two fully connected layers, where the first, third, and fifth convolutional layers are followed by the pooling layer. The size of convolution kernels in the convolutional layers are illustrated over each layer in Fig. 2. Both the kernel size and stride size in the pooling layer are three. In the forward propagation stage, the transformation function from $(l-1)^{th}$ layer to the lth can be formulated as two different formulas:

$$x_l^1 = \sigma(W_{l-1}^{1,1}x_{l-1}^1 + b_{l-1}^{1,1} + W_{l-1}^{1,2}x_{l-1}^1 + b_{l-1}^{1,2}), 1 < l \leq 4 \tag{1}$$

where $\sigma(*)$ is the activation function, $\sigma(x) = x$ when $x > 0$ and 0 otherwise. $W_{l-1}^{1,i}(i = 1, 2)$ refers to the weights from $l-1$ layer of the ith pathway to the l layer of the first pathway, and $b_{l-1}^{1,i}$ is the corresponding bias.

$$x_l^2 = \sigma(W_{l-1}^1 x_{l-1}^1 + b_{l-1}^1), 4 < l \leq 7 \tag{2}$$

where W_{l-1}^1 refers to the weights from the $(l-1)^{th}$ layer to the lth layer, and b_{l-1}^1 is the bias. The final output $\tilde{d}$ is defined as:

$$\tilde{d} = softmax(\sigma(W_7^1 x_7^1 + b_7^1)) \tag{3}$$

where $softmax(*)$ is a softmax function.

Similar to the dish pathway, we use the same type of layers and model parameters in the restaurant pathway, but the connections have a little difference. In addition to the last two layers, all the other layers in the restaurant pathway are connected to the previous layers and they are formulated as follows:

$$x_l^2 = \sigma(W_{l-1}^{2,1}x_{l-1}^2 + b_{l-1}^{2,1} + W_{l-1}^{2,2}x_{l-1}^2 + b_{l-1}^{2,2}), 1 < l \leq 5 \tag{4}$$

The final output $\tilde{r}$ is defined as:

$$\tilde{r} = softmax(\sigma(W_7^2 x_7^2 + b_7^2)) \tag{5}$$

2.2 Training

For each dish image, we expect the output $\tilde{d}_i$ and $\tilde{r}_i$ to get close to the goal classification vector d_i and r_i respectively. In our dataset, both the dish and restaurant label have 100 classes. Therefore, d_i and r_i are a 100-D vector with one-shot representation. The loss function for dish classification can be defined as:

$$L_1 = \frac{1}{2}\sum_{i=1}^N \left(d_i - \tilde{d}_i\right)^2 + \frac{\lambda}{2}\sum_{l=1}^3 \left(\|W_l^{11}\|_F^2 + \|W_l^{12}\|_F^2\right) + \frac{\mu}{2}\sum_{l=4}^7 \|W_l^1\|_F^2 \tag{6}$$

where $\tilde{d}_i$ is the output in Eq. 3 for image I_i; λ and μ are the factors to balance the loss and regularization to previous over-fitting.

For the restaurant pathway, we define the loss function for restaurant classification as L_2, which can also be computed according to the loss function of regression:

$$L_2 = \frac{1}{2}\sum_{i=1}^{N}(r_i - \tilde{r}_i)^2 + \frac{\lambda}{2}\sum_{l=1}^{4}\left(\|W_l^{21}\|_F^2 + \|W_l^{22}\|_F^2\right) + \frac{\mu}{2}\sum_{l=5}^{7}\|W_l^2\|_F^2 \quad (7)$$

We select a batch of dish images in the dataset and use L_1 to update the weights W_1 in the dish pathway, and use L_2 to update the weights W_2 in the restaurant pathway. We repeat the two operations until the errors converge.

For one image I_i, we can obtain the dish and restaurant labels simultaneously based on the trained PAMT-CNN.

3   Experiment

3.1   Datasets and Implementation Details

Since none of existing food datasets has the restaurant information, we need to build our food dataset. Specifically, we crawled the food images from Dianping with the dish name and the restaurant information. For preprocessing, we firstly discarded the dish with less than 20 images, and then removed the restaurants with less than 3 dishes and the dishes contained by less than 3 restaurants. The number of the resulted dataset is 24,690 with 100 classes of dishes and 100 classes of restaurants. Each dish image in our dataset belongs to both one of the hundred dishes and one of the hundred restaurants. Figure 3 shows the number of images per restaurant and dish, respectively. For space consideration, we use Arabic numerals to denote restaurants and the dishes. Figure 4 shows some examples from our food dataset [15].

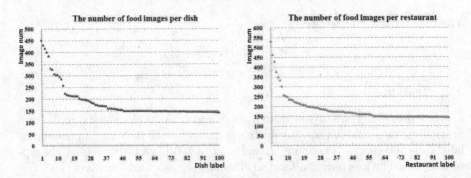

Fig. 3. The distribution of food images per dish and restaurant. For space consideration, we use Arabic numerals to denote restaurants and dishes.

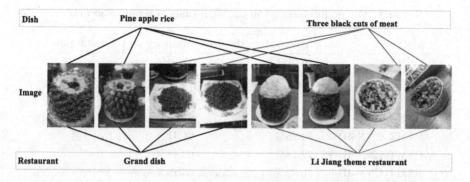

Fig. 4. Some examples of our food dataset. There are two kinds of dishes: Pine apple rice and Three black cuts of meat and two classes of restaurants: Grand dish and Li Jiang theme restaurant

For parameter settings, following AlexNet [11], each image is resized to 256×256, and five 224×224 crops are cropped from the center and the four corners of the resized image. The dropout rate is 0.5 in the last two fully connection layers in each task. The learning rate starts from 0.01 for all layers and is divided by 10, when the error rate stops reducing. It is trained on a single GeForce GTX 780 Ti with 3 GB memory.

3.2 Dish and Restaurant Recognition

To assess our models on the food image dataset, the data set is split into three subsets: 18,626 cases as the training set, 1,122 cases as the validation set and 4,942 cases as the testing set. We adopt classification accuracy as the evaluation metric and choose the following baselines for comparison: (1) CNN-ST: CNN-SingleTask. This baseline trains the dish pathway and the restaurant pathway separately in a single-task way. (2) amtCNN [12]: Each layer of the restaurant pathway is guided by the layer from the dish pathway. (3) amtCNN-Inv: Each layer of the dish pathway is guided by the layer from the restaurant pathway. (4) CNN-MT [2]: This baseline adopts the traditional multi-task deep architecture and each layer between two pathways influences each other. (5) PAMT-CNN-4D: The first fourth layers between two pathways interact with each other while the last remaining layers are separate. (6) PAMT-CNN-4D-2S: The first fourth layers between two pathways interact with each other and the following two layers from the restaurant pathway are guided by the layer from the dish pathway. The last layer between two pathways are separate. (7) PAMT-CNN-4D-3S: The first fourth layers between two pathways interact with each other and the remaining layers from the restaurant layer are guided by the layers from the dish pathway.

The experiment results are shown in Table 1. From these comparison results, we can see that: (1) The interaction between two kinds of information contributes to both dish recognition and restaurant recognition. Therefore, the performance of all the multi-task deep model methods is better than CNN-

Table 1. The performance of all the algorithms in terms of accuracy.

Method	Accuracy on the dish	Accuracy on the restaurant
CNN-ST	70.01 %	56.16 %
amtCNN [12]	70.65 %	59.89 %
amtCNN-Inv	73.72 %	56.21 %
CNN-MT [2]	72.97 %	63.06 %
PAMT-CNN-4D	73.25 %	61.41 %
PAMT-CNN-4D-2S	72.78 %	63.48 %
PAMT-CNN-4D-3S	70.92 %	63.19 %
PAMT-CNN	**74.87 %**	**64.75 %**

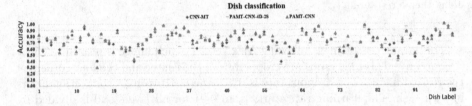

Fig. 5. Comparison of different algorithms over 100 classes of dishes in terms of accuracy. For space consideration, we use Arabic numerals to denote the dishes.

ST. (2) amtCNN in restaurant recognition and amtCNN-Inv in dish recognition has nearly 3 % improvement. These results demonstrate the effectiveness of the guidance from the other pathway. (3) Our method PAMT-CNN outperforms all other baselines. PAMT-CNN in dish recognition and restaurant recognition both has 1 % improvement compared with the best baselines. The reasons are as follows: Firstly, the lower fourth layers of CNN mostly learns generic features [13]. Therefore, interaction with these lower layers between two pathways enables more robust lower layer features. Secondly, the higher layers from the dish pathway learn semantically meaningful dish features. Since the restaurant identity depends on the dish semantics. The guidance from fourth layer of the dish pathway leads to more robust restaurant-oriented features. In addition, the performance of PAMT-CNN is better than PAMT-CNN-3D-2S and PAMT-CNN-3D-3S. The possible reason is that the guidance of higher-level features from the sixth and seventh layer of the dish pathway leads to larger weight of dish-oriented features and thus affect of the performance in restaurant recognition. The detailed comparisons among better baselines CNN-MT, PAMT-CNN-3D-2S and our method PAMT-CNN over each individual class for two tasks are illustrated in Figs. 5 and 6, respectively.

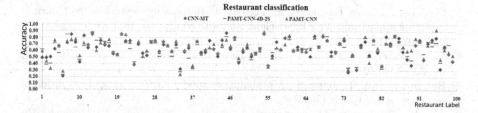

Fig. 6. Comparison of different algorithms over 100 classes of restaurants in terms of accuracy. For space consideration, we use Arabic numerals to denote the restaurants.

4   Conclusion

In this paper, we have proposed a Partially Asymmetric Multi-Task Convolutional Neural Network (PAMT-CNN) model to address the problem of simultaneous dish and restaurant recognition from food images. PSMT-CNN makes the restaurant's identity learned from both the restaurant pathway and the dish pathway to constitute the partially asymmetric shared network architecture. The experiments have justified the effectiveness of our PAMT-CNN. In the future, we plan to investigate the following research directions: (1) We can utilize the correlation among the food images, the dish label and restaurant information learned from the model to conduct novel applications, such as dish and restaurant topic visualization. (2) We will add the user dimension for personalized restaurant recommendation.

Acknowledgements. This work was supported in part by the National Basic Research 973 Program of China under Grant No. 2012CB316400, the National Natural Science Foundation of China under Grant Nos. 61532018 and 61322212, the National High Technology Research and Development 863 Program of China under Grant No. 2014AA015202, China Postdoctoral Science Foundation under Grant No. 2016M590135, Beijing Science And Technology Project under Grant No. D161100001816001. This work is also funded by Lenovo Outstanding Young Scientists Program (LOYS).

References

1. Beijbom, O., Joshi, N., Morris, D., Saponas, S., Khullar, S.: Menu-match: restaurant-specific food logging from images. In: Applications of Computer Vision, pp. 844–851 (2015)
2. Bengio, Y.: Learning deep architectures for ai. Mach. Learn. **2**(1), 1–127 (2009)
3. Bettadapura, V., Thomaz, E., Parnami, A., Abowd, G.D., Essa, I.: Leveraging context to support automated food recognition in restaurants. In: Applications of Computer Vision, pp. 580–587 (2015)
4. Bossard, L., Guillaumin, M., Gool, L.: Food-101 – mining discriminative components with random forests. In: Fleet, D., Pajdla, T., Schiele, B., Tuytelaars, T. (eds.) ECCV 2014. LNCS, vol. 8694, pp. 446–461. Springer, Heidelberg (2014). doi:10.1007/978-3-319-10599-4_29

5. Cordeiro, F., Bales, E., Cherry, E., Fogarty, J.: Rethinking the mobile food journal: exploring opportunities for lightweight photo-based capture. In: Proceedings ACM, pp. 3207–3216 (2015)
6. Ge, M., Ricci, F., Massimo, D.: Health-aware food recommender system. In: ACM, pp. 333–334 (2015)
7. Herranz, L., Xu, R., Jiang, S.: A probabilistic model for food image recognition in restaurants. In: ICME (2015)
8. Jia, Y., Shelhamer, E., Donahue, J., Karayev, S., Long, J., Girshick, R., Guadarrama, S., Darrell, T.: Caffe: Convolutional architecture for fast feature embedding. In: ACM MM, pp. 675–678 (2014)
9. Kadowaki, T., Yamakata, Y., Tanaka, K.: Situation-based food recommendation for yielding good results. In: ICMEW, pp. 1–6 (2015)
10. Kawano, Y., Yanai, K.: Foodcam-256: a large-scale real-time mobile food recognitionsystem employing high-dimensional features and compression of classifier weights. In: Proceedings ACM MM, pp. 761–762 (2014)
11. Krizhevsky, A., Sutskever, I., Hinton, G.E.: Imagenet classification with deep convolutional neural networks. In: Advances in NIPS, pp. 1097–1105 (2012)
12. Liu, S., Cui, P., Zhu, W., Yang, S.: Learning socially embedded visual representation from scratch. In: Proceedings of ACM MM, pp. 109–118 (2015)
13. Zeiler, M.D., Fergus, R.: Visualizing and understanding convolutional networks. In: Fleet, D., Pajdla, T., Schiele, B., Tuytelaars, T. (eds.) ECCV 2014. LNCS, vol. 8689, pp. 818–833. Springer, Heidelberg (2014). doi:10.1007/978-3-319-10590-1_53
14. Meyers, A., Johnston, N., Rathod, V., Korattikara, A., Gorban, A., Silberman, N., Guadarrama, S., Papandreou, G., Huang, J., Murphy, K.P.: Im2calories: towards an automated mobile vision food diary. In: Proceedings of ICCV, pp. 1233–1241 (2015)
15. Wang, S., Jiang, S.: Instre: a new benchmark for instance-level object retrieval and recognition. ACM Trans. Multimedia Comput. Commun. Appl. 11(3), 1–21 (2015)
16. Xu, R., Herranz, L., Jiang, S., Wang, S., Song, X., Jain, R.: Geolocalized modeling for dish recognition. IEEE TMM 17(8), 1187–1199 (2015)
17. Yang, L., Cui, Y., Zhang, F., Pollak, J.P., Belongie, S., Estrin, D.: Plateclick: bootstrapping food preferences through an adaptive visual interface. In: Proceedings of KSEM, pp. 183–192 (2015)
18. Yang, S., Chen, M., Pomerleau, D., Sukthankar, R.: Food recognition using statistics of pairwise local features. In: CVPR, pp. 2249–2256 (2010)

A Real-Time Gesture-Based Unmanned Aerial Vehicle Control System

Leye Wei, Xin Jin$^{(\boxtimes)}$, Zhiyong Wu, and Lei Zhang

Shenzhen Key Lab of Broadband Network and Multimedia, Graduate School at Shenzhen,
Tsinghua University, Beijing, China
weily14@mails.tsinghua.edu.cn,
{jin.xin,zywu,zhanglei}@sz.tsinghua.edu.cn

Abstract. Unmanned aerial vehicles (UAVs) are playing important roles in many fields for their stability and flexibility. However, controlling a UAV by its remote-controller is very difficult especially for the beginners. In this paper, we propose a real-time UAV control system that only exploits shape and movements of the user's hands. A set of gestures that map the hand actions to all motions of the UAV is designed based on subjective experience assessment. 94.898 % of motion accuracy can be achieved with only 0.19 s of latency on average. Compared with other systems, our system reduces 40.625 % and 36.667 % in the latency. To the best of our knowledge, our control system is the first one to realize all motions of the UAV in the actual experiments by only utilizing hand motions.

Keywords: UAV · RealSense · Gesture-based · Control system

1 Introduction

Unmanned aerial vehicles (UAVs) have been increasingly used in many aspects of our daily life. Based on their stable and flexible features, UAVs are used rapidly in dangerous environments, typically in places where are hard for human to arrive at [1, 2]. Due to their complex activities, the control system should be intelligent enough to satisfy the demand of the users. Unfortunately, the existing way to control the UAV by a remote-controller is hard to learn and does not conform to the requirements of the users for controlling. It's necessary to change the original method to other simple, convenient and intelligent methods which are easy to learn [3].

In 1995, Kesslcr et al. proposed that we could communicate with the UAV by a glove which was equipped with 18 sensors to capture the movements of fingers [4]. Similarly, a glove is built at UC Berkeley in 2000 [5]. While the glove and sensors were inconvenient and damageable. Guo et al. explored interaction with an UAV by using tangible device such as Wii-mote [6]. This device changed traditional input devices to motion controllers, but it was uncomfortable for the users to hold such devices for a long time. Sugiura et al. implemented a smartphone to operate an UAV via finger movements [7]. Different taps and swipes on the screen represent different actions of the UAV. It was

© Springer International Publishing AG 2016
E. Chen et al. (Eds.): PCM 2016, Part I, LNCS 9916, pp. 529–539, 2016.
DOI: 10.1007/978-3-319-48890-5_52

convenient to use a smartphone as controller, but it was dangerous because phone calls might disturb the control signal. In [8–11], the Kinect enabled users to interact with their computers through a natural user interface using the positions and angles among user's arms and body [12]. This method was accurate but needed the whole body to appear in front of the Kinect. So it needed a large space and it was also uncomfortable for the users to stand for a long time.

In order to eliminate these restrictions and improve the enjoyment and effectiveness of controlling, a series of gestures have been designed according to the user preferences. Based on these gestures, we build a real-time control system which consists of a communication network made up of a RealSense sensor, a smartphone, a laptop and a microcontroller. One part of the control system is the RealSense sensor, which has many image sensors that can be utilized to discern hand shapes and movements in real time [13]. Overall, the contributions of this study are mainly in three aspects:

1. A new system is built to control the movements of the UAV just rely on gestures instead of holding some sensors or getting the whole body involved. Green-hands can do well in controlling the UAV after an easy training.
2. A set of new gestures that map the hand actions to all motions of the UAV is designed based on subjective experience assessment.
3. The response time of the control system is reduced significantly to satisfy the demand of real-time.

The remainder is structured as follows. The real-time control system is introduced in Sect. 2. Experiments are conducted to verify the effectiveness and latency in Sect. 3. Finally, we conclude the paper in Sect. 4.

2   Control System

2.1   Structure of the Control System

The control system consists of four main parts. The first part is an Intel RealSense sensor, which is a platform for implementing gesture-based Human-Machine interaction techniques. The second part is a laptop which acts as a ground station to process those photos taken by the RealSense. A GUI (Graphics User Interface) in the laptop is used to show the actions of gestures. The third part is a 32-bit Cortex M4 microcontroller STM32F407, which sends commands to the UAV. The forth part is a smartphone that connects to the UAV via repeaters to get the real-time flight data and video stream. User's gestures are tracked by the RealSense, which is connect to the laptop via USB (Universal Serial Bus); gestures are recognized by an Intel RealSense SDK (Software Development Kit) and sent to the microcontroller in the form of related commands via RS-232 (Recommended standard-232) port; commands are switched to PWM (Pulse Width Modulation) signals. Then those signals are sent via a 2.4 G module to control the UAV; flight data and video stream are transferred to the smartphone by Wi-Fi via the repeaters. The structure of the control system is shown in Fig. 1.

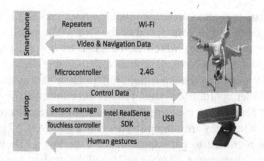

Fig. 1. Structure of the control system.

2.2 Gesture Design

The interaction technology based on gestures is more desirable than methods that require touch or wearable devices because it is easier to reconfigure and program [14]. Gestures that satisfy user preferences will bring much more convenience to the process of controlling. According to this conclusion, we design many series of gestures and make a research to pick up a sort of gestures to meet the needs of controlling the UAV. The designed candidate gestures are shown in Fig. 2.

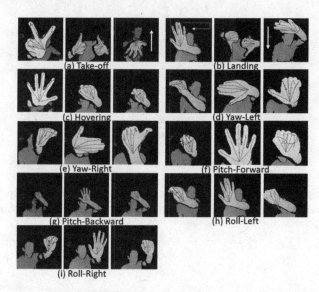

Fig. 2. Gestures we designed for the entire actions of the UAV. From left to right: "V" sign, double thumb-up, raise palm of (a) is about taking-off; wave, double thumb-down, fall palm of the (b) is about landing; spread-fingers, fist, full-pinch of (c) is about hovering; full-pinch and palm towards left (right), thumb-left (thumb-right) of (d) (e) is about yaw-left (yaw-right); full-pinch, palm and fist move forward, backward, left, right of (f) to (i) are about pitch-forward, pitch-backward, roll-left and roll-right.

The UAV consists of 4 arms. Every arm holds a rotor on its end. The motion of the UAV can be changed by varying the speed of the rotors. The whole movements of the UAV include: take-off (landing) which is the same as upward (downward) means increasing (decreasing) the speed of all motors with the same average; hovering means controlling the UAV to fly at a fixed position; roll, pitch or yaw means rotating with X, Y or Z axis of the Euler coordinate system [15]. X axis indicates the nose of the UAV.

The goal of our design is to measure performance of these gestures and get parameters from the users when they are attempting to control the UAV. 17 students (14 males and 3 females) are recruited to participate in the experiment. They are all graduate students. The ages of them range from 22 to 26 and the median age is 24. All of them have used tele-controllers to control toy cars before. Only 1 has used tele-controllers to control an UAV before. None of them has used the RealSense sensor or gestures to control some robots before.

In order to conduct this experiment, a test space is designed in the center of a playground with no obstacles. The length and width of the test space are 10 m. Participants and the RealSense are located at the outside of the test space. Participants need to finish these missions one by one in different series of gestures. The top view of this test space is shown in Fig. 3.

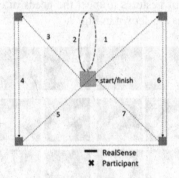

Fig. 3. Top view of the test space.

The participants need to grade those gestures according to their experience after using all interaction techniques with a 5-point Likert scale where 1 represents strong

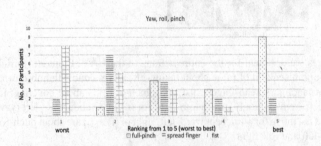

Fig. 4. Histogram of user rankings of moving.

dislike while 5 is very fond of it. After the study, a histogram of user rankings for interaction technique about moving is shown in Fig. 4.

According to the Fig. 4, 9 participants prefer full-pinch to other gestures but none of them grades full-pinch the worst to indicate the moving. Conversely, none of them prefers fist to other gestures and 8 participants grade fist the worst to indicate the moving. So the most suitable gesture for moving is full-pinch. Based on these scores, expectations and variances of all gestures are shown in Table 1.

Table 1. Expectations and variances of different actions

Action	Gesture	Expectation	Variance
Take-off	"V" sign	3.2941	1.8456
	Double thumb-up	3.2941	1.8456
	Raise palm	4.1765	1.0296
Hovering	Spread-finger	4.2941	0.8456
	Full-pinch	3.2353	1.3162
	Fist	3.5882	1.2574
Landing	Wave	4.5882	0.3824
	Double thumb-down	3.5882	0.7574
	Fall palm	3.8235	0.6544
Movements	Full-pinch	4.1765	1.0294
	Spread-finger	2.7059	1.4706
	Fist	1.8235	0.9044

According to the results of the expectations shown in Table 1, the final selected gestures for the quadrotor UAV actions are shown in Fig. 5.

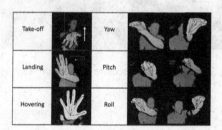

Fig. 5. Relationship between gestures and actions.

Some gestures are designed to act as interaction techniques to control the UAV. The result of the study shows users prefer those gestures that are easy to pose. Raise palm is about taking-off; wave is about landing; spread-fingers is about hovering; full-pinch towards left (right) is about yaw-left (yaw-right); full-pinch moves forward, backward, left, right are about pitch-forward, pitch-backward, roll-left and roll-right.

2.3 Steps of Data Exchange, Hardware and Software

The control system is aiming at translating the gestures to the related commands. Steps of the data exchange process are shown in Fig. 6.

Fig. 6. Steps of data exchange.

First, the depth and color information about gestures are tracked by the RealSense and sent to the laptop; second, shapes and movements of hands are received with the support of the Intel RealSense SDK which includes many APIs to deal with photo information on the laptop; third, according to the relationship between gestures and actions, the related commands are sent to the microcontroller from the laptop; forth, commands are translated into different control signals by the microcontroller. At the same time, an App in the smartphone acts as a GUI so as to show the flight height, angles, battery information and real-time video streams from the on-board camera via Wi-Fi. Moreover, a GUI in the laptop allows the users to watch the effects of the gestures.

Hardware architecture of the control system is shown in Fig. 7. It is mainly constructed with five parts, including a RealSense, a laptop, a microcontroller, an UAV

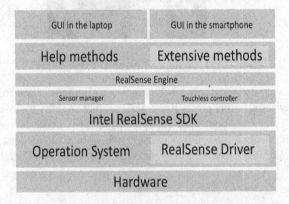

Fig. 7. Hardware architecture of the control system.

Fig. 8. Software architecture of the control system.

and a smartphone. Software architecture of the control system is shown in Fig. 8. With the support of the RealSense Driver and Operation System, Intel RealSense SDK acts as the main part of the system to recognize the gestures. Touchless controller and sensor manager are used to allocate resources to the RealSense engine to finish all computing tasks. Extensive methods allow users to design and implement their special demands. GUIs provide interfaces for users to watch the current situations of the UAV.

3 Experimental Results

3.1 Verification of the Control System

15 cases including different permutations and combinations of those actions are designed to verify the effectiveness of the control system in different environments. The results of the experiments in an indoor environment #1 and a special outdoor environment #2 during a cloudy dusk are shown in Table 2. In those cases, TO, U, F, B, L, R, TL, TR, D and LO mean sending the take-off, upward, forward, backward, left, right, turn-left, turn-right, downward and landing command. Hovering appears between every two actions so we omit it. Unfinished motions are marked by overstrikes for #1 and underline for #2. Snapshots from the experiment are shown in Fig. 9.

Table 2. Experience and variance of different actions

Case	Scenario	#1	#2
1	TO U F D LO	5/5	5/5
2	TO U B D LO	5/5	5/5
3	TO U L <u>D</u> LO	5/5	4/5
4	TO <u>U</u> R D LO	5/5	4/5
5	TO U TL ~~D~~ LO	4/5	3/5
6	TO U <u>TR</u> D <u>LO</u>	5/5	3/5
7	TO U <u>F</u> B D LO	6/6	4/6
8	TO <u>U</u> B <u>F</u> D ~~LO~~	5/6	3/6
9	TO U <u>L R</u> D LO	6/6	4/6
10	TO U R L D LO	6/6	6/6
11	TO U TL ~~TR~~ D LO	5/6	4/6
12	TO U TR TL D LO	6/6	6/6
13	TO U F <u>B</u> L R <u>TL</u> ~~TR~~ D LO	9/10	7/10
14	TO U <u>TL</u> L R F B <u>TR</u> F B R ~~TR~~ LO	12/13	8/13
15	TO U <u>L R</u> F B <u>TL</u> B F <u>TR</u> R <u>TL</u> F B LO	15/15	10/15
	Final result of an environment	93/98	76/98

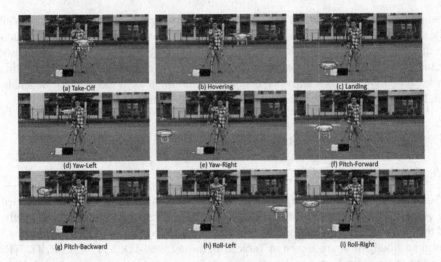

Fig. 9. Snapshots from an experiment, in which a user is controlling a quadrotor.

The flight data can be got by reading the UAV's memory card. The latency of the control system delay between the users and the UAV can be measured by analyzing the video sequence and counting the number of frames elapsed between the users and the UAV movements [12]. The ratio of finishing individual actions in an indoor environment successfully is 93/98 and the final result of a special outdoor environment is 76/98. In order to summarize the latency, we get the data about altitude and angle from the memory card. Figure 10 shows plots about altitude and angle for case No. 12. The time of changing gestures is marked as the red dotted line and the time of changing position is marked as the blue solid line. This script takes movements as the following order: take-off, upward, turn-right, turn-left, downward, and landing.

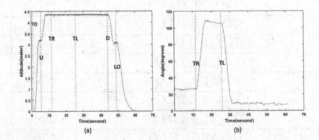

Fig. 10. Plot of the altitude and angle over time during trial #12.

The quadrotor UAV takes related actions successfully when the commonds are transferred to it. Figure 10(a) shows the altitude of the quadrotor UAV over around 65 s. When it gets the take-off command and the altitude of the quadrotor UAV changes from 0 m to 3.24 m. Then it is hovering at this altitude and waiting for the next command. The exact time about those movements can be acquired according to the video sequence.

For example, the gesture about take-off is posed at 2.27 s, and the movement of the quadrotor UAV starts at 2.43 s. The latency of the interaction about take-off is 0.16 s. The angles of the orientation will change when we make turn-left and turn-right commands. Plot of the UAV's angle over time during experiment No.12 is shown in Fig. 10(b). For example, gestures about turn-right is posed at 11.51 s, the UAV starts this action at 11.72 s. The latency of this movement is 0.21 s.

3.2 Discussion of the Control System

We make 15 cases to verify the accuracy and latency of the control system in two different kinds of environments. We have implemented our method using C# on a desktop with four-core Intel Core i5-3470 processor running at 3.20 GHz with 8 GB of RAM. Every case has different interactions to realize. As listed in Table 2 in an indoor environment, 15 cases have 98 motions, and the control system responds to 93 of them successfully. 94.898 % of motion accuracy can be achieved with 0.19 s of latency on average. As listed in Table 2, same motions are tested in a special outdoor environment during a cloudy dusk. The control system responds to 76 of them successfully and the motion accuracy is 77.55 %. There are two systems based on the postures of the whole body to control the UAV had tested the average latency [12, 16]. Compared with other control systems, results of average latency about them are shown in Table 3. But their articles did not provide experiment results about the accuracy so that we can not compare ours with the previous experiments. Our method reduces 40.625 % and 36.667 % in the latency compared with other methods.

Table 3. Compare latency with other control systems

Control system	Average latency
Kinect. Whole body [12]	0.32 s
Kinect. Whole body [16]	0.30 s
Proposed RealSense. Gestures	0.19 s

As marked by the overstrikes in Table 2 of the indoor experiment, the control system fails to respond to 5 motions and 3 of them are turn-right. The gesture of turn-right is full-pinch and twists the hand to the right. Posing this gesture differently leads to the wrong identification results of the RealSense sensor. Except for the turn-right and turn-left in case 12, other motions about turn-right and turn-left are fail in the outdoor experiment. At the same time, the accuracy of the outdoor experiment is lower than the accuracy of indoor experiment due to the illumination variation. The control system also has some failures when the users pose the gestures inaccurately or the users change the gestures too fast to be confirmed by the RealSense sensor during the interaction. Although the control system can recover from these failures, its instability in a short time forces the users to wait. After some practice, the users can perform very well in the interaction. At the beginning of designing this control system, we are aiming at designing a system which is easy to learn for the green-hands. After those experiments, we find that a bit of user training can bring a quite obvious improvement for the users in the interaction with the control system.

4 Conclusion and Future Work

This paper presents a control system based on real-time Human-Machine interface whereby a user can only use gestures to control an UAV. A user study with green-hands involved is made to find a series of gestures that meet the demands and preferences of the users. Controlling the UAV by gestures is really natural and interesting according to the positive feedback of these participants. In a series of cases, the UAV gets more than 94.898 % correct execution of the user's intentions. The latency of the control system is 0.19 s on average. Future work will focus on improving the precision of the control, which means the control system can adapt to more kinds of speed to control the UAV according to the speed of moving gestures.

Acknowledgments. This work was supported by the project of NSFC 61371138 and NSF project of Guangdong 2014A030313733, China.

References

1. Ackerman, E.: Japan earthquake: global Hawk UAV may be able to peek inside damaged reactors. In: IEEE Spectr. **17** (2011)
2. Adams, S., Friedland, C., Levitan, M.: Unmanned aerial vehicle data acquisition for damage assessment in hurricane events. In: Proceedings of the 8th International Workshop on Remote Sensing for Disaster Management, Tokyo, Japan, vol. 30 (2010)
3. Hays, R.T., Jacobs, J.W., Prince, C., Salas, E.: Flight simulator training effectiveness: A meta-analysis. Mil. Psychol. **4**(2), 63 (1992)
4. Kessler, G.D., Hodges, L.F., Walker, N.: Evaluation of the CyberGlove as a whole-hand input device. ACM Trans. Comput.-Hum. Interact. (TOCHI) **2**(4), 263–283 (1995)
5. Hollar, S.E.A.: Cots dust (2000)
6. Guo, C., Sharlin, E.: Exploring the use of tangible user interfaces for human-robot interaction: a comparative study. In: Proceedings of the SIGCHI Conference on Human Factors in Computing Systems, pp. 121–130. ACM (2008)
7. Fernando, C.L., Igarashi, T., Inami, M., Sugimoto, M., Sugiura, Y., Withana, A.I., Gota, K.: An operating method for a bipedal walking robot for entertainment. In: ACM SIGGRAPH ASIA 2009 Art Gallery & Emerging Technologies: Adaptation, pp. 79–79. ACM (2009)
8. Stowers, J., Hayes, M., Bainbridge-Smith, A.: Altitude control of a quadrotor helicopter using depth map from Microsoft Kinect sensor. In: 2011 IEEE International Conference on Mechatronics (ICM), pp. 358–362. IEEE (2011)
9. Asiimwe, R., Anvar, A.: Automation of the Maritime UAV command, control, navigation operations, simulated in real-time using Kinect sensor: a feasibility study. World Acad. Sci. Eng. Technol. **72** (2012)
10. Boudjit, K., Larbes, C., Alouache, M.: Control of flight operation of a quad rotor AR. drone using depth map from Microsoft Kinect sensor. Int. J. Eng. Innovative Technol. **3**, 15–19 (2008)

11. Sanna, A., Lamberti, F., Paravati, G., Manuri, F.: A Kinect-based natural interface for quadrotor control. Entertainment Comput. **4**(3), 179–186 (2013)

12. Mashood, A., Noura, H., Jawhar, I., Mohamed, N.: A gesture based kinect for quadrotor control. In: 2015 International Conference on Information and Communication Technology Research (ICTRC), pp. 298–301. IEEE (2015)

13. http://www.intel.com/content/www/us/en/architecture-and-technology/realsense-overview.html

14. Lambrecht, J., Kleinsorge, M., Krüger, J.: Markerless gesture-based motion control and programming of industrial robots. In: 2011 IEEE 16th Conference on Emerging Technologies & Factory Automation (ETFA), pp. 1–4. IEEE (2011)

15. Walid, M., Slaheddine, N., Mohamed, A., Lamjed, B.: Modeling and control of a quadrotor UAV. In: 2014 15th International Conference on Sciences and Techniques of Automatic Control and Computer Engineering (STA), pp. 343–348. IEEE (2014)

16. Sanna, A., Lamberti, F., Paravati, G., Manuri, F.: A Kinect-based natural interface for quadrotor control. Entertainment Comput. **4**(3), 179–186 (2013)

A Biologically Inspired Deep CNN Model

Shizhou Zhang, Yihong Gong$^{(\boxtimes)}$, Jinjun Wang, and Nanning Zheng

Institute of Artificial Intelligence and Robotics, Xi'an Jiaotong University,
Xi'an 710049, People's Republic of China
shizhouzhang@stu.xjtu.edu.cn, {ygong,jinjun,nnzheng}@mail.xjtu.edu.cn

Abstract. Recently, the Deep Convolutional Neural Networks (DCNN) have achieved state-of-the-art performances with many tasks in image and video analysis. However, it is a very challenging problem to devise a good DCNN model as there are so many choices to be made by a network designer, including the depth, the number of feature maps, interconnection patterns, window sizes for convolution and pooling layers, etc. These choices constitute a huge search space that makes it impractical to discover an optimal network structure with any systematic approaches. In this paper, we strive to develop a good DCNN model by borrowing biological guidance from the human visual cortex. By making an analogy between the proposed DCNN model and the human visual cortex, many critical design choices of the proposed model can be determined with some simple calculations. Comprehensive experimental evaluations demonstrate that the proposed DCNN model achieves state-of-the-art performances on four widely used benchmark datasets: CIFAR-10, CIFAR-100, SVHN and MNIST.

Keywords: DCNN · Bio-inspired · Network design · Visual cortex

1 Introduction

Although Deep Convolutional Neural Networks (DCNN) have achieved state-of-the-art performances with many applications in image and video analysis, such as image classification [6,21,25,27], object detection [1,18], segmentation [9,16], etc., it is a very challenging task to devise a good DCNN model as there are so many choices to be made by a network designer, including the depth of the network, the number of feature maps in each layer, interconnection patterns between two adjacent layers, window sizes for each convolution and pooling layers, etc. These choices are critical to the ultimate network performance, and it requires profound knowledge and experiences, as well as many trials and errors to build a DCNN model that achieves state-of-the-art performances. Nowadays, the common practice in the field is that researchers adopt one of the state-of-the-art DCNN models, such as AlexNet [6], ZFNet [27], VGGNet [21], make certain modifications if necessary, and use it to solve their own problems. It is interesting to note that even the configuration of AlexNet, the winner of the ImageNet ILSVRC 2012 competition, was proved to be not the best one. For example, in [27] Zeiler and Fergus modified several parameters of AlexNet,

© Springer International Publishing AG 2016
E. Chen et al. (Eds.): PCM 2016, Part I, LNCS 9916, pp. 540–549, 2016.
DOI: 10.1007/978-3-319-48890-5_53

e.g. the size and stride of the receptive window in the first convolution layer were changed from 11×11 to 7×7, 4 to 2, respectively, and was able to improve its image classification accuracy by 1.7 % on the ImageNet ILSVRC 2012 dataset.

Many research studies in the literature have revealed that a deeper network structure, a smaller convolution window, and more feature maps per layer generally result in a network model with a better performance accuracy. Besides these, there is not much generally applicable guidance which we can learn from the literature. However, these and other network design choices, together with all their possible combinations, constitute a huge search space that makes it impractical to discover an optimal network structure with any systematic approaches. This is especially true for large scale DCNN models because it often takes days if not weeks to train such models with a large image dataset. Therefore, devising a state-of-the-art DCNN model is largely a craftman's work that requires both profound knowledge, experiences and many trials and errors.

In this paper, we strive to develop a good DCNN model with state-of-the-art performances by borrowing biological guidance from human visual cortex. In recent decades, multi-disciplinary research efforts from neuroscience, physiology, psychology, etc., have discovered that object recognition in visual cortex is modulated via the ventral stream [3,13,15,19], starting from the primary visual cortex (V1) through extrastriate visual areas I (V2) and IV (V4), to the inferotemporal cortex (IT), and then to the PreFrontal Cortex (PFC). The diagrammatic sketch of ventral stream can be seen in Fig. 1. Through this layered structure, raw neuronal signals from the retina are gradually transformed into higher level representations that are discriminative enough for accurate and speedy object recognition. The dimensionality of each layer's input and output changes significantly, and the processing time also varies with different layers. Although we know very little about the processing details inside, and the internal representations abstracted by each of these layers, the dimensionality of each layer's input and output, and their relative processing times do serve as an important guidance to design our own DCNN model.

We propose a new DCNN model by making an analogy between the proposed model and the human ventral stream. Taking cues from the ventral stream, the proposed DCNN model consists of four convolution layers. The number of feature maps in each layer is determined according to the ratio of the input and output dimensions of the corresponding layer in the ventral stream. We speculate that the relative processing time of each layer in the ventral stream reflects its internal computational complexity, which motivates us to introduce convolution layers with varied complexity. Traditionally, a convolution layer processes its input by using linear filters followed by a nonlinear activation function. The linear filters can be generalized to more complex, nonlinear ones to increase the feature abstraction power of the convolution layer. In the proposed model, we borrow the idea from the NIN model [12] to add multi-layer perceptrons into each convolution layer, and accomplish convolution layers of varied complexity by adding a different number of perceptron sub-layers to a different convolution layer. The appropriate number of perceptron sub-layers to be added to a convolution layer is determined by the relative processing time of the corresponding layer in the ventral stream. By borrowing biological guidance from human visual cortex, many critical design choices of the proposed DCNN model can be determined with some simple calculations. Through comprehensive experimental evaluations, we demonstrate that the proposed DCNN model achieves state-of-the-art performances on all of the four benchmark test sets CIFAR-10, CIFAR-100, SVHN and MNIST.

The remainder of this paper is organized as follows. Section 2 describes details of the proposed DCNN architecture, Sect. 3 reveals experimental evaluation results, and Sect. 4 draws the conclusion of the paper.

2   Bio-inspired DCNN Model

In this section, we describe our biologically inspired DCNN architecture. Firstly, we review the structure of the human ventral stream which motivates us to propose our DCNN model.

2.1   Structure of Human Ventral Stream

Multi-disciplinary research studies from neuroscience, physiology, psychology, etc., have discovered that the ventral stream in human visual cortex houses key circuits for object recognition [3,13]. The ventral stream has a layered structure, starting from the primary visual cortex (V1) through extrastriate visual areas I (V2) and IV (V4), to the inferotemporal cortex (IT), and then to the PreFrontal Cortex (PFC) (see Fig. 1). The IT layer reveals a more complex structure, and can be further divided into three sub-layers: pIT, cIT, and aIT. It is believed that through this layered structure, raw neuronal signals from the retina are gradually transformed into higher level representations, and that at the IT layer,

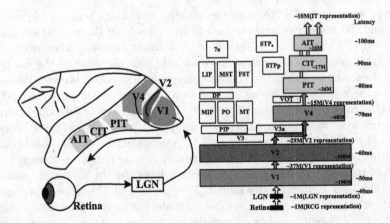

Fig. 1. The human ventral stream cortical area locations and the flow of neuronal signals from retina.

pattern representations have achieved a great amount of invariance to those identity-preserving image transformations (e.g. changes in position, scale, pose, view angle, lighting condition, etc.), by which object identity of the input signal becomes available [10,17,20]. The dimensionality of each layer's input and output changes significantly, and the processing time also varies with different layers. As shown in Fig. 1, when visual stimulus is received by human eyes, the retina outputs neuronal signals with about one million dimensions. The Lateral Geniculate Nucleus (LGN) area takes retina's outputs, and performs certain preprocessing to deal with variance in luminance and contrast within the visual input. Its output has about the same dimensionality as that of retina. For the V1 layer, the dimensionality of its output is expanded more than 30-fold to about 37 millions. In subsequent layers, the dimensionality of output signals reduces gradually, from 29M to 15M, and to 10M at the IT layer.

In addition, the processing time from LGN to V4 is almost the same, with $\sim$10 ms for each layer. In contrast, the processing time at the IT layer is about $\sim$30 ms, three times as much as that of the other layers. We speculate that the relative processing time of each layer in the ventral stream reflects its internal computational complexity, and therefore, when taking these cues from ventral stream to design our own DCNN model, it is necessary to develop convolution layers with varied complexity.

Although research outcomes from the areas of neuroscience, physiology, psychology, etc., have revealed very little about the processing details and the internal representations for each of these layers, the dimensionality of each layer's input and output, and their relative processing times do serve as an important guidance to design our own DCNN model. In the following part of this section, we propose a new DCNN model that simulates the V1 to IT layers of the human ventral stream with respect to their input-output dimensionality ratios and computational complexities.

2.2 Convolution Layers with Varied Complexity

As stated above, it is necessary to develop convolution layers with varied complexity to develop our biologically inspired DCNN model. To achieve this, we adopt the multi-layer perceptron (MLP) as in NIN [12], and add a different number of MLP sub-layers to a different convolution layer.

A traditional convolution layer generates feature maps by using linear filters followed by a nonlinear activation function, e.g. sigmoid, tanh, rectifier linear unit, etc. Taking the rectifier linear unit as an example, the feature maps can be calculated as follows:

$$f_{i,j,k} = max(\mathbf{w}_k^T \cdot \mathbf{x}_{i,j} + b_k, 0), \tag{1}$$

where (i, j) denotes the spatial location on feature maps, k the feature map index, $\mathbf{x}_{i,j}$ the input patch centered at (i, j), and $\mathbf{w}_k^T$, b_k the filter coefficient vector and the bias of the k_{th} feature map, respectively.

We generalize traditional convolution layers to convolution layers with varied complexity by utilizing an MLP instead of a linear filter. When an MLP is used, the feature maps can be calculated as follows:

$$f^1_{i,j,k_1} = max(\mathbf{w}^{1T}_{k_1} \cdot \mathbf{x}_{i,j} + b_{k_1}, 0),$$
$$f^2_{i,j,k_2} = max(\mathbf{w}^{2T}_{k_2} \cdot \mathbf{f}^1_{i,j} + b_{k_2}, 0),$$
$$\vdots$$
$$f^n_{i,j,k_n} = max(\mathbf{w}^{nT}_{k_n} \cdot \mathbf{f}^{n-1}_{i,j} + b_{k_n}, 0). \tag{2}$$

In Eq. (2), the subscript (i, j) denotes the spatial location on feature maps, $k_1, \cdots, k_n$ the node indexes of the MLP hidden layers $1, \cdots, n$, respectively, the superscripts $1, \cdots, n$ the MLP layer indexes, $\mathbf{x}_{i,j}$ the input patch centered at location (i, j), $\mathbf{f}^l_{i,j}$ the output vector of the l-th MLP layer, where $\mathbf{f}^l_{i,j} = \{f^l_{i,j,k_l}\}$. $\mathbf{w}^m_{k_m}$ denotes the vector of the connection weights between the inputs and the k_m node in the m-th hidden layer and b_{k_m} is the corresponding bias. By adjusting n in Eq. (2), we can obtain convolution layers with varied complexity.

Note that Eq. (2) is equivalent to cascaded cross channel parametric pooling, and the cross channel parametric pooling is also equivalent to a convolution layer with 1×1 convolution kernel [12] (In the next subsection, this kind of layers are denoted as cccp layers). In other words, a generalized convolution layer using an MLP to scan the input is equivalent to a traditional convolution layer using a linear filter followed by several traditional convolution layers with 1×1 convolution kernel.

2.3   The Proposed DCNN Model

In this subsection, we propose a new DCNN model which simulates the V1 to IT layers of the human ventral stream, and develop the model by using the building blocks of the convolution layers with varied complexity.

According to the input-output dimensionality ratios and computational complexities of the V1 to IT layers in the human ventral stream, we develop the BIC-A on all the three datasets CIFAR-10 [5], CIFAR-100 [5] and SVHN [14]. As images in these datasets all have the dimensions of $32 \times 32 \times 3$, BIC-A's configuration can be shared among these three datasets. Since Images in the MNIST dataset [7] have the dimensions of $28 \times 28 \times 1$, we develop the BIC-B to change the model configuration accordingly. The detailed configuration of BIC-A and BIC-B is listed in Table 1.

Both BIC-A and BIC-B are configured by making an analogy between the conv1, conv2, conv3 layers of the models and the V1, V2, V4 layers in the human ventral stream. Take BIC-A as an example. As each input image is $32 \times 32 \times 3$, according to V1's input-output ratio (which is 37), the conv1 layer should be $32 \times 32 \times 3 \times 37 = 32 \times 32 \times 111$. For computational efficiency we scale up the number of feature maps to 128, a multiple of 16. As a result, the output size of the conv1 layer is set to $32 \times 32 \times 128$. Similarly, output sizes of the conv2 and conv3

Table 1. The detailed configuration of BIC-A and BIC-B.

Layer name	Padding	Filtersize/stride	Output size(BIC-A)	Output size(BIC-B)
conv1	2	$5 \times 5/1$	$128 \times 32 \times 32$	$48 \times 28 \times 28$
relu1			$128 \times 32 \times 32$	$48 \times 28 \times 28$
cccp1	0	$1 \times 1/1$	$96 \times 32 \times 32$	$32 \times 28 \times 28$
relu_cccp1			$96 \times 32 \times 32$	$32 \times 28 \times 28$
pool1	0	$3 \times 3/2$	$96 \times 16 \times 16$	$32 \times 14 \times 14$
drop1			$96 \times 16 \times 16$	$32 \times 14 \times 14$
conv2	2	$5 \times 5/1$	$384 \times 16 \times 16$	$160 \times 14 \times 14$
relu2			$384 \times 16 \times 16$	$160 \times 14 \times 14$
cccp2	0	$1 \times 1/1$	$256 \times 16 \times 16$	$96 \times 14 \times 14$
relu_cccp2			$256 \times 16 \times 16$	$96 \times 14 \times 14$
pool2	0	$3 \times 3/2$	$256 \times 8 \times 8$	$96 \times 7 \times 7$
drop2			$256 \times 8 \times 8$	$96 \times 7 \times 7$
conv3	1	$3 \times 3/1$	$768 \times 8 \times 8$	$320 \times 7 \times 7$
relu3			$768 \times 8 \times 8$	$320 \times 7 \times 7$
cccp3	0	$1 \times 1/1$	$384 \times 8 \times 8$	$160 \times 7 \times 7$
relu_cccp3			$384 \times 8 \times 8$	$160 \times 7 \times 7$
cccp4	0	$1 \times 1/1$	$192 \times 8 \times 8$	$80 \times 7 \times 7$
relu_cccp4			$192 \times 8 \times 8$	$80 \times 7 \times 7$
cccp5	0	$1 \times 1/1$	$10 \times 8 \times 8$	$10 \times 7 \times 7$
relu_cccp5			$10 \times 8 \times 8$	$10 \times 7 \times 7$
pool3	0	$8 \times 8/1$	$10 \times 1 \times 1$	$10 \times 1 \times 1$

layers are set to $16 \times 16 \times 384$ and $8 \times 8 \times 768$, respectively. Note that although the dimensionality of the IT layer is $\sim 10M$, the dimensionality of BIC-A's final layer is determined by the number of categories in the dataset. As a result, cccp5 should be $8 \times 8 \times 10$, and finally pool3 is $1 \times 1 \times 10$ for the CIFAR-10 dataset (For CIFAR-100, cccp5 is $8 \times 8 \times 100$ and pool3 is $1 \times 1 \times 100$ as it has 100 categories).

To simulate the relative computational complexity of the human ventral stream, one cccp layer (which is a 1×1 convolutional layer [12]) is stacked after conv1 and conv2, while three cccp layers are utilized after conv3. Note that stacking n cccp layers means that setting the number of MLP layers to $n + 1$. The rectified linear unit function is used after each convolution and cccp layer. Two pooling layers with a 3×3 window and 2 pixel stride are used before the conv2 and conv3 layers. Finally, a global average pooling layer with a 8×8 pooling region is used to generate 10 output nodes which is the number of the categories for CIFAR-10 (for CIFAR-100, finally 100 feature maps are used to generate 100 output nodes). In addition, two dropout layers are used after the pool1 and pool2 layers to prevent overfitting. Similar to BIC-A, BIC-B is devised accordingly.

2.4 Comparison with the NIN Model

Because the NIN model achieves the state-of-the-art performances on all the four image datasets used in our experimental evaluations, we provide a detailed comparison between the proposed BIC and the NIN models with respect to the model structure and processing time (although the recent DSN [8] model outperforms NIN, it does not change NIN's model structure and only changes the model's training strategy). Firstly, for clarity, we name the NIN model for CIFAR-10 dataset as NIN-A and that for MNIST dataset as NIN-B. The detailed configurations of the NIN-A and NIN-B models are listed in [12]. We compare BIC-A with NIN-A and compare BIC-B with NIN-B from the following three aspects.

The model depth. Both BIC-A and BIC-B contain eight weight layers: conv1, cccp1, conv2, cccp2, conv3, cccp3, cccp4, cccp5, while NIN-A and NIN-B contain nine weight layers: conv1, cccp1, cccp2, conv2, cccp3, cccp4, conv3, cccp5, cccp6. BIC-A and BIC-B stack convolution layers with varied complexities, *i.e.* from simple to complex, while NIN-A and NIN-B simply stack two cccp layers after each traditional convolution layer.

The number of parameters. BIC-A and BIC-B contain about 3.2M, 0.49M parameters, respectively, while NIN-A and NIN-B contain about 0.97M, 0.35M ones, respectively. Although BIC-A and BIC-B have more parameters than NIN-A and NIN-B, their depth is less than that of latter. As the computation in the same layer can be easily parallelized on the concurrent devices, e.g. GPUs, the total processing time is not strictly proportional to the number of parameters during the forward or backward process.

Processing time in forward and backward process. We test the processing time for BIC-A, BIC-B and the corresponding NIN models. The same hardware platform which contains a 3.4G Hz CPU, 32GB RAM and a GTX 980Ti GPU is adopted. The Caffe package [4] is used as the software platform. 1,000 images are used and the average processing time is calculated and listed in Table 2. As can be seen, both the forward and backward processing times of BIC-B are less than those of NIN-B. Although NIN-A's forward processing time is less than that of BIC-A, its backword processing time is more than that of BIC-A. In total, the processing time of one iteration (one forward process plus one backward process) of BIC-A is more or less the same as that of NIN-A.

Table 2. Processing time comparisons between BIC-A and NIN-A, BIC-B and NIN-B.

Process	CIFAR-10		MNIST	
	BIC-A	NIN-A	BIC-B	NIN-B
Forward	103.1 ms	**91.6 ms**	**53.9 ms**	66.1 ms
Backward	**154.0 ms**	160.0 ms	**83.6 ms**	97.1 ms
In total	257.1 ms	**251.3 ms**	**137.5 ms**	163.3 ms

3   Experiments

In this section, we first compare the performances of BIC-A and BIC-B with state-of-the-art models in the literature using four datasets: CIFAR-10, CIFAR-100, SVHN, and MNIST. Then, we make some arbitrary modifications to BIC-A, and test these BIC-A variants on CIFAR-10 dataset. These experiments serve to verify the optimality of the proposed BIC model.

3.1   Performance of BIC-A and BIC-B

Datasets. The CIFAR-10 dataset is composed of 10 classes of color images, with 6,000 images per class. There are a total of 50,000 training images and 10,000 test images in the dataset. Each image is 32×32 in size and in RGB format. The CIFAR-100 dataset is the same in image size and format as the CIFAR-10 dataset, but contains 100 classes. The number of images in each class is only one tenth of that of CIFAR-10. The SVHN dataset is obtained from the house numbers in the Google Street View images. It contains 630,420 32×32 color images, including training set, testing set and an extra set. The MNIST dataset consists of 0–9 hand written digits which are 28×28 gray images. There are 60,000 training and 10,000 testing samples in total.

Experimental Settings and Results. For fair comparison, we strictly follow the training and testing protocols in [8,12]. The preprocessing of input images also follows that in [8,12].

As Table 3 shows, the proposed BIC models achieve the state-of-the-art accuracy on CIFAR-10, CIFAR-100 and MNIST datasets. The proposed BIC-A achieves a comparable but not better result (2.05 %) with DSN(1.92 %) on SVHN. Note that DSN is a generic method to improve the performance of DCNN models, when BIC-A is combined with deeply supervised information, it could get better performance.

Table 3. Test top-1 error rate on four datasets.

Algorithm	CIFAR-10	CIFAR-100	SVHN	MNIST
Learned Pooling [11]	-	43.71	-	-
Stochastic Pooling [26]	15.13	42.51	2.80	0.47
CNN+Spearmint [22]	14.98	-	-	-
Maxout Networks [2]	11.68	38.57	2.47	0.45
Prob. Maxout [23]	11.35	38.14	2.39	-
Tree Based Priors [24]	-	36.85	-	-
NIN [12]	10.41	35.68	2.35	0.47
DSN [8]	9.78	34.57	1.92	0.39
BIC-A(BIC-B)	**9.10**	**34.33**	**2.05**	**0.26**

Table 4. Test set error rates for the variants of BIC-A on CIFAR-10 dataset.

layer	×2	×0.5
conv1	9.12	10.08
conv2	9.71	9.69
conv3	9.63	9.81

3.2 BIC-A Variants

To verify how optimal the proposed model structure is, we make arbitrary modifications to BIC-A. More specifically, we randomly select one of BIC-A's three convolution layers, expand or reduce its number of feature maps by a specified scaling factor, and test the modified model using the CIFAR-10 dataset. The modified variants of BIC-A are named as BIC-A-conv x-$\times y$, where x denotes the convolution layer 1, 2, or 3, and y the scaling factor of 2 or 0.5.

Table 4 shows the comparison results of the BIC-A variants. Note that BIC-A achieves 9.10 % test error rate on this dataset. Clearly, all the BIC-A variants obtained test error rates that are inferior to that of the original BIC-A. It is interesting to note that when expanding the number of feature maps the performance does not get boosted. These experimental results serve as a valid verification that our proposed BIC model has indeed a near optimal structure and configuration.

4   Conclusion

In this paper, we propose a novel DCNN model which simulates the V1, V2, V4 and IT visual cortexes with respect to their input-output dimensionality ratios and computational complexities. By borrowing biological guidance form human visual cortex, many critical design choices of the proposed DCNN model can be determined with some simple calculations. Comprehensive experiments demonstrate that the proposed DCNN model achieves state-of-the-art performances.

Acknowledgments. This work is supported by National Basic Research Pro- gram of China (973 Program) under Grant No. 2015CB351705, and the National Natural Science Foundation of China (NSFC) under Grant No. 61332018.

References

1. Girshick, R., Donahue, J., Darrell, T., Malik, J.: Rich feature hierarchies for accurate object detection and semantic segmentation. In: CVPR (2014)
2. Goodfellow, I.J., Warde-Farley, D., Mirza, M., Courville, A., Bengio, Y.: Maxout networks. In: ICML (2013)
3. Gross, C.G.: How inferior temporal cortex became a visual area. Cereb. Cortex 4(5), 455–469 (1994)

4. Jia, Y., Shelhamer, E., Donahue, J., Karayev, S., Long, J., Girshick, R., Guadarrama, S., Darrell, T.: Caffe: Convolutional architecture for fast feature embedding. In: ACM MM (2014)
5. Krizhevsky, A., Hinton, G.: Learning multiple layers of features from tiny images (2009)
6. Krizhevsky, A., Sutskever, I., Hinton, G.E.: Imagenet classification with deep convolutional neural networks. In: NIPS (2012)
7. LeCun, Y., Bottou, L., Bengio, Y., Haffner, P.: Gradient-based learning applied to document recognition. Proc. IEEE **86**(11), 2278–2324 (1998)
8. Lee, C.Y., Xie, S., Gallagher, P., Zhang, Z., Tu, Z.: Deeply-supervised nets. In: AISTATS (2015)
9. Long, J., Shelhamer, E., Darrell, T.: Fully convolutional networks for semantic segmentation. In: CVPR (2015)
10. Majaj, N., Hong, H., Solomon, E., DiCarlo, J.: A unified neuronal population code fully explains human object recognition. Cosyne Abstracts (2012)
11. Malinowski, M., Fritz, M.: Learnable pooling regions for image classification. In: ICLR 2013 workshop
12. Lin, M., Qiang Chen, S.Y.: Network in network. In: ICLR (2014)
13. Miyashita, Y.: Inferior temporal cortex: where visual perception meets memory. Ann. Rev. Neurosci. **16**(1), 245–263 (1993)
14. Netzer, Y., Wang, T., Coates, A., Bissacco, A., Wu, B., Ng, A.Y.: Reading digits in natural images with unsupervised feature learning. In: NIPS workshop on deep learning and unsupervised feature learning (2011)
15. Orban, G.A.: Higher order visual processing in macaque extrastriate cortex. Physiol. Rev. **88**(1), 59–89 (2008)
16. Pinheiro, P.H., Collobert, R.: Recurrent convolutional neural networks for scene parsing. In: ICML (2014)
17. Pinto, N., Majaj, N., Barhomi, Y., Solomon, E., DiCarlo, J.: Human versus machine: comparing visual object recognition systems on a level playing field. Cosyne Abstracts (2010)
18. Ren, S., He, K., Girshick, R., Sun, J.: Faster r-cnn: Towards real-time object detection with region proposal networks. In: NIPS (2015)
19. Rolls, E.T.: Functions of the primate temporal lobe cortical visual areas in invariant visual object and face recognition. Neuron **27**(2), 205–218 (2000)
20. Serre, T., Oliva, A., Poggio, T.: A feedforward architecture accounts for rapid categorization. Proc. Natl. Acad. Sci. **104**(15), 6424–6429 (2007)
21. Simonyan, K., Zisserman, A.: Very deep convolutional networks for large-scale image recognition. In: ICLR (2015)
22. Snoek, J., Larochelle, H., Adams, R.P.: Practical bayesian optimization of machine learning algorithms. In: NIPS (2012)
23. Springenberg, J.T., Riedmiller, M.: Improving deep neural networks with probabilistic maxout units. In: ICLR Workshop Track (2014)
24. Srivastava, N., Salakhutdinov, R.R.: Discriminative transfer learning with tree-based priors. In: NIPS (2013)
25. Szegedy, C., Liu, W., Jia, Y., Sermanet, P., Reed, S., Anguelov, D., Erhan, D., Vanhoucke, V., Rabinovich, A.: Going deeper with convolutions. In: CVPR (2015)
26. Zeiler, M.D., Fergus, R.: Stochastic pooling for regularization of deep convolutional neural networks. In: ICLR (2013)
27. Zeiler, M.D., Fergus, R.: Visualizing and understanding convolutional networks. In: Fleet, D., Pajdla, T., Schiele, B., Tuytelaars, T. (eds.) ECCV 2014. LNCS, vol. 8693, pp. 818–833. Springer, Heidelberg (2014). doi:10.1007/978-3-319-10590-1_53

Saliency-Based Objective Quality Assessment
of Tone-Mapped Images

Yinchu Chen[✉], Ke Li, and Bo Yan

Shanghai Key Laboratory of Intelligent Information Processing,
School of Computer Science, Fudan University, Shanghai, China
{14210240038,15110240012,byan}@fudan.edu.cn

Abstract. High Dynamic Range (HDR) image is an imaging or photographic technique that can keep more intensity information than Low
Dynamic Range (LDR) image. Based on the features of HDR images,
we describe a technique for the saliency detection of HDR images, and
further combine it for objectively assessing the quality of Tone-mapping
operators. We propose a Tone-mapping quality index which is more similar to subjective quality scores ranked by human being. We use saliency
map of the HDR images to adjust the differences of structural fidelity.
Experimental results demonstrate that our proposed method can get
relatively high score by comparing with the subjective scores.

Keywords: High dynamic range image · Tone-mapping operators ·
Quality assessment

1 Introduction

The advanced development of computer technology makes possible the wide
application of computer image technology in such fields as video surveillance,
medical research and satellite remote sensing, and results in the demand for
high quality of computer images.

Human senses are extremely sensitive to luminance information. After the
optic nerve in the retina perceives the intensity of light, the human eye can
perceive more by adjusting. As a digital camera can only receive a certain range
of illumination, if one of the pixel of the photo exceeds the camera's dynamic
range, it tends to wash out to white, or become black. Then the photo will not
show all the details in the real world.

High Dynamic Range (HDR) Image is an imaging or photographic technique
used to protect more luminance information in the photo. The amount of information it can obtain is quite close to that of human senses can get. HDR images
can represent a greater range of luminance levels than traditional Low Dynamic
Range (LDR) images and provide much larger contrast characteristics.

As the HDR technique gets more popular, it is imperative for display of HDR
images on LDR display equipment. The technique to convert HDR images to
LDR images is called Tone-mapping operators (TMOs). Because HDR images

© Springer International Publishing AG 2016
E. Chen et al. (Eds.): PCM 2016, Part I, LNCS 9916, pp. 550–558, 2016.
DOI: 10.1007/978-3-319-48890-5_54

contain more luminance information than LDR images, the main aim of tone mapping technology is to retain the maximum amount of important information and abandon some information which is not easy to be noticed while compressing and quantifying HDR images. The compressed images can be displayed on the LDR display equipment.

Tone Mapping Operators aim to transform HDR images to LDR images, while keep as much as details as possible. Dozens of different operators have been proposed these years. Generally speaking, TMOs fall into two categories: global TMOs and local TMOs. Global method [1] is to map the intensity of each pixel of the HDR image to the corresponding LDR image, regardless the position of the pixel. The advantage of this approach is simplicity and quick operation. Its shortage is that the same brightness will be mapped to the same values, regardless of the context information like the positions of the pixels in the image. As a result, the difference in the intensity of brightness between neighbor pixels of the generated LDR image will be limited. Global tone mapping operators usually use exponential function and logarithmic function as the mapping function. The compression curve of global operators is the same over the whole image, while in local operators the curve is adaptive to each pixel. Local tone mapping method can simulate the characteristics of human eyes that the eyes can change the intensity of the visible light received. The intensity of brightness of the pixel will be adjusted according to the information of neighboring pixels. Drago et al. [2] introduced a bias power function with adaptively varied logarithmic bases. With the change of the bases of the logarithmic function, the images can be changed according to the overall brightness of the scene, thus improving the contrast in bright area and dark area. Durand et al. [3] presents a technique by de-composing the image into a base layer and a detail layer, and only the base layer has its contrast reduced. It can keep the details of the HDR images well. Local operator can be adaptive to different situations, and can usually get better result, but it is computationally more expensive.

As different TMOs will lead to different results, we propose a Tone-mapping quality index in order to get the quality score of TMOs. There are two standards to assess the tone mapping operators. One is whether the generated image retains the structure of the original HDR image, especially the most important parts that human eye will pay attention to, for example, the human portrait and the key object. The other is whether the generated image preserves the texture of the background and whether the whole image looks natural on the premise that the details of the important objects are kept well. These two conflicting factors need to be weighed to achieve the best desirable result.

In this paper, we firstly review related work in Sect. 2. Then in Sect. 3, we propose our quality assessment method. Experimental results demonstrated in Sect. 4 prove that our method is able to provide better performance than other state-of-the-art technique. Finally, we draw our conclusions in Sect. 5.

2   Related Work

2.1   Objective Quality Assessment

Image quality assessment is a basic issue in the research of computer image. In the process of digital image compression, transmission, processing and storage, image data may change, resulting in the loss of image information. If the quality of the image cannot meet the requirements, it may cause errors, such as errors in target identification. As different compression methods will lead to different results, we need a quality assessment metric to select a better method.

Quality assessment can either be the subjective method in which viewers grade LDR images or the objective method, in which computers grade LDR images by analyzing the characteristics of the images. Subjective assessment may be a valid one, but a large amount of time and manpower will be needed, and the rating may be affected by some external factors such as experimental environment and equipment, and it is not suitable for large volumes of data.

A Viewer can evaluate an LDR image by his or her subjective standard easily, but it has been a difficult problem for a computer to do the same work. Compared with subjective assessment, objective assessment may yield errors. The consistency between objective and subjective assessment can be used to measure the accuracy of the objective assessment.

One of the evaluation factors is the structural fidelity of the HDR image and the LDR image. The SSIM [4] approach is a useful method for predicting the structural fidelities between LDR images, but it is not suitable for HDR images. HDR-VDP [5] is one of the metrics to predict visually significant differences, but it needs complex calibration. The other HDR image quality index is TMQI [6], which modifies the factors relevant to luminance and defines the local structural fidelity as

$$S_{local}(x,y) = \frac{2\sigma'_x 2\sigma'_y + c_1}{\sigma'_x{}^2 + \sigma'_y{}^2 + c_1} \cdot \frac{\sigma'_{xy} + c_2}{\sigma'_x \sigma'_y + c_2} \tag{1}$$

where x, y and xy are the local standard deviations and cross correlation between the two corresponding patches x and y in HDR and LDR images, and c_1 and c_2 are positive stabilizing constants. The local structural fidelity measure S_{local} uses a sliding window that runs across the image space. This step is applied to multiple scales, which means the original image is repeatedly filtered and subsampled to generate a sequence of reduced resolution images and the local structural fidelity map is generated from each image. The final score is an average of all the scores of each scale [6]:

$$S_l = \frac{1}{N_l} \sum_{N_l}^{i=1} S_{local}(x_i, y_i) \tag{2}$$

where x_i and y_i are the i-th patches in the HDR and LDR images being compared and N_l is the number of patches in the l-th scale. Finally, scores in different scales are combined to get an overall score [6]:

$$S = \prod_{L}^{i=1} S_l^{\beta_l} \tag{3}$$

where L is the total number of scales and β_l is the weight assigned to the l-th scale. In the paper $\beta_l = 0.0448, 0.2856, 0.3001, 0.2363, 0.1333$ according to the psychophysical experiment results [7]. Besides, TMQI also uses a statistical naturalness model simply built on statistics of a certain amount of natural images to generate the statistical naturalness measure N. Finally, TMQI combine the structural fidelity measure S and the statistical naturalness measure N [6]:

$$Q = aS^\alpha + (1 - a)N^\beta \tag{4}$$

where the parameters $a = 0.8012$, $\alpha = 0.3046$, and $\beta = 0.7088$, that are tuned to best fit the subjective evaluation data [8].

2.2 Saliency Detection

Digitized photographs always contain some redundant information, and the most attractive parts usually occupy certain areas. The saliency of an item is the state or quality by which it stands out relative to its neighbors. Saliency detection is used to measure which part of an image attractive to human visual system, for example, for people pictures, people is always more attractive to the viewers than the background.

Saliency detection algorithm is usually achieved by using the local or global contrast, or segmenting the important objects and the background into two parts. The first few saliency detection algorithms use elementary features, such as color, orientation, direction of movement, disparity etc. Koch et al. [9] extends the idea and proposes an application of saliency detection.

As computer can hardly get the high level knowledge of an image, saliency detection methods are mainly depend on priors that the different properties of objects and backgrounds. In this paper, we assume that the contrast values between the background patch and the object patch are high, while the contrast values inside the background patch and the object patch are low. This is widely used in saliency detection methods [10,11].

In this paper, we refer to Geodesic Saliency (GS) [12] to get our saliency map. GS builds an undirected weighted graph $G = V, E$, whose vertices are all image patches P_i plus a virtual background node B. The virtual background node is connected to the image boundary patches. Then the geodesic saliency of a patch is the accumulated edge weights along the shortest path from it to background node on the graph [12]:

$$Saliency(P) = \min_{P_1=P,P_2,\ldots,P_n=B} \sum_{i=1}^{n-1} weight(P_i, P_{i+1}), s.t.(P_i, P_{i+1}) \in E \tag{5}$$

where the weight of the edges of G are set as the difference between the mean colors of two patches (in LAB color space). After the saliency values of all patches in the image are generated, GS [12] can get a complete saliency map of the target image.

3   Our Method

When HDR images are converted into LDR images, some of the information is lost due to the different capacity of the information they can store. For the purpose of preserving the most important information, we tend to select and retain the details of the regions which have a high saliency value because human eyes are very sensitive to the loss of the information of these regions.

When we use GS [12] with original weight function to calculate the saliency map of the HDR images, we usually get poor results that only a very small portion of the salient regions get high value while the other important items are lost. As a result, traditional image saliency detection algorithm cannot be directly applied to HDR images, which have a greater dynamic range than LDR images.

Using LDR images converted by tone mapping operators as the input of the saliency detection, we can get a much better saliency map. However, some information lost in the process of conversion from HDR images to LDR images. So we cannot ensure the tone mapping operator we choose to convert HDR images is a reliable one. In this section, we present a method of computing the saliency map of HDR images derived from Geodesic Saliency [12] in which HDR images are directly used as the input.

Figure 1 shows the results obtained with traditional saliency detection algorithm. In the girl portrait, the left part of her face is lost. And even worse, in the two pictures of the lamp, only the glittering part is selected. These examples suggest that direct computation of HDR images usually lead to poor results that only a small region of the images is chosen as salient region, while the other attractive parts are ignored.

The first step in computing saliency map is to determine the weight of each patch, i.e., the similarity of each patch. Due to the difference in the nature of the brightness quantity of HDR images and LDR images, previous researches on image saliency detection are not so suitable for HDR images. Therefore, the computing method of weight of each patch should be modified accordingly. We found that biological sensors are sensitive to contrasts rather than absolute differences, so we extend the assessment

$$d_l(x, y) = \frac{|l_x - l_y|}{l_y} \tag{6}$$

where x and y is two patches in the input HDR images, l_x and l_y is the mean luminance of the patch. We replace the luminance component in the LAB color space of the weight in Eq. (5) with Eq. (6). After get the similarity between patches, we use Geodesic Saliency [6] introduced in Sect. 2.2 to calculate the saliency map. Figure 1 shows the results of our saliency detection algorithm. Compared with the saliency map generated by using color histogram directly, more salient regions are retained in the saliency map generated by our method. Then we will include the results of HDR image saliency detection into TMO quality assessment. We propose that the structural fidelity of more important

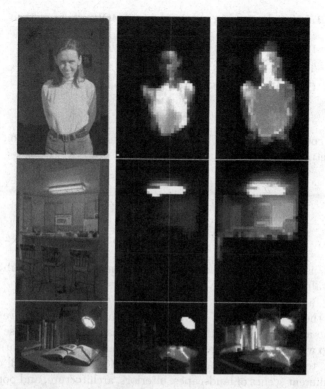

Fig. 1. Left: Original images. For HDR images cannot be displayed, we use TMO to translate them to LDR images. Middle: Saliency map computed by GS using original weight function. Right: Our method.

part of the image has a larger impact on the quality of the image, for example, we care more that the human in the image was blurred, but we cannot even discover that the background has some change. The saliency map is one way to express the importance of one item in the image. Combined with the original algorithm, we get:

$$S_{local}(x, y) = \frac{2\sigma'_x 2\sigma'_y + c_1}{\sigma'^2_x + \sigma'^2_y + c_1} \cdot \frac{\sigma'_{xy} + c_2}{\sigma'_x \sigma'_y + c_2} \cdot Saliency(x) \tag{7}$$

where $Saliency(x)$ is the saliency of the patch computed by our method introduced above. We replace Eq. (1) with Eq. (7) to generate $S_{local}(x, y)$. Then we follow TMQI [6] introduced in Sect. 2.1 to generate our final quality index.

4   Results

The performance of our method is evaluated by comparing our objective quality assessment results with subjective data. We use Spearmans rank-order

Table 1. Performance evaluation of TMQI and our method

Database1	SRCC	KRCC	Database2	SRCC	KRCC
TMQI	0.8223	0.6905	TMQI	0.7882	0.5897
OurMethod	0.8503	0.7143	OurMethod	0.7936	0.5897

correlation coefficient (SRCC) and Kendalls rank-order correlation coefficient (KRCC) metric which is given as follow:

$$SRCC = 1 - \frac{6 \sum_{i=1}^{N} d_i^2}{N(N^2 - 1)} \tag{8}$$

$$KRCC = \frac{N_c - N_d}{\frac{1}{2} N(N - 1)} \tag{9}$$

where d_i is the difference between the i-th images ranks in subjective and objective evaluations, N_c and N_d are the numbers of concordant and discordant pairs in the data set.

To test the performance of our approach, we need an objective evaluation to verify the algorithm. The subjective quality assessment database is the best criterion. So we select two different subjective quality assessment databases with MOS scores to test our tone mapping quality index. Database1 [13] contains 15 classes of different scenes of landscapes, interiors, architecture, and portraits with 8 images for each class. Database2 [14] contains 3 classes with 14 images for each class, and these 3 classes of images consist of photos taken in bright daylight, dim light and normal light. Images in the same class are converted from the same HDR image by different TMOs. We test the TMQI without extending by the saliency map and with the saliency map.

From Table 1, we can see that our method can get higher SRCC and KRCC in most instances, which means that our method can get closer to the subjective quality assessment scores ranked by human.

Figures 2 and 3 show two classes of images in the Database1 [13]. According to the subjective scores, the right image has a better quality than the left one in the

Fig. 2. Subjective (1 means the best and 8 means the worst): (a) 3.9 (b) 3.05. TMQI (1 means the best and 0 means the worst): (a) 0.9476 (b) 0.9476. Our Method (1 means the best and 0 means the worst): (a) 0.6434 (b) 0.6513

Fig. 3. Subjective (1 means the best and 8 means the worst): (a) 5.6 (b) 4.45. TMQI (1 means the best and 0 means the worst): (a) 0.9121 (b) 0.9080. Our Method (1 means the best and 0 means the worst): (a) 0.6385 (b) 0.6592

two classes. Our method shows the same result while TMQI shows the opposite. That means our method can get relatively similar result with the subjective scores for these images.

5   Conclusions

This paper has introduced a tone mapping operator quality assessment which fits the characteristics of HDR images. By combining the quality assessment with HDR image saliency detection, we can get the scores closer to those of the subjective quality assessment. The proposed method can also be integrated into the tone mapping operator for the purpose of parameter optimization.

This method still has certain limitations. When too much attention is focused on salient items, whether details in the background are preserved may not be our first concern, thus resulting in the loss of some of the background details people are actually interested in. Besides, for lack of databases of objective image saliency detection data for HDR images, we still do not have very definite standard to select the parameters in our saliency detection.

References

1. Qiu, G., Guan, J., Duan, J., Chen, M.: Tone mapping for HDR image using optimization - a new closed form solution. In: International Conference on Pattern Recognition, vol. 1, pp. 996–999 (2006)
2. Drago, F., Myszkowski, K., Annen, T., Chiba, N.: Adaptive logarithmic map-ping for displaying high contrast scenes. View Issue TOC **22**, 419–426 (2003)

3. Durand, F., Dorsey, J.: Fast bilateral filtering for the display of high-dynamic-range images. ACM Trans. Graph. **21**, 257–266 (2002)
4. Wang, Z., Bovik, A.C., Sheikh, H.R., Simoncelli, E.P.: Image quality assessment: from error visibility to structural similarity. IEEE Trans. Image Process. **13**, 600–612 (2004)
5. Mantiuk, R., Joong, K., Allan, K., Rempel, G., Heidrich, W.: HDR-VDP-2: a calibrated visual metric for visibility and quality predictions in all luminance conditions. In: SIGGRAPH 2011 ACM SIGGRAPH (2011)
6. Yeganeh, H., Wang, Z.: Objective quality assessment of tone-mapped images. IEEE Trans. Image Process **22**, 657–667 (2013)
7. Wang, Z., Simoncelli, E.P., Bovik, A.C.: Multi-scale structural similarity for image quality assessment. In: Signals, Systems and Computers (2004)
8. Song, M., Tao, D., Chen, C., Bu, J., Luo, J., Zhang, C.: Probabilistic exposure fusion. IEEE Trans. Image Process **21**, 341–357 (2012)
9. Koch, C., Ullman, S.: Shifts in selective visual attention: towards the underlying neural circuitry. Hum. Neurobiol. **4**, 219–227 (1985)
10. Cheng, M.M., Warrell, J., Lin, W.Y., Zheng, S., Vineet, V., Crook, N.: Efficient salient region detection with soft image abstraction. In: IEEE International Conference on Computer Vision (2013)
11. Klein, D., Frintrop, S.: Center-surround divergence of feature statistics for salient object detection. In: IEEE International Conference on Computer Vision (2011)
12. Wei, Y., Wen, F., Zhu, W., Sun, J.: Geodesic saliency using background priors. In: Fitzgibbon, A., Lazebnik, S., Perona, P., Sato, Y., Schmid, C. (eds.) ECCV 2012. LNCS, vol. 7574, pp. 29–42. Springer, Heidelberg (2012). doi:10.1007/978-3-642-33712-3_3
13. Subject-rated image database of tone-mapped images. https://ece.uwaterloo.ca/~z70wang/research/tmqi
14. Cadik, M.: Evaluation of tone mapping operators (2005). http://www.cgg.cvut.cz/members/cadikm/tmo

Sparse Matrix Based Hashing for Approximate Nearest Neighbor Search

Min Wang[1], Wengang Zhou[1(✉)], Qi Tian[2], and Houqiang Li[1]

[1] University of Science and Technology of China, Hefei, China
wm123@mail.ustc.edu.cn, {zhwg,lihq}@ustc.edu.cn
[2] University of Texas at San Antonio, San Antonio, USA
qitian@cs.utsa.edu

Abstract. Binary hashing has been widely studied for approximate nearest neighbor (ANN) search with its compact representation and efficient comparison. Many existing hashing methods aim at improving the accuracy of ANN search, but ignore the complexity of generating binary codes. In this paper, we propose a new unsupervised hashing method based on a sparse matrix, named as Sparse Matrix based Hashing (SMH). There are only three kinds of elements in our sparse matrix, *i.e.*, $+1$, -1 and 0. We learn the sparse matrix by optimizing a new pair-wise distance-preserving objective, in which the linear projection on the Euclidean distance and the corresponding Hamming distance is preserved. With the special form of the sparse matrix, the optimization can be solved by a greedy algorithm. The experiments on two large-scale datasets demonstrate that SMH expedites the process of generating binary codes, and achieves competitive performance with the state-of-the-art unsupervised hashing methods.

Keywords: Hashing · Binary code learning · Unsupervised hashing · Image retrieval

1 Introduction

Approximate nearest neighbor search is an important research topic and has attracted considerable attention in computer and multimedia fields. In recent years, binary hashing has been extensively explored for approximate nearest neighbor search [19–25]. Using binary hashing, each original high dimensional data vector is mapped to a low dimensional binary code. The resulted binary codes significantly reduce the memory cost, and the distance in Hamming space can be efficiently computed by modern CPUs. With these merits, binary hashing has become more and more popular.

Existing binary hashing methods can be categorized as data-independent and data-dependent methods according to whether the training data is involved. As the representative data-independent hashing methods, Locality Sensitive Hashing (LSH) [1] and its variants [2,3,18] have been widely used in practice.

E. Chen et al. (Eds.): PCM 2016, Part I, LNCS 9916, pp. 559–568, 2016.
DOI: 10.1007/978-3-319-48890-5_55

Recently, lots of research efforts are devoted to data-dependent hashing methods, in which training dataset is used to learn more compact binary codes. Data-dependent methods can be divided into three categories according to whether label or class information is involved in the training process: unsupervised [4,5,8], semi-supervised [14], and supervised hashing methods [15–17]. Although in many literature, semi-supervised and supervised hashing methods have been demonstrated with much better performance than unsupervised ones, label or class information for training data is usually unavailable in many scenarios. In this paper, we only focus on unsupervised binary hashing.

Most existing hashing methods focus on improving the accuracy of ANN search, but ignore the complexity of generating binary codes. The process of generating binary codes often involves one or more matrix multiplications in the original space or kernel space, or even more complicated forward propagations of multi-layered neural networks and convolutional neural networks. For instance, Iterative Quantization (ITQ) [4] learns an orthogonal rotation matrix by minimizing the quantization loss while mapping the data preprocessed by PCA projections to binary code. Spherical Hashing (SPH) [5] exploits that hypersphere-based hashing function maps spatially coherent data points to similar binary codes. It involves computing the distance between the query sample and a series of center points of hyperspheres. In [6], a novel neural network is developed to seek multiple hierarchical non-linear transformations to learn binary codes to preserve the non-linear relationship of samples. The process of generating binary codes in [6] involves forward propagation of a multi-layer neural network, which essentially comprises the multiplications of multiple matrices. Although these unsupervised methods achieve promising performance, the process of generating binary codes can be expedited to boost the efficiency of hashing in both the off-line database processing and on-line query, so as to adapt to many computation sensitive scenarios.

To expedite the process of generating binary codes, we propose a new unsupervised hashing method based on a sparse matrix, named as Sparse Matrix based Hashing (SMH). There are only three kinds of elements in our sparse matrix, i.e., +1, −1, and 0. The sparse matrix is mainly occupied by the element 0, which largely decreases the number of multiplication operations. And the non-zero elements in the sparse matrix are +1 and −1, which converts the multiplication into addition operations. These two aspects promote SMH to generate binary codes faster compared with general hashing methods.

SMH learns the sparse matrix by optimizing a new pairwise distance-preserving term, minimizing the point-wise quantization loss, and keeping the balance property of binary codes simultaneously. The proposed pairwise distance-preserving term aims to keep the linear relationships between the Euclidean distance and the Hamming distance of data points. Since the sparse matrix only contains three kinds of special elements, the learning problem can be efficiently solved by a greedy optimization algorithm, in which only addition operations are involved. The experiments on two large-scale datasets demonstrate that SMH expedites the process of generating binary codes, and achieves comparable performance with the state-of-the-art methods.

2   Related Work

In this section, we review the existing unsupervised hashing methods. These methods learn hash functions with training data points without any label or class information. They aim at the distance preservation across the original space and the Hamming space. The hash functions are usually formulated as some fixed forms, such as linear or kernelized linear projection based one projection matrix, or more complex nonlinear projection based on neural networks or other classifiers.

Spectral Hashing (SH) [8] formulates the hash function learning problem as a particular form of graph partition to seek a binary code with balanced and uncorrelated bits. It generates binary codes by computing the values of eigen-functions of the weighted Laplacian. K-means Hashing (KMH) [7] simultaneously performs k-means clustering and learns the binary indices of the quantized cells. The process of generating binary codes in KMH is involved with computing the distance between data points and the centroids of the quantized cells. Binary Reconstructive Embedding (BRE) [9] utilizes pairwise relations between samples and minimizes the squared error between the normalized Euclidean distance and the normalized Hamming distance. Matrix multiplications in kernel space are involved in the process of generating binary codes in BRE. Our SMH also uses a pairwise distance preserving objective, and the objective of BRE can be seen as a special case of our objective. Minimal Loss Hashing (MLH) [10] adopts a pair-wise hinge-like loss function and minimizes its upper bound to learn binary codes. It involves matrix multiplication in the original space to generate binary codes. [11] focuses on the binary autoencoder model, which seeks to reconstruct a data point from the binary code produced by the hash functions. Forward propagation is involved in the process of computing binary codes, which essentially contains the multiplications between multiple pairs of matrices. Compared with these hashing methods, our SMH method computes binary codes based on a sparse matrix, in which only a small fraction of addition operations are involved.

3   Our Method

In this section, we first describe our hashing method based on the learned sparse matrix. Then, we discuss the objective function used to learn the sparse matrix. After that, we present the learning algorithm of our SMH method.

3.1   Sparse Matrix Based Hashing

Given a dataset $\mathbf{X} \in \mathbb{R}^{n \times D}$, each row of $\mathbf{X}$ is a high dimensional data vector $\mathbf{x}_i \in \mathbb{R}^D$. The Euclidean distance between the original data vector $\mathbf{x}_i$ and $\mathbf{x}_j$ is computed by L_2-norm, $d(\mathbf{x}_i, \mathbf{x}_j) = \|\mathbf{x}_i - \mathbf{x}_j\|_2$, and we denote it as $d_{i,j}$ for concise.

The usual paradigm of binary hashing is to first map each data point into a low dimensional space, then quantize the mapped data point to a binary vector. We discuss a simplest case of mapping function, *i.e.*, taking the linear projection as the mapping function. Let $\mathbf{W} = [\mathbf{w}_1, \mathbf{w}_2, \ldots, \mathbf{w}_L] \in \mathbb{R}^{D \times L}$ be the learned projection matrix, where L is the required bit length. Then the mapping of $\mathbf{X}$ can be obtained as $\mathbf{U} = \mathbf{X}\mathbf{W}$, which is further binarized to obtain the binary codes as follows:

$$\mathbf{B} = (sgn(\mathbf{U}) + 1)/2 = (sgn(\mathbf{X}\mathbf{W}) + 1)/2, \tag{1}$$

where $sgn(\cdot)$ is an element-wise sign function.

In the proposed Sparse Matrix based Hashing (SMH) method, we adopt a sparse matrix as the mapping function. Let $\mathbf{W} \in \{0, +1, -1\}^{D \times L}$ be the learned sparse matrix. There are only three kinds of elements in the sparse matrix. The elements 0 occupy the most locations in the sparse matrix, which results in the decline of number of operations. And the remaining locations of the sparse matrix are occupied by the elements $+1$ and -1, which converts the multiplication into addition operations. These two aspects largely expedite the process of generating binary codes. The result of k-th mapping function on $\mathbf{x}_i$ can be obtained as $\mathbf{u}_{i,k} = \sum_{j=1, \mathbf{w}_{k,j}=1}^{D} \mathbf{x}_{i,j} - \sum_{j=1, \mathbf{w}_{k,j}=-1}^{D} \mathbf{x}_{i,j}$, which only involves a few of addition operations. After the mapping, the binary codes are obtained as Eq. (1).

3.2   Learning Objective

In this section, we describe the details to learn the sparse matrix. The main methodology of unsupervised hashing methods is distance-preserving across the original Euclidean space and Hamming space, *i.e.*, $h_{i,j} \propto d_{i,j}$. To achieve the distance-preserving objective, we propose to keep the linear projection relationship of the two distances between pairwise data points. This objective can be achieved by minimizing the following function:

$$\Phi(\mathbf{W}, a, b) = \|\mathbf{H} - a\mathbf{E} - b\|_2^2, \tag{2}$$

where a and b[1] are the parameters of linear distance transformation, and implicitly impact the selection of the projection matrix $\mathbf{W}$. $\mathbf{E}$ and $\mathbf{H} \in \mathbb{R}^{N_p \times 1}$, where N_p denotes the number of selected pairs from data points. Each element in $\mathbf{E}$ denotes the L_2 distance between a pair of data points in the Euclidean space, while each element in $\mathbf{H}$ denotes the Hamming distance between the corresponding binary codes of the pair of data points in the Hamming space.

To get better binary codes for ANN search, we simultaneously consider minimizing the quantization loss and keeping the expected balance property

---

[1] a, b are scalars, the multiplication between a and $\mathbf{E}$ is element-wise multiplication between a and each element of $\mathbf{E}$, and the subtraction to b is also element-wise, we omit the $\mathbf{1}$ vector for concise.

for binary codes into our learning objective. The final optimization function is described as follows:

$$\min_{\mathbf{W},a,b} \ \alpha \|\mathbf{H} - a\mathbf{E} - b\|_2^2 + \lambda |N_1 - \frac{N}{2}| + \beta \|\mathbf{U} - sgn(\mathbf{U})\|_F^2,$$
$$s.t. \ \mathbf{W} \in \{-1, +1, 0\}^{D \times L}, \|\mathbf{W}\|_0 = L \cdot D \cdot S, \tag{3}$$

where $\| \cdot \|_F$ denotes Frobenius norm. The second term denotes the balance property of the binary codes, and the third term describes the quantization loss. N_1 denotes the number of bit '1' in all the binary codes, and N is equal to the number of bits in all the binary codes. If the balance property is strictly preserved, $N_1 = N_0 = \frac{N}{2}$. The second constraint on $\mathbf{W}$ controls the number of the non-zero elements, and S denotes the required sparseness for the matrix. $\| \cdot \|_0$ counts the number of non-zero elements in a matrix. We use three parameters α, β, and λ to easily control the ratio of different terms in the whole optimization objective.

3.3 Learning Algorithm

Simultaneously optimizing the Eq. (3) with respect to $\mathbf{W}, a$ and b is difficult. We propose an alternative scheme to solve this objective function. First, we fix the sparse matrix $\mathbf{W}$, and optimize Eq. (3) with respect to a and b. Then we fix the linear projection parameters a and b, and optimize Eq. (3) with respect to $\mathbf{W}$. The above two steps are repeated until convergence. In the following, we discuss the learning process in details.

a,b-step: With $\mathbf{W}$ fixed, the optimization in Eq. (3) becomes

$$\min_{a,b} \ \|\mathbf{H} - a\mathbf{E} - b\|_2^2. \tag{4}$$

This is a Linear Regression problem, which can be directly solved by Least Square method.

W-step: With a, b fixed, the optimization in Eq. (3) becomes

$$\min_{\mathbf{W}} \ \alpha \|\mathbf{H} - a\mathbf{E} - b\|_2^2 + \lambda |N_1 - \frac{N}{2}| + \beta \|\mathbf{U} - sgn(\mathbf{U})\|_F^2,$$
$$s.t. \ \mathbf{W} \in \{-1, +1, 0\}^{D \times L}, \|\mathbf{W}\|_0 = L \cdot D \cdot S. \tag{5}$$

Directly solving the objective function in Eq. (5) is not easy because of the non-smooth resulted by the binary codes. But in our SMH method, $\mathbf{W}$ is a sparse matrix, and only contains three kinds of elements. Inspired by [12], these constraints result in an efficiently greedy solution to Eq. (5). And in the greedy algorithm, only some addition operations are involved. The difference between [12] and our SMH method lies in that [12] only involves a simple distance-preserving objective like that of BRE [9], which minimizes the squared error between the normalized Euclidean distance and the normalized Hamming distance. The main contribution of [12] is to devise a fast feature descriptor for real time applications. In contrast, our SMH method considers a more general distance-preserving objective, and simultaneously reduces the quantization loss and keeps balance property into the final objective.

Finally, we summarize the whole learning algorithm for our SMH method in Algorithm 1.

Algorithm 1. Sparse Matrix based Hashing

Input:
  Training data matrix $\mathbf{X}$, the number of training pairs N_p, the required length L of binary code, and the required sparseness of the matrix S.
Output:
  The sparse matrix $\mathbf{W}$.
1: **Initialization:**
  Randomly generate N_p training pairs $\mathbf{P}$, and compute the $L2$ distance $\mathbf{E}$ for these training pairs;
  Randomly generate a sparse matrix $\mathbf{W}$, in which $L \cdot D \cdot (1 - S)$ elements are 0, and the others are randomly set as $+1$ or -1.
2: **Repeat:**
3:    Generate binary codes for $\mathbf{X}$, and compute the Hamming distance $\mathbf{H}$ for the training pairs.
4:    Compute a, b in Eq. (4) using Least Squared method.
5:    **Repeat:**
6:        Randomly pick two elements from $\mathbf{W}$, denoted by $\mathbf{w}_{u,v}$ and $\mathbf{w}_{p,q}$.
7:        Update $(\mathbf{w}_{u,v}, \mathbf{w}_{p,q})$ for each of the following cases:
8:          If both $(\mathbf{w}_{u,v}, \mathbf{w}_{p,q})$ are non-zero, check four kinds of pairs, *i.e.*, $(-1, 1)$, $(-1, -1)$, $(1, 1)$, and $(1, -1)$, and take the one that best minimizes the Eq. (5);
9:          If one of $(\mathbf{w}_{u,v}, \mathbf{w}_{p,q})$ is non-zero, check four kinds of pairs, *i.e.*, $(-1, 0)$, $(0, -1)$, $(0, 1)$, and $(1, 0)$, and take the one that best minimizes the Eq. (5);
10:         If both $(\mathbf{w}_{u,v}, \mathbf{w}_{p,q})$ are zeros, continue.
11:   **until** convergence
12: **until** convergence

This greedy optimization algorithm preserves the number of non-zero elements in $\mathbf{W}$, but allows the adjustment on the element locations and signs. Although this algorithm cannot guarantee to converge to a global minimum, it usually ensures a local minimum, which can give enough satisfying results in the experiments.

4   Experiments

We evaluate our SMH method on two large-scale datasets:

- ANN_SIFT1M [13]: this dataset consists of 10,000 query vectors, 1,000,000 base vectors, and 100,000 training vectors, with each vector corresponding to a 128-D SIFT feature. The groundtruth for each query corresponds to its 100 nearest neighbors ordered by increasing Euclidean distance.

- ANN_GIST1M [13]: this dataset consists of 1,000 query vectors, 1,000,000 base vectors, and 500,000 training vectors, and each vector is a 960-D GIST feature. The grountruth for each query contains its 100 nearest neighbors ordered by Euclidean distance in ascending order.

Since our method is unsupervised, we compare it with five representative unsupervised hashing methods, including LSH [1], BRE [9], SPH [5], ITQ [4], and MLH's unsupervised version [10]. In our experiments, we use the implementations of all these five hashing methods released by their authors with the default parameters. Since our SMH method learns the sparse matrix with a random initialization, all the results are averaged over three repeated experiments. And we set the parameters $\alpha = 128.0/L$, and $\lambda = 1$ for all the experiments. For the parameter β, we set $\beta = 1/2$ for the experiments on ANN_SIFT, and set $\beta = 1$ for the experiments on ANN_GIST. The sparseness of our sparse matrix is set as $S = 0.2$, which means eighty percent of elements in the sparse matrix are the elements 0.

In this paper, we use binary codes to perform approximate nearest neighbor search based on hash code ranking strategy, which sorts the binary codes by increasing Hamming distance. Based on this strategy, we use two evaluation metrics to measure the performance of different methods in this paper:

- Recall@K: it counts the percentage of true neighbors among all the ground-truth in the retrieved K samples.
- mAP (mean Average Precision): it is obtained by computing the area under the Precision-Recall curve.

In Table 1, the mAP comparisons between our SMH method and other representative methods are listed. From these results, we can find that our SMH method achieves better or comparable performance with the state-of-the-art methods only with a very sparse matrix (80 % elements in the matrix are 0). In Fig. 1, we show the recall@K comparisons for different methods on the two datasets.

Table 1. Comparison on mAP(%). The bold numbers indicate the best result under the same bit length setting. SMH denotes our proposed Sparse Matrix based Hashing method.

Dataset	Code length(bits)	Approaches					
		LSH [1]	BRE [9]	MLH [10]	SPH [5]	ITQ [4]	**SMH**
ANN_SIFT1M	16	0.55	0.54	0.49	0.93	0.88	**1.00**
	32	1.94	1.88	2.34	3.38	3.27	**3.85**
	64	6.70	4.84	6.41	9.50	9.20	**9.92**
	128	15.67	11.29	12.95	18.92	19.77	**19.90**
ANN_GIST1M	16	0.15	0.50	0.33	0.45	0.62	**0.62**
	32	0.48	1.24	1.08	1.28	1.77	**1.77**
	64	1.45	2.65	2.65	3.24	3.50	**3.69**
	128	3.31	4.81	4.57	**6.58**	5.65	6.35

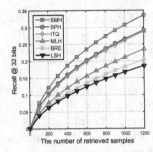 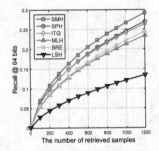

Fig. 1. Recall@K comparison on ANN_SIFT and ANN_GIST. Left: ANN_SIFT, Right: ANN_GIST

Table 2. Comparison on the time of generating binary codes for the two testing datasets (including all the query vectors and base vectors). Time:seconds

Dataset	Code length(bits)	Approaches					
		LSH [1]	BRE [9]	MLH [10]	SPH [5]	ITQ [4]	**SMH**
ANN_SIFT1M	16	0.44	12.45	1.50	3.87	0.64	0.55
	32	0.94	19.29	1.80	5.45	1.15	0.92
	64	1.84	37.59	2.11	8.40	2.20	1.43
	128	3.65	70.23	3.17	14.64	4.53	2.95
ANN_GIST1M	16	2.00	12.37	3.56	14.90	1.98	1.69
	32	3.06	22.39	3.74	17.43	3.29	2.51
	64	5.10	41.61	4.19	24.36	5.59	3.96
	128	8.99	78.61	5.03	34.06	10.30	7.34

Finally, we make an analysis on the time complexity of generating binary codes in SMH. SMH first uses Principal Component Analysis (PCA) to preprocess the dataset as that of ITQ [4]. The time complexity of PCA in SMH is the same as that in ITQ, $i.e.$, $O(N \cdot L \cdot D)$, where N is the number of all the data in the dataset, L is the required bit length, and D is the dimension of the original data. After PCA preprocessing, we multiply the preprocessed data by the learned sparse matrix, in which the time complexity is $O(N \cdot S \cdot L^2)$, where S is the required sparseness for the sparse matrix. (Note that if one carefully devises the matrix multiplication for our special sparse matrix, lower time complexity can be expected.) The theoretically optimal complexity is $N \cdot S \cdot L^2$ addition operations. But we finally implement this step by the matrix multiplication in Matlab for easy, which declines the efficiency of our method in a way. Finally, SMH binarizes the mapping data with the time complexity equal to $O(N \cdot L)$. So the whole time complexity of generating binary codes in SMH is $O(N \cdot L \cdot (D + S \cdot L + 1))$. In Table 2, we list the time of generating binary codes for the testing datasets (including all the query vectors and base vectors) in SMH and the compared methods. Our PC is configured with dual-core 2.00 GHz CPU.

The time listed for SMH contains the time for PCA. From Table 2, we can easily find that SMH effectively expedites the process of generating binary codes even if it involves a PCA preprocessing.

5 Conclusion

In this paper, we propose a novel hash method based on sparse matrix, named as Sparse Matrix based Hashing (SMH). The sparse matrix only contains three kinds of elements: $+1$, -1, and 0. The element 0 occupies most of locations in the sparse matrix, which effectively decreases the number of computational operations. And the other locations in the sparse matrix are occupied by the elements $+1$ and -1. These two kinds of special elements convert the multiplication into addition operations, which further expedites the process of generating binary codes. We learn the sparse matrix by optimizing a new pair-wise distance-preserving objective, in which the linear projection with respect to the Euclidean distance in the original space and the Hamming distance in the Hamming space is preserved. To make our SMH method more effective, we integrate the quantization loss and the balance property of binary codes into the final objective. The experiments on two large scale datasets demonstrate that SMH achieves competitive performance with the state-of-the-art unsupervised hash method, and efficiently expedites the process of generating binary codes.

In our future work, we will extend our SMH method in a supervised way, and explore better objective function for the SMH method to improve the performance of approximate nearest neighbor search.

Acknowledgments. This work is supported in part to Prof. Houqiang Li by the 973 Program under Contract 2015CB351803 and the National Natural Science Foundation of China (NSFC) under Contract 61390514 and Contract 61325009, and in part to Dr. Wengang Zhou by NSFC under Contract 61472378, the Natural Science Foundation of Anhui Province under Contract 1508085MF109, and the Fundamental Research Funds for the Central Universities.

References

1. Datar, M., Immorlica, N., Indyk, P., Mirrokni, V.S.: Locality-sensitive hashing scheme based on p-stable distributions. In: Proceedings of the Twentieth Annual Symposium on Computational Geometry, pp. 253–262. ACM (2004)
2. Kulis, B., Grauman, K.: Kernelized locality-sensitive hashing. PAMI **34**, 1092–1104 (2012)
3. Raginsky, M., Lazebnik, S.: Locality-sensitive binary codes from shift-invariant kernels. In: NIPS, pp. 1509–1517 (2009)
4. Gong, Y., Lazebnik, S.: Iterative quantization: a procrustean approach to learning binary codes. In: CVPR, pp. 817–824 (2011)
5. Heo, J., Lee, Y., He, J., Chang, S., Yoon, S.: Spherical hashing. In: CVPR, pp. 2957–2964 (2012)
6. Erin Liong, V., Lu, J., Wang, G., Moulin, P., Zhou, J.: Deep hashing for compact binary codes learning. In: CVPR, pp. 2475–2483 (2015)

7. He, K., Wen, F., Sun, J.: K-means hashing: an affinity-preserving quantization method for learning binary compact codes. In: CVPR, pp. 2938–2945 (2013)
8. Weiss, Y., Torralba, A., Fergus, R.: Spectral hashing. In: NIPS, pp. 1753–1760 (2009)
9. Kulis, B., Darrell, T.: Learning to hash with binary reconstructive embeddings. In: NIPS, pp. 1042–1050 (2009)
10. Norouzi, M., Fleet, D.J.: Minimal loss hashing for compact binary codes. In: ICML, pp. 353–360 (2011)
11. Carreira-Perpinán, M.A., Raziperchikolaei, R.: Hashing with binary autoencoders. In: CVPR, pp. 557–566 (2015)
12. Ambai, M., Yoshida, Y.: CARD: compact and real-time descriptors. In: ICCV, pp. 97–104 (2011)
13. Jegou, H., Douze, M., Schmid, C.: Product quantization for nearest neighbor search. PAMI **33**, 117–128 (2011)
14. Wang, J., Kumar, S., Chang, S.: Semi-supervised hashing for large-scale search. PAMI **34**, 2393–2406 (2012)
15. Liu, W., Wang, J., Ji, R., Jiang, Y., Chang, S.: Supervised hashing with kernels. In: CVPR, pp. 2074–2081 (2012)
16. Xia, R., Pan, Y., Lai, H., Liu, C., Yan, S.: Supervised hashing for image retrieval via image representation learning. In: AAAI (2014)
17. Zhang, M., Shen, F., Zhang, H., Xie, N., Yang, W.: Hashing with inductive supervised learning. In: PCM, pp. 447–455 (2015)
18. Xie, H., Chen, Z., Liu, Y., Tan, J., Guo, L.: Data-dependent locality sensitive hashing. In: Ooi, W.T., Snoek, C.G.M., Tan, H.K., Ho, C.-K., Huet, B., Ngo, C.-W. (eds.) PCM 2014. LNCS, vol. 8879, pp. 284–293. Springer, Heidelberg (2014). doi:10.1007/978-3-319-13168-9_32
19. Li, P., Wang, M., Cheng, J., Xu, C., Lu, H.: Spectral hashing with semantically consistent graph for image indexing. TMM **15**(1), 141–152 (2013)
20. Zhou, W., Yang, M., Wang, X., Li, H., Lin, Y., Tian, Q.: Scalable feature matching by dual cascaded scalar quantization for image retrieval. PAMI **38**(1), 159–171 (2016)
21. Zhou, W., Li, H., Hong, R., Lu, Y., Tian, Q.: BSIFT: towards data-independent codebook for large scale image search. TIP **24**(3), 967–979 (2015)
22. Zhou, W., Yang, M., Li, H., Wang, X., Lin, Y., Tian, Q.: Towards codebook-free: scalable cascaded hashing for mobile image search. TMM **16**(3), 601–611 (2014)
23. Liu, Z., Li, H., Zhou, W., Zhao, R., Tian, Q.: Contextual hashing for large-scale image search. TIP **23**(4), 1606–1614 (2014)
24. Zhou, W., Lu, Y., Li, H., Tian, Q.: Scalar quantization for large scale image search. In: MM (2012)
25. Zhou, W., Lu, Y., Li, H., Song, Y., Tian, Q.: Spatial coding for large scale partial-duplicate web image search. In: MM, pp. 131–140 (2010)

Piecewise Affine Sparse Representation via Edge Preserving Image Smoothing

Xuan Wang[(✉)], Fei Wang, and Yu Guo

Xi'an Jiaotong University, Xi'an, China
xwang.cv@gmail.com

Abstract. We show a new image editing method, which can obtain the sparse representation of images. The previous methods obtain the sparse image representation by using first-order smooth prior with l_0-norm. A type of incorrect structure will be preserved due to the so called staircasing effects, which usually occur in the region where the image changes gradually. In this paper, we propose the model formed with the data fidelity and the new regularization preserving the gradient at the salient edges and penalizing the magnitude of second-order derivative at all of the other pixels. To obtain the sparse representation, we iteratively minimize the model. In each iteration, the salient edges are re-extracted and the weight of regularization becomes larger than previous. Our iterating smoothing scheme yields the sparse representation, and avoids the incorrect structure caused by staircasing. The experiments illustrate our method outperforms the state of the arts.

Keywords: Image smoothing · Sparse representation · Second-order regularization · Image editing

1 Introduction

Obtaining the image sparse representation via image smoothing is an interesting issue and can be used as the key technique in many applications. To get the sparse representation of image, previous methods use the image denoising model with l_0 regularization. It's well known that the first-order smoothness, e.g. TV, favors the piecewise constant functions and therefore leads to staircasing effects. Consequently, the l_0 gradient minimization method designed for the first-order smoothness will preserve the incorrect structures, especially in region where the image signals change gradually.

The method in this paper is designed to obtain the sparse representation of image, meanwhile to remove the staircasing effects. The original l_0 gradient minimization uses the splitting scheme by introducing auxiliary variables. Using the l_0 gradient minimization with second-order smoothness usually produces meaningless results. Especially when the weight of regularization is relatively large, preserving the second-order derivatives often leads to incorrect function, which is quite different from the input. In the proposed approach, we use the

© Springer International Publishing AG 2016
E. Chen et al. (Eds.): PCM 2016, Part I, LNCS 9916, pp. 569–576, 2016.
DOI: 10.1007/978-3-319-48890-5_56

Fig. 1. Sparse representation via image smoothing. Our proposed method yields the sparse representation of image, meanwhile preserves the details belonging to the saliency structures.

strategy that preserves the gradient at the edges belonging to the dominate structures and penalize the magnitude of second-order derivatives at all of the other pixels. To get the sparse representation, the weight of regularization keep increasing from the initial one to the predefined max value (Fig. 1).

To evaluate our method, we show that the results from our method can be used in many applications and can achieve better performance than the baseline approaches. Besides, the sparsity of the results can be controlled by adjusting the weights configuration. Although our method is designed for the sparse representation, it still can be applied to the image denoising and show the good capacity of preserving the edges, if we reduce the requirement of the sparsity. We also make the quantitative comparisons against the baselines for this issue.

2 Related Works

Two main technique categories are related to our method. First is sparse representation of image. Second is image denoising. The main goal of both issues is to preserve the features (e.g. salient edges) and remove the noise simultaneously.

Obtaining the sparse representation of images is a technique pursuing the sparsity of the image by image smoothing technique. The original L_0 gradient minimization is proposed in [1]. A new strategy is used to confine the discrete number of intensity changes among neighbouring pixels, which links to the l_0 norm of the image gradient. [2] proposed the region fusion based minimization approach that converges fast and gets a better approximation of l_0 norm. Our strategy is similar to [1], but makes improvements by adopting the second-order smoothness.

Image denoising is the fundamental problem in multimedia. The noise is one of the most important source of the image perturbation. Recovering the original image from the noise-polluted image is an ill-posed problem. The digital image can be regarded as a 2-D function encoded as a matrix of grey levels or color values. To better constrain this problem, kinds of regularization are proposed, e.g. ROF model, TV-L_1 model and Huber ROF model. The most broadly used one is total variation, which penalizes the image gradient and can preserve the edges successfully. Another advantage is that it can be solved efficiently in a primal-dual optimization framework. Refer to [5] and [3,7] for more details about the image denoising and TV respectively.

Although there are lots of approaches, to pursuit the sparsity of the result meanwhile avoid the staircasing is still challenging. In most existing methods, the first-order smoothness is used, including the Total Variation. Generally speaking, the first-order smoothness favors the piecewise constant function, and the second-order smoothness favors piecewise affine function [8]. However, preserving the second-order derivatives during pursuing the sparsity usually produces the incorrect result, especially when the weight of regularization is too large. To solve this problem, we propose a strategy that preserves the gradient at the details belonging to the main structures, and penalize the magnitude of the second-order derivatives at anywhere else. In the iterating smoothing scheme, the method produces a sparse representation of the image with the increasing weight of regularization.

In the remainder of this paper, we describe the details of our method, and show the experiments that prove the effectiveness.

3   Proposed Method

In this section, we show how the proposed method obtain the sparse smoothed result and prevent the incorrect structure caused by staircasing. Given the input image $Z(p), p \in \Omega$, and assume the desired sparse representation is denoted as S, in iteration k, the S_k can be updated by minimizing the following energy.

$$S_k = \arg\min_S \int_\Omega E_d(p)dp + \beta \left(\int_{\Omega_s} E_{r_1}(p)dp + \int_{\Omega \backslash \Omega_s} E_{r_2}(p)dp \right) \quad (1)$$

$$E_{r_1}(p) = \|\nabla S(p) - \nabla S_{k-1}(p)\|_2^2 \quad (2)$$

$$E_{r_2}(p) = \|\Delta S_{k-1}(p)\|_2^2 \quad (3)$$

$$E_d(p) = (S(p) - Z(p))^2 \quad (4)$$

E_d, E_{r_1} and E_{r_2} are the data fidelity, regularization for preserving gradient, and the second-order smoothness regularization respectively. ∇ is the nabla operator, Δ is the Laplace operator, and Ω_s is the set, including the salient edges extracted in current iteration k. For the salient edges detection, the criterion is as follows.

$$\Omega_s = \{p | \|\nabla S(p)\|_2^2 > \lambda/\beta\} \quad (5)$$

Since β keeps increasing across the iterations, the thresholds used to detect the salient edges are not same in different iterations. In discrete setting, assuming

S_k and Z are encoded as the column vectors, we can re-define the above equations for simplicity.

$$S_k = \arg\min_S |S - Z|_2^2 + \beta(|D_{r_1}S - D_{r_1}S_{k-1}|_2^2 + |D_{r_2}S|_2^2) \qquad (6)$$

Since (6) is convex, the minimum can be easily obtained by solving the least square problem.

$$S_k = (I_{n \times n} + \beta(D_{r_1}^T D_{r_1} + D_{r_2}^T D_{r_2}))^{-1}(Z + \beta D_{r_1}^T D_{r_1} S_{k-1}) \qquad (7)$$

where $I_{n \times n}$ is the identity matrix and n is the number of pixels. So far, we showed how to obtain the minimum of the proposed energy function. Then the sparse representation of image can be obtained by the complete algorithm showed in Algorithm 1.

Algorithm 1. Sparse Representation via Image Smoothing

   Input: I, β, k_{max}, λ, τ
   Output: S_k
1 $k = 1$, $S_0 = I$;
2 **while** $k \leq k_{max}$ **do**
3   Update Ω_s using (5);
4   Construct D_{r_1} and D_{r_2} according to Ω_s;
5      $S_k = (I_{n \times n} + \beta(D_{r_1}^T D_{r_1} + D_{r_2}^T D_{r_2}))^{-1}(Z + \beta D_{r_1}^T D_{r_1} S_{k-1})$;
6      $\beta = \tau\beta$;

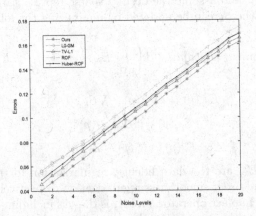

Fig. 2. Quantitative comparison of image denoising. Noised images are created in 20 noise levels. The results are plotted in different colors and the error is mean of the absolute color value difference. (Color figure online)

4   Experiments

Just as what stated in [1], the yielded sparse representation can be used in many applications. Thanks to the second-order smooth regularization, our method reaches a better performance, as shown in the remaining part of this section. For comparison, we select the broadly used baseline methods, such as TV-L1 [7], ROF [6], Huber-ROF [7], and the l_0 gradient minimization denoted as L0-GM [1]. Thanks to the available implementations [1,4], we can make comparisons easily.

Image Denoising. Although our method is to discover the sparse representation of the image, that is to say, only to find the main structure, it still can be applied to noised image. Here we show the ability to discover the sparse representation, even from a highly noised image.

Given a clean image, we generate noised images by adding Gaussian noise with different variances, which change from 0.1^2 to 0.2^2 uniformly. Note that the color values in rgb channels are normalized in $[0, 1]$. Then we apply our method, TV-L1, ROF, Huber-ROF and L0-GM to the noised images. To evaluate the denoising performance, we calculate the mean of absolute color value (rgb) error of all the pixels, see Fig. 2.

Sparse Representation. To illustrate the sparsity of our result, we plot the landscapes of the results obtained by L0-GM and our method which are designed to pursue the sparsity. We use the same images used in the image denoising, and plot the landscape of those images (Fig. 4). We only display the ellipse region in the centre of the image to illustrate how can our method achieve a better result than L0-GM. For simplicity, we convert the color images to grey-level matrices. In the ellipse, there is a gradual changing which can lead to the staircasing. As shown in Fig. 4, L0-GM fails to preserve the main structure of the image due to the staircasing. It's obvious that L0-GM leads to a piecewise constant function; however, our method favors the piecewise affine function.

Besides, we also apply our method to the natural images, and it also proves to be effective. The results can also be used to extract the image abstraction since only the salient structures are preserved in result.

Edge Extraction. The sparse representation of the images can be used in many applications. The edge extraction perhaps is the most intuitive one. During the process of our method, the dominate structures are preserved, meanwhile the subordinate structures are removed. We can easily extract the edges from the sparse image (Figs. 3 and 5).

Parameters. The parameters used in this paper is to control the sparsity of the result. We set $\beta_0 = \lambda$ and $\beta_{max} = 1e5$. For λ, it controls the sparsity of the smoothed result. From Fig. 6, we can see that the value of λ determines how sparse the result is.

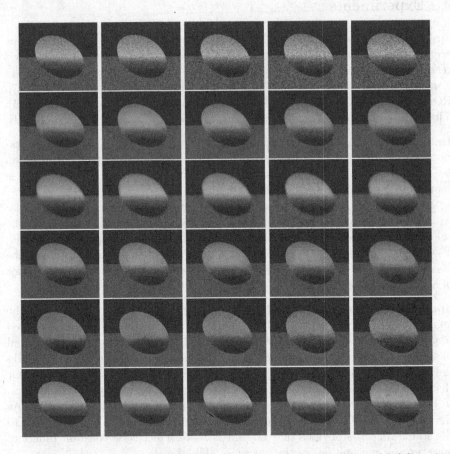

Fig. 3. Results of image denoising. The top row shows the images being added Gaussian noise in different levels (1, 5, 10, 15, 20). From the second row to the bottom, the images are the results denoised by ROF, Huber-ROF, TV-L1, L0-GM and ours method respectively.

Fig. 4. Landscapes of images. Landscape of the clean image, noised image, denoised image by L0-GM and result of our method are displayed from left to right. (Color figure online)

Fig. 5. Edge extraction. Left column shows the original image above and the edge image extracted from it below. Right column shows the smoothed image by our method above and the edge extracted from it below. The same edge extractor is applied to both images.

Fig. 6. Sparsity controlled by λ. Different sparsity of the images are showed. The results obtained by L0-GM and ours are placed side by side, left column is from L0-GM and right one is from ours. Except for the original images in the first row, λ changes from 0.01 to 0.5 uniformly from second row to bottom row.

5   Conclusion

We have proposed a new method obtaining the sparse representation of the image. It uses the second-order smoothness, which favors the piecewise affine function rather than piecewise constant. Consequently, it avoids the incorrectness caused by staircasing. Besides, the proposed method can remove low-amplitude structures and globally preserve and enhance salient edges, even if they are boundaries of very narrow objects.

Sometimes our method will yield over-sharpen results. To cope with this, we plan to design a more robust strategy to determine salient edges in future.

Acknowledgement. This work is funded, in part by Natural Science Foundation of China (No. 61231018, No. 61273366), National Science and technology support program (2015BAH31F01) and Program of introducing talents of discipline to university under grant B13043.

References

1. Xu, L., Lu, C., Xu, Y., Jia, J.: Image smoothing via L_0 gradient minimization. In: SigGraph Asian (2011)
2. Nguyen, R.M.H., Brown, M.S.: Fast and effective L_0 gradient minimization by region fusion. In: ICCV (2015)
3. Chambolle, A., Caselles, V., Novaga, M.: An introduction to total variation for image analysis. Technical report (2009)
4. http://gpu4vision.icg.tugraz.at/index.php?content=downloads.php
5. Buades, A., Coll, B., Morel, J.M.: A review of image denoising algorithms, with a new one. Technical report (2005)
6. Rudin, L., Osher, S.: Total variation based image restoration with free local constraints. In: ICIP (1994)
7. Handa, A., Newcombe, R., Angeli, A., Davison, A.: Applications of Legendre-Fenchel transformation to computer vision problems. Technical report (2011)
8. Bredies, A., Kunisch, K., Pock, T.: Total generalized variation. SIAM J. Imaging Sci. (2010)

Author Index

Printed in the United States
By Bookmasters